EUROPEAN FINANCIAL REGULATION

Mirroring the long-established structure of the financial industry, EU financial regulation as we know it today approaches banking, insurance and investment services separately and often divergently. In recent decades however, the clear separation between financial sectors has gradually evaporated, as business lines have converged across sectors and FinTech solutions have emerged which do not fit traditional sector boundaries.

As the contours of the traditional tripartition in the financial industry have faded, the diverging regulatory and supervisory treatment of these sectors has become increasingly at odds with economic reality.

This book brings together insights developed by distinguished researchers and industry professionals in a series of articles analysing the main areas of EU financial regulation from a cross-sectoral perspective. For each specific research theme – including prudential regulation, corporate governance and conduct of business rules – the similarities, as well as gaps, overlaps and unjustifiable differences between banking, securities and insurance regulation, are clearly presented and discussed. This innovative research approach is aimed at informing lawmakers and policymakers on potential improvements to EU financial regulation whilst also supporting legal and compliance professionals applying the current framework or looking to streamline compliance processes.

European Financial Regulation

Levelling the Cross-Sectoral Playing Field

Edited by
Veerle Colaert
Danny Busch
and
Thomas Incalza

·HART·
OXFORD · LONDON · NEW YORK · NEW DELHI · SYDNEY

HART PUBLISHING

Bloomsbury Publishing Plc

Kemp House, Chawley Park, Cumnor Hill, Oxford, OX2 9PH, UK

1385 Broadway, New York, NY 10018, USA

HART PUBLISHING, the Hart/Stag logo, BLOOMSBURY and the Diana logo are
trademarks of Bloomsbury Publishing Plc

First published in Great Britain 2019

A catalogue record for this book is available from the British Library.

Library of Congress Cataloging-in-Publication data

Names: Colaert, Veerle, editor. | Busch, Danny, editor. | Incalza, Thomas, editor.

Title: European financial regulation : levelling the cross-sectoral playing field /
[edited by] Veerle Colaert, Danny Busch, Thomas Incalza.

Description: Chicago : Hart Publishing, an imprint of Bloomsbury Publishing, 2019. |
Includes bibliographical references and index.

Identifiers: LCCN 2019044171 (print) | LCCN 2019044172 (ebook) | ISBN 9781509926459 (hardback) |
ISBN 9781509926473 (Epub)

Subjects: LCSH: Financial institutions—Law and legislation—European Union countries. |
Financial services industry—Law and legislation—European Union countries. | Banking law—
European Union countries. | Securities—European Union countries.

Classification: LCC KJE2188 .E98 2019 (print) | LCC KJE2188 (ebook) | DDC 346.24/08—dc23

LC record available at https://lccn.loc.gov/2019044171

LC ebook record available at https://lccn.loc.gov/2019044172

ISBN: HB: 978-1-50992-645-9
       ePDF: 978-1-50992-646-6
       ePub: 978-1-50992-647-3

Typeset by Compuscript Ltd, Shannon
Printed and bound in Great Britain by CPI Group (UK) Ltd, Croydon CR0 4YY

MIX
Paper from
responsible sources
FSC   FSC® C013604
www.fsc.org

To find out more about our authors and books visit www.hartpublishing.co.uk.
Here you will find extracts, author information, details of forthcoming events
and the option to sign up for our newsletters.

PREFACE

This book is the result of an ambitious research project, spanning more than two years and bringing together researchers from eight different Member States. The project was formally kicked-off in February 2017 with a two-day round-table session at KU Leuven University. Academics – both lawyers and economists – met with stakeholders from the banking, insurance and investment sectors, representing both industry and consumer interests. The aim of the conference was to discuss, on the basis of a series of preliminary outlines and presentations, the feasibility and desirability of establishing a book project featuring an entirely novel approach to financial regulation: instead of examining the different sectors of the financial industry separately, this project would engage in a *cross-sectoral comparison* of all the main areas of EU financial regulation.

The project's scope was vast; the enthusiasm of those present at the conference astounding. In order to move the project forward, the group of academics involved had to be enlarged. Finally, no less than 28 academics and practitioners have contributed to this book so as to ensure that the most important areas of EU financial regulation would be adequately covered, comparing the EU regulatory regime applicable in the banking, investment and insurance industry.

In order to streamline the focus and research method of the book project and to ensure that the different contributions would not overlap, a second international conference was organised at the Radboud University, Nijmegen on 15 and 16 October 2018. At that occasion first drafts of each paper were presented and thoroughly discussed with both members of the research group and external discussants.

The result of the authors' joint research effort is a fundamentally different book on EU financial regulation, which is both an informative tool for legal practice and scientifically groundbreaking. This book will therefore be of use to readers with very different perspectives.

First, comparing regulation which tackles very similar problems in the three financial sectors is illuminating for legal practitioners, who are increasingly confronted with the limitations and inefficiencies of sectoral legislation. This book unearths the myriad similarities and differences in sectoral financial legislation and helps in comprehending to what extent similar processes, structures and procedures apply across the financial industry, and where the rules differ. All too often very similar problems result in different regulatory solutions in the banking, securities and insurance fields, whereas many financial institutions are part of a group which provides a broad range of banking, securities *and* insurance services. For lawyers who need to implement and ensure compliance with EU financial regulation, it is therefore extremely useful to gain an insight into how the regulator deals with the same problem in different pieces of regulation in each of those sectors. Greater clarity on the similarities and differences in regulatory approach with regard to the same problem, makes it easier to streamline compliance processes, procedures and tools across financial products and services.

Second, this book provides invaluable guidance on how to improve the current framework, since for each specific topic, the gaps, overlaps and unsubstantiated differences between banking, securities and insurance regulation are brought to light. This may inform future policy decisions in this quickly evolving area. From this perspective, the book can be situated in the much wider context of the EU Interinstitutional Agreement on better law-making.[1]

Finally, also from an educational perspective, this book will prove particularly valuable to practitioners, policymakers and academics working in this field. Most of them typically specialise in one of the three sectors – banking, securities or insurance. The inter-sectoral comparison of the main themes of financial regulation gives each of them a point of departure to widen their knowledge and understanding of other sectoral regulation and to easily grasp the similarities and differences of the legislative and regulatory framework governing the other sectors.

We hope that the reader will learn as much from this book as we did when reading and editing the manuscript.

The editors are particularly grateful to the Fund of Scientific Research of Flanders for support-ing this project with a four-year research grant, allowing Thomas Incalza to contribute to this project. We also extend special thanks to Radboud University Nijmegen, which granted its Excel-lence Initiative Professorship to Veerle Colaert on the basis of this project, in order to support its efficient coordination and development in cooperation with Danny Busch and the Radboud Institute for Financial Law.

One of the goals of the Fund of Scientific Research of Flanders and the main motivation for establishing the Radboud Excellence Initiative has been to encourage international collaboration between outstanding academics. This project has proven very fruitful in this respect. The book has, indeed, benefitted tremendously from the discussions at the Leuven and Nijmegen confer-ences and the input of those present at those meetings. We would like to express special gratitude to the esteemed discussants of the papers presented at those conferences: Kern Alexander, Filippo Annunziata, John Armour, Lilli Bialluch, Herman Cousy, Meinrad Dreher, Peter De Proft, Anne-Christine Fornage, Katarzyna Hanula-Bobbitt, Sebastiaan Hooghiemstra, Sanne Jansen, Olav Jones, Ernst de Klerk, Katja Langenbucher, Iain MacNeil, Dorota Masniak, Denisa Mularova, Iris Palm-Steyerberg, Andrea Perrone, Peter Rott, Mardina Smayel, Kristien Smedts, Jo Swyngedouw, Annick Teubner, Alex Toscano, Caroline Van Schoubroeck and William Vidonja.

Most of all, however, we are much indebted to all the authors of this book for their dedication to this project and its particular research method, and for their commitment to drafting (and redrafting) outstanding papers in order to produce the excellent book that we are honoured to present to you today.

Leuven and Nijmegen
1 July 2019
Veerle Colaert, Danny Busch and Thomas Incalza

---

[1] Interinstitutional Agreement of 13 April 2016 between the European Parliament, the Council of the European Union and the European Commission on Better Law-Making, OJ L123, 12 May 2016, https://eur-lex.europa.eu/legal-content/EN/TXT/PDF/?uri=CELEX:32016Q0512(01)&from=EN, especially paras 20–24 on the ex post evaluation of legislation, and paras 46–48 on simplification of legislation.

TABLE OF CONTENTS

PART III
CONSUMER PROTECTION

PART IV
SUPERVISION AND INTERNAL MARKET

PART V
SUMMARY AND CONCLUSIONS

LIST OF CONTRIBUTORS

Gilian Bens is FWO Project Researcher at KU Leuven, Belgium.

Jens-Hinrich Binder is Professor of Private Law, Commercial Law, Company and Securities Law at Eberhard Karls University Tübingen, Germany.

Danny Busch is Professor of Financial Law and Founding Director of the Institute for Financial Law at Radboud University Nijmegen, the Netherlands, and a Fellow of the Commercial Law Centre, University of Oxford, United Kingdom.

Veerle Colaert is Professor of Financial Law at KU Leuven, Belgium, Excellence Initiative Professor at Radboud University Nijmegen, the Netherlands, and chair of the ESMA Stakeholder Group.

Sofie Cools is Professor of Company Law at KU Leuven, Belgium.

Victor de Serière is Professor of Securities Law of the Institute for Financial Law, Business and Law Research Centre at Radboud University in Nijmegen and attorney-at-law in Amsterdam, the Netherlands.

Carmine Di Noia is Commissioner at Consob, Italy.

Guido Ferrarini is Emeritus Professor of Business Law at the University of Genoa, Department of Law and Director of the Centre for Law and Finance, Genoa, Italy, and Visiting Professor at Radboud University Nijmegen, the Netherlands.

Matteo Gargantini is Assistant Professor of European Economic Law at the University of Utrecht, the Netherlands.

Geneviève Helleringer is Professor at ESSEC Business School Paris-Singapore, IECL Lecturer at the Law Faculty of Oxford University, United Kingdom, and ECGI Research Fellow.

Thomas Incalza is Postdoctoral FWO Researcher and Visiting Professor of Business and Company Law at KU Leuven, Belgium.

Bart Joosen is Extraordinary Professor of Financial Law at the VU University of Amsterdam, the Netherlands, associated with the ZIFO Institute for Financial and Corporate Law and working in private practice as a solicitor in Amsterdam.

Peter Laaper is an Assistant Professor at Utrecht University, the Netherlands, and is affiliated with the Dutch law firm Keijser Van der Velden.

Kitty Lieverse is Professor of Financial Regulatory Law of the Institute for Financial Law, Business and Law Research Centre at Radboud University in Nijmegen and attorney-at-law in Amsterdam, the Netherlands. She is also a deputy judge at the Court of Appeal in The Hague.

Eugenia Macchiavello is Assistant Professor in Business and Banking Law at the University of Genoa and Senior Research Fellow at the Genoa centre for Law and Finance, Italy.

Monika Marcinkowska is Professor of Banking and Director of the Institute of Finance at the Faculty of Economics and Sociology of the University of Łódź, Poland.

Luís Morais is Jean Monnet Professor of EU Law and Financial Law at Lisbon Law University (FDL), Portugal, Founder and Chair of the Lisbon-based Research Centre on Regulation and Supervision of the Financial Sector (CIRSF), attorney-at-law, and Vice-Chair of the Appeal Panel of the Single Resolution Board (SRB).

Katrien Morbee is Lecturer in Banking and Finance Law at the Centre for Commercial Law Studies of Queen Mary University of London and PhD Candidate in Law and Finance at Balliol College, University of Oxford, United Kingdom.

Maarten Peeters is PhD in Law, KU Leuven, Belgium, and Project Manager at KBC Bank.

David Ramos is Professor of Commercial Law at Universidad Carlos III de Madrid, Spain, Visiting Scholar at University of Bologna, Italy, and Alternate Member of the Appeal Panel of the Single Resolution Board.

Wolf-Georg Ringe is Director of the Institute of Law & Economics at the University of Hamburg, Germany, and Visiting Professor at the University of Oxford, United Kingdom.

Michele Siri is Full Professor of Business Law and holds a Jean Monnet Chair on EU Financial and Insurance Markets Regulation at the University of Genoa, Italy.

Arthur van den Hurk is Senior Regulatory Counsel with Aegon N.V. and Fellow at the Institute for Financial Law, Business and Law Research Centre at Radboud University Nijmegen, the Netherlands.

Emanuel van Praag is attorney-at-law with HVG Law LLP Amsterdam and Senior Fellow at the Erasmus School of Law Rotterdam, the Netherlands.

Mirik van Rijn is PhD Researcher and Financial Law Lecturer at the Institute for Financial Law of Radboud University, the Netherlands.

Tom Vos is PhD Researcher at the Jan Ronse Institute for Company and Financial Law at KU Leuven, Belgium.

Marc-David Weinberger is Research Assistant with the Economic Law Unit of the Centre for Private Law at the Université libre de Bruxelles, Belgium, and practicing attorney at the Brussels Bar.

Marieke Wyckaert is Professor of Company Law at KU Leuven, Belgium, and practicing attorney at the Brussels Bar.

Eddy Wymeersch is Professor at Ghent University, Belgium.

LIST OF ABBREVIATIONS

AIFMD	Directive 2011/61/EU of the European Parliament and of the Council of 8 June 2011 on Alternative Investment Fund Managers and amending Directives 2003/41/EC and 2009/65/EC and Regulations (EC) No 1060/2009 and (EU) No 1095/2010 [2011] OJ L174/1
AIFMR	Commission Delegated Regulation (EU) No 231/2013 of 19 December 2012 supplementing Directive 2011/61/EU of the European Parliament and of the Council with regard to exemptions, general operating conditions, depositaries, leverage, transparency and supervision [2013] OJ L83/1
BRRD	Directive 2014/59/EU of the European Parliament and of the Council of 15 May 2014 establishing a framework for the recovery and resolution of credit institutions and investment firms and amending Council Directive 82/891/EEC, and Directives 2001/24/EC, 2002/47/EC, 2004/25/EC, 2005/56/EC, 2007/36/EC, 2011/35/EU, 2012/30/EU and 2013/36/EU, and Regulations (EU) No 1093/2010 and (EU) No 648/2012, of the European Parliament and of the Council [2014] OJ L173/190
CCD	Directive 2008/48/EC of the European Parliament and of the Council of 23 April 2008 on credit agreements for consumers and repealing Council Directive 87/102/EEC [2014] OJ L133/66
CRA Regulation	Regulation (EC) No 1060/2009 of the European Parliament and of the Council of 16 September 2009 on credit rating agencies [2009] OJ L302/1
CRD IV (Directive)	Directive 2013/36/EU of the European Parliament and of the Council of 26 June 2013 on access to the activity of credit institutions and the prudential supervision of credit institutions and investment firms, amending Directive 2002/87/EC and repealing Directives 2006/48/EC and 2006/49/EC [2013] OJ L176/338
CRR	Regulation (EU) No 575/2013 of the European Parliament and of the Council of 26 June 2013 on prudential requirements for credit institutions and investment firms and amending Regulation (EU) No 648/2012 [2013] OJ L176/1

CSD Regulation	Regulation (EU) No 909/2014 of the European Parliament and of the Council of 23 July 2014 on improving securities settlement in the European Union and on central securities depositories and amending Directives 98/26/EC and 2014/65/EU and Regulation (EU) No 236/2012 [2014] OJ L257/1
DGS Directive	Directive 2014/49/EU of the European Parliament and of the Council of 16 April 2014 on deposit guarantee schemes [2014] OJ L173/149
DMD	Directive 2002/65/EC of the European Parliament and of the Council of 23 September 2002 concerning the distance marketing of consumer financial services and amending Council Directive 90/619/EEC and Directives 97/7/EC and 98/27/EC [2002] OJ L271/16
Draft Crowdfunding Regulation	Proposal for a Regulation of the European Parliament and of the Council on European Crowdfunding Service Providers (ECSP) for Business, Interinstitutional File: 2018/0048(COD)
EBA Regulation	Regulation (EU) No 1093/2010 of the European Parliament and of the Council of 24 November 2010 establishing a European Supervisory Authority (European Banking Authority), amending Decision No 716/2009/EC and repealing Commission Decision 2009/78/EC [2010] OJ L331/12
EIOPA Regulation	Regulation (EU) No 1094/2010 of the European Parliament and of the Council of 24 November 2010 establishing a European Supervisory Authority (European Insurance and Occupational Pensions Authority), amending Decision No 716/2009/EC and repealing Commission Decision 2009/79/EC [2010] OJ L331/48
EMIR	Regulation (EU) No 648/2012 of the European Parliament and of the Council of 4 July 2012 on OTC derivatives, central counterparties and trade repositories [2012] OJ L201/1
ESMA Regulation	Regulation (EU) No 1095/2010 of the European Parliament and of the Council of 24 November 2010 establishing a European Supervisory Authority (European Securities and Markets Authority), amending Decision No 716/2009/EC and repealing Commission Decision 2009/77/EC [2010] OJ L331/84
ESRB Regulation	Regulation (EU) No 1092/2010 of the European Parliament and of the Council of 24 November 2010 on European Union macro-prudential oversight of the financial system and establishing a European Systemic Risk Board [2010] OJ L331/1

ICS Directive	Directive 97/9/EC of the European Parliament and of the Council of 3 March 1997 on investor-compensation schemes [1997] OJ L84/22
IDD	Directive (EU) 2016/97 of the European Parliament and of the Council of 20 January 2016 on insurance distribution (recast) [2016] OJ L26/19
IDD Delegated IBIPs Regulation	Commission Delegated Regulation (EU) 2017/2359 of 21 September 2017 supplementing Directive (EU) 2016/97 of the European Parliament and of the Council with regard to information requirements and conduct of business rules applicable to the distribution of insurance-based investment products [2017] OJ L341/8
IFD	Proposal for a Directive of the European Parliament and of the Council on the prudential supervision of investment firms and amending Directives 2013/36/EU and 2014/65/EU, Interinstitutional File: 2017/0358(COD), (Presidency Compromise proposal of 19 March 2019)
IFR	Proposal for a Regulation of the European Parliament and of the Council on the prudential requirements of investment firms and amending Regulations (EU) No 575/2013, (EU) No 600/2014 and (EU) No 1093/2010 (Interinstitutional File: 2017/0359(COD), (Presidency Compromise proposal of 19 March 2019)
IMD	Directive 2002/92/EC of the European Parliament and of the Council of 9 December 2002 on insurance mediation [2003] OJ L9/3
IORP I	Directive 2003/41/EC of the European Parliament and of the Council of 3 June 2003 on the activities and supervision of institutions for occupational retirement provision [2003] OJ L235/10
IORP II	Directive (EU) 2016/2341 of the European Parliament and of the Council of 14 December 2016 on the activities and supervision of institutions for occupational retirement provision (IORPs) [2016] OJ L354/37
MCD	Directive 2014/17/EU of the European Parliament and of the Council of 4 February 2014 credit agreements for consumers relating to residential immovable property and amending Directives 2008/48/EC and 2013/36/EU and Regulation (EU) No 1093/2010 [2014] OJ L60/34
MiFID I	Directive 2004/39/EC of the European Parliament and of the Council of 21 April 2004 on markets in financial instruments amending Council Directives 85/611/EEC and 93/6/EEC and Directive 2000/12/EC of the European Parliament and of the Council and repealing Council Directive 93/22/EEC [2004] OJ L145/1

MiFID I Implementing Directive   Commission Directive 2006/73/EC of 10 August 2006 implementing Directive 2004/39/EC of the European Parliament and of the Council as regards organisational requirements and operating conditions for investment firms and defined terms for the purposes of that Directive [2006] OJ L241/26

MiFID II   Directive 2014/65/EU of the European Parliament and of the Council of 15 May 2014 on markets in financial instruments and amending Directive 2002/92/EC and Directive 2011/61/EU [2014] OJ L173/349

MiFID II Delegated Directive   Commission Delegated Directive (EU) 2017/593 of 7 April 2016 supplementing Directive 2014/65/EU of the European Parliament and of the Council with regard to safeguarding of financial instruments and funds belonging to clients, product governance obligations and the rules applicable to the provision or reception of fees, commissions or any monetary or non-monetary benefits [2017] OJ L87/500

MiFIR   Regulation (EU) No 600/2014 of the European Parliament and of the Council of 15 May 2014 on markets in financial instruments and amending Regulation (EU) No 648/2012 [2012] OJ L173/84

PEPP Regulation   Regulation (EU) No 2019/1238 of the European Parliament and of the Council of 20 June 2019 on a pan-European Personal Pension Product (PEPP) [2019] OJ L198/1

PRIIPs Regulation   Regulation (EU) No 1286/2014 of the European Parliament and of the Council of 26 November 2014 on key information documents for packaged retail and insurance-based investment products (PRIIPs) [2014] OJ L352/1

PSD II   Directive (EU) 2015/2366 of the European Parliament and of the Council of 25 November 2015 on payment services in the internal market, amending Directives 2002/65/EC, 2009/110/EC and 2013/36/EU and Regulation (EU) No 1093/2010, and repealing Directive 2007/64/EC

Solvency II   Directive 2009/138/EC of the European Parliament and of the Council of 25 November 2009 on the taking-up and pursuit of the business of Insurance and Reinsurance (Solvency II) [2009] OJ L335/1

SRM Regulation   Regulation (EU) No 806/2014 of the European Parliament and of the Council of 15 July 2014 establishing uniform rules and a uniform procedure for the resolution of credit institutions and certain investment firms in the framework of a Single Resolution Mechanism and a Single Resolution Fund and amending Regulation (EU) No 1093/2010 [2014] OJ L225/1

SSM Regulation	Regulation (EU) No 468/2014 of the European Central Bank of 16 April 2014 establishing the framework for cooperation within the Single Supervisory Mechanism between the European Central Bank and national competent authorities and with national designated authorities (SSM Framework Regulation) [2014] OJ L141/1
TEU	Consolidated version of the Treaty on European Union [2012] OJ C326/13
TFEU	Consolidated version of the Treaty on the Functioning of the European Union [2012] OJ C326/47
UCITS Directive	Consolidated version of Directive 2009/65/EC of the European Parliament and of the Council of 13 July 2009 on the coordination of laws, regulations and administrative provisions relating to undertakings for collective investment in transferable securities (UCITS) Directive (recast) [2009] OJ L302/32
UCPD	Directive 2005/29/EC of the European Parliament and of the Council of 11 May 2005 concerning unfair business-to-consumer commercial practices in the internal market and amending Council Directive 84/450/EEC, Directives 97/7/EC, 98/27/EC and 2002/65/EC of the European Parliament and of the Council and Regulation (EC) No 2006/2004 of the European Parliament and of the Council ('Unfair Commercial Practices Directive') [2005] OJ L149/22
UCTD	Council Directive 93/13/EEC of 5 April 1993 on unfair terms in consumer contracts [1993] OJ L95/29

PART I

Conceptual Framework

1

Regulating Finance in a Post-Sectoral World: Setting the Scene

VEERLE COLAERT AND DANNY BUSCH

I. Problem Statement

Financial regulation[1] as we know it today mirrors the traditional structure of the financial industry. In most legal systems, it is thus divided into banking, insurance and investment services law.[2] In recent decades however, the clear separation between financial sectors has gradually evaporated, as business lines have converged across sectors.[3] This evolution has been noticeable at the level of service providers, products and distribution channels. In the current environment, credit institutions, investment firms and insurance companies are typically vying for the same customers with similar products and through an identical set of distribution channels.[4] Specific terminologies have been created to capture this phenomenon: 'Allfinanz'-strategies and -products, 'bancassurance', 'assurfinance' and even 'bancassurfinance'.[5]

As the contours of the traditional *tripartition* in the financial industry faded, the diverging regulatory and supervisory treatment of these sectors has become increasingly at odds with economic reality. This has caused certain marked inefficiencies. In a sectorally organised regulatory model the qualification of a particular institution, product or service as either a banking, investment or insurance institution, product or service is the decisive determinant to establish the applicable legal framework. Different rules may thus apply to institutions, products or services based solely on their classification in one of the traditional sectors, without each of these

---

[1] In this contribution and in the conclusion, we use the term European 'regulation' as encompassing both formal legislation (European regulations and directives) and supervisory guidance (such as guidelines from the European Supervisory Authorities). Similarly the term 'regulator' refers both to the formal legislator and the supervisor issuing supervisory guidance.

[2] Part of this introduction is based on a previous contribution, which features more detail and a historic overview. See V Colaert, 'European banking, securities and insurance law: cutting through sectoral lines?' (2015) *Common Market Law Review* at 1579–1583.

[3] Basel Committee on Banking Supervision, 'The Joint Forum Core Principles. Cross-Sectoral Comparison' (November 2001), www.bis.org/publ/joint03.pdf at 8–9.

[4] E Ferran, N Moloney, J Hill and J Coffee, *The Regulatory Aftermath of the Global Financial Crisis* (Cambridge, CUP, 2012) at xvii.

[5] Among others: Colaert, 'European banking, securities and insurance law: cutting through sectoral lines?' (fn2) at 1583; M Schüler, 'The emerging role of single financial authorities – Germany', in D Masciandaro (ed), *Handbook of Central Banking and Financial Authorities in Europe* (Cheltenham, Edgar Elgar, 2005) 292; M Tison (ed), *Bancassurfinance (cahiers AEDBF/EVBRF-Belgium)* (Bruylant 2000) 3.

differences necessarily being substantiated from an economic point of view. For financial institutions offering a wide range of products or services, such a regulatory approach is not efficient as different processes will need to be implemented depending on the formal sector in which the product or service is to be classified. For retail customers, it may moreover be confusing if different standards are applicable to very similar situations. Unjustified differences between banking, investment services and insurance legislation, which do not correspond to differences in the economic characteristics of the institution, product or service, finally also create a fertile breeding ground for regulatory arbitrage, meaning that market participants exploit gaps and inconsistencies in different sets of regulation applicable to economically very similar situations, with a view to avoiding the stricter regulatory framework.[6] In France, for instance, sales of unit-linked life insurance have increased following the implementation of the Markets in Financial Instruments Directive 2004 (MiFID), to the detriment of direct sales of units in investment funds.[7] For the sale of units in investment funds the strict MiFID conduct of business rules applied, whereas the sale of unit-linked life insurance products was subject to the much lighter regime of the Insurance Mediation Directive.[8] The so-called 'shadow banking' sector has also been cited as engaging in 'bank-like' credit intermediation without being subject to the strict rules that apply to banks.[9]

In addition, the financial industry is continuously developing new ways of intermediation (such as crowdfunding, P2P lending and other FinTech techniques) and new financial products and services (eg in relation to virtual currencies). Regulators are struggling to determine whether those new techniques and products are already covered by existing regulation and, if not, whether they should be, and if so, how.[10] One of the problems is that such new techniques and products are not always easily qualified as banking, investment or insurance platforms, products or services, which results in gaps and inefficiencies.

It follows from the above that the current sectoral approach has some clear inefficiencies. It raises the question whether a more cross-sectoral approach to (a number of areas of) EU financial regulation would be feasible[11] and more efficient.[12]

---

[6] J Kremers, D Schoenmakers and P Wierts, 'Cross-sector supervision: Which model?' in R Herring and R Litan (eds), *Brookings-Wharton Papers on Financial Services* (Washington DC, Brookings Institution Press, 2003), 241; E Avgouleas, *Governance of Global Financial Markets: The Law, the Economics, the Politics* (Cambridge, CUP, 2012) at 311.

[7] European Commission, 'Open Hearing on Retail Investment Products' (2008) at 11; see also at 17, where several examples of regulatory arbitrage in the Netherlands are given, and at 16, where Eddy Wymeersch, chairman of CESR at the time, argued that regulatory arbitrage has been seen on a massive scale through the growth of the certificate market. See for other concrete examples: N Moloney, *EU Securities and Financial Markets Regulation* (Oxford, OUP, 2014) at 780, fn 71.

[8] Directive 2002/92/EC of the European Parliament and of the Council of 9 December 2002 on insurance mediation [2003] OJ L9. This Directive has in the meanwhile been replaced by the Insurance Distribution Dir (EU) 2016/97 of the European Parliament and of the Council of 20 January 2016 on insurance distribution (recast) [2016] OJ L26.

[9] See Financial Stability Board, 'Shadow Banking: Scoping the Issues' (12 April 2011) at 5; Financial Stability Board, 'Shadow Banking: Strengthening Oversight and Regulation. Recommendations of the Financial Stability Board' (27 October 2011) at 13; Communication from the Commission to the Council and the European Parliament, 'Shadow Banking – Addressing new sources of risk in the Financial Sector' (COM/2013/0614 final).

[10] See, eg, European Commission, 'Consultation on Crowdfunding in the EU – exploring the added value of potential EU action' (3 October 2013); EBA, 'Opinion on lending-based crowd-funding' (EBA/Op/2015/03, 26 February 2015); European Commission, 'FinTech Action plan: For a more competitive and innovative European financial sector' (COM/2018/109final, 8 March 2018). See also the national reports on P2P lending, published in the Journal of European Markets and Consumer Law ((2016), issue 4 (at 181–190) and issue 5 (at 222–228)), evidencing very divergent interpretations on the applicability of the traditional regulatory framework to P2P lending.

[11] The feasibility test seeks to determine whether similarities between problems, risks and regulatory answers in the various financial sectors can be established and translated into a cross-sectoral regulatory approach.

[12] The efficiency test seeks to answer the question of whether the (long-term) benefits of a cross-sectoral approach outweigh the cost, including both the potential adverse effects of a cross-sectoral approach, and the (one-off) costs of a regulatory overhaul. The authors would like to thank Georg Ringe for bringing into the debate the need to also take into account the costs of a regulatory overhaul.

II. State of the Art

A. Structure of Financial Supervision

In academic literature the question of whether financial supervision should be structured in a sectoral or cross-sectoral manner has been the topic of a heated debate. In view of the blurring lines between the traditional sectors and the gaps and overlaps resulting from sectoral supervision, pleas have been made to discard the sectoral supervisory model, ie a separate supervisor for the banking, securities and insurance sectors. Alternatives include the single supervisory model, with one supervisor for the entire financial industry, or the so-called twin peaks supervisory model with two functionally competent supervisors: one conduct of business supervisor for the entire financial industry and one prudential supervisor for the entire industry.[13] Several Member States have indeed reformed their supervisory structure to ensure a consistent level of supervisory scrutiny across the financial sectors and to avoid supervisory arbitrage.[14] The European System of Financial Supervision (ESFS), however, remains structured along sectoral lines, mimicking the sectoral nature of EU financial regulation.[15] The only exception to the sectoral approach to financial supervision at EU-level, is the macro-prudential supervisor, the European Systemic Risk Board, which is competent across the entire financial industry.

Recently, there has been renewed attention for this topic in view of the EU review of the European Supervisory Authorities,[16] which called for a thorough re-assessment of the structure of financial supervision. In the end this review has, however, not produced major changes, and not led to an abolishment at the EU-level of a supervisory structure organised along sectoral lines.

B. Structure of Financial Regulation

Only limited attention has been devoted to the question of whether financial regulation should be structured in a more cross-sectoral or holistic manner.[17] This is surprising, as reform of the

---

[13] See, among others, J Kremers, D Schoenmakers and P Wierts, 'Cross-sector supervision: Which model?' in R Herring and R Litan (eds), *Brookings-Wharton Papers on Financial Services* (Washington DC, Brookings Institution Press, 2003), 241; E Wymeersch, 'The Structure of Financial Supervision in Europe: About single, twin peaks and multiple financial supervisors' (2007) *EBOR* 237–305; J de Luna Martinez and T Rose, 'International Survey of Integrated Financial Sector Supervision' (World Bank Policy Research Working Paper 3096, July 2003) 44; R Herring and J Carmassi, 'The Structure of Cross-sector Financial Supervision' (2008) 17 *Financial Markets, Institutions & Instruments* 51–76; O Erdélyi, *Twin Peaks for Europe. State-of-the-Art Financial Supervisory Consolidation: Rethinking the Group Support Regime Under Solvency II* (Cham, Springer, 2016); Colaert, 'European banking, securities and insurance law: cutting through sectoral lines?' (fn 2) at 1584–1594.

[14] For an overview of supervisory structure in the different Member States, see European Central Bank, 'Recent developments in supervisory structures in the EU Member States (2007–2010)', Oct 2010. Since this document was published, supervisory structures in several Member States have been reformed again. Belgium, Germany and the UK are, for instance, still mentioned in this study as adhering to the integrated supervisory model, but have since evolved towards a twin peaks model.

[15] As part of the European System of Financial Supervision three European Supervisory Authorities (ESAs) have been established, one for each of the financial sectors: the European Banking Authority (EBA), the European Insurance and Occupational Pensions Authority (EIOPA) and the European Securities and Markets Authority (ESMA). These Authorities however work together in a 'Joint Committee on cross-sectoral matters'. See also Colaert, 'European banking, securities and insurance law: cutting through sectoral lines?' (fn 2) at 1589.

[16] European Commission, 'Public consultation on the operations of the European supervisory authorities. DG for Financial Stability, Financial Services and Capital Markets Union' (21 March 2017) https://ec.europa.eu/info/sites/info/files/2017-esas-operations-consultation-document_en.pdf.

[17] See J Armour et al, *Principles of Financial Regulation* (Oxford, OUP, 2016) 10–11; Colaert, 'European banking, securities and insurance law: cutting through sectoral lines?' (fn 2) at 1583–1584.

supervisory architecture can only have limited efficacy as long as financial legislation does not take the same approach.

i. *The International Scene*

Almost two decades ago the Basel Committee on Banking Supervision, the International Organization of Securities Commissions (IOSCO) and the International Association of Insurance Supervision (IAIS), undertook a cross-sectoral comparison of their Core Principles in order to identify common principles and understand differences where they arose.[18] This comparison indicated an important common ground in the principles applying to the three sectors of the financial industry, alongside substantial differences. However, these international organisations did not take the next step, ie to draft joint principles for the entire financial industry. A similar exercise has not been undertaken ever since.

However, with regard to a more limited aspect of financial regulation – resolution of financial institutions – the Financial Stability Board (FSB) has taken a cross-sectoral approach. In 2011 it published 12 cross-sectoral key attributes for resolution of financial institutions of all types that would create systemic risk in case of failure.[19] The initial key-attributes were further refined in 2014. While the 12 key attributes were considered to remain the umbrella-standard for resolution regimes covering financial institutions of all types, further guidance has been developed, inter alia, with a view to accommodating sector-specific considerations.[20]

ii. *The EU and its Member States*

In 2002 the Netherlands was one of the first jurisdictions to introduce the so-called 'twin peaks' *supervisory* model. In 2006 the legislator aligned Dutch financial *legislation* with this cross-sectoral supervisory model.[21] It introduced one financial code for the entire financial industry, applicable since 1 January 2007, and structured this code in a functional rather than a sectoral manner.[22] This attempt for a more functional approach to financial regulation was, however, seriously hampered by the sectoral approach of European directives, which the Netherlands had to implement in their national financial code.[23] In 2016, after a public consultation with regard to the question of

---

[18] Basel Committee on Banking Supervision, 'The Joint Forum Core Principles. Cross-Sectoral Comparison' (November 2001), www.bis.org/publ/joint03.pdf.

[19] FSB, 'Key Attributes of Effective Resolution Regimes for Financial Institutions' (October 2011), www.fsb.org/wp-content/uploads/r_111104cc.pdf.

[20] FSB, 'Key Attributes of Effective Resolution Regimes for Financial Institutions' (15 October 2014), www.fsb.org/wp-content/uploads/r_141015.pdf. The authors would like to thank Jens Binder for bringing those Key Attributes to the attention of the authors at the KU Leuven kick-off meeting of this book project on 6 and 7 February 2017.

[21] Act of 28 September 2006 on financial supervision. See for a thorough overview: C Grundmann-van de Krol, *Koersen door de wet op het financieel toezicht* (Boom Juridische Uitgevers 2012). The author explains at p 14 that this legislative overhaul represented a second step in the evolution needed to adapt Dutch financial law to the functional structure of financial supervision.

[22] For an overview of other Member States that took a partially cross-sectoral approach in their national financial legislation, see ch 5 of this book.

[23] C Grundmann-van de Krol, 'Betere Europese regelgeving – een nieuwe opzet van de Wft in het verschiet?' (2007) *Ondernemingsrecht*, 549–550; A J A D van den Hurk, Een toekomstbestendige en inzichtelijke Wft, *Tijdschrift voor Financieel Recht* 2015, 365–366.

whether the Dutch financial code is futureproof the Dutch Ministry of Finance decided to leave the functional structure of the Dutch financial code unchanged.[24]

Several other Member States took more limited cross-sectoral measures in the field of product information,[25] in order to tackle problems of regulatory arbitrage. The result was an un-level playing field in the EU, with different product information measures applying to similar products in different Member States. EU intervention was therefore almost inevitable.[26]

In its reaction, the EU legislature explicitly recognised the limits of sectoral financial regulation and announced that it would take steps towards a more cross-sectoral approach in respect of (i) product information and (ii) conduct of business regulation.[27] With the Regulation on Packaged Retail Investment and Insurance-based Products (PRIIPs Regulation)[28] the EU indeed opted for a more cross-sectoral approach to product information, requiring the same key information document for structured deposits (banking product), insurance-based investment products (insurance product) and packaged financial instruments (investment product). This regulation has however been criticised for being too limited in scope.[29] In respect of conduct of business rules, no single cross-sectoral piece of legislation has been introduced. Although the scope of the MiFID II Directive has been widened to provide the same level of retail client protection for structured deposits (banking product) as for financial instruments (investment product),[30] insurance products remained out of the scope of MiFID II and are subject to a separate sectoral directive. The Insurance Distribution Directive (IDD) has, nevertheless, explicitly based its retail client protection rules for the sale of insurance products on the MiFID II standard.[31] However, many unsubstantiated differences remain between MiFID II and IDD.[32] The relevant level 2 and 3 measures diverge even further as a result of the fact that there is little cooperation between the European Supervisory Authorities (ESAs) which are principally responsible for the content of the MiFID II and IDD level 2 and 3 measures. It is questionable whether all these differences are indeed substantiated by the economic differences between the institutions, products and services covered by MiFID II and IDD respectively.[33]

A second EU battlefield against regulatory arbitrage has been a range of phenomena collectively referred to as the shadow banking system. After the crisis, the European Commission

---

[24] Ministerie voor Financiën, 'Herziening van de Wft: verkenning. Consultatiedocument' (22 November 2016) www.internetconsultatie.nl/herzieningwft/details, 37 p. See for an in-depth discussion of the consultation and the results: Chapter 5 of this book, especially at 97–98.

[25] See, eg, European Commission, 'Feedback Statement on contributions to the call for evidence on "substitute" retail investment products' (March 2008) 33–34; V Colaert, 'Investor Protection in the Capital Markets Union' in D Busch, E Avgouleas and G Ferrarini, Capital Markets Union in Europe (Oxford, OUP, 2018) at para's 16.16 and 16.17.

[26] See Colaert, 'European banking, securities and insurance law: cutting through sectoral lines?' (fn 2) at 1594.

[27] European Commission, 'White Paper Financial Services Policy 2005–2010' (5 December 2005) at 6–7; Financial Services Committee, 'Report of the FSC on Long-Term Supervisory Issues' (FSC/4162/08, 10 March 2008) in particular at 47–48.

[28] PRIIPs Regulation, [2014] OJ L352/1.

[29] V Colaert, 'Regulation of PRIIPs: Great Ambitions, Insurmountable Challenges?' (2016) 2(2) *Journal of Financial Regulation*, at 205–210.

[30] Article 1 (4) of Dir (EU) 2014/65 of the European Parliament and of the Council on markets in financial instruments and amending Dir 2002/92/EC and Dir 2011/61/EU, [2014] OJ L173/349.

[31] IDD, [2016] OJ L26/19.

[32] V Colaert, 'MiFID II in relation to other investor protection regulation: Picking up the crumbs of a piecemeal approach' in D Busch and G Ferrarini, *Regulation of the EU Financial Markets: MiFID II and MiFIR* (Oxford, OUP, 2017) at 590–599.

[33] Ibid. See on this question, Chapters 14A, 14B and 15 of this book.

described and assessed the problem in a Communication.[34] This has been followed up by a number of changes in existing legislation,[35] but has not sparked a fundamental debate on the scope and structure of EU financial regulation at large. As a result, no steps have been taken to tackle unsubstantiated differences in governance rules, prudential regulation, resolution regimes, etc.

A third EU initiative worth mentioning in this context is the European Commission's 'cross-sectoral study on terminology as defined in the EU financial services legislation'.[36] This study was very broad in scope in terms of the directives and regulations included, but only focused on a limited number of definitions. Moreover, the study is now largely outdated as it appeared prior to the avalanche of post-crisis regulation.

Fourth, in September 2015, the European Commission initiated a comprehensive review of the cumulative impact and coherence of the financial legislation adopted in response to the financial crisis. The purpose of this review was to assess the overall coherence of the existing framework.[37] This review, however, explicitly aimed at 'specific and targeted change', rather than a fundamental rethinking of EU financial regulation as a whole.[38]

Finally, in a most recent development, the European legislator is implementing its 2018 Sustainable Finance Action Plan. While many cross-sectoral pieces of financial regulation are being amended, Parliament and Council have also agreed on a new cross-sectoral Regulation on sustainability-related disclosures in the financial services sector.[39]

C. FinTech

The relatively recent FinTech revolution has created new challenges for both legislators and financial supervisors. In the absence of a clear EU regulatory response with regard to the question of whether different types of FinTech are covered by existing pieces of EU financial regulation,[40] Member States have made their own interpretations, and sometimes introduced national rules to cover FinTech techniques.[41]

The European Commission recognised this situation in its Action Plan on FinTech and has decided to invite the European Supervisory Authorities (ESAs) to start a mapping exercise

---

[34] European Commission, 'Communication to the Council and the European Parliament. Shadow Banking – Addressing New Sources of Risk in the Financial sector' (Brussels, 4 September 2013, COM(2013) 614 final).

[35] Regulation (EU) 2015/2365 of the European Parliament and of the Council of 25 November 2015 on transparency of securities financing transactions and of reuse and amending Regulation (EU) No 648/2012.

[36] European Commission, 'Cross-sectoral study on terminology as defined in the EU financial services legislation' (2009).

[37] European Commission, Communication to the European Parliament, the Council, the European Economic and Social Committee and the Committee of the Regions – Project Plan on Building a Capital Markets Union Brussels (30 September 2015, COM(2015) 468 final).

[38] The intended research for this project will, nevertheless, benefit from the overview of the incoherencies and inefficiencies which are brought to light by this Commission review. See in this regard: European Commission, 'Communication on the call for evidence: EU regulatory framework for financial services' (COM(2016) 855 final, 23 November 2016).

[39] Regulation of the European Parliament and of the Council on sustainability-related disclosures in the financial services sector (2018/0179 (COD)), final text agreed on 23 October 2019, not yet published in Official Journal. In view of its very recent adoption, this Regulation has not been dealt with in more detail in this book.

[40] See fn 10.

[41] See in respect of P2P lending, the divergent national interpretations of whether, among other things, the national implementation of the Capital Requirements Directive and of the Consumer Credit Directive are applicable, and whether that Member State has taken specific measures: the national reports on P2P lending, published in the Journal of European Markets and Consumer Law ((2016), issue 4 (at 181–190) and issue 5 (at 222–228)).

in respect of current authorising and licensing approaches for innovative FinTech business models.[42] The European Commission has, moreover, presented a proposal for an EU Regulation on crowdfunding service providers (ECSP) for business, aiming at establishing a European label for investment- and lending-based crowdfunding platforms that enables cross-border activity and seeks to address risks in a proportionate manner.[43]

Lately, much research has been devoted to the question of whether particular FinTech techniques are covered by specific pieces of EU financial regulation.[44] However, the question of whether a more cross-sectoral approach to regulation would be part of the answer to the question of whether and how to regulate innovative products, services and intermediaries, has not yet been raised.[45]

D. Gap in the Literature

Several policy documents have discussed the problem of regulatory arbitrage in specific areas[46] and FinTech as such is an important new area of research. Apart from a more general article in the *Common Market Law Review*,[47] EU financial regulation has not yet been thoroughly examined from the perspective of a cross-sectoral level playing field. The goal of this book is to fill this gap. Subject by subject this book establishes to what extent it would be feasible and useful to redesign EU financial regulation and supervision in a cross-sectoral manner.

III. Research Method

In order to answer this question – ie whether a more cross-sectoral approach to EU financial regulation would be feasible and useful – the main areas of EU financial regulation will be analysed from a cross-sectoral perspective. For each specific theme, similarities as well as gaps, overlaps and unjustifiable differences between banking, securities and insurance regulation will be charted. This approach will increase insight into the regulatory answers to similar problems across sectors, making it easier to streamline compliance processes and providing a solid basis for a number of normative conclusions on the way forward for EU financial regulation. The ultimate goal is (i) to reveal common principles applicable to the entire industry and (ii) to determine to what extent, on top of those common principles, differentiation is necessary for specific institutions, products and services.

This research method is different from the traditional legal analysis with respect to financial regulation: instead of examining and interpreting the rules sector per sector and directive per

---

[42] European Commission, 'FinTech Action Plan' (fn 10) at 7.

[43] Proposal for a Regulation of the European Parliament and of the Council on European Crowdfunding Service Providers (ECSP) for Business (COM(2018) 113 final), Explanatory Memorandum at 2. The Council issued a heavily amended compromise proposal on 24 June 2019 (Council 10557/19).

[44] Apart from the references in fn 10, see also in respect of virtual currencies, R Böhme, N Christin, B Edelman and T Moore, 'Bitcoin: Economics, Technology, and Governance (2015) 29 (2) *Journal of Economic Perspectives* 213–238; N Vandezande, *Regulating virtual currencies* (accepted for publication: Intersentia, 2018).

[45] An exception should be made for non-financial regulation, such as the General Data Protection Regulation and the Anti-Money Laundering Directive, which is explicitly mentioned in the Commission's FinTech Action Plan as applicable to FinTech. See European Commission, 'FinTech Action Plan' (fn 10) at 2–3. See Chapter 4 of this book for an answer to the research question.

[46] See fn 9.

[47] V Colaert, 'European banking, securities and insurance law: Cutting through sectoral lines?' (fn 3) at 1579–1616.

directive, EU financial regulation will be approached – in line with the research hypothesis – in a cross-sectoral and functional manner. After an examination of the fundamental conditions of a cross-sectoral approach, the research will thus be structured on the basis of the main areas which are typically regulated in financial regulation: (i) prudential regulation; (ii) consumer protection; and (iii) financial supervision.

For each area the existing sector- and institution-specific legislation will be examined in order to detect on the one hand common concepts and principles and on the other hand the differences in concepts and rules. Differences will be thoroughly examined in order to distinguish between (i) differences which are useful in view of different functions, characteristics or risks of the regulated entities, services or products; and (ii) unsubstantiated differences which cannot be justified on the basis of different functions, characteristics or risks in the regulated entities, services or products.

IV. Research Hypothesis

The research hypothesis of this project is that there is a sufficient degree of similarity in functions, problems and regulatory goals, to make it feasible to apply a number of common concepts and principles across the financial industry, even though certain differences in functions, characteristics and risks of financial institutions, products and services may still require different detailed requirements, on top of, or even deviating from, common concepts and principles.

V. Overview of this Book

This book has been set up as follows.

The ***first part*** lays down the *foundations* of a cross-sectoral approach to financial regulation in order to find an answer to the question of whether there are indeed sufficient similarities in functions and goals in the different sectors of the financial industry to allow for a meaningful cross-sectoral approach. This part includes research into the different functions of the financial industry, the configuration of goals of financial regulation in each of the sectors, an evaluation of whether, and to what extent, (sectoral) regulation appropriately covers different types of financial innovation (FinTech), and a study of the problems and limitations encountered by the Dutch attempt to restructure financial regulation in a more cross-sectoral manner.

In the ***second part*** different aspects of EU *prudential regulation* are systematically compared in order to assess what differences are substantiated on the basis of different functions, characteristics or risks of those institutions and what differences are accidental, unjustified and potentially detrimental to efficiency. This part features chapters on macro-prudential stability, capital requirements, corporate governance, recovery and resolution requirements, guarantee systems and outsourcing.[48]

---

[48] Financial regulation typically serves both stability and customer protection objectives. It is usually clear, however, what the main objective of a certain rule is, and what is the more indirect objective. In respect of the rules on outsourcing it is more difficult to decide what is the main objective. We have decided to place this chapter in the part on financial stability, since it is closely related to corporate governance, which is typically considered to primarily be part of prudential regulation.

In the ***third part*** EU financial regulation dealing with *customer protection* is compared across the sectors of the financial industry, ie assessing what differences are substantiated and what differences are accidental, unjustified and potentially detrimental to efficiency. This part also draws the link with general consumer law. It includes chapters on the scope of protection of EU financial regulation, product information, regulatory duties of care, assist-your-customer requirements, conflicts of interest and inducements, and product intervention.

The ***fourth part*** deals with supervision and the internal market. A first chapter examines the different models for an *institutional architecture* of financial regulation and supervision. Taking into account the research results of the previous parts, this chapter attempts to establish (i) which model of financial supervision would be the most appropriate for the EU, and what the chances are for it to actually be adopted; (ii) what are the possible alternatives to improve the current EU system of financial supervision if the ideal model proves difficult to attain in practice, and (iii) how different institutional models at EU Member State level and at EU (supranational) level can coexist. A second chapter assesses how cross-border activities are regulated in different directives.

In the ***last part***, we provide a summary of the book, with conclusions for each part, in order to conclude to what extent our initial research hypothesis has been confirmed or refuted.

2

Functioning of the Financial Industry

MONIKA MARCINKOWSKA

I. Introduction

This chapter will offer a general presentation of the functions of the financial industry. The starting point will be the definition of the financial system and its components. We will present a general overview of the functions of the financial system and the risks to which it is exposed, after which we will discuss the exact activities, functions and risks of the main financial institutions – banks, insurance companies, investment funds, and pension funds – and of the less regulated shadow banking system and FinTech.

The purpose of this chapter is to combine a functional approach with an institutional perspective, in order to determine how and to what extent different types of financial institutions perform the same functions.

Our research hypothesis is that to a certain extent the activities of different types of institutions overlap, and fulfil similar functions of the financial system. This chapter will therefore present the scope of activities of the different financial institutions, as well as the risks undertaken by them. Changes to the nature and structure of the financial system – stemming from financial and technological innovations – will also be signalled. This should provide a solid basis for a discussion of the desired goals and structure of future financial regulations.

II. Financial System and Institutions – Functions and Risks

A. Definition and Structure of the Financial System

The financial system is a complex structure consisting of:[1]

- financial markets,
- financial institutions (intermediaries), and
- financial authorities (regulators and supervisors).

---

[1] See also FJ Fabozzi and PP Drake, *Finance. Capital markets, Financial Management, and Investment Management* (Hoboken, John Wiley & Sons, 2009) 4.

In a narrow sense, the financial system's role is to facilitate the transfer of resources from savers or investors ('surplus units') to borrowers who need funds ('deficit units').[2] The financial system transforms savings of households, companies and governments into funds available for investment (or consumption). More broadly speaking, the financial system serves to execute any financial transaction, including payments, settlements, hedging, etc.

A financial market is defined either in terms of players (market participants), or as a place (an infrastructure). In the first meaning a financial market is a collection of traders who compete to buy financial products (debt, equities, currencies, derivatives) offered by issuing entities (companies, central and local governments and others). Any entity can be a market participant: individuals (natural persons), companies, central and local governments, or non-government organisations.

In the second meaning a financial market is a 'place' where financial instruments are exchanged (traded).[3] This also includes the infrastructure, needed to execute transactions.[4] The financial market infrastructure includes: payment systems, central securities depositories, securities settlement systems, central counterparties, and trade repositories.[5]

Financial markets can be seen as a platform for a direct exchange of funds between trusted parties. However, due to several market frictions – the most important ones being information asymmetry and high transaction costs[6] – financial intermediaries are necessary. These institutions create more favourable transaction terms than could be realised by lenders (investors) and borrowers dealing directly with each other.[7] They obtain funds from surplus units (savers, lenders, investors) and invest them in deficit units (borrowers). The funds that a financial intermediary acquires are its liabilities. The funds lent or invested by a financial intermediary are its assets.

Financial intermediaries can be narrowly or broadly defined, depending on one's view of a financial market. Financial intermediaries in the narrow sense are traditional 'bank-like' intermediaries. These firms borrow from large numbers of agents (using debt contracts) and lend to large numbers of clients (also using debt contracts).[8] As the borrowing and lending groups are large – and therefore substantial granularity (fragmentation) takes place – the intermediary institution diversifies its assets and liabilities. It should be noted that the claims issued to borrowers and to lenders have different state contingent payoffs,[9] resulting in the transformation of funds' size, terms, currency, etc.[10] Financial intermediaries therefore have an important role to play in alleviating trade frictions between borrowers and lenders.[11]

The broadest definition of financial intermediaries includes all financial institutions that mediate in the execution of a financial transaction, including both regulated financial institutions

---

[2] AWA Boot and A Thakor, 'Financial System Architecture' (1997) 10 *The Review of Financial Studies* 693; Z Bodie, RC Merton, *Finance* (Upper Saddle River: Prentice Hall, 1998) 23.

[3] Fabozzi and Drake, *Finance* (2009).

[4] This is consistent with the broader meaning of a financial system.

[5] CPSS and IOSCO *Principles for financial market infrastructures. Disclosure framework and Assessment methodology* (BIS and OICU-IOSCO, 2012) 1.

[6] Asymmetry of information occurs when due to one's party's insufficient knowledge about the other party of the transaction makes it impossible to make accurate decisions when conducting the transaction, and leads to adverse selection and moral hazard problems. FS Mishkin, *The Economics of Money, Banking and Financial Markets*, 9th edn (Boston, Pearson, 2010) 174.

[7] Fabozzi and Drake, *Finance* (2009) 114.

[8] G Gorton and A Winton 'Financial intermediation', *NBER Working Paper series* 2002–8928.

[9] Different preferences over payoffs at the initial date and different state contingent payoffs in the future; payoffs may include amounts of different sizes, in different dates, different currencies, etc.

[10] Gorton and Winton *Financial intermediation*.

[11] LD Spajić, *Financial intermediation in Europe* (New York, Springer Science+Business Media LLC, 2002), 62.

and non-bank financial intermediaries (shadow banks).[12] They include the following institutions, performing the following functions:

- depository institutions – accept deposits and make loans; they include commercial banks, saving and loans associations, mutual savings banks and credit unions;
- contractual savings institutions – acquire funds at periodic intervals on a contractual basis and pay agreed benefits; they include insurance companies and pension funds;
- investment intermediaries – include investment firms, investment funds (collective investment funds, mutual funds), money market mutual funds (a special type of fund offering deposit-type accounts, which is therefore also categorised as a depository financial institution), investment banks (their intermediation is not based on deposits, as they intermediate in the issuance of securities) and financial vehicle corporations / special purpose entities (carrying out securitisation transactions);
- financial corporations engaged in lending – including captive finance companies,[13] money lenders (consumer credit companies), leasing and factoring companies, companies facilitating credit creation, credit insurance companies and financial guarantors.

The above catalogue is complemented by financial auxiliaries, being corporations and quasi-corporations which are engaged primarily in activities closely related to financial intermediation, but do not themselves perform an intermediation role.[14] They include companies engaged in financial transaction processing and settlement (including payment institutions), financial advisors, brokers and dealers, trustee, fiduciary and custody services, etc.

Besides the traditional financial institutions it is also worth noting the FinTech subsector, consisting of a wide range of companies offering either products and services complementary to those created by traditional financial institutions (competing with them by directly serving their customers) or tools for financial markets participants facilitating their functioning. Some technological innovations can be used by financial institutions as well as supervisors, while others can successfully replace intermediaries and financial markets, enabling direct execution of transactions. This is a substantial change for the structure and functioning of the financial system.

The last component of a financial system are authorities: regulators and supervisors.[15] They establish the rules according to which financial institutions and markets function, and control law enforcement. Their role is to ensure the efficient and effective functioning of financial markets and institutions, minimising the threat of financial crises (or at least reducing their negative effects), and thus ensuring that the financial system performs its functions (including efficient transfer of funds, promoting economic growth and reducing poverty).[16] While traditional financial institutions (banks, insurance companies, investment companies) are subject to regulations and supervision, some intermediaries are not, or only subject to partial regulation of

---

[12] See, eg, FS Mishkin, SG Eakins, *Financial Markets and Institutions*, 6th edn (Boston, Pearson, 2009) 29, www.ecb.europa.eu/stats/html/index.en.html, Financial Stability Board, *Strengthening Oversight and Regulation of Shadow Banking. Policy Framework for Strengthening Oversight and Regulation of Shadow Banking Entities*, August 2013.

[13] Specialised subsidiaries of manufacturing companies – eg car manufacturers – that finance retail purchases of parent company clients.

[14] https://stats.oecd.org/glossary/detail.asp?ID=962.

[15] In a broader sense: financial safety net.

[16] For further discussion see, eg, H Davies and D Green, *Global Financial Regulation: The Essential Guide* (Cambridge, Polity Press, 2008); JR Barth, G Caprio Jr, R Levine, *Rethinking Bank Regulation. Till Angels Govern*, (Cambridge, Cambridge University Press, 2006); obviously political will is also a necessary element – see, eg, A Admati, M Hellwig, *The bankers' new clothes: what's wrong with banking and what to do about it* (Princeton, Princeton University Press, 2013).

their activities (eg some 'shadow banks' and FinTechs). This influences the behaviour of financial institutions which may be tempted to use regulatory arbitrage, especially given the fact that they compete with less regulated or unregulated institutions offering products that may be a substitute for theirs.

The summary of the description of the financial system is shown in Figure 1, which presents its components (with the arrows indicating the flow of funds).[17] As pointed out above, FinTechs (F-T) change the structure of the system: they can either be intermediaries themselves or play an auxiliary role, co-creating market infrastructure (supporting financial institutions in customer service, enabling better use of financial markets, or creating the possibility of direct transactions by market participants, for example P2P or B2B).[18]

Figure 1   Components of the financial system

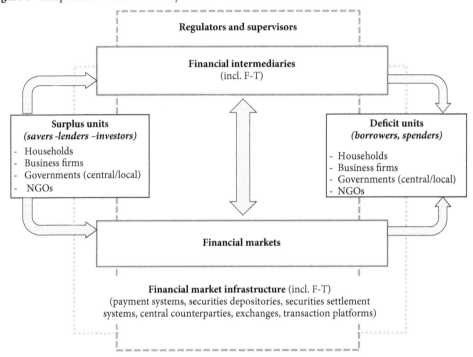

The importance of financial markets and financial intermediaries differs across countries and therefore we observe different financial system structures, depending on the history of their economies and their legal and institutional frameworks.[19] However, through financial innovation,

---

[17] The figure extends the diagrams proposed by Bodie and Merton, *Finance* 23 and Mishkin, *The Economics of Money, Banking and Financial Markets* (2010) 26.

[18] Mishkin distinguished indirect and direct finance (the first performed using intermediaries, the second on the financial market). Some types of operations offered by FinTech can be treated as new types of financial markets (new infrastructure, platforms enabling execution of transactions), or even as bypassing financial markets, ie technology-enabled direct (social) finance; the examples are P2P lending, crowdfunding, etc.

[19] See, eg, F Allen and D Gale, *Comparing Financial Systems* (Cambridge, The MIT Press, 2001) and J de Haan, S Oosterloo, D Shoenmaker, *European Financial Markets and Institutions* (Cambridge, Cambridge University Press, 2009). E Neave, *Modern Financial Systems. Theory and Applications* (Hoboken, John Wiley & Sons, 2009), 7.

technological changes, globalisation trends and the consolidation tendency (resulting in the dominance of financial conglomerates that provide a full catalogue of financial services), those structures also evolve and the differences decrease.

For the purposes of this chapter, we will not consider alternative financial institutions, in particular social banks[20] and Islamic financial institutions,[21] since they are subject to different overriding principles and behavioural and organisational factors.

B. Functions of the Financial System

According to Robert Merton, financial intermediation can be analysed either from an institutional perspective, or from a functional perspective. The first point of view concentrates on the efficiency of financial institutions (banks, insurance companies, investment companies, etc) in performing their particular intermediation services. The alternative approach starts from the functions to be performed by financial institutions and looks for the best institutional solutions.[22] The functional approach rightly recognises that the functions of the financial system must be performed regardless of existing institutional structures. Structures (institutions) are easier to adjust. Additionally, competition enforces changes in institutional structures to achieve greater efficiency in the performance of the functions of the financial system. Merton and Bodie therefore treat financial functions as exogenous factors and the institutional structure as endogenous.[23] This assumption is of critical importance in making postulates about the shape of the financial system and the regulation of its operations. It means that various financial institutions can fulfil the same or similar functions through their products and services. In other words, different products and services can be substitutes if they fulfil the same functions.[24] It is therefore important to perform a closer analysis of the functions of the financial system.

As already stated, the basic role of a financial system is to transfer funds from surplus units to those who have a deficit of funds, ie to efficiently allocate and deploy economic resources (in time and space, in an uncertain environment). Based on this, Merton formulated six core functions performed by the financial system:[25]

(1)   Providing a payments system for the exchange of goods and services.
(2)   Providing a mechanism for the pooling of funds to undertake a large-scale indivisible enterprise.
(3)   Providing a way to transfer economic resources across time and geographic regions and industries.
(4)   Providing a way to manage uncertainty and control risk.

---

[20] See, eg, R Benedikter, *Social Banking and Social Finance. Answers to Economic Crisis* (New York, Springer, 2011).
[21] See, eg, N Alam, L Gupta, B Shanmugam, *Islamic Finance. A Practical Perspective* (Cham, Palgrave Macmillan, 2017).
[22] RC Merton, 'A Functional Perspective on Financial Intermediation' (1995) 24 *Financial Management* 23.
[23] Institutional structure includes financial institutions, financial markets, products, services, organisation of operations, and supporting infrastructure (regulatory rules, the accounting system). RC Merton and Z Bodie, 'Design of Financial Systems: Towards a Synthesis of Function and Structure' (2005) 3 *Journal of Investment Management* 1.
[24] A simple comparison of the financial services industry (based on the products sold) over the decades leads to the conclusion that – despite the formal separation between the various operations performed by financial institutions – the products sold and the risks faced by modern financial institutions have become similar. See A Saunders, MM Cornett, *Financial Institutions Management. A Risk Management Approach* 6th edn (Boston, McGraw Hill/Irwin, 2008) 27–28.
[25] Merton, *Functional Perspective on Financial Intermediation* (1995). See also SB Crane et al, *The global financial system: a functional perspective* (Boston, Harvard Business School Press, 1995) 4.

(5) Providing price information that helps to coordinate decentralised decision-making in various sectors of the economy.
(6) Providing a way to deal with the asymmetric-information and incentive problems when one party to a financial transaction has information that the other party does not.

Those functions are developed in some more detail below.

The first function concerns clearing and settling payments. A payment order requiring one agent to pay another, is executed by a third party who effects a transfer of funds from the payer's to the payee's institution.[26] An efficient payment system should be timely, accessible, easy to integrate with other processes and easy to use, safe and reliable, affordable and transparent.[27] This function is (traditionally and currently) the basic function of a financial system. Efficient payment execution is fundamental to the functioning of the economy, for both enterprises and individuals. Perhaps this is why at present we are observing many innovations that contribute to the improvement and dissemination of this function.[28]

Pooling and transferring resources is the essence of every financial intermediary. As described in Figure 1, financial intermediaries gather the funds – mainly from households, but also from companies and governments – and then lend them – mainly to companies and governments, but also households. Savers and investors use the financial system to invest their wealth. A financial system should provide the opportunity to involve resources at a risk commensurate with the expected rate of return.[29] An important feature is that pooled resources can be transferred geographically (to different entities in different locations, and to different sectors) and in time. This may, in particular, mean that short-term borrowings of one financial market participants group (eg households) will be used over a long period by another group (eg business firms).

The fourth function concerns risk, which is present at every moment in the functioning of each entity. Risk management is necessary to limit its negative consequences while achieving the benefits related to its positive aspects. The very essence of financial institutions is risk management. Each financial institution takes risks and may also expose its clients to risk. The manner and scope of using this function depends on the risk appetite of an entity (it can tailor risk exposure to its preferences). One of risk management's techniques is risk transfer, where risk is allocated from one party to another (eg through insurance contracts or financial instruments like guarantees, derivatives etc).

The last two functions concern information. Financial institutions provide information which is used for decision-making. This is connected with the efficient market hypothesis, which states that if markets are perfectly competitive and there are no market frictions, then asset prices (especially the prices of securities) will be at an equilibrium that fully reflects all available information.[30]

The last function is connected to this. In real life there are usually informational differences (one party has private information that can put the other one at a disadvantage). It has already been mentioned that information asymmetry is an everyday reality of financial markets,

---

[26] EH Neave, *Modern Financial Systems* (Hoboken, Wiley, 2009) 16.

[27] Reserve Bank of Australia, *Submissions to the Financial System Inquiry*, March 2014. BIS Committee on Payment and Settlement Systems and IOSCO formulated the principles for financial market infrastructures, including standards for payment systems that are systemically important.

[28] Current regulations are to contribute to further increase innovation and foster competition in this market – they expand the circle of entities that can provide payment services.

[29] Neave, *Modern Financial Systems* (2009) 18.

[30] EF Fama, 'Efficient Capital Markets: A Review of Theory and Empirical Work' (1970) 25 *The Journal of Finance* 383.

which means that decisions are not optimal. The two basic problems arising from information asymmetry are adverse selection and moral hazard.[31] Financial intermediaries have sufficient expertise in screening potential borrowers to alleviate those problems and identify profitable lending (investment) opportunities.[32]

C. Risks of Financial Institutions

The quintessence of the functioning of any financial institution is its exposure to risk. This results directly from the functions performed by the institution, each of which directly involves making, sharing and transferring risk. As a consequence, the essence of managing a financial institution is risk management.

It should, however, be clearly noted that the often-used terms 'risk incurred by a financial institution' and 'institution's exposure to risk' are largely imprecise. Indeed, an institution takes on risk, but it can transfer it to its customers or counterparties to a significant degree. In addition, the stakeholders of the financial institution (clients, creditors, owners) would feel the serious consequences of its potential bankruptcy but are often unaware of the risks associated with relationships with financial intermediaries.[33] Therefore in consideration of the functioning of financial institutions the risk issue must be taken into account.

Risk is usually characterised by reference to the probability of an event and its consequences.[34] The risk for a financial institution arises from any transaction or business decision that entails uncertainty about the results.[35]

Risk management is a central part of a financial institution's strategic and operational management. It is the process whereby 'organisations methodically address the risks attaching to their activities with the goal of achieving sustained benefit within each activity and across the portfolio of all activities'.[36]

---

[31] JE Stiglitz and A Weiss, 'Credit Rationing in Markets with Imperfect Information' (1981) 71 *The American Economic Review* 393 and DW Diamond, 'Financial Intermediation and Delegated Monitoring' (1984) 51 *Review of Economic Studies* 393.
    Asymmetric information can create two problems:

  – before the transaction occurs: adverse selection – it may occur because the lender is not sure of the precise circumstances surrounding the loan and associated project and may select projects which are wrong (they offer a lower chance of meeting the outcomes specified by the borrower than loans for other more viable projects which are rejected); because adverse selection makes it more likely that loans might be provided to bad borrowers (with high credit risk), lenders may decide not to make any loans even though there are good potential borrowers (with low credit risk);
  – after the transaction occurs: moral hazard – is the risk (hazard) that the borrower may engage in activities that are undesirable (immoral) from the lender's point of view (reducing the probability of the loan being repaid).

See also: Mishkin, *The Economics of Money, Banking and Financial Markets* (2010) 41; K Matthews and J Thompson *The Economics of Banking* (Hoboken, Wiley, 2005) 41.
[32] X Freixas and J-Ch Rochet, *Microeconomics of Banking* (Massachusetts Institute of Technology, 1999) 29; D Diamond, 'Financial Intermediation and Delegated Monitoring' (1984) 51 *The Review of Economic Studies* 393.
[33] ISO/Guide 73 defines exposure in the broader context of stakeholders, as an 'extent to which an organization and/or stakeholder is subject to an event' – see *ISO/Guide 73 Risk management – Vocabulary*, 2009, www.iso.org/obp/ui/#iso:std:iso:guide:73:ed-1:v1:en.
[34] *ISO/Guide 73 Risk management.*
[35] G Schroeck, *Risk management and value creation in financial institutions* (Hoboken, John Wiley & Sons, 2002) 25.
[36] The Institute of Risk Management (2002) *A Risk Management Standard.*

The risk to which the entity is exposed may result from factors both external and internal to the organisation. External factors include exchange rates, interest rates, customer demand, competition, industry changes, regulations, natural events, etc. Internal factors are connected with products and services, employees and intellectual capital, internal structure and procedures, information systems, liquidity, etc.[37]

We can distinguish specific risk and market-wide (systematic, aggregate) risk.[38] The former is specific to the entity or the industry in which it operates. The latter is undiversifiable risk, which is inherent to the entire market, as it is caused by macroeconomic factors.[39]

Market-wide risk can result in systemic risk. 'Systemic financial risk is the risk that an event will trigger a loss of economic value or confidence in, and attendant increases in uncertainly about, a substantial portion of the financial system that is serious enough to quite probably have significant adverse effects on the real economy'.[40]

In addition, we can distinguish between continuous risk (caused by a factor constantly affecting the unit, eg interest rates, FX rates) and event risk (caused by a specific, discontinuous incident, eg customer/counterparty bankruptcy, asset damage, theft, cyber-attack, natural disaster).[41]

There are many types of risk, some of which are specific to a given sector. Examples of risks occurring in each financial institution (although to a different extent) are as follows:[42]

– Business risk – possibility of loss related to an incorrect business model, inherent in the institution's environment (eg competition) and operations;

– Strategic risk – the possibility of losses as a result of making unfavourable or wrong strategic decisions, lack of or improper implementation of the adopted strategy, and external environment changes and improper response to those changes;

– Country / sovereign risk – the risk that repayments to foreign lenders or investors may be interrupted because of restrictions, intervention, or interference from foreign governments;

– Market risk – the risk that changes in market prices will reduce the value of the financial institution's positions (affect the income); this includes interest rate risk, currency risk, equity risk, commodities risk etc;

– Credit risk – the risk that promised cash flows from loans and securities held by a financial institution may not be paid in full or within an agreed term;

– Liquidity risk – the risk that a sudden surge in liability withdrawals may require a financial institution to liquidate assets in a very short period of time and at less than fair market prices, or to get funding;

– Off-balance-sheet risk – the risk incurred by a financial institution as the result of activities related to its contingent assets and liabilities held off the balance sheet;

– Operational risk – the risk of loss resulting from inadequate or failed internal processes, people and systems, or from external events;

[37] Ibid.
[38] Schroeck *Risk management* (2002).
[39] Systematic risk is described as 'unknown unknowns'.
[40] Group of Ten, *Report on consolidation in the Financial Sector* 2001, 126.
[41] Schroeck *Risk management* (2002).
[42] M Crouhy, F Galai, R Mark, *Risk Management* (New York, McGraw-Hill, 2001) 34; Saunders and Cornett, *Financial Institutions Management*; UKNF, *Methodology of risk assessment framework (BION) for insurance and reinsurance undertakings*, 2018; BCBS, *Principles for the Sound Management of Operational Risk*, 2011.

- Reputational risk – the possibility of loss due to negative reception of the entity's image by its stakeholders;

- Insolvency risk – the risk that an FI may not have enough capital to offset a sudden decline in the value of its assets.

The types of activities of financial institutions (operations performed, products offered) result in a different risk profile (the degree of severity of a given type of risk).

Financial institutions need to determine their appetite for different types and levels of risk, carefully taking into consideration their organisational capacity to manage such risk.[43] Prudent risk management is a basic requirement for financial institutions. It is therefore emphasised that risk culture should have a central role in those organisations.[44]

III. Banks

A. Activities

Besides insurance, banking is the most regulated industry. Banks are licenced institutions (a bank charter is necessary to conduct certain banking activities). The regulations limit the scope of the bank's activities; some banking activities may be performed only by banks, some may also be performed by other entities subject to regulations and supervision, and some are not subject to restrictions.

Bank funding relies mainly on debt (their funding structure is characterised by high leverage). Traditionally banking is based on deposit-taking and loan-making.[45] Banks mainly acquire funds by collecting deposits and issuing debt obligations. Based on that they acquire income-earning assets, which are mainly loans and securities.[46]

The liabilities of banks include:

- term deposits (from individuals, companies, local governments, NGOs);

- current (à vista) deposits (on saving, personal and current accounts; the latter two are of transactional nature as they are used to make payments with the use of payment cards and other payment instruments);

- wholesale funding (instruments such as large denomination certificates of deposits, repurchase agreements, etc);

- bonds issued;

- borrowings from other institutions (central banks, other banks, non-financial corporations).

---

[43] International Finance Corporation, *Standards on Risk Governance in Financial Institutions*, 2012.

[44] A Caretta, F Fiordelisi, P Schwizer, *Risk culture in banking*, (Cham, Palgrave Macmillan, 2017) 18.

[45] CRR defines credit institution as 'an undertaking the business of which is to take deposits or other repayable funds from the public and to grant credits for its own account'. Regulation (EU) No 575/2013 of the European Parliament and of the Council of 26 June 2013 on prudential requirements for credit institutions and investment firms and amending Regulation (EU) No 648/2012; [2013] OJ L176/1.

[46] For broader presentation of bank activities see, eg, Mishkin *The Economics of Money, Banking* (2010); Fabozzi & Drake *Finance* (2009); Saunders and Cornett *Financial Institutions Management* (2008).

The majority of banks assets are:

- loans granted (to companies, local governments, households, NGOs);
- securities (mainly debt instruments; in some jurisdictions banks are not allowed to hold stock; the main issuers are state and local governments, other banks, and to a much smaller extent companies).

Among their assets, banks also have reserves (banks are required to maintain a certain portion of accepted deposits as a reserve on a central bank account), and deposits at other banks (usually at a 'correspondent bank'; also as interbank deposits).

Banks also conduct many off-balance-sheet activities (their scale is sometimes bigger than the bank's balance sheet), including guarantees, letters of credit, loan commitments. Those products have an insurance underwriting element, as they make future commitments to lend. Another group of off-balance-sheet items is a consequence of the bank's engagement in derivatives transactions (eg options, swaps, futures, forwards). They are usually used to actively manage risk (ie to hedge risk or to consciously expose the bank to it, in order to earn money).

The composition of a bank's assets and liabilities differs, depending on the type of banking institutions, type of clients served, historical and economic conditions, and the scope of competition in the financial sector. Commercial banks rely on retail deposits which are supplemented by wholesale funding; in some cases, non-deposit sources of funds can also be substantial. Their assets side is usually dominated by loans granted (and the range of types of loans is quite wide, consisting of consumer, commercial, and real estate loans); those banks also hold a considerable portion of securities. The majority of commercial banks are universal banks – their offers are addressed to individual clients, SMEs, enterprises, local government units, and include a wide range of products. Some banks specialise in a particular group of products or – more often – a particular group of customers (eg corporates). In the latter case their offer is adequately adjusted (eg can include project finance, specialised lending, etc). The main source of funding of mortgage banks are asset-backed securities (debt securities closely related to the assets held by these banks, mainly mortgage loans, but also treasury bonds). Community banks, cooperative banks and saving and loans associations concentrate on deposits and loans (they do not use wholesale funding, but to a certain degree issue bonds). The spectrum of their products is narrower and they concentrate on retail and consumer banking. Investment banks (as already pointed out are treated not as deposit-taking institutions but as investment intermediaries) assist their customers (companies, central and local governments and government agencies) in raising funds on the market. They also assist investors as brokers or dealers in secondary market transactions.

It is worth noting that the balance sheet of banks has changed over time. Traditionally banks used deposits to fund the loans and they kept those loans until maturity. When the demand for loans rose, banks first expanded their sources of funding, and in a next step started selling loans granted to clients before, to clear their balance sheet and gain the possibility to grant more loans. Changing the traditional originate-to-hold model of lending into the originate-to-distribute model accelerated the development of non-bank financial intermediaries buying those loans and repackaging them to sell complex products to investors.[47]

---

[47] N Cetorelli, BH Mandel, L Mollineaux, 'The Evolution of Banks and Financial Intermediation: Framing the Analysis' (2012) 18 *Federal Reserve Bank of New York Economic Policy Review* 1; VM Bord, JAC Santos, 'The Rise of Originate-to-Distribute Model and the Role of Banks in Financial Intermediation' (2012) 18 *Federal Reserve Bank of New York Economic Policy Review* 21. They describe the shadow credit intermediation mechanism as: after loan origination and warehousing, the processes of pooling and structuring loans into asset-backed securities and further securitisation – CDOs. They present data showing a drop in the share of loans originated (mortgage and corporate) in the portfolios

Another important issue is that in the 1980s, the trend of creating financial conglomerates started (usually banks bought insurance companies and/or investment companies).[48] This allowed them to extend their offer to intermediation in the sale of insurance and investment products as well. Currently, most large banks have comprehensive financial services (they sell their own products and act as an intermediary in the sale of other financial products, like insurance policies, pension funds, investment funds, asset management, etc, – and even offer non-financial products).[49] Banks that are able to sell a bundle of services can gain a competitive advantage over other financial intermediaries.[50] In addition to standard products (from either financial sector), banks offer innovations that combine the features (and risks) of products from various financial subsectors. Examples are reverse mortgages (which combine a bank loan and annuity and are subject to actuarial risk) and structured deposits (which combine a bank deposit and derivatives and are subject to many kinds of market risk).

B. Functions

Banks fulfil all of the functions of the financial system.[51] The most important ones are connected with the essence of banking activities, namely taking deposits and granting loans. Banks gather deposits and wholesale funding, issue debt securities, but also sell mutual funds and offer trust services and thus 'provide a mechanism for the pooling of funds to undertake large-scale indivisible enterprise'. By granting loans they 'provide a way to transfer economic resources' through time (eg they transform short-term deposits into long-term loans) and across geographic regions and industries (eg deposits from individuals are transformed into loans for companies, or funds raised from bonds purchased by large enterprises are designated for loans to small enterprises, enterprises from other industries, etc). Banks also 'provide a way to manage uncertainty and control risk' directly – they sell risk management services – and indirectly – the characteristics of their product offerings (different terms of deposits and loans, broad range of derivatives etc) reduce the uncertainty associated with default, liquidity, and market risk (interest rate, exchange rate).

By providing payment services, transfers from checking accounts, debit and credit cards and access to cash through ATMs they 'provide a payments system for the exchange of goods and services'.

In addition, they also indirectly fulfil the other two functions of the financial system. They 'provide price information that helps coordinate decentralised decision-making in various sectors of the economy', as they provide various record-keeping services involving the processing, storing, and dissemination of financial information (eg banks have a lot of information on customers' financial behaviour that can be used for credit scoring or individual offer design). Furthermore, by pricing their products (eg interest rates of deposits and loans) they provide information about the expected levels of market interest rates; by pricing derivatives they provide information about the expected levels of market prices of the underlying assets, etc.

---

of banks and an increase in the share of non-bank investors in the credit market. The study shows that although banks could create collateralised loan obligations using loans they originated, they prefer to use, eg investment management companies.

[48] Neave *Modern Financial Systems* (2009).

[49] S Heffernan, *Modern Banking in Theory and Practice* (Chichester, John Wiley and Sons, 1996) 24.

[50] This tendency is called 'one-stop-finance', 'one-stop shop' or 'all-finance'.

[51] See JF Sinkey Jr., *Commercial Bank Financial Management in the Financial-Services Industry* 6th edn (Upper Saddle River, Prentice Hall, 2002) 5; Crane *The global financial system*; Neave *Modern Financial Systems*.

Banks 'provide a way to deal with the asymmetric-information and incentive problems': they monitor borrowers' creditworthiness[52] and they provide guarantees such as a banker's acceptance, etc. Thus by granting loans or giving guarantees they send signals to the market that their customer is creditworthy (if the price is disclosed they also give additional information about the risk premium).

C. Risks

Banks' activities expose them primarily to the following types of risk:[53]

– Credit risk – in a narrow sense this is connected with loans and guarantees granted by a bank. It includes the risk to standalone facilities (its components are default risk, migration risk, future exposure risk, recovery risk, counterparty risk) and portfolio risk (correlation and concentration risks). In a broad sense, it relates to the risk of the value of any assets, including in particular securities and also includes a transaction risk and portfolio risk (and the components are issue risk, issuer risk and counterparty risk).

– Liquidity risk – as the main function of a bank is the transformation of deposits (and other funds) into loans (and other assets), liquidity risk is at the centre of its interest. This type of risk has two dimensions, namely funding liquidity risk and trading-related liquidity risk; both are related to market liquidity.

– Market risk – results from the volatility of market prices (parameters). Its components are interest rate risk (which includes trading risk, general market and specific risk, and gap risk), currency risk, equity risk and commodity risk;

– Operational and legal (compliance) risk.

IV. Insurance Companies

A. Activities

Apart from banking, insurance is the most regulated industry. Insurance companies are licenced institutions and regulations limit the scope of their activities. The primary function of insurance companies is to protect policyholders (individuals, companies, etc) from adverse events. For a certain price (the premium), insurers promise policyholders compensation if certain specified events occur.[54] In this manner, insurance companies help their clients in managing uncertainty and controlling risk.

There are several types of insurance, and as a consequence, different types of insurance companies. First of all it is necessary to distinguish social and private insurance. Social insurance is based on the notion that economic agents are facing fundamental risks which they cannot

---

[52] It should however be noted that in the originate-to-distribute model the banks' incentives to screen and monitor credit risk have decreased.

[53] See, eg, Crouhy, Galai and Mark *Risk Management* (2001); J Bessis, *Risk Management in Banking* 4th edn (Chichester, Wiley, 2015).

[54] Saunders and Cornett *Financial Institutions Management* (2008).

afford to deal with by themselves (social insurance refers to the inability to generate income resulting from, for example, age, illness or disability). It is therefore in many states organised by the government and / or compulsory. Its operating rules (including benefits and financing methods like taxes or premiums) are often determined by law; the programme provides for explicit accountability of benefit payments and income. Private insurance consists of voluntary (with several exceptions) insurance coverage for particular risks.[55]

Within the private insurance sector there are two major groups: primary insurers (companies issuing the insurance contracts, direct insurers) and reinsurers (secondary insurers, ie companies assuming part of the risk covered under a contract issued by a primary insurer). There are two types of primary insurance:[56]

(1) Life and health (L&H) insurance – provides protection against the possibility of untimely death, illnesses, and retirement. This group also includes annuities, which are the reverse of life insurance activities.[57]

(2) Property and casualty (P&C) insurance – protects owners from the impact of risk associated with owning property, as well as against personal injury, and liability such as accidents, theft, and fire. This group also includes insurance obligations concerning financial aspects like insolvency, credit, and direct and indirect suretyship.

Regulations divide these two groups. The insurer can provide services only in one of them, but often twin entities are created in one group: one providing services in the field of L&H and the other in the field of P&C.[58]

Except for the types of insurance mentioned above, insurers also sell a variety of banking and investment products, either as a bundle combining an insurance contract (usually life insurance) with elements of investment,[59] or as a simple intermediation in the sale of investment and banking products. As mentioned, the cross-selling of financial products from the three main sectors (banking, insurance and investment) is nowadays quite widespread, although its scale differs in different countries. With regard to insurance companies an important factor is the distribution channel. Generally three main channels are used: insurance agents, insurance brokers and direct writers; cross-selling is easier through own and captive channels (eg tied agents), and limited in advice-based channels (brokers and advisors).[60]

[55] However, this classification is not unambiguous, as some 'private' insurance is sold by the government, not all compulsory insurance is social insurance, and part of the social insurance can be implemented by private entities (as a complement to the state system). See JF Outreville, *Theory and Practice of Insurance* (New York, Springer Science+Business Media, 1997) 199.

[56] For a broader presentation of insurance activities see, eg, JF Outreville, *Theory and Practice of Insurance* (1997); Mishkin & Eakins *Financial Markets and Institutions* (2009); Saunders and Cornett *Financial Institutions Management* (2008).

[57] An annuity (rent) is a stream of regular payments (for an initial fixed sum or stream of payments the insurance company pays the beneficiary a fixed amount). It is a form of saving product, used for retirement needs and – in case of specific tax legislation – to defer income for tax reasons.

[58] In some jurisdictions the division is slightly different, distinguishing between life and non-life insurance (health insurance is separated from life insurance).

[59] Eg, through unit-linked and index-linked products, insurance companies may then sell financial securities under the form of insurance products, see A Beltratti and G Corvino, 'Why are Insurance Companies Different? The Limits of Convergence Among Financial Institutions' (2008) 33 *The Geneva Papers* 363.

[60] For further discussion of distribution models see, eg, M Eckardt, *Insurance Intermediation. An Economic Analysis of the Information Services Market* (Heidelberg, Physica-Verlag, 2007).

The fundamental elements of financial management of insurance companies are:[61]

(1) reflected in the profit and loss account:
- premiums – these are the price for insurance security (an adequate portion of it is ceded to reinsurers). Payment is made before a service is provided. The premiums should cover the expected loss to be paid by insurer,[62] as well as commissions and administrative expenses (and it should be the source of insurer's profit).
- losses/claims (non-life) and benefits (life) paid to policy-holders (beneficiaries).

(2) reflected in the balance sheet:
- technical and insurance provisions (reserves) – they are a liability of an insurer and are made obligatory to cover current and future liabilities resulting from insurance contracts; they include reserves for unearned premiums, reserves for losses and expenses, future policy holders' benefits, deposits and other outstanding claims of policyholders, reserves for catastrophic events.
- investments (securities, real estate, loans granted, bank deposits etc) – they should provide funds for the payment of benefits and compensation. Their types and structure (in particular maturity) must therefore be adapted to the types of insurance offered: life insurers, having mainly long-term liabilities, concentrate their investments on longer maturity and more profitable items (bonds, equities, real estate); non-life insurers, having more uncertain payouts on their insurance contracts, must include assets that can be easily liquidated.

The very nature of insurance is based on the laws of probability and the estimates of the risk of loss,[63] so the actuarial function is essential in insurance to measure the probability and risk severity of future events. This is necessary in order to price premiums adequately, as well as to calculate adequate provisions.

The specific methods of financial management will depend in the first place on the type of insurance (life/non-life), but also on the legal status of the insurer (stock company or mutual insurance company).

B. Functions

Insurance companies also fulfil the majority of the functions of the financial system.[64] Their most important function is the provision of 'a way to manage uncertainty and control risk' – it is the essence of insurance. Insurance eliminates (or at least reduces) losses resulting from uncertainty. Insurance contracts serve as value protection (and thus provide economic agents with a more stable basis for their planning); they provide compensation when the risk materialises (clients sell risk to insurers); insurance companies can share this risk with reinsurers; furthermore insurers mitigate losses also thanks to the preventive function (insurance conditions cause greater awareness and care of the insured and insurers may play the role of technical supervisors).

Insurers gather insurance premiums, may issue debt securities, and sell mutual funds and offer trust services – and thus 'provide a mechanism for the pooling of funds to undertake

---

[61] P Zweifel and R Eisen, *Insurance Economics* (Heidelberg, Springer, 2012) 152; Outreville *Theory and Practice of Insurance* (2009).

[62] Pricing is based on the analysis of the estimated loss and the probability of its occurrence. It is therefore pointed out that the insurance policy premiums are put option premiums (insurance companies write put options on insured parties' assets and sell the puts to their clients) – Neave, *Modern Financial Systems* (2009).

[63] S Laiming, 'Insurance: Minimizing Your Loss and Managing Risk' (1989) 2 *The Bottom Line* 14.

[64] See also: Crane *The global financial system* (1995); Neave *Modern Financial Systems* (2009); Zweifel and Eisen, *Insurance Economics* (2012); Neave *Modern Financial Systems* (2009).

large-scale indivisible enterprise'. By investing the premiums collected they 'provide a way to transfer economic resources through time across geographic regions and industries': money from collected premiums is invested in financial instruments of different types, like maturities, and issued by companies and governments in different locations.

Insurance companies play an important role in information economics. They 'provide price information that helps coordinate decentralised decision-making in various sectors of the economy'. First of all, risk management is based on information, so information gathering, processing and dissemination is crucial (for estimating probabilities etc).[65] Furthermore, as premium calculation is based on the perception of risk, by pricing the insurance products they provide information on probability and potential severity of losses. They also 'provide a way to deal with the asymmetric-information and incentive problems': based on information they possess, insurance companies decide whether to underwrite (and at what price). By setting certain conditions in a policy, they can raise awareness and give incentives to the insured to take better care of his property, health and life (this applies, for example, to the exclusion of the insurer's liability, the bonus-malus system, franchise etc). In certain financial insurance products (eg insolvency, credit, direct and indirect surety-guarantee) they monitor insured entities' creditworthiness – thus by giving insurance guarantees, credit insurance or granting loans they send signals to the market that their customer is creditworthy.

Insurance companies do not perform the first function of a financial system – they do not 'provide a payments system for the exchange of goods and services'.[66]

C. Risks

Insurers' activities expose them primarily to the following types of risk:[67]

- underwriting risk – is the basic risk associated with underwritten insurance contracts, and may be the effect of inadequate pricing and provisioning assumptions, product design, underwriting process, claims larger than expected, overly high retention, policyholder behaviour, etc; specific kinds of risk are connected with specific lines of business (eg mortality, longevity, disability, catastrophe etc);

- credit risk – is a risk of default (or at least the change in credit quality) of issuers of securities (in an insurer's investment portfolio), counter-parties (eg reinsurers, deposit-takers, derivate contract counterparties) and intermediaries; sovereign and concentration risk are also included in this category;

- market risk – results from the volatility of market prices, and is associated with the insurer's investments and includes interest rate risk, currency risk, equity risk, commodity risk, reinvestment risk;

- liquidity risk – is exposure to loss in the event that insufficient liquid assets will be available among the assets supporting the policy obligations to meet the cash flow requirements of policyholders' obligations when they are due (therefore it means asset/liability mismatch);

- operational, conduct and legal (compliance) risk.

---

[65] Eckardt, *Insurance Intermediation* (2007).

[66] However, the PSD2 Directive creates an opportunity for insurers in the context of payment initiation (PIS), but most of all the account information (AIS); they can integrate payments with their products, and gain knowledge on customers from their payment data, and use it to better design or price their products.

[67] International Actuarial Association, *A Global Framework for Insurer Solvency Assessment* (2004).

V. Investment Funds

A. Activities

Investment funds – referred to as investment pools or collective investment vehicles – are financial intermediaries that typically pool the financial resources of many small investors (individuals and companies) and invest in diversified portfolios of assets. In that way those investors obtain benefits from lower transaction costs (the fund gets volume discounts on brokerage commissions), high diversification of investment (and thus lower risk) and do not have to have professional expertise and spend time analysing the market and making investment decisions.[68] The profits (or losses) regarding that investment are divided proportionally among all shares (participation units/investment certificates).

The main forms of investment funds are open-ended and closed-ended funds:[69]

– Open-ended funds sell and re-purchase their units on a continuous basis, at their current net assets value (NAV); the value is calculated on daily basis. The objective of open-ended schemes is to generate long-term capital appreciation.

– Closed-ended funds are open for subscription only during a specified period (the fixed number of nonredeemable units is issued at the initial offering); investors can invest in the scheme at the time of the initial public issue, and thereafter they can buy or sell the units of the scheme on the stock exchange where they are listed. If the investors want to redeem the units they can do so after the maturity period.

There are many types of investment funds, which can be distinguished on the basis of their investment strategy (ie the classes of assets in which they invest). The main types are: equity funds, bond funds, hybrid funds, money market funds and real estate investment trusts. The investment strategy of a fund can be active or passive.

Investment funds charge investors a price or fee for the services they provide (ie, management of a diversified portfolio of financial securities). Two types of fees are incurred: entry / exit fees (one-time up-front fees or commission charges on the initial investment in or on the exit out of an investment fund) and fund operating expenses (management fee charged as a per cent of the fund assets; investors bear that fee indirectly, as it is paid out of the fund's assets).

B. Functions

Investment funds fulfil the majority of functions of the financial system.[70] Their main function is 'the pooling of funds to undertake large-scale indivisible enterprise': they gather funds from many small investors and invest them on the market.

By investing the funds gathered from investors they 'provide a way to transfer economic resources through time and across geographic regions and industries', as they offer different types of investments (short and long term, in different classes of assets from different industries).

---

[68] Saunders and Cornett *Financial Institutions Management* (2008); Mishkin & Eakins *Financial Markets and Institutions* (2009).
[69] R Pozen and T Hamacher, *The Fund Industry. How Your Money Is Managed* (Hoboken, Wiley, 2011); BVS Sekhar, *The Management of Mutual Funds* (Cham, Palgrave Macmillan, 2017).
[70] See also: Crane *The global financial system* (1995); Neave *Modern Financial Systems* (2009).

They 'provide a way to manage uncertainty and control risk', as they allow for portfolio diversification and a choice of investment strategy consistent with investor's risk tolerance. In addition, they provide liquidity thanks to the possibility of the redemption of units (in the case of open-end funds), can deliver hedging, and provide professional portfolio management services, which gives investors the opportunity to benefit without having to analyse the market on their own.

They 'provide price information that helps coordinate decentralised decision-making in various sectors of the economy': in making portfolio management decisions they gather, process and disseminate information concerning financial instruments and the whole economy and its sectors.

They 'provide a way to deal with the asymmetric-information and incentive problems': they monitor the issuers and market of financial instruments (financial standing of assets in which they invest) and by investing in certain assets (or issuers) they send a signal that they see their value growth potential (individual investors tend to copy institutional investors); sometimes they engage actively in a company in which they have invested (eg they appoint a board member) and thus directly influence its activities and incentives.

Investment funds do not perform, however, the first function of a financial system: they do not 'provide a payments system for the exchange of goods and services'.

C. Risks

Insurers' activities expose them primarily to the following types of risk:

- liquidity risk – inability to exit market position, lack of funds to support operations;
- market risk – results from the volatility of market prices and affects the value of the investment portfolio of an investment fund, eventually reducing commission income (based on net asset value);
- credit risk – a risk of default of issuers of securities, counter-parties, or sovereign; concentration risk;
- operational (especially technological), conduct and legal (compliance) risk.

VI. Pension Funds

A. Activities

Pension funds are a special kind of financial intermediary, as they combine features of a life insurance company and an investment fund. A pension fund (or plan) is a part of a pension (social insurance) system. There can be public and private pension funds, depending on the country's regulations. A private-sector pension fund represents employee savings accumulated to a financial payment of retirement benefits.[71] A pension plan is established by a plan sponsor, who can be:[72]

- a private business entity (on behalf of its employees) – a corporate employee retirement plan, private plan;

---

[71] Neave, *Modern Financial Systems* (2009).
[72] Fabozzi & Drake *Finance.*

- a state and local government (on behalf of its citizens) – a public plan;
- a union (on behalf of its members);
- an individual – an individually sponsored plan.

Institutional arrangements vary across countries and include separate government agencies, separate private entities (funds like mutual funds), plans managed internally (by the sponsor's staff) or externally (by an insurance company, investment fund or asset management company).
    There are three main types of pension plans:[73]

(1) Defined-benefit pension plan – employees are promised a specified amount of benefit when they retire. The playout is usually determined with a formula using the numbers of years worked and the employee's final salary. Defined-benefit plan's pension obligations are a debt obligation of the sponsor of the plan (who may face the risk that the plan is underfunded).
(2) Defined-contribution pension plan – no specific amount is guaranteed at retirement; the plan specifies only what will be contributed to the fund (usually expressed as a percentage of the employee's salary and/or a percentage of the employer's profits). The benefits are not defined and they depend on the value of collected contributions and earnings of the fund (growth of the plan's assets).
(3) Hybrid form, eg defined-contribution pension plan with capital guarantee.

The management of the pension fund assets depends on its characteristics, but it includes some elements that are easy to predict (especially in the defined-contribution system): the investment period is either strictly defined (retirement age) or can be longer; regular contributions are made. Depending on the plan's condition the benefits may be paid out once, as an annuity for a specified period, or (in case public pension plans) for a lifetime. In managing the fund therefore, asset management skills of an investment fund are necessary, and during the pay-out period – the actuarial skills of an insurer (in case of defined-benefit plans, which are rarely used nowadays, actuarial skills are necessary during the whole period of a pension plan).

B. Functions

Being a specific mix of a life-insurance company and investment fund, a pension plan performs the same functions as those institutions.

C. Risks

Pension funds are exposed primarily to the following types of risk:

- actuarial risk – connected with calculation of benefits – in case of defined-contribution plans (except for one-off pay out) or contributions – in case of defined-benefit plans;
- credit risk – a risk of default of issuers of securities, counter-parties, sovereign; concentration risk;

---

[73] Mishkin & Eakins *Financial Markets and Institutions* (2009); Fabozzi & Drake *Finance* (2009). For a broader presentation of different types see, eg, C Hertrich, *Asset Allocation Considerations for Pension Insurance Funds. Theoretical Analysis and Empirical Evidence* (Wiesbaden, Springer Gabler, 2013).

–   market risk – results from the volatility of market prices, is associated with the investments and includes interest rate risk, currency risk, equity risk, commodity risk, and reinvestment risk;

–   operational, conduct and legal (compliance) risk;

–   liquidity risk – is exposure to loss in the event that insufficient liquid assets will be available to meet the cash flow requirements of persons entitled to a pension (this risk is minimal, given the defined time of retirement).

VII. Investment Firms

A. Activities

European legislation also regulates 'investment firms'. There are two broad groups of activities that can be performed by them:[74]

(1)   the provision of investment services to third parties (clients) – mainly: reception and transmission of orders in relation to financial instruments, execution of orders on behalf of clients, portfolio management, investment advice, underwriting or placing of financial instruments (with or without a firm commitment basis);

(2)   the performance of investment activities (on a professional basis) – mainly: dealing on own account or operation of a multilateral trading facility (MTF) or an organised trading facility (OTF).

In both cases the subject of the service or activity are financial instruments, mainly: equity and debt securities, derivatives, units in collective investment undertakings, etc.[75]

The practice and literature on the subject distinguishes between investment banks (or more broadly: investment banking activities) and securities firms (brokers and dealers).[76] In general, investment banks mainly assist in the sale of securities on the primary market, and securities brokers and dealers assist in the trading of securities in the secondary markets. Investment banks specialise in originating, underwriting, and distributing issues of new securities (are intermediaries that help corporations and other institutions raise funds), but also advise companies on equity sales (sale of companies or corporate divisions), mergers and acquisitions and restructuring (eg capital structure, industrial strategy etc). Securities firms specialise in the purchase, sale, and brokerage of existing securities, or provide a platform for customers to trade without the intermediation of a broker.

Investment firms usually also provide additional services ('ancillary services'), including: investment research (in order to issue recommendations relating to transactions in financial instruments), and safekeeping and administration of financial instruments for the account of clients (custody services and cash or collateral management). It is also quite common practice

---

[74] See Annex I, A to Dir 2014/65/EU of the European Parliament and of the Council of 15 May 2014 on markets in financial instruments and amending Dir 2002/92/EC and Dir 2011/61/EU, [2014] OJ L173/349 ('MiFID II'). See also D Busch, 'MiFID II: Stricter Conduct of Business Rules for Investment Firms' (2017) 3 *Capital Markets Law Journal*, 340.

[75] Annex I, C to Dir 2014/65/EU.

[76] See, eg, Saunders and Cornett, *Financial Institutions Management* (2008); Mishkin & Eakins *Financial Markets and Institutions* (2009).

to provide clients with loans or credit in order to allow them to carry out transactions on financial instruments.[77]

B. Functions

The activity of investment firms can be very diverse, so it is not possible to create a uniform list of functions performed by them. Some investment firms provide 'bank-like' services, so we can directly refer to the functions performed by banks / shadow banks. In addition, some investment services allow for the performance of certain functions performed by investment funds.

In general, the main function of investment firms is to 'provide a way to transfer economic resources in time and geographic regions and industries'; this function is performed by all firms, eg through securities trading (both the execution of orders on behalf of clients and dealing on own account) or providing a trading facility (MTF or OTF).

Underwriting or placing of financial instruments are examples of 'providing a mechanism for the pooling of funds to undertake a large-scale indivisible enterprise'.

Investment firms 'provide a way to manage uncertainty and control risk', as they provide professional portfolio management services, investment research and recommendations, which gives investors the opportunity to benefit without having to analyse the market on their own. They also allow for portfolio diversification and a choice of investment strategy consistent with investor's risk tolerance. In addition, they provide liquidity (especially securities dealers, but also other firms through certain underwriting schemes or the placing of financial instruments on a firm commitment basis) and deliver hedging (eg via derivatives or short sale).

They 'provide price information that helps coordinate decentralised decision-making in various sectors of the economy': in making portfolio management decisions they gather, process and disseminate information concerning financial instruments and the whole economy and its sectors. By pricing their services they may provide information about the expected levels of market prices of the underlying assets.

They 'provide a way to deal with the asymmetric-information and incentive problems': they monitor the issuers and market of financial instruments (financial standing of assets in which they invest) and by investing in certain assets (or issuers) they send a signal that they see their value growth potential or by granting loans they send signals to the market that their customer is creditworthy (if the price is disclosed they also give additional information about the risk premium).

Investment firms do not perform the first function of a financial system: they do not 'provide a payments system for the exchange of goods and services'.

C. Risks

The risk profile of an investment firm may vary considerably, depending on whether and, if so, to what extent it engages in investments on its own account or provides underwriting of financial instruments,[78] and – in the case of securities trading – whether it is a broker or dealer.[79] Its risk

---

[77] See Annex I.B Dir 2014/65/EU.

[78] The scale of risk also differs with a form of underwriting – ie an investment bank may buy an entire issue outright, offer a guaranteed price a few days before the securities are issued, or offer a best-efforts distribution in which it attempts to raise as much money as possible from the security sale (Neave *Modern Financial Systems* (2009) 388).

[79] Brokers act as agents for investors in the purchase or sale of securities (they match buyers with sellers). Dealers hold securities purchased from customers who want to sell and hold inventories of securities, which they sell to customers

profile is mainly determined by the scale of exposure to market risk (position risk). This kind of risk is connected with the price of financial instruments (depending on the position in those securities – long or short – the firm is exposed to losses when prices fall or rise, respectively), credit risk (non-payment of principal and interests in debt issues), and interest rate and foreign exchange risk, depending on the nature of the financial instruments involved. The level of position risk is also related to the level of concentration of investments in a single issue or issuer (or a group of connected entities) – ie, the lack of appropriate diversification.

The basic credit risk occurs, of course, if the investment firm grants the clients loans or credits, enabling them to enter into transactions involving financial instruments.

Counterparty risk (the risk that a party to a financial contract will not perform on its obligations) is an important type of risk to which an investment firm is exposed. In the case of securities firms it is mainly connected with settlements (the settlement risk depends to a large extent on the design of the clearing and settlement system).

All of the above types of risk affect the liquidity risk of the investment firm.

As in the case of other financial intermediaries, investment firms are also exposed – to a significant degree – to operational, conduct and legal (compliance) risk.

VIII. Shadow Banks (Non-Bank Financial Intermediation)

A. Activities

Shadow banking is a broad term without a precise definition. It is referred to as 'non-bank financial intermediation',[80] 'unregulated financial intermediation', or 'market-based finance'. Shadow banking can be described as 'instruments, structures, firms, or markets which, alone or in combination, replicate, to a greater or lesser degree, the core features of commercial banks: monetary or liquidity services, maturity mismatch, and leverage',[81] 'but are exempt from both the onerous regulatory environment and from its mainly consumer protective reimbursements in the event of losses'.[82]

The main reason for creating such entities and structures is precisely the desire to avoid regulatory burdens.[83] Even though such entities face a higher cost of capital, they have lower compliance costs, since they are not subject to regulation or only subject to less stringent regulation benefits.[84]

The FSB uses a broad and narrow concept of shadow banking. The first covers all financial institutions that are not central banks, banks, insurance corporations, pension funds, public financial institutions, or financial auxiliaries. The latter include 'non-bank financial entity types that authorities have assessed as being involved in credit intermediation that may pose financial

---

who want to buy (and therefore their risk is substantially higher). See, eg, Mishkin & Eakins *Financial Markets and Institutions* (2009) 600.

[80] In 2018 the Financial Stability Board decided to replace the term 'shadow banks' with 'non-bank financial intermediation' in its communications.

[81] P Tucker, *Shadow banking, financing markets and financial stability* (2010) Remarks at a BGC Partners Seminar, London.

[82] RJ Girasa, *Shadow Banking. The Rise, Risks, and Rewards on Non-Bank Financial Services'* (Cham, Palgrave Macmillan, 2016) xxiii (the author quotes other definitions).

[83] Regulatory burdens raised costs and limited the scope of products that traditional banks can provide. G Buchak, G Matvos, T Piskorski, A Seru, *Fintech, Regulatory Arbitrage, and the Rise of Shadow Banks*, NBER Working Paper 23288 (2018).

[84] D Martinez-Miera and R Repullo, *Markets, Banks and Shadow Banks*, CEPR Discussion Paper No 13248 (2018).

stability risks, based on the FSB's methodology and classification guidance'.[85] The narrow concept is based on defined economic functions or activities that can give rise to financial stability risks of shadow banking; those functions are:[86]

(1) Management of collective investment vehicles with features that make them susceptible to runs – money market funds, fixed income funds, mixed funds, credit hedge funds, real estate funds.
(2) Loan provision that is dependent on short-term funding – finance companies, leasing/factoring companies, consumer credit companies.
(3) Intermediation of market activities that is dependent on short-term funding or on secured funding of client assets – broker-dealers, securities finance companies.
(4) Facilitation of credit creation – credit insurance companies, financial guarantors, monolines.[87]
(5) Securitisation-based credit intermediation and funding of financial entities – securitisation vehicles, structured finance vehicles, asset-backed securities.

Our assessment of shadow banking is ambiguous. On the one hand, shadow banking is useful in dispersing or transferring risk. On the other hand, it also contributes to increasing the overall risk.[88]

B. Functions

As a sector, shadow banking performs all but one of the functions of the financial system (they do not provide payment services). The quintessence is that these entities provide services mirroring key banking or investment funds services (although they mirror different institutions to a different extent). The most important of these is the collection and transformation of funds (the second and third functions are thus implemented). The nature of the transactions makes it possible to limit or allocate various risks and therefore fulfil the fourth function. As a majority of shadow banking operations are market-based, they facilitate the provision of price information in respect of assets, and thus fulfil the fifth function. In certain cases this function is, however, disrupted because the complicated structures of products (less standardised, or a combination of various instruments, transferring of funds and risk between multiple entities), impede proper pricing. As a result, so relying on the market price can be misleading. The sixth function – dealing with the asymmetric-information and incentive problems – is controversial. Froot argues that innovations within the financial system provide new ways of managing incentive problems. At the same time he admits that 'incentive problems arise because parties to financial contracts cannot easily observe or control one another, and because contractual enforcement mechanisms are not

---

[85] FSB, *Global Shadow Banking Monitoring Report 2017* (2018).
[86] Ibidem and FSB, *Strengthening Oversight and Regulation of Shadow Banking* (2013).
[87] A monoline insurance company provides guarantees to issuers, often in the form of enhancements intended to support the issuer's credit.
[88] See, eg, N Gennaioli, A Shleifer, RW Vishny, 'A Model of Shadow Banking' (2013) 68 *The Journal of Finance* 1331; A Moreira, A Savov, 'The Macroeconomics of Shadow Banking' (2017) 72 *The Journal of Finance* 2381; CL Culp, AMP Neves, 'Shadow Banking, Risk Transfer, and Financial Stability' (2017) 29 *Journal of Applied Corporate Finance* 45; R Irani, R Iyer, R Meisenzahl, and J-L Peydró, *The Rise of Shadow Banking: Evidence from Capital Regulation*, CEPR Discussion Paper No 12913 (2018).

costless to invoke'.[89] It must therefore be stressed that shadow banking involves diverse institutions and products, so the differences in performance of this function will be substantial. In the case of simple products mirroring banking or insurance products (consumer credit, leasing, guarantees, monolines), or even slightly complex products mirroring investment funds (money market funds, fixed income funds, mixed funds, real estate funds), this function is performed the same way as in those core financial institutions. However, more complex structures (hedge funds, securitisation, etc) may be extremely opaque and fragile and susceptible to incentive problems.

C. Risks

Due to the big diversity and heterogeneity of shadow banks, it is not possible to indicate a uniform classification of the risks they incur. However, given that their nature – to a certain extent – is comparable to banks it is possible to point out the most important risks, namely: counterparty risk, liquidity risk, credit risk, market risk and operational risk. The main specific risk factors are: counterparty default, roll over risk, contamination risk (errors in the mix of assets and in warehousing),[90] tail risk (remote negative events), sustainability risk (lack of margins), runs (unexpected reimbursement requests), hidden leverage, mispricing (mistakes in the evaluation), organisational and governance risk.[91]

IX. FinTech Companies

A. Activities

As was already mentioned, financial systems are invaded by FinTech companies. The FSB defines FinTech as 'technologically enabled innovation in financial services that could result in new business models, applications, processes or products with an associated material effect on financial markets and institutions and the provision of financial services'.[92]

Two major categories of FinTechs can be distinguished, offering:[93]

(1)   products and services that can be directly offered to customers practically in all areas of financial intermediation, including:

   –   payments, clearing, settlements – retail and wholesale payments, foreign exchange financial market infrastructure;

---

[89] KA Froot, 'Incentive Problems in Financial Contracting' in SB Crane et al, *The global financial system: a functional perspective* (Boston, Harvard Business School Press, 1995) 225.

[90] Warehousing is an intermediate step in securitisation: assets (loans or securities) are kept in a balance sheet and financed temporarily (warehoused) until the target amount (the critical mass needed) is reached. See: JJ de Vries Robbé, *Securitization Law and Practice. In The Face of Credit Crunch* (Alphen aan den Rijn, Kluwer Law International, 2008) 13.

[91] V Lemma, *The Shadow Banking System: Creating Transparency in the Financial Markets* (Houndmills, Palgrave Macmillan, 2016) 134.

[92] www.fsb.org/work-of-the-fsb/policy-development/additional-policy-areas/monitoring-of-fintech/.

[93] BCBS, *Sound Practices: Implications of fintech developments for banks and bank supervisors* (2018); FVB, *Financial Stability Implications from Fin Tech* (2017). For examples of ecosystems see, eg, www.businessinsider.com/fintech-ecosystem-report?IR=T.

- cryptocurrencies;
- deposits, lending and capital raising;
- investment management, personal finance management;
- insurance;

(2) market support services – data aggregators and data applications (big data analysis, machine learning, predictive modelling), distributed ledger technology, security (customer identification and authentication), ecosystems (infrastructure, open source, APIs), cloud computing, omnichannel, Internet of things and Internet of body, artificial intelligence (bots, automation, algorithms), accountancy.

The FinTech sector is not uniform – it consists of small, innovative companies (usually start-ups), but also big established corporations. Many of them concentrate on one line of business (sometimes even one solution) or technological area, but some have a broader offer. Some FinTechs compete with traditional financial institutions (directly servicing customers) and some cooperate with them (offering their services through financial companies).

A considerable percentage of FinTechs are not subject to any regulatory regime. Some are subject to some regulations (mainly concerning payment and investment services), and some are subject to a national authorisation or registration regime (the percentage of companies in individual areas of activity varies significantly).[94] There are cases where companies operating outside the regulated financial sector have gradually expanded their business to eventually apply for a licence (eg banking).

B. Functions

As a sector, Fintech performs all the functions of the financial system, however, individual companies – usually operating only in a selected area of financial finance – implement only a part of them.

It is important to observe that FinTech companies modify the way the financial system functions. In particular, some FinTech solutions enable the direct execution of financial transactions (they contribute to the 'democratisation' of finance). Traditional financial intermediaries are becoming less important, as the use of technology makes it possible to eliminate or limit the main market frictions that were the reason of existence of financial intermediaries: FinTech enables the acquisition and processing of information (limit information asymmetry) and significantly reduce transaction costs.[95]

C. Risks

Due to the huge diversity and heterogeneity of FinTech companies, it is not possible to indicate a uniform classification of the risks they incur. They depend on the business line in which they operate (and the scope of activities). The risks are therefore the same as in the case of traditional financial institutions in a given business line. The most important risk seems to be operational

---

[94] EBA, *Discussion Paper on the EBA's approach to financial technology (Fin Tech)*, (2017).
[95] It is even suggested, that in the digital age financial systems can be built without financial banks. See J McMillan, *The end of banking. Money, Credit, and the Digital Revolution* (Zurich, Zero/One Economics 2014).

risk, including most of all technological risk, as this industry is based on technological innovations, and the risk of customer service. Due to regulatory uncertainty, legal and conduct risks may also pose a threat.

X. Conclusion

As we have shown, both regulated and unregulated financial institutions (or institutions performing financial activities) perform – to a different degree and in different ways – three basic economic functions: the collection, allocation, and deployment of capital. By doing that they enable uncertainty and risk control and decentralised decision-making coordination. Information asymmetry is also addressed.

The changes within financial institutions, new financial products and new market facilities, and improved ITC technology have led to huge and rapid changes in the structure of global financial markets and institutions.[96]

Contemporary financial institutions are essentially engaged in cross-sectoral activity. The trend towards 'one-stop-finance' transform financial institutions into conglomerates offering products that fulfil the same functions.[97] Furthermore, part of their activity is transferred from these institutions to entities not covered by the regulations. Supported by modern technology, finance is now everywhere, and economic functions can be performed even without the intermediation of financial institutions.

Along with the increased complexity of financial products and the increasing links between financial products, the risk for customers is also growing. Attention should also be paid to the growing interconnectedness between financial institutions and financial sectors, as those links can be the channels of risk contagion. Interdependence can be caused by the provision of combined services (institutions are in the same intermediation chain), but also by cross (mutual)-ownership and by the fact that most regulated institutions maintain similar assets as collateral.[98]

Effective regulation must take into account the changes described. Financial regulation should therefore be based on the system's underlying economic functions rather than on any specific financial architecture, as functions change less than institutions and structures.[99]

Essentially, any institution performing the same activities, should be covered by the same regulations regardless of its affiliation to the given financial sector. The current 'regulatory patchwork' is the result of a series of amendments and supplements to regulations once established for specific financial institutions or specific financial products. Those changes were caused by both changes in the financial sector (eg new products, new ways of providing services, new institutions), and the ineffectiveness and gaps discovered in existing regulations. Firms are looking for ways to circumvent regulation or at least reduce the compliance costs. Inconsistent regulations, and non-uniform regulatory and supervisory requirements not only results in different conditions for various entities, leading to an unlevel playing field, but also creates incentives to seek

---

[96] RC Merton, Z Bodie, 'Design of Financial Systems: Towards a Synthesis of Function and Structure' (2005) 3 *Journal of Investment Management* 1.

[97] Sometimes these are complex products or a bundle of products.

[98] FSB, *Global Shadow Banking Monitoring Report 2017* shows the trends in interconnectedness among financial sectors.

[99] RC Merton, 'Operation and Regulation in Financial Intermediation: A Functional Perspective' in P Englund (ed) *Operation and Regulation of Financial Markets* (Stockholm, Ekonomiska rådet, 1993) 17; SL Schwarcz, 'Regulating Financial Change: A Functional Approach' (2016) 100 *Minnesota Law Review* 1441.

regulatory arbitrage. As a consequence, both the risk of the institutions and markets may grow, but above all the risk of stakeholders of these institutions, especially customers, increases. As shown in this chapter, risk is an inherent feature of every type of financial institution, and one of their basic functions is risk management. To avoid that this risk is eventually transferred to clients of financial institutions, prudential regulations are imposed on these entities, forcing them to ensure an adequate level of security and stability. Again, if different types of institutions perform similar functions with the same types of risk, it would be desirable to harmonise the regulatory approach with regard to each type of risk.

3

Objectives of Financial Regulation and their Implementation in the European Union

EDDY WYMEERSCH

I. Introduction

Financial activity in all its diversity and complexity is subject to an elaborate system of regulation and supervision. It is one of the most heavily regulated industries in our economies, as it touches on so many interests, whether at the individual level, or as part of the functioning of our economic systems and more generally, in today's worldwide economic and political relations. Interdependence of these different levels of regulation is an important feature and requires regulatory conditions to be analysed from different perspectives. The analysis in this chapter should therefore first deal with the objectives of financial regulation in general, to be further supplemented and detailed with respect to the specific objectives in the European financial markets.

Describing the goals of financial regulation is therefore a quite complex, multidimensional exercise, whereby the objectives of each level should be connected to the other levels.[1]

One could state that the overall objective of financial regulation aims at guaranteeing the efficient and effective functioning of the financial system and this in the interest of society in general and of all participants in particular. Efficiency aims at allocating the available means to the most productive, or highly rated uses, as defined by the economic and political system. This includes the optimal generation of savings and their use for maximum value-adding investments as the instruments for achieving efficiency. Both sides of this balance are realised through market mechanisms, which are supposed to achieve optimal outcomes on the basis of perfect competition. Regulation influences this mechanism by creating the conditions for optimal competition, while correcting its functioning for other goals aimed as insuring fair distribution or avoiding damaging externalities. The latter objective calls for regulatory measures, which may limit the benefits of perfect competition.

Financial regulation attempts to establish a balance between these objectives. An essential precondition is however that the participants have sufficient confidence in the system, allowing them to take part in it, to safely entrust their savings to the intermediary institutions, and belief in the promises made. These objectives are pursued by a diversity of instruments: consumer

---

[1] See for a systematic overview and analysis: J Armour, D Awrey, P Davies, L Enriques, J Gordon, C Mayer and J Payne, *Principles of Financial regulation* (Oxford, OUP, 2016); Lamandini and Ramos, *EU Financial Law, An Introduction* (Wolters Kluwer, 2016).

and investor protection, transparency, efficiency, enforceability, public interest, financial stability, competition, judicial protection, all aim at ensuring the effectiveness of the regulation and are present, at different intensities, in the different components of the financial system. In most cases they are supported by, or are the outcome of regulatory provisions and processes, addressing the behaviour of the market participants, and more particularly regulating the conduct of the financial institutions on which the functioning of the system is based.

A. General Objectives of Financial Regulation

The financial activity of markets participants[2] takes places within the context of different levels of legal provisions, some of which are contractual hence voluntary, other regulatory, hence mandatory. These provisions establish a multi-level legal regime aimed at protecting the efficiency of the financial system and its participants.

The first layer governs the relationship of a market participant with an institution: the latter can be a bank, an investment firm, a financial market infrastructure, a collective savings entity, an insurance company, a pension fund or residually a non-categorised institution.[3] The relationship will firstly be contractual, and therefore be embedded in national law. To a certain extent, freedom of contract will apply, and choice of law will allow for flexibility. But regulatory provisions will often intervene, dictating certain behaviour or imposing certain prohibitions. This is quite frequently the case in order to safeguard fairness and avoid negative externalities not only for the protection of the contractual parties but more generally for defending the confidence in the individual institutions or more generally in the financial system as a whole. The rules on investor protection, on financial disclosure, on certain types of transactions – eg the distribution of credits – on market transparency, on payments, are examples of provisions serving in different degrees the mentioned individual and collective objectives. These regulatory provisions are embedded in local traditions, in local legal provisions relating to the conduct of market participants, but also in specific national market structures. The internationalisation of the market has resulted in an increasing number of similar requirements being applicable in the national, but also applicable in a cross-border context.

The second layer of regulatory provisions addresses the position of the financial institutions, as such, whether individually or as a class of similar institutions. Although there are significant differences between the type of institutions and their obligations – banks, insurance companies, investment firms, investment funds, etc – the base objective and obligation are their ability to meet their obligations at all times.

At the level of the individual institution, a whole range of measures apply, essentially aimed at ensuring that objective, here referred to as the 'solvency' of the institution, but more precisely, the ability to honour their obligations. These measures are mostly imposed by government regulation as a counterbalance for the privilege of 'receiving funds' from the public, in fact for the financial institution to deal with the public for financial matters. Therefore, public confidence becomes a public good and deserves to be strongly protected as the basis for collective trust and stability. This protective regime is often – but imprecisely – called prudential regulation: it refers

---

[2] For a detailed analysis of the different functions in the financial systems, their legal status and resulting risks, see ch 2 in this volume.

[3] Formerly 'shadow banking', but better called resilient market-based finance, see: Financial Stability Board, 'Transforming Shadow Banking into Resilient Market-based Finance: An Overview of Progress', 12 November 2015.

to a complex set of regulatory provisions aimed at securing the institution's ability to meet its obligations.

The prudential regime is composed of a wide range of prescriptions among which their own fund requirements, the governance rules, the management rules, including risk management and the remuneration restrictions play the main role. Respecting the provisions applicable according to the first transaction-related layer, will often be relevant in the application of the second layer: lack of respect of depositors' rights may be a warning signal for the institutions' solvency. Proper accounting and auditing are instruments that allow communication with market participants, but also to inform supervisors of deficiencies or illegal activities. Supervision is exercised on a stand-alone basis, for company groups complemented by a consolidated approach. In many cases, supervision will also serve to enforce the regulatory provisions applicable under the first layer of objectives.

The position of an institution will normally depend on its own proper characteristics, essentially its business model and its solvency. However, there is a collective dimension which should not be neglected: the financial problems affecting one bank may reverberate on other banks in the same jurisdiction, in the same branch of activity, or further in the financial system in general. Reputation and contagion risks are external factors which are very difficult to control. Events on one stock exchange, or in one class of assets, may reverberate worldwide. The suspension of redemptions in one investment fund initially triggered the 2007 financial crisis. Individual risks become collective risks.

In these cases, the shock to confidence leads to calls for collective protection mechanisms: a collective safeguard is to be found in the deposit guarantee or insurance systems, based on the contributions or liabilities of the participating institutions. Less known is the liquidity support granted by the central banks. Recovery and resolution mechanisms are important instruments supporting confidence in the financial system: by eliminating institutions which may not be able to meet their liabilities, the development of further risks is avoided, parts of the insolvent firm rescued, while market participants previously at risk may be protected, whether by obtaining a privileged treatment, or by being able to avail themselves of the deposit guarantee system, or other support systems. For securities business, investors enjoy protection by an investor-compensation scheme.

Financial stability crises are most of the time local and have been effectively dealt with by the local supervisory authorities, often with Treasury intervention. Depending on the nature of the deficiencies, they may become international: excessive risk exposures, supervisory weaknesses, deficiencies in some market segments or a general confidence crisis may explain the root causes of international financial crises. In these cases, few legal mechanisms are available. International financial cooperation, based on agreements between central banks, or between resolution authorities may help to mitigate some of the consequences, often with the help of international financial institutions such as the International Monetary Fund, central banks, the World Bank. At the end of the analysis, only governments are able to shoulder the consequences of the downfall.

In a more regulatory approach, financial stability is approached from a Europe-wide and international angle, developing instruments or models to avoid wider financial crises. At the EU level, measures have been adopted to ensure the orderly resolution of a failing bank, further implemented for the euro area in the context of a single resolution mechanism. Support to Member States or indirectly to individual financial institutions will also be made available by the European Stability Mechanism.[4]

---

[4] It is planned that the European Stability Mechanism will be the common backstop to the Single Resolution Fund; see: EUROSUMMIT 2 TSGC 9, 29 June 2018, euro 502IS.

The analysis presented above essentially applies to the banking sector: it is the most sensitive in terms of risks and liabilities – especially in terms of liquidity as deposits are generally on sight or on a very short term, while concentrated risks may accumulate on the asset side. But the phenomenon is also present in other parts of the financial system, such as the securities markets or in the collective investment or pension funds sector.

This multiple level structure is also applicable to the insurance sector: the contract terms for most insurance products are subject to quite detailed regulation and national law, while some of their assets – eg as part of their lending activity – are subject to the same contractual provisions as applicable to banks. The activity of insurance companies is subject to extensive regulation aimed at safeguarding their long-term solvency, while reinsurance will offer an instrument for introducing a collective coverage for certain risks, broadening the basis on which the liabilities can be established. In some jurisdictions there are also insurance guarantee systems in place.

This three-layered system identifies the individual's interest, the position of the intermediary institution and the societal interest: it captures the basic scheme and interests pursued by the regulatory regimes. It stands for the overall framework, within which the detailed models and regulations will operate. Each of the layers has its own objectives, its own dynamics. It is important to point to the relationship between the three layers, as they support each other in an organic way.[5] They all form part of the single financial system which is of crucial importance to our economies and our societies.

This scheme is common to most financial systems. It is also the central framework on which EU regulation is based and shapes a large part of its regulatory and supervisory structure. Fundamental changes such as a shift from micro to macro supervision and the consequences of the internationalisation of the financial and economic activity are the main drivers which created the principal characteristics of today's financial regulatory system.[6]

B. Regulation in the European Union

In the EU, as in all large financial markets, the above principles are largely applied, with the necessary differences, with the Union covering 28 or 27 different Member States and different markets, and their different financial and legal traditions. However, the operation of these principles in the EU takes place through an interactive mechanism of political, structural and regulatory systems, which lead to an overall quite complex outcome and shapes the form and the content of the regulatory provisions. This diversity gives a unique twist to the implementation of the above principles.

II. The Integration of the EU Financial Market as an Overall Objective

The objectives as outlined above have to be developed on the background of an overarching political objective which is the creation of a Europe-wide integrated financial market. Due to

---

[5] Whether this three-pillar approach with its regulatory and institutional implications is the only, even the right way to organise financial supervision is debatable, as it limits oversight of cross-sectoral matters, may extend risks throughout the system while preventing efficiency in dealing with common issues.

[6] See The fundamental principles of financial regulation, Geneva Reports on the World Economy 11, 2009, www.princeton.edu/~markus/research/papers/Geneva11.pdf, dealing essentially with systemic risk, its causes and characteristics. In the same sense see Armour, Awrey et al, Conclusion (n 1).

the historical structure of the EU, this market is a composite structure, with 28 (27 after Brexit) Member States: one of the objectives of the creation of the Union has been the integration of their economies including their national markets into one single market, in this case a single financial market. This objective presupposes a certain number of prerequisites, the most important ones being free access to each other's national markets, and equal rights to offer products on these markets. For goods, this has been decided since the landmark ECJ decision of *Cassis de Dijon*.[7] In the financial field the same principles apply and are further rooted in the Treaty's freedom of capital movements and freedom of establishment, or of services.[8] The basic reasoning is that if freedom of access to the neighbour's markets has to be achieved, access restrictions have to be eliminated to the greatest extent possible and operators have to abide by the same rules in all jurisdictions, and this is to satisfy the general objectives of financial regulation as outlined above, mainly in terms of investor protection, solvency and financial stability. At the same time, adequate measures have to guarantee that the regulations are effectively applied and the objectives achieved. The legal and administrative processes through which these objectives are pursued are quite complex due to the multinational and cross-border aspects of the subject matter.

Access to the financial market was historically governed by national regulations which determined the conditions of establishment of intermediaries but also outlines the characteristics of the products or services on offer. These requirements served to secure the solvency, financial stability and investor or consumer interests. Access to another EU market would normally require operators to meet the requirements of that market: this would result in operators meeting the regulations of 28 states, clearly contrary to the integration objective. Therefore, starting in the mid-1990s, a technique was developed, called 'mutual recognition' whereby operators meeting the conditions in one Member State – the 'home' state – could access other states without meeting substantial additional conditions: only the rules of the 'home' state would suffice. This system has been designated as the 'European passport' which offers free access to all Member States. The passport for financial services only applies to activities which are subject to EU regulation, and are effectively supervised in the home state. As the regulation primarily aims at pursuing the general objectives of financial regulation, complying with the passport conditions implies that the operators will also conform to the said general objectives. At the same time, the EU financial market will, legally at least, become fully operational as an internal market, guaranteeing the same protection to depositors and investors.

In order to become operational, this free access regime applies to activities which are subject to EU regulation, and for which the necessary authorisations have been granted by the home state supervisor. These conditions will guarantee that the same legal regime is applicable in all EU states and that the market participants can expect the same protection as in their home state. The EU regulations take the form of directives – which being addressed to the national legislators – have to be transposed into national laws and EU regulations which are directly applicable in the national legal order, and therefore are directly binding on the national supervisors and the entities subject to their supervision. Freedom of access is guaranteed by these legal instruments: for financial intermediaries, this takes the form of freedom to access the other states' markets by whether opening a branch in that market, of by providing services. In both cases, the passport would allow financial intermediaries to undertake these activities without an authorisation procedure in the host state: only some information procedures between supervisors will apply.

---

[7] ECJ, Case 120/78. *Rewe-Zentral AG v Bundesmonopolverwaltung für Branntwein* ('*Cassis de Dijon*') [1979] ECR 649.
[8] TFEU, Arts 49,56,63.

Different from branches, subsidiaries are separate legal entities[9] and therefore separate authorisation procedures will have to be followed, but once authorised the subsidiary, recognised as a local operator, will be entitled to prevail itself of the passport. These facilities have resulted in financial institutions, especially banks, to be present in many EU Member States, thereby guaranteeing that the objectives of the integrated market are achieved.

Non-EU operators can also become active in the EU: in many cases they establish a subsidiary which will be governed by the rules applicable in the state of establishment. These rules will be governed by the EU regulations and therefore will put the operator at the same level as any other local entity, also in terms of authorisation and supervision. The same freedom does not apply to branches: here the authorisation can only be granted by the local supervisor, and according to its conditions. Also, the activity of the branch is limited to the host state.

III. Equal Regulation and Competition

The passport regime is conditioned by the strict application of the EU regulation which by being similarly applicable in all Member States, will create equal conditions (a level playing field objective) and will avoid competition between regulatory systems (regulatory competition and regulatory arbitrage concerns). This is one of the core internal market objectives pursued by the EU regulations and directives, in the latter case by the national laws transposing these directives. It is essential that the application of the EU regulation and the application of the national transposing laws should – effectively – be the same in all Member States. Whether this result is achieved depends on many factors. With respect to regulations, this effect is largely guaranteed by the principles of EU law,[10] as regulations are directly applicable in the national legal systems and this with the same authority as national law. The principle also applies to national laws transposing EU directives, although in the transposition, due to the national freedom of formulation, local characteristics may appear, such as additional conditions, complementary supervisory processes, language or translation differences, and in some cases more substantial differences, because directives may allow Member States the choice between different options for the transposition.[11] Some of these differences may be based on the intention of the national regulator to better protect investors in its jurisdiction, but they may also cover the intention to make access to its market more difficult, or more attractive, leading to a form of fragmentation which is not compatible with the integrated EU financial market. This is often referred to as 'gold plating'.

Differences between national and European legal regimes may also be due to diversity at the level of the underlying approaches to contract, company, bankruptcy and other parts of national law. In many fields, national laws remain applicable to private law relations, possibly creating tension with the EU requirements. These conflicts are probably more frequent in the fields of

---

[9] Capital Requirements Regulation, Art 11 and Capital Requirements Dir IV, Art 111 outline the rules applicable to consolidated supervision.

[10] TFEU, Art 288.

[11] These are the 'options and discretions'. See on the Options and Discretions in the banking field: Regulation (EU) 2016/445 of the European Central Bank of 14 March 2016 on the exercise of options and discretions available in Union law (ECB/2016/4); ECB Guide on options and discretions available in Union law, Consolidated version, November 2016. Recommendation of the ECB of 4 April 2017 on common specifications for the exercise of some options and discretions available in Union law by national competent authorities in relation to less significant institutions (ECB/2017/10). Guideline (EU) 2017/697 of the ECB of 4 April 2017 on the exercise of options and discretions available in Union law by national competent authorities in relation to less significant institutions (ECB/2017/9).

regulated contracts, eg consumer credit or payment services, although recent ECJ cases illustrate a similar phenomenon in company and banking law.[12] This observation indicates that there may be three layers of legal provisions applicable: EU regulations, national legislation transposing directives, and general national law. Nevertheless, all should meet the requirements of applicable EU law.

Differences between national law and the directives will be identified by the national supervisors, or may be the subject of remarks formulated by the European Supervisory Authorities or by the Commission, the latter having the right to bring the case before the ECJ.[13] The ECJ case law makes it clear not only that this conformity check is not limited to differences in the formulation between these two levels, but the overall purpose of the EU regulatory provisions has to be compared, and may ultimately prevail.[14]

The optimal solution for creating a fully integrated European financial market might consist of having all Member States adopt the same legal system, not only in terms of regulation but also as far as private law is concerned. Except perhaps in the wholesale financial markets, which function on a worldwide basis, this solution is unachievable. It does not mean however that one should not strive for more uniformity, starting with offering similar or identical solutions in the different regulations for largely identical matters.[15]

IV. The Structure of the EU Financial Supervision

The implementation of the legal requirements applicable to the different categories of financial institutions and transactions is supervised by public bodies, the so-called National Competent Authorities (NCAs). They are structured along the same lines as the regulations, ie banking, insurance and securities regulations are addressed by different supervisory bodies, not necessarily housed in the same institutions: in some jurisdictions, one supervisor is in charge of the three domains, in several states, insurance and securities are supervised by one entity, in a limited number of states there is a supervisor per type of financial activity. Their total number is difficult to determine and has substantially changed over time, especially as a consequence of the decision to centralise banking supervision in the euro area.[16] This wide diversity is mainly due to differences in the subject matters to be supervised, but also to historical factors, while different national policies may play a role in maintaining their historical structure.

At the European level, the activity of the NCAs is coordinated by the ESAs, the European Supervisory Authorities, each of which is active in one of the three pillars of financial activity. Their creation in 2010 was intended to deal with the 'shortcomings in the areas of cooperation, coordination, consistent application of Union law and trust between national supervisors'.[17]

---

[12] See also ECJ, C 604-11, 30 May 2013. Genil, and the analysis by D Busch, 'The private law effect of Mifid I and Mifid II: the Genil case and beyond', in D Busch and G Ferrarini, (eds), *Regulation of the EU financial markets, Midif II and Mifir* (Oxford, OUP, 2017).

[13] TFEU, Art 258. The state will have to comply with the ECJ decision, and if not the Commission can impose a penalty: TFEU, Art 260.

[14] See, eg, in ECJ Case T-133/16 to T-136/16, 24 April 2018, Caisses regionales, where the decision was based on the rationale of the provision. The Court refrained from interpreting national law.

[15] See also R Smits and N Badenhoop 'Towards a Single Standard of Professional Secrecy for Financial Sector Supervisory Authorities; A Reform Proposal', (2019) *European Law Review*.

[16] See E Wymeersch, 'The Structure of Financial Supervision in Europe: About Single Financial Supervisors, Twin Peaks and Multiple Financial Supervisors' (2007) *European Business Organization Law Review*, 237.

[17] ESMA, Reg Recital 2. The three ESAs were originally created by three identical EU regulations. Later on, some amendments have introduced some changes.

The ESAs are mainly in charge of developing similar overall policies in their respective sectors, contributing to the drawing up of regulatory standards, coordinating the supervisory activities of the NCAs and supporting the respect of EU law, and when needed, resolving conflicts between NCAs. From the angle of integrating financial markets, the ESAs develop an indispensable action in formulating common instruments to be used in actual supervision, and striving at convergence of national supervisory practices.[18] They have become leading players in their respective fields, contributing to the development of common approaches and more coherence in their attributed fields of action.

Notwithstanding the terminology used, the ESAs generally are not engaged in the actual supervision or addressing individual financial firms, but exercise their supervisory tasks in a more general, sectoral approach. Most of these activities are limited to their respective sector of financial institutions, or transactions, coordinating the activities of their members, the NCAs, and advising the Commission on related regulatory initiatives. They have significantly stepped up their efforts in the development of supervisory convergence activities[19] and in the development, monitoring, assessment and implementation of common guidelines.[20] Cross-sectoral activities have been reported by each of the ESAs.[21]

Of the three ESAs, ESMA has been the one which, after the financial crisis, was put in charge of the supervision of specific activities which previously were outside its remit, ie the supervision of the credit rating agencies and of the trade repositories, ie bodies to which derivatives transactions have to be notified. The ESA regulation allows it to act in cases of a breach of EU law by an NCA.[22] Proposals to extend a centralised supervisory function per domain have not been successful.[23]

---

[18] Joint Guidelines on the convergence of supervisory practices relating to the consistency of supervisory coordination arrangements for financial conglomerates, 22 December 2014: https://eiopa.europa.eu/publications/eiopa-guidelines/guidelines-on-the-conv-of-supervisory-practices-rltng-to-theconsistency-of-supervisory-coord. Guidelines on Facilitating an Effective Dialogue between Insurance Supervisors and Statutory Auditors, 2 February 2017: https://eiopa.europa.eu/Pages/Guidelines/Guidelines-on-Facilitating-an-Effective-Dialogue-between-Insurance-Supervisors-and-Statutory-Auditors.aspx. EIOPA Joint Guidelines Compliance Table, 22 December 2015, JC 2015, 087.

[19] EBA published an annual report on supervisory practices: see REPORT ON THE CONVERGENCE OF SUPERVISORY PRACTICES EBA/GL/2019/03 6 March 2019, dealing inter alia., with the SREP guidelines (SREP guidelines Supervisory Review and Evaluation process) EBA-Op-2017-14, of 21 November 2017. Report on the functioning of supervisory colleges in 2017, 16 March 2018, dealing inter alia with the EBA College monitoring activity. EIOPA Annual report, 2017, 'Strengthening supervisory convergence, enhancing consumer protection and maintaining financial stability were the focus of our activities in 2017.'

[20] See for the list of Peer Reviews, the EBA Review Panel.

[21] See as recent examples: Final Report of the Joint Committee following joint consultation paper concerning amendments to the PRIIPs KID, 8 February 2019, and COMMISSION DELEGATED REGULATION (EU) …/… of …. amending Delegated Regulation (EU) 2017/653 supplementing Regulation (EU) No 1286/2014 of the European Parliament and of the Council on key information documents for packaged retail and insurance-based investment products (PRIIPs) by laying down regulatory technical standards with regard to the presentation, content, review and revision of key information documents and the conditions for fulfilling the requirement to provide such documents, 8 March 2019, submitted by the Joint Committee. Report on FinTech: Regulatory sandboxes and innovation hubs, JC 2018, 74. ESAS Joint Opinion on the risks of money laundering and terrorist financing affecting the Union's financial sector (JC-2017-07). The cross-selling of financial products – request to the European Commission to address legislative inconsistencies between the banking, insurance and investment sectors, 26 January 2016, ESAs 2016-07.

[22] Allowing the ESA to directly address itself to a financial institution in case the NCA does not take action within the specific period of time (Art 17 (4) ESA reg).

[23] See, however, with respect to CCPs, Proposal for a REGULATION OF THE EUROPEAN PARLIAMENT AND OF THE COUNCIL amending Regulation (EU) No 1095/2010 establishing a European Supervisory Authority (European Securities and Markets Authority) and amending Regulation (EU) No 648/2012 as regards the procedures and authorities involved for the authorisation of CCPs and requirements for the recognition of third-country CCPs, providing a new

The way financial regulation has been framed in each of the respective three fields is to a certain extent comparable. The basic provisions have been laid down in a regulation, or in one or several directives. These have been further implemented in a series of regulations, adopted whether by the Parliament and Council, the Union legislator,[24] or by the Commission pursuant to a delegation by the legislator. Further levels of more detailed regulation are the regulatory or implementing technical standards, which have been prepared by the respective ESAs and formally adopted by the Commission as regulations. In addition, the ESAs may develop 'guidelines and recommendations' which are binding on a 'comply-and-explain" basis.[25] They may also develop 'Q & As' and opinions establishing a common view which, although not legally binding, may under peer pressure result in some de facto harmonisation.

V. EU Sectoral Financial Regulation and Supervision

The EU system of regulation and supervision is carried out in a clearly defined model in which the three main financial activities have been subject to their own specific regulatory regimes. Although these regimes may appear to be different, they share a considerable number of common issues, and structural challenges.

A. In the Banking Field

In line with the international standards, banking regulations and supervision essentially deal with the solvency of individual banks, thereby supporting the financing of the economies. To secure the banks' solvency, a complex system of regulations and directives have been adopted following the international guidelines as developed on the basis of standards developed by the Basel Committee on Banking Supervision. The national banking supervisors exercise their prudential supervision on a largely comparable basis applying the EU rules and some the additional national provisions. This feature inspires confidence to depositors and investors in each of the Member States. The supervision of the institutions is organised on a national basis, the NCAs coordinating their action at the level of the European Banking Authority (EBA). The EBA has developed an 'interactive single rulebook' in which the main regulatory instruments and their implementing regulations have been included.

On the other hand, banking supervision is less involved in the surveillance of the individual transactions of bank clients: the EBA regulation describes its missions relating to 'consumer protection and financial activities', by referring to tasks which are more in line with its prudential objectives than the protection of the individual position of consumers. Also, its powers to prohibit or restrict certain financial activities are related to the orderly functioning of the markets and their stability, not to the protection of the individual investor.[26]

---

supervisory function for ESMA. Compare for a different pattern: Commission, Strengthening the Union framework for prudential and anti-money laundering supervision for financial institutions, Brussels, 12.9.2018 COM(2018) 645 final.

[24] Specifically for the SSM regulation, in which the Parliament was technically not involved.

[25] EBA reg, Art 16.

[26] EBA reg, Art 9. Compare the recent decisions on binary option and contracts for difference, adopted by ESMA, in July 2018 and repeatedly renewing, the relevant decision. As national authorities have introduced similar or more stringent bans, ESMA did not renew the temporary prohibition from 1 July 2019, the previous decisions having expired.

The supervisory structure has been considerably modified in the field of banking supervision when on 3 November 2013, the European Central Bank was put in charge of banking supervision in the now 19 euro area Member States within the framework of the Single Supervisory Mechanism on the basis of a Council Regulation.[27] From then on, the ECB will exercise direct banking supervision on the larger banks in the euro area, while the smaller institutions (the Less Significant Institutions v the significant ones[28]) will continue to be supervised by the NCAs in charge of – mostly local – banking supervision, however under the overall guidance of the ECB.[29] The non-euro area banks will remain subject to their own national banking regulatory regime which will be largely similar and subject to the same EU regulations.

With respect to the application of Union law, the ECB will be governed by all relevant Union law and especially the SSM regulation in which its supervisory tasks have been listed.[30] It will apply the EU regulations, including the regulations developed by the EBA, and its Guidelines and Recommendations, including its European Supervisory Handbook.[31] On the other hand, the ECB has limited regulatory power of its own, the SSM regulation confining its regulatory action to the tasks which that regulation conferred to it, being the main domains of prudential supervision.[32] Up to now the ECB has adopted a prudent approach to developing its own regulations in the field of supervision, although many of its 'opinions' cannot be disregarded as indications of its supervisory action.[33]

This specific approach has been conceived to guarantee the level playing field between the institutions, irrespective of the supervisory regime, thereby avoiding the supervision of Significant Institutions to become a different or a superior one. This view is also expressed in the statement that the ECB shall be considered, as appropriate, the competent authority for the tasks of prudential supervision in the euro states.[34] By tying the supervisory action of the ECB to the regulatory and other developments at the EBA level – where the national supervisors are the decision makers – one may wonder whether on the longer term that approach establishes the right balance with most of the EBA members also being members in the ECB's Supervisory board, and the non-Eurozone members not likely to become representative leaders in the field of prudential supervision. One day, this structure will be up for reform.

At the same time, the NCAs will *assist* the ECB with respect to the preparation and implementation of supervisory acts relating to *all* credit institutions.[35] The LSIs will be supervised by the NCA of the state where the institution has its registered office or head office,[36] but the ECB has a

---

[27] Council regulation 1024/2013, of 15 October 2013, SSM Reg.

[28] Usually referred to as SIs and LSIs. These are defined on the basis of the criteria mentioned in the SSM, eg, Art 6(4), the most important one being total value of assets, exceeding 30bn euros.

[29] ECJ, Case T 122/15 of 16 May 2017 (53) *Landeskreditbank Baden Wurtemberg – Forderbank v ECB*, /n 38 and further stating: 'the SSM is not a system of distribution of competences but allow the exclusive competences delegated to the ECB to be implemented within a decentralized framework' (54) …. 'the NCAs are assistants the ECB, but do not exercise autonomous competences' (58). Confirmed by Court decision: C 450/17: 8 May 2019. Also: Bundesverfassungsgericht, 30 Juli 2019, 2 BvR 1685/14, 2 BvR 2631/14.

[30] SSM reg, Art 4(1; see Art 9(1) where the ECB is considered 'the competent authority … in the member States as established by relevant Union law'.

[31] On the basis of EBA reg, Art 8(1)(aa). EBA has developed common standards, but not yet a Handbook.

[32] As mentioned in SSM reg, Art 4(1). It means that the ECB will be treated as an NCA foe the application of the provisions of Art 4(1) and 4(2) and 4 (2), the latter dealing with macroprudential issues.

[33] See ECB: All ECB opinions.

[34] SSM reg, Art 9(1). The ECJ stated in *Landeskreditbank*, nt 29: 'that direct prudential supervision by the national authorities under the SSM was envisaged by the Council of the European Union as a mechanism of assistance to the ECB rather than the exercise of autonomous competence.' (58).

[35] SSM reg, Art 6(3).

[36] CRD IV, Art 13(2).

'higher' right of supervision, allowing it to adopt 'regulations, guidelines and general instructions' addressed to the NCAs or to take over direct supervision of an individual institution in case the 'consistent application of standards' raises the need for the ECB to exercise direct supervision.[37] This relationship between the two levels of supervision has been defined by the European Court of Justice as follows: 'the [ECB] shall be exclusively competent to carry out, for prudential supervisory purposes, the following tasks in relation to *all* institutions established in the participating member States ....'.[38] This list of tasks has been detailed in the SSM regulation,[39] and includes almost all activities relevant to banking supervision.

The introduction of centralised banking supervision has contributed to the integration of the European financial markets as all institutions are subject to the same rules, applied in the same manner. Moreover, the ECB analyses the way the NCAs apply the rules with respect to the LSIs subject to their supervision. Only the ECB is entitled to appreciate whether the decisions by NCAs have rightly been adopted,[40] subject to ECJ review.[41] On the other hand the ECB is only involved in prudential supervision: matters relating to protection of consumers or investors have been left in the hand of the NCAs, with the ECB cooperating with them.[42]

In the field of recovery and resolution, a comparable regulatory structure as in prudential supervision applies. In the euro area a separate institution – the Single Resolution Board – has been designated to adopt resolutions decisions for significant institutions, while the NCAs will remain further in charge of the LSIs.

Financial stability objectives are of paramount importance in banking: the EBA, acting with the European Systemic Risk Board, has been mandated to identify criteria for the identification and measurement of systemic risk, undertake the necessary stress testing and develop effective instruments to determine the resilience of financial institutions. Risks of this nature may be addressed by the resolution mechanism and the deposit guarantee or insurance scheme – although both first serve to protect the individual bank client. Special powers have been granted to the NCAs and the ECB to adopt macroprudential measures with a view of avoiding financial stability risks, or if needed, systemic developments.[43]

B. In the Securities Field

The approach to regulation and supervision in the securities field is to facilitate the financing of mostly long-term investments, with a view of stimulating economic welfare, mainly through

---

[37] SSM reg, Art 6(5)(a) and (b); in fact this relates to cases in which the NCA has not, or has not been able to implement the banking supervisory principles and regulations.

[38] ECJ, Case T-122/15 of 16 May 2017 (53) *Landeskreditbank Baden Wurtemberg – Forderbank v ECB*. See also the quote in n 29.

[39] SSM reg, Art 4(1).

[40] See ECJ, Case C-219/17, *Silvio Berlusconi and Another v Banca d'Italia*, 19 December 2018.

[41] See ECJ, Case T-757/16 of 13 July 2018, *Société générale* v ECB and *Banque postale v ECB*, case T-733/16 of 13 July 2018 where the Court annulled the ECB decision on the basis of an error of law, the provision of the French law being clear.

[42] See Rec 28, SSM reg indicating these fields of on cooperation on securing a high level of consumer protection and on AML In a certain number of court cases, the conflict between national law and EU law was raised: ECJ, UBS Judgments, 13 September 2018, Cases C-358/16 *UBS Europe and Others v A. Hondequin* and others and in C-594/16 *Enzo Buccioni v Banca d'Italia*, where the court analysed the professional secrecy in civil proceedings obligation should be interpreted on the basis of the claimant's position and his rights of defence and the relevance in the proceedings. In other cases, the NCA was not involved: ECJ, Case C 156/15 of 10 Nov 2016, *Private Equity Insurance Group SIA v Swedbank* AS [2016] ECJ, Case C-51/17 20 September 2018, *OTP Bank Nyrt. and OTP Faktoring Követeléskezelő Zrt. v Teréz Ilyés and Emil Kiss*.

[43] See EBA reg, Art 22 et seq, SSM reg, Art 5.

facilitating the creation of an efficient market for financing through securities issues, in competition with bank lending.

Substantially different from the banking field is the risk distribution: in the securities field, the risks are ultimately supported by the investor, not by the intermediary who intervened in the issuance or the trading of the security. Therefore, the regulations pay much attention to the conditions in which the investors acquire the securities, ie by providing adequate information, at issuance in the prospectus, or by providing continuous disclosure afterwards. The conditions of trading, and especially of safekeeping are also strictly regulated: trading is widely concentrated in regulated markets, eg on stock exchanges, while the depositories are held to strict segregation. In comparison with banking regulation, in securities matters, safety wins from solvency. Also different from the banking sector is the diversity of the institutions intervening in the securities business: each function in this market is the subject of a specific regulation, often carried on by different specialised institutions, subject to a broad range of different legal regimes. Furthermore, there is separation of retail and wholesale activity in which mainly professionals intervene, and where the risk distribution is organised differently, often by offsetting risks against liabilities of other intermediaries.[44]

The investment funds are an important group of participants in the securities business: they hold and trade securities for numerous individual investors who are the beneficial owners of the common portfolio which legally belongs to the fund, a separate legal entity. There are many forms of investment funds: actively managed, index funds, exchange traded funds, money market funds, private equity or hedge funds, etc. Some of these funds offer insurance coverage, others are used as pension funds, triggering the application of the insurance or pension fund regulations. The regulations applicable to these different types of intermediaries aim at avoiding or reducing risks for the beneficiaries, often by holding a diversified portfolio. Regulation will therefore determine how the portfolios have to be invested and managed.

Differently from the banking field, there is no overarching regulatory system: the main instrument deals with markets in financial instruments,[45] but for many topics, or for different classes of intermediaries, separate regulations have been enacted. Most of these regulations have been adopted at the EU level, some on the basis of comparable international standards (IOSCO) as the activity addressed is often of a very international nature. These regulations will be applied by the national supervisors, their supervisory activity being coordinated at the ESMA level, where the 27 (still 28) national authorities are represented. The large diversity of regulations will make it quite difficult to put together a single rulebook. Actual practices may lead to more diversity.

The supervisory structure is based on the intervention of national securities supervisors, in each of the 27 Member States; there is no separate regime for the euro Member States, as there is – with some exceptions – no central supervisory authority. ESMA plays a significant role in coordinating the implementation by the NCAs, and developing common guidelines or standards allowing to better harmonise their action.

Financial stability issues in the securities business come in a different format: they often manifest themselves as market developments, resulting in a sudden lack of trust, leading to great imbalances in the markets, and creating a scare in the entire financial system. Resilience of the systems, orderly trading, adequate liquidity provision instruments are among the objectives of this part of the regulation. Market supervisors will have the power to stop trading or to

---

[44] See for the CPPs: EMIR, Art 4, Mifir, Art 29.
[45] Mifid II.

impose restrictive measures. Specific measures are being considered for the derivatives which are transferred to CCPs to reduce risks for the parties to the derivative.

C. Insurance

The third pillar of EU financial regulation relates to insurance activities. The basic regulatory scheme is based on an elaborate prudential regime, laid down in the 2009 Directive Solvency II, applicable since 2016.[46] These measures lay down the core capital requirements, risk management rules and the supervisory regime including the authorisation conditions and procedures. It includes winding up of insurance undertakings. These measures apply to the different activities in the field of insurance, such as life and non-life insurance, and reinsurance. A directive has laid down the regime on institutions for occupational retirement provision (IORP).[47] The Commission has adopted a long list of implementing and delegated acts dealing with numerous, especially technical aspects of the insurance regime.[48] In parallel to the prudential regime, another directive deals with the distribution of insurance products.[49] A regulation has been issued by the Commission listing in detail the items on which the subscribers of insurance have to be informed.[50] In the fields of PRIIPs, a regulation establishes a comparable questionnaire such as requirements for insurance-based investment products.[51]

Institutionally, the supervisory regime for the insurance activity is based on the presence of multiple national supervisory bodies, who often exercise their functions alongside the national ministries of finance or of economic affairs.[52] In a few jurisdictions, the central bank is involved as well.[53] Strikingly, the European Central Bank is not involved in the insurance activities nor in their supervision, due to an exception in the TFEU.[54]

Comparable to the two other sectors, an ESA – the European Insurance and Occupational Pensions Authority (EIOPA) – is in charge of dealing with insurance and occupational pensions

---

[46] Solvency II Directive (Dir 2009/138/EC [recast]) was adopted in November 2009, and amended by Dir 2014/51/ EU of the European Parliament and of the Council of 16 April 2014 (the so-called 'Omnibus II Directive'; Commission Delegated Regulation (EU) 2015/35 of 10 October 2014 supplementing Dir 2009/138/EC of the European Parliament and of the Council on the taking-up and pursuit of the business of Insurance and Reinsurance (Solvency II).

[47] Directive (EU) 2016/2341 of 14 December 2016 on the activities and supervision of institutions for occupational retirement provision (IORPs). See: implementing and delegated act 634/2014; https://ec.europa.eu/info/sites/info/files/ iorp-directive-level-2-measures-full_en.pdf.

[48] See; https://ec.europa.eu/info/sites/info/files/solvency2-directive-level-2-measures-full_en.pdf.

[49] Directive 2016/97 on insurance distribution; with implementing and delegated acts; https://ec.europa.eu/info/law/ insurance-distribution-directive-2016-97-eu/amending-and-supplementary-acts/implementing-and-delegated-acts_nl; https://ec.europa.eu/info/sites/info/files/idd-level-2-measures-full_en.pdf.

[50] Commission Implementing Regulation (EU) 2017/1469 of 11 August 2017 laying down a standardised presentation format for the insurance product information document.

[51] Commission Delegated Regulation (EU) 2017/653 of 8 March 2017 supplementing PRIIPs Regulation by laying down regulatory technical standards with regard to the presentation, content, review and revision of key information documents and the conditions for fulfilling the requirement to provide such documents. It is equally applicable to investment funds. A regulation has been issued by the Commission listing in detail the items on which the subscribers of insurance have to be informed. In the fields of PRIIPs, a regulation establishes a comparable questionnaire like requirement for insurance-based investment products.

[52] See: List of insurance and pension authorities https:/ /ec.europa.eu/info/business-economy-euro/banking-and-finance/insurance-and-pensions/insurance-pensions-authorities-and-organisations_nl.

[53] Only in seven Member States, does the central bank exercise direct supervisory powers.

[54] The TFEU excludes the ECB to deal with insurance supervision, see TFEU, Art 126(6). The ECB is not represented on the Board of EIOPA. EBA and ESMA are.

issues coordinating the action of the NCAs.[55] EIOPA has defined its mission mostly in terms of protection of consumers, while by strengthening regulation, supervision and harmonisation, the development of a common supervisory culture is being pursued.[56] EIOPA stated that it intends to pay stronger priority to supervisory convergence than to regulatory convergence. Significant work is undertaken on convergence in conduct, and on the conduct related risk. Common templates for PRIIPs are being considered.[57]

The relevance of insurance in terms of financial stability has been recognised by including the EIOPA in the European Systemic Risk board[58] and is receiving additional attention at the Council level.

There is no EU wide insurance protection scheme, but some states have introduced local guarantees schemes.[59] To be mentioned is the creation of a Pan-European Personal Pension Product (PEPP), which is seen as a tool to activate and support financing of European enterprises.[60]

Another workstream deals with consumer protection issues related to monetary incentives and remuneration between providers of asset management services and insurance undertakings.[61] EIOPA has published an opinion on this subject, on the basis of an EU wide thematic review. This general mission is based on provisions in the ESA regulation[62] and on its specific duties under the PRIIPs regulation and the IDD Directive. EIOPA's concerns relate essentially to the choice of an insurance undertaking for investment vehicles on the basis of the highest remuneration for the insurance undertaking, thereby neglecting the consumers' interests.

VI. Diversity and Coordination

Regulatory diversity is relatively high in the EU financial regulatory system, while harmonisation of the regulatory requirements is now pursued very actively. Diversity can be attributed perhaps less to the lack of harmonisation than to the divided structure of the supervisory system.

A significant harmonisation effort has been undertaken in the past with the intention to replace the diverse existing national laws or regulation by Union legal acts, thereby reducing

---

[55] See EIOPA governed by a largely identical regulation as applicable to EBA and ESMA.

[56] See EIOPA, A Common Supervisory Culture; Key characteristics of high-quality and effective supervision culture, issues of consistent application of Union law and developing trust between national supervisors are elements of this debate https://eiopa.europa.eu/Publications/Speeches%20and%20presentations/A%20Common%20Supervisory%20 Culture.pdf, 2017. EIOPA's Strategy for Conduct of Business Supervision – next Steps, 23 April 2018. https://eiopa.europa. eu/Publications/Speeches%20and%20presentations/A%20Common%20Supervisory%20Culture.pdf.

[57] Opinion on monetary incentives and remuneration between providers of asset management services and insurance undertakings; EIOPA-BoS-17-064 26 April 2017.

[58] See ESRB Regulation 1092/2010 of 24 November 2010.

[59] See: https://ec.europa.eu/info/system/files/insurance-guarantee_schemes-oxera-study_en.pdf: Oxera: Insurance guarantee schemes in the EU November 2007.

[60] See Regulation (EU) 2019/1238 of the European Parliament and of the Council of 20 June 2019 on a pan-European Personal Pension Product (PEPP) [2019] OJ L198/1 ('PEPP Regulation').

[61] Opinion on monetary incentives and remuneration between providers of asset management services and insurance undertakings; fn 57.

[62] EIOPA reg, Art 9(1); and Product Oversight and Governance requirements under the IDD, Art 25(1) and Arts 5 and 7 of the Commission Delegated Regulation (EU) 2017/2358 of 21.9.2017 supplementing Dir (EU) 2016/97 of the European Parliament and of the Council with regard to product oversight and governance requirements for insurance undertakings and insurance distributors (C (2017) 6218 final), as endorsed by the European Commission.

the wide diversity that existed between the Member States. These efforts were undertaken in the numerous harmonisation directives, in fields such as banking law or company law, to name a few. This streamlining eliminates the most significant distortions, but inevitably left many issues open as no agreement could be reached among the Member States for a single common approach. Some of these issues are still on the agenda today, and lead to distortions in the level playing field which should not be expected in an integrated internal market. In order to reduce this diversity, the Union legislature is now almost exclusively using regulations, but differences have subsisted.

Streamlining the requirements in specific fields is also the result of the activity of the ESAs in preparing the draft technical or implementing standards. These are the result of the consultations on the proposed actions and the subsequent collective efforts of the NCAs within the ESAs: they will normally result in common positions, or even in common decisions. As the standards have to be adopted by the Commission, changes to the ESA draft should not intervene except after prior coordination. These and other procedural guarantees[63] should ensure that the regulation adopting the standards generally meet the majority views of the NCAs concerned. A similar streamlining effect is likely to be achieved in the ex post monitoring of the implementation of the standards through the peer reviews. These not only reveal differences in implementation and practice but give an overview of the state of compliance – of non-compliance – of the individual NCAs; peer reviews are therefore powerful instruments to achieve the overall objectives of the regulation.

Apart from diversity between the Member States, there is also diversity in the EU regulatory instruments, and diversity in the implementation of these instruments. Different solutions are formulated in EU instruments for dealing with the same or similar questions: coherence should be an objective. Diversity also occurs in the way the NCAs apply the provisions for which they are responsible: these differences may be due to differences in national laws transposing directives, or in general national law – eg company law, contract law, which remains applicable to the underlying legal structures or to contractual relations. In the present status of development of European financial regulation, single concepts or rules are included in European harmonisation directives or in regulations which may be interpreted in different ways at the national level: one can refer to examples as different formulations of the 'fit and proper' test in prudential regulations,[64] or the conditions to be respected under the PRIIPs regime.[65] These differences negatively influence the integration of the financial markets, leading to national bias or regulatory competition.

Also, differences in national laws applicable to the entities supervised – eg national company law – or to the contractual relations governed by an EU regulation – consumer credit, payments, etc – often lead to a type of diversity which is not neutralised in the applicable financial regulations. It reduces cross-sectoral comparability, or leads to cross-border differences, negatively – and often surreptitiously – influencing market participants' choices intending to engage in cross-sectoral or cross border activity. But any appreciation of these differences will always be subject to a check on its conformity with the higher European standard.[66]

---

[63] See ESA reg, Art 10.

[64] See chapter 8A of this book; ECJ, Case T-133/16 to T-136/16, *Crédit Agricole v ECB*, 24 April 2018; comp. Case T-712/15, *Crédit mutuel Arkéa* v *ECB*, 13 December 2017; Joint ESMA and EBA Guidelines on the assessment of the suitability of members of the management body and key function holders, applicable to bank and investment firms, 21 March 2018, ESMA71-99-598; Decision (EU) 2017/933 of the ECB of 16 November 2016 on a general framework for delegating decision-making powers for legal instruments related to supervisory tasks (ECB/2016/40). See: 0 Voordeckers, 'How to Handle Normative Divergence within a Single Rulebook? An Analysis of the Implementation of Fit and Proper Requirements within the Single Supervisory Mechanism', EBI 2019 Conference.

[65] See chapter 13 of this book.

[66] See ECJ, Case T-133/16 to T-136/16, *Crédit Agricole v ECB*, 24 April 2018, on the basis of the separation of executive and non-executive or oversight function.

The causes of diversity may go deeper and be due to the diverse structure of supervision: for most financial regulations, the implementation is in the hands of the NCAs who often develop their own interpretation of the regulation, or add national application provisions, and this notwithstanding the principle of direct effect of the regulations. In other cases, NCAs have a genuine different reading of a regulatory provision: this practice is not strictly incompatible with EU law, provided the EU rule is respected.

Introducing additional local requirements to regulations or even applying additional local supervision may lead to diversity and possibly to fragmentation of the market: but local require-ments are sometimes imposed to better protect local investors or consumers. However, these additional requirements may bar access to investors from other EU jurisdictions, if some of these local requirements eg on additional disclosure have not been met. Therefore, EU supervisors should keep a close watch on these practices, and test the genuineness of the reasoning and the rationale for introducing these additional conditions. Cases of discrimination on the basis of nationality have been reported. Keeping a close watch should essentially be the task of the ESAs, who have been empowered with the necessary instruments and contribute to realise this part of the level playing field, without however endangering the fundamental characteristics of the regulation, eg, in terms of investor protection. They might also become points of contention trig-gering litigation, especially if the national rule conflicts with the European one.

For reducing these types of diversity, several solutions can be considered. The action of a central authority, with powers to impose a single interpretation, is the approach followed in the SSM, although not without difficulty. Another one, found in regulatory practice, is a wider appli-cation of the home state rule: by declaring that the applicable regulatory regime will be the one of the home state, it makes the same regulation – including its interpretation – applicable wher-ever the financial transaction or business is located. This regime has been successfully applied in passporting, eg for branches of banks, of investment firms, investment funds, but also for prospectuses, etc. Delegation of tasks and responsibilities among NCAs could also contribute to develop a commonality in the rules to be applied.[67]

Due to the role of the NCAs as members of the ESAs boards, the ESAs play an important role in developing common sectoral views. They determine the decisions and policies developed by the NCAs, and in so doing contribute to develop common views on subjects nationally dealt with by the ESA. This experience is further contributing to the preparatory work for Commission regulations. The development of common standards or methods with respect to their supervi-sory actions have contributed to streamlining the supervisory practices and the creation of a more level regulatory playing field. The cross-sectoral cooperation was first developed in the field of financial conglomerates, involving supervision of banking and insurance groups. Since then cooperation between the three ESA has been stepped up.

Conflicts between European law, and national provisions or interpretations will sometimes lead to judicial action, depending on the case, first to be decided at the national level,[68] and then further to be submitted to the ECJ by way of a preliminary ruling. In the SSM context, some of these cases in which national law confronted EU law, are the direct consequence of decisions of the ECB as the EU supervisory authority with direct supervisory powers. In these cases, the ECB was challenged by the supervised institution with respect to the position which the financial

---

[67] See EBA reg, Art 8(1)(c); also ESA reg, Art 28, for delegation among NCAs and to ESAs. This instrument has not been frequently used.

[68] Published national case law indicates that a certain number of cases are submitted to the national supreme courts. Preliminary review applications seem to be rather rare.

institution had adopted in reliance of the NCAs analysis, but the NCA is not a party to the litigation.[69] Indirectly the procedures have the effect of an appeal of the NCA decision. Recently, the number of cases so decided has increased,[70] pointing towards more interaction between the NCAs and the ECB. These cases stand for important steps in the roll-out of the Single Supervisory Mechanism towards a more homogenous regulatory system.

This unifying role could probably also be exercised by the ESAs by using their powers in case of breach of Union law by an NCA.[71] The ESA could investigate the breach on its own initiative, or act pursuant to a request from the Union institutions.[72] On the basis of this investigation of the breach, and if the NCA does not act to address the recommendations of the ESA, the Commission could issue a formal opinion to the NCA urging it to comply. Only if non compliance with the directly applicable act takes place, may the ESA address a decision to the individual financial institution. This decision could be challenged before the Joint ESA Board of Appeals. In a case in which a plaintiff objected to the appointment of bank directors for not being 'fit and proper', stating that the EBA refused to investigate the case, the plaintiff appealed to the ECJ from the decision of the Board of appeal, but was dismissed on the basis that as an individual, he had no locus standi not belonging to one of the categories entitled to request action from the ESA, while action was within the discretion of the ESA ('may').[73]

The ESAs have been empowered to play an important role in pursuing a more homogeneous regulatory regime and have received ample competences to that effect. The ESA regulations provide that they have been mandated to 'contribute to the establishment of high quality common regulatory and supervisory standards' and to 'contribute to the consistent application of legally binding Union acts ...'.[74] This would include the verification of the extent to which these additional national requirements are (in)-compatible with the Union standards or as the case may be, do not contribute to the overall objectives of the internal market. As mentioned above, the ESAs could also start an enforcement procedure for breach of Union law by an NCA. However, this procedure is quite complicated, requiring the initiative of other EU institutions and a formal Commission opinion. In several cases, plaintiffs were dismissed for not having the required capacity under Article 17(2), ESA regulation. The Commission would also be entitled to exercise this 'disciplinary mission' against a Member State which is 'failing to fulfil a Treaty obligation'.[75]

The regulatory diversity could also be approached by using the existing instruments provided in the ESA regulation which may lead to reduce diversity or if possible to common positions. The ESAs regulation provide for several instruments to enhance the coordination of the supervisory activity, not only among their constituent members, the NCAs, but also with the other ESAs and their members, the other NCAs. Among the techniques which may contribute to higher consistency in the regulatory practice one could mention the development of 'guidelines

---

[69] Compare the *Societe generale* and *Banque Postale* cases at fn 41, in fact opposing the ECB to the French ACPR.

[70] See ECJ, Case T-712/15*Crédit mutuel Arkéa v ECB, 13 December 2017*; ECJ, Case T-122/15, *Landeskreditbank Baden Wurtemberg – Forderbank v ECB* at fn 29.

[71] See ESA reg, Art 17.

[72] Parliament, Council, Commission, but also the Stakeholders group of the ESA, but not interested third parties.

[73] EBA reg, Arts 17(6), 18 and 19 of Regulation No 1093/2010 ECJ, 9 September 2015. ECJ, Case T-660/14, *SV Capital OÜ v EBA*; Board of Appeal. BoA 2014- C1-02 of 14 July 2014; see for the cases rendered by the Joint ESA Board of Appeal, https://eba.europa.eu/about-us/organisation/joint-board-of-appeal/decisions. Many of these cases were unsuccessful. See, however, BoA, 27 February 2019, where the Board considered that the different Nordic banks involved had not acted negligently on Nordic banks for having published credit assessments, in accordance with their national tradition, and having been unaware of t the application of the CRA regulation. These cases started with ESMA imposing fines for circulating ratings without authorisation: see ESMA: Convergence – enforcement actions.

[74] ESA reg, Art 8(1), (a) and (b).

[75] See TFEU, Art 258.

and recommendations with a view of establishing consistent, efficient and effective supervisory practices' not only among the NCAs active in the ESA but on an EFSF[76] wide basis, including with the other supervisory bodies.[77] These guidelines and recommendations apply on a 'comply-and-explain' basis: the ESAs have adopted many of these instruments.[78] In addition, the ESAs will develop a general 'coordination function' in order to be able to deal jointly with 'adverse' situations.[79] The regulations set up a 'Joint Committee of the ESAs', a forum dealing inter alia with selected list of subjects, and developing joint positions and common acts, to be adopted in parallel by the three ESAs.[80] Finally, a joint Board of Appeal has been created for the three ESAs.[81]

Inconsistency may also be the consequence of the continued application of national law resulting in conflicts with EU law. The resulting conflicts are first decided at the national level[82] and may be submitted by the parties to the ECJ by way of a request for a preliminary ruling, in fact opposing a decision adopted by an NCA or by the ECB in its supervisory capacity. Recently the number of cases so decided have increased, contributing to the uniform interpretation of Union law where the national legal provision is incompatible with the ECB's reading of Union law, but also pointing to stronger enforcement willingness of the ECB.

VII. The Effect of Regulation on the Integration of the EU Financial Markets

What is the effect of the regulatory and supervisory system on the integration of the EU financial markets? Would a different regulatory scheme, or changes in the present scheme improve cross–border integration? To what extent is the present regulatory scheme enabling stronger and faster integration of the EU markets?

Theoretically, if the conditions under which market participants could engage in financial affairs were increasingly similar in the EU Member States, they would be able to compare the services offered in the different jurisdictions and after comparison, take advantage of the better conditions offered in another state. This is what happens continuously in other markets segments, eg for foodstuff or drinks. If that facility would be offered, competition would play a stronger role,

---

[76] The ESFS comprises, according to Art 2 of the ESA regulation, the three ESAs, the ESRB, the Joint Committee, the ECB, and the other 'competent or supervisory authorities' referred to in other Union acts. Its mission 'shall be to ensure that the rules applicable to the financial sector are adequately implemented to preserve financial stability and to ensure confidence in the financial system as a whole and sufficient protection for the customers of financial services.'

[77] See about the composition of the EFSF, Art 2 of the EBA reg; 'and this with a view of common, uniform, and consistent application of union law'.

[78] Different institutions have different definitions of guidelines and recommendations. According to ESMA, guidelines aim to ensure a 'common, uniform and consistent implementation….': they also aim to achieve a convergent approach in the supervision '… and lead to improved investor protection (consumer outcomes). See for the guidelines// the recommendations defined by the Commission as 'allowing the EU institutions to make their views known and to suggest a line of action without imposing any legal obligation on those to whom it is addressed. They have no binding force'. See on the EBA guidelines and recommendations: ECB compliance with EBA guidelines and recommendations, www.bankingsupervision.europa.eu/legalframework/regulatory/compliance/html/index.en.html.

[79] See ESMA reg, Art 31.

[80] Article 54 et seq, with special reference to the Joint Committee dealing with financial conglomerates, created by the CRD IV Directive, consolidated version. This was one of the first cross-sectoral committees. There is also an Anti-Money Laundering Committee, a subcommittee of the Joint Committee of the three ESAs.

[81] Article 58; see for its decisions: https://eba.europa.eu/about-us/organisation/joint-board-of-appeal/decisions; see fn 66.

[82] Published national case law indicates that a certain number of cases are submitted to the national supreme courts, in some cases leading to preliminary review applications.

and market integration would result in more efficiency, offering a wider choice most of the time at more favourable conditions. Generally, the overall objectives of financial regulation would be better served. The first question is therefore, what has been the impact of the present regulatory system on the structure of banking, and to what extent have financial consumer reacted on the evolving regulatory system? In the present state of available information, to measure this impact is an exercise of approximation.

In banking, the composition of the population might give some indication about the regional footprint of the largest banks. Of the 119 significant institutions supervised by the ECB,[83] most focused their activity on the jurisdiction of the parent company, although the largest banking groups[84] are more active through subsidiaries located in other states, mostly their neighbouring states. The largest groups show a net preference for locating subsidiaries in Luxembourg with some interest for Belgium, Germany and Italy. The picture is however imprecise as it only refers to subsidiaries in the SSM jurisdictions.

As to cross-border transactions, it seems likely that these are most developed in the field of cross-border payments, a field which is receiving attention from the European Commission.[85] Many payments are executed through other means, especially by using credit card and through other third-party intermediaries. The involvement of the banks is therefore cross-border in a bank-to-bank sense.

In the investment fund sector, available data indicate that the cross-border activity is quite substantial, as illustrated by the information on the in- and outflows from investment funds, with Luxembourg (+62 billion) and Ireland (+47 billion) attracting the largest volumes of incoming investment in 2018.[86] Per hypothesis, these flows represent cross-border net investments. In terms of assets, these trends have resulted in considerable, total asset positions for the investment funds domiciled in the same countries: Euro 4.065 billion for Luxembourg and Euro 2.421 billion for Ireland, followed by the UK at 1.493 billion.[87] These figures give some idea about the volumes of cross border financial flows in the two jurisdictions where largely comparable regulations have been adopted.

More precise information on individual behaviour can be derived from a Commission led research, as part of its Consumer Financial Services Action Plan, conveying some insights on the factual situation per regulatory domain.

In a study of April 2016,[88] the European Commission published a large-scale public opinion survey about the use of financial products in the different Member States, including their use in a cross-border context. The Eurobarometer[89] survey related to the following products or

[83] See for the 2018 list see: www.bankingsupervision.europa.eu/ecb/pub/pdf/ssm.list_of_supervised_entities_201802.en.pdf.

[84] Eg, the Dutch, French, Spanish banking groups seem to have established more subsidiaries in other jurisdictions.

[85] Commission: Consumer Financial Services Action Plan: Better Products, More Choice, COM/2017/0139 final, 23 March2017; see also: Summary of contributions to the Green Paper on retail financial services: Better products, more choice and greater opportunities for consumers and businesses COM(2015) 630 final, http://ec.europa.eu/finance/consultations/2015/retail-financial-services/docs/summary-of-responses_en.pdf.

[86] See EFAMA, Net Sales by Country of Domiciliation and Investment Type, p 5 www.efama.org/Publications/Statistics/Quarterly/Quarterly%20Statistical%20Reports/190308_Quarterly%20Statistical%20Release%20Q4%202018.pdf.

[87] EFAMA, Net Assets by Country of Domiciliation, 2018, UCITS Directive and AIFs; in euro. The use of ISIN codes in each of these jurisdictions is likely to confirm these figures.

[88] Special Eurobarometer 446 – April 2016 'Financial Products and Services', EV-04-16-507-EN-N.

[89] See about the Eurobarometer, starting 1974, and its methodology: http://ec.europa.eu/commfrontoffice/publicopinion/index.cfm; compare for payment services: Commission, Consumer Financial Services Action Plan, 2017, factsheet-consumer-financial-services-action-plan-23032017_en.pdf; www.google.com/search?client=safari&rls=en&q=Commission,+Consumer+Financial+Services+Action+Plan,++2017,+factsheet-consumer-financial-services-action-plan-23032017_en.pdf&ie=UTF-8&oe=UTF-8, with an action plan for 2018, pointing to the need for a deeper Single Market for consumer credit.

services: current bank accounts, car insurance, savings accounts, credit cards, life or private health insurance, mortgage or personal loans, shares or bonds, investment funds, and other insurance products and services. The use of these products by individuals in all Member States was analysed, identifying significant differences between the Member States for all products and services tested. With respect to the cross-border use, the research indicated that 7 per cent of all respondents have used a product or service in another Member State, younger users or higher educated users being more active, and certain progress being noted with the previous 2011 survey.[90] The more active users were located in Luxembourg, Ireland and Romania, with the lowest percentages for Denmark, the Netherlands, France, Spain and Greece. Per product, the interest for life insurance, investment funds[91] or mortgage loans were found to be very small (between 0 per cent and 3 per cent).[92] Noteworthy are the reasons for this limited interest for foreign services and products: most answers indicated that users did not see the need for going abroad, their needs being met locally (33 per cent). Other explanations were: the absence of information (17 per cent), concern about fraud or crime (16 per cent), concerns about the way to deal with possible problems (13 per cent) and the language barrier (12 per cent). Complexity, extra costs, lack of consumer protection, too high fees, and the refusal to contract with a party from another state are also mentioned. The firms from their side pointed to the negative effects of local regulations, with differences of consumer protection requirements, gold plating, tax laws, local networks for insurance claims and divergent interpretations of money laundering requirements. Consumer organisations suggested focusing on better enforcement of existing EU consumer protection rules. Better access to cross-border financial services including portability of products including cross-border; transparency and comparability of products; access to bank accounts abroad and no unjustified discrimination on the grounds of residence; insurance protection schemes in insolvency cases and better access to compensation.

The report attributes to the lack of cross-border competition that investors and consumers do not get the best deal in these cases.

As evidenced by the figures comparing 2011 to 2016, it is likely that the interest in cross-border financial activity has further increased. It is important to mention that the survey relates to the conduct of individual citizens in the different Member States and not to the action of commercial firms which are likely to have a different approach, more focused on cross-border activity.

This factfinding overview could be read as evidence for the lack of interest for more uniformity in financial regulation in a cross-border context but points to a week interest as far as consumers are concerned. However, this view does not respond to todays need for a more efficient financial system, an important support for the activity of the economic actors who should be enabled to operate on a Europe-wide basis. As the financial activity becomes increasingly based on information technology, more transparent, with a wider offering of products, less dependent on localisation and widely available throughout the Union, the reliance on a more uniform legal regime – including the contractual conditions under national law – would contribute to the development of the EU internal market, and support the cross-border exchange of goods and services. At the same time, more competition, better safeguards for participants, but also more attractive fees would strengthen this evolution and increase its benefits. As is already the case, language differences are less relevant due to already available translations, and if not, of on the

---

[90] There are no data available from more recent surveys.
[91] The figure for investment funds seems difficult to reconcile with the data made available by the fund sector itself.
[92] Table Q c 1.

spot automated translation. In order to eliminate the remaining distrust from users,[93] a more uniform legal regime in which users could expect to have the same legal position and the same protection, while producers of financial services could take advantage of the uniform requirements. These elements would be a significant factor in strengthening the EU's internal market, while rendering EU financial services more attractive to non-EU based users.

With respect to the subjects discussed here, the Commission drew a double conclusion: (a) increase consumer trust and empower consumers (b) reduce legal and regulatory obstacles affecting businesses.

VIII. Conclusion

This overview of the financial regulatory system in Europe conveys a message of complexity, a characteristic which is not proper to the EU, if one compares with the similarly if not more complex American regulatory landscape.

Europe's financial regulatory system, like all comparable systems in developed economies, generally succeeds at meeting the general objectives of financial regulation, and in most fields, it has been quite successful. These objectives are embedded in a complex framework aimed at integrating the financial markets in the 27 Member States, allowing participants to have equal access to all markets and services in the Union. The structure developed to achieve this objective has significantly influenced the structure of the applicable regulation, which is based on at least two superimposed layers – European and the 27 national legal systems – applicable with some differences in the three sectors of financial activity – banking, insurance and securities. Notwithstanding these considerable differences in regulatory characteristics, these sectoral regulations have largely achieved the general objectives of regulation. Inevitably, the outcome has been sometimes been quite confusing, based on different formulation for identical issues, thereby rendering their application unpredictable, and needing considerable administrative – and judicial – efforts and costs. It is important to mention that this unsatisfactory status of the European financial regulation is largely due to its organisational structure and to the difficulty to coordinate between the different decision-making levels. Considerable efforts are now being undertaken to achieve a higher level of convergence and coherence between the different supervisory bodies who are daily confronted with the resulting complexity, and these efforts should be strongly supported.

But changes are necessary. A first series of changes may consist of better organising the regulatory function and its accessibility. At present financial regulation in the EU is spread over thousands of pages, with documents of different legal status, available on many websites at the Commission, at the ESAs, the ECB, the ESRB etc. The idea of the 'Single Rulebook' in its widest sense has long since been lost: it should be replaced by 'the common rulebook', made accessible in an interactive website where the different levels of regulations are accessible through links. The individual instruments should be made available in a coordinated format, and at least available on the sites of the bodies which are expected to apply them, as unfortunately, this is not always the case today. Duplicate or largely similar provisions should be merged, and differences in the

---

[93] Under the heading of increasing trust the Commission mentioned in its press release 'we want to make it easier for drivers to take their no-claims bonus ('bonus-malus') abroad. We also want to reduce fees for cross-border transactions involving non-Euro currencies and we will be taking steps towards more transparent pricing of car rental insurance', It also proposed to 'Reduce legal and regulatory obstacles affecting businesses when seeking to expand abroad. This will include working on common creditworthiness assessment criteria and facilitating the exchange of data between credit registers.'

numerous definitions brought together in one single definitions article, of course after having been checked as to their content. The sanctioning or secrecy provision, for example, are also among the candidates for coordination, touching on Human Rights issues.[94]

Substantive coordination is not absent from the agenda of the ESAs, as they are more engaged in regulatory convergence and in Joint Committee work, but a wider, Commission-led initiative would be welcome: the confusion is some fields – the PRIPPs being an example – should be clarified by following a more integrated approach. Coordination is especially important when fundamental changes are introduced: repositioning a well known product in a new perspective calls for special attention in terms of coherence.[95,96]

The NCAs from their side could also contribute on a regional basis, especially if they belong to the same legal tradition: harmonisation of national law, eg provisions of contract law or negligence rules should be considered, to safeguard the level playing and avoid jurisdictional arbitrage. The latter question leads to a more fundamental issue: in fields which are the subject of tight regulation, especially for reasons of investor protection, is it acceptable that different national contract rules still apply, and should these not be replaced by a common Uniform Financial Contracts code?[97] These could offer better protection and shield against unilateral, or divergent interpretations. In the wholesale markets, this outcome is largely achieved by having standard contracts referring to uniform contract rules, made by professional organisations (ISDA).

Therefore, the present initiative to identify further regulatory similarities and propose how these can be harmonised is a step in the right direction. It would be useful to broaden the perspective to subjects for which uniform regulatory provisions could be developed and this across the entire regulatory spectrum. The further pursuit of this project should preferably be undertaken with the support of the ESAs, and their constituent members. The general objectives of financial regulation should remain fully applicable.

In some fields, a common core of identical provisions could be developed: there are several types of investment funds, and these are governed by largely identical provisions. Why not develop a common core of rules, to be supplemented by specific provisions for the different types of funds? More ambitiously, could one not try a similar exercise for the provisions on credit institutions and investment firms, which share many characteristics, governance being a well-known example? A comparable analysis may be undertaken for the company disclosure rules, or the rules governing the distribution of financial products. Developing common legal provisions would lead to common administrative practices and contribute to simplify the application of this complex regulatory apparatus.

---

[94] See: ECJ, Case C-358/16, *UBS Europe SE and Alain Hondequin a.o v. DV a.o*, 13 September 2018. See nt 15.

[95] This is the case with the extension of the planned prudential regime to certain investment funds: see: Opinion Of The European Central Bank of 22 August 2018 on the review of prudential treatment of investment firms (CON/2018/36)/; Directive Of The European Parliament And Of The Council on the prudential supervision of investment firms and amending Dirs 2013/36/EU and 2014/65/EU, 20 December 2017, COM(2017) 791 final; Proposal for a Regulation Of The European Parliament And Of The Council on the prudential requirements of investment firms and amending EU Regulations CRR, MiFIR and EBA, COM(2017) 790 final; EFAMA: EFAMA calls for legal certainty and a compatible approach between the provisions of the new regime for investment firms and relevant existing provisions already applying to investment firms. The European Supervisory Authorities (ESAs) submitted to the European Commission, draft regulatory technical standards to amend the Delegated Regulation covering the rules for the Key Information Document (KID) for Packaged Retail and Insurance-based Investment Products (PRIIPs).

[96] EFAMA welcomes the preliminary agreement in trilogue on the proposal on facilitating cross-border distribution of funds.

[97] Compare the success of the UCC in the US.

Over time, deeper reforms are necessary. The relationship between national and EU law has become a point of contention. Most ECJ cases in these fields are driven by the technical diversity of national law, and the ECB's overriding reading of the general purpose of EU prudential supervision. This tension is unlikely to go away as long as the relationship between the ECB and the NCAs remain based on an unclear form of codecision. But more efficient and speedy ways of solving these tensions may be developed, whereby protection of individual rights might usefully be strengthened.

The core question in this field has been the restructuring of the ESAs, which has recently been hotly debated. As the question was posed in terms of centralisation, the answer was inevitably negative, less from the ESAs but mainly from the NCAs. This failure is partly due to the too ambitious nature of the objectives pursued. At the same time, alternatives to more efficiency should be considered: the home country technique as a centralising technique was mentioned above. The ESAs themselves should investigate where they can cooperate without losing their specificity to the extent that this is linked to their different missions. Centralisation could be started with some functions, eg on data collection or integrating parts of their internal organisation, but also coordination of decision making could help reduce the burden, and be beneficial to their budgets. One could see a mandate by the Commission to investigate the fields in which effective coordination could help simplify the present structure.

These few remarks should not reduce the merit of the distance which has been covered in EU financial regulation, especially in supervision over about the last 20 years.

4

FinTech Regulation
from a Cross-Sectoral Perspective

EUGENIA MACCHIAVELLO

I. Introduction: FinTech and Regulation

The reciprocal chase between financial innovation and regulation ('regulatory dialectic') is not a new phenomenon in the financial sector.[1] Nonetheless, the intense technological progress characterising the last few years has intensified the recourse to technology in the financial industry and accelerated such chase, leading to the identification of a new market segment called 'FinTech', seen as a sub-category of financial innovation.[2] The sector has exponentially grown since then, despite the initial blame on financial innovation after the financial crisis.[3]

At first, the term FinTech referred to start-ups and new market entrants applying technology to finance, thus innovating products, services, processes or the distribution of the same traditionally provided by banks, investment firms and insurance firms and creating alternatives to the traditional financial sector.[4] Classical examples are crowdfunding platforms, virtual currencies and InsurTech (ie usage-based, on-demand or P2P insurance).[5] More recently, official

---

[1] About financial innovation and 'regulatory dialectic', see E Kane, 'Interaction of Financial and Regulatory Innovation', (1988) 78(2) *Surprises from Deregulation* 328; D Llewellyn, 'Financial innovation: a basic analysis', in H Cavanna (ed), *Financial Innovation*, (London, Routledge, 1992), 14ff. For further references, see E Macchiavello, 'Financial-Return Crowdfunding and Regulatory Approaches in the Shadow Banking, Fintech and Collaborative Finance Era', (2017) 14(4) *European Company and Financial Law Review* 662.

[2] P Amstrong, 'Financial Technology: The regulatory tipping points', FMA's FinTech conference – Liechtenstein (27 September 2016), www.esma.europa.eu/sites/default/files/library/2016-1420_financial_technology_the_regulatory_tipping_points_by_patrick_armstrong_0.pdf; DW Arner, J Barberis and RS Buckley, 'FinTech, RegTech, and the Reconceptualization of Financial Regulation', (2017) 37(3) *NWJILB* 371; Basel Committee on Banking Supervision (BCBS), 'Sound Practices: implications of Fintech developments for banks and bank supervisors', (February 2018), 13–14, www.bis.org/bcbs/publ/d431.pdf; Commission, 'FinTech Action Plan: For a more competitive and innovative European financial sector', (Communication) (8 March 2018), COM(2018) 109 final.

[3] On the evolution of FinTech, see in particular DW Arner, J Barberis and RP Buckley, 'The Evolution of FinTech: A New Post-Crisis Paradigm?', (2016) 47 *Georgetown Journal of International Law* 1271, 1272–73.

[4] See, eg, PwC, 'Blurred lines: how FinTech is shaping the Financial services industry', (2016), www.pwc.de/de/newsletter/finanzdienstleistung/assets/insurance-inside-ausgabe-4-maerz-2016.pdf; S Darolles, 'The rise of fintechs and their regulation', (2016) 20 *Financial Stability Review* 85.

[5] About InsurTerch: OECD, 'Technology and innovation in the insurance sector', (2017), www.oecd.org/pensions/Technology-and-innovation-in-the-insurance-sector.pdf; EIOPA, 'Report on best practices on licencing requirements,

definitions underline the widespread use of technology in the provision of financial services also by incumbents (especially online and mobile technology, biometrics and, potentially, big data, cloud computing and machine learning). The FSB, in fact, defines FinTech as 'technology-enabled innovation in financial services that could result in new business models, applications, processes or products with an associated material effect on the provision of financial services'.[6] International Authorities have been recently discussing not only risks and benefits of the new FinTech entrants,[7] but also the scenarios for incumbents and the financial market in general deriving from the use of technology in the financial sector by regulated operators.[8]

The FinTech world has in fact raised several regulatory issues.[9] In particular, difficulties have emerged in applying traditional categories to such new activities, which tend to resort to business models not conceivable by regulators at the time when principles and rules were set (eg machines and algorithms substituting humans in trading and management;[10] online platforms and block-chain instead of markets to exchange financial products). Furthermore, the use of technology might create new risks requiring specifications or new requirements. Significant differences between FinTech activities and traditional ones, potential benefits and lower level of risks (especially systemic) of FinTech might justify exemptions, adaptations, sandboxes (ie experimental regimes) and special regulations but with potential regulatory arbitrage and un-level playing field effects.

Finally, technology has the potential to overcome territorial and sectoral borders, adding complexity to the analysis. In particular, FinTech presents cross-sectoral issues per se: it has spread among all financial sectors, with the same technology deployed in different (economic, not only financial) sectors and contexts; it has taken advantage of grey areas between sectoral regulations or of the lack of clarity and over-lapping of rules and authorities' competences, therefore calling for the attention of all financial regulators.[11]

---

peer-to-peer insurance and the principle of proportionality in an Insurtech context, (27 March 2019), https://eiopa. europa.eu/Publications/EIOPA%20Best%20practices%20on%20licencing%20March%202019.pdf.

[6] FSB, 'Financial Stability Implications from FinTech. Supervisory and Regulatory Issues that Merit Authorities' Attention', (27 June 2017), 7, www.fsb.org/wp-content/uploads/R270617.pdf; EBA, 'Fintech Roadmap. Conclusions from the Consultation on the EBA's Approach to Financial Technology (Fintech)', (15 March 2018) 9, www.eba.europa.eu/documents/10180/1919160/EBA+FinTech+Roadmap.pdf; EBA, 'Discussion Paper on the EBA's approach to financial technology (FinTech)', (4 August 2017), EBA/DP/2017/02, 4–6, www.eba.europa.eu/documents/10180/1919160/EBA+Discussion+Paper+on+Fintech+%28EBA-DP-2017-02%29.pdf; IAIS, 'FinTech Developments in the Insurance Industry', (21 February 2017), www.iaisweb.org/file/65625/report-on-fintech-developments-in-the-insurance-industry.

[7] See, among many others: FSB (n 6); Committee on the Global Financial System (CGFS) and FSB, *FinTech Credit. Market structure, business models and financial stability implications*, (BIS, Basel, 2017); IOSCO, 'Research Report on Financial Technologies (Fintech)', (February 2017), www.fsb.org/wp-content/uploads/CGFS-FSB-Report-on-FinTech-Credit.pdf; World Economic Forum (WEF), 'The Future of Financial Services. How disruptive innovations are reshaping the way financial services are structured, provisioned and consumed', (2015), www3.weforum.org/docs/WEF_The_future__of_financial_services.pdf; EBA, 'Discussion' (n 6).

[8] See BCBS (n 2); FSB, 'FinTech and market structure in financial services: Market developments and potential financial stability implications', (14 February 2019), www.fsb.org/wp-content/uploads/P140219.pdf; EBA, 'Report on the prudential risks and opportunities arising for institutions from FinTech', (3 July 2018), www.eba.europa.eu/documents/10180/2270909/Report+on+prudential+risks+and+opportunities+arising+for+institutions+from+FinTech.pdf.

[9] See C Brummer and D Gorfine, 'FinTech: Building a 21st-Century Regulator's Toolkit', (2014), http://assets1c.milkeninstitute.org/assets/Publication/Viewpoint/PDF/3.14-FinTech-Reg-Toolkit-NEW.pdf; M Fenwick, WA Kaal and EPM Vermeulen, 'Regulation Tomorrow What Happens When Technology is Faster than the Law', (2017) 6 *American University Business Law Review* 561.

[10] See C Brummer, 'Disruptive Technology and Securities Regulation', (2015) 84 *Fordham Law Review* 997.

[11] See European Parliament, 'FinTech: the influence of technology on the future of the financial sector', Resolution of 17 May 2017 (2016/2243(INI)).

FinTech also underlines some important shortcomings in the existing system of financial regulation, suggesting the need of rethinking financial regulation towards a more proportionate and function-based model, before creating separate frameworks for un-traditional models.

In this chapter, after a brief description of the FinTech sector, I will discuss the main regulatory issues related to the same, with special regard to whether and what regulation is needed and to cross-sectoral aspects. Examples, especially from the financial-return crowdfunding (FRC) and crypto-assets areas, will be provided. Finally, I will identify useful components of a proposal about FinTech regulation, as a part of a more general reconceptualisation of financial regulation, taking into account the variety and complexity of the FinTech universe and therefore the lack of a 'one-fits-all' solution.

II. The FinTech World: Characteristics and Effects on the Financial Sector

A. FinTech Size, Drivers and Categorisations

The FinTech sector is exponentially expanding every year, especially in Asia.[12] Among the reasons for such fast development the following are generally listed:[13] the recent jump in technological development leading to increased computing power, broader accessibility and lower costs (eg smartphones, shopping online, etc); the partial withdrawal of traditional financial institutions also related to the post-crisis increased regulatory burden and compliance costs; the post-crisis distrust towards traditional financial providers; change in customers' (especially the 'millennials') expectations, preferences (in terms of speed and convenience) and needs because of the experience with Big-Tech in other areas of consumption.[14]

It represents a very diverse world, encompassing different sectors and technologies but mainly occupying the traditional areas of lending, payments and personal and SME banking, while also currently expanding in the areas of asset management and insurance.[15] However, even existing categorisations struggle to provide a clear picture of the FinTech universe. Some of them try to reconnect the new services/products to the traditional sub-sectors of payments (eg mobile payments, digital wallet), lending and financing (crowdfunding, invoice trading, innovative credit scoring), financial management and exchanges (robo-advisory, brokerage platforms, exchange-based platforms, social trading) and insurance (InsurTech, P2P insurance). However, most recent

---

[12] From 2013 to 2016, the Alternative Finance sector (the main area of the Fintech sector) has expanded, in Europe, from €1.1 billion to €7.7 billion, in the Asian-Pacific region, from €4.13 billion to €221.6 billion and in the Americas, from €3.2 billion to €31.8 billion: T Ziegler et al, 'Expanding Horizon – The 3rd European Alternative Finance Industry Report', (2018), www.jbs.cam.ac.uk/fileadmin/user_upload/research/centres/alternative-finance/downloads/2018-ccaf-exp-horizons.pdf and Id, 'Shifting Paradigms – The 4th European Alternative Finance Benchmarking Report', (2019), www.jbs.cam.ac.uk/fileadmin/user_upload/research/centres/alternative-finance/downloads/2019-04-4th-european-alternative-finance-benchmarking-industry-report-shifting-paradigms.pdf (with updated data); for data about global private investments in FinTech companies, see also KPMG International, 'The Pulse of FinTech Q4 2017', (2018), https://assets.kpmg.com/content/dam/kpmg/xx/pdf/2018/02/pulse_of_fintech_q4_2017.pdf.

[13] Capgemini, 'World Fintech Report 2017', (2018), www.capgemini.com/service/introducing-the-world-fintech-report-2017/; IOSCO, 'Research Report'; FSB (n 6) 15ff.

[14] EBA, 'Report on the impact of Fintech on incumbent credit institutions' business models', (3 July 2018), 9.

[15] See data in Citi GPS, 'Digital Disruption. How FinTech is Forcing Banking to a Tipping Point', (March 2016), https://ir.citi.com/D%2F5GCKN6uoSvhbvCmUDS05SYsRaDvAykPjb5subGr7f1JMe8w2oX1bqpFm6RdjSRSpGzSaXhyXY%3D; PwC (n 4); BCBS (n 2).

works have created the additional category of market support services (eg data management, financial data and service aggregators, comparison websites, AI, cloud computing, cyber-security, Distributed-Ledger Technology-DLT[16]) and underlined the use of the same technology or innovation in different areas (eg big data and machine learning both for credit scoring in crowdfunding platforms and InsurTech; DLT in online marketplaces, payments and InsurTech).[17]

B. Benefits and Risks of FinTech and its Effects on the Financial Sector

FinTech is believed to channel a varied range of benefits:[18] lower costs and a consequent financial inclusion effect;[19] increased competition, innovation and service quality (with also incumbents forced to provide faster, more personalised and higher-quality services, in a transparent way); resilience and diversification in a traditionally concentrated and highly inter-related sector.

Nonetheless, such benefits obviously do not come without risks.[20] First, FinTech has been associated with a disruptive effect on the financial sector, challenging traditional operators in their most profitable operational segments and therefore their stability,[21] although current analyses present a still low level of disruption and scenarios of collaborations and mergers between incumbents and new entrants ('fintegration').[22] Systemic risks have been generally put aside because of the limited size of the FinTech sector compared with the traditional one. However, studies have more recently pointed at some specific micro-prudential risks, such as liquidity, maturity, volatility, operational (cyber, legal, outsourcing, etc) risks and at the systemic risk deriving from its exponential expansion, increased interconnectedness also with the traditional sector and complexity of the sector as well as new critical economic functions or market infrastructure, changes to customer loyalties and the consequent effect on stability and regulatory arbitrage.[23]

---

[16] DLT allows the creation of a "a multi-party system in which participants reach agreement over a set of shared data and its validity, in the absence of a central coordinator" (M Rauchs et al, 'Distributed Ledger Technology Systems: A Conceptual Framework', 2018, www.jbs.cam.ac.uk/fileadmin/user_upload/research/centres/alternative-finance/downloads/2018-10-26-conceptualising-dlt-systems.pdf). Blockchains are distributed and shared registries recording in chronological sequence all transactions ('blocks') in an irreversible way. There are differences between DLT and block-chain and many types of the same (eg permission-less, private, federated, etc) with varied legal and technical implications. See ibid and D Lee and RH Deng, *Handbook of blockchain, digital finanancem ad inclusion – vol 2*, (London, Academic Press, 2018).

[17] See IOSCO (n 7); BCBS (n 2).

[18] European Parliament (n 11); CGFS-FSB (n 7); BCBS (n 2) 22ff.

[19] For references about financial inclusion and Fintech, E Macchiavello, *Microfinance and Financial Inclusion. The Challenge of Regulating Alternative Forms of Finance*, (Routledge, London, 2017); DW Arner et al., 'Fintech for Financial Inclusion: A Framework for Digital Financial Transformation', (4 September 2018), UNSW Law Research Paper No 18–87, https://ssrn.com/abstract=3245287; UNSGSA FinTech Working Group and CCAF, 'Early Lessons on Regulatory Innovations to Enable Inclusive. FinTech: Innovation Offices, Regulatory Sandboxes, and RegTech', (2019), 10ff, www.jbs.cam.ac.uk/fileadmin/user_upload/research/centres/alternative-finance/downloads/2019-early-lessons-regulatory-innovations-enable-inclusive-fintech.pdf.

[20] Ibid; BCBS (n 2) 24ff.

[21] Although FinTech remains a small sector compared to the traditional one, it presents incredibly high growth rates and has developed in the most profitable segments for banks (eg payments, settlements and retail banking): see Citi GPS, (n 15); PwC (n 4); Capgemini (n 13); CGFS-FSB (n 7).

[22] See Capgemini (n 13); BCBS (n 2); EBA (n 14), 11ff, 25ff.

[23] FSB (n 6); M Carney, 'The Promise of FinTech – Something New Under the Sun?', speech at Deutsche Bundesbank G20 conference 'Digitalising finance, financial inclusion and financial literacy', Wiesbaden, 25 January 2017, www.bankofengland.co.uk/-/media/boe/files/speech/2017/the-promise-of-fintech-something-new-under-the-sun.pdf?la=en&hash=0C2E1BBF1AA5CE510BD5DF40EB5D1711E4DC560F; BCBS (n 2) 5ff; BaFin, 'Big Data meets artificial

Therefore, the attention has been mostly focused on consumer protection issues, which are only partially shared among certain FinTech segments. For instance, the use of big data[24] and algorithms for credit scoring or insurance underwriting presents risks as regards data protection, accessibility (ability to access data and challenge their reliability), portability (because of data ownership), interoperability, wrongful assessment (because of the data inaccuracy or errors in the algorithm design), opacity (lack of transparency about the evaluation process) and related opportunity for discrimination, granular segmentation and lower comparability (caused by the extreme personalisation of the evaluation).[25]

Other risks, instead, depend on the characteristics of each FinTech and specific business model. For example, robo-advice platforms present the risk of clients not understanding the diversity from the regulated investment advice and the importance of the information provided; possible errors in the underlying algorithm or limited ability to cover the specificities of all customers, especially the ones with complicated financial needs; difficulties in liability attribution (especially between the service provider and developer).[26] Virtual currencies (VC, in particular, cryptocurrencies)[27] present high volatility, scarce liquidity and higher risk of fraud because of the anonymity of its system and lack of legal protections compared with legal tender.[28] FRC poses at risk crowd-lenders/investors as regards capital loss (for both platform and recipient's default), agency costs and asymmetric information, illiquidity, investment concentration, lack of adequate and not-misleading information; the recipient, as regards the risk of concealed high cost and over-indebtedness, unfavourable contractual terms, privacy issues; the system, with reference to the risk of fraud, money-laundering and financing terrorism.[29] P2P insurance might expose customers to the risk of hidden costs, lack of coverage or of claim payments.[30]

intelligence', (2018), 13ff, www.bafin.de/dok/11250046 (also pointing out that a new form of systemic risk might result from the use of the same technology – AI).

[24] European Institutions refer to 'big data' as 'high volumes of different types of data produced with high velocity from a high number of various types of sources are processed, often in real time, by IT tools (powerful processors, software and algorithms)'. They can consist in personal data such as name, citizenship, date and place of birth, gender, marital status, contact details, education, job and income, hobbies, etc or data use such as browsing history, log data, call and messaging activity and provided in aggregated and anonymous form or not. Sources can be social media, internet provider, e-commerce, etc. See Joint Committee, 'Discussion Paper on the Use of Big Data by Financial Institutions', (2016), www.esma.europa.eu/sites/default/files/library/jc-2016-86_discussion_paper_big_data.pdf; Id, 'Final Report on Big Data, (15 March 2018), JC 2018/04, www.esma.europa.eu/sites/default/files/library/jc-2018-04_joint_committee_final_report_on_big_data.pdf; Commission, 'Data Driven Economy', (Communication), COM(2014)442 final.

[25] Ibid; BaFin (n 23).

[26] Joint Committee of ESAs, 'Report on automation in financial advice', (2016), https://esas-joint-committee.europa.eu/Publications/Reports/EBA%20BS%202016%20422%20(JC%20SC%20CPFI%20Final%20Report%20on%20automated%20advice%20tools).pdf.

[27] 'Virtual Currency' means a 'digital representation of value that is not issued or guaranteed by a central bank or a public authority, is not necessarily attached to a legally established currency and does not possess a legal status of currency or money, but is accepted by natural or legal persons as a means of exchange and which can be transferred, stored and traded electronically' (Art 3(16) V AML/CT Directive; European Central Bank-ECB, 'Virtual Currency Schemes – A Further Analysis', ECB, Frankfurt, 2015). Cryptocurrencies are bi-directional and decentralised virtual currencies. About different types of virtual currencies, see N Vandezande, *Virtual Currencies: A Legal Framework*, (Cambridge, Intersentia, 2018). The term crypto-assets is more recently used to refer to both virtual currencies and tokens: see EBA, 'Report with advice for the European Commission on crypto-assets', (9 January 2019); ESMA, 'Initial Coin Offerings and Crypto-Assets. Advice', (9 January 2019), ESMA50-157-1391, 1.

[28] ECB, 'Virtual currency' (2015).

[29] Commission, 'Unleashing the potential of Crowdfunding in the European Union', (Communication) COM(2014) 172 final 2. For further references, see Macchiavello, 'Financial-return'.

[30] EIOPA (n 5) 27.

III. FinTech: Main Regulatory Issues

A. Traditional Legal Categories, Activity-Based versus Entity-Based Regulation and the Challenges Raised by the Technology Evolution

FinTech, as mentioned, does not only challenge the traditional financial sector but also regulators as FinTech techniques often do not fit into traditional legal categories.[31]

Many financial innovations cannot be easily placed within existing legal frameworks and the picture is complicated by the interaction with other innovations, not exclusive of the financial sector, such as the new collaborative economy. The flourishing of online platforms, allowing the interface and contractual relationships between private users (peer-to-peer), has blurred the distinction between consumers and providers, professional and non-professional providers, employed and self-employed workers, which are categories traditionally used to define the scope of application of certain rules.[32]

As regards the financial sector, as discussed in other parts of this book, current EU financial regulation requires specific and differentiated authorisations to carry out certain relevant activities, namely the banking activity (reception of reimbursable funds from the public and provision of credit), investment services (certain services as identified in the Markets in Financial Instruments Directive – MiFID – II No 2014/65/EU and pertaining to financial instruments), payment services and insurance activities. The rationale of such activity-based regulation and 'regulated activities' approach is, first, to subject to the same regulation activities presenting similar characteristics and risks, irrespective of the type of entity performing them, thus preserving competition. Second, to subject certain relevant and systemically important activities to public controls at the entry stage as well as during their functioning. An entity-based regulation, instead, would incentivise regulatory arbitrage, favouring the escape towards unregulated areas. However, there are certain entity-based correctives. Systemically important institutions deserve, in fact, special rules for their potential to negatively affect the entire system and the real economy, as evidenced during the financial crisis. Prudential regulation in general has entity-based grounds, related to systemic risk aspects (eg interlinkages).[33]

Nonetheless, the possibility – facilitated by technology – to parcel out the activity and services in different segments and then externalise or distribute the same among different operators might anyway exclude the identification of a regulated activity with reference to a single operator.[34] For instance, in P2P lending and certain P2P insurance models, the typical lending or insurance activity is offered by non-professional people, potentially acting at the same time as customers, while other related (managing/technical) services are offered by an online platform.[35]

---

[31] See Commission, 'FinTech Action Plan', 5; W Kaal and EPM Vermeulen, 'How to Regulate Disruptive Innovation-From Facts to Data, (2017) 57 *Jurimetrics Journal* 169. About 'regulatory disruption', N Cortez, 'Regulating Disruptive Innovation', (2014) 29 *Berkeley Technology Law Journal* 175, 183ff.

[32] See Commission, 'A European agenda for the collaborative economy', (Communication) COM(2016) 356 final; Id., 'Online Platforms and the Digital Single Market. Opportunities and Challenges for Europe', (Communication), (25 May 2016), COM(2016) 288 final; C Busch, 'The Rise of the Platform Economy: A New Challenge for EU Consumer Law', (2017) 5 *Journal of European Consumer and Market Law* 3.

[33] EBA (n 6) 'Roadmap', 10–11.

[34] See Carney (n 23): 'FinTech's true promise springs from its potential to unbundle banking into its core functions of: settling payments, performing maturity transformation, sharing risk and allocating capital'.

[35] In the P2P insurance context, anyway, most business models require the platform to obtain an authorisation as an insurance firm (when offering – at least partially and residually – insurance coverage) or broker (when also distributing others' insurance products for residual coverage): EIOPA (n 5) 26ff.

Furthermore, fundamental legal concepts (eg issuer, market, securities, insurance) – conceived in a scenario of physical financial markets, branch-based services and central role of traditional intermediaries – are hardly applicable to new phenomena and anyway suffers from wide differences among Member States. Consequently, despite the prevalent activity-based regulation, many FinTech end-up unregulated or subject to inadequate regulations (ie not adequately responding to the risks posed).[36]

For instance, one central concept in EU financial regulation is the notion of 'financial instruments' (one of the conditions to apply to MiFID, Market Abuse and Transparency Directives, Prospectus Regulation, etc), which is defined in EU legal texts only through a reference to a list of financial instruments in an annex (cf Article 4(1)(15) MiFID II). However, a broad interpretation would allow regarding such a list as open and consider financial instruments for any financial product (ie investment of money with expectation of return based on the underlying risk) characterised by 'negotiability' – ie, based on the Commission's interpretation, transferability and ability to be the object of transactions taking place in contexts where buying and selling interests in securities meet.[37] Interpreters tend also to require the standardisation of the conditions attached to the product (to facilitate the creation of a 'market').[38] Nonetheless, national implementations and interpretations significantly vary in identifying financial instruments and further defining the same. In fact, many require, in addition, the 'similarity' to the financial instruments mentioned in the annex, in terms of the rights attached (see below).[39] Different definitions also exist as regards single investment services (eg reception and transmission of orders, placement, etc).

Consequently, for instance, although some investment-based (IBC) and lending-based crowd-funding (LBC) business models echo certain investment services (eg reception and transmission of orders, placement without guarantee, management of MTF/OTF or, based on other business models,[40] investment advice, portfolio management), EU financial regulation might not find application. In fact, IBC platforms have often been resorting to business models involving products not considered financial instruments and/or services not considered investment services (both cumulative conditions for the application of MiFID) under certain national interpretations, therefore escaping the applicability of MiFID authorisation requirements and discipline, despite the similarities with investment services and the transferability or even negotiability feature of the products.[41] Similarly, LBC platforms conduct an activity similar to credit intermediation but with a more decisive role in selecting borrowers, in setting the contractual terms of the loan and

---

[36] See EBA (n 6) 'Discussion' (signaling significant differences in regulatory approaches to FinTech among Member States and the prevalent un-regulated nature of FinTech businesses).

[37] Commission, 'Questions on Single Market Legislation' – Definitions, 'transferable securities', Art 4(1)(18) of Dir 2004/39/EC, ID 150 (Internal reference 2) and ID 285 (Internal reference 115); European Securities Market Expert Group, 'Financial Instruments – Impact of definitions on the perimeter of FSAP Directives', 4 (2008), http://ec.europa.eu/internal_market/securities/docs/esme/fin-instruments-050308_en.pdf; G Castellano, 'Towards a General Framework for a Common Definition of "Securities": Financial Markets Regulation in Multilingual Contexts', (2012) 17(3) *Uniform Law Review* 449.

[38] P Hacker and C Thomale, 'Crypto-Securities Regulation: ICOs, Token Sales and Cryptocurrencies under EU Financial Law', forthcoming in *European Company and Financial Law Review*, https://ssrn.com/abstract=3075820.

[39] Ibid; ESMA (n 27).

[40] Eg, implying the use on many peer-to-peer lending platforms of automatic and algorithm-based systems diversifying loans from a single lender among multiple borrowers according to the risk profiles and preferences of borrowers and the lender.

[41] Ie, participations in private limited companies in Hungary and silent partnerships in Italy and Germany are considered financial instruments while this is not the case in other countries (eg silent partnerships in Austria and participations in private limited companies in Italy). See Macchiavello (n 1); G Ferrarini and E Macchiavello, 'Investment-based Crowdfunding: Is MiFID II enough?', in D Busch and G Ferrarini (eds), *Regulation of EU Financial Markets: MiFID II* (Oxford, OUP, 2017).

often in influencing crowd-lenders' decisions (as in investment services). However, they have often ended-up unregulated or regulated, at most, as payment institutions, therefore subject to a regime responding to the needs and aims of protection of client funds and cyber-security but not to the aspects related to the platform's conduct, due diligence checks and information to clients about risks and recipients' reliability.[42]

As regards VC, the decentralised nature of the system for Bitcoin creation/emission ('mining') – therefore the absence of a natural/legal person recognisable as the issuer or market manager – has so far prevented the application, among others, of investment services, markets and prospectus regulations to cryptocurrencies emissions. Instead, platforms operating cryptocurrency exchanges and wallet service operators in principle might be considered providing investment or payment or e-money services but the legal qualification of cryptocurrencies is complex and varies remarkably worldwide, even within the same country.[43] For instance, the US Inland Revenue Service qualifies the Bitcoin as property, the Commodity Futures Trading Commission as commodity and certain US courts as money. A SEC official has recently denied the qualification as securities of cryptocurrencies because of their decentralised nature (failing to meet the 'common enterprise' and 'profits from the efforts of others' features of the *Howey* test and not representing a claim against an identifiable issuer).[44] The BaFin considers Bitcoin as a financial instrument, in particular, 'units of account', only under the German Banking Act (not the Financial Markets Act – *WpHG* – or MiFID), which means that commercially dealing in virtual currencies might require a national authorisation (not a MiFID one);[45] in any case, German courts seem not to share this view.[46]

---

[42] In other countries, as investment service, credit intermediation, lending or reception of repayable funds, with very different regulatory consequences: Macchiavello (n 1) and Id, 'Peer-to-Peer Lending and the "Democratization" of Credit Markets: Another Financial Innovation Puzzling Regulators', 21(3) (2015) *Columbia Journal of European Law* 521; G Ferrarini and E Macchiavello, 'FinTech and Alternative Finance in the CMU: The Regulation of Marketplace Investing', in D Busch and G Ferrarini (eds), *Capital Markets Union in Europe*, (Oxford, OUP, 2018); Commission, 'Final report: Identifying market and regulatory obstacles to crossborder development of crowdfunding in the EU', (December 2017), https://ec.europa.eu/info/sites/info/files/171216-crowdfunding-report_en.pdf; Id., 'FinTech'; DA Zetzsche e C Preiner, 'Cross-Border Crowdfunding – Towards a Single Crowdfunding Market for Europe', European Banking Institute Working Paper Series 2017 – No 8, https://ssrn.com/abstract=2991610.

[43] Cryptocurrencies are generally not regarded as money, lacking the main features of the latter as recognised under the main theories. In fact, they are not a legal tender, nor accepted as a general mean of payment: Vandezande, *Virtual*, 137ff but see also different theories in RM Lastra and JG Allen, 'Virtual Currencies in the Eurosystem: Challenges Ahead', 30ff, www.europarl.europa.eu/committees/en/econ/monetary-dialogue.html.

[44] For references, see D Zuluaga, 'Should Cryptocurrencies Be Regulated like Securities?', CMFA Briefing Paper No 1 (25 June 2018), www.cato.org/publications/cmfa-briefing-paper/should-cryptocurrencies-be-regulated-securities# endnote-016; P Athanassiou, *Digital Innovation in Financial Services: Legal Challenges and Regulatory Policy Issues* (London, Kluwer Law International, 2018), 102.

[45] In fact, the qualification of a virtual currency as a financial instrument also under German securities law (derived from MiFID) will instead depend, on a case-by-case basis, on whether that particular VC or token is transferable, negotiable, embodies a right and it is not an instrument of payment (security) or it can be qualified as units of a collective investment or capital investment (profit participation or subordinated loan, etc): Bafin, 'Supervisory classification of tokens or cryptocurrencies underlying 'initial coin offerings' (ICOs) as financial instruments in the field of securities supervision', Advisory Letter Ref. No. WA 11-QB 4100-2017/0010, www.bafin.de/SharedDocs/Downloads/EN/Merkblatt/WA/dl_hinweisschreiben_einordnung_ICOs_en.pdf;jsessionid=47741C233E9A50ED71B9 B1596A01F0B5.2_cid290?__blob=publicationFile&v=2; see also www.bafin.de/EN/Aufsicht/FinTech/VirtualCurrency/virtual_currency_node_en.html and www.bafin.de/SharedDocs/Veroeffentlichungen/EN/Fachartikel/2018/fa_bj_1803_ICOs_en.html. An Italian Court qualified bitcoin as a financial instrument but only in order to apply the Italian Consumer law about the distance marketing of financial services to consumers to the service of bitcoin-euro exchange in view of a crowdfunding operation (without motivating on such qualification): Tribunale di Verona, 24 January 2017, No 195 available at www.dirittobancario.it/sites/default/files/allegati/tribunale_di_verona_24_gennaio_2017_n._195.pdf.

[46] The Berlin Court of Appeal has recently denied to bitcoin the nature of financial instrument under German banking law: *Kammergericht Berlin*, 25 September 2018, reference No (4) 161 Ss 28/18 (35/18).

Instead, tokens issued in Initial Coin Offerings – ICOs – (ie offering of tokens in exchange for fiat currency financing an enterprise)[47] with certain characteristics (eg transferability, negotiability and similarity with existing financial instruments in terms, for instance, of rights embodied, contractual structure and transferability rules) and cryptocurrency derivatives tend to be considered by many Member States and US authorities as financial instruments, therefore on a case-by-case[48] analysis but each identifying different relevant factors.[49]

The ECB has so far excluded the qualification of typical cryptocurrencies also as e-money (in particular, for not being 'issued upon receipt of funds' but 'mined')[50] but not proposed alternative categories. Under certain – isolated – interpretations cryptocurrencies might be qualified as 'funds' under Article 4(25) of the Payment Service Directive – PSD2 (No 2015/2366)[51] but this does not seem to reflect the current EU position[52] and anyway leads to assimilate cryptocurrencies with generally accepted methods of payments, which they are not (at least at present). The European Court of Justice has qualified bitcoin as a 'contractual means of payment', not comparable with securities, but only with reference to VAT law and to recognise a VAT exemption.[53]

More recently, the EBA and ESMA have asserted that a crypto-currency or token, while generally not qualifying as e-money or funds under PSD2, might come under the notion of e-money or financial instrument depending on the specific characteristics of the same and, as regards the latter, national interpretations and implementations of MiFID II.[54]

---

[47] Cf the definition in ESMA, 'ESMA alerts investors to the high risks of Initial Coin Offerings (ICOs)', Statement, (13 November 2017), www.esma.europa.eu/sites/default/files/library/esma50-157-829_ico_statement_investors.pdf. About ICOs and different types of tokens (currency, utility and investment), P Maume and M Fromberger, 'Regulation of Initial Coin Offerings: Reconciling US and EU Securities Laws', forthcoming in *Chicago Journal of International Law*, available at https://ssrn.com/abstract=3200037; Hacker and Thomale (n 38); Lastra and Allen (n 43), 21ff; ESMA (n 27).

[48] The ESMA has warned firms to verify whether tokens issued qualify as financial instruments since this would trigger the application of several EU laws concerning regulated activities: ESMA, 'ESMA alerts firms involved in Initial Coin Offerings (ICOs) to the need to meet relevant regulatory requirements', (13 November 2017), www.esma.europa.eu/sites/default/files/library/esma50-157-828_ico_statement_firms.pdf.

[49] Maume and Fromberge (n 47), 17ff, 41ff. Because of the closed list in Art 211-1 *CMF*, the French AMF considers equity tokens and transferable securities only when recognising to investors a share of capital of a commercial company: AMF, 'Discussion paper on Initial Coin Offerings', (26 October 2017), www.amf-france.org/en_US/Publications/Consultations-publiques/Archives?docId=workspace%3A%2F%2FSpacesStore%2Fa2b267b3-2d94-4c24-acad-7fe3351dfc8a. The British FCA considers the simple expectation of the rise in value and of profit from a resale on the secondary market not enough to qualify tokens as transferable securities but requires rights comparable to shares (profit but also voting right on relevant/strategic issues) or bonds, negotiability and presentation as investment: FCA, 'Guidance on cryptoassets', (23 January 2019), www.fca.org.uk/publication/consultation/cp19-03.pdf. The Spanish CNVM has more widely identified, as indicators, the existence of an expectation of profit *or* the attribution of rights equivalent to financial instruments *or* the presentation of the product as similar to financial instruments as regards profits or liquidity, even when utility token: CNVM, 'Considerations on cryptocurrencies and ICOs addressed to market professionals', (8 February 2018), www.cnmv.es/Portal/verDoc.axd?t=%7b62395018-40eb-49bb-a71c-4afb5c966374%7d. On the nature of Bitcoin in comparative perspective see also A Blandin et al, *Global Cryptoasset Regulatory Landscape Study*, (Cambridge, Cambridge University Press, 2019), www.jbs.cam.ac.uk/faculty-research/centres/alternative-finance/publications/cryptoasset-regulation/#.XN6vQegzbIV; Vandezande (n 27); N Vardi, 'Bit by bit: Assessing the Legal Nature of Virtual Currencies', in G Gimigliano, *Bitcoin and mobile payments; constructing a European Union Framework*, (Basingstoke, Palgrave MacMillan, 2016), 61; S Shcherbak, 'How should Bitcoin be regulated?', (2014) 7(1) *European Journal of Legal Studies* 45, 56.

[50] EBA, 'Opinion on virtual currencies', EBA/Op/2014/08, 11. Instead e-money is 'electronically, including magnetically, stored monetary value as represented by a claim on the issuer which is issued on receipt of funds for the purpose of making payment transactions [...], and which is accepted by a natural or legal person other than the electronic money issuer' (Art 2(2) e-money Dir No 2009/110).

[51] Shcherbak (n 49) 57.

[52] ECB (n 27) 30; Vandezande (n 27) 323ff.

[53] CJEU, *Hedqvist* case, C-264/14, EU:C:2015:718, para 42.

[54] EBA (n 27) 12ff; ESMA (n 27).

Robo-advice falls within the MiFID perimeter when consisting in a personalised recommendation, presented as adequate for the recipient and pertaining to financial instruments[55] and a similar definition exists also for insurance advice as regards insurance investment products (Article 2(1)(15), IDD). However, in fully-automatised systems, it might be difficult to recognise the typical discretion of advisors and apply conduct rules. Anyway, in force of the 'technological neutrality' principle (see section III.B below), the EU considers automatic services equivalent to human-lead ones.[56] Furthermore, some business models, structured as comparative websites but expressing evaluations based on client preferences, might be qualified as mere intermediation (or insurance distribution).[57]

Finally, certain regulations (not entailing an authorisation for conducting specific activities) but protecting interests other than stability and investor confidence also present entity-based grounds and therefore end up not applying to unregulated FinTech. For instance, the Consumer Credit Directive (No 2008/48) only applies to credit agreements between professional lenders and consumers. Therefore, the absence of the professional character in the lending activity of peer-to-peer lenders excludes its application to P2P loans despite the presence of consumer-borrowers and of the platform acting professionally as an intermediary between the parties (providing standard contracts and conducting checks on parties). Similarly, previous AML/CT Directives used only to apply to credit institutions and certain other financial institutions (insurance undertakings and intermediaries, investment firms, collective investment undertakings, branches, PI/e-money institutions, currency exchange officers), therefore excluding unregulated online platforms (eg LBC, virtual currencies exchange platforms, etc) but subsequent revisions have progressively expanded their scope.[58] The V AML/CT Directive has explicitly included among the obliged entities VC exchange platforms and custodian wallet providers.[59] The same Directive has also introduced, moreover, the obligation for such new operators to register, have fit and proper managers and beneficial holders as well as adopt measures for customer verification. However, this obviously appears as only partial regulation, leaving uncovered many other risks, as underlined by EBA, which also fears that the inclusion within the Directive's scope might give the false impression of the existence of certain (actually inexistent) safeguards.[60] Similarly, general consumer protection rules (eg e-commerce and consumer rights Directives) only apply where not excluded by the

---

[55] See Art 9 Commission Delegated Regulation No 565/2017; W-G Ringe and C Ruof, 'A Regulatory Sandbox for Robo Advice', (May 31, 2018), EBI Working Paper Series 2018 No 26, https://ssrn.com/abstract=3188828; IOSCO (n 7) 25.

[56] Art 54(1) Commission Delegated Regulation 2017/565; ESMA, 'Guidelines on certain aspects of the MiFID II suitability requirements – Final Report', (28 May 2018). About discretion in automated execution of orders, ESMA, 'Questions and Answers. On MiFID II and MiFIR market structures topics', (19 November 2018), question No 21, www.esma.europa.eu/sites/default/files/library/esma70-872942901-38_qas_markets_structures_issues.pdf.

[57] Ringe and Ruof (n 56); IOSCO (n 7) 31; EIOPA (n 5).

[58] The IV AML/CT Directive includes as obliged entities also gambling services, legal and natural persons acting in the exercise of their professional activities (auditors, external accountants, tax advisors, notaries, legal professionals, trusts and company service providers, estate agents, etc). Crowdfunding platforms are therefore not subject to AML/CT when not falling under any of such categories. Instead, as regards virtual currency, not only their providers are not easily assimilated with existing obliged entities but even cryptocurrencies cannot be easily qualified as 'funds' or 'property' under current EU and national regimes. About difficulties in extending, by means of interpretation, AML/CT regime to cryptocurrencies platforms and exchanges, see Vandezande (n 27) 298ff; C Kaiser, 'The Classification of Virtual Currencies and Mobile Payments in Terms of the Old and New European Anti-Money Laundering Frameworks', in Gimigliano (n 51) 214–215.

[59] The original draft of the European Parliament resolution on the V AML/CT Directive aimed at covering, as obliged entities, all virtual currency providers (including issuers, administrators, distributors and intermediaries) but, also considering the difficulties in applying such rules to the decentralised nature of most cryptocurrencies, the article was amended in the final resolution.

[60] EBA, 'Opinion on the EU Commission's proposal to bring Virtual Currencies into the scope of Directive EU', 2015/849 (4AMLD), EBA-Op-2016-07, 5.

lack of subjective (consumer/professional) or objective requirements. For instance, the Distance Marketing of Consumer Financial Services Directive No 2002/65 applies in the case of a service with banking, payment, insurance, personal pension fund or investment nature and provided by a person acting in his professional capacity and counterparty of the consumer.[61]

B. The FinTech Regulatory Dilemma and Current Approaches: New Regulatory Instruments and Regulatory Arbitrage

In facing the above-mentioned issues, regulators around the world have showed differentiated responses to the FinTech regulation problem. In particular, the alternatives have been: a) subjecting FinTech to existing regulations – thanks to flexible and wide definitions and scopes of the latter – possibly creating incubators or Innovation Hubs to help enterprises navigate the regulatory landscape (UK, Singapore, Canada, Australia); b) adapting existing law to the specificities or needs of FinTech even through guidelines and warnings (more flexible and fast to adopt than legislative reforms[62]); c) creating case-by-case exemptions through no-action letters or dispensations, etc (in the long-term, a very expensive and opaque process with potentially discriminatory outcomes; USA); d) resorting to new regulatory instruments, creating sandboxes or new ad hoc regulation (eg UK, Netherlands, Switzerland, Hong Kong, Singapore, Malaysia, Australia); e) leaving it unregulated, recognising the activities as falling outside the regulatory perimeter (China).[63] This last option might appear difficult in a post-crisis and shadow banking fear scenario[64] but it is not so uncommon. Finally, some have introduced experiments in deploying technology also in regulatory compliance and supervision, in order to reduce costs (RegTech and SuperTech).[65]

Technology per se does not change the structure or principles of financial regulation, therefore the EU has assertively adopted a 'technologically-neutral' – as well as activity-based and proportionate – approach in financial regulation, in order to ensure a level-playing field between incumbents and new entrants.[66] Therefore, irrespective of the use of technology, carrying out a regulated activity requires a licence and the respect of certain rules. However, as already mentioned, technology might complicate the task of ascribing certain activities to traditional categories.

Furthermore, technology can create new risks,[67] therefore potentially requiring special measures to contain the same. For instance, online banking is exactly the same activity as traditional

---

[61] The Directive requires the provider to inform the consumer about himself, the service provided (including the total price and whether financial instruments with special risks are involved) and the contract (duration, withdrawal right in 14 days, redress measures, applicable law).

[62] T Wu, 'Agency Threats', (2011) 60 *Duke Law Journal* 1841, 1841–42 (Essay); Cortez (n 29) 185–86.

[63] For a partially different categorisation and a deep comparative analysis of the alternatives, see DA Zetzsche, RP Buckley, JN Barberis, DW Arner, 'Regulating a Revolution: From Regulatory Sandboxes to Smart Regulation', (2017) 23 *Fordham Journal of Corporate & Financial Law* 31; Brummer and Gorfine (n 9). See also UNSGSA FinTech Working Group and CCAF (n 19) 26ff.

[64] IH-Y Chiu, 'Fintech and Disruptive Business Models in Financial Products, Intermediation and Markets – Policy Implications for Financial Regulators', (2016) 21 *Journal of Technology Law and Policy*. 55.

[65] About RegTech and SupTech, V Colaert, 'RegTech as a Response to Regulatory Expansion in the Financial Sector' (June 2018), https://ssrn.com/abstract=2677116; Arner et al (n 2). About the need of new trainings for supervisors' staff, see BCBS (n 2) 6; L Enriques, 'Financial Supervisors and Regtech: Four Roles and Four Challenges', in (2017) *RTDF* 53, https://ssrn.com/abstract=3087292; DW Arner, DA Zetzsche, RP Buckley and JN Barberis, 'Fintech and Regtech: Enabling Innovation While Preserving Financial Stability', (2017) 18(3) *Georgetown Journal of International Affairs*. 47.

[66] European Parliament (n 11); EBA (n 6) 'Roadmap'; Id., 'Discussion' (n 6); Commission (n 2); EIOPA (n 5) 10, 13, 15.

[67] See, involving other sectors, EU actions in the related Digital Economy, Cyber-security and Data Protection areas (see Commission (n 2) 2).

banking but carried out with different instruments, therefore presenting new risks such as a lower level of depositor fidelity, more competition, and, consequently, increased liquidity risk and stability risks.[68] However, current risk-based requirements are easily adapted to technology-based activities (eg through guidelines), simply requiring that all risks are efficiently managed by financial service providers.

Nonetheless, the ECB, despite in principle supporting the technologically-neutral approach, seems to impose on FinTech banks (eg banks where the production and delivery of banking products and services are based on technology-enabled innovations) new requirements, often justified by certain elements not exclusive of FinTech banks but shared with any start-up bank (eg small depositor base, limited statistical data, etc).[69]

As regards to robo-advice, the ESMA, in its final guidelines on suitability,[70] has decided to subject robo-advisors to the same rules as traditional investment advisors (while in the first draft references were made to the need of 'additional rules'), simply indicating specifications in case of use of AI and algorithms (in particular, governance and risk management requirements, more than disclosure).

Adaptations might anyway be needed when a technologically-neutral approach is not able to respond to the specific risks raised by FinTech or hinder the creation of new business models channelling relevant benefits (eg requirements implying the physical presence of the client and of the financial operator or paper-based information block innovation).[71]

A different approach entailing special regulations and exemptions might appear instead discriminatory, especially when only targeting new alternative entrants, therefore damaging non-FinTech small companies. Nonetheless, it might be justified in certain cases, in consideration of the significant differences between certain FinTech and traditional businesses in terms of functions and risks (see below about FRC)[72] and of the need of an alternative sector to

---

[68] Arner et al (n 3) 12–13. About fingerprint recognition and related legal and ICT security risks, EBA (n 8) 15ff.

[69] In the ECB guide on FinTech banks, the main shareholders of FinTech banks are required to have, contrary to traditional banks' (but see Joint Committee, 'Joint Guidelines on the prudential assessment of acquisitions and increases of qualifying holdings in the financial sector – Final report', 20 December 2016, JC/GL/2016/01, 10.23ff) technical and professional experience in banking and the ECB justifies this choice with the assumption that FinTech banks have presumably few shareholders and IPOs represent a rare option. Moreover, supervisors will have to monitor the data and methodology used for credit scoring and loan management by FinTech banks – contrary to traditional banks – since they presumably cannot rely on a long historical set of data being a start-up. FinTech banks need to present an exit plan, in addition to the business plan, justified by their start-up condition and therefore lack of historical data. Also, minimum capital and liquidity reserves are set higher because the ECB is concerned with the high initial IT investment coupled with competition, volatility – and therefore more expensive interbank financing – and customer mobility. See ECB, 'Guide to assessments of licence applications – Licence applications in general', (March 2018), www.bankingsupervision.europa. eu/ecb/pub/pdf/ssm.201803_guide_assessment_credit_inst_licensing_appl.en.pdf; Id., 'Guide to assessments of fintech credit institution licence applications', (March 2018), www.bankingsupervision.europa.eu/ecb/pub/pdf/ssm.201803_ guide_assessment_fintech_credit_inst_licensing.en.pdf.

[70] ESMA (n 57). See also Recital 86 and Art 54(1) Commission Delegated Regulation (UE) No 2017/565.

[71] Ringe and Ruof (n 56). Some issues had been already raised and addressed in the Commission, 'Staff Working Document on the Call for Evidence – EU regulatory framework for financial services', (23 November 2016), SWD(2016) 359 final, 77–78; EIOPA (n 5) 15.

[72] Commission, 'FinTech: a more competitive and innovative European financial sector', (Consultation document) (2017), https://ec.europa.eu/info/sites/info/files/2017-fintech-consultation-document_en_0.pdf; CGFS-FSB (n 7); Commission (n 72) 80:

'There are clear advantages associated with being a regulated financial institution, such as access to central bank liquidity and deposit guarantees. Accordingly, level-playing field arguments must be looked at in a holistic way. The nature of the entity and the risk of its business, including its size and interconnectedness, may also determine the set of applicable rules.'

advance financial inclusion while protecting customers. Furthermore, the absence of an un-level playing field might be ensured by the absence of a competition in the same market or of the substitutability of products.[73]

Some countries (eg UK, Singapore and Japan) have created regulatory sandboxes, ie 'safe places' where businesses can experiment new products and services with real customers in a controlled environment 'without immediately incurring all the normal regulatory consequences of engaging in the activity in question'.[74] The extent of the exemption or of the suspension of the application of existing regulations depends on the type of sandbox, type of activities and supranational obligations (eg EU law mandating the application of certain rules to the entities conducting a certain activity, saved for discretions and application of the proportionality principle).[75] Regulatory sandboxes respond to the aim of better knowing the innovative business and allowing the development of the same before regulating it, as well as removing barriers to entry and reducing concentration in the market, while, at the same time, limiting the potential harm to consumers.[76] However, sandboxes are not downside free: commentators underline the lack of a level-playing field, its resource-intensive nature, the risk of model convergence and lack of transparency as well as the complexities in creating sandboxes within the restricted limits set by EU law.[77]

C. Regulatory Issues Related to Cross-Border Activity

The diffusion of the internet and other similar technologies has reduced distances but, at the same time, has also facilitated the existence of legally-complex situations, where subjects from different countries are involved and multiple regulations from different countries potentially apply.[78] In fact, existing conflict between rules (in Rome I Regulation No 593/2008 for contracts or in sectoral regimes), are subject to national interpretations, are partially national (international private law) or not easily applicable in a technology-driven context, often presenting sectorial-based differences which can lead to lack of clarity and over-lapping. In fact, also depending on the qualification, additional foreign laws might apply, making it difficult for both providers and clients to understand which rules are applicable.

---

[73] Some reports seem to attest the absence of direct competition between incumbents and new entrants and this would also be the case when products and services are different: see EBA (n 14) 37; A Fraile Carmona et al, 'Competition issues in the Area of Financial Technology (FinTech) Policy', (July 2018), www.europarl.europa.eu/RegData/etudes/STUD/2018/619027/IPOL_STU(2018)619027_EN.pdf.

[74] FCA, 'Regulatory sandbox', (November 2015), www.fca.org.uk/publication/research/regulatory-sandbox.pdf. An entry-test generally assesses whether a true innovation exists, the same benefits consumers and the market, it enhances or does not endanger financial stability, measures to protect consumers are in place (eg right to complain, restriction to sophisticated customers) and existing regulations are not able to adequately regulate the activity. See Ringe and Ruof (n 56) 40ff; Zetzsche et al (n 64) 30ff.

[75] See also European Supervisory Authorities (ESAs) – Joint Committee, 'FinTech: Regulatory sandboxes and innovation hubs – Report', (7 January 2019) JC/2018/74, 18, www.esma.europa.eu/sites/default/files/library/jc_2018_74_joint_report_on_regulatory_sandboxes_and_innovation_hubs.pdf.

[76] See Ringe and Ruof (n 56); Zetzsche et al (n 64); Commission (n 2); FSB (n 6) 28.

[77] To overcome national regulatory differences, some authors have hypothesised the creation of a sandbox at EU level or to facilitate it at EU level but then leave the creation of the sandbox to Member States: Ringe and Ruof (n 56).

[78] DR Johnson and DG Post, 'Law and Borders – The Rise of Law in Cyberspace', (1996) 48(5) *Stanford Law Review* 1367.

For instance, both credit institutions and investment firms can conduct in other Member States the activities admitted to mutual recognition and for which they have been authorised in their home country, also through branches, and subject to home country regulation and supervision, except for certain requirements imposed on branches by the host country for the 'general interest'. However, the conduct and product rules that apply are these of the host country in case of banks and those of the home state in case of investment firms.[79] Parties might decide which law is applicable to the contract but without prejudice to the protection recognised by the law of the country where the consumer has his/her habitual residence (which anyway apply) (Articles 3, 4(b) and 6, Rome I Regulation). However, in the insurance sector, the applicable law is always the one of the country where the insured risk is located (Article 7, Rome I Regulation).[80]

Furthermore, especially in the case of digital services, it might not be clear when a services is provided in the territory of another Member State. As a general rule, an activity is considered conducted in a certain country when at least a part of the 'characteristic performance' (ie the essential supply for which payment is due) takes place in that country.[81] However, such principle has been formally affirmed only with reference to the banking sector (therefore contested in the investment services sphere), and in the insurance sector the Commission has deployed a partially different criterion: an insurance activity is considered conducted in a state when the risks covered or the commitments are situated in such a state.[82]

Also in the area of the offering of transferable securities (prospectus Regulation), the home country (where the issuer has its registered office) rule is in force but other Member States' rules might apply as regards the marketing of securities (or even of investment products other than financial instruments) addressed to their citizens. The picture is complicated by the existence of significant differences among States in the exemption thresholds and prospectus liability regimes.[83] Moreover, other Member States' rules might apply as regards investment firms and investment services in the distribution chain of such securities.

Finally, as mentioned above, there are significant differences among Member States in interpreting fundamental concepts for the applicability of EU law, such as 'financial instruments', 'investment services', 'funds' and in the implementation of consumer protection directives, resulting in very different regulatory treatment also depending on the applicable law.

All this creates regulatory arbitrage, different investor protection across countries and difficulties in cross-border supervision but also disincentives for cross-border activity, underlying an incomplete harmonisation. Also, consequently, only few FinTech companies operate in multiple jurisdictions saved for the payment sector.[84]

---

[79] See N Moloney, *EU Securities and Financial Markets Regulation*, (Oxford, OUP, 2014), 396ff; G Walker and R Purves, *Financial Services Law*, (Oxford, OUP, 2014), 120ff.

[80] Commission, 'Green Paper on retail financial services – Better products, more choice, and greater opportunities for consumers and businesses', COM(2015) 630 final, 25–26.

[81] See Commission, 'Freedom to provide services and the interest of the general good in the Second Banking Directive', (Communication), 97/C 209/04.

[82] Commission, 'Freedom to provide services and the general good in the insurance sector', (Communication) 2000/C 43/03 (where the offering of insurance services to clients situated in other Member States requires a notification to the host State, contrary to the banking regime).

[83] For instance in the UK, where offering financial products to British citizens as well as inviting businesses to issue securities account as regulated activities: see T Aschenbeck-Florange et al, 'Regulation of Crowdfunding in Germany, the UK, Spain and Italy and the Impact of the European Single Market', (June 2013), 18, www.osborneclarke.com/media/filer_public/51/b3/51b3007b-73aa-4b9a-a19d-380fc1d6ff35/regulation_of_crowdfunding_ecn_oc.pdf.

[84] BCBS (n 2).

IV. Regulatory Issues Deriving from Flaws of the Current Approach in Financial Regulation and Supervision in General

A. The Effect of the Financial Crisis and of the Shadow Banking Fear. Post-Crisis Over-Regulation Effect, Lack of Proportionality and Regulatory Arbitrage

Some issues in FinTech regulation come from, more generally, flaws in existing financial regulations, as discussed in this book, but appear more evident in the FinTech context.

Many commentators believe that existing financial regulation is sufficiently flexible and proportionate to adequately regulate most FinTech businesses.[85]

The financial crisis has had two main effects on the financial regulation framework: we have witnessed, first, an exponential increase in the number and strictness of requirements imposed on regulated firms (see CRD IV/CRR package; MiFID II; Solvency II Directive), disregarding the effects on small providers and SMEs financing and with little consideration to proportionality.[86] The EU is currently showing efforts towards a more proportionate approach, having the Commission recently proposed, for instance, to simplify and lower requirements for small banks (cf CRD V/CRR 2 proposals) as well as capital requirements for certain investment firms.[87]

However, such raising of the bar and focus on systemic risk have also reduced the differences among activities and operators, causing increasing homogeneity and reduced proportionality. As an example, traditionally, banks have been highly prudentially regulated because of their special functions (eg maturity transformation, liquidity creation, monetary belt, payment system, etc) at the bank's own risk and 'depositor run' risk with, consequently, potentially relevant systemic implications. Instead, the regulation of investment firms – which conduct activities at investors' risk – used to focus on conduct and transparency requirements in order to reduce agency costs and market-based supervision.[88] Such framework has changed because of the evolution of the

---

[85] ESMA, 'Licensing of Fintech business models – Report', (12 July 2019), 4–5, 8, 21ff, www.esma.europa.eu/sites/default/files/library/esma50-164-2430_licensing_of_fintech.pdf (only DLT, crypto-assets, ICOs and marketplace lending are identified as not easily covered by existing regimes); EBA, 'Regulatory perimeter, regulatory status and authorisation approaches in relation to FinTech activities – Report', (18 July 2019), https://eba.europa.eu/documents/10180/2551996/Report+regulatory+perimeter+and+authorisation+approaches.pdf.

[86] Moloney (n 80); DW Arner, 'Adaptation and Resilience in Global Financial Regulation', (2011) 89 *North Carolina Law Review* 1579. The principle of proportionality in embedded in EU law (Art 5(4) TFEU) and in particular in EU financial law and supervisory processes but of difficult application in case of detailed and rigid rules.

[87] See Regulation (EU) 2019/876 of the European Parliament and of the Council of 20 May 2019 amending the Capital Requirements Regulation as regards the leverage ratio, the net stable funding ratio, requirements for own funds and eligible liabilities, counterparty credit risk, market risk, exposures to central counterparties, exposures to collective investment undertakings, large exposures, reporting and disclosure requirements (CRR II) and Directive (EU) 2019/878 of the European Parliament and of the Council of 20 May 2019 amending the Capital Requirements Directive IV as regards exempted entities, financial holding companies, mixed financial holding companies, remuneration, supervisory measures and powers and capital conservation measures (CRD V); Commission, 'Call for Evidence – EU regulatory framework for financial services', (Communication), 23 November 2016, COM(2016) 855 final; Id., 'Follow up to the Call for Evidence – EU regulatory framework for financial services', (Report), COM(2017)736 final; Id., 'Proposal for a Regulation of the European Parliament and of the Council on the Prudential Requirements of Investment Firms', COM(2017) 790 final.

[88] See chs 2 and 3 in this book; CJ Benston and CW Smith, 'A transaction cost approach to the theory of financial intermediation', (1976) 31(2) *Journal of Finance* 215; AM Santomero, 'Modeling the Banking Firm: A Survey', (1984) 3(1) *Journal of Money, Credit, Banking* 576, 576–79; S Bhattacharya and AV Takor, 'Contemporary Banking Theory', (1993) 3 *Journal of Financial Intermediation* 2; A Pacces, 'Financial Intermediation in the Securities Markets: Law and Economics of Conduct of Business Regulation', (2000) 20 *International Review of Law and Economics* 279, 481–482; I Chiu, 'Securities Intermediaries in the Internet Age and the Traditional Principal-Agent Approach Model of Regulation', (2007) 2 *Journal*

financial system (with investment firms competing with banks in the investment area)[89] and the effect of the global financial crisis (negative consequences of systemic crises can be huge, originate from operators other than banks and affect public confidence towards the system as a whole). Therefore, investment firms have been subjected to significant prudential rules. More recently, even payment institutions – introduced in EU law with the objective of breaking the banking monopoly over payments and through the creation of new operators subject to a lighter regime in consideration of the different functions and activities performed[90] – have witnessed an increase in their regulation through PSD2, in terms of own funds and governance (in addition to cyber-security).

This is also expression of the so called 'shadow banking fear', inducing concern for 'a system of intermediaries, instruments, entities or financial contracts generating a combination of bank-like functions but outside of the regulatory perimeter or under a regulatory regime which is either light or addresses issues other than systemic risks, and without guaranteed access to central bank liquidity facility or public sector credit guarantees'.[91] Shadow banking raises the Commission's concerns when entailing systemic risk, in consideration of its economic function, size and interconnectedness with the banking sector, and when not already covered by the CRD IV/CRR or MiFID, UCITS Directive, AIFMD/EuVECA/EuSEF, PSD2 or e-money, occupational pension funds and insurance directives.[92] The most recent categorisation by the FSB restricts shadow banking to financial intermediaries with certain economic functions[93] and susceptible to depositors/customers' runs, in order to cover only operators creating systemic risk, also in consideration of their interconnectedness with the banking sector, and therefore to be monitored for stability reasons, in line with FSB's macro-prudential focus.

Because of such 'fear', the EU law has recently progressively extended its reach to certain shadow banking entities or simply alternative providers[94] but not always coherently with the economic functions and related risks (eg new rules for PIs with stricter capital adequacy and

---

of International Commercial Law and Technology 138; JA Burke, 'Re-examining Investor Protection in Europe and the US', (2009) 16(2) *Murdoch University Electronic Journal of Law* 1, 6ff.

[89] Eg, bank activities have exponentially expanded to other areas such as investments, new operators have started offering activities similar to banks (lending, payments, securitisation) and company groups involving banks and investment firms have flourished.

[90] See recital 11 PSD.

[91] See European Parliament, 'Resolution of 20 November 2012 on Shadow Banking', 2012/2115(INI) and FSB, 'Shadow Banking: Strengthening Oversight and Regulation-Recommendations of the Financial Stability Board', (2011), www.financialstabilityboard.org. The sector includes entities transforming maturities or liquidity and transferring credit risk (eg Special Purpose Vehicles –SPVs- in securitisations), receiving funds from the public with deposit-like instruments (eg money-market mutual funds), using financial leverage (eg exchange traded funds, hedge funds and private equity funds or reinsurance firms). See Commission, 'Shadow Banking–Addressing New Sources of Risk in the Financial Sector', (Communication) COM/2013/0614 final, 3.

[92] Commission (n 90) 3-4, 16–17; EBA, 'Guidelines. Limits on exposures to shadow banking entities which carry out banking activities outside a regulated framework under Article 395(2) of Regulation (EU) No 575/2013', EBA/GL/2015/20.

[93] The five economic functions are: 1) management of collective investment vehicles involving maturity/liquidity transformation or leverage and so susceptible to runs; 2) loan provision dependent on short-term funding (eg consumer credit or leasing companies); 3) intermediation of market activities that is dependent on short-term funding or on secured funding of client assets (eg broker/dealers and securities finance companies); 4) facilitation of credit creation (eg financial guarantors); 5) securitisation-based credit intermediation and funding of financial entities (SPVs): FSB, 'Global Shadow Banking Monitoring Report 2015', (2015), 1, 7–8, 14ff, www.fsb.org/wp-content/uploads/global-shadow-banking-monitoring-report-2015.pdf.

[94] See Alternative Investment Fund Managers Directive (AIFMD, No 2011/61); Regulation No 648/2012 on OTC derivatives, central counterparties and trade repositories (EMIR); Regulations on credit rating agencies No 1060/2009 (CRA I), 513/2011 (CRA II) and No 462/2013 (CRA III); Regulation No 236/2012 on short selling. See Moloney (n 80) 40, 212–215; N Moloney, 'The legacy effects of the financial crisis on regulatory design in the EU', in E Ferran et al (eds), *The Regulatory Aftermath of the Global Financial Crisis*, (Cambridge, CUP, 2012), 126, 171; Arner (n 87) 1579.

governance rules). The PSD2 has included Payment Initiation Services Providers (PIS) and Account Information Service (AIS) Providers ('third party payment service providers') within its scope but subjecting the same to a partially lighter regime (based on transparency, client money protection and governance requirements to ensure cyber security) compared to PIs, in consideration of the difference in types of services (information services or technical ones) and the lack of holding of client funds (therefore excluding the application of segregation and capital requirements or minimum capital rules, adding instead the requirement of a professional insurance).

Finally, financial regulation has increased in complexity, being composed of an exponential number of legislative texts, at different levels (eg EU/national; Lamfalussy level 1, 2 or 3), with overlapping spheres of application and supervision[95] and with different aims (cf privacy, cyber security, stability, competition, protection of the weak party and of consumers, etc), making it extremely complex navigating applicable regimes by regulated entities.

All this has increased the potential for regulatory arbitrage and created incentives towards moving away from the regulatory perimeter (platforms and ICOs instead of traditional intermediaries and trading venues). Therefore, this might lead us to recognise the need, before finding solutions specifically for FinTech regulation, to re-think financial regulation in a more proportionate, functional and risk-based way.

B. Cross-Sectoral Issues and FinTech

As discussed across this book, existing EU financial regulation tends to be structured in separate sectoral regulations, presenting varied differences in regimes applicable to banks, investment firms and insurance firms. Some of those have originated from the diversity of functions of traditional intermediaries and might still be justified, although challenged by new models of business and new forms of intermediation, which reduce such differences and might create new functions (see above).

Other differences find justification in the limited EU competence, which is grounded in the principle of conferral and, in the internal market area, limited by the subsidiary and proportionality principles. Therefore, EU law has so far targeted only services and products considered the most dangerous for EU citizens and the market (see below for instance PRIIPs, where the EU has limited its attention only to certain complex financial products). Furthermore, the fragmentation and limitation of European Supervisory Authorities' competence (restricted to certain legislative acts identified in Article 1(2) ESAs Regulations and to the powers identified in level 1 acts) seems to impede sectoral authorities to adopt a broader view and effective guidance and rules for cross-sectoral issues.[96] The recent EC proposal to reinforce the Joint Committee role, in particular in the investor protection area,[97] might only partially solve this problem.

The EU has recently showed some attempts to react to cross-sectoral innovations but not in an organic and coherent manner. For instance, verifying the existence of new investment

---

[95] Because of the application of multiple laws of different authorities, need of increased and improved cooperation: BCBS, (n 6) 33ff.

[96] Ie, the EBA and ESMA have issued separate opinions about crowdfunding and cryptocurrencies/ICOs, only discussing the regulatory issues falling within their restricted and separate purview.

[97] See Commission, 'Proposal for a Regulation of the European Parliament and of the Council Amending Regulation (EU) No 1093/2010, No 1094/2010, No 1095/2010 establishing a European Supervisory Authority [...]', (20 September 2017), COM(2017) 536 final (further amended in September 2018). The ESAs will be also required to – separately – coordinate national policies in the FinTech area and create a Financial Innovation Committee each.

products and delivery methods putting at risk investors, has decided, through PRIIPS Regulation (No 1286/2014) and MiFID II, to extend traditional securities protection (MiFID-like conduct rules and product intervention powers) to structured deposits and linked insurance products,[98] although pertaining to different sectors or not traditionally considered financial instruments.[99] However, the Commission's declared holistic approach in retail investor protection, despite reducing the distance between different sectors and products,[100] is limited only to certain products considered the most complex and risky,[101] leaving out significant aspects and still shielding investors with different degrees of protection depending on the type of products, creating confusion and lack of clarity.[102]

FinTech simply makes such shortcomings more evident. In fact, some risks might manifest across sectors because of the deployment of the same technology in different areas (eg DLT deployed by VC platforms for issuance and payment transactions, by InsurTechs in claim satisfaction and by market exchanges for investment products; AI and algorithms for robo-advice applied to financial management, pension, lending and insurance[103]) or of its 'asset agnostic' nature (eg DLT, in principle, can be used to transfer any type of assets, eg software, securities, virtual currencies, insurance, etc, every time triggering different regulations).[104] Digital platforms even exist across all economic sectors, raising similar issues (eg network effects, interoperability, transparency, data use) and might receive in the near future a regulatory treatment on their own.[105] Furthermore, Big-Techs, with their data-based competitive advantage, have started expanding across sectors, including financial, offering a varied range of financial services (becoming 'Tech-Fin') but potentially subject to partially different rules and raising relevant anti-trust and macro-prudential issues.[106] Finally, the difficult qualification of FinTech (see above) tends to

---

[98] About the attempt by the European Regulator to reduce the distances in investor protection among the banking, securities and insurance sectors, see V Colaert, 'European banking, securities and insurance law: cutting through sectoral lines?, (2015) 52 *CML Rev* 1579.

[99] See N Moloney, *How to Protect Investors: Lessons from the EC and the UK*, (CUP, Cambridge, 2010), 201–2.

[100] Eg, PRIIPs Regulation only refers to pre-contractual information and insurance investment products and structured retail deposits (term deposits with return based on underlying assets) when the amount repayable is subject to fluctuations because of investors' exposure to reference values or performance of assets not directly purchased by them.

[101] The Commission had considered the opportunity to cover with PRIIP all investment products sold to retail investors. However, it eventually decided not to, claiming it would be difficult to identify the same requirements for so widely different investment products, while recognising in packaged investment products a level of complexity and risk requiring protective measures for retail investors: Commission, 'Consultation by Commission Services on legislative steps for the Packaged Retail Investment Products initiative', (2010), 6, http://ec.europa.eu/finance/consultations/2010/prips/docs/consultation_paper_en.pdf.

[102] See Colaert (signalling unrealised comparability among products and differences and overlapping among authorities' product intervention powers). Critically examining traditional sectoral separations, see HE Jackson, 'Regulation in a Multi-sectored Financial Services Industry: An Exploratory Essay', (1999) 77(2) *Washington University Law Quarterly*. 319; Moloney (n 80) 779ff; Id. (n 100) 184ff.

[103] And we can find different definitions of advice and requirements depending on the sector: ESAs, 'Report on automation in financial advice', (16 December 2016), https://esas-joint-committee.europa.eu/Publications/Reports/EBA%20BS%202016%20422%20(JC%20SC%20CPFI%20Final%20Report%20on%20automated%20advice%20tools).pdf.

[104] See Athanassiou (n 44) 38.

[105] See Commission, 'Proposal for a Regulation of the European Parliament and of the Council on promoting fairness and transparency for business users of online intermediation services', (26 April 2018), COM/2018/238 final; see also N Srnicek, *Platform Capitalism* (Cambridge, CUP, 2017), 49ff; A Wiewiórowska-Domagalska, 'Online Platforms: How to Adapt Regulatory Framework to the Digital Age?', www.europarl.europa.eu/ReqData/etudes/BRIE/2017/607323/IPOL BRI(2Q17)607323 EN.pdf; M Finck, 'Digital Co-Regulation: Designing a Supranational Legal Framework for the Platform Economy', LSE Legal Studies Working Paper No 15/2017, forthcoming in *EL Rev* 2018, https://ssrn.com/abstract=2990043; C Busch, 'Towards a 'New Approach for the Platform Ecosystem: A European Standard for Fairness in Platform-to-Business Relations', (2017) 6 *Journal of European Consumer and Market Law* 227.

[106] The term 'Big Tech' refers to five Technology companies (Google, Amazon, Facebook, Apple and Microsoft) expanding to other sectors taking advantage of the information and data acquired from users and with a potential relevant force

place certain FinTech businesses in grey areas across different sectors, potentially subjected to no regulation or, at the opposite, to multiple regimes.

V. Proposals and Conclusions: Need for a More Functional, Proportional and Cross-Sectoral Approach

Some regulatory issues discussed in relation to FinTech arise for any type of start-up or new products, irrespective of its FinTech nature or not. Therefore, they can be solved through a general rethinking of financial regulation, instead of ad hoc regulations for FinTech.[107] In particular, there is a need for a tiered (ie progressive, with escalating requirements depending on the activity/function), functional (calibrating requirements, especially prudential ones, to the operators' functions)[108] and proportionate (to risks)[109] system, with a simplified authorisation process and regime for providers of basic financial activities with simple models and small operations as well as for SMEs securities' offering.

RegTech, SupTech and forms of 'compliance by design' (embedding rules into platforms' or systems' design) could help balance investor and client protection (and its recent 'assist-your-customer' trend[110]), risk management with financial inclusion and cost reduction objectives, allowing for instance the use of technology in the area of information transmission to the supervisory authority, know-your-customer rules and tests, demands and needs test, responsible lending, product governance, etc.

Finally, a more cross-sectoral approach would reduce regulatory arbitrage (including in respect to Big Techs) and differences in qualifications and consequent treatment. In particular, also in order to avoid loopholes or over-lapping in investor protection, we might introduce a standard and synthetic informative document – based on the KID model – to be provided to consumers by any person proposing to consumers in the course of his/her business (even as intermediary between peers) products deploying the latter's money with an expectation of financial return or saving objective. This would contain, in a clear, simple and not misleading way, information about the proponent (also whether regulated or not and how), product/service, with a focus on costs, risks, role of the provider, warnings and redress instruments. Then, additional sections and specifications (or even additional documents, eg in case a long Prospectus is required under the Prospectus Regulation) would depend on the sector, regulated

---

to disrupt the financial sector more than FinTechs: see FSB, 'FinTech and market structure in financial services: Market developments and potential financial stability implications', (14 February 2019), www.fsb.org/wp-content/uploads/P140219.pdf. On Tech-Fin and Big Tech, see also Arner et al (n 3); DA Zetzsche, RP Buckley, DW Arner and JN Barberis, 'From FinTech to TechFin: The Regulatory Challenges of Data-Driven Finance', (April 28, 2017), EBI Working Paper Series 2017/6, forthcoming *NYU Journal of Law and Business*, https://ssrn.com/abstract=2959925; BaFin, 'Digitalisation. Impact on financial markets, supervision and regulation – Part I', (2018), 15, www.bafin.de/SharedDocs/Downloads/EN/BaFinPerspektiven/2018/bp_18-1_digitalisierung_en.pdf?__blob=publicationFile&v=9; BaFin (n 23) 9ff; FSB (n 8); WEF (n 7).

[107] Zetzsche et al (n 64); Macchiavello (n 1).

[108] About functional approach to regulation: RC Merton, 'A Functional Perspective of Financial Intermediation', (1995) 24(2) *Financial Management* 23; J Armour et al, *Principles of Financial Regulation*, (Oxford, OUP, 2017); SL Schwarcz, 'Regulating Financial Change: A Functional Approach', (2016) 100 *Minnesota Law Review* 1441.

[109] See Commission, 'Follow up'; Commission, 'Summary of contributions to the Public Consultation on FinTech: a more competitive and innovative European financial sector', (2017), https://ec.europa.eu/info/sites/info/files/2017-fintech-summary-of-responses_en.pdf.

[110] See ch 14B in this book.

nature or not of the proposing party, type of activity and product, etc. Another similar standard informative document might be conceived for loans to consumers (and perhaps micro/small enterprises), even when provided by non-professional lenders but with the intermediation of a professional, again with additions and specifications based on the particular type of the same (see consumer and residential loans). This would substitute the information to be provided under the Directive 2002/65 and allow the capture of some FinTech products and other 'grey areas', now escaping existing regulations, ensuring a minimum level of client protection. Cross-sectoral responses to certain common issues raised by certain technology would also simplify regulation (eg technology interoperability, access and ownership of big data and results of algorithms, liabilities issues in case of AI or permission-less DLT systems).

Instead, other regulatory issues remain and, aware of the very diverse nature of the FinTech universe and the consequent inadequacy of one-fits-all solutions, we need to consider the differences in FinTech activities, their functions and risks, compare these with traditional ones and calibrate the regulatory response to such risks and functions.

Therefore, firstly, in case of same activity and function compared to traditional ones (eg online banking; certain robo-advice and insurTech), FinTech should be subjected to traditional financial regulation, with certain adaptations through level 2 rules or guidelines to remove obstacles (eg physical presence requirement) and clarify the response to specific risks (eg low level of client loyalty, more intense competition and, therefore, higher level of liquidity and stability risks), benefits or other relevant features but, as mentioned, it would also benefit from the proposed tiered, proportional and functional regulatory approach for financial regulation.

Secondly, in other cases, where the function and activities are close to traditional ones but differ instead under significant aspects in terms of risks, structure, customer expectations and reliance, a special regulation becomes preferable (even preceded by a sand-box). Nonetheless, such regulation would mimic the traditional regulation corresponding to the activity and functions that most resemble FinTech's ones, also in consideration of each law's policy objectives.

For instance, marketplace lending/investing (FRC) has not realised a true disintermediation of traditional activities but simply innovated intermediation. Some forms of FRC, such as marketplace investing (or IBC), resembles traditional brokerage, markets or placement. Therefore, when also involving financial instruments (in the terms that should be specified by the Commission under Article 4(2), MiFID II and ESMA), exemptions/facilitations are hardly acceptable but might be anyway grounded on the creation of an alternative (clearly separated from the traditional one and therefore not involving investor trust or systemic implications), innovative (in terms of firms' evaluation, signalling and investors' decisions, co-investing with Venture Capitalist or Business Angels, etc),[111] riskier but simple market, conducive of more financial inclusion (eg more financing for SMEs) and diversification (avoiding model convergence), therefore responding to partially different functions. Instead, marketplace lending (or LBC), under the basic business model, significantly differs from banking (ie receiving reimbursable funds from the public to lend on its own risk), not involving maturity or liquidity transformation, therefore deserving a different regulatory treatment. However, such platforms represent a new form of credit intermediation (connecting private people and offering related information services) with investment aspects, performing also in this case functions similar to, depending on the particular business model, brokerage, markets, portfolio management or placement but of financial products (generally other than financial instruments), contributing to information

---

[111] See for references Macchiavello (n 1) 677–78.

asymmetry reduction. Therefore, a regulation following the traditional regulatory model for investment activities but simplified (in consideration of the different type of assets and business models) and taking into account the need to also protect SME and consumer crowd-borrowers (eg through transparency obligations, warnings about over-indebtedness and other risks, withdrawal right) appears reasonable.[112] The recent Commission Proposal for a European Crowdfunding Services Providers Regulation (ECSP)[113] seems only to partially reflect these guiding principles. In fact, it respects such principles through the creation of an ad hoc regime, in exemption from MiFID, for both IBC and LBC (cross-sectoral), centred around a simple authorisation, disclosure (in particular, a simple and synthetic document, the KIIS, similar to the KID), conduct (including a 'entry knowledge test', a sort of appropriateness test but only regarding crowdfunding in general and crowdfunding services, not specific investments/products) and flexible organisational rules. On the other hand, it fails at creating a functional and proportionate framework by disregarding certain products (consumer loans and financial products other than transferable securities), completely assimilating LBC and EBC in the regime[114] as well as professional and retail investors, resorting to MiFID (which, by the way, does not apply) to identify and define crowdfunding activities and products (despite the mentioned differences and legal fragmentation among Member States), creating a 'patchwork' regime (a 'one-fits-all' regime mixing OTF, reception and transmission and placement regimes, irrespective of the type of service provided), requiring ECSPs to check only the completeness and clarity of the KIIS and lacking specific protective measures for recipients. The recent European Parliament Resolution (preceded by a similar ECON Committee report),[115] while improving certain aspects (eg explicitly allowing more complex and widespread models, subjecting the same to stricter rules, adding a professional insurance among the authorisation requirements and a transparency obligation also about performance), it falls short in designing an optimal regulation. In fact, firstly, it explicitly introduces a due diligence obligation of ECSPs in selecting borrowers only in terms of AML/CT checks; secondly, it increases the 'patchwork' effect and potentially investor confusion (eg moving the 'knowledge' test closer to a suitability test – collection of information also about the investor's financial situation and investment objectives – not in line with certain types of services listed – eg reception and transmission of orders and placing, using interchangeably both the terms 'appropriate' and 'suitable' but leaving unchanged the consequences in case of a negative result, which still consists in only a warning; further assimilating ECSP regime and terminology with MIFID, etc); thirdly, it misses the opportunity to introduce more innovative safeguards to counterbalance the lighter regime (eg investment limits) or supranational supervision (taking

---

[112] Macchiavello (n 1); Ferrarini and Macchiavello (n 41).

[113] 'Proposal for a Regulation of the European Parliament and of the Council on European Crowdfunding Service Providers (ECSP) for Business', (8 March 2018), COM(2018)113. For a first comment see E Macchiavello, 'Feedback on the European Commission "Proposal for a Regulation on European Crowdfunding Service Providers (ECSP) for business"', (11 May 2018), https://ec.europa.eu/info/law/better-regulation/initiatives/ares-2017-5288649/feedback/F11570_en?p_id=181605.

[114] See instead Macchiavello (n 1) and Ferrarini and Macchiavello (n 41) about differences between EBC and LBC and consequently suggested differentiated rules under certain respects.

[115] European Parliament, 'Legislative resolution of 27 March 2019 on the proposal for a regulation of the European Parliament and of the Council on European Crowdfunding Service Providers (ECSP) for Business', (COM(2018)0113 – C8-0103/2018 –2018/0048(COD)), www.europarl.europa.eu/RegData/seance_pleniere/textes_adoptes/provisoire/2019/03-27/0301/P8_TA-PROV(2019)0301_EN.pdf; European Parliament – Committee on Economic and Monetary Affairs, 'Report on the proposal for a regulation of the European Parliament and of the Council on European Crowdfunding Service Providers (ECSP) for Business', (9 November 2018), www.europarl.europa.eu/sides/getDoc.do?pubRef=-//EP//NONSGML+REPORT+A8-2018-0364+0+DOC+PDF+V0//EN.

supervisory powers away from ESMA in favour of national competent authorities under a home country control principle). The compromise version of the Proposal recently published by the Council shows an even different view.[116] The Council, in fact, in addition to making the regime mandatory (instead of optional), seems to be willing to limit crowdfunding to execution-only types of services (eg prohibiting more complex services, auto-bid and bulletin boards similar to markets) but then inconsistently designs a stricter and rigid regime, closer to other types of services and incumbents' regulations (prudential requirements and more detailed and strict organisational rules), despite anyway filling some gaps in the original proposal (eg introducing the distinction between sophisticated and non-sophisticated investors, benefiting from differentiated protective measures – eg for the latter, withdrawal right and national investment limits – expanding the scope regime to the shares of limited liability companies not considered financial instruments under national law and extending disclosure to credit scoring methods and default rates). In conclusion, the resulting regime appears excessively strict and disproportionate (when compared to existing or soon-to-be-approved regimes for executive-only services without clients' money or financial instruments handling), at least as regards business models involving loans and products other than financial instruments and limited to sophisticated investors (for whom KIIS and simulation of loss mechanisms appear useless but costly), as well as fragmented (allowing wide Member States' discretions a regards, eg, retail investment limits and maximum size of the offer).

To this second FinTech sub-group belong also certain ICOs of tokens (eg investment tokens or hybrid tokens), resembling IPOs of financial instruments but resorting to new structures (decentralised and disintermediated systems) and atypical rights attached, making existing regulation unfit. In fact, while DLT per se does not justify regulation (but cross-sectoral specifications about, eg, GDPR and AML/CT application and liability attribution might be useful), certain applications of the same to financial markets or payments (traditional and reserved functions in reason of their systemic importance) do require adaptations of the law since its decentred and disintermediated nature (in case of true decentralized systems – unlike permissioned or power-centred blockchains and recent 'Initial Exchange Offerings' where permissioned and private blockchain platforms perform the 'offeror' role) makes traditional regulations (all assuming the existence of an intermediary or central manager) unfit to regulate the same and might require moving to forms of 'compliance by design' or 'by code'.[117]

Finally, on the other end of the spectrum, there are FinTechs representing true new businesses. For example, smart contracts, innovative forms of automatic contract execution (therefore with a function partially different from traditional contracts), might require certain ad hoc rules (eg not only about validity, applicable laws, jurisdiction, ADRs but also developers and promoters' duties), especially when involving consumers. Similarly, VC and utility tokens in ICOs represent new products escaping traditional categories and functions and cannot be functionally assimilated to, respectively, fiat currency or financial instruments/mere services, although presenting aspects of payment and investment functions (see above). Such cases, when involving

---

[116] Council of the European Union, 'Proposal for a Regulation of the European Parliament and of the Council on European Crowdfunding Service Providers (ECSP) for Business and amending Regulation (EU) No 2017/1129 – Mandate for negotiations with the European Parliament – Compromise proposal', (24 June 2019), https://data.consilium.europa.eu/doc/document/ST-10557-2019-INIT/en/pdf.

[117] See Chiu (n 65) 86–87; Athanassiou (n 44) 39, 52–53; TCW Lin, 'Infinite Financial Intermediation', (2015) 50 *Wake Forest Law Review* 643, 655ff, https://ssrn.com/abstract=2711379; FSB, 'Decentralised financial technologies – Report on financial stability, regulatory and governance implications', (6 June 2019), www.fsb.org/wp-content/uploads/P060619.pdf.

users' investment of money, would be captured under the proposed 'minimum disclosure regime' but, in the long run, might require sandboxes and ad hoc regimes based on the functions performed, in line with the proposed tiered-approach (with, eg, prudential requirements only in case of certain functions and public trust; additional obligations – such as disclosure, data and cyber security rules, conflict of interest policy, minimum organisational requirements, redress measures, client money protection and AML/CT – depending on the activities and risks).

5

A Cross-Sectoral Approach to Regulation and a Twin Peaks System of Supervision: The Netherlands

KITTY LIEVERSE AND VICTOR DE SERIÈRE

I. Introduction

The topic of this chapter is the national system of legislation that is applied for the regulation of the financial sector. The starting point of the analysis in this chapter is the assumption that a national system of legislation to regulate the financial sector may be structured in different ways. Based on the systems of legislation for the regulation of the financial sector as these are in use in different Member States of the European Union, a distinction[1] may be made between: (a) a sectoral approach, with separate legislation for the different sectors, such as the banking sector, the insurance business and the investment services industry; and (b) a cross-sectoral approach, where at least some parts of the legislation equally apply to different sectors.

The system of legislation is to be distinguished from the system of supervision. With regard to the latter, reference is made to the manner in which supervision and enforcement of financial sector legislation is organised. Based on the practice in different Member States, a distinction can be made between various supervisory systems, including: (a) a so-called Twin Peaks model,[2] (b) a sectoral model,[3] and (c) a model with one single supervisor for all sectors and functions (which we refer to as the integrated model).

There is no structural link between the system of legislation and the system of supervision. A sectoral approach to legislation for example may be combined in respect of the structure of

---

[1] This is a distinction in very general terms only, without regard to any details or specifics that would provide a nuance to this distinction.

[2] In a Twin-Peaks model a distinction is made between: (i) topics of market behaviour including consumer protection, and (ii) prudential supervision. There are two different supervisors appointed for each of these two distinctive topics. In this chapter, the analysis in respect of prudential supervision is focused on the supervision at the level of individual financial institutions, so-called micro-prudential supervision (rather than macro–prudential supervision).

[3] In a sectoral model of supervision, there are different supervisors appointed for each sector, such as the banking sector, the insurance industry and the provision of investment services.

supervision with a twin-peaks model, a sectoral model or an integrated model. This can be deducted from the following overview of the approach in various Member States:[4]

	Financial sector legislation	System of supervision
Belgium	Sectoral legislation	Twin Peaks
Germany	Sectoral legislation	Integrated
France	One Codex, consisting of separate laws + mixed functional/sectoral structure	Twin Peaks
Italy	Sectoral legislation	Sectoral
Spain	Sectoral legislation	Twin Peaks
United Kingdom	Mixed functional/sectoral[5]	Twin Peaks
Cyprus	Sectoral legislation	Sectoral
Hungary	Sectoral legislation	Integrated
Austria	Sectoral legislation	Integrated
Romania	Sectoral legislation	Sectoral
Slovenia	Sectoral legislation	Sectoral
The Netherlands	Mixed functional/sectoral	Twin Peaks

At the (supra-national) level of the EU the approach for both legislation and supervision can be qualified as sectoral. This is true for the investment services industry that is regulated by the Markets in Financial Instruments Directive (MiFID) II[6] and Markets in Financial Instruments Regulation (MiFIR).[7] It is also true for managers of alternative investment funds regulated by the Alternative Investment Fund Managers Directive (AIFMD)[8] and/or the European Venture Capital Funds (EuVECA),[9] the European Social Entrepreneurship Funds (EuSEF),[10] the European Long-Term Investment Funds (Eltif),[11] and the Money Markets Funds (MMF)[12] Regulations, and Undertakings for Collective Investment in Transferable Securities (UCITS) Directive and their managers as regulated by the UCITS Directive.[13] It is further true for offerors of consumer credit (regulated by the Consumer Credit Directive (CCD)[14]) and the Mortgage Credit Directive (MCD[15]). It is somewhat less true, however, for the banking sector, regulated by the Capital Requirements Directive IV (CRD IV),[16] the Capital Requirements Regulation (CRR)[17] and the

---

[4] This overview is based on Box 4, p 27, of the consultation document on a contemplated revision of the Dutch system of financial supervision legislation: *Herziening van de Wft: verkenning, Consultatiedocument*, published 22 November 2016.

[5] In the UK there is a combination of the Financial Services and Markets Act 2000 that applies on a cross-sectoral basis on the one hand, and a number of laws that apply to a particular sector only on the other hand. Further, there are extensive handbooks that have been published by the two supervisors, the Prudential Regulatory Authority (PRA) and the Financial Conduct Authority (FCA).

[6] MiFID II, [2014] OJ L173/349.

[7] MiFR, [2014] OJ L173/84.

[8] AIFMD, [2011] OJ L174/1.

[9] EuVECA, [2013] OJ L115/1.

[10] EuSEF, [2013] OJ L115/18.

[11] Eltif, [2015] OJ L123/98.

[12] MMF, [2017] OJ L169/8.

[13] UCITS Directive, [2009] OJ L302/32.

[14] CCD, [2008] OJ L133/66.

[15] MCD, [2014] OJ L60/34.

[16] CRD IV, [2013] OJ L176/338.

[17] CRR, [2013] OJ L176/1.

Single Supervisory Mechanism (SSM)-regulations,[18] which also cover a specific part of the investment services industry (but this will largely change upon the Investment Firms Directive (IFD)[19] and the Investment Firms Regulation (IFR)[20] becoming effective, to which reference is made in footnote 50). The Solvency II Directive[21] and Regulation[22] are specific to the insurance industry, but they also cover entities for risk-acceptance. The second Payment Services Directive (PSD II)[23] mainly regulates payment services providers, but is also relevant to e-money institutions, which in addition have their 'own' e-money Directive.[24] Other pieces of European legislation, however, are even more 'cross sectoral' such as the Insurance Distribution Directive (IDD)[25] (relevant to insurers, advisors and intermediaries in respect of insurance products) and Packaged Retail and Insurance-based Investment Products Regulation (PRIIPs)[26] (relevant to insurers, investment firms, managers of investment institutions and advisors and intermediaries of insurance products that qualify as PRIIPs). The division of tasks between the European Securities and Markets Authority (ESMA), European Insurance and Occupational Pensions Authority (EIOPA) and European Banking Authority (EBA) runs to a large extent parallel to the mostly sectoral approach of the legislation, with ESMA as dedicated authority for the securities markets, EIOPA for the insurance industry and EBA as banking sector supervisor.

The research question of this chapter focusses on the Dutch system of legislation for the financial sector. As will be discussed in more detail below, this system has cross-sectoral elements to it. This legislative system is 'hybrid' in the sense that most financial legislation is concentrated in one statute, the Financial Supervision Act (*Wet op het financiële toezicht*, (FSA)). Within this statute, however, as we will discuss below, there is a mixture between generally applicable provisions and provisions which are organised per sector. This chapter discusses the challenges to the largely cross-sectoral approach of the Dutch legislation, while the underlying European legislation is predominantly arranged on a sectoral basis, combined with the Twin Peaks model of supervision. This chapter aims to provide a response to the question of whether that cross-sectoral approach to legislation is sufficiently resilient to address the challenges that the financial sector may provide.

II. The Dutch Approach on Financial Sector Regulation and Supervision

A. The Traditional Approach in the Netherlands

Traditionally, financial sector legislation in the Netherlands has been organised on a sectoral basis, with separate pieces of legislation for the banking sector, the insurance industry, the provision of investment services and the occupational pensions sector. This meant that until their absorption

---

[18] SSM, [2013] OJ L287/63; Regulation (EU) 468/2014, [2014], OJ L141/1.

[19] Reference is made to the proposal for a Directive of the European Parliament and of the Council on the prudential supervision of investment firms and amending Dirs 2013/36/EU and 2014/65/EU, COM/2017/0791 final – 2017/0358 (COD).

[20] Reference is made to the proposal for a Regulation of the European Parliament and of the Council on the prudential requirements of investment firms and amending Regulations (EU) No 575/2013, (EU) No 600/2014 and (EU) No 1093/2010, COM/2017/0790 final – 2017/0359 (COD).

[21] Solvency II, [2009] OJ L335/1.

[22] Delegated Regulation (EU) 2015/35, [2015] OJ L12/1.

[23] PSD II, [2015] OJ L337/35.

[24] Directive 2009/110/EC, [2009] OJ L267/7.

[25] IDD, [2016] OJ L26/19.

[26] PRIIPs, [2014] OJ L352/1.

by the FSA, there were not less than eight separate statutes covering various sectoral financial activities. The consistency, inter-action and efficiency of this approach left much to be desired. In this connection, important contributing factors were the emergence of detailed European directives and regulations requiring implementation and adjustment of these statutes, as well as an increasing need to cater for better protection of clients as the financial industry expanded both in terms of volume and complexity of products. Until 2002, this sectoral approach to the legislation was largely mirrored in the system of supervision. There were separate supervisors for the different sectors within the financial sector.[27]

B. The Restructuring of the Supervisory Structure

As of 2002,[28] the supervisory structure was revised, with the introduction of a Twin Peaks model. This made the Dutch Central Bank (DCB) responsible for prudential supervision on inter alia banks, insurers and investment firms. In the pensions sector, the separate pensions supervisor (the *Pensioen- en Verzekeringskamer*) was merged into DCB in 2004, so that DCB also became the prudential supervisor for the occupational pensions sector. The Authority for Financial Markets (AFM) became responsible for supervising market conduct of all financial sector participants, including the pensions sector.[29] At that time the sectoral approach to the legislation was maintained.

C. Revision of the Legislative Structure

As of 2007, the system of legislation was fundamentally revised, however, adopting a more cross-sectoral approach. All sectoral laws were abandoned and a single code for the supervision of the financial sector was introduced, the FSA.[30]

The drivers for this change in the set-up of the legislation as can be deducted from the parliamentary documents[31] were as follows. First of all, the aim was to increase transparency in the system by clearly distinguishing between common parts of financial supervision generally applicable to the different sectors on the one hand and specific sectorally applicable provisions on the other hand. It was thought that a cross-sectoral approach would be better able to cope with regulating financial instruments with cross-sectoral features, such as mortgage loans coupled to insurance investment contracts (*beleggingshypotheken*), PRIIPs and securities financing transactions (SFT). In addition, it was felt that a cross-sectoral approach of legislation would support the

---

[27] Dutch Central Bank (DCB, *De Nederlandsche Bank*) was appointed as supervisor for banks and investment institutions. The Pension and Insurance Chamber (*Pensioen- en Verzekeringskamer*) was appointed as supervisor for the insurance business and the supervision on the investment services industry and the stock exchanges was attributed to the STE (*Stichting Toezicht Effectenverkeer*), currently named the Authority for the Financial Markets (AFM, *Stichting Autoriteit Financiële Markten*).

[28] Reference is made to the parliamentary documents with reference 28122 (*Kamerstukken II*, 2001-2002, 28122) on the financial sector reforms.

[29] This includes the financial institutions subject to prudential supervision by DCB and also of those financial institutions that are not subject to prudential supervision such as financial service providers (advisors and intermediaries in respect of insurance and consumer credit products, for example).

[30] *Wet op het financieel toezicht*, reference is made to the parliamentary documents with reference 29507 (*Kamerstukken II*, 2003-2004, 29507). The text of the FSA can be found at https://wetten.overheid.nl/BWBR0020368/2019-01-01.

[31] Reference is made to fn 30.

functional model for supervision, with separate parts to cover prudential supervision and market conduct supervision. Finally, the aim was to be market-oriented and to support the financial sector with a level playing field on a cross-sectoral basis. The legislator's goal to arrive at an integrated, efficient and clear set of legislation did however not materialise (see below).

D. The Occupational Pensions Sector

Oddly enough, an important part of the financial sector, the pensions sector, was not included in this cross-sectoral legislation. The pension sector remained the subject of separate legislation, even though prudential supervision continued to be carried out by DCB and the AFM continued to exercise market conduct supervision. It was thought that the specific and very different features of the Dutch pensions system warranted separate legislation.[32] The governance provisions, giving recognition to the interests of different classes of stakeholders with different interests, the need for complicated calibration of pension liabilities, the associated pensions coverage requirements and prudential risk control provisions, and more generally the social sensitivities of the pensions system in the Netherlands, all warranted a separate, specialised approach. Also, including pensions in the FSA would have made that Act even more complicated than it already was. In hindsight, this has proven to be a wise approach.

E. The Current Supervisory Structure

The current structure of supervision is as follows. There are two main supervisors, DCB and the AFM. These two supervisors have distinctive tasks. Prudential supervision is entrusted to DCB, and market conduct supervision to the AFM. Prudential supervision is defined in Article 1:24, FSA as supervision aimed to ensure the solidity of financial institutions and the stability of the financial system. Market conduct supervision is defined in Article 1:25, FSA as aimed to ensure orderly and transparent financial markets processes, the integrity of the relationship between market participants and the fair treatment of clients. This latter definition mentions that market conduct supervision should also take into account the importance of maintaining the stability of the financial sector. The joint basis for exercising the supervisory authority by DCB and the AFM lies in the FSA.[33] In addition to these two supervisors, the Minister of Finance has some limited specific tasks and functions separate from those of these two supervisors.[34] For instance, the Minister of Finance is entrusted with licensing regulated securities markets established in the Netherlands, and with supervising Central Securities Depositaries (CSDs), established in the Netherlands.[35] As stated under F. below, the Minister of Finance also has the function of indirect supervision over the AFM.

---

[32] *Kamerstukken II*, 2001-2002, 28122, nr 3, p 7/8.

[33] Articles 1:24 et seq. FSA. As far as DCB is concerned, the legal basis for its monetary and regulatory functions and authorities is also to be found in the Banking Act 1998 (https://wetten.overheid.nl/BWBR0009508/2019-01-01).

[34] It is not always evident why certain authorities have not been delegated to the two supervisory agencies, but have been retained by the Minister of Finance. Certainly the public policy aspect of the areas concerned, which relates to financial infrastructure, has been a driver. In this chapter, we will not elaborate on these specific functions of the Minister of Finance.

[35] This is currently only Euroclear Nederland.

F. Independence of the Supervisory Authorities

Whilst DCB is independent, the AFM is not. DCB is a private company (a public limited liability company, an NV) with the state as its sole shareholder. The directors of DCB are appointed and dismissed by Royal Decree, and must be independent. The state has no authority to give instructions to the directors of the DCB in respect of monetary policy matters (but obviously the European Central Bank (ECB) does). There is a supervisory board with one state appointed member. The remainder of the members of the supervisory board are independents appointed by the state as the sole shareholder on the basis of binding nominations by the board itself (in other words by way of co-optation). The law requires there to be a binding functional description to which all members of the two boards must conform. That functional description is subject to the approval of the Minister of Finance, and in this (limited) way there is some (indirect) control over the functionalities of the two boards. The powers of the state as the sole shareholder are rather limited. A number of important decisions of the directors are subject to supervisory board approval. In addition, there is a Bank Council (*Bankraad*) which has an advisory and consultative function in the policy making process of DCB. We will not in this chapter discuss how the functions of DCB are affected by the European SSM and SRM[36] regimes.[37]

The independence of the AFM is limited.[38] The AFM is organised as a separate foundation, a legal entity under Dutch law. There is a board of directors and a supervisory council. The directors are appointed by Royal Decree (with the supervisory council having a non-binding right to propose new members), and can be dismissed by Royal Decree. The Minister of Finance may suspend directors. The supervisory council has wide powers (including for instance approval of the budget and the annual accounts). All members of this council are appointed by the Minister of Finance. In addition to the management board and the supervisory council, there is a so-called advisory panel, consisting of representatives of financial undertakings that are supervised by the AFM and certain other parties. The advisory panel has no actual authorities of its own, it is established purely for consultative purposes.

III. The Act on Financial Supervision

The FSA is the main piece of national legislation that regulates the financial sector.[39] It consists of different parts. Part 1, General, contains the definitions that apply for all parts of the Act, unless a specific part or chapter provides otherwise. Further, Part 1 sets out the tasks of the supervisors, provisions on cooperation between supervisors, and also provisions on supervision and enforcement. Part 2 relates to market access. This part contains provisions on licence requirements and the requirements to obtain or use a passport by financial institutions. The provisions on

---

[36] SRM, [2014] OJ L225/1.

[37] The above is a very brief summary of the detailed provisions relating to the governance of DCB. Those provisions are basically to be found in the Banking Act 1998, the Articles of Association of DCB and Art 1:27a, FSA. Internal DCB regulations give further implementation to the governance and operational structure.

[38] Again, this is a brief summary. The relevant provisions are basically to be found in Arts 1:26 et seq. FSA and in the Articles of Association of the AFM. There are also internal regulations further detailing the governance and operational structure.

[39] As set out above, this does not include the pension sector, which is regulated via separate legislation. In addition, it is noted that the FSA is the basis for an extensive set of further regulations issued by means of a Decree, regulations issued by the Minister of Finance and regulations issued by DCB or the AFM.

market access within this Part 2 are arranged per type of institution or business. This entails that the licence requirements for (for example) banks, insurance companies, investment firms and management companies for investment institutions are listed separately. Part 3 sets out prudential requirements. These prudential requirements are to a large extent clustered per topic. For example, the requirements in respect of suitability and trustworthiness of managing directors and supervisory directors of all entities subject to prudential supervision are combined in one provision that equally applies to all these entities. The same principle applies for the rules in respect of own funds, liquidity and solvency requirements. These prudential requirements are stated in very broad terms in the FSA. Details of these requirements are *in extenso* set out in implementing regulations. In these implementing regulations distinctions per type of business are made to the extent the requirements of CRDIV, CRR and Solvency II for different categories of institutions vary.[40] Part 3A contains provisions on recovery and resolution of banks and certain investment firms as a result of the implementation of the BRRD.[41] Further, Part 3A also contains the Dutch national regime[42] on recovery and resolution of insurance companies. Part 4 provides for requirements for financial institutions when it comes to market conduct. Comparable to Part 3, the topics are clustered to the extent the same requirements apply for different types of businesses and are further elaborated on in lower level regulations. This is true, for example, for the requirements in respect of the suitability and trustworthiness of managing directors and supervisory directors of financial institutions that are primarily supervised by the AFM. This principle also applies, for example, for rules in respect of the business organisation, outsourcing and complaints handling. In addition thereto, separate provisions per type of business are provided to the extent there are specific requirements for a certain type of business. This includes for example product specific transparency requirements or inducement rules that are specific to certain types of businesses, such as the investment services industry and financial services in respect of consumer credit. Part 5 has a distinctive position within the FSA, as its applicability does not concern financial institutions as such. Part 5 basically provides market conduct rules in respect of the financial markets for any participant thereto, including investors, issuers and shareholders of listed companies. It contains, for example, the implementing provisions in respect of the Prospectus Regulation,[43] covering the prospectus requirements for public offerings or listings of securities.[44] Part 6 contains a national regime in respect of special measures that may be taken by the Minister of Finance in the event of a clear and present danger to certain parts of the financial sector. This Part 6 enables the Minister of Finance to nationalise financial institutions such as banks and insurance companies. The only instance this authority was used relates to the failing of SNS Bank, where certain assets in relation to the SNS Reaal NV group were expropriated in 2013.[45]

Based on the contents of the various Parts of the FSA, it is too simple to label the FSA as cross-sectoral. Part 1 for example contains provisions on the supervisory powers of the DCB and AFM, such as their authority to make enquiries and to take enforcement measures.

---

[40] Eg, an additional provision in respect of the management and supervision within a bank is included to cater for specific requirements resulting from Art 91, CRD IV.

[41] BRRD, [2014], OJ L173/190.

[42] This regime was promulgated in 2018 in the absence of (and in anticipation of) a European framework on the recovery and resolution of insurers. The structure of this regime is broadly aligned to the structure as set out in the BRRD and the SRM Regulation.

[43] Regulation (EU) 2017/1129 of the European Parliament and of the Council of 14 June 2017 on the prospectus to be published when securities are offered to the public or admitted to trading on a regulated market, and repealing Directive 2003/71/EC [2017] OJ L168/12.

[44] As of 21 July 2019, the chapter of the FSA in respect of the prospectus requirement has been revised, with a view to the full effectiveness of the Prospectus Regulation as of that date.

[45] This Part 6 will not be discussed further.

As a starting point, these provisions apply equally to all sectors and businesses. Nevertheless, distinctions have been made, in particular, if underlying European legislation provides for special authorities for certain types of businesses or activities. This includes, for example, special provisions in respect of investment firms based on MiFID II and in respect of banks and certain investment firms in the context of recovery and resolution, based on the Bank Recovery and Resolution Directive (BRRD). Part 2 on market access is in fact arranged on a strictly sectoral basis. Apart from a distinction per sector, the provisions on market access are arranged by using two additional types of distinctions. The first one concerns access to the Dutch market versus access to foreign markets. The second one is the distinction whether DCB (or the ECB) or the AFM is authorised to grant licences. Part 3 on prudential supervision and Part 4 on market conduct have a mixed cross-sectoral and sectoral character. Similar types of provisions have been clustered as much as possible. This means, for example, that the fit and proper requirements for directors of financial institutions and the requirements on outsourcing and other items of business organisation are mainly stated on a cross-sectoral basis. Again, however, carve outs and special provisions are made for certain sectors if dictated by European legislation. On this basis, for example, additional provisions on the fit and proper requirements are stipulated for significant banks. Part 4 on market conduct in particular is for a large part structured on a sectoral basis. For instance, although AIFMs[46] are subject to organisational requirements that are mainly stipulated on a cross sectoral basis, they are in addition subject to certain requirements in respect of the prevention of asset stripping that are specific to AIFMs only. On the same basis, separate chapters within Part 4 apply only to certain financial services, such as the offering and intermediation of credit and the provision of investment services. Part 5, finally, is arranged on a topical basis, as dictated by the underlying European regulations and directives, such as prospectus requirements[47] and transparency requirements for listed companies and their shareholders.

IV. Challenges to the Cross-Sectoral Approach of Legislation

As follows from sections II and III above, the FSA cannot be labeled as being fully cross-sectoral. Rather, the FSA is based on the concept that rules that are more or less common to different types of financial institutions or their business, are clustered. At the same time, rules that apply to specific financial institutions or types of business only, are stated separately.

The main challenge to the cross-sectoral approach of the FSA, without a doubt, is its relation to European legislation. In the cross-sectoral approach of the FSA, the content of the rules is the focal point. Clustering has the effect that as a starting point, market participants operating in different sectors but conducting more or less comparable businesses, are subject to the same rules. At the same time, however, the European system of legislation for the financial sector has a very different approach. European legislation is typically structured by type of enterprise, type of activity, service or product and this impacts on the effectiveness[48] of the cross-sectoral provisions

---

[46] This refers to managers of alternative investment funds that are subject to the AIFMD.

[47] Based on the full effectiveness of the Prospectus Regulation as of 21 July 2019, the Part 5 provisions on prospectus requirements are limited to some implementing provisions as required by the Prospectus Regulation.

[48] The use of this terminology reflects the drivers for the cross-sectoral approach, to the extent possible, as set out in section II of this chapter.

of the FSA. The mainly sectoral approach at the European level is illustrated by the following overview:[49]

Type of financial enterprise	Market access & governance	Prudential supervision	Market conduct		
Bank	CRDIV/CRR	CRDIV/CRR			
Insurer	Solvency II	Solvency II	Solvency II	IDD	PRIIPs
Investment firm	MiFID II/MiFIR/ CRDIV	CRDIV/CRR[50]	MIFID II/MiFIR	PRIIPs	
Investment institutions/ managers	AIFMD/UCITS Directive	AIFMD/UCITS Directive	AIFMD/UCITS Directive	PRIPPs	
Payment institution	PSD2	PSD2	PSD2		
Insurance intermediary	IDD		IDD	PRIIPs	

European directives and regulations for different sectors of the financial industry typically have topics in common that could be very suitable for a cross-sectoral implementation.[51] However, in practice such joint topics are not arranged in exactly the same consistent manner at the European level. New directives may have been inspired on former directives, but they tend to reflect the most recent insight on a topic which may then differ from the former directive in another sector. As a result, there is an increasing tension if a Member State such as the Netherlands aims to implement such comparable but not similar provisions on a cross-sectoral basis. If the cross-sectoral approach is used to implement at the level of the highest standard, this leads to gold plating. This has the benefit of national cross-sectoral consistency. However, it has the downside of disturbing the European sectoral level playing field. In addition hereto, regardless of the clustered approach for implementation of various European directives, the need to honor the principle of interpretation in accordance with relevant Union rules may entail that certain requirements that are stated in exactly the same wording in the FSA on a cross-sectoral basis may nevertheless have to be interpreted differently, depending on to which financial sector such requirements relate.

Another development with an impact on the effectiveness of the cross-sectoral approach to be noted here, is the increasing number of directly applicable European regulations, including delegated regulations. For example, next to the main sources for regulation of the investment services industry consisting of MiFID II and MiFIR, there are no less than 42 delegated regulations[52] providing for regulatory and implementing technical standards to MiFID II and MiFIR. A number of rules, implementing MiFID II and its implementing directive[53] remain contained in the FSA and lower level decrees and regulations. The vast majority of the implementing rules and

---

[49] This overview is a simplified version of Appx 3, p 37, of the consultation document on a contemplated revision of the Dutch system of financial supervision legislation: *Herziening van de Wft: verkenning, Consultatiedocument*, published 22 November 2016.

[50] Currently, the system of prudential supervision for investment firms is subject to review. It has been proposed by the European Commission to introduce an Investment Firm Directive (IFD) and an Investment Firms Regulation (IFR). The IFR and IFD would introduce a new prudential regime for investment firms that will no longer be in scope of CRDIV and CRR. The investment firms that will be in scope of the new prudential regime for investment firms, will be divided in two categories: Class 2 and Class 3. Class 1 investment firms would remain subject to the CRDIV/CRR regime.

[51] These topics could by the way also be suitable for cross-sectoral legislation at Union level, but Brussels does not appear to be organised to cater for that approach.

[52] Reference is made to the overview provided by ESMA on its website.

[53] MiFID II Delegated Directive, [2017] OJ L87/500.

the related guidance, however, can no longer or only partially found in this national implementation. This set of rules has to be traced via delegated regulations, ESMA guidelines and opinions and Q&A's.

In addition to the hard and soft law rules mentioned here specifically in respect of the investment services industry,[54] there are a multitude of guidelines, interpretations, legal opinions, supervisory expectations and the like, issued by European regulators in relation to other financial industry sectors, and various other publications by European regulators which have an informal status but which these regulators nevertheless expect financial institutions to abide by. In addition, there are soft law rules that are issued by Dutch regulators implementing or interpreting hard (or soft) European rules. However, the majority of European soft law rules are not as such 'translated' into national soft law rules, but are directly applied by the national regulators as if constituting hard law. The emergence of a large body of soft law on the European level leads to the following results. One can no longer rely on national rules reflecting European law. National rules gradually begin to lose their relevance. In addition, in order to determine what the legal position is practitioners and regulators will more and more have to resort to European soft law, which is not always easily accessible. National regulators tend to regard European soft law as hard law, and are loath to deviate from soft law even if that leads to questionable or unreasonable results. If European soft law allows for differing interpretations, national regulators will tend to adhere to the most conservative approach. At the same time, financial institutions are reluctant to challenge soft law, which means there is no meaningful judicial oversight with respect to the validity of soft law. The (quasi)regulating power of the ESAs and the national regulators thus remains 'unchecked'.

Clearly, this is not a topic unique to national cross-sectoral regulation, but it does pose an additional challenge to maintain transparency and accessibility of the full scope of national and European legislation. This is largely attributable to the fact that the technique of cross-sectoral national legislation entails that provisions of a directive that needs to be implemented are basically scattered around in the national legislation to be included in those parts of the cross-sectoral legislation they can be clustered with. It is generally difficult if not impossible to arrive at a holistic logical legislative approach.

It is further noted that some EU legislation, notably on consumer protection rules, applies cross-sectorally by nature. UTCD[55] on unfair contract terms is a case in point. We will not further discuss European consumer protection legislation in this chapter.

The impact of European legislation on the FSA can be further illustrated by the following numbers.[56] Between 2007 and 2017, the FSA has been revised 75 times. More than one-third of these revisions was triggered by changes in European legislation. It is interesting to note that in addition quite a few revisions were triggered by the fact that the Dutch legislator/regulator in first instance did not correctly or not properly systematically implement the European rules. This clearly illustrates how difficult it is to integrate these European rules in cross-sectoral national legislation. In addition, between 2007 and 2017, the number of types of financial institutions regulated by the Act on financial supervision increased from 9 to 19. A considerable number of these new types of financial institutions subjected to regulation were introduced by European regulation. This includes reinsurers and entities for risk-acceptance (2007), payment service

---

[54] Clearly, similar comments can be made for the banking industry, the insurance sector, the investment institutions and the management thereof, the payment services industry, etc.

[55] UTCD, [1993] OJ L95/29.

[56] These figures have been derived from the consultation document on a contemplated revision of the Dutch system of financial supervision legislation: *Herziening van de Wft: verkenning, Consultatiedocument*, published 22 November 2016.

providers (2009), electronic money institutions (2011), and managers of alternative investment funds and depositaries of such funds (2013).

There has not just been an increased number of revisions to the underlying European legislation and an extension of scope by adding new types of regulated entities and activities. The complexity has increased as well. This can be illustrated by comparing the implementation of the Reinsurance Directive[57] (2007) and the BRRD/SRM (2015). The Reinsurance Directive could basically be implemented in the FSA by extending the definition of the insurer with that of a reinsurer. Until such time, life and non-life insurers were regulated. The new regulation on reinsurers could be implemented by adding reinsurers to the scope of this supervision and catering for any specialties in this regard by a limited number of separate provisions. An example of such special provision for reinsurers are the rules on capital for a captive reinsurer. The BRRD/SRM on the other hand appeared to add such a level of complexity that it could *not* be implemented in the cross-sectoral system of the FSA. This was resolved as a practical matter by basically adding a separate chapter on the implementation of the BRRD and the SRM as a new Part 3A of the Act on financial supervision, entitled *Special measures and provisions for financial institutions*. By the way, implementation of the BRRD was made more complex because the Dutch legislator pre-empted on the European Directive by introducing a national law covering the same topics in advance of this Directive being promulgated.[58] The Directive's provisions had then to be integrated into the existing deviating national framework. This complication is likely to arise again if and when a European directive on the recovery and resolution of insurance companies will be introduced. The Dutch legislator has already pre-empted on that forthcoming directive as well.[59]

V. Revisions to the Cross-Sectoral Approach of the FSA?

The challenges to the cross-sectoral approach of the FSA, and its complicated relationship with European legislation, have led to a market consultation, on the occasion of the tenth anniversary of the Act in 2016, to establish whether or not and if so how the FSA ought to be thoroughly overhauled, possibly abandoning the largely cross-sectoral approach adopted in 2007.[60] The market was presented with five basic options to choose from. These varied from a zero-option in which nothing would change to an option to return to a strict sectoral approach with separate laws for each separate sector. In May 2019, the Minister of Finance has communicated that for the time being the consultation will not result in a formal follow up and a determination whether or not the cross-sectoral system of legislation will be revised. The reasoning for this non-action approach is based on the burden in time and costs that an overhaul of the legal system for the financial sector would entail, combined with ongoing national and international developments which would make it even more difficult to conduct such operation. This outcome was predictable, based on the responses to the consultation from which the following conclusions can be drawn.

First of all, it is clear that the vast majority of the respondents agree on the challenges that the FSA poses. This includes, in particular, lack of transparency and accessibility and the tension between the cross sectoral approach of the FSA and the mainly sectoral approach of the European

---

[57] Directive 2005/68/EC, [2005] OJ L323/1 (this directive is no longer in force since Solvency II).
[58] *Stb.* 2012/241.
[59] *Stb.* 2018/489.
[60] *Herziening van de Wft: verkenning, Consultatiedocument*, published 22 November 2016.

legislation. There also seems to be a strong (albeit far from unanimous) consensus on the best way forward, namely: to revise the system of the FSA from a largely cross-sectoral to a more strictly sectoral approach, based on the choices that the European legislator makes.

At the same time, several parties who have responded to the consultation have expressed their doubts and concerns on the feasibility of such an overhaul of the system of the FSA, considering inter alia the fact that the European legislation as a tracker would be a moving target in any event. It is also clear that such overhaul will generate a multitude of interpretation issues, causing undesirable uncertainty in the financial sector. Furthermore, such overhaul will in practice mean an invitation to Parliament to reconsider politically sensitive issues, such as for instance to take the opportunity to further improve customer protection rules and to set further strict standards on remuneration in the sector. The financial industry is of course not hugely enthusiastic about that prospect.

As stated above, it has been confirmed by the Minister of Finance, who took the initiative to the consultation in question, that for the time being there will be no revision of the FSA. Instead, the Minister will, going forward from time to time, initiate legislative changes aimed at improving the accessibility and transparency. If there is no substantive revision and the legislative system will remain largely 'as is' (ie, integrated, and 'hybrid' with a strong emphasis on a sectoral approach), we are left with the complications noted above, particularly in relation to the way in which European rules laid down in directives and regulations are absorbed in Dutch law. In summary, going forward these complications lead to (at least) the following possible approaches at the national level:

(a)   The first approach would be a one-on-one implementation in the FSA and/or lower Dutch regulations of European directives, reflecting the exact wordings of the directives concerned. In this approach there would be no gold plating. EU regulations and delegated EU Commission regulations which are directly applicable clearly would not be part of that implementation process.[61] This necessarily results in European legislation being partly reflected in the FSA and/or lower regulations, partly in European regulations and delegated regulations that apply directly. The FSA and/or the lower regulations accordingly would not contain the complete legislative framework for the rules in question. The division of rules between the two legislative systems is not always based on logic. This constitutes a substantial challenge for financial institutions and their advisers to track and trace applicable legal provisions in specific cases.

(b)   Another possible approach going forward would be the implementation of European directives by adjusting existing Dutch rules to align with the European rules rather than by way of 'faithful translation' on a one-on-one basis.[62] This may lead to intended or unintended gold plating. EU regulations and delegated EU Commission regulations (which are all directly applicable) would typically not be part of that implementation process. Again, this would result in European legislation being partly reflected in the FSA and/or lower regulations, not always recognisable as such, and partly in European regulations and delegated regulations. Also in this case the FSA no longer provides the complete legislative framework for the rules

---

[61] Although certain provisions of EU regulations may require national implementation, eg to decide on Member State options that have been provided.

[62] The implementation of the BRRD and the SRMR into Dutch law, by way of introducing a new Part 3A in the FSA, is a good example of absorption of Union rules on the basis of existing legislation rather than on a one-on-one basis. The Union rules in this instance were not as detailed and clear-cut as one might hope, and in Part 3A the Dutch legislator made an attempt to fill in gaps and remove uncertainties. Nevertheless many uncertainties remain, which in practice will have to be addressed by the resolution authorities concerned, the SRB and DCB.

in question. A possibly additional complicating factor here is that the European rules that are implemented into national law by way of interpretative alignment will be subject to interpretation in accordance with the European rules and their respective intents and purposes. That may result in FSA rules that have a (slightly, or possibly even substantially) different portent than the Dutch text thereof indicates. There is also the possibility that implementation is incomplete or incorrect. This is the approach that the Dutch legislators have so far adopted.

(c) A third possible approach would be the adjustment of the FSA and/or lower regulations to accommodate and absorb all relevant EU law, including directly applicable EU regulations and delegated regulations. This would of course be a virtually impossible exercise (at least in so far as existing European legislation is concerned), in any event an exercise of daunting proportions. It would lead to the somewhat confusing situation that the FSA would be made to contain both directly applicable European rules and national rules. To the extent both are fully interrelated and consistent with each other, this should not be a problem. But that is not always the case. To the extent national rules conflict with or deviate from the directly applicable regulations, they would be ineffective. To the extent there is room for interpretation, that interpretation must conform to the European rules and their respective intents and purposes. The impracticalities and the undesirable consequences of this approach would appear to make this option unworkable, notwithstanding that one might then end up having one all-encompassing legislative instrument.

(d) Now and then, when European rules permit (basically whenever there is no maximum harmonisation requirement), there can be deliberate gold plating on the national level. This leads to the possible complication that the gold-plated rules must be partly interpreted in accordance with the European rules concerned and their intents and purpose, and partly (to the extent of the gold plating itself) interpreted according to Dutch law. Gold plating is likely to lead to distortion of the European level playing field. It can also have unintended negative consequences. The remuneration rules applicable in the Netherlands which are stricter than Union law requires,[63] may serve as an example. That gold-plating exercise has had unintended and unexpected consequences in that these strict rules have proven to be a severe handicap in the Union-wide competition for financial sector business as a consequence of Brexit.

(e) In respect of both directly applicable European regulations and directives, European supervisory authorities frequently issue guidelines, interpretations, opinions, supervisory expectations, etc ('soft law'). These filter through into Dutch laws and regulations, and thus affect the interpretation and application of the Dutch implementing rules; the ability to rely on the texts of the FSA and lower Dutch regulations that have a European origin or connection is thereby jeopardised.

(f) As stated above, Dutch supervisory authorities are at times seen to be applying European 'soft law' rules fully as if they were directly applicable 'hard' rules of European law. There is a certain tendency of Dutch supervisory authorities to be rather unappreciative of market parties' arguments that this may in circumstances actually not be the correct or appropriate approach.

(g) In addition to the 'soft law' mentioned in (e) and (f) above, there are guidelines, interpretations and opinions, etc issued by the Dutch supervisory authorities. This soft law of Dutch origin is not necessarily limited to purely Dutch rules of law, but can also cover European rules, providing market parties with a Dutch interpretation of the meaning of directives

---

[63] This is especially true for the 20% bonus cap of Art 1:121, FSA.

and regulations. These interpretations are not necessarily always fully in conformity with Union law or the interpretations thereof that the European supervisory authorities provide, and may cause confusion. Sometimes there is separate Dutch soft law that reflects or duplicates or expands on European soft law. Usually, Dutch guidance or interpretation faithfully follows the European soft law. But sometimes one will see that the Dutch guidance and interpretation is based on a (not always necessarily correct) conservative translation of corresponding European soft law. This may lead to intended or unintended gold plating. For market parties, this may lead to complex issues, particularly if there is reason to doubt whether the European soft law itself is fully in accordance with the European regulation or directive concerned.

All in all, the complicated relationship between national rules and national implementation of European legislation on the one hand and directly applicable European regulations and delegated regulations on the other hand, supplemented with national and European 'soft law' and topped-up with the potential of gold plating, form a far from ideal but perhaps unavoidable legislative puzzle. There are however mitigating developments. One of these is the tendency of the European legislator more and more to opt for maximum harmonisation through the issuance of regulations rather than directives, or to use a combination of directives and regulations to achieve maximum harmonisation and to ensure uniform application of rules. Another is that the Dutch legislator appears to be more and more willing to choose one-on-one implementation of Union rules, rather than absorbing them into and adapting them to pre-existing legislation. This trend however cannot be discerned where maximum harmonisation does not stand in the way in respect of topics that are politically charged. As stated above, one sees a trend whereby practitioners in advising financial institutions more and more prefer to rely on actual European sources of national law rather than on the manner of their implementation into national law.

Would the picture be fundamentally different if legislation were strictly organised on a sectoral basis? The difficulties identified above would undoubtedly not be resolved by a sectoral approach of national legislation. A sectoral approach may however help make the national and European law rules substantially better aligned and more accessible and user friendly. On the other hand, different rules for different sectors of the financial industry may result in unnecessary and unhelpful compartmentalisation, not only of the rules themselves, but possibly also in their practical application by national supervisory authorities and market parties.

VI. The Cross-Sectoral Approach of the FSA and the Twin Peaks Model: Does it Work?

In this section, a test case is discussed. This is presented in an attempt to arrive at an answer to the question of whether the cross-sectoral approach of the FSA, combined with the Twin Peaks model, works in practice. In other words, whether a cross-sectoral approach to legislation combines well with a Twin Peaks supervisory system.

The test case concerns DSB Bank. This bank, in pre-SSM times, had obtained a licence from DCB. Its business mainly consisted of providing mortgage and consumer credit, with relatively low interest rates. These were subsidised by rather high earnings of the bank acting as an insurance intermediary for payment protection policies and other insurance products. The financing of the bank's business was obtained through securitisations of credit portfolios and through deposits taken from the public, including deeply subordinated deposits that were permitted to count as core capital of the bank. An unusual feature of the bank's organisation was the fact that it was owned by the CEO. Ultimately, the business model appeared to pose a high risk from a duty of care perspective. Breaches of the duty of care and resulting customer claims led to the loss of trust by deposit-holders of the bank, an increasing risk of a bank run, culminating ultimately in the bankruptcy of DSB Bank.

In this test case, there were arguably certain conflicting interests between the intents and purposes of prudential supervision by DCB on the one hand and those of market conduct supervision by the AFM on the other hand. An illustration of that conflict between prudential and market conduct rules can be found in the issuance of subordinated bonds to the public. Issuance of these instruments helped strengthen the regulatory capital of the bank, and therefore were seen to be acceptable and desirable from a prudential regulatory standpoint. At the same time, these instruments constituted a concern from a consumer protection point of view. This was because these instruments, being core capital instruments of the bank, constituted complex securities with a default risk profile difficult to understand by retail customers. In a judgment of the Court of Appeals in Amsterdam,[64] it was confirmed that in this case, the AFM as a market conduct supervisor had not been required to take any additional measures to safeguard the position of retail investors. A question that arises in this context is whether the AFM should have discouraged the issue of these instruments to retail customers (or perhaps should have insisted upon rather stronger caveats in the issue documentation, resulting in these instruments becoming less attractive). It is actually unclear whether the AFM at the time had statutory authority to block the issuance of these instruments to the public (basically deposit holding clients of DSB Bank), but if it had and if it had used this authority, that would clearly have run counter to DCB's prudential interests in ensuring that the bank maintained as strong a core capital position as was practically feasible. In the case of DSB Bank, it would probably not have been possible to replace these capital instruments with core capital attracted in the regular capital markets.[65] On this topic, one could therefor conclude that at least from a theoretical perspective, the division of tasks between supervisors in a Twin Peaks mode prevents that market conduct supervision would become subordinated to prudential supervision, simply because each supervisor may be expected to be primarily focused on its own task. It is debatable whether any form of subordination or derogation should be permissible. It is to be noted, as stated in this chapter above, that market conduct supervision includes safeguarding financial stability.[66] The AFM may therefore not have a mono-focus on market conduct aspects without considering the impact on financial stability. Clearly, market conduct supervision issues can ultimately lead, as it did here, to prudential issues, namely the bankruptcy of DSB Bank.

A further, and in the context of this chapter perhaps more important, question is whether the supervisory authorities should have intervened at an earlier stage in the operations of DSB Bank, and whether such intervention, if indeed it should have been carried out at an earlier stage, was impeded by the Twin Peaks model. In other words, was the separation of prudential

---

[64] Court of Appeals Amsterdam, judgment dated 26 March 2013, *JOR* 2013/173, ECLI:NL:GHAMS:2013:BZ5509.

[65] Similar issues with respect to comparable capital instruments have arisen for instance in the context of the failure of SNS Bank in the Netherlands and Banco Popular Espanyol in Spain. In the latter case, measures were taken, with some help of 'white knight' Banco Santander, to ensure that retail investors in these instruments would not suffer from bail-in, even though these instruments, being part of the regulatory capital of these banks, would strictly speaking have been eligible for bail-in directly in line after the so-called Core Equity Tier 1 capital of these banks. In the case of SNS Bank, retail holders of subordinated debt instruments, also counting as core capital, were also given beneficial treatment. In this case, there was a concern that these retail holders could, in lieu of a claim under their subordinated debt, claim as concurrent creditors for damages on the basis of mis-selling. The beneficial treatment was given them even though the validity of their concurrent claim in tort was not tested in the courts.

[66] Article 1:25, para 2, FSA.

and market conduct authority in this case a possible cause for the 'failure' of the two supervisory authorities to prevent the failure of DSB Bank? It is debatable whether more effective supervision could have been achieved if an integrated supervision model had been chosen, whether or not combined with a sectoral legislative approach. In hindsight it is certainly conceivable that under such a different system the national supervisor(s) would have achieved better coordination among themselves and on that basis might have intervened at an earlier stage.

Another potential conflict between the two supervisors in the Twin Peaks model arose in respect of the fit and proper testing of one of the directors of the bank. DCB approved a certain candidate from its prudential perspective, while the AFM had made objections to the same person from a market conduct perspective. To prevent such conflict from re-occurring, an additional provision was introduced in the FSA[67] to safeguard that in such case a given candidate cannot be appointed if either of the two supervisory authorities voice objections.[68]

In addition to the test case concerning DSB Bank, one could perhaps also mention the failure of SNS Bank as an illustrative example here. These two bank failures bear little resemblance to each other. Whilst it could be said that the root causes for the demise of DSB Bank were both of a prudential and a market conduct nature (market conduct issues actually being the main drivers), the root causes of the insolvency of SNS Bank were predominantly to be found in prudential requirements applicable to SNS Bank: that bank failed to timely strengthen its capital base in accordance with requests to that effect made by DCB as the prudential supervisor. The nationalisation of the SNS Reaal Group, to which SNS Bank belonged, occurred in February 2013. The nationalisation decree issued by the Minister of Finance on 1 February 2013 contains an elaborate overview of events leading to the demise of SNS Bank.[69] In addition, the Report of the Evaluation Commission on the Nationalization of SNS Bank (often referred to as the Report of Hoekstra & Frijns), published in 2014, contains a detailed analysis and evaluation of these events.[70] If one examines these documents, one can conclude that the inter-action and cooperation between DCB (as the prudential supervisory authority) and the Minister of Finance (as the authority empowered by statute to nationalise financial institutions) at times left much to be desired. In the events leading up to this nationalisation, the AFM was not involved in any significant way. Hence it is not possible to draw conclusions from the demise of this bank for the effectiveness of the Twin Peaks model. One could perhaps speculate whether a more incisive involvement of the AFM in the events leading up to the failure of this bank might have made a difference, even though the underlying causes in this case were more of a prudential nature than a matter of market conduct. We note that at the time of the demise of SNS Bank, the BRRD and the SRM Regulation had not yet been promulgated; the nationalisation was the first (and remains the only) instance in which nationalisation powers were used by the Minister of Finance. Had the BRRD and the SRM Regulation then already been in place, it is fair to assume that the bank would have been resolved rather than nationalised.

---

[67] Article 1:47c, Act on financial supervision.

[68] Clearly, it would be interesting to see how these cooperation provisions would work in practice in the event of a significant bank where the fit and proper testing is in the hands of the ECB. This adds a complication to the Twin Peaks model. On this topic: AA van Gelder en P Teule, *Gedragstoezicht en het SSM: op weg naar een nieuwe balans*, (TvFR, 2014), p 462-468.

[69] The decree, Nr FM/2013/213M, dated 1 February 2013 can be found at http://old.findinet.nl/~uploads/newsModule/sns_onteigeningsbesluit.pdf.

[70] To be found at http://old.findinet.nl/~uploads/newsModule/snsreaalnationalisatierapport.pdf.

VII. Conclusion

The largely cross-sectoral approach that the Dutch legislator embraced is not ideal, but it seems to work reasonably well. The downsides to the cross-sectoral approach are clear, but supervisors, financial institutions and their advisors have generally learned to cope with these downsides. In any event, the growing importance of directly applicable European law (hard and soft), on a strict sectoral basis, makes the question which of the various possible legislative approaches is preferable more and more irrelevant.

One could also say that the clarity of the distinction made in the legislation between prudential supervision and market conduct (basically the Twin Peaks model) serves in particular supervisory authorities rather better than market participants. The supervisors can easily track and trace their tasks and authority. Market participants, however, have to make a considerable effort to keep track of their obligations that are arranged on a cross-sectoral basis.

A revision of the FSA into a sectoral model would probably make life significantly easier for regulators, financial institutions and their advisors, and it is likely to lead better, more precise implementation of European rules (with less gold plating). But revision would also be a dauntingly complicated exercise, which has quite a few downsides. Hence the hesitation to embark on this exercise as expressed by market participants and professionals in the consultation on the future of the FSA.

The interaction between the cross-sectoral legislative structure and the Twin Peaks model of supervision seems to work well. There have been no significant failures of supervision that could definitively be attributed to flaws in that interaction. The DSB Bank failure could in any event not definitively be so attributed. The effectiveness of said interaction is to a large extent dependent upon cooperation and consultation between DCB, AFM and the Minister of Finance. The duty to consult and cooperate is in part embedded in the FSA (perhaps with room for further improvement). This statutory basis is crucial to make the interaction work properly.

PART II

Stability of the Financial System

6

Regulating Systemic Risk: A Cross-Sectoral Approach

DANNY BUSCH AND MIRIK VAN RIJN[1]

I. Introduction

This chapter seeks to contribute to the discussion on the development within the European Union (EU) of a regulatory regime which adequately addresses and mitigates the risk to financial stability posed by non-bank systemically important financial institutions (non-bank SIFIs).

Section II highlights the relevance of the problem by reiterating lessons learned from the global financial crisis, especially in respect of the systemic risk posed by non-bank financial institutions. Sections III–VI consider the existing body of EU financial regulation. We assess what has already been accomplished since the global financial crisis and provide context to our proposed regime of non-bank SIFI supervision and resolution. Section VII makes suggestions and explores legal possibilities for enhancing the existing body of EU financial regulation by including designation, supervision and resolution of non-bank SIFIs at the European level. Section VIII contains our concluding remarks.

II. Systemic Risk

The global financial crisis painfully demonstrated deficiencies in the regulation, supervision and resolution of financial institutions. Not only in the traditional banking sector but also in other parts of the financial system. Indeed, systemic risk manifested itself to a large degree outside the traditional banking sector, especially in the lightly regulated shadow banking sector. The latter refers, quite ominously, to market-based credit intermediation outside the banking sector. Due to a lack of comprehensive regulation and supervision, banks increasingly shifted activities to the shadow banking sector in order to avoid tax, disclosure and capital requirements.[2]

---

[1] This chapter was completed on 12 March 2019. No account could be taken of developments since that date. It is based in part on the authors' article 'Towards Single Supervision and Resolution of Systemically Important Non-Bank Financial Institutions in the European Union', (2018) *European Business Organisation Law Review* 301–363.

[2] See, eg, T Adrian, AB Ashcraft, N Cetorelli, 'Shadow bank monitoring' in AN Berger, P Molyneux, JOS Wilson (eds) *The Oxford handbook of banking* (2nd edn) (Oxford, Oxford University Press, 2015), pp 378–407, p 392.

Such behaviour, which is designed to evade more stringent regulation and supervision or to evade regulation and supervision altogether, is known as regulatory arbitrage. The exploitation of regulatory gaps, however, creates risks to financial stability and erodes the notion of a level playing field.

To strengthen financial stability, we propose that non-bank financial institutions which are systemically relevant should be subjected to European prudential regulation and to a European supervisor and a European resolution authority.[3]

Our proposals exclude banks as they are already subject to stricter prudential regulation under the Capital Requirements Directives (CRD IV) and Capital Requirements Regulation (CRR) and, within the Member States participating in the European Banking Union (EBU), are subject to the Single Supervisory Mechanism (SSM) and the Single Resolution Mechanism (SRM). Within the SSM, significant banks are directly supervised by the ECB and resolved by the Single Resolution Board (SRB).[4]

In accordance with the approach of the Financial Stability Board[5] and drawing inspiration from the US Dodd-Frank reforms,[6] we advocate that the EU's sectoral approach to financial regulation, supervision and resolution be complemented by a more risk-based identification, regulation, supervision and resolution of non-bank systemically important financial institutions. Any non-bank financial institution[7] which could pose a threat to financial stability – referred to as non-bank systemically important financial institutions (non-bank SIFIs) – should therefore be subject to commensurate supervision, regulation and resolution, regardless of the legal categorisation of the non-bank financial institution.[8] This would entail partial reform and extension of supervision, regulation and resolution of financial institutions in the EU, which is presently organised largely along sectoral lines, and a move towards a more pan-sectoral regime for non-bank SIFIs. A cross-sectoral supervisory and resolution regime for non-bank SIFIs would correspond with the increasingly blurred distinction between markets, financial institutions and products.[9] It would also help to reduce regulatory arbitrage activities and gaps in coverage, as it would ensure that the risks posed by a non-bank SIFI are subject to commensurate regulation, regardless of the legal form of the entity. In order to properly identify non-bank SIFIs, robust monitoring of the entire European financial sector is necessary.

---

[3] More broadly, it is also questionable whether a sectoral model of supervision is sufficient and indeed future-proof in the increasingly interconnected financial sector. See, ie, E Ferran, 'Institutional design: the choices for national systems' in N Moloney, E Ferran, J Payne (eds), *The Oxford Handbook of Financial Regulation* (Oxford, Oxford University Press, 2015) pp 97–128, p 101; D Awrey 'Law, financial instability, and the institutional structure of financial regulation' in A Anand (ed), *Systemic risk, institutional design, and the regulation of financial markets* (Oxford, Oxford University Press, 2016), pp 61–96. However, this chapter does not seek to revisit the make-up of the supervisory model in the EU as a whole but rather to supplement the existing framework with a robust holistic approach for the identification, supervision, regulation and resolution of non-bank SIFIs. Moreover, while our proposal concerns institution-based regulation and supervision this does not detract from the need for market and product-based regulation as essential complements to entity-based regulation.

[4] As regards the European Banking Union, see, eg, D Busch, G Ferrarini (eds), *The European Banking Union* (Oxford, Oxford University Press, 2015).

[5] Financial Stability Board (2011b) Policy measures to address systemically important financial institutions. 4 November 2011, www.fsb.org/wp-content/uploads/r_111104bb.pdf?page_moved=1, para 3.

[6] 12 US Code, s 5323.

[7] 'Financial institution' should be understood as a broad term encapsulating all financial sector entities.

[8] The FSB defines SIFIs as 'financial institutions whose distress or disorderly failure, because of their size, complexity and systemic interconnectedness, would cause significant disruption to the wider financial system and economic activity'.

[9] E Ferran 'Institutional design: the choices for national systems' in N Moloney, E Ferran, J Payne (eds), *The Oxford Handbook of Financial Regulation* (Oxford, Oxford University Press, 2015), pp 97–12; RH Huang, D Schoenmaker (eds), *Institutional structure of financial regulation: theories and international experiences* (Abingdon, Routledge, 2014).

The proposed regime is in line with financial reform proposals issued by the Financial Stability Board (FSB), which call for a level of supervision proportionate to the potential destabilisation risk that a financial firm poses to the financial system.[10] Additionally, the FSB requires an effective resolution regime for all financial institutions which could be systemically significant or critical if they fail.[11]

For the development of such a regime we draw on the experiences in the United States. Although the Trump administration intends to reverse the course of US financial regulation, non-bank financial companies have in the past been designated as systemically important.[12] Such designation puts them under federal supervision and, reflecting their importance to the financial system, makes them subject to specific prudential and living will requirements. Additionally, non-bank financial institutions posing a systemic risk may be subjected to a specialised resolution regime.

The global financial crisis highlighted a number of structural weaknesses in the worldwide financial system and economies. One of the most important lessons was the, generally unforeseen, possibility of systemic risk originating from non-bank financial institutions.

Systemic risk is the risk that a national, regional or the global financial system breaks down.[13] Systemic risks manifest where a localised shock – such as the failure of a financial institution – has repercussions that adversely affect the broader economy.[14] It thus poses a threat to financial stability.[15] Systemic risk may manifest in many different forms and within a range of financial institutions. As noted by Anabtawi and Schwarcz, systemic risks do not distinguish between financial market participants.[16] Systemic risk should therefore be regarded as an elusive concept, not confined to certain institutions, markets or products.[17] Accordingly, financial regulation should have an equally flexible and open scope.

Despite the regulatory focus, it turned out that systemic risk was not confined to the (retail) banking sector. Non-bank financial institutions such as Long-Term Capital Management (LTCM), American International Group (AIG) and Reserve Primary proved equally capable of creating systemic risk. This realisation is reflected in the European Systemic Risk Board Regulation, which

---

[10] Financial Stability Board, 'Progress and next steps towards ending 'too-big-to-fail' (TBTF)' (2013). Report of the Financial Stability Board to the G-20. 2 September 2013. www.fsb.org/wp-content/uploads/r_130902.pdf?page_moved=1, p 18.

[11] Financial Stability Board, 'Key attributes of effective resolution regimes for financial institutions' (2011a), October 2011. www.fsb.org/wp-content/uploads/r_111104cc.pdf.

[12] The Financial Stability Oversight Council (FSOC) designated American International Group (AIG), General Electric Capital Corporation, Prudential Financial and MetLife to be non-bank financial companies whose material financial distress could pose a threat to US financial stability. Changes in the business of GE Capital Global Holdings (successor to General Electric Capital Corporation), AIG, and Prudential Financial subsequently led the FSOC to rescind their designations in, respectively, 2016, 2017 and 2018. Metlife successfully appealed its designation at the Federal District Court for the District of Columbia. The US Court of Appeal dismissed the appeal on 23 January 2018, on a motion to this effect filed jointly by Metlife and FSOC. See *Metlife, Inc. v Financial Stability Oversight Council*, CA No 15-0045 (D.D.C. 30 March 2016).

[13] HS Scott, 'Reducing systemic risk through the reform of capital regulation', (2010) 13(3) *Journal of International Economic Law* 763–778, 764.

[14] I Anabtawi, SL Schwarcz, 'Regulating systemic risk: towards an analytical framework' (2011) 86 *Notre Dame Law Review* 1349–1412, 1351. See also SL Schwarcz SL (2008) 'Systemic Risk', (2008) 97 *Georgetown Law Journal* 193–249, 203.

[15] RM Lastra, 'Systemic risk & macro-prudential supervision' in N Moloney, E Ferran, J Payne J (eds), *The Oxford handbook of financial regulation* (Oxford, Oxford University Press, 2015), pp 309–333, p 312.

[16] I Anabtawi, SL Schwarcz, 'Regulating systemic risk: towards an analytical framework' (2011) 86 *Notre Dame Law Review* 1349–1412, fn 10.

[17] Indeed, the creation of suitable regulation of markets and financial products – for example by increasing market transparency and through product approval processes – is essential for the safeguarding of financial stability. However, this article focuses mainly on the regulation of entities, specifically non-bank SIFIs.

acknowledges that all types of financial intermediaries, markets and infrastructure may potentially be systemically important to some degree.[18] Additionally, both the legislative proposal of the European Commission (Commission) on a framework for the recovery and resolution of central counterparties (CCPs)[19] and its proposal for the creation of a new supervisory mechanism for CCPs aim to regulate and supervise the systemic risk posed by CCPs.[20] This illustrates our premise that non-bank financial institutions are equally capable of posing systemic risks.[21] Asset management activities are another example of a potential source of non-bank systemic risk which has recently attracted attention.[22]

The Commission's proposal for the establishment of a Capital Markets Union (CMU) is also of interest as the envisaged growth of non-bank credit intermediation makes overarching checks on systemic risks even more pressing.[23] Designed to increase the supply of alternative sources of financing – thereby reducing dependence on funding through the banking sector – the CMU proposal looks to increase the role of non-bank financial intermediaries.[24] Such diversification of funding improves the allocation of capital and diversification of risk and thereby strengthens the European financial system. At the same time, as recognised by the 'Five Presidents' Report', closer integration of capital markets and gradual removal of remaining national barriers necessitates an expansion and strengthening of the available tools to manage financial players' systemic risks prudently (macro-prudential toolkit) and to strengthen the supervisory framework to ensure the solidity of all financial actors.[25] This should, according to the report, ultimately lead to a single European capital markets supervisor.[26]

This shows that systemic risk can occur in different sectors, or indeed across different sectors, and have a variety of distinct characteristics. Hence, it might be difficult to identify such risks.

---

[18] Regulation (EU) No 1092/2010 (ESRB Regulation), Art 2, sub (c).

[19] Recognising the central and growing systemic importance of CCPs – resulting from the G20 commitment to clear additional classes of over-the-counter derivatives with CCPs – the European Commission proposed recovery and resolution measures to safeguard financial stability. See Proposal for a Regulation on a framework for the recovery and resolution of central counterparties and amending Regulations (EU) No 1095/2010, (EU) No 648/2012, and (EU) 2015/2365, COM(2016) 856 final.

[20] See on the supervision of CCPs, section V below.

[21] At the same time, CCPs have very specific market infrastructural functions which, in their case, might warrant a specific, sectoral, approach to their regulation and supervision. As our chapter focuses on bank-like risks occurring in non-bank financial institutions, CCPs fall outside the scope of our proposed regulatory reforms owing to their specific activities.

[22] See Financial Stability Board, 'Policy recommendations to address structural vulnerabilities from asset management activities' (2017), 12 January 2017. www.fsb.org/wp-content/uploads/FSB-Policy Recommendations-on-Asset-Management-Structural-Vulnerabilities.pdf; N Doyle, L Hermans, PA Molitor, C Weistroffer 'Shadow banking in the euro area: risks and vulnerabilities in the investment fund sector' (2016) European Central Bank Occasional Paper Series No 174. www.ecb.europa.eu/pub/pdf/scpops/ecbop174.en.pdf?2cc4d889706adbcb918c06de4e5df144. The FSB found that the worldwide assets under management rose from $53.6 trillion in 2005 to $76.7 trillion in 2015, equating to 40% of global financial system assets. It identified a number of potential financial stability risks in asset management activities.

[23] See also, N Véron, GB Wolff, 'Capital Markets Union: a vision for the long term' (2016) 2(1) *Journal of Financial Regulation* 139–153; K Alexander K, 'Capital Markets Union from the perspective of the banking industry and prudential supervision', (2015) 9(3) *Law and Financial Markets Review* 191–195.

[24] European Commission, 'Building a capital markets union' (2015). Green paper, COM(2015) 63 final.

[25] J-C Juncker, D Tusk, J Dijsselbloem, M Draghi, M Schulz M, 'Completing Europe's economic and monetary union' (2015). Five Presidents' Report. www.ecb.europa.eu/pub/pdf/other/5presidentsreport.en.pdf, p 12.

[26] Ibid. See on ESMA as a single European capital markets supervisor: E Avgouleas, G Ferrarini G, 'A single listing authority and securities regulator for the CMU and the future of ESMA' in D Busch, E Avgouleas, G Ferrarini (eds), *Capital Markets Union in Europe* (Oxford, Oxford University Press, 2018), pp 55–78. See on CMU in a general sense: D Busch, E Avgouleas, G Ferrarini (eds), *Capital Markets Union in Europe* (Oxford, Oxford University Press, 2018); D Busch D (2017), 'A Capital Markets Union for a Divided Europe'. (2017) 3(2) *Journal of Financial Regulation* 262–279.

It is therefore of great importance for jurisdictions to have a broad monitoring system in place, capable of identifying systemic risk throughout the entire financial sector.

III. European Banking Union

In the EU, the policy response to the global financial crisis and the European sovereign debt crisis has remained organised largely along sectoral lines. The most notable reform has been the creation of a European Banking Union (EBU) which entailed an extensive overhaul and transfer of bank supervision and resolution to the EU level.[27] Because the creation of the Banking Union is the single most important response to the manifestation of systemic risk in the eurozone, a short account of its institutional make-up and scope, is in order. This will also allow us to assess the feasibility of expanding its scope to capture systemically important shadow banking entities. EBU consists of three pillars.

A. Single Supervisory Mechanism (SSM)

The first pillar is the Single Supervisory Mechanism (SSM), which came into force on 4 November 2014. This has resulted in a historical shift of powers from the national level to the EU level. Since that date, the European Central Bank (ECB) in Frankfurt has been the direct prudential supervisor with respect to the 'significant' banks (and some other institutions) in the Eurozone.[28] Within EBU, direct prudential supervision with respect to 'less significant' banks in the Eurozone remains in the hands of the national prudential supervisors.[29] The ECB and the national prudential supervisors operate on the basis of a European Single Rulebook, consisting of the Capital Requirements Directive IV (CRD IV) and the Capital Requirements Regulation (CRR).[30] These rules do not only apply within the Eurozone but across the entire EU.

B. Single Resolution Mechanism (SRM)

The second pillar is the Single Resolution Mechanism (SRM), which came into force on 1 January 2016. Since then, the Single Resolution Board (SRB) in Brussels has been in charge of the resolution of the 'significant' banks in the Eurozone. Mirroring the division of labour within the SSM, the national resolution authorities remain the competent authorities with respect to the resolution of non-significant banks in the Eurozone.[31] The SRB and the national resolution authorities

---

[27] On EBU, see, eg, D Busch, G Ferrarini (eds), *The European Banking Union* (Oxford, Oxford University Press, 2015).

[28] Article 6(4) of Council Regulation (EU) No 1024/2013 (SSM Regulation). However, the ECB is responsible, regardless of size or systemic significance of the institution, for the granting and withdrawal of banking licences, and for assessing the suitability of bank owners. See Art 4(1)(a) and (c) and Art 6(4), SSM Regulation. Non-eurozone EU Member States can participate to the SSM by entering into a 'close cooperation agreement' with the ECB. See SSM, Arts 2(1) and 7.

[29] Article 6(4) SSM Regulation. However, the ECB can always 'call up' direct supervision for such other Eurozone banks when necessary to ensure consistent application of high supervisory standards. See Art 6(5)(b), SSM Regulation.

[30] Directive 2013/36/EU. Capital Requirements Directive (CRD IV); Regulation (EU) 575/2013, Capital Requirements Regulation (CRR).

[31] Regulation (EU) No 806/2014, (SRM Regulation).

operate on the basis of the Bank Recovery and Resolution Directive (BRRD), which does not only apply within the Eurozone but across the entire EU.[32]

C. European Deposit Insurance Scheme (EDIS)

The third pillar of EBU is the European Deposit Insurance Scheme (EDIS), but this pillar has not yet been erected. The Commission made, in November 2015, a proposal for a regulation setting up a EDIS for bank deposits in the euro area, however, as of yet, no agreement has been reached.[33] The EDIS proposal builds on the system of national deposit guarantee schemes (DGS) regulated by Directive 2014/49/EU. This system already ensures that all deposits up to €100 000 are protected through national DGS all over the EU. EDIS would provide a stronger and more uniform degree of insurance cover in the euro area. This would reduce the vulnerability of national DGS to large local shocks, ensuring that the level of depositor confidence in a bank would not depend on the bank's location and weakening the link between banks and their national sovereigns. EDIS would apply to deposits below €100 000 of all banks in the banking union. When one of these banks is placed into insolvency or in resolution and it is necessary to pay out deposits or to finance their transfer to another bank, the national DGS and EDIS will intervene. The scheme will develop in different stages and the contributions of EDIS will progressively increase over time. At the final stage of the EDIS set up, the protection of bank deposits will be fully financed by EDIS, supported by a close cooperation with national DGS.[34]

D. Assessment

EBU is an ambitious and vigorous overhaul of banking supervision and resolution in the Eurozone. Unfortunately, EBU is restricted to direct prudential supervision by the ECB of large and international Eurozone banks. Other systemically important financial institutions such as large insurance companies and market infrastructure providers are excluded. Also, the shadow banking sector is left unaffected by EBU, thus creating risks of regulatory arbitrage and, ultimately, the build-up of systemic risk.

However, for the sake of clarity, its scope does extend to certain non-bank entities and groups. The SSM also captures parent undertakings which are a financial holding or mixed financial holding. The resolution mechanism also extends to 730k investment firms and financial institutions that are covered by the consolidated supervision of the parent undertaking by the ECB. This creates a complicated legal patchwork where certain non-bank financial entities are also affected by the regime created by EBU. Whether and, if so, to what extent an entity falls within the scope of EBU depends on its legal classification (eg the perimeter or definition of credit institution) and the nature of the group to which it belongs. The partial supervision of financial groups, which *excludes* solo supervision of non-bank entities within a group, but *includes* supervision of their parent holding, risks gaps in supervision. Similarly, resolution at group level can be triggered only if strict conditions are met, with the health of the group's bank subsidiary being decisive.

---

[32] Directive 2014/59/EU, Bank Recovery and Resolution Directive (BRRD).

[33] See, eg, A Enria, 'Supervising banks – Principles and priorities' (2019). Speech 7 March 2019, Frankfurt am Main.

[34] Proposal for a Regulation 806/2014 in order to establish a European Deposit Insurance Scheme, COM(2015) 586 final (24 November 2015).

This could encourage regulatory arbitrage activities as groups might escape supervision and resolution under EBU by changing the make-up of their group.

Although EBU is an ambitious and vigorous overhaul of banking supervision in the Eurozone, it risks being inflexible and setting a non-future proof regulatory perimeter due to the rigid scope of its application.[35]

E. Direct Prudential Supervision by the ECB of Systemic Investment Firms within the Eurozone

But the regulatory perimeter of EBU may well expand in the near future, albeit in a modest way. On 20 December 2017 the Commission published its proposals for more proportionate and risk-sensitive rules for investment firms.[36] Alongside banks, EU capital markets rely on several thousands of small and large investment firms which give advice to clients, help companies to tap capital markets, manage assets, and provide market liquidity, thereby facilitating investments across the EU.

The proposal includes: (i) new and simpler prudential rules for the large majority of investment firms which are not systemic, without compromising financial stability; and (ii) amended rules to ensure that large, systemic investment firms which carry out bank-like activities and pose similar risks as banks are brought under the same supervisory regime as significant credit institutions.

The proposal further defines as credit institutions those systemic investment firms which carry out certain bank-like activities (ie underwriting and dealing on own account) and have assets over €30 billion. These systemic firms will be fully subject to the same treatment as banks. This means that their operations in Member States participating in EBU will be subject to direct prudential supervision by the ECB within the SSM.[37]

IV. Other Sectoral Reform in the EU

Besides the European Banking Union, the European legislators have adopted numerous reform measures for the financial sector.[38] These can largely be divided into regulation, either of markets or financial institutions, and supervisory infrastructure. Both are organised mainly along sectoral lines. Many of the regulatory reforms have, at least partially, a financial stability objective. This reduces the potential for regulatory arbitrage, at least in regard to the applicable entities.

---

[35] Posen and Véron also note that 'The exclusion of smaller banks and non-banks from direct supervision at European level could lead to harmful regulatory arbitrage'. See A Posen, N Véron, 'Europe's half a banking union' (2014). http://bruegel.org/2014/09/europes-half-a-banking-union/.

[36] Proposal for a Regulation on the prudential requirements of investment firms and amending Regulations (EU) No 575/2013, (EU) No 600/2014 and (EU) No 1093/2010, COM(2017) 790 final 9 (20 December 2017); Proposal for a Directive on the prudential supervision of investment firms and amending Dirs 2013/36/EU and 2014/65/EU, COM(2017) 791 final (20 December 2017).

[37] A political agreement on this proposal was reached by the European Parliament and Member States on 26 February 2019. See European Commission, 'Capital Markets Union: Agreement simplifies rules for investment firms to support open and vibrant capital markets' (2019). Press release. 26 February 2019, Brussels.

[38] For an overview of the more than 50 European Commission proposals for legislative and non-legislative measures, see https://ec.europa.eu/info/business-economy-euro/banking-and-finance/financial-reforms-and-their-progress/progress-financial-reforms_en.

A. Investment Funds

For instance, investment funds are subject to increased regulation under the 'undertakings for collective investment in transferable securities' (UCITS) Directive[39] or the Alternative Investment Fund Managers Directive (AIFMD).[40] Both directives have the effect of reducing liquidity risks in investment funds. The UCITS Directive requires investment funds to hold liquid assets only. Alternative investment funds (AIFs), other than unleveraged closed-ended AIFs, must employ appropriate liquidity management and monitoring procedures for liquidity risks.[41] The liquidity profile of the investments must comply with the AIF's underlying obligations.

The UCITS Directive places direct restrictions on the use of leverage. A UCITS Directive may only borrow up to 10 per cent of its assets.[42] Additionally, synthetic leverage, which is acquired through derivatives and securities lending and measured in 'global exposure', must not exceed the fund's total net asset value.[43] The AIFMD, in contrast, does not provide regulatory limits on the amount of leverage. Instead, the AIFM has to demonstrate the leverage limits set by it, for each AIF it manages, are reasonable and that it complies with them at all times. National authorities are competent to impose leverage limits on an AIF in its jurisdiction where they deem this necessary in order to ensure the stability and integrity of the financial system.[44] Furthermore, additional regulation is applicable to money-market funds to preserve the integrity and stability of the internal market.[45]

B. Insurance Sector

In regard to the insurance sector, the EU legislator adopted the Solvency II Directive, harmonising EU insurance regulation.[46] The Solvency II Directive requires Member States to ensure that their supervisory authorities can protect policyholders and, second, to contribute to the stability of the financial system as a whole.[47] Solvency II therefore requires insurers and regulators to take account of the asset-side risks, as capital needs to be held against market risks.

---

[39] This Directive concerns EU-based, open-ended collective investment arrangements which invest in a diverse portfolio of transferable securities or specific other liquid financial assets and offers participation to the public. See Directive 2009/65/EC (UCITS Directive), Arts 1 and 3(b).

[40] AIFs are collective investment undertakings which are offered to a number of investors and invest their collective assets in accordance with a defined investment policy without requiring authorisation as a UCITS Directive. This broad definition captures all non-UCITS Directive. See Dir 2011/61/EU (AIFMD), Art 4(a). For a detailed discussion of the AIFMD, see L Van Setten, D Busch (eds), *Alternative Investment Funds in Europe* (Oxford, Oxford University Press, 2014); D Zetzsche (ed), *The alternative investment fund managers directive*, (2nd edn) (Alphen aan den Rijn, Kluwer Law International, 2015).

[41] AIFMD, Art 16.

[42] UCITS Dir, Art 83.

[43] UCITS Dir, Art 51(3). Global exposure can be calculated according to the standard 'commitment approach', in which case a total market exposure of 200% of NAV is permitted. Alternatively, global exposure may be calculated according to the value-at-risk model. This model is recommended by ESMA for funds with more complex investment strategies. Under this model the total value-at-risk has to stay below 20% of the net asset value, which potentially allows for more leverage.

[44] AIFMD, Art 25(3).

[45] The regulation allows for constant net asset value (CNAV) for short-term MMFs investing in government debt. A new category is introduced as low volatility net asset value (LVNAV), which may maintain a constant NAV within certain perimeters. All other MMFs have to convert into variable net asset value (VNAV). The regulation also introduced liquidity requirements: CNAC and LVNAV must have 10% of NAV daily maturing and 30% of NAV weekly maturing. For VNAV funds these percentages are 7.5 and 15.5 respectively. See Regulation (EU) 2017/1131 on money market funds.

[46] Directive 2009/138/EC (Solvency II).

[47] M Everson, 'Regulating the Insurance Sector' in N Moloney, E Ferran, J Payne (eds), *The Oxford handbook of financial regulation* (Oxford, Oxford University Press, 2015), pp 409–452, p 433.

C. OTC Derivatives Clearing

A third example with an obvious financial stability objective is the European Market Infrastructure Regulation (EMIR).[48] EMIR is a centrepiece of the legislation introduced in the wake of the financial crisis to make financial markets safer and more transparent. A key pillar of EMIR is the requirement for standardised OTC (over-the-counter) derivatives contracts to be cleared through a Central Counterparty (CCP).[49] A CCP is a market infrastructure that reduces systemic risk and enhances financial stability by standing between the two counterparties to a derivatives contract (ie acting as buyer to the seller of risk and seller to the buyer of risk) and thereby reducing the risk for both.[50] EMIR also introduced strict prudential, organisational and business conduct requirements for CCPs and established arrangements for their prudential supervision to minimise any risk to users of a CCP and to underpin systemic stability.[51]

D. Assessment

Notwithstanding the increase of sectoral regulation, the potential for regulatory arbitrage remains. The ESRB, for instance, notes in its 2017 shadow banking report that hedge funds should be closely monitored as they are not subject to leverage limits if regulated under the AIFMD.[52] More importantly, such an approach to financial regulation remains calibrated on 'form over function'; in other words, the legal label of a financial institution is decisive for the applicable regulation and supervisor. In consequence, new financial market participants (eg FinTech entities) or formally different institutions performing similar activities may fall into regulatory gaps, thus creating systemic risk.[53]

V. The European Supervisory Agencies (ESAs)

A. Sectoral Approach

From a financial stability perspective it is important to note that the institutional supervisory structure provided at the EU level mimics the sectoral approach in EU regulation. The European

---

[48] Regulation (EU) No 648/2012 on OTC derivatives, central counterparties and trade repositories.

[49] See for the clearing obligation, Art 4 in conjunction with Art 5, EMIR.

[50] See for the definition of 'CCP' Art 2(1), EMIR.

[51] See Art 16 and Arts 40–50 (prudential requirements), Arts 26–39 (organisational and business conduct requirements).

[52] European Systemic Risk Board, 'EU Shadow Banking Monitor' (2017). No 2/May 2017. www.esrb.europa.eu/pub/pdf/reports/20170529_shadow_banking_report.en.pdf, p 18. For a discussion of the macroprudential elements and gaps in existing EU regulation, see European Systemic Risk Board, 'Macroprudential policy beyond banking: an ESRB strategy paper' (2016). July 2016. www.esrb.europa.eu/pub/pdf/reports/20160718_strategy_paper_beyond_banking.en.pdf.

[53] Recent examples of different institutions performing functionally equivalent services are inter alia apparent from ABN AMRO's prospectus. Risk factor 8 notes that ABN AMRO's competition for products and services 'consists of traditional large banks, smaller banks, insurance companies, pension funds, niche players, nonfinancial companies that offer credit and savings products (such as car lease companies) as well as technology firms and other new entrants. Insurance companies and pension funds, for instance, are increasingly active in the mortgage market. Not all of these parties are subject to the same regulatory controls imposed on banks.' See ABN AMRO (2015) Prospectus. 10 November 2015, p 78, available at: www.abnamro.com/en/investor-relations/equity-investors/ipo/prospectus/index.html. ESMA also finds that the evolving loan origination by investment funds, has the potential for additional systemic risks. ESMA therefore argues that it should fall under a suitable regulatory framework such that 'systemic risk is mitigated, and, in any case, is no higher than that posed by bank lending'. More specifically, regulation should mitigate risks stemming from liquidity

Supervisory Authorities (ESAs) were created in 2010 and consist of (i) the European Banking Authority (EBA), (ii) the European Securities and Markets Authority (ESMA) and (iii) the European Insurance and Occupational Pensions Authority (EIOPA).[54]

B. Few Direct Supervisory Powers

Referring to the ESAs as supervisors is slightly misleading, as they mainly assist the European Commission in law-making. Of the three ESAs, only ESMA currently has direct supervisory powers, namely over Credit Rating Agencies (CRAs) and Trade Repositories (TRs), otherwise the national supervisors are still competent – except for significant banks in the Eurozone where the ECB is in charge (see section III above).

C. Data Reporting Services Providers, Funds, Benchmarks

However, as far as the Commission is concerned, especially ESMA, should be endowed with more direct supervisory powers. In its proposal of 20 September 2017, the Commission proposes to grant ESMA additional direct supervisory powers with respect to (i) data reporting services providers; (ii) approval of certain prospectuses; (iii) certain harmonised collective investment funds; and (iv) benchmarks.[55]

D. PEPP Providers

In addition, the European Parliament and Council have recently adopted a new Regulation on a pan-European Personal Pension Product (PEPP). PEPP providers will be supervised by the national competent supervisors, but a PEPP may only be manufactured and distributed in the Union where it has been authorised by EIOPA.[56]

E. Crowdfunding Service Providers

Furthermore, there is the 8 March 2018 Commission Proposal for a Regulation on European Crowdfunding Service Providers (ECSP) for Business.[57] The proposal seeks to establish uniform rules on crowdfunding at EU level. It does not replace national rules on crowdfunding where they exist. A crowdfunding service provider can choose to (i) either provide or continue providing services on a domestic basis under applicable national law (including where a Member

---

and maturity transformation and risks related to imprudent lending. See ESMA, 'Opinion – Key principles for a European framework on loan origination by funds' (2016). ESMA/2016/596, 11 April 2016.

[54] See Regulation (EU) No 1095/2010 (ESMA Regulation), Regulation (EU) No 1093/2010 (EBA Regulation) and Regulation (EU) No 1094/2010 (EIOPA Regulation).

[55] Proposal for a Regulation, COM(2017) 536 final (20 September 2017).

[56] Regulation (EU) 2019/1238 of the European Parliament and of the Council of 20 June 2019 on a pan-European Personal Pension Product (PEPP) [2019] OJ L198/1 ('PEPP Regulation')

[57] Proposal for a Regulation on European Crowdfunding Service Providers (ECSP) for Business, COM(2018) 113 final (8 March 2018); Proposal for a Directive amending Dir 2014/65/EU on markets in financial instruments, COM(2018) 99 final (8 March 2018).

State chooses to apply MiFID II to crowdfunding activities); or (ii) seek authorisation to provide crowdfunding services under the proposed regulation.

In the latter case, (i) authorisation allows crowdfunding service providers to provide crowdfunding services under a passport across all Member States; (ii) a legal person that intends to provide crowdfunding services shall apply to ESMA for authorisation as a crowdfunding service provider; and (iii) crowdfunding service providers shall provide their services under the supervision of ESMA. Please note that the Regulation does not apply to crowdfunding services that are provided by project owners that are consumers. But the persons at the other end, ie those who grant loans or acquire transferable securities through a crowdfunding platform (investors) are also captured by the regulation if they are consumers.

F. OTC Derivatives Clearing

Last, but certainly not least, the Commission's proposal of 13 June 2017 is noteworthy. It proposes amendments to the European Market Infrastructure Regulation (EMIR) and the ESMA Regulation, with a view to regulating and supervising the systemic risk posed by CCPs and strengthening the role of ESMA.[58] In order to avoid risks of regulatory and supervisory arbitrage the 'CCP executive session' – established within the European Securities and Markets Authority (ESMA) – will be responsible for a more coherent and consistent supervision of CCPs. To this effect, ESMA may determine a third-country CCP to be systemically important, thereby subjecting it to stricter requirements. Acting on a recommendation from ESMA, the Commission may also determine a third-country CCP to be substantially systemically important. Subsequent to such a determination, the Commission may declare that the CCP may provide services in the Union only if it is authorised in the EU.[59] The determination of systemic importance of CCPs by ESMA shows clear parallels with our proposed non-bank SIFI determination.

G. Assessment

In conclusion, two elements in the make-up of the European Supervisory Agencies stand out. First, despite some coordination efforts, it is based on a sectoral approach to supervision.[60] As sectoral lines increasingly blur and new institutions outside the traditional institutional regulatory perimeter perform equivalent activities, an institutionally based layout of the supervisory organisation may risk regulatory gaps. An institutional approach to financial regulation and supervision encourages regulatory arbitrage. It is therefore of eminent importance that an institutional approach to financial regulation is supplemented by the existence of an authority with robust, financial sector-wide, monitoring powers and, if deemed necessary, the power to

---

[58] European Commission, Proposal for a Regulation No 648/2012, (13 June 2017) (EMIR Commission Proposal 13 June 2017). Recognising the central and growing systemic importance of CCPs as a result of the G20 commitment to clear additional classes of over-the-counter derivatives with CCPs, the Commission previously proposed recovery and resolution measures for CCPs in order to safeguard financial stability. See European Commission, Proposal for a Regulation on a framework for the recovery and resolution of central counterparties, COM(2016) 856 final (28 November 2016).

[59] See in more detail, D Busch, 'A stronger role for the European Supervisory Authorities in the Eu27' in D Busch, E Avgouleas, G Ferrarini (eds), *Capital Markets Union in Europe* (Oxford, Oxford University Press, 2018), pp 28–53.

[60] See also, D Awrey, 'Law, financial instability, and the institutional structure of financial regulation' in A Anand (ed), *Systemic risk, institutional design, and the regulation of financial markets* (Oxford, Oxford University Press, 2016), pp 61–96, p 86.

pull systemically important financial institutions inside a suitable regulatory and supervisory perimeter. As discussed in the following section, the European Systemic Risk Board is responsible for monitoring the financial system within the EU and identifying systemic risk. Its powers, however, are rather limited.

A second important element in the functioning of the ESAs is their limited powers of direct prudential supervision of financial institutions.[61] Instead, national authorities are responsible for day-to-day prudential supervision. Systemically important institutions expand, however, across many jurisdictions. Much the same arguments that underpin the creation of direct ECB supervision over significant banks therefore apply also to non-bank SIFIs. This line of reasoning is now familiar, for example because a European authority is better placed to ensure a smooth and sound overview of the entire non-bank SIFI and its overall health and would reduce the risk of different interpretations and contradictory decisions at the level of the individual entity, thereby enhancing market integration. In our proposal, designated non-bank SIFIs, like significant banks, should therefore be placed under direct prudential supervision by an EU authority. The intended reforms of the ESAs may therefore provide a connection with our proposal. They illustrate a developing inclination to endow the ESAs with more direct supervisory powers. Supervision of designated non-bank SIFIs by the most relevant ESA, as determined by the nature and activities of the non-bank SIFI, is in line with these developments.

VI. The European Systemic Risk Board (ESRB)

The De Larosière Group envisaged a Union body charged with overseeing risk in the financial system as a whole.[62] This led to the creation, in November 2010, of the European Systemic Risk Board (ESRB).[63] It is tasked with exercising 'macroprudential oversight of the financial system within the Union, in order to contribute to the prevention or mitigation of systemic risks to financial stability in the Union'.[64] Its oversight has a broad scope as the ESRB Regulation recognises that all types of financial intermediaries, markets and infrastructure may potentially be systemically important to some degree.[65]

As a consequence of the global financial crisis, microprudential supervision of financial institutions has become increasingly complemented by a macroprudential dimension. The latter's objective is to limit the distress of the financial system as a whole in order to protect the overall economy from significant losses in real output.[66] Macroprudential supervision focuses on systemic risks arising from the common exposure of many financial institutions to the same risk factors. In other words, whereas microprudential supervision focuses on the tree, macroprudential

---

[61] As stated, only ESMA performs direct supervision, namely of credit rating agencies and trade repositories.

[62] 'The Group believes that to be effective macro-prudential supervision must encompass all sectors of finance and not be confined to banks, as well as the wider macro-economic context. This oversight also should take account of global issues.' See J de Larosière, L Balcerowicz, O Issing, R Masera, CM Carthy, L Nyberg, J Pérez, O Ruding, ('The High Level Group on Financial Supervision in the EU' (2009). Report 25 February 2009. Brussels. http://ec.europa.eu/internal_market/finances/docs/de_larosiere_report_en.pdf, (De Larosière report) p 39.

[63] Regulation (EU) No 1092/2010 on European Union macro-prudential oversight of the financial system and establishing a European Systemic Risk Board (ESRB Regulation).

[64] ESRB Regulation, Art 3(1).

[65] ESRB Regulation, Art 2 sub (c). In the Regulation 'systemic risk' is defined as 'a risk of disruption in the financial system with the potential to have serious negative consequences for the internal market and the real economy'.

[66] J De Larosière, L Balcerowicz, O Issing, R Masera, CM Carthy, L Nyberg, J Pérez, O Ruding 'The High Level Group on Financial Supervision in the EU' (2009). Report 25 February 2009. Brussels. http://ec.europa.eu/internal_market/finances/docs/de_larosiere_report_en.pdf, p 38.

supervision is all about the forest. In accordance with its macroprudential tasks, the ESRB monitors and assesses risks and, if necessary, adopts warnings and recommendations.

Pursuant to its monitoring tasks the ESRB may request information from the European System of Central Banks (ESCB), the ESAs, the national supervisory authorities or the national statistics authorities. If information remains unavailable the ESRB may request it from the Member States.[67] The request may be of either a general or a specific nature and must be addressed in particular to the Union as a whole or to one or more Member States, or to one or more of the ESAs, or to one or more of the national supervisory authorities.

When the ESRB identifies significant risks to financial stability it must provide warnings and, where appropriate, issue recommendations for remedial action.[68] Warnings and recommendation may be of a general or a specific nature and must be addressed in particular to the Union as a whole or to one or more Member States, or to one or more of the ESAs, or to one or more of the national supervisory authorities.[69] As the ESRB has no formal legal powers its warnings and recommendations are non-binding, but they are subject to a 'comply-or explain' procedure. In consequence, addressees of recommendations have to inform the ESRB and the Council of the actions undertaken in response and must provide adequate justification for any inaction.[70] A warning or recommendation may be made public when two-thirds of the General Board agree to this.[71]

The ESRB does not have legal personality or its own budget. It has a complicated organisational structure consisting of a General Board, a Steering Committee, an Advisory Technical Committee (ATC) and an Advisory Scientific Committee (ASC). The General Board is the principal decision-making body of the ESRB. Of its 67 (!) members, 38 have a voting right. These are the President and Vice-President of the ECB, the Governors of the 28 national central banks, a Member of the Commission, the Chairperson of each of the European Supervisory Authorities, the ATC Chair, the ASC Chair and the two ASC Vice-Chairs. The non-voting members consist of one representative per Member State of the competent national supervisory authorities and the President of the Economic and Financial Committee.

All in all, as it currently stands, the ESRB is a rather weak institution with few powers and a small budget.

VII.   More is Needed in Europe to Address Systemic Risk

A.   Addressing Systemic Risk: The Institutional Structure

Financial institutions falling outside the regulatory perimeter of traditional financial entities may engage in equivalent activities without being subjected to adequate regulation. In the same vein, sectoral supervisors can only monitor the build-up of systemic risk within their competence and thus, by definition, lack a comprehensive overview of the financial sector. The institutional financial supervisory structure in the EU should, therefore, be supplemented by an institution charged with monitoring systemic risk build-up in any financial institution and, when necessary, bring them within an adequate regulatory and supervisory perimeter.

---

[67] ESRB Regulation, Art 15(5).
[68] ESRB Regulation, Art 16(1).
[69] ESRB Regulation, Art 16(2).
[70] ESRB Regulation, Art 17(1).
[71] ESRB Regulation, Art 18(1).

As demonstrated in sections II–V above, an institutional approach is still prevalent in the EU's financial regulatory structure. Because such an approach is especially susceptive to regulatory gaps, it needs to be complemented by a robust monitoring mechanism which has an activity-based approach of detecting systemic risk across the entire financial sector. In the EU, the ESRB provides for monitoring of systemic risks, but lacks substantial formal legal power. The US, in contrast, has equipped the Financial Stability Oversight Council (FSOC) with substantial systemic risk monitoring powers and the competence to bring systemically important financial institutions within an adequate regulatory and supervisory perimeter.[72] An expansion of the ESRB's powers, providing it, in imitation of the FSOC, with the competence to designate financial institutions as systemically important and, in consequence, bring them within prudential super-vision or enhanced supervision, would be in order.

Given the dual legal orders of the EU and its Member States, it is submitted that prudential supervision should be performed at the EU level by an EU institution. As systemically impor-tant financial institutions operate across national borders, regulation and supervision should not be confined within such borders. This brings to mind what Dirk Schoenmaker has called the 'financial trilemma': increased financial integration due to globalisation and, more specifically, to the creation of a European internal market is not compatible with both financial stability and national financial policies.[73] National supervision of non-bank SIFIs has proved inadequate.[74] This is in part due to inherent jurisdictional limitations and the corresponding fragmentised view of the supervised institution.[75] Moreover, national authorities might be tempted to practise forbearance in regard to financial institutions perceived as national champions.[76]

Similarly, the resolution of non-bank SIFIs can best be achieved by a Union institution. Much the same arguments as for European supervision apply. Lacking a comprehensive view of a non-bank SIFI's business causes suboptimal resolution decisions. Moreover, national authori-ties have strong incentives to minimise the impact of failing non-bank SIFIs on their economy.[77] This can result in unilateral measures such as requiring higher capital and liquidity buffers or limiting intra-group transfers. Maintaining financial stability is not the prime aim of such measures. Consequently, they have the potential to cause unnecessary destruction of the non-bank SIFI's value and distort the functioning of the internal market.

---

[72] 12 US Code, s 5323.

[73] D Schoenmaker, *Governance of international banking: the financial trilemma* (Oxford, Oxford University Press, 2013).

[74] In consequence, the De Larosière report found that Europe should be equipped with a standard set of rules and that strengthened international collaboration in the supervision of large complex cross-border financial groups is of crucial importance. See J de Larosière, L Balcerowicz, O Issing, R Masera, CM Carthy, L Nyberg, J Pérez, O Ruding, 'The High Level Group on Financial Supervision in the EU (2009). Report 25 February 2009. Brussels. http://ec.europa.eu/internal_market/finances/docs/de_larosiere_report_en.pdf.

[75] The Commission, for instance, notes in its consultation on the reform of the European Supervisory Agencies that stakeholders confirmed that the understanding and supervision of investment funds is very different among National Competent Authorities, which ultimately limits the uptake of these funds. See European Commission, 'Public consulta-tion on the operations of the European supervisory authorities' (2017), p 17. Similarly, recital (5) of the SSM Regulation grants that the creation of the SSM was prompted by the conviction that 'Coordination between supervisors is vital, but the crisis has shown that mere coordination is not enough, in particular in the context of a single currency. In order to preserve financial stability in the Union and increase the positive effects of market integration on growth and welfare, integration of supervisory responsibilities should therefore be enhanced'. This holds similarly true for the supervision of non-bank SIFIs.

[76] N Véron, 'Banking nationalism and the European crisis' (2013). Remarks before a symposium of the European Private Equity and Venture Capital Association, Istanbul, 27 June 2013.

[77] This is also cited as a basis for the creation of the SRM. See recital (9), SRM Regulation.

B. Monitoring Systemic Risk

The global financial crisis exposed the integrated nature, both cross-sectoral and cross-border, of financial markets and institutions. This warrants an integrated approach to the monitoring of financial risks. In the EU the ESRB is tasked with systemic risk monitoring. The ESRB's powers, however, are limited to monitoring and assessing systemic risks and, where appropriate, issuing warnings and recommendations. It does not have formal powers and instead has to rely on systemic risk warnings and non-binding recommendations to EU members, which can be punctuated by a 'comply or explain' mechanism.

In regard to the collection of information, it is of interest to note that the ESRB may request information of the ESA's, the ECB, the Commission and national supervisors, statistics authorities and Member States.[78] However, as the information provided has to be in aggregate form, it is impossible to distinguish individual firms. If, as we propose below, the ESRB is to be able to make non-bank SIFI designations comparable to the FSOC designations, this limitation has to be removed.

In the US, the FSOC is charged with identifying risks to the financial stability of the US, promoting market discipline, and responding to emerging risks to the stability of the US financial system. Its powers include the designation of non-bank financial institutions and financial market utilities to be supervised by the Federal Reserve Board. It may issue recommendations on heightened prudential standards to supervisory authorities. Moreover, it makes recommendations on jurisdictional disputes and reports on regulatory gaps to Congress.

C. Non-Bank SIFI Designation

It is submitted that the ESRB be equipped with powers similar to those of the FSOC to designate non-bank financial companies as systemically important and, consequently, deserving of additional prudential regulation and supervision. This would go a long way towards alleviating systemic risks by creating a mechanism to ensure non-bank SIFIs are subjected to a regulatory perimeter consistent with the risks they pose. Such a designation would be an important instrument in preventing regulatory arbitrage. Indeed, echoing the designation process of the FSOC, we would note that the level of regulatory scrutiny to which a non-bank SIFI is subjected is an important factor when deciding on a designation.

The ESRB could be given the power to designate non-bank SIFIs under Article 114 of the Treaty on the Functioning of the EU (TFEU), as it aims to improve the functioning of the internal market by helping to provide financial stability. Indeed, the very goal of such a designation is to make sure that such non-bank SIFIs are regulated to an extent consistent with the level of systemic risk they pose. Consequently, the power to make such a designation is conditional on whether it addresses a threat to financial stability and whether such a designation would alleviate the threat.

---

[78] The European Commission, in its consultation document on the Review of the EU Macro-Prudential Framework, provides that the ESRB could benefit from additional own analytical resources, especially in areas where there is less pre-existing knowledge such as systemic risk outside the banking sector. See European Commission (2016) 'Consultation document review of the eu macro-prudential policy framework' (2016) pp 1–8. http://ec.europa.eu/finance/consultations/2016/macroprudential-framework/docs/consultation document_en.pdf.

However, such a power of designation for the ESRB might be subject to legal constraints on the delegation of discretionary powers to agencies. The EU Member States have delegated powers to the EU through the Treaties. In turn, the Union legislature may decide to delegate some of these powers to an agency in cases where the Treaties provide for this possibility either in a specific provision or in the form of a general competence such as Article 114 TFEU.

The degree to which such delegation is allowed was addressed by the Court of Justice of the European Union (CJEU) in its *Meroni* ruling.[79] The CJEU distinguished between two types of delegation. Whereas purely executive powers may be delegated as their exercise can be reviewed against objective criteria specified by the delegating authority, powers involving a wide margin of discretion in determining economic policy may not be delegated. Such delegation would replace the choices of the delegating authority by those of the delegatee and bring about an actual transfer of responsibility.[80] As a transfer of responsibility of this kind would alter the balance of power between the EU institutions, it would be incompatible with the Treaties.[81]

In its *Short Selling* judgment[82] the CJEU revisited and revised its *Meroni* doctrine. First, the CJEU emphasised that the contested delegation in *Meroni* concerned delegation to an entity governed by private law, whereas the contested delegation in the *Short Selling* case was to ESMA, which had been established pursuant to an EU regulation. The Court went on to note that ESMA's power to prohibit or impose conditions on the entry by natural or legal persons into a short sale or require them to notify a competent authority or to disclose to the public details of net short positions[83] does not confer any autonomous power that goes beyond the boundaries of the regulatory framework established by the ESMA Regulation.[84] Furthermore, and unlike the circumstances in *Meroni*, ESMA's discretionary powers in regard to short selling are circumscribed by various conditions and criteria.[85] The CJEU therefore held that the powers available to ESMA in regard to short selling are precisely delineated and amenable to judicial review in the light of the objectives established by the delegating authority. Accordingly, it found that those powers comply with the requirements laid down in *Meroni*. Consequently, those powers do not imply that ESMA is vested with a 'very large measure of discretion' that is incompatible with the Treaties.[86]

In line with the *Short Selling* ruling it could be argued that granting the ESRB the power to designate non-bank financial institutions as systemically important is not in breach of the *Meroni* constraints. Much the same conditions and restraints applicable to ESMA's short selling powers would be applicable to the designation procedure as the ESRB too has to make an assessment of a possible threat to the stability of the whole or part of the financial system. The Commission could provide conditions detailing how such an assessment should be made in a delegated regulation. Judicial review of a designation would also be possible as a designation is of direct and individual concern to the subject institution, opening up proceedings, under Article 263 TFEU, before the CJEU.

---

[79] Case 9-56, *Meroni & Co., Industrie Metallurgiche, SpA v High Authority of the European Coal and Steel Community,* ECLI:EU:C:1958:7 *(Meroni).*

[80] *Meroni,* p 152.

[81] Ibid.

[82] Case C-270/12, *The United Kingdom of Great Britain and Northern Ireland v European Parliament and the Council of the European Union,* ECLI:EU:C:2014:18 *(Short Selling).*

[83] As provided for under Art 28 of the Short Selling Regulation. See Regulation (EU) No 236/2012 on short selling and certain aspects of credit default swaps.

[84] *Short Selling,* paras 43–44.

[85] *Short Selling,* paras 45–53.

[86] *Short Selling,* paras 53 and 54.

At the same time, we concede that in order to have in place a forward-looking system for the monitoring and designation of systemically important institutions, it is vital for the ESRB to have a degree of discretion. As the financial sector is ever evolving, the ESRB should not be subject to extremely detailed conditions limiting its ability to review and determine systemic relevance. As the FSOC too notes in its final rule and interpretive guidance on non-bank SIFI designation, a determination decision cannot be reduced to a formula.[87]

In order to loosen possible *Meroni* constraints, final determination could be subjected to validation by the Commission (or by non-objection within an appropriate time frame). As the Commission has a direct basis in the Treaties, it is not subjected to *Meroni* constraints. Such an arrangement has, for the same reasons, been used in the context of the Single Resolution Mechanism, where resolution decisions by the Single Resolution Board are validated by the Commission. Additionally, in the recent legislative proposal on supervision of CCPs, ESMA may make a request to the Commission that a CCP may be of such systemic importance that it will be able to provide services in the Union only if it establishes itself in the EU. Again, the Commission, officially, makes the final determination.

Alternatively, the ESRB or a newly created institution could be endowed with designation powers in the Treaty. This might be the preferable option as it would provide a strong legal basis, without complicating the governance structure by including the Commission. However, as it would require a Treaty change it seems politically unfeasible. On the other hand, political realities could turn out to fluctuate more than the financial markets.

Furthermore, designations must of course comply with fundamental principles of EU law, including the principle of proportionality and subsidiarity.[88] Accordingly, a designation must be necessary to achieve the goal of financial stability and must not exceed the limits of what is necessary to achieve this. It should be noted that in our proposal a proportionality test is ingrained in the designation procedure. A non-bank SIFI designation should only take place after establishing deficiencies in the current regulation and/or supervision of the institution, and in order to alleviate these deficiencies. Allocating responsibility for designations to an EU authority is also in line with the subsidiarity principle. After all, establishing whether a designation is prudent requires an in-depth overview of its activities and current regulatory and supervisory regime which likely extends across multiple national jurisdictions. This cannot be sufficiently achieved by national authorities whose powers stop at the border.

D. Non-Bank SIFI Supervision

New prudential regulation in the US rearranged and expanded financial regulation, supervision and resolution. FSOC-designated 'systemically important' financial institutions are subject to the prudential regulations set out in Title I of the Act and are supervised by the Board of Governors of the Federal Reserve System (FRB). The latter has the discretion to impose additional, tailor-made prudential standards and disclosure requirements.[89]

---

[87] The FSOC further states that '[e]ach determination will be made based on a company-specific evaluation and an application of the standards and considerations set forth in section 113 of the Dodd-Frank Act, and taking into account qualitative and quantitative information that the Council deems relevant to a particular nonbank financial company'. Financial Stability Oversight Council, 'Authority to require supervision and regulation of certain nonbank financial companies' (2012). Federal Register 77(70), pp 21367–21662, p 21642.

[88] As provided in Art 5(3) and (4) of the Treaty on European Union. Likewise, other fundamental principles, such as the right to good administration, must also be secured.

[89] 12 US Code, § 5365.

Following the example set by the FSOC, a designation by the ESRB should have the consequence of pulling a financial institution within an appropriate prudential regulatory perimeter and related supervision. This is not to say that a one-size-fits-all approach should be taken in determining prudential requirements. Instead, regulators should have the discretion to set specific requirements reflecting the specific business of a regulated entity. Following the example set by Dodd-Frank,[90] this should include requirements in relation to capital, leverage limits, liquidity, risk management, resolution planning and credit exposure reporting. Again, following the US model, the prudential standards should be tailored, on an individual basis or by category, to the designated institution. Such standards should reflect the institutions' capital structure, riskiness, complexity, financial activities (including the financial activities of their subsidiaries), size and any other risk-related factors. In consequence, the resulting tailored prudential requirements address the systemic risks while providing a fair regulatory burden, taking into account the specific nature and activities of the institution.[91]

European supervision could be realised by having designated non-bank SIFIs fall within the scope of the Banking Union. In addition to supervising significant eurozone banks, the ECB would then also be charged with supervising of non-bank financial institution designated by the ESRB as systemically important.[92] In this scenario it would be most sensible to have the ECB determine adequate prudential requirements for the designated institution. Of interest, in this regard, is the 2017 Commission proposal to amend the definition of 'credit institution'. Pursuant to the proposal, systemic investment firms which engage in dealing on own account and/or underwriting or placing instruments on a firm commitment basis and have assets over EU 30 billion, will fall under the definition of credit institution.[93] As a consequence, the ECB, would supervise such systemic investment firms in the Banking Union. This shows a certain willingness, at least on part of the Commission, to expand the perimeter of credit institution and, in effect, bring systemic investment firms under the scope of the SSM.

Alternatively, another EU entity could be charged with supervision. A possible connection could be made with the intended or successive reforms of the European Supervisory Agencies. Pursuant to a non-bank SIFI designation by the ESRB, the ESA which has most affinity with the designate institution would operate as direct prudential supervisor. Direct supervision by an ESA is not unprecedented as ESMA already has direct supervisory tasks. Some would prefer this option as it would remove the perception that designated institutions are regulated and supervised as banks by the ECB. Moreover, as the ECB, arguably, already has a conflict of interest between monetary policy and prudential supervisory objectives, this would be even more the case if it were also to supervise non-bank SIFIs.[94] At the same time, the ECB could profit from

---

[90] Ibid.

[91] The proposed rules of the FRB regarding capital requirements for supervised institutions significantly engaged in insurance activities in the US, follows a similar approach. See Federal Register, 'Capital Requirements for Supervised Institutions Significantly Engaged in Insurance Activities', Vol 81, No 114, 14 June 2016, p 38635.

[92] The ECB could in this process profit from experience gained in the course of the Supervisory and Review Evaluation Process, in which the ECB has to ensure that credit institutions have adequate arrangements, strategies, processes and mechanisms as well as capital and liquidity to ensure a sound management and coverage of their risks, including risks institutions may pose to the financial system. See CRD IV, Art 97.

[93] European Commission, Proposal for a Regulation No 600/2014, (20 December 2017), Art 60(2).

[94] A conflict of interest could occur, for example, if the ECB were tempted to set interest rates beneficial to ailing banks, thus making improper use of a monetary policy instrument. Conversely the Governing Council might be inclined to include monetary policy interests in determining its approval of supervisory decisions, such as the withdrawal of a credit institution's authorisation. Schoenmaker and Véron, however, found in their review on the functioning of SSM during

the resources and experiences gained in the context of the European Banking Union and from a comprehensive overview of the financial sector. We will limit ourselves to the more fundamental contention that the prudential supervision of non-bank SIFIs, subject to a determination by the ESRB, should be performed by an EU authority as opposed to a national authority. It is, however, important to note that the scope of ECB supervision in the context of the European Banking Union currently coincides with that of the Eurozone as no additional Member States have acceded. This is more limited than the scope of the ESAs which operate throughout the EU. We would prefer a broader scope.

This touches upon an important, additional benefit of our proposed designation and supervision scheme for systemically important institutions. As Schwarcz and Zaring point out, the benefits of a non-bank SIFI identification and supervisory scheme extend beyond the systemic risk mitigation of the supervised institution. First, the possibility to take over or provide additional supervision of designated firms deters the initial supervisors (if any, of course) of the non-bank institutions from applying lax supervisory standards or neglecting to take proper account of systemic risk.[95] This dimension is of extra importance in the context of the EU where non-bank financial regulation largely depends on national administration. As stated, national supervisors are not well equipped to address systemic risks in cross-border financial institutions. They are ill-positioned to have a comprehensive overview of the risks present in a cross-border financial institution and are predominantly mandated to address national (stability) concerns. National supervisors might also feel tempted to practise supervisory forbearance by giving national champions a competitive advantage. In such cases, the looming threat of losing supervisory control to an EU authority would provide a strong incentive for national supervisors to redouble their efforts. Moreover, an instruction from EU authorities such as the ESRB itself or other agencies to national supervisors would have even greater impact if non-compliance could lead to a non-bank SIFI designation by the ESRB.

Another benefit of the designation regime is that it compels financial institutions to exercise self-restraint when confronted with the threat of being designated as a non-bank SIFI. Since, as already noted, the existing level of regulatory scrutiny is an important factor for a non-bank SIFI determination, financial institutions which add value through regulatory arbitrage activities might be deterred from engaging in these activities if they knew that this might bring them within the scope of a non-bank SIFI designation. In other words, the possibility of being designated as systemically important curbs the risk appetite of institutions. These effects are already apparent in the US where General Electric has greatly reduced its risk profile in a successful effort to have its non-bank SIFI status rescinded.

---

its first 18 months that supervisory tasks have not been distorted or softened by the ECB's monetary policy objectives. See D Schoenmaker, N Véron (eds), *European banking supervision: the first eighteen months*, vol 25. (Brussels, Bruegel Blueprint Series, 2016). http://bruegel.org/wp content/uploads/2016/06/Blueprint-XXV-web.pdf, p 25.

[95] Schwarcz and Zaring indicate that the threat of designation incentivises primary regulators of non-banks to implement reform aimed at limiting systemic risk and take proper account of changes in financial markets which warrant a change in their regulatory approach. See D Schwarcz, DT Zaring, *Regulation by threat: understanding Dodd-Frank's regulation of systemically significant non-bank financial companies* (2016) (preliminary version). www.law.ox.ac.uk/sites/files/oxlaw/regulation_by_threat_nov_6_-_zaring.pdf, p 41. The probability of different priorities in supervision is also acknowledged, and lies at the basis of, the FRB's proposed capital requirements for institutions significantly engaged in insurance activities. The proposed rules set capital requirements for the consolidated institution focusing inter alia on 'enhancing financial stability, and complement the primary mission of state insurance supervisors, which tends to focus on the protection of policyholders'. See Federal Register, 'Capital Requirements for Supervised Institutions Significantly Engaged in Insurance Activities', Vol 81, No 114, 14 June 2016.

The scope of the SSM will have to be expanded in order to bring supervision of designated non-bank SIFIs within the scope of the European Banking Union. However, the scope of the SSM is subject to Treaty limitations.

Article 127(6) TFEU grants the Council the power to confer specific tasks upon the ECB concerning policies relating to the prudential supervision of credit institutions and other financial institutions with the exception of insurance undertakings. It follows that although the basic Treaty provision allows for a broader scope than merely credit institutions, the SSM does not reflect this. Instead the design of the SSM was determined by the need to break the link between sovereigns and banks, as joined supervision paved the way for the mutualisation of bank bailouts.[96]

It is therefore possible to expand the scope of the SSM to include other financial institutions, provided they do not qualify as insurance undertakings. It could, perhaps, be argued that the term insurance undertaking should be narrowly defined to exclude institutions that deal in bank-like products, as AIG did when it took large positions in credit default swaps.

However, a more legally satisfying approach, albeit perhaps a politically less feasible one, would be to amend the TFEU. The primary function of such an amendment would be to confer on a European body the power to supervise all non-bank SIFI designated entities. Logically, this would be the same body as is in charge of supervision under the SSM.

Alternatively, a European Supervisory Agency could be tasked with the direct prudential supervision of designated non-bank SIFIs. To this end, the EU legislators could adopt a regulation on based on Article 114 TFEU in which they delegate these tasks to a European agency. Article 114 TFEU provides a suitable legal basis as EU supervision harmonises the supervisory practices and thereby improves the conditions for the establishment and functioning of the internal market. This is also in compliance with the principle of subsidiarity and proportionality since the execution of supervision at the EU level is motivated, precisely because, fragmentised supervision at the national level has proven inadequate. Additionally, proportionality is an important element in the determination whether or not to designate a financial institution as a non-bank SIFI and placing it under direct supervision.

In view of the *Short Selling* judgment, direct prudential supervision by an EU agency seems legally possible when the execution of supervision is circumscribed by various conditions and criteria which limit the agency's discretion and the possibility of judicial protection against the agency's acts. However, while the CJEU's 'relaxing' of *Meroni* through the *Short Selling* case provides a legal window to task supervision of non-bank SIFIs with an EU agency, the associated legal uncertainty is troublesome. Furthermore, the fact that no regulatory powers may be conferred to the agency renders it impossible for the agency to adopt tailored prudential requirements for non-bank SIFIs without approval by an EU institution with a Treaty basis.

E. Non-Bank SIFI Resolution

A credible resolution regime for non-bank SIFIs is of paramount importance in order to create a credible alternative to publicly funded bailouts and help safeguard financial stability by providing for orderly liquidation and allowing for the continued operation of systemically important business processes. Such a regime subjects non-bank SIFIs to market discipline as it cancels out their Too-Big-To-Fail status and associated implicit guarantees.

---

[96] N Moloney, (2014) 'European Banking Union: assessing its risks and resilience', (2014) 51(6) *Common Market Law Review* 1609–1670, 1624.

The European Banking Union (EBU) provides a resolution regime for banks and, subject to certain conditions, their parent companies if they are a financial holding company or mixed financial holding company. Additionally, 730k investment firms and financial institutions' subsidiaries may also fall within the resolution scope of EBU. This creates a complicated and opaque resolution regime with some entities within a group falling within the resolution scope and others not. The scope of resolution is governed not by the systemic risk posed by an institution and whether this may be mitigated by placing it under resolution but instead by inflexible and arbitrary legal norms.

This leads to regulatory gaps, regulatory arbitrage, an unlevel playing field and an incomplete toolbox for addressing systemic risk, which may manifest itself in different and to some extent unknown forms. A resolution regime needs to reflect this. Therefore non-bank SIFIs should also qualify for liquidation under a European resolution mechanism. This creates a more flexible, open-ended and forward-looking approach aimed at preventing the next crisis, not the last one.

Inspiration can, again, be drawn from the resolution regime created by the Dodd-Frank Act in the US. This regime, known as the Orderly Liquidation Authority (OLA), captures any non-bank financial institution whose failure would seriously impact financial stability in the US.[97]

A possible way of strengthening the European resolution regime and mitigating the systemic risks stemming from non-bank entities would be to widen the scope of the SRM to include all financial institutions that pose systemic risk.

It should be remembered that the legal basis of the SRM is Article 114 TFEU, which provides a basis for the adoption of measures for the approximation of the provisions in Member States which have as their object the establishment and functioning of the internal market.

According to the European Court of Justice (CJEU), measures under Article 114 TFEU must genuinely have as its object the improvement of the conditions for the establishment and functioning of the internal market.[98]

A centralised European resolution authority aims to ensure a uniform application of resolution rules. This enhances the proper functioning of the internal market, specifically in the field of financial services as it eliminates, national, fragmentised resolution rules and thus improves the level playing field. Additionally, its main objective is to strengthen financial stability in the EU: an essential prerequisite for the functioning of the internal market.

This leads to the conclusion that a resolution scheme for non-bank SIFIs or an expansion of the SRM to include such entities does not need Treaty change. Instead, it can be established in accordance with the ordinary legislative procedure on the basis of Article 114 TFEU.

VIII. Conclusion

The global financial crisis revealed that the migration of financial activities outside the traditional banking sector was accompanied by a huge and unchecked build-up of systemic risk. National and/or sectorally organised regulation and supervision proved insufficient owing to the continued integration and interconnectedness of financial markets, institutions, products and services. Gaps in the coverage of regulation and supervision led to an inconsistent regulatory treatment of equivalent products and/or services. This in turn caused an unlevel playing field and encouraged

---

[97] 12 US Code, s 5381 ff.
[98] See Case 376/98, *Germany v European Parliament and Council*, ECLI:EU:C:2000:544, para 84.

regulatory arbitrage behaviour, which caused a migration of activities and a build-up of systemic risk in the less regulated or unregulated parts of the financial system.

We propose that equivalent financial products and/or services should be subject to an integrated European regulatory and supervisory approach. Above all, institutions that pose systemic risk should be brought within a regulatory perimeter consistent with the risk they pose to financial stability.

A European body should therefore be in charge of monitoring financial institutions active in the EU, and should identify institutions which pose systemic risk. It should, subsequently, have the discretion to designate a non-bank financial firm as a non-bank SIFI. Such designation would ensure a level of regulation and supervision consistent with the risks to financial stability posed by a financial institution. Given its current tasks, the European Systemic Risk Board seems best suited for this task.

After an institution has been designated as non-bank SIFI, it comes under (stricter) European supervision. As such a regime has been created for banks in the form of the European Banking Union, designated non-bank SIFIs could be brought within the perimeter of EBU. While the Treaties exclude insurance companies, other financial institutions can be brought under supervision of the ECB without the need for Treaty change. The ECB would then be able to supervise and impose enhanced prudential standards on designated non-bank SIFIs. Alternatively, another EU entity could be charged with supervision, for example the relevant ESA. It is, however, important to note that the scope of ECB supervision in the context of EBU currently coincides with that of the eurozone as no additional Member States have acceded. This is more limited than the scope of the ESAs which operate throughout the EU. We would prefer a broader scope.

In keeping with the second pillar of EBU, a regime should also be in place to ensure that non-bank SIFIs can be resolved without causing systemic risk. This would resolve the Too-Big-To-Fail dilemma and subject the institutions concerned to market discipline. A connection could be made with the EBU's second pillar by expanding the scope of the SRM to include designated non-bank SIFIs. Such an inclusion could be based on Article 114 TFEU, as the alleviation of systemic risk greatly improves the functioning of the internal market.

The development of such a regime could be based on the example of the US, where the Dodd-Frank Act provides for the designation of non-bank SIFIs and their regulation, supervision and possible resolution.

Ensuring that non-bank SIFIs are properly regulated, supervised and, if necessary, resolved would help to eliminate supervisory and regulatory gaps, reduce regulatory arbitrage activities, enhance the level playing field and contribute to the stability of the financial system as a whole.

7

A Cross-Sectoral Analysis of Micro-Prudential Regulation

ARTHUR VAN DEN HURK AND BART JOOSEN

I. Introduction

In this chapter, we discuss the micro-prudential supervision on banks, investment firms and insurance companies, from the perspective of the research subject of this book. These businesses are a heterogeneous group of undertakings, with very different business models, type of activities and territorial scope of their undertakings. A preliminary conclusion is that 'levelling the playing field' and drive to cross-sectoral convergence will appear to be less relevant or necessary. A small, local insurance company, investment firm or bank may not benefit from such a process and may unnecessarily be confronted with 'spill-over-effects' from other sectors. An internationally active conglomerate that is compelled to apply rules stemming from different sectoral frameworks anyway to parts of its group (solo-supervision) and to the entire group (group or consolidated supervision) must apply different rules for a reason.[1]

We will start the chapter with an outline of the typical elements of banks', investment firms' and insurance companies' business models to explore as to whether or not similarities exist and the circumstances in which rules aiming at the micro-prudential stability of those institutions must be organised. These observations will highlight the different dynamics that apply in respect of risks accruing, more particularly the occurrence of such risks and the way to mitigate them with measures of a micro-prudential nature. This analysis will emphasise the relation to the horizon in time of the risk environment and impact to stakeholders. In view of this, we consider

---

[1] However, there appears to be room for better alignment of the different forms of sectoral and cross-sectoral consolidated supervision, to avoid overlap and inconsistencies. For instance, the insurance sectoral framework, Solvency II (Dir 2009/138/EC), appears in some respects to be more encompassing than the CRR (Regulation (EU) 575/2013) framework, in particular in terms of scope by including in its scope of supplemental supervision entities from other parts of the financial sector or non-financial entities. The regulatory requirements on consolidated supervision pursuant to CRR are, on the other hand, more elaborate (including liquidity requirements, as well as recovery and resolution requirements). For further reading on the Financial Conglomerates Directive, reference is made to, eg, M Siri and AJAD van den Hurk, "Financial Conglomerates in the Banking Union", in D Busch and G Ferrarini (eds) '*European Banking Union*', 2nd edn, (Oxford, Oxford University Press (forthcoming)). S Illegems, "Het prudentieel toezicht op financiële conglomeraten onder het Single Supervisory Mechanism" in R Houben and W Vandenbruwaene (eds) '*Het nieuwe bankentoezicht, the new Banking Supervision*', (Cambridge, Intersentia Cambridge, 2016). M Gruson, "Supervision of Financial Conglomerates in the European Union", www.imf.org/external/np/leg/sem/2004/cdmfl/eng/gruson.pdf, International Monetary Fund, 2004.

whether supervisory and regulatory convergence would adequately contribute to the increased protection of stakeholders as an important objective of public authority intervention and scrutiny. Subsequently, we will describe the micro-prudential requirements applicable to each of the different types of undertakings, including reflections on the sector-specific context in which these requirements need to be placed. Furthermore, we will analyse the differences in the regulatory approaches, and discuss their justification in relation to their different business models.

Important themes in our analysis are the fundamental bases on which the different regulatory frameworks are founded, such as in particular the 'Three Pillar' approaches, as well as the balance sheet approaches and the role of capital and capital requirements in relation to the business dynamics of the different types of undertakings.

II. Roles and Functions of Banks, Investment Firms and Insurance Companies

A. Banks: Maturity Transformation, Protection of Bank Depositors and Systemic Risk

Bank's business models may vary. And banking business may be conducted within legal entities or organisations that are not regulated and supervised as banks. Particularly if businesses choose not to raise funds from retail depositors as a means of financing their business, it is generally assumed that such businesses are not subject to bank supervision. For instance, a consumer credit business fully financed by means of equity capital of its shareholders, would typically not fall within the remit of the definition of 'credit institution' (hereinafter also referred to as 'bank') within the meaning of the Capital Requirements Regulation (CRR).[2] We may take this even a step further: in Europe numerous businesses are active that conduct business which could be considered or perceived to be 'universal banking' or 'investment banking'. Such businesses provide loans and credit facilities, they are active in the capital markets by underwriting and guaranteeing placement of securities (for instance at the occasion of an initial public offering), they maintain a large trading portfolio dealing on the financial markets for their own risk and account with the aim to benefit from market price arbitrage, they provide investment advice and carry out most of the investment services as listed in Annex I to the Markets for Financial Instruments Directive (MiFID II).[3] And still, these businesses are thus far not regulated as a bank. However, they do hold a licence as an investment firm.

Banks are regulated in Europe already from early days of the creation of the internal market. The prevailing definition of what constitutes the business of a 'credit institution' dates from the first banking directive of 1972[4] and has not been made subject to change since then.[5]

---

[2] 'Capital Requirements Regulation' refers to Regulation (EU) No 575/2013 of the European Parliament and of the Council of 26 June 2013 on prudential requirements for credit institutions and investment firms and amending Regulation (EU) No 648/2012, [2013] OJEU L176, of 27 June, pp 1–337. The definition of credit institution may be found in Art 4(1)(1), CRR.

[3] 'MiFID II' stands for Markets in Financial Instruments Directive II, being Dir 2014/65/EU of the European Parliament and of the Council of 15 May 2014 on markets in financial instruments and amending Dir 2002/92/EC and Dir 2011/61/EU Text with EEA relevance [2014] OJEU L173, of 12 June, pp 349–496.

[4] First Council Dir 77/780/EEC of 12 December 1977 on the coordination of the laws, regulations and administrative provisions relating to the taking up and pursuit of the business of credit institutions [1977] OJEC L322, of 17 December, pp 30–37.

[5] As noted this will now change with the introduction of the new prudential regime for investment firms.

That definition encompasses the following activities: 'to take deposits or other repayable funds from the public and to grant credits for its own account'[6]

As explained above, the core driver for regulating businesses as a bank is the deposit taking business or the raising of other repayable funds from the public. These are generally assumed to result in liabilities of the (bank) business to the group of individuals and businesses that are considered to form part of the 'public'. Should these individuals or businesses fund the business with equity capital only, there would not be a qualification as a bank. And, evidently, should the individuals and businesses not form part of the public whilst providing debt financing, then the business being funded in such manner is not likely to qualify as a bank. It is important to note, therefore, that the supervision of banks was first and foremost driven by protecting all counterparties of businesses that raised their funding by means of a deposit taking activity and activities of a similar nature. The catch-all expression 'other repayable funds' as comprised in the definition 'credit institution' was meant to widen the scope of the type of liabilities arising when counterparties provided funding to a business but where the 'product definition' would not make such liabilities to constitute a 'deposit'.

It would be wrong, however, to analyse the definition of what is a bank out of the context of the other element of the definition, being the activity of credit granting. Rather, it is because of the potential impact of the credit granting business on the ability of depositors to recover and reclaim monies deposited with or lent to a business that justifies regulation and supervision of a business as a bank. It is the combination of raising funds and utilising such funds for the credit granting process that constitutes the so-called 'maturity mismatch' risk which banks are required to manage. Depositors and anybody providing short-term loans to a bank expect that their counterparty is able to repay them at the shortest possible notice, even within a day. Banks, however, typically lend monies for longer periods to their clients. For instance, if a bank is in the business of granting mortgage loans, such loans will typically have maturities of at least 20 years. The mismatch of maturities (short-term liabilities versus long-term receivables), is a typical element of the banking business and the ability to adequately manage the risks concerning this mismatch forms an important element in the supervision of such businesses.

A typical differentiating aspect of banking business compared to other businesses is the aspect of, what we call 'extreme liquidity'. When we argue that a depositor or financier must be able to trust that claims are to be repaid by the counterparty, this would generally be true for any type of counterparty. Banks are different, in a way that they are expected to be able to respond at any time and at the shortest possible notice to requests or claims for repayment, and furthermore that creditors (depositors or other financiers) may rely on the ability to do so. If somebody provides a loan to a non-bank, the agreed upon terms between lender and borrower will usually cater for delays or terms of repayment of the loan and acceptance that the borrower will utilise the monies borrowed to achieve certain objectives (for instance the purchase of an asset or the funding of business working capital needs). The negotiated permitted utilisation of the loan will also determine the schedule of the repayments of the loan to the lender. The longer the borrower may take to pay the loan back, the higher this risk to the lender. This risk will be taken into account in the price that the borrower will need to pay for such a loan (interest or other lender compensation).

Lehman Brothers & Co's bankruptcy in September 2008 led to the articulation of the need to factor in another main policy objective of the supervision of banks, being the avoidance of financial instability caused by contagion effects of ailing banks. Lehman Brothers was not materially exposed to the risk we described in the previous paragraph. This bank did not have a large retail

---

[6] See the current definition comprised in Art 4(1)(1), CRR.

client base and the funding of the bank was not predominantly raised by means of retail deposits. This bank was rather depending on wholesale funding raised from institutional investors. The bank's interconnectedness with a very large group of US, Asian and European banks confirmed that the bank was systemically important. But it was only after the collapse of the bank, that such systemic importance was identified and experienced by the devastating chain reaction the bankruptcy caused across the global financial markets.

Henceforth, such systemic risk was required to be managed in a better fashion and, furthermore, the resilience of banks should be improved in order to enable them to withstand shocks caused by external developments in the markets, including the failure of one or more systemically important banks. The focus of the policy initiatives after the financial crisis of 2007/2008 was therefore not restricted to the identification of systemically important banks and measures for such institutions. Rather, the entire banking sector has been exposed to a fundamental review of the existing supervisory framework and requirements. This broad scope and comprehensive approach was necessary and justified, as the contagion effect of the systemic crisis also impacted banks that, based on the then prevailing norms, could be considered to be relatively healthy and strong.

B. Roles and Functions of Investment Firms and the Rationale for their Micro-Prudential Supervision

In Europe, investment firms carry out a wide variety of functions in the financial markets, each of those functions requiring different approaches as to their prudential supervision. Firstly, the most common functions of investment firms relate to their roles as intermediaries in securities trades executed on behalf of their clients. Secondly, investment firms may be involved in asset management functions for and on behalf of their clients. Thirdly, investment firms may be active, dealing on own account, in the financial markets when trading in financial instruments,[7] either in capacities as market maker on the markets, or to achieve arbitration results when dealing in such instruments. Investment firms may be authorised to fulfil roles in the distribution of securities in the context of primary market transactions, acting as placement agents whether or not with a placement guarantee. Finally, a peculiar element of the European regime for investment firms relates to the organisation and supervision of trading platforms. Apart from the supervisory regime applicable to regulated markets which are separate and distinct organisations required to obtain and uphold a specific authorisation, alternative trading platforms are supervised by requiring such platforms to be conducted by a licensed investment firm or market operator. This is the case for so called multilateral trading platforms (MTF) and organised trading platforms (OTF).

In certain cases one or more of these roles are combined in one single organisation, for instance an asset manager that also fulfils a role as intermediary broker in order to introduce orders on the private or public markets, typically will obtain an authorisation to carry out such a different role. The authorisation scheme for investment firms is laid out in[8] MiFID II. This Directive provides in Annex I, Section A for a catalogue of investment services and investment activities for which the authorisation requirements apply. Furthermore, investment firms may provide 'ancillary services'

---

[7] As this concept is defined in MiFIID II and amending IMD and AiFMD [2014] OJEU L173, 12 June, pp 349–496.
[8] Titel II, Ch 1 of MiFID II, see for a full reference to this Directive fn 9.

alongside the investment services and activities within the scope of their authorisation. Such ancillary services are carried out in the context of the product and services offering of investment firms to their clients.

From a micro-prudential point of view, European investment firms have traditionally been subject to stricter requirements then their counterparts on other continents. As will be explained in section VI B below, the European legislator has considered that the application of micro-prudential rules for banks on an equal basis for certain investment firms was necessary to create an optimal level playing field. This was particularly the case for investment firms that carried out similar functions on the capital markets as banks, for instance in the field of dealing on own account or acting as placement agent for new to be launched financial instruments guaranteed to the issuer of such financial instruments.

In later instances, investment firms' activities in respect of the safe custody of client monies and assets obtained a particular interest of the regulator where, alongside the organisational requirements stemming from MiFID II (and its predecessors), such activities (customarily they fit in the definition of an ancillary services within the meaning of Annex I, Section B, MiFID II) are subject to capital requirements. The reasoning has been that in order to protect the interests of clients owning cash or financial instruments placed in safe custody with the investment firm, capital buffers are necessary to shield the client's interests against insolvency of the investment firm.

Micro-prudential rules of the CRR text work with an incremental model of capital requirements for investment firms, depending on the type of investment services or investment activities carried out by such firms. In summary, capital requirements for investment firms fulfil *three objectives*.

Firstly, such requirements are imposed on firms with similar activities on the capital markets as banks in order to level the playing field. This is particularly true for investment firms dealing on own account and those firms placing financial instruments with placement guarantee. It is difficult to conclusively analyse the reason for imposing these requirements, as in many instances investment firms carrying out the aforementioned roles do not create or amplify financial risks for clients or on the financial markets requiring strict micro-prudential supervision.[9]

Secondly, capital requirements are imposed on investment firms for which, by nature of their activities, the occurrence of operational risk represent an increased risk for the provision of services to their clients. Typically, such investment firms must quantify the sum of damages that may occur in such instances, and maintain capital buffers against such quantified sum. The buffers serve to increase the resilience of the investment firms against the potential fallout effects of the operational risk becoming manifest, for instance to compensate clients for damages.[10] Capital requirements for operational risk are particularly relevant for investment firms exploiting an MTF or OTF or those firms with important activities in the field of brokerage services for clients dealing on the financial markets, for instance firms providing direct electronic access (DEA) to customers or firms operating large scale online (execution only) broker platforms.

---

[9] A firm dealing on own account usually does not have clients whose interests must be protected against insolvency. Investment firms offering the services of placement activities with guarantee may not fund themselves with (retail) deposits (because the investment firm would need to be authorised as a bank in such case), henceforth the risks resulting from the placement guarantee (which may indeed increase the probability of financial difficulties if the placement process goes wrong) is to be borne by its shareholders in any event.

[10] Investment firms benefit in most instances from a mitigated regime to capitalise operational risk, in a rule specifically designed for this type of institutions: the fixed overhead rule of Art 97, CRR. This simplified quantification method allows the firm to maintain capital based on a straightforward and simple formula of calculation, being a quarter of the annual fixed costs of the firm concerned.

Thirdly, and most importantly, capital requirements are imposed on firms that carry out custodian services for their clients' assets and monies. Such custodian services may, in certain European Member States,[11] result with the firm holding such assets (financial instruments) or monies in its own name, whether permanently or temporarily. Capital requirements intend to mitigate the risks accruing when client assets and monies comingle with those of the firm. Financial distress with the firm can result in losses of client assets and monies and damages for clients if the overall financial position of the firm falls short to honour all the claims of the clients.

Micro-prudential rules for investment firms, therefore, serve different objectives and may also result into considerably different rules applicable to such firms. As we will discuss briefly in further paragraphs, certain requirements imposed on banks (for instance the strict regime for liquidity management) are customarily not applied to investment firms, as the objectives of such rules are not relevant in the context of the business of investment firms generally.

C. Risk Pooling, Risk Transfer, Risk Transformation and the Potential for Systemic Risk in Insurance

Insurance is an ancient activity,[12] and is essentially a mechanism for the management of risk.[13] In its earliest forms, insurance typically emerged in the form of mutualisation of risk within a group, such as the mutualisation of losses of cargo among traders, mutualisation of losses due to fire damage and the mutualisation of individual disability through joint funds by guilds and friendly societies. A crucial shift in the evolution of insurance is formed by the failure of such self-help funds and their replacement by commercial insurance.[14]

Through insurance, risks are transferred from economic actors that are not willing or able to bear these risks to actors who are prepared to bear these risks. Risks are spread by pooling individual risks in a larger pool of aggregate and less correlated risks, and risks are priced by attributing a premium to the transfer of risk to each transferor, thereby distributing risks and returns to each actor appropriately. Insurance is the business of accepting insurable risks, managing them, and providing compensation for possible losses.[15] As we will explain in more detail in section VI D, this specific character of insurance has profound implications for the way in which insurers manage risks. The presence of a sufficiently diversified pool of uncorrelated risk is essential for the insurance model.

---

[11] It is with an intention that we refer to 'certain European Member States', as in certain Member States (such as the Netherlands), investment firms that are not authorised as a bank, are simply prohibited to hold client assets and monies in their own name or comingle such assets or monies in the estate of the investment firm. Asset segregation rules imposed on such firms, alleviate the need for strict capital requirements for such firms.

[12] Early forms of insurance can be traced backed to ancient China (3000 BC), Phoenecians, Greek and Roman times, See, eg, C Thimann, 'What is insurance?', in F Hufeld, RSJ Koijen, C Thimann, *The economics, regulation and systemic risk of insurance markets*, (Oxford, Oxford University Press, 2017), para 1.3.2; M Everson, 'Regulating the insurance sector', in N Moloney, E Ferran and J Payne (eds), *Oxford Handbook of Financial Regulation*, (Oxford, Oxford University Press, 2015), ch 14; M Clarke, 'An introduction to insurance contract law', in: J Burling and K Lazarus (eds), *Research handbook on international insurance law and regulation*, (Cheltenham, Edward Elgar, 2011), para 3.

[13] M Clarke, o.c., para 1.

[14] See M Everson, o.c., ch 14.

[15] Thimann, o.c., para 1.2.1. Thimann describes this definition, distinguishing three qualifications: (1) Insurance risks are faced by policyholders but beyond their control. They are not systematic but subject to the law of large numbers; and they are non-financial – that is, not directly related to the economic or financial cycle; (2) the managing of risks takes place through pooling or mutualisation or takes place through cession and diversification; and (3) compensation takes place for losses that have actually occurred, not for hypothetical losses nor for events that may have caused losses.

The liabilities of insurers are fundamentally different from the liabilities of banks, that we have described in section II A.[16] Where the core driver of bank liabilities is deposit taking and raising of repayable funds from the public and from businesses, insurers accept insurance risk against a premium, to be paid by the policyholder and invest that premium income in order to meet obligations towards policyholders over time.

The investment of insurance premiums is inherent to the insurance business model. Life insurance obligations are typically long-term obligations with limited ability of early withdrawal of funds. It is essential for insurers to match assets and liabilities as much as possible. Unlike banks, insurers try to minimise an asset-liability mismatch as much as possible in order to be able to meet obligations to policyholders at all times. This means that insurers tend to pursue a well-diversified investment portfolio and may enhance asset-liability matching through the use of derivatives. The investment strategy of insurers is driven by the duration and predictability of the insurance liabilities. Given the long-term character of many life insurance obligations, and consequently their illiquidity, the investment portfolio of life insurers may consist of a larger proportion of illiquid investments than banks are able to hold. Non-life insurance obligations obviously require more liquid investments to meet the less predictable insurance obligations, but investments play a different role for non-life insurers, compared to life insurers. For non-life insurers, investments provide additional revenues that might be used to determine premiums. Life insurance provides protection against the financial consequences of death and morbidity, as well as long-term savings and pension solutions.[17] Investments and investment income are being used to meet policyholder obligations and form a key component of many life insurance products.

In section VI D we will address the question, of what the characteristics of insurance, as described in this paragraph, mean for the prudential requirements that insurers are subject to.

As explained in section II A, since the 2007/2008 financial crisis, starting with the Lehman Brothers bankruptcy, the case for a more prominent articulation of macro-prudential policy objectives in bank supervision has become clear and important steps have been taken in bank regulation since then, in particular with the aim to avoid financial instability through contagion by ailing banks. Although it seems clear that systemic risk is not, per se, restricted to the banking sector, the manner in which insurance is able to create or to amplify systemic risk and the question if the existing regulatory framework is sufficient to address potential macro-prudential concerns or additional tools are needed is still subject to substantial debate at international and European level and in literature.[18] For a more detailed description and analysis, we refer to chapter 6 on macro-prudential regulation by Danny Busch and Mirik van Rijn. In this chapter, we limit ourselves to the elements of macro-prudential regulation that are relatively closely linked to micro-prudential regulation.

Very recently, the European Insurance and Occupational Pensions Authority (EIOPA) has published a discussion paper on macro-prudential policy in insurance.[19] Specifically,

---

[16] See in detail the Insurance Europe publication: 'Why insurers differ from banks', Brussels, October 2014, available at www.insuranceeurope.eu.

[17] Insurance Europe, 'Why insurers differ from banks', October 2014, p 12.

[18] See, eg, J Monkiewicz and M Małecki (eds), *Macroprudential supervision in insurance*, (Basingstoke, Palgrave MacMillan, 2014), A Georgosouli and M Goldby (eds) *Systemic Risk and the future of insurance regulation*, (Abingdon, Taylor and Francis 2016), F Hufeld, RSJ Koijen and C Thimann (eds) *The economics, regulation and systemic risk of insurance markets*, (Oxford, Oxford University Press, 2017).

[19] EIOPA, Discussion Paper on 'Systemic Risk and Macroprudential Policy in Insurance', EIOPA-BoS-19/131, https://eiopa.europa.eu/Publications. This paper builds on a series of three earlier papers, published by EIOPA titled: 'Systemic risk and macroprudential policy in insurance,' 'Solvency II tools with macroprudential impact' and 'Other potential

the European Commission has asked EIOPA, as part of a call for advice in the context of the Solvency II 2020 review, to assess whether the existing provisions of the Solvency II framework allow for an appropriate exercise of macro-prudential supervision. Should EIOPA conclude that such is not the case, EIOPA is requested to advise on how to improve the following closed list of items:

(a)   the own-risk and solvency assessment;
(b)   the drafting of a systemic risk management plan;
(c)   liquidity risk management planning and liquidity reporting;
(d)   the prudent person principle.

This assessment should, according to the European Commission, be based on strong supporting evidence, also assessing the possible impact of such additional specifications of insurers' behaviour and possible interactions with other Solvency II instruments.[20] While the request to EIOPA is focused on macro-prudential supervision, the list of items selected by the European Commission is closely connected to the micro-prudential Solvency II framework.

It may seem somewhat surprising that liquidity risk is being considered as part of macro-prudential measures in insurance, considering the long term and the generally illiquid nature of insurance liabilities. At the same time, insurers are not immune to liquidity risk, be it in a different manner and (perhaps with a less severe) magnitude as banks are. The micro-prudential framework for insurers typically does not include quantitative liquidity requirements, but it is a relevant topic in the own risk and solvency assessment that insurers need to undertake in pillar 2 (see section V for a further outline of the Three Pillar Framework). In section VI G we will discuss in more detail the role of liquidity. Apart from liquidity requirements to meet insurance liabilities, insurers also need to take into account the liquidity aspects of their investments, and as such, need to reflect this in the application of the prudent person principle for their investments and other assets (covering capital requirements).

As stated, the debate on systemic risk in the insurance sector is still ongoing. It does appear that the manner in which insurers might contribute to systemic risk is not identical to the manner in which banks may contribute to systemic risk. To the extent this contribution to systemic risk is for instance related to the provision of pensions or other income in (local) markets, or the availability of insurance cover in certain (niche) markets, it could be argued that micro-prudential measures also address macro-prudential concerns. Furthermore, the reasons why and manner in which insurers invest is distinctly different from the manner in which other market participants may invest, given the nature of their liabilities and their goal of matching assets and liabilities. This also may have implications for the contribution of insurers to systemic risk and financial stability. In fact, the contribution to financial stability may, in many circumstances, be positive.

III.   International Standard Setters

Soon after the collapse of Lehman Brothers in 2008, the G-20 political leaders[21] gathered to discuss the severe crisis occurring in the global financial markets. In the November 2008

---

macroprudential tools and measures to enhance the current framework,' published by EIOPA in the period 2017–2018, available at the website of EIOPA: www.eiopa.europa.eu.

[20] Formal request to EIOPA for technical advice on the review of the Solvency II Directive, 11 February 2019. FISMA/D4/SR/et/ARES(2019)865485, https://ec.europa.eu/info/files.

[21] From its establishment by the G-7 finance ministers and central bank governors in September 1999, 'the G-20' has meant the finance ministers and central bank governors of the 19 member countries, plus an equivalent-level

Washington summit of the G-20, the global political leaders agreed upon an action plan to introduce drastic changes to the worldwide institutional arrangements for supervision of the financial sector and the necessary regulatory initiatives. This agenda purported to address the widespread crisis in the financial sector and focussed in first instance on addressing the systemically important institutions' role in the development of the crisis. The G-20 agreed to an agenda for fundamental reform. Barth et al. (2013) summarise it as follows:

> As from their first summit in Washington, D.C., in November 2008, G-20 leaders have pursued a broad and ambitious agenda, first to stabilize, and then to repair and reform, the global financial system. One of their main targets has been the risks posed by the largest, most complex, and most interconnected financial firms, in particular banking companies.[22]

With the broad political support provided by the G-20 the existing standard setting bodies started their ambitious work to firstly adapt existing standards to address the new reality as this became prominently visible in the aftermath of the crisis in 2007/2008. More importantly, new concepts and methodologies have been developed by the standard setting bodies, to first identify the root causes of the financial crisis and second to develop regulation and supervisory practices that aim to mitigate the risks and issues that became apparent. Important roles were given to the Basel Committee on Banking Supervision (BCBS)[23] and the International Monetary Fund (IMF) in first instance. The role of the standard setting bodies in the early days of the financial crisis was important, and many initiatives taken by such bodies ultimately ended up in overhauled new legislation across the globe.

Standard setting bodies are not carrying out their work on the basis of mandates comprised in international treaties or similar international binding frameworks. These bodies:

> are politically and legally independent groups of regulatory and supervisory authorities from member countries whose purpose is to "set out what are widely accepted as good principles, practices, and guidelines" under which firms and supervisory authorities in a given economic or financial sector should operate.[24]

Standards as developed by these bodies necessarily are required to be translated to binding laws in the jurisdictions that wish to endorse and adopt such standards. In Europe, the standards as developed by the international standard setting bodies are typically translated to coordinated European wide legislation. In most cases, standard implementation occurs at the level of European legislation where individual Member States usually refrain from deviating from such uniform and coordinated legislation.[25] It can be concluded that the important work of the

---

representative of the EU. That would be either the president of the European Council or the head of the European Central Bank, serving on a rotating basis. The G-20 defines itself as the 'premier forum for international cooperation on the most important issues of the global economic and financial agenda', see: www.g20.org/docs/about/about_G20.html. See: James R Barth, Chris Brummer, Tong Li, and Daniel E Nolle, 'Systemically Important Banks in the Post-Crisis Era, The Global Response and 135 Countries' Responses', September 2013.

[22] Barth et al., (2013), o.c. p 10.

[23] The Basel Committee on Banking Supervision (BCBS) is the primary global standard setter for the prudential regulation of banks and provides a forum for regular cooperation on banking supervisory matters. Its 45 members comprise central banks and bank supervisors from 28 jurisdictions.

[24] See: Financial Stability Board, 'What Are Standards?' and 'Who Are the Standard-Setting Bodies?' at www.fsb.org.

[25] This is perhaps with the exception of the UK, that, particularly after the severe crisis in the banking sector developing in 2008 and further years, tended to adapt the European body of law to introduce certain elements that were derived from the international standards, but which were not transposed at European level. An example concerns the bank ringfencing rules where the largest UK banks must separate core retail banking from investment banking. Ring-fencing was the central recommendation of the Independent Commission on Banking chaired by Sir John Vickers and was introduced through the Financial Services (Banking Reform) Act 2013. See: www.gov.uk/government/publications/ring-fencing-information/ring-fencing-information.

international standard setting bodies that was produced to execute the reform agenda set by the G-20 has been translated to the European legislative and supervisory environment to a great extent. If deviations occurred in adapting the standards to legislation, such deviations aimed at introducing stricter rules or rules that supplemented the globally agreed upon standards.[26]

The standard setter for the insurance sector, the International Association of Insurance Supervisors (IAIS) develops, however, as a continuing exercise, a set of core principles for effective insurance supervision (ICP) and as such, aims to provide a globally accepted framework for the supervision of the insurance sector. The first version of the ICPs was adopted in 2003, and subsequently updated in 2007 and 2013. With the ICPs, the IAIS intends to develop a framework for insurance supervision, using a risk-based methodology including both quantitative and qualitative elements for capital adequacy, governance, market conduct and disclosure, both at the level of the insurance entity and at group level. Furthermore, it provides principles for effective supervision and supervisory actions. While the IAIS does not prescribe one specific method for the calculation of capital adequacy of (re)insurers and (re)insurance groups, it does promote the translation of insurers' 'risk exposure as far as practicable into quantitative measures which provide a sound and consistent basis for the setting of premium levels, determining technical provisions and deciding on the economic capital it finds optimal from its risk management perspective.'[27]

IV. Micro-Prudential Regulation in Europe

A. CRR-CRD IV Framework for Banks and Investment Firms

Basel III-Capital[28] and Basel III-Liquidity[29] as adopted by the BCBS in December 2010 have been quickly endorsed by the European legislator. Initially, there has been broad support for the concepts developed by the BCBS and the European legislator envisaged a swift implementation process of the revised standards for capital requirements and the new liquidity management standards. It is important to note that the implementation efforts of the European legislator to adopt Basel III coincided with the ambition to introduce a Single Rule Book for banks as had been recommended in February 2009 by the High Level Committee chaired by Jacques De Larosière.[30]

---

[26] An example of a typical European concept that supplemented the international standards is the 'systemic risk buffer' for banks and certain investment firms as first introduced in 2013 in the CRD IV (Dir 2013/36/EU). Such a systemic risk buffer aims at imposing a banking sector-wide additional capital buffer on those firms that are considered to be potentially contributing to systemic risk within Member States of the EU. The framework for systemic buffers is introduced in addition to the capital buffers for systemically important banks which rules are based on the work of the BCBS and FSB and the methodologies developed by such standard setting bodies.

[27] The IAIS 'Common Structure of the Assessment of Insurer Solvency' (2007).

[28] BCBS, 'Basel III: A global regulatory framework for more resilient banks and banking systems', December 2020 (revised June 2011).

[29] BCBS, 'Basel III: International framework for liquidity risk measurement, standards and monitoring', December 2010, subsequently revised by BCBS, Liquidity Coverage Ratio (January 2013) and BCBS Net Stable Funding Ratio (October 2014).

[30] Report: 'The High Level Group on Financial Supervision in the EU', 25 February 2009 to be consulted via http://ec.europa.eu/economy_finance/publications recommended as to the single rule book in point 109 on p 29: 'The European Institutions and the level 3 committees should equip the EU financial sector with a set of consistent core rules. Future legislation should be based, wherever possible, on regulations (which are of direct application). When directives are used, the co-legislator should strive to achieve maximum harmonisation of the core issues. Furthermore, a process should be launched to remove key-differences stemming from the derogations, exceptions and vague provisions currently contained in some directives (see chapter on supervision).'

We will leave the developments concerning the Single Rule Book for what they are, and focus on the substantive rules introduced with the new regulatory framework.

Most of the substantive prudential requirements for banks and for investment firms are contained in the CRR and the level 2 body of regulations adopted by the European Commission based on the preparatory work of the EBA and the European Systemic Risk Board (ESRB). Furthermore, level 3 guidance in the form of guidelines, recommendations and Questions & Answers supplement this massive body of law. In aggregate the CRR and all the further regulatory technical standards, implementing technical standards and level 3 guidance are contained in legal texts that may very well exceed 10,000 pages. By far, this legislative framework is the most significant piece of legislation at European level setting forth rules for the financial sector. CRR regulates the following topics:

1. The substantive rules for consolidated supervision on groups of banks and investment firms.
2. Qualitative capital requirements determining the legal requirements which must be met in order for equity instruments and debt instruments to qualify as so-called 'regulatory capital'.
3. Capital requirements for credit risk, market risk and operational risk.
4. Liquidity management requirements introducing two new ratios that must be met by banks in order to maintain sufficient liquidity buffers, being the Liquidity Coverage Ratio (LCR) and the Net Stable Funding Ratio (NFSR).
5. The Credit Risk Mitigation framework.
6. The Securitisation framework.
7. The leverage ratio requiring banks (and certain investment firms) to maintain capital based on a non-risk weighted measure of the balance sheet.
8. Reporting and disclosure requirements.

Furthermore, mainly because of political reasons and certain limitations stemming from the European Treaties, the CRR legislative body is supplemented by the Capital Requirements Directive IV of 2013 (CRD IV).[31] CRD IV deals with the market access processes for banks, the organisation of the supervisory and review process by the competent authorities, cooperation between competent authorities in respect of groups of banks and investment firms operating on a cross border basis, harmonised rules concerning sanctions and enforcement by competent authorities.

Furthermore and, quite typically, CRD IV comprises rules on the regime for Global Systemically Important Institutions (GSII), Other Systemically Important Institutions (OSII), the capital conservation buffer, the countercyclical capital buffer and the systemic risk buffer. We referred to the latter topics as being 'quite typically' regulated in CRD IV. The inclusion of these topics at directive level is caused by a fierce political debate among the Member States about the preservation of sovereignty of the Member States to deal with certain topics that had been considered of national interest. Therefore, the most logical way of organising the rules on these specific topics by including them in the CRR where the 'other' capital requirements are regulated, was rejected by the Member States in the final compromise to adopt the CRR-CRD IV text in 2013.

As has been highlighted in section II B, the requirements as currently in place based on the CRR and CRD IV framework apply for credit institutions and investment firms on more or less

---

[31] CRD IV, amending Directive 2002/87/EC and repealing Directives 2006/48/EC and 2006/49/EC, [2006] OJEU L176, p 338.

the same manner. With the new regime of Investment Firm Regulation[32] (IFR) and Investment Firm Directive[33] (IFD) this will change in the forthcoming years.

B. Prudential Regime for Investment Firms

In Europe, the micro-prudential supervision of investment firms has for a considerable period of time been aligned, for a large number of businesses operating in the sector, to the rules for banks. With the adoption of the first Capital Adequacy Directive[34] in 1993, investment firms had been made subject to identical rules for the quantification and capitalisation of market risk, being the risk of losses occurred in the firms' own trading portfolio as a result of price movements on the markets for financial instruments. Such equal treatment has been explained by the legislator to create a level playing field between the various types of businesses active on the money and capital markets and the risk they incur when trading in financial instruments.[35]

For a relatively long period of almost 25 years, investment firms have been subject to the same micro-prudential rules as banks, and, therefore, it is fair to say that cross-sectoral regulation in this field has been the main conceptual design of the regulatory framework as well as the supervisory approach to apply and enforce rules to both sectors.

It is in the context of the adoption of CRR and CRD IV[36] in 2013 that the European legislator has launched an evaluation concerning the desirability to continue such cross-sectoral regulation. This evaluation has been conducted at the request of the European Commission by the European Banking Authority (EBA) from 2015 until 2017. In its proposals, the EBA has redesigned the entire framework for prudential supervision of investment firms overhauling the rules for this sector into a bespoke system and with its own rules. EBA motivated such proposals as follows:

> As was concluded in the EBA Report, there is a clear need to develop a single, harmonised set of requirements that are reasonably simple, proportionate, and more relevant to the nature of investment business, to cover the broad range of all types of investment firms.[37]

With the introduction of the new prudential regime for investment firms as contemplated by the European institutions it is envisaged to define in the CRR a new category of 'credit institutions'

---

[32] Proposal for a Regulation of the European Parliament and of the Council on the prudential requirements of investment firms and amending CRR, MiFIR and EBA (Interinstitutional File: 2017/0359(COD), (Presidency Compromise proposal of 19 March 2019).

[33] Proposal for a Directive of the European Parliament and of the Council on the prudential supervision of investment firms and amending CRD IV and MiFID II, Interinstitutional File: 2017/0358(COD), (Presidency Compromise proposal of 19 March 2019).

[34] Council Directive 93/6/EEC of 15 March 1993 on the capital adequacy of investments firms and credit institutions, [1993] OJ L141, of 11 June, pp 1–26.

[35] See: Recitals (7), (8) and (9) of Directive 93/6/EEC: 'Whereas common basic standards for the own funds of institutions are a key feature in an internal market in the investment services sector, since own funds serve to ensure the continuity of institutions and to protect investors; Whereas in a common financial market, institutions, whether they are investment firms or credit institutions, engage in direct competition with one another; Whereas it is therefore desirable to achieve equality in the treatment of credit institutions and investment firms.'

[36] CRD IV, amending Directive 2002/87/EC and repealing Directives 2006/48/EC and 2006/49/EC, [2013] OJ L176, of 27 June, pp. 338–436.

[37] EBA, Discussion Paper, 'Designing a new prudential regime for investment firms', EBA/DP/2016/02 of 4 November 2016.

which are addressed in the proposals of the European Commission for an IFR as carrying out 'bank like' activities. In this proposal, it is stated:

> The largest and most interconnected investment firms have business models and risk profiles that are similar to those of significant credit institutions – they provide "bank-like" services and underwrite risks on a significant scale.[38]

These largest investment firms are classified as Class 1 investment firms and will be regulated and supervised as if they were credit institutions. For the remainder of the approximately 8,000 investment firms a bespoke and separate (and therefore non-cross sectoral) regime will apply, distinguishing the firms in two classes, where Class 2 firms will be subject to the full requirements of the prudential regime and Class 3 firms to a lighter touch regime.

On 16 April 2019 the European Parliament voted in its plenary session on the adoption of the new regime for prudential supervision of investment firms consisting of the IFR and IFD. It is expected that the final text of the IFR and IFD will be published in the Official Journal of the EU yet in the first half year of 2019. With the transition provisions of this new regime taken into account, this will mean application of the new rules from 1 January 2021 and the final abolishment of the cross-sectoral approach for credit institutions and investment firms.

C. Solvency II Framework for Insurance Companies

The current Solvency II prudential regulatory framework for insurance companies in Europe is relatively new.[39] Unlike the CRR-CRD IV framework, Solvency II capital requirements are not based on international capital standards.[40] The Solvency II framework can however be considered the European implementation of the ICPs developed by the IAIS (see below).

The Solvency II framework entered into force on 1 January 2016, replacing earlier generations of EU insurance directives and introducing, conceptually, a market consistent prudential framework, that is intended to be more sensitive to the risks faced by insurance companies than the previous frameworks. Similar to the Basel and CRD framework, its design reflects a three-pillar structure (see section V A for a discussion of this concept), complemented by a layer of group supervision, that can be described as the roof, on top of the three pillars.

The Solvency II approach to micro-prudential supervision is based on an economic, total balance sheet approach, a departure from and improvement, compared to, the earlier generations of EU insurance regulatory frameworks. In terms of capital requirements, not only insurance risks are considered, and slightly more broadly, not only the risks at the liability side of the insurance company's balance sheet, but also the risks at the asset side of the balance sheet. This means that for instance risks, such as market[41] and counterparty risk, are considered as well in the capital requirements.[42]

---

[38] See: Art 60 of the proposal for the Investment Firm Regulation amending the definition of 'credit institution' of Art 4(1)(1), CRR to comprise the large investment firms to qualify as a 'credit institution'.

[39] Although the history of the Solvency II reform is long, dating back from 1998. See, eg, A V Guccione, 'From Solvency to Omnibus. Historical Origins and Normative Evolution', in M Andenas and others (eds), *Solvency II: A dynamic Challenge for the Insurance Market, Il Mulino Strumenti*, (Bologna, 2017).

[40] Efforts are ongoing at international (IAIS) level to come to international capital standards for insurers, as well as a common framework for internationally active insurance groups.

[41] Market risk comprises interest rate risk, equity and currency risk.

[42] However, it should be noted that these risks can have an effect on both the asset and liability side of the balance sheet. An important source of market risk, for example, are product features in insurance contract that allow policyholders to exercise certain rights under their insurance contracts, See H Duverne, 'Managing Risk', in F Hufeld et al. (eds), *The economics, regulation and systemic risk on insurance markets*, (Oxford, Oxford University Press, 2017), p 57.

Furthermore, Solvency II has also introduced more interaction between the various pillars of the framework, in particular pillar 1 and 2. Quantitative requirements cannot be seen separately from qualitative requirements in the framework. This means, as an example, that the so-called prudent person principle and the principle of freedom of investment, that have replaced more static investment limits in previous frameworks, have both quantitative elements, as well as qualitative elements. The prudent person principle is as much the principle that guides how insurance companies need to invest from a quantitative perspective, but is also a behavioural and governance standard.[43]

Solvency II has also introduced market valuation of the insurance balance sheet. At the same time, due to the long-term character of parts of the insurance business (in particular life insurance) adjustments were considered necessary for the right calibration of the framework. This explains for instance the introduction of the long-term guarantee or LTG measures, a set of measures that addresses the need for adjustments in the framework, for long-term investment products in order to avoid undue volatility in the requirements. The reason for the acceptability of such adjustments, that are specific to the insurance sector, is the nature of these insurance liabilities (illiquid and/or for the account of the policyholder).

An important improvement that Solvency II has brought as well is a more advanced form of group supervision, compared to the supplementary sectoral requirements in the earlier Insurance Groups Directive.[44]

V. Three Pillar Approach

A. Three Pillar Approach as Important Innovation of Basel II in 2004

With the adoption of Basel II in 2004,[45] the Basel Committee introduced the three-pillar approach for banking supervision. The three pillars are as follows:

PILLAR 1	PILLAR 2	PILLAR 3
• Quantitative and qualitative capital and liquidity requirements	• Internal Capital and Liquidity Adequacy Assessment Processes (ICAAP, ILAAP) and Supervisory Review and Evaluation Process (SREP)	• Market discipline, disclosures

Pillar 1 defines the capital and liquidity requirements that must be met by banks as a minimum standard, based on the applicable rules for, firstly, quantification of risk (risk weighting) related to on balance and off balance sheet items and the operation of the business and, secondly, providing for rules for qualitative requirements for bank capital (see for a further discussion of

---

[43] EIOPA, 'Final Report on Public Consultation No. 14/017 on Guidelines on system of governance', para 2.136, EIOPA-BoS-14/253, Frankfurt, 28 January 2015.

[44] Directive 98/78/EC of the European Parliament and of the Council of 27 October 1998 on the supplementary supervision of insurance undertakings in an insurance group, [1998] OJEC, L330/1.

[45] BCBS, 'International Convergence of Capital Measurement and Capital Standards; A Revised Framework', June 2004.

the qualitative capital requirements section VI B). Measurement of the level of required capital is made either on the basis of a standardised approach (where the rules are based on common rules) or on the basis of bank's internal models.

Pillar 2 defines the supervisory review and evaluation process (SREP) in which the supervised bank and the supervisory authority engage in a, in principle, annual review process of the bank's own assessment of adequacy of its capital and liquidity.[46] Should the outcome of SREP point out that the bank's capital and liquidity as maintained based on pillar 1 rules are insufficient to cover for all the risks identified in the SREP-process, banks may have imposed further (pillar 2) requirements as a result of an iterative process between the institution and the supervisory authority.

Pillar 3 defines the market discipline rules, based on the assumption that disclosure of the risk management approach upheld by the bank and its key prudential ratios (in addition to the ordinary financial reports banks must publish based on the corporate law rules) will drive banks to benchmark their performance, capital ratios and liquidity management with competitors in the market. Such benchmark-processes should incentivise bank's management to align own risk management strategies to market standards. This approach considers the ability of banks to remain attractive for investors in its capital instruments.

In balance, the three pillar approach introduced an overhaul of the requirements imposed on banks in respect of the organisation of risk management and the supervisory engagement model. The requirements following from the pillar 2 ICAAP and ILAAP processes, enhance the requirements for banks to properly organise frequent and in-depth evaluation of the existing risk management environment in order to identify potential flaws or impediments on adequate risk management. Where needed, banks are required to measure the existing levels of capital and liquidity maintained to fulfil the ordinary pillar 1 requirements, in order to supplement these levels of capital or liquidity commensurate to the additional risks identified in the pillar 2 process. As regards supervisory engagement, the pillar 2 processes increase the pro-active approach by the supervisory authorities. This enables them to anticipate in a better fashion potential future adverse developments in respect of the bank supervised, and where necessary to address these future risks with concrete measures implemented by the bank, either based on an iterative dialogue or, where this dialogue does not produce adequate results, based on imposed measures. In both instances, banks will be required to hold additional capital or enhance the ability to address liquidity outflows in stressed circumstances. These additional measures are often referred to as 'pillar 2 capital' or comparable expressions to clarify that such measures are additions to the ordinary pillar 1 requirements.

As regards pillar 3, the market discipline following from disclosure of the details of the risk definition and risk management processes and key prudential ratio's, one could be more pessimistic about the beneficial effect these rules have brought. Clearly, the lack of harmonised standards for the disclosures has contributed to the great variety of methods of disclosures, where individual institutions may make very different choices in the establishment of reports and publication of the same. It is fair to say that, as regards the banking industry, there is misalignment of requirements in this respect, resulting in failures to create an appropriate basis for true benchmarking of the disclosed data by the different banks. The comparison is often between apples and oranges, therefore it is challenging for the market and investors to make an adequate analysis of the risk

---

[46] This annual 'Internal Capital Adequacy Assessment Process (ICAAP)' and (in later stages introduced) 'Internal Liquidity Adequacy Assessment Process (ILAAP)' requires banks to prepare annual reports to the supervisory authorities, in which the bank evaluate the appropriateness of the levels of capital and liquidity held (based on pillar 1 requirements and supplemented with capital and liquidity to be maintained for other risks not captured in pillar 1 rules).

profile and capital and liquidity adequacies with different banks. As we will discuss in section VI E, Solvency II has brought about more consistency across Europe in pillar 3 disclosures of European insurance companies and insurance groups, which can, at least in part, be explained by the manner in which the Solvency II framework has been structured. With the revisions to the Capital Requirements Regulation[47] that will enter into force on 1 January 2021, further harmonisation of Pillar 3 disclosures will occur for banks too.

B. Analogous Application of Three Pillar Approach to Investment Firms

As from the point in time that the capital requirements regulations implementing Basel II became effective and applicable in Europe (2007), the pillar 3 regime became also applicable to certain investment firms. The relevant rules have been introduced with the adoption of Directive 2006/48/EC, that was required to be implemented on 1 January 2007 at the latest in the national laws of the Member States. In view of the scoping requirements of this Directive, certain smaller and non-complex investment firms have not been made subject to the three pillar model. However, the larger and more complex such an investment firm was, the more likely is the application of the three pillar model. The fact that there has been a differentiated application of the relevant rules across Europe is explained by the discretionary powers exercised by the competent authorities as to whether or not to apply the SREP-process wholly or partially to investment firms.

In practice, only a few Member States applied the three pillar approach to investment firms to the fullest extent possible. The processes concerning this supervisory engagement model have been applied most extensively by the UK, German and Dutch authorities which are also the home of most of the investment firms in Europe. In other Member States functions executed by investment firms in the aforementioned Member States have rather been fulfilled by businesses holding a banking licence.[48]

In the new prudential regime for investment firms that will enter into force in 2021 once the provisions of the IFR become applicable and the IFD provisions have been transposed to national law, investment firms will be subject to a very similar three pillar approach as is currently the case for firms subject to the provisions of CRR and CRD IV. The relevant rules are set forth in Chapter 2 of the IFD (*Internal Capital Adequacy and Risk Assessment Process*). It is fair to say, that in this respect a cross-sectoral approach has been followed for investment firms to follow the same patterns of required risk management organisation and evaluation and the supervisory scrutiny exercisable in pillar 2. So, in this respect, there is commonality in respect of principles.

But if one takes a closer look at the technical implementation of the principles, there are major differences to be observed for both types of institutions. These differences can be summarised as follows. Whereas banks are required to observe pillar 2 capital requirements as an ex ante

---

[47] Regulation (EU) 2019/876 of the European Parliament and of the Council of 20 May 2019 amending CRR as regards the leverage ratio, the net stable funding ratio, requirements for own funds and eligible liabilities, counterparty credit risk, market risk, exposures to central counterparties, exposures to collective investment undertakings, large exposures, reporting and disclosure requirements, and EMiR, [2019] OJ*EU* L150 of 7 June.

[48] See for further background: EBA, Discussion Paper, 'Designing a new prudential regime for investment firms', EBA/DP/2016/02 of 4 November 2016.

mandatory requirement, pillar 2 capital for investment firms rather works as an extraordinary measure imposable by the supervisory authorities in times of distress. So for the latter type of firms pillar 2 is rather a sanction than an ordinary measure, whereas for banks pillar 2 serves rather as an ordinary requirement, not necessarily related to stressed or contentious circumstances. We therefore see commonalities in the template and principles of the three pillar approach, but great diversity in the normative embedding of the rules for the two types of institutions.

C. Three Pillar Approach in Solvency II

As indicated in section IV C and similar to the Basel and CRR framework, the Solvency II design reflects a three-pillar structure, complemented by a layer of group supervision. The three-pillar structure of Solvency II is comparable to the three-pillar structure of CRR, but there are nuanced differences. The three pillars can be depicted as follows:

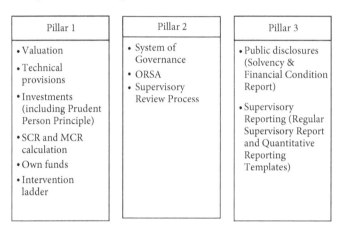

Pillar 1	Pillar 2	Pillar 3
• Valuation • Technical provisions • Investments (including Prudent Person Principle) • SCR and MCR calculation • Own funds • Intervention ladder	• System of Governance • ORSA • Supervisory Review Process	• Public disclosures (Solvency & Financial Condition Report) • Supervisory Reporting (Regular Supervisory Report and Quantitative Reporting Templates)

The first pillar of Solvency II consists of quantitative requirements, imposed on insurance companies, in particular the capital requirements (that can be calculated either through the application of a full or partial internal model (developed by the insurance company and the use of which should be approved by the supervisor), own fund requirements, valuation rules, rules relating to the calculation of technical provisions, and rules relating to investments (general requirements and more specific requirements for investments backing the technical provisions and backing the different levels of capital requirements, the MCR and SCR). The second pillar consists of qualitative requirements, including enhanced requirements with respect to the system of governance, including the risk management system and internal control framework, key functions, remuneration, outsourcing, the requirement to undertake an own risk and solvency assessment (ORSA) and the supervisory review process. The third pillar consists of confidential supervisory reporting and public disclosure.

As already mentioned in section IV C, the three pillars in Solvency II should not be considered in isolation but are interdependent. The assessment of risk by the insurance company, including the calculation of capital requirements, should be supported by strong risk governance and internal controls, while freedom of investment, while considering the prudent person principle, is reflected both in the quantitative requirements and in governance requirements.

D. Comparison of the Three-Pillar Structure in Bank, Investment Firm and Insurance Regulation

While structurally, through the three-pillar structure, the Solvency II framework bears significant resemblance to the Basel and CRR framework, the three pillar-structure in the Solvency II framework also has its distinct features. The calculation of capital requirements in Solvency II takes place almost entirely in pillar 1, on the basis of the total economic balance sheet of the insurer and taking into account interaction and diversification between risk categories, while for banks the calculation of required capital is essentially a combination of pillar 1 and pillar 2 requirements, whereby required capital, as a percentage of total risk-weighted assets, is calculated separately for the three main areas of risk and an additional pillar 2 requirement might be added through the ICAAP and SREP, while the Own Risk and Solvency Assessment (ORSA) is used to assess overall solvency needs and the ability of the insurer to meet solvency capital requirements, the outcome of the ORSA is not used to calculate or recalculate the SCR.[49] In exceptional circumstances capital add-ons might be imposed by the supervisory authorities as a temporary measure, but these capital add-ons should not be seen as an additional capital requirement. This is similar to the pillar 2 approach of the investment firm regime, as explained in paragraph 5.3 and is different from the Basel and CRR regime. Under Solvency II capital add-ons serve as an extraordinary measure, not as a part of the regular process of calculating capital requirements, as is the case in the Basel and CRR framework.

VI. Specific Features of Banking and Insurance

A. Different Business Models Require a Sectoral Approach

In previous paragraphs we have briefly touched upon the typical risks concerning banks, requiring bespoke arrangements from a regulatory and supervisory perspective. This chapter focuses on some of the micro-prudential rules for financial institutions and forms part of the overall analysis of this Book dealing with the fundamental question as to whether or not convergence of rules towards a cross-sectoral approach is possible to achieve and would make sense. From the perspective of micro-prudential regulation of banks, investment firms and insurance companies, we do not believe that common rules and common frameworks across the financial sector would be possible or justified. In this paragraph we will highlight some issues and constraints that support this conclusion. In making this analysis, we have made some choices as to the topics covered. Many other topics could have been included that would enhance the findings set forth herein.

B. Qualitative Capital Requirements – Tiering of Capital Components

Until the adoption of Basel III-Capital, there have been only few internationally harmonised rules on so-called qualitative capital requirements. Qualitative capital requirements purport to

---

[49] In fact, the ORSA process is not limited to the same confidence level (one-year horizon) that is used in the capital calculation but instead, should take into account a prospective, longer term perspective, as well as risks that are not covered in pillar 1, such as (eg) strategic and reputational risk.

enhance the (legal) characteristics of regulatory capital, in order to ensure that raised and available capital fulfils the essential functions of such capital components. In brief, regulatory capital raised by prudentially supervised businesses must enable them to meet the objectives of prudential supervision. These objectives are for banks: protection of deposit holders and avoidance of systemic risk. For insurance companies these objectives must be placed in the perspective of policyholder protection, and in certain cases management of systemic relevance.[50] In order to meet such objectives the following main characteristics must be met for banks, investment firms and insurance companies alike:

(1)   Regulatory capital must represent the most fully subordinated claim [in liquidation of a prudentially supervised business].
(2)   Regulatory capital must be permanently available.
(3)   Investors may not delay committed contributions of regulatory capital.
(4)   Regulatory capital must have the ability to absorb losses.
(5)   (Preferred) distributions of dividends and interest must be aligned to the requirements of mandatory levels of regulatory capital.
(6)   The quality of regulatory capital may not be diluted as a result of intra-group support.
(7)   The Regulated business' creditors may not accelerate repayment by the bank of capital instruments before the (long term) maturity date.[51]

The definition of these characteristics is set out in the relevant rules of CRR and Solvency II for banks, investment firms and insurance companies. Clearly, such qualitative capital requirements must be translated to the concrete (civil and corporate) law features of the relevant regulatory capital instruments issued by prudentially supervised businesses. This requires careful drafting of the relevant documentation implementing such terms and conditions and in many instances, a supervisory review process must be followed in order to test the eligibility of (to be issued) capital instruments with the statutory qualitative capital requirements.[52] Whereas the relevant main characteristics of regulatory capital may be considered to be common principles applicable to all types of prudentially regulated businesses (banks, insurance companies and investment firms[53]) differences occur as regards the relative and absolute levels (the amount) of regulatory capital and the creation of various tiers within the regulatory capital volume to be maintained.

For the purposes of ordinary capital requirements imposed on banks, a relatively large proportion of regulatory capital must be held in the form of long term (as permanent as possible)

---

[50] It should be noted, however, that Solvency II thus far does not include additional capital buffers for systemic relevance of insurance companies. In a recent discussion paper, EIOPA includes (for discussion) the potential introduction of a capital surcharge for systemic risk, as a possible macro-prudential tool. EIOPA Discussion Paper on Systemic Risk and Macroprudential Policy in Insurance, EIOPA-BoS-19/131, March 29, 2019, para 5.4. In this context, reference is made as well to the Request from the European Commission to EIOPA for technical advice on the review of the Solvency II Directive, February 11, 2019, Ref. Ares(2019)782244 – 11/02/2019, para 3.10.

[51] See for an elaborate analysis of these characteristics: Bart P M Joosen, 'Regulatory Capital Requirements and Bail in Mechanisms', ch 9 in: *Research handbook on Bank Crisis Management*, M Haentjens and B Wessels (eds), (Cheltenham, Edward Elgar Publishing, 2015).

[52] For instance, Art 26(3), CRR prescribes an *ex ante* clearing by the competent authority of the prospective issue of CET1 capital instruments. Oddly enough, such requirements do not exist for AT1 and Tier 2 instruments. This is odd, as it is particularly in respect of these complex debt capital instruments that debate can arise as to the eligibility of the debt capital issue for regulatory capital purposes. A straightforward share capital issue can hardly be structured and engineered to avoid the eligibility of these instruments as CET1. This may not necessarily be true for AT1 and Tier 2 instruments.

[53] For investment firms this follows until the entry into force and application of IFR and IFD from the fact that the relevant CRR provisions apply equally to investment firms as they apply to banks. After the applicability of the rules of IFR and IFD, investment firms will remain to be subject (for the time being) to the same CRR rules on qualitative capital requirements by the cross reference to the definitions of Common Equity Tier 1, Additional Tier 1 and Tier 2 capital of chs 2, 3 and 4 of Title 1 of Part Two CRR in Art 9(1)(i), IFR.

liabilities of the bank in the form of share capital, retained earnings and certain qualifying reserves (Common Equity Tier 1, 'CET1') capital instruments. Lesser amounts may be held in the form of absolutely perpetual and deeply subordinated debt instruments (additional Tier 1, 'AT1') capital instruments. The smallest proportion of the regulatory capital (being 25 per cent) may be held in the form of subordinated medium-term capital instruments (Tier 2). Before the introduction of Basel III-Capital in 2010 (and its implementation in CRR in 2013), banks and investment firms were permitted to maintain a small portion of regulatory capital in the form of Tier 3 instruments, being subordinated short term liabilities of the entity, which Tier 3 capital was intended to fund positions in the so-called trading portfolio. Basel III abolished the permissibility of Tier 3 capital instruments, and has driven the relative proportions of longer term, deeply subordinated regulatory capital to higher levels. Furthermore, as we will discuss in section VI C, additional capital buffer requirements (mainly those to address macroeconomic and systemic risks) are to be met with CET1 capital only, which amplifies the trend towards a greater and robust portion of the bank regulatory capital to meet the stricter qualitative requirements as set out hereabove.

In essence, tiering of bank regulatory capital means that the higher tier of the regulatory capital must observe the strictest capital requirements, for instance the requirement on permanency, whereas lower tiers may apply the qualitative requirements to a lesser extent. For instance CET1 capital is supposed to be provided on a permanent (ie perpetual) basis and may not be paid back, redeemed or otherwise reimbursed to the capital provider by the bank, whereas for Tier 2 instruments banks are permitted to agree terms with the Tier 2 financiers on repayment of the instruments within a medium term (which should in any event exceed five years). The permanency requirement means that banks are deriving assurance from the long-term availability of such capital instruments, and the ability to use the same in case there is a need to absorb losses.

In respect of the absolute levels of the tiers of bank capital, the outcome of the transformation of the bank capital rules as a result of Basel III-Capital, has ended up in the creation of a larger cushion of the CET 1 capital and a lesser amount of Tier 2 capital. For example, a bank that is subject to the ordinary capital requirements set out in Article 92, CRR, shall be required to maintain a proportion of 75 per cent in Tier 1 and 25 per cent in Tier 2 capital instruments. Within the Tier 1 capital component, 75 per cent must consist of CET1 capital and 25 per cent may be filled with AT1 instruments only. However, such a bank will also be exposed to so called 'combined buffer requirements' as defined in Article 128, CRD IV. We will give two examples of such combined buffer requirements in section VI C hereinafter. Such combined buffers must be met with CET1 capital components only, and this will mean that the bank concerned will be required to fill much larger proportions of its regulatory capital, with the highest quality capital components, being share capital, retained earnings and similar capital components.

Insurance companies' regulatory capital components, referred to as 'own funds', are also structured into three tiers. Similar to banks, Tier 1 capital constitutes the highest quality of capital and Tier 3 the lowest quality. The characteristics of the own fund items determine in which tier they can be placed. In particular this is the case with respect to the extent to which the own fund items are permanently available to absorb losses and, consequently, their level of subordination. In addition, thresholds are placed on the percentages that Tier 2 and Tier 3 items can make up of total own funds, in a similar way as is the case for banks. Own fund items that meet the characteristics of (eg) Tier 2 basic own funds but exceed the thresholds of Tier 2, can often be used to qualify as Tier 3 capital. At least 50 per cent of the (higher) Solvency Capital Requirement (which is equal to the first supervisory intervention level[54]) must be covered with Tier 1 basic own funds.

---

[54] Supervisory intervention levels are an innovation of Solvency II. In essence, insurance companies have to comply with two different capital requirements, being the Solvency Capital Requirement (SCR) that must be seen as the requirements

The (lower) minimum capital requirement (at which level a smaller buffer remains above the level of the technical provisions and a more imminent threat to policyholder rights exists) should be covered for at least 80 per cent with Tier 1 capital. Another distinction made is between basic own funds and ancillary own funds. Basic own funds are on balance sheet items, ancillary own funds are off balance sheet items, that can be called upon when needed and represent contingent liabilities of the supplier of the relevant own fund item or they accrue as and when the relevant item fulfils the 'realisation test'. Ancillary own fund items (a typical feature of the qualitative capital requirements for insurance companies not applied for banks or investment firms) can only be used, within thresholds, as Tier 2 and Tier 3 items and cannot be used to cover Minimum Capital Requirements.[55]

The undisputed availability of bank regulatory capital is furthermore enhanced with a complex system of prudential filters and capital deductions. For example, bank's deferred tax assets (ie future claims on the tax authorities in the event a bank has overpaid (corporate) taxes in a certain year) are required to be deducted from bank regulatory capital.[56] This odd system of cross booking of an asset to the liability side of the balance sheet is a typical measure for banks. For insurance companies, because of the different function of insurance company regulatory capital and the longer-term perspective of utilisation of insurance capital to absorb losses, this works in a completely different way. Deferred tax assets may, in the case of insurance companies, serve as component of the regulatory capital, rather than that these assets serve as a deduction from such capital. Furthermore, deferred tax *liabilities*, that may arise due to valuation differences between Solvency II and the insurance company's commercial accounts, may, in some circumstances, result in a decrease of the capital *requirements*.[57]

The assessment of the level of subordination and permanent availability is largely comparable to the assessment under the Basel III-Capital framework as outlined hereabove in this subparagraph. Article 93(2) of the Solvency II Directive sets out at high level, the following features for that assessment:

(a)   sufficient duration;
(b)   absence of incentives to redeem;
(c)   absence of mandatory servicing costs;
(d)   absence of encumbrances.

More detailed requirements are provided, in particular, in the Solvency II Delegated Regulation.[58] Although it is interesting to observe that after the implementation in CRR in 2013 of the Basel III accord, Tier 3 capital items are no longer recognised as regulatory capital for banks, essentially reducing the number of tiers to two, and instead Solvency II introduced, as of 2016, for

---

for insurance companies on a going concern basis. Secondly, insurance companies must comply with the Minimum Capital Requirement (MCR). The latter requirements are setting a minimum threshold to be observed by the insurance company to remain authorised to conduct its business. If the insurance company would hold capital below this minimum threshold, it would lose its authorisation to act as insurance company, and the business will be brought under control of the insurance supervisory authority. If an insurance company faces pressures to meet its SCR requirements, this will result in intervention by the competent authority, requiring the insurance company to develop a recovery plan and to outline the planning towards restoration of the required SCR-level. This may be considered to be the 'first step' on the intervention ladder. The second step being intervention in the event of a breach of the MCR requirement.

[55] See for a brief explanation on the different capital requirements fn 55.

[56] See for this particular deduction: Art, 36 CRR.

[57] A similar concept, that we will not discuss in detail, is included in Solvency II for the loss-absorbing capacity of technical provisions, that might be embedded in the possibility of insurance companies to reduce non-obligatory discretionary profit-sharing features in insurance products.

[58] Commission Delegated Regulation (EU) 2015/35 of 10 October 2014 supplementing Solvency II, [2015] OJEU L12, of 17 January, pp 1–797.

the first time at European level a clear distinction of own fund items into 3 tiers, we believe it is more relevant to focus on the substance, rather than the number of tiers. To begin with, as explained above, Tier 3 capital of banks and investment firms could only serve as a buffer for a specific part of the banks' balance sheet (capitalisation of the short-term exposures of the trading book). Tier 3 capital of insurance companies is not linked to specific assets on the insurance companies' balance sheet and the capitalisation of losses that may accrue in respect of such assets. It should be noted that the activities of insurance companies are much more restricted than the activities of banks, and do not have a comparable asset (and risk profile) as the trading book of banks. Furthermore, the nature of the assets (in general terms less liquid) explains the acceptability of own funds that would not be capable of achieving sufficient loss absorption and are to a lesser extent permanently available if they would have to serve a regulatory capital of banks (and investment firms that are dealing on own account).

The illiquid nature of insurance liabilities also helps to explain, as mentioned before, why capital items such as deferred tax assets (resulting from accrued tax losses) are more suitable to cover regulatory capital requirements of insurance companies, than they would be to cover the capital requirements of banks. Insurance companies have a higher expectation of realising the value of these tax assets with future results, arguably even to some extent in a going concern scenario, whereby insurance companies are resolved in a prolonged resolution (run-off) process, that may take many years, in order to avoid policyholder detriment by a forced sale of investments, backing the insurance liabilities.

Own fund items under Solvency II rely to a lesser extent than regulatory capital for banks and investment firms on prudential filters. In this context, it should be pointed out that the fact that a separate Solvency II balance sheet is prepared, based on Solvency II requirements, reduces the need for such adjustments under the Solvency II framework (see section VI D). Whilst in general terms characteristics of insurance own funds and bank and investment firm regulatory capital are comparable, differences do exist. A more detailed analysis might uncover some further divergence that would exist between the different sectoral regimes as regards qualitative capital requirements. We, however, believe that most differences can be explained on the basis of structural differences of the business models of the sectors. In the next section we will discuss an example of such a typical difference that is stemming from the different business model of banks as compared to insurance companies (or investment firms for that matter).

C. Different Capital Buffers

Capital buffers, whether based on pillar 1 or pillar 2 requirements, are imposed on banks, investment firms and insurance companies for different reasons, but effectively they operate in the same fashion. However, it must be emphasised that the major differences between the reasons to impose various buffers also point out the differences in the business models between these regulated institutions. These differences may be explained with two examples of capital buffers introduced in Europe implementing the Basel III-Capital accord.

The examples given are the capital conservation buffer and the countercyclical capital buffer. Both buffers apply, in principle, to banks only (see below in respect for the regime applicable to investment firms). The buffers are not included in the micro-prudential rules for insurers, as these buffers primarily relate to the management of risks for banks in connection with credit granting and the consequences of losses in loan portfolios in the event of an economic downturn. Although insurance companies may, as part of their investment strategy, invest in loan portfolios originated by other businesses, we believe it would be in conflict with the rules on restrictions for insurers to carry out non-insurance business that they would make lending part of the core business offering. For banks, granting loans is their core business.

The capital conservation buffer has been introduced by the Basel Committee as one of the measures of Basel III-Capital. The fundamental objective of this capital buffer is to ensure banks increase the levels of high-quality regulatory capital, in order to improve the resilience of banks to withstand economic shocks. Such shocks have immediate repercussions for the quality of the loan portfolios held by banks, and the probability that losses in loan portfolios increase. The manner of calculating the buffer is based on straightforward principles: the buffer requires banks to hold an additional 2.5 per cent capital measured on the total risk exposure amount calculated from time to time by the bank. There is no profound academic research on the effectiveness of this additional capital buffer or the percentage number established by the Basel Committee. There is also hardly empirical evidence that the 2.5 per cent is set at the correct level. It is fair to say, that when developing the relevant standard shortly after the global financial crisis in 2008/2009, the Basel Committee had to strike a balance between an acceptable major increase of capital buffer requirements (the 2.5 per cent must be related to the 8 per cent original BIS-ratio[59] that still applies for banks) and the ability of banks to successfully implement strategies to meet the new capital buffer requirements. In Europe the capital conservation buffer has been introduced in 2014 with the adoption and application of the provisions of Article 129, CRD IV. The capital conservation buffer was to be build up in stages, the last stage towards a fully loaded capital conservation buffer was reached on 1 January 2019.

The countercyclical capital buffer operates in a different way. This additional capital buffer purports to increase the capital requirements for banks active in certain market segments which, due to macroeconomic developments, present an increased risk of future downturn. Such downturn may result in the development of specific losses in loan portfolios of banks that are active in such market segments. Also, the countercyclical buffer aims to stimulate saving in good time to address problems in bad times. The buffer is 'countercyclical' as its requirements are activated at the discretion of the competent authorities at a point in time that the relevant market segment is prospering, in other words lending in the relevant market segment is subject to low thresholds and it is easy for potential borrowers to obtain loans. By countering the relevant loan practices with an increased capital buffer, the lenders are required to set aside additional capital to address potential risks that may accrue in the portfolio they build up in the 'good times'. Typically, introducing the relevant buffer requirements is a discretionary competence of the authorities concerned and they are country specific. In the European legislation the rules for countercyclical buffers are set forth in the provisions of Article 130, CRD IV. The rules of this provision are complex, as they regulate the adoption of decisions of national competent authorities in the EU Member States that are required to address developments in their national markets. The rules go beyond the 'home state-host state' control mechanism, as national competent authorities are authorised to adopt decisions affecting banks that are active in their markets generally, whether or not these banks are established in the country itself. For instance if the competent authorities of a Member State want to address the developments in the residential real estate market in their country, they may introduce a countercyclical buffer for all the banks active in that market, also banks that operate from another Member State on a cross border basis. The countercyclical capital buffer may be introduced up to the level of 2.5 per cent of the total risk exposure amount. As is evident from the brief description of this buffer requirement, it is a bank specific requirement that focusses on the core business of banks.

---

[59] 'BIS-ratio' refers to the Bank for International Settlements in Basel, Switzerland. The BIS is conducting the professional secretariat of the Basel Committee on Banking Supervision which introduced the BIS-ratio in Basel I in 1988.

That the above buffer requirements may not necessarily be relevant for investment firms (and therefore that cross-sectoral application of these requirements is not desirable), has been recognised by the European legislator. Firstly, the scope of application of these buffer requirements is restricted to a very small subset of investment firms performing the activity of dealing on own account or providing the service of placement of financial instruments with a placement guarantee. See Article 128, last paragraph CRD IV. Secondly, in the second paragraphs of both Articles 129 and 130, CRD IV a generic exemption rule is introduced for small and medium-sized investment firms (those firms that are subject to the requirements and not excluded from the application thereof based on the last paragraph of Article 128, CRD IV). This generic exemption rule has been applied by a significant number of Member States in the EU.[60] Therefore, the additional buffer requirements as discussed in this section have hardly any relevance for the sector of investment firms.

Whereas in this section we discussed the origin of the typical combined buffer requirements for banks, we also found that significant differences may be derived from the different risk management approaches to be followed by banks, insurance companies and investment firms. In the following section we will outline the main elements of the risk management framework for insurance companies. This discussion will highlight the major differences in the approaches followed in the different sectors, which arises from the typic differences of the business models of such institutions.

D. Risk Management of Insurance Requires a Sectoral Approach

As explained in sections II C and II D, insurers accept and manage insurable risks and provide compensation to policyholders and other beneficiaries for potential losses. Risks that might be difficult or impossible to be borne by individual policyholders are transformed into (more) affordable, predictable (periodic) payments. A crucial condition for the effectiveness of insurance is a sufficient level of uncorrelated risk. The resilience of insurance companies' exposure to risk not only depends on the law of large numbers (more ability to absorb losses due to the mere size of the risk pool), but also on the composition of the pool, in the sense that the risks in the pool behave sufficiently differently between them and do not occur in a similar way at the same time. Therefore, insurers seek to diversify the portfolio of risks they are exposed to. Diversification can take place in different ways: different products, geographical areas, markets, characteristics of the policyholders, etc. A high level of diversification increases the likelihood that an insurer is able to cover the actual losses it has expected it to occur, based on the assumptions it has made in determining the technical provisions (the provisions it has calculated to cover the insurance liabilities). The more accurate the assumptions are, the less likely it is that an insurer needs to rely on the capital buffers it maintains in addition to the investments it holds to cover its insurance liabilities. Therefore, the level of diversification in the insurance portfolio is an important factor for the determination of the capital buffers it needs to hold. Obviously there are other risks that insurers may face as well and these are relevant to determine the capital requirements, in particular underwriting risk, market risk, credit risk, counterparty default risk and operational risk.[61]

---

[60] The ESRB published from time to time the notifications received from the Member States based on the system of Artis 129 and 130, CRDIV. If a Member State wishes to apply the generic exemption for investment firms, this must be notified to the ESRB and such notifications are of public record. See: www.esrb.europa.eu/national_policy for an overview of the application of the relevant generic exemptions by Member States.

[61] These risks are the minimum risks that need to be taken into account by an insurer in accordance with the standard formula for calculating the solvency capital requirement in accordance with Solvency II.

Furthermore, in order to mitigate the risks in the insurance portfolio, insurers make use of risk transfer techniques, such as reinsurance and derivatives for hedging purposes. Speculative use of derivatives is typically not allowed for insurers. In fact, the activities an insurer is allowed to undertake are usually restricted in various ways. Ancillary activities that insurers are allowed to undertake are limited and generally speaking, should be connected to the core insurance activity. The combination of life insurance and non-life insurance is generally not allowed either, or is limited to supplementary insurance.[62] These factors differentiate insurers from banks, that may be allowed to undertake a broader range of activities. This adds to the differences in the prudential risks that insurers and banks are exposed to.

The two main types of insurance are non-life insurance and life insurance. The purpose of non-life insurance is to protect the policyholder against the negative financial consequences of adverse events. The emphasis for non-life insurers is on the correct segmentation and pricing of risk, pooling and diversification of risk and optimising operating costs. As explained in section II C, investments are typically relevant in a different manner to non-life insurers than they are to life insurers. For non-life insurers, investments provide additional revenues that might be used to determine premiums. Life insurance provides protection against the financial consequences of death and morbidity, as well as long-term savings and pension solutions.[63] Investments and investment income are being used to meet policyholder obligations and form a key component of many life insurance products.

As explained before, insurers rely for their business on their ability to properly assess and underwrite risk, diversify risk and match insurance liabilities and assets. Balance sheets of insurers are economically stable, as assets and liabilities are matched, unlike banks, that engage in maturity transformation and on average, have assets with a longer duration than their liabilities. There is no need for insurers to be 'hyper-liquid' in stressed circumstances in the manner as banks need to be.[64] As a consequence, the focus of prudential supervision of insurers is primarily on the assessment of risks they are exposed to and on capital. Liquidity requirements generally do not form part of the quantitative prudential requirements to which insurers are subject and the nature of their liabilities allows insurers to take into account other forms of capital than would be suitable to cover the capital needs of banks.[65] Furthermore, insurers do not have access to central bank liquidity. As a consequence, there is no direct sovereign link for insurers.

Like banks, insurers also have a specific role in society, albeit a different one, compared to banks. Through the protection that insurers offer to policyholders and in their role as institutional investors, they contribute to the functioning of the economy in various ways. Consequently, trust in insurers is important, but in a different manner than trust in banks is important. This translates into a more diverse picture with respect to the availability of insurance guarantee schemes, compared to deposit guarantee schemes[66] and the absence of access for insurers to central bank liquidity.

---

[62] With the exception of reinsurance, that can be conducted on a composite basis.

[63] Insurance Europe, 'Why insurers differ from banks', October 2014, p 12.

[64] Even if insurers are faced with an asset-liability mismatch, they typically have a prolonged period of time to manage that mismatch over time, due to the long-term nature of their liabilities and the low likelihood that policyholders cancel their insurance policies, even in periods of stress.

[65] In particular, the loss absorbing capacity of deferred taxes may be a relevant form of capital for some insurers, because of the likelihood of their ability to compensate tax losses from the past with future profits, thus reducing the future tax burden.

[66] This might be explained in particular because of the perceived low risk of a 'run' on an insurer, compared to a 'bank run' and (or in combination with) high preferential rights of policyholders in insolvency.

A distinct risk to the insurance business is underwriting risk that might be caused by an inaccurate assessment of the insured risks or by unforeseen circumstances, beyond the insurers' control.[67] Essential to the successful mutualisation of insurance risk, risk pooling, is the completeness of information and the exactness of actuarial assumptions. Essential to insurance is the management of information asymmetries.[68] More broadly speaking, the insurance market, like banking, is characterised by market imperfections, including the limited ability of many policyholders to understand the insurance contract, to assess the fairness of premiums and the ability of the insurance company to meet claims. On the other hand, the challenge for insurance companies is to obtain adequate information to assess the risks that the insured poses.[69]

The nature of insurance activity – covering risks for the economy, financial and corporate undertakings and households – has both differences and similarities when compared to the other financial sectors. Insurance, unlike most financial products, is characterised by the reversal of the production cycle insofar as premiums are collected when the contract is entered into and claims arise only if a specified event occurs. Insurers intermediate risks directly.[70] Thimann distinguishes insurance risk, as being non-financial in nature, from financial risk, that is related to the economic or financial cycle.[71]

Obviously, the differences in business models of banks and insurers have an impact on the types of risks they are faced with and, to the extent the risks they are exposed to are similar, impact the manner which they are exposed to such risks. As mentioned before, generally speaking, an insurers' balance sheet is economically stable, in the sense that insurers aim to match their liabilities, specifically insurance liabilities, with assets that match the duration of these liabilities. In essence, insurers do not engage in maturity transformation, as a consequence of which the average duration of most banks' assets is longer than the average duration of their liabilities.[72] As follows from the above, insurers invest the insurance premiums they receive in order to be able to pay the claims under the insurance policies when these claims materialise and in order to cover operational and funding costs.

Some authors point out that there is a difference between the liabilities of banks, compared to insurance liabilities, being the level of loss absorption of the liabilities. They argue that bank liabilities generally provide little or no loss-absorbing capacity, while insurance liabilities provide more ability for loss-absorption, which results in insurers being less exposed to liquidity risk than banks.[73] We do not concur with this analysis. In general, the loss absorbing capacity of bank liabilities has been enhanced fundamentally with the introduction of the Basel III-Capital standards. Furthermore, whilst we do not debate this at length in this chapter, the new resolution regime for banks introducing the Total Loss Absorbing Capacity rules as developed by the Financial Stability Board,[74] further enhance banks' loss absorbing capabilities to a large extent. It is fair to say that prior to Basel III-Capital the loss absorbing capacity of banks would be rather

---

[67] Insurance Europe, 'Why insurers differ from banks', October 2014, www.insuranceeurope.eu.

[68] M Everson, o.c., ch 14.

[69] See: L Steinberg. 'International organisations: their role and interconnectivity in insurance regulation', in J Burling and K Lazarus (eds), *Research handbook on international insurance law and regulation*, (Cheltenham, Edward Elgar, 2011), p 277.

[70] IAIS, 'Insurance Core Principles, Standards, Guidance and Assessment Methodology', October 2011, p 3.

[71] Thimann, o.c. para 1.2.1.

[72] Insurance Europe, 'Why insurers differ from banks', Brussels, October 2014, available at www.insuranceeurope.eu.

[73] A Al-Darwhish and others, o.c., para 124.

[74] See: Financial Stability Board, 'Principles on Loss-absorbing and Recapitalisation Capacity of G-SIBs in Resolution. Total Loss-absorbing Capacity (TLAC) Term Sheet', 9 November 2015, see: www.fsb.org.

restricted to some 2 to 3 per cent of its balance sheet. Nowadays, some larger banks must organise minimum loss absorbing capacity in the range of 25–30 per cent of the balance sheet total.

Micro-prudential risks of insurers are obviously not only mitigated through requirements such as capital requirements or governance standards. The scope of activities that insurance companies are allowed to perform under their licence tends to be more strictly regulated than is the case for example banks., as explained earlier in this section.

E. Total Balance Sheet Approach for Insurers

The Solvency II approach to micro-prudential supervision is based on an economic, total balance sheet approach, a departure from earlier generations of EU insurance regulatory frameworks and an improvement of these earlier frameworks. In terms of capital requirements, not only insurance risks are considered,[75] but risks at both sides of the balance sheet. Consequently, risks, such as market and counterparty risk, are considered as well in the capital requirements. Furthermore, Solvency II takes into account the interaction between risks on the balance sheet.

Solvency II has introduced market valuation of the insurance balance sheet. At the same time, due to the long-term character of parts of the insurance business (in particular life insurance) adjustments were considered necessary for the right calibration of the framework. This explains for instance the introduction of the Long Term Guarantee (LTG) measures, a set of measures that addresses the need for adjustments in the framework, for long term investment products in order to avoid undue volatility in the requirements. The reason for the acceptability of such adjustments, that are specific to the insurance sector, is the nature of the insurance liabilities (illiquid and/or for the account of the policyholder). Under Solvency II, insurers are required to prepare a separate, regulatory, balance sheet, distinct from the statutory accounts. Valuation principles are included in the Solvency II framework.

The CRR framework itself does not include valuation rules. The regulatory balance sheet is prepared, taking the statutory accounts as starting point, using the applicable accounting standards and valuation principles for these accounts, not specifically for the preparation of regulatory accounts. To translate these statutory accounts into a regulatory balance sheet, the CRR framework uses prudential filters. Due to the fact that under Solvency II the regulatory balance sheet is prepared separately and the requirements for preparing this regulatory balance sheet are embedded in the Solvency II framework, the use of prudential filters is not necessary and therefore, Solvency II does not contain such prudential filters. We believe this helps to explain that under Solvency II, more consistency is achieved throughout the EU in the pillar 3 disclosures of insurance companies, compared to banks.

Furthermore, Solvency II has also introduced more interaction between the various pillars of the framework, in particular pillar 1 and 2. Quantitative requirements cannot be seen separately from qualitative requirements in the framework. This means, as an example, that the so-called prudent person principle and the principle of freedom of investment, that have replaced more static investment limits in previous frameworks, have both quantitative elements, as well as qualitative elements. The prudent person principle is as much the principle that guides how insurance companies need to invest from a quantitative perspective, but is also a behavioural and governance standard.

---

[75] Insurance liabilities typically form the most important liability on an insurers' balance sheet.

F. Group and Consolidated Supervision

An important improvement that Solvency II has brought is a more advanced form of group supervision, compared to the supplementary sectoral requirements in the earlier EU Insurance Groups Directive.[76] With respect to group supervision, a notable difference between CRR consolidated supervision and Solvency II group supervision is the scope of consolidation of the two frameworks. CRR consolidated supervision focuses primarily on credit institutions and investment firms (institutions) and entities that undertake similar or related activities (financial institutions and ancillary services undertakings)[77] whereas Solvency II group supervision essentially encompasses the entire group.[78] For the purpose of the calculation of group solvency in accordance with Solvency II, participations of the insurance group in entities such as credit institutions, investment firms, financial institutions, UCITS Directive or AIF managers and IORPS are usually taken into account applying the solvency requirements, as well as own funds in accordance with relevant sectoral requirements.[79] Instead, as indicated above in the consolidated CRR capital calculation, participations in (eg) insurance undertakings are usually[80] not included in the consolidated CRR calculation.

The absence of a specifically prescribed method for the calculation of capital adequacy at international level leads to specific challenges for the calculation of available capital at group level of (re)insurers operating in different jurisdictions or regions. The rules under which available capital at group level is calculated might come from a different framework than the requirements that apply to (some of) the (re)insurance subsidiaries in the group. This could result in more onerous requirements for such groups, compared to locally active groups. This is one of the reasons why Solvency II group supervision includes the regulatory technique of 'equivalence', whereby eligible regulatory frameworks have been assessed by the European Commission and some have been found (in whole or in part) equivalent to Solvency II. As a result, local capital adequacy requirements can be used for the purpose of the group capital calculation in respect of the (re)insurance subsidiaries established in such equivalent jurisdictions.[81]

CRR rules on consolidated supervision of bank groups with headquarters in Europe, however, do regulate to a certain extent extraterritorial effects of the CRR rules to businesses located outside the EU. The relevant rules require banks whose financial holding companies are located in the EU and where subsidiaries of the group are located outside the EU, if such subsidiaries conduct a banking business, to apply the same CRR rules on such non-EU banks. Consequently, the consolidated supervision applies to the entire group in respect of the entire banking business, whether or not the business is carried out in the EU. This significant difference between

---

[76] Directive 98/78/EC of the European Parliament and of the Council of 27 October 1998 on the supplementary supervision of insurance undertakings in an insurance group, [1998] OJEC, L330/1.

[77] Article 18 CRR, see also eg, Single Rulebook Q&A, 2013_383, www.eba.europa.eu, question and answer on the inclusion of insurance undertakings in prudential consolidation.

[78] Article 212 and further Solvency II Directive.

[79] As a general rule, these participations are not included in the group solvency calculation using the accounting-consolidation method, but instead using deduction and aggregation. This has consequences for the diversification that can be achieved in the group solvency between the insurance entities and other entities in the group.

[80] Unless an alternative approach is used, available under the so-called Danish compromise. See, eg, Van den Hurk and Siri, o.c.

[81] Due to the international Basel framework for banks, the recognition of different standards applied throughout the continents for the purpose of the calculation of capital adequacy on a consolidated basis is less relevant in the banking sector.

banks and insurance groups may also be given as an example of diverging rules for both sectors. For groups that are exclusively comprised of investment firms, whether or not located in the EU or outside the EU, a specific exemption rule applies based on Article 15, CRR, permitting such groups to apply the relevant rules on consolidated supervision in a mitigated way. The varying scope of applicability of the rules on consolidated supervision for banks and investment firms versus supplemental supervision for insurance businesses, may in our view, be explained by the progress internationally to create worldwide standards for solvency supervision. With the Basel Accords, one could say that such international standards have been developed further than is the case for the insurance industry.

G. Liquidity Rules

Apart from capital regulation, a crucial element of bank regulation are liquidity requirements. An important driver for liquidity requirements of banks is the inherent risk related to the business model of banks, engaging in maturity transformation, accepting short-term deposits and investing these in long-term, often less liquid assets.

With the introduction of Basel III-Liquidity in 2010, a new and for the first time harmonised comprehensive set of rules was developed to create quantitative and qualitative rules for liquidity management. The quantitative rules, firstly, encompass the requirement for banks to meet two new ratios. On the one hand, the so-called Liquidity Coverage Ratio (LCR) is geared to measure the ability of banks to withstand shocks in stressed circumstances and the ability to meet potential increased liquidity outflows with a sufficiently robust liquidity buffer. On the other hand, the so-called Net Stable Funding Ratio (NSFR) introduces a mid-term perspective as regards the bank's funding models. The NFSR requires banks to organise their funding structure in such a way, that mid-term calls on fulfilment of its liabilities towards clients and other external parties, can be met with sufficiently available (stable) funding.

Secondly, the qualitative liquidity management requirements introduce strict rules on the organisation of the risk management and treasury functions, and governance arrangements commensurate to the required needs of the organisation in the context of the liquidity management. Since the introduction of these rules, banks are subject to strict rules on the accountability in respect of the liquidity management upheld, in the pillar 2 process. The introduction of the so-called 'Internal Liquidity Adequacy Assessment Process' (ILAAP) is a new structural element in the entire pillar 2 process where banks are required to make thorough assessments on the internal organisation and risks of the business carried out, and report on the relevant assessment and evaluation of the same by the competent supervisory authority in the SREP process.[82]

Insurers on the other hand, accept insurance liabilities that are often long-term in nature and invest the premiums in assets, that match the liabilities as much as possible. When early surrender by policy holders of insurance policies is possible, the terms and conditions under which policies are surrendered are strictly regulated. Early surrender of policies is often also subject to

---

[82] For investment firms, we briefly point out that in view of the deviating business model of such firms, liquidity supervision hardly plays a role in the micro-prudential regulatory and supervisory framework. Most investment firms currently benefit from generic waivers of application of such rules based on Art 6(4), CRR. In the future IFD and IFR regime, a very limited liquidity supervision regime will apply, which is in no respect to be compared to the strict and elaborate regime applicable to banks.

a number of disincentives[83] that reduce the risk for the insurer of early surrender of the policy. Furthermore, compared to banks, the activities that insurance companies are allowed to undertake in a licensed insurance entity are generally more limited than banks are allowed to undertake under a banking licence.

These features of the insurance business reduce to a large extent the potential emergence of liquidity risk, in a similar way as liquidity risk emerges in banks. At the same time, liquidity risk is also present in insurance companies and insurers manage liquidity risk as well. In particular, in the context of the Solvency II framework, liquidity risk is managed through the prudent person principle, that applies to investment of assets (covering both the technical provisions, assets covering the minimum and the solvency capital requirement and assets in general) as well as through the own risk and solvency assessment, that should also cover the assessment of liquidity risk.[84] The inclusion of liquidity risk in the ORSA seems to have a similar, but insurance-specific purpose as the ILAAP under CRR, while the inclusion of liquidity risk in the prudent person principle seems to achieve a commensurate alternative for liquidity requirements under the CRR framework.

VII. Conclusion

Is cross-sectoral and uniform regulation of banking and insurance businesses useful and productive? We tend to believe that it is not. The different business models, other stakeholder interests and requirements to provide for protection of such interests constitute impediments to the convergence of regulation. This conclusion is without prejudice, however, to the idea that supervisory convergence may be a productive and useful route to follow and, as has been outlined in the chapter, we conclude that this actually resulted in similar concepts and similar practices being pursued both in the banking and insurance industry.

Differences in stakeholder interests require different approaches to the substantive rules for banks and insurance companies. We have outlined the main differences in this chapter, by highlighting the different conceptual viewpoints in the capital adequacy and liquidity management rules. Whereas banks are typically required to comply with the 'hyper-liquidity' standards to address the legitimate claims of depositors to be repaid at the shortest possible notice, policyholders will be able to exercise different claims, usually in a much longer timescale. Liquidity rules for banks differ therefore from those of insurance companies, certainly if it concerns life insurers.

From a macroeconomic view, the impact of developments in the economy may have direct consequences for rights and obligations of banks' customers, whereas the same developments obviously impact the insurance company's investment basis and policies. But correlations between claims and (payment) obligations of policyholders and macroeconomic developments are at least very remote, if not non-existent. This could perhaps be different for insurance products

---

[83] For instance, receiving only the surrender value of the policy, forfeiting the benefit of guarantees, embedded in the product, paying a surrender charge, adverse tax consequences, reduced ability to obtain insurance coverage elsewhere, contractually allowed delay of payment by the insurer, see H Duverne, 'Managing Risk', in F Hufeld, RSJ Koijen and C Thimann (eds), *The economics, regulation and systemic risk of insurance markets*, (Oxford, Oxford University Press, 2017), p 72.

[84] In the context of potential additional macro-prudential measures, EIOPA has also included, for consideration, certain additional measures aimed at liquidity risk. It should be noted that EIOPA had initially also considered liquidity requirements as a potential tool, but is not further considering this tool, EIOPA, discussion paper on systemic risk and macro-prudential policy in insurance, EIOPA-BoS-19/131, March 29, 2019, chs 5.5–5.7 and Annex A.2.

designed to support retirement schemes. In this field, we wish to point out that such insurance products tend to contain more 'banking and investment' features, which can result in such products converging more to the qualification as a banking product than as an insurance product. This characterisation may even be stronger for so-called 'unit-linked' insurance products, which entitle the policyholder to track and trace the developments on the capital markets as a definition of the ultimate distribution in respect of the (life insurance) product held.

Conversely, certain banking products may contain typical insurance elements, such as guarantee features or credit default swaps. Notwithstanding these similarities, it is however a common rule and understanding that such banking products are to be made subject to banking regulation only, without introducing insurance supervisory elements in the relationship between the bank and the protection buyer.

Where business models and typical products offered by banks and insurance companies require different approaches to regulation, we do believe that there is more convergence in respect of the organisation of supervisory engagement and application of supervisory practices in both sectors. We outlined the important development of introducing in 2016 the Three Pillar Model for the organisation of supervision for insurance companies pursuant to the Solvency II framework. This Three Pillar Model has been directly derived from the similar concepts introduced for banks pursuant to Basel II in 2007. This is perhaps the strongest example of convergence and alignment of supervisory methodologies between the two sectors.

Also, the concept of differentiating supervisory engagement and rules in respect of banks and insurance companies qualifying as being systemically important may be considered to be based on similar policy objectives and similar stakeholder protection in which the scope of the supervision has been widened to manage and regulate the contagion effects that may be caused by systemically important institutions. This topic emphasises the need to avoid that the focus of supervision (and regulation) should be of micro-prudential nature only. Macro-prudential objectives have been introduced in both sectors since the financial crisis of 2007/2008 and these are now embedded in the overall architecture of the regulation and supervision of both the insurance and banking sectors. It is fair to say that this particular element of regulation and supervision constitutes a more or less common and harmonised overlay of the micro-prudential regulatory and supervisory frameworks. We do believe that this is notwithstanding the continued different approaches as regards the substantive micro-prudential regulation for both sectors.

Our main comparison has been the discussion of differences between the insurance and bank sectors. However, we also discussed parts of the prudential supervision regime for investment firms in Europe. We have pointed out that for decades the main micro-prudential rules for investment firms had been embedded in the regulatory framework for banks. Based on recommendations made by the EBA to the European Commission, there will be a fundamental shift to creating a distinct prudential regime applicable for banks on the one hand and investment firms on the other hand. The development of a bespoke prudential regime for investment firms and the considerable effort of the European legislator made in this respect has been explained and justified by the fact that bank prudential rules were considered to be inadequately addressing the typical risks accruing in businesses of investment firms. This lack of appropriateness of the bank prudential rules for investment firms, is therefore another example of the increasing divergence of regimes, rather than a convergence trend. However, it should be noted that in certain areas, cross-sectoral principles are still being applied, especially in relation to the engagement between supervisory authorities and individual firms, which continues to be based on the Three Pillar approach, as discussed in more detail in this chapter. This is particularly relevant for the organisation of risk management by individual firms and the supervisory scrutiny exercisable in pillar 2.

8

Corporate Governance

8A

A Cross-Sectoral Analysis
of Corporate Governance Provisions:
About Forests and Trees[1]

TOM VOS, KATRIEN MORBEE,* SOFIE COOLS
AND MARIEKE WYCKAERT

I. Introduction

In the aftermath of the 2008 financial crisis, regulators have strengthened and re-oriented the regulatory framework of financial institutions, including the provisions on their governance. For the present chapter, we use a straightforward and basic, but generally accepted definition of corporate governance: 'the system by which companies are directed and controlled'.[2]

Corporate governance in financial institutions has been a largely neglected topic until the 2008 financial crisis.[3] For a long time, it was mostly assumed that corporate governance in financial institutions is not fundamentally different from corporate governance generally.[4] Prudential regulation was deemed a sufficient answer to the specific characteristics of financial institutions.[5] This changed drastically with the 2008 financial crisis. The Basel Committee Report of 2010 marked the beginning of a wave of reports and research on corporate governance in financial institutions.[6] While it was initially exclaimed that poor corporate governance was a cause of the

---

* The author would like to thank the Economic and Social Research Council [ES/J500112/1], the Oxford-Man Institute of Quantitative Finance, Balliol College – University of Oxford, and the Scatcherd European Scholarship for financial support.

[1] This chapter is dated 14 June 2019. The authors would like to thank Veerle Colaert for her thoughtful comments and guidance during the broader project, as well as Thomas Incalza, Arthur van den Hurk and the participants in the conference 'Regulating Finance: Levelling the Cross-Sectoral Playing Field' at the Radboud University Nijmegen.

[2] A Cadbury, *Report of the Committee on the Financial Aspects of Corporate Governance* (Gee 1992).

[3] Jonathan R Macey and Maureen O'Hara, 'The Corporate Governance of Banks' (2003) 9 *FRBNY Economic Policy Review* 91; Peter O Mülbert, 'Corporate Governance of Banks' (2009) 10 *European Business Organization Law Review* 411, 415–418.

[4] Eg, Grant Kirkpatrick, 'The Corporate Governance Lessons from the Financial Crisis' in OECD (ed), *Financial Market Trends 2009* (2008). See, however, Ross Levine, 'The Corporate Governance of Banks: A Concise Discussion of Concepts and Evidence' [2004] World Bank Policy Research Working Paper 3404.

[5] John Armour, 'Bank Governance' in Jeffrey N Gordon and Wolf-Georg Ringe (eds), *The Oxford Handbook of Corporate Law and Governance* (Oxford, OUP, 2018) 1109.

[6] Klaus J Hopt, 'Corporate Governance of Banks after the Financial Crisis' in Eddy Wymeersch, Klaus J Hopt and Guido Ferrarini (eds), *Financial Regulation and Supervision* (Oxford, OUP 2012) 338–341.

financial crisis,[7] it soon appeared that banks with what was until then considered 'good' corporate governance, actually fared worse during the crisis.[8] Consequently, the realisation set in that the corporate governance model for non-financial firms cannot simply be transposed to banks.[9]

The post-crisis debate focused on problems with the governance of *banks*. Policy[10] and academic[11] literature have proposed specific changes to the governance of banking institutions, tailored to their business model and to the type of systemic risk they pose. In light of this, the Capital Requirements Directive IV (CRD IV) adopted new governance rules applicable to banks ('credit institutions') in the European Union. Some rules are only applicable to 'significant'[12] banks. CRD IV rules aim to (i) ensure the effectiveness of the board of director's risk oversight, (ii) improve the status of risk management, and (iii) ensure effective supervision.[13]

Regulators worldwide have also intervened in the governance of non-bank financial institutions. The financial crisis indeed made clear that a variety of non-bank financial institutions can perform functions similar to banks through market-based intermediation and arguably should therefore be put under similar regulatory scrutiny.[14] The EU, for example, adopted new or revised existing governance rules for a variety of non-bank financial institutions, such as investment firms (CRD IV,[15] Markets in Financial Instruments Directive II (MiFID II)), insurance companies (Solvency II), pension funds (Occupational Pension Funds Directive), UCITS fund managers (UCITS Directive), and alternative investment fund managers (AIFMD). In December 2017, the Commission proposed a review of the prudential rules for investment firms aiming at simplifying life for smaller investment firms, while keeping the largest (mostly systemic) firms under the same regime as European banks under CRD IV.[16] For example, smaller investment

---

[7] Grant Kirkpatrick, 'The Corporate Governance Lessons from the Financial Crisis' in OECD (ed), *Financial Market Trends 2009* (2008); High Level Group on Financial Supervision in the EU, Report on the future of financial supervision in the EU, 25 February 2009, 29.

[8] Andrea Beltratti and René M Stulz, 'The Credit Crisis Around the Globe: Why Did Some Banks Perform Better?' (2012) 105 *Journal of Financial Economics* 1; Renée Birgit Adams, 'Governance and the Financial Crisis' (2012) 12 *International Review of Finance* 7. See also the studies cited further in this paragraph. See, however, Andrey Zagorcheva and Lei Gao, 'Corporate Governance and Performance of Financial Institutions' (2015) 82 *Journal of Economics and Business* 17.

[9] Klaus J Hopt, 'Corporate Governance von Finanzinstituten' [2017] *Zeitschrift für Unternehmens- und Gesellschaftsrecht* 438, 444.

[10] See, eg, European Commission, 'Green Paper. Corporate Governance in Financial Institutions and Remuneration Policies' (2010) COM(2010) 284 final; Senior Supervisors Group, *Observation on Risk Management Practices during the Recent Market Turbulence* (Financial Stability Board); David Walker and others, 'A Review of Corporate Governance in UK Banks and Other Financial Industry Entities' www.theqca.com/article_assets/articledir_38/19306/QCAResponse_WalkerReview_Oct09.pdf.

[11] See, eg, John Armour and Jeffrey N Gordon, 'Systemic Harms and Shareholder Value' (2014) 6 *Journal of Legal Analysis* 35; Lucian A Bebchuk and Holger Spamann, 'Regulating Bankers' Pay' (2009) 98 *Georgetown Law Journal* 247; Saule T Omarova, 'Bank Governance and Systemic Stability: The 'Golden Share' Approach' (2017) 68 *Alabama Law Review* 1029; Joel Shapiro, Alan Morrison and Hamid Mehran, 'Corporate Governance and Banks: What Have We Learned from the Financial Crisis?' in Mathias Dewatripont and Xavier Freixas (eds), *The crisis aftermath: new regulatory paradigms* (Centre for Economic Policy Research 2012).

[12] The term 'significant' is defined further in section III.

[13] Commission, 'Proposal of 20 July 2011 for a Directive of the European Parliament and of the Council on the access to the activity of credit institutions and the prudential supervision of credit institutions and investment firms and amending Dir 2002/87/EC of the European Parliament and of the Council on the supplementary supervision of credit institutions, insurance undertakings and investment firms in a financial conglomerate' COM(2011) 453 final, 8 (after 'Proposal CRD IV').

[14] John Armour and others, *Principles of Financial Regulation* (Oxford, OUP, 2016) 433.

[15] The rules in CRD IV also apply to certain types of investment firms as defined by MiFID, see further section III.

[16] Proposal COM(2017) 791 final of 20 December 2017 for a Directive of the European Parliament and of the Council on the prudential supervision of investment firms and amending CRD IV and MiFID II [2017]; Proposal COM(2017) 790 final of 20 December 2017 for a Regulation of the European Parliament and of the Council on the prudential requirements of investment firms and amending CRR, MiFIR and EBA.

firms that have limited proprietary trading will not be subject to additional remuneration and governance rules. With some amendments, these proposals have been approved by the European Parliament.[17] In this chapter, we discuss the text as adopted by the European Parliament which is the version of the proposals that we also discuss.

Some argue that these governance provisions for non-bank financial institutions are not based on a thorough analysis of the business model and the systemic risk threats these institutions present. BINDER, eg, claims that the governance rules applicable to investment firms under MiFID II consist of barely more than an extension of the requirements under CRD IV. These governance rules were adopted without a careful analysis of the similarities and differences between investment firms and banks or any evidence of the existence of a governance failure in investment firms.[18] CÂMARA makes a similar argument in the context of AIFMD. He labels the governance rules in AIFMD as a 'quack' intervention disregarding empirical and finance literature. Governance intervention 'should be confined to areas that present clear examples of market failure or to cases in which public interests are at stake'.[19] One could draw a conclusion from such studies that the European legislator – at least in some sectors – has gone too far in drafting corporate governance provisions in the same way across all sectors.

It is true that the EU regulator has not always been clear about the market failure intended to be remedied or the public interest intended to be protected by its governance rules. Financial stability has been a prominent driver for regulatory intervention in governance, especially since the financial crisis. Even though corporate governance failures may not have directly triggered this crisis, it is believed that the lack of effective checks on risk-taking in financial institutions prior to the crisis facilitated it happening.[20] In their preamble, both CRD IV[21] and MiFID II[22] clearly link corporate governance failure and systemic stability. UCITS V Directive[23] and AIFMD[24] are less specific but do mention financial stability as a key rationale for regulation more generally. Solvency II points to financial stability as a secondary objective of the regulation, but states that it should not undermine the main objective of protecting policy holders and beneficiaries.[25] The protection of investors and beneficiaries is found as a rationale in other legislation as

---

[17] European Parliament legislative resolution of 16 April 2019 on the proposal for a directive of the European Parliament and of the Council on the prudential supervision of investment firms and amending CRD IV and MiFID II (COM(2017)0791 – C8-0452/2017 – 2017/0358(COD)) (2019) P8_TA-PROV(2019)0377 ('Investment Firms Directive'); European Parliament legislative resolution of 16 April 2019 on the proposal for a regulation of the European Parliament and of the Council on the prudential requirements of investment firms and amending CRR, MiFIR and EBA (COM(2017)0790 – C8-0453/2017 – 2017/0359(COD)) (2019) P8_TA-PROV(2019)0378 ('Investment Firms Regulation').

[18] See, eg, Binder with regard to investment firms in MiFID, Jens-Hinrich Binder, 'Governance of investment firms under MiFID II' in Jens-Hinrich Binder and Guido Ferrarini (eds), *Regulation of the EU financial markets MiFID II and MiFIR* (Oxford, OUP, 2017) 60. See also more generally: Jens-Hinrich Binder, 'Corporate Governance of Financial Institutions: In Need of Cross-Sectoral Regulation? A Comparative Analysis of Banks, Investment Firms, Asset Managers, and Pension Funds' in D Busch, G Ferrarini and G van Solinge (eds), *Governance of financial institutions* (Oxford, OUP, 2019) 9.

[19] Paulo Câmara, 'The AIFM's Governance and Remuneration Committees: The Impact of the AIFMD' in Dirk Zetzsche (ed), *The alternative investment fund managers directive* 2nd edn (Zuidpoolsingel, Kluwer Law International, 2015) 308.

[20] European Commission (n 2).

[21] Preamble (53) and (54) CRD IV.

[22] Preamble (5) MiFID II.

[23] Preamble (8) UCITS Directive.

[24] Commission, 'Proposal of 30 April 2009 for a directive of the European Parliament and the Council on Alternative Investment Fund Managers and amending Directives 2004/39/EC and 2009/.../EC' COM(2009) 207 final, 2–3 (after 'Proposal AIFMD').

[25] Preamble (16) Solvency II.

well, be it specifically for justifying the governance rules (eg in AIFMD,[26] CRD IV,[27] IORPS,[28] MiFID II[29]), or more generally (eg UCITS Directive[30]). Other rationales include consistency of governance requirements across sectors[31] and even mobility of workers.[32]

This chapter compares the governance rules adopted in these various EU instruments. Where the rules differ, we examine whether there are indications that such differences are indeed grounded in a market failure that is not present in other institutions; where the rules are the same, we examine whether this similarity is justified. This approach should allow us to identify the possibility and desirability of a cross-sectoral governance regime in the EU. The focus will be on the systemic risk rationale for corporate governance regulation, even though the other rationales put forward by the EU regulator will be addressed in passing. The chapter contributes to the literature by expanding both the scope of institutions covered[33] and the level of detail covered.[34] More specifically, we discuss the regimes of banks (CRD IV), investment firms (CRD IV, MiFID II and the new Investment Firms Directive and Investment Firms Regulation), insurance companies (Solvency II), pension funds (Occupational Pension Funds Directive), UCITS Directive management companies[35] (UCITS Directive), and alternative investment fund managers (AIFMD). Moreover, we compare the rules on institutional level 1, level 2 and level 3. The result of this comparative exercise can be found in the table in the annex and is summarised in the following sections.

We do not purport to engage in a critical analysis of the role of corporate governance regulation to address market failures in general[36] or financial stability in particular,[37] nor to evaluate the content of the corporate governance rules, which we take as a given. Instead we focus on the question: as the legislator believes that corporate governance rules are important for achieving certain objectives, what should be their scope of application and can we discern consistency behind this scope?

Finally, we note that there are some limits to our chapter. We do not study the regulation of remuneration in financial institutions, also an important part of corporate governance, because

---

[26] Proposal AIFMD, 2–3.

[27] Commission, 'Proposal for a Directive of the European Parliament and of the Council on the access to the activity of credit institutions and the prudential supervision of credit institutions and investment firms and amending Directive 2002/87/EC of the European Parliament and of the Council on the supplementary supervision of credit institutions, insurance undertakings and investment firms in a financial conglomerate' COM(2011) 453 final, 8.

[28] Preamble (52) IORPS.

[29] Preamble (5) MiFID II.

[30] Preamble (8) UCITS Directive.

[31] Proposal Solvency II, 8.

[32] Preamble (4) IORPS.

[33] Previous work is more limited as regards the scope of institutions covered, see, eg, Jens-Hinrich Binder, 'Corporate Governance of Financial Institution in Need of Cross-sectoral Regulation' in Danny Busch, Guido Ferrarini and Gerard Van Solinge, *Governance of Financial Institutions* (Oxford, OUP, 2019), who does not cover insurance companies. Our research also covers the recent Investment Firms Directive and Investment Firms Regulation, which we consider a good example of a proportionate approach to cross-sectoral financial regulation.

[34] A paper that takes a very similar approach to ours, but only studies the fit & proper tests, is: Danny Busch and Iris Palm-Steyerberg, 'Fit and proper requirements in EU financial regulation. Towards more cross-sectoral harmonisation?' in Danny Busch, Guido Ferrarini and Gerard Van Solinge, *Governance of Financial Institutions* (Oxford, OUP, 2019).

[35] Since the rules applicable to UCITS Directive management companies generally apply *mutatis mutandis* to UCITS Directive investment companies, we only study the former.

[36] On the use of corporate governance reforms for a variety of policy problems, see Mariana Pargendler, 'The Corporate Governance Obsession' (2016) 42 *The Journal of Corporation Law* 359.

[37] The role of corporate governance regulation to address systemic risk has not been uncontested, see Guido Ferrarini, 'Understanding the Role of Corporate Governance in Financial Institutions: A Research Agenda' [2017] ECGI Working Paper Series in Law 1.

this is dealt with in another chapter in this book.[38] In addition, we leave to future research the study of the implementation of the governance requirements at the level of the Member States,[39] and, where relevant, by the national supervisors.

Three conclusions can be drawn from our analysis of the corporate governance provisions across the financial sectors. Firstly, many of the differences between the regimes seem the result of a lack of coordination in adopting the various instruments, rather than of a thorough analysis of diverging identified market failures and their remedies. Secondly, some of the governance mechanisms used are of such a general nature that – even assuming significant differences in governance needs – it can validly be assumed that they would benefit the governance of all types of financial institutions. Thirdly, where differences in the regulatory framework are necessary, these differences can be found as much within sectors as across sectors. The systemic threat posed by different types of asset managers and their funds, eg, varies greatly. However, the existing governance regime focuses on the cross-sectoral divide, rather than on the differences within sectors.

The chapter proposes the idea of European cross-sectoral rules applicable to systemically important financial institutions, ideally via a high-level cross-sectoral directive or regulation based on – eg, as they seem most worked out in adequate detail – the governance rules in CRD IV. We appreciate that there may be a need to distinguish between the different business models and the way they present systemic risk and suggest that this can be achieved through technical implementation measures at level 2 taken by the Commission. This proposal complements other proposals[40] for financial regulation specific to systemically important institutions. In the US, for example, the Financial Stability Oversight Council (FSOC) has authority to designate non-bank financial institutions as 'systemically important' and subject them to higher prudential standards under the supervision of the Federal Reserve.[41] In this chapter, we contribute to the literature by focusing on the role of corporate governance provisions.

The chapter proceeds as follows. First, we analyse why financial institutions need specific corporate governance rules. Second, we discuss the scope of the different legislative instruments. Third, we engage in a thorough comparison between the different governance regimes. Finally, we propose a new framework for corporate governance in financial institutions, based on a cross-sectoral approach. As mentioned above, at the end of this chapter the reader also finds a summarising table, outlining the similarities and differences between the governance regimes in the different financial institutions, which should be read together with the second part. The third part will not reference the relevant articles in the legal instruments, except to the extent that they cannot be found in the table.

---

[38] See the contribution of Guido Ferrarini and Michele Siri further in this book.

[39] In Belgium, where the financial crisis struck particularly hard, the national legislator, looking forward to CRD IV, has in several instances made the deliberate choice to go further than what CRD IV imposes. Examples are the mandatory two-tier system (Art 21, §1, 1° Bank Law of 25 April 2014), or the prior approval of the regulator of so called 'special operations' (strategic decisions, substantial investments outside the banking sector, mergers and splits, transfer of businesses between banks (Art 77, Bank Law). In other instances, the Belgian legislator opted for a stricter interpretation, eg of the notion 'group' for purposes of calculating the maximum number of mandates a board member can assume (Art 62, Bank Law) or for the approval of loans to related parties of board members (Art 72, Bank Law).

[40] See, eg, Danny Busch and Mirik BJ van Rijn, 'Towards Single Supervision and Resolution of Systemically Important Non-Bank Financial Institutions in the European Union' (2018) 19 *European Business Organization Law Review* 301.

[41] Section 113 Dodd-Frank Act of 2010. Over time, four institutions have been designated as such. All four are now de-designated (www.treasury.gov/initiatives/fsoc/designations/Pages/default.aspx).

II. Why Do We Need a Special Governance Regime for Financial Institutions?

Corporate governance traditionally steers companies towards promoting shareholders' interests, which, in listed companies, can easily be measured by the company's stock price. The assumption is that doing so will maximise the aggregate welfare of all parties affected by the company's activities. Shareholders are supposed to have a financial interest in increasing the pie for all parties involved because, as the company's residual claimants, they receive all (and no more than) what is left after the company has paid its dues to other parties.[42] Yet, shareholders are seldom in a position to manage the company themselves and thus appoint directors and, indirectly, managers, to manage the company in their stead. One of the main challenges of corporate law is then to ensure that managers and directors do not prioritise their own interests over the shareholders' interests. This can, among other things, take the form of shirking responsibilities and stealing, but it can also manifest itself in unwarranted risk avoidance, given that their (human capital) investment is undiversified while tied up in the company.[43] In order to entice managers to maximise the stock price and not to avoid risk too much, corporate law deploys a wide range of strategies, including equity based executive remuneration, the presence of independent directors and shareholder approval requirements.[44]

Ironically, it was precisely such 'good' corporate governance mechanisms, ie those aimed at aligning the interests of managers and shareholders, that led bank managers to take too many risks in the run up to the financial crisis. To understand this, a consideration of the specific characteristics of financial institutions is indispensable. These are most salient in banks, where they include a maturity mismatch between assets and liabilities, systemic importance, explicit and implicit government guarantees, high leverage ratios and complex, opaque and easily substitutable assets, but are to a certain extent also present in non-bank financial institutions.

A. Maturity Transformation, Deposit Insurance and Implicit Guarantee

Liquidity production is the essence of banks' (and shadow banks'[45]) business model: banks provide illiquid loans to long-term borrowers on the basis of deposits for which depositors have liquid claims – they can withdraw their deposits at par value at any time.[46] For this maturity transformation, banks can charge a premium: borrowers who take a long-term loan from the bank will pay a higher interest rate than deposit holders will receive on their bank account. However, the maturity mismatch also risks causing a collective action problem among depositors. If large funds are withdrawn unexpectedly, individual depositors face a so-called 'prisoners' dilemma'. Collectively, they are usually better off if everyone leaves his or her money in his or her

---

[42] John Armour, Henry Hansmann, Reinier Kraakman and Mariana Pargendler, 'What is the Goal of Corporate Law?' in Reinier Kraakman et al. (eds), *The Anatomy of Corporate Law* 3rd edn (Oxford, OUP, 2017) 22–24.

[43] John Armour and Jeffrey N Gordon, 'Systemic Harms and Shareholder Value' (2014) 6 *Journal of Legal Analysis* 36.

[44] John Armour, Henry Hansmann and Reinier Kraakman, 'Agency Problems and Legal Strategies' in Reinier Kraakman et al. (eds), *The Anatomy of Corporate Law* 3rd edn (Oxford, OUP 2017) 29–30.

[45] FSB, Consultative Document. A Policy Framework for Strengthening Oversight and Regulation of Shadow Banking, 18 November 2002, ii.

[46] Christa HS Bouwman, in Allen N Berger, Philip Molyneux, and John OS Wilson (eds) *Oxford Handbook of Banking* 2nd edn (Oxford, OUP, 2014) 185–189.

bank account. However, depositors are unable to coordinate their reactions and hence they rush to withdraw their money before the bank's cash reserves are drained, knowing that banks keep only a fraction of deposits on reserve and will not be able to effect the last withdrawals.[47] Even the most solvent banks would not survive a bank run. To prevent this destructive mechanism from setting into motion, states organise a system of bank deposit insurance. Thus, depositors can rest assured that, no matter what, they will recover (at least part of) their money.

Deposit protection is, however, a double-edged sword. It weakens the incentives for creditors to properly monitor the bank's activities and constrain risk-seeking behaviour,[48] thus creating a problem of moral hazard on the part of the shareholders. In the absence of creditor monitoring, shareholders are encouraged to engage in even riskier activities and even to 'gamble for resurrection' in extreme situations for which normally no funding would be available (but for which it is now, thanks to deposit protection).[49] The financial crisis has indeed demonstrated that managers' performance-based remuneration incites them to seek excessively risky strategies as this increases the stock price.[50] Admittedly, deposit protection is mostly capped at a rather low amount and hence relevant only for small depositors, who would in any case have neither the habit nor the capacity to monitor efficiently.[51] The fact that bank debt is largely diffuse creates a collective action problem for scattered and small depositors.[52] More important, therefore, is the implicit deposit guarantee, which follows from the practice of states and central banks to save 'too big to fail' financial institutions (and financial institutions that governments do not want to fail for other, eg political reasons), to the extent this is still possible under BRRD. Non-depositor creditors anticipate such bailouts and content themselves with lower interest rates, which do not include full compensation for risk. Paradoxically, what is meant as a safety net thus increases risk taking,[53] although the move from bail-out to bail-in mechanisms should mitigate this effect. Moreover, the measures to contain problems in too big to fail institutions yield incentives to create, and effectively did create, even bigger financial institutions.[54]

Maturity transformation, the risk of a run and depositor insurance are less or not at all present in other financial institutions, but there are exceptions. Investment firms neither take deposits nor make significant or long-term loans, but mainly deal with financial instruments which cannot be withdrawn at short notice at par value.[55] The insurance business model does not involve short term funding or liquidity transformation, as the insured's claim is contingent on the materialisation of – mostly – idiosyncratic risk.[56] A drop in value of the investments by asset

---

[47] Douglas W Diamond and Philip H Dybvig, 'Bank Runs, Deposit Insurance, and Liquidity' (1983) 91 *Journal of Political Economy* 401; Jonathan R Macey and Maureen O'Hara, 'The Corporate Governance of Banks' (2003) 9 *FRBNY Economic Policy Review* 91, 97.

[48] Ross Levine, 'The Corporate Governance of Banks: A Concise Discussion of Concepts and Evidence' [2004] World Bank Policy Research Working Paper 3404.

[49] Marco Becht, Patrick Bolton and Ailsa Röell, 'Why Bank Governance is Different' (2011) 27 *Oxford Review of Economic Policy* 445.

[50] Lucian A Bebchuk and Holger Spamann, 'Regulating Bankers' Pay' (2020) 98 *Georgetown Law Journal* 247.

[51] Peter O Mülbert, 'Corporate Governance of Banks' (2009) 10 *European Business Organization Law Review* 411, 426.

[52] Luc Laeven, 'Corporate Governance: What's Special About Banks?' (2013) 5 *Annual Review of Financial Economics* 71–72.

[53] Allen N Berger, Richard J Herring and Giorgio P Szegö, 'The Role of Capital in Financial Institutions' (1995) 19 *Journal of Banking & Finance* 393; Hamid Mehran, Alan Morrison and Joel Shapiro, 'Corporate Governance and Banks: What Have we Learned from the Financial Crisis?' [2011] Federal Reserve Bank of New York Staff Report No 502, 4.

[54] Mark J Roe, 'Structural Corporate Degradation Due to Too-Big-to-Fail Finance' (2014) 162 *University of Pennsylvania Law Review* 1419; Saule T Omarova, 'The "Too Big To Fail" Problem' [2019] Cornell Law School research paper No 19-06, 3.

[55] Commission, Proposal for a Regulation on the prudential requirements of investment firms and amending IFR, MiFIR and EBA, 20 December 2017, COM(2017) 790 final, 2.

[56] Armour and others (n 15) 494.

managers is usually borne by the investors, thus preventing that withdrawal demands exceed available assets. However, open-ended funds, which offer short-term liquidity, are increasingly investing in illiquid assets, which in certain circumstances may render them prone to liquidity shortage in case of unanticipated large redemptions.[57] Also, hedge funds may find their investors withdrawing in the scenario where they would be forced to sell off assets rapidly, but this assumes that they are highly leveraged, invested in relatively illiquid assets, and not contractually limiting withdrawal rights – which they usually do.[58] Investors in private equity funds are usually locked in for the duration of the fund, thus preventing them from initiating a run on the fund.[59] Asset managers that offer immediate liquidity *and* fixed returns for investors are mainly to be found in the shadow banking system (eg money market funds), in which case, as stated above, the same reasoning applies as for traditional banking.[60] Similarly, investment banks that also transform liquid short-term funds into illiquid long-term assets are also subject to liquidity issues.[61]

B. Complexity, Opacity and Substitutability of Assets

A second special feature of banks are their notoriously complex and opaque balance sheets. The quality of bank loans and other bank investments (such as collateralised debt obligations) are not as easily observable to outsiders as the quality of assets of generic firms. This difficulty played a major role in the 2008 financial crisis and the crash of the interbank market, which showed that even banks were not in a position to assess other banks' levels of risk accurately.[62] In addition, banks can also rapidly modify the composition of their asset portfolio in comparison to regular firms, which mostly make more firm-specific investments. Even if the financial asset itself cannot be easily liquidated, such as long-term loans and mortgages, banks can transform them into liquid assets by means of securitisation.[63] Consequently, outsiders and even bank directors have a hard time keeping up to date with changes in a bank's risk profile.[64] This information asymmetry hampers creditors' ability to monitor the risk a bank has assumed and creates opportunities for risk-shifting.[65] Complexity and opacity also complicate the task of correctly calibrating

---

[57] ESRB, 'Macroprudential Policy Beyond Banking: An ESRB Strategy Paper', July 2016, 11; FSB, 'Policy Recommendations to Address Structural Vulnerabilities from Asset Management Activities' (2017) 11–12.

[58] Armour and others (n 15) 490.

[59] Ibid, 491.

[60] Armour and others (n 15) 478; Christoph Van der Elst, 'Corporate Governance and Banks: How Justified is the Match?' [2015] ECGI Law Working Paper No 284, 7.

[61] The investment bank Lehman Brothers, eg, financed its investments – such as securitised mortgages – with short-term wholesale funding. When this short-term funding dried up during the crisis, it was forced to sell off illiquid assets at fire sale prices, which led to its crash (FGB Graaf and RA Stegeman, *Regulering van de OTC-Derivatenmarkten in de EU en de VS* (Deventer, Kluwer, 2011) 35–37).

[62] Peter O Mülbert, 'Corporate Governance of Banks' (2009) 10 *European Business Organization Law Review* 411, 420–421.

[63] Marco Becht, Patrick Bolton and Ailsa Röell, 'Why Bank Governance is Different' (2011) 27 *Oxford Review of Economic Policy* 445; Peter O Mülbert, 'Corporate Governance of Banks' (2009) 10 *European Business Organization Law Review* 411, 424–425.

[64] Ibid, 438.

[65] Luc Laeven, 'Corporate Governance: What's Special About Banks?' (2013) 5 Annual Review of Financial Economics 67; Ross Levine, 'The Corporate Governance of Banks: A Concise Discussion of Concepts and Evidence' [2004] World Bank Policy Research Working Paper 3404.

incentive pay for executives.[66] Inversely, both complexity and the rapid transformability of a financial portfolio allow managers and shareholders to mold a bank's risk profile so as to increase managers' performance based remuneration respectively to shareholder returns.[67]

Most other financial institutions generally do not feature the same degree of complexity and opacity of assets as banks.[68] Information asymmetry is a real issue, however, in insurance firms, due to the combination of complexity of the business and dispersion of and little insurance expertise among policyholders and insurance beneficiaries (except in the reinsurance business).[69] Complexity has also been increasing in the financial world generally, including not only shadow banking activities,[70] but also for instance in the asset management business,[71] which may render them more complex than the least convoluted banks.

C. High Leverage Ratio

A third special characteristic of banks is that they are highly leveraged, although they have significantly deleveraged under pressure of stricter Basel III capital requirements. The proportion of equity on their balance sheet is multiple times smaller than in other industries.[72] This inherently follows from the business model of banks, which consists of transforming short-term deposits into long-term loans and thus presupposes numerous investments by depositors and bondholders.[73] Moreover, leverage is stimulated by government guarantees since – as explained above – it makes debt a cheap source of financing. High leverage significantly distorts the incentives of shareholders and management towards inordinate risk-taking. Due to high leverage, shareholders stand to lose even less upon failure than is already the case in regular companies as a consequence of limited liability. Hence, it is rational for them to gamble upon a risky strategy which will bring in more revenue if it turns out well, while most of the costs will be borne by the creditors if it fails.[74] Similarly, for managers with equity based remuneration, a high degree of leverage increases the incentive to take risk.[75]

---

[66] John Armour, 'Bank Governance' in Jeffrey N Gordon and Wolf-Georg Ringe (eds), *The Oxford Handbook of Corporate Law and Governance* (Oxford, OUP, 2018) 1114.

[67] Peter O Mülbert, 'Corporate Governance of Banks' (2009) 10 *European Business Organization Law Review* 411, 425.

[68] Jens-Hinrich Binder, 'Corporate Governance of Financial Institution in Need of Cross-sectoral Regulation' in Danny Busch, Guido Ferrarini and Gerard Van Solinge, *Governance of Financial Institutions* (Oxford, OUP, 2019) 38.

[69] OECD Guidelines on Insurer Governance (2017) 44–46; Donald P Morgan, 'Rating Banks: Risk and Uncertainty in an Opaque Industry' (2002) 92 *American Economic Review* 874–875; Arthur Van den Hurk and Michele Siri, 'Comparative Regulation of Corporate Governance in the Insurance Sector' in Danny Busch, Guido Ferrarini and Gerard Van Solinge, *Governance of Financial Institutions* (Oxford, OUP, 2019), 65.

[70] Jaime Caruana, 'Financial Regulation, Complexity and Innovation', 2014 www.bis.org/speeches/sp140604.htm.

[71] See Claire Célérier and Boris Vallée, 'What Drives Financial Complexity? A Look into the Retail Market for Structured Products' [2013] HEC Research Paper Series No 1013.

[72] Christoph Van der Elst, 'Corporate Governance and Banks: How Justified is the Match?' [2015] ECGI Law Working Paper No 284, 10.

[73] John Armour, 'Bank Governance' in Jeffrey N Gordon and Wolf-Georg Ringe (eds), *The Oxford Handbook of Corporate Law and Governance* (Oxford, OUP, 2018) 1112.

[74] Guido Ferrarini, 'Understanding the Role of Corporate Governance in Financial Institutions: A Research Agenda' [2017] ECGI Law Working Paper No 347.

[75] Marco Becht, Patrick Bolton and Ailsa Röell, 'Why Bank Governance is Different' (2011) 27 *Oxford Review of Economic Policy* 446.

High leverage ratios are also typical of investment banks[76] and hedge funds,[77] but less so of other financial institutions.[78] The average leverage ratio in the investment funds sector is many times lower than in the banking sector,[79] as a consequence of differences in both their activities and regulatory constraints[80] on balance sheet leverage.[81] The insurance business model does not involve leverage either: as a consequence of their inverted production cycle, insurers instead receive premiums well before liabilities will be paid or even known or realised.[82] Yet, there are exceptions in both directions. For instance, not all hedge funds use leverage, while some other types of funds do resort to significant leverage.[83] Leverage positions do not only yield incentives to take more risk, but can also increase the risk of fire-sales,[84] which brings us to the next feature: systemic risk.

D. Systemic Importance and Fragility

All three of the above factors induce a bank to take more risks. Regulators are particularly concerned about this in financial institutions where risk can take on a systemic dimension. In contrast to idiosyncratic risk, which affects only a single institution or asset (and the involved parties), systemic risk implies that the failure of one firm causes a chain of failures of other firms.[85] As a consequence of the interconnection of the financial system (liabilities of one financial firm are assets on the balance sheet of another) as well as the importance of trust in the entire sector, difficulties of one single firm can spread through contagion to other financial institutions. An exacerbating factor is that, as a consequence of their maturity transformation business model, many banks are particularly vulnerable to spikes in liquidity demand or drops in the value of their liquid assets. The real economy is also likely to be affected, because of banks' role as creditors to the real economy and the importance of liquidity and the payment system. This is a classic example of externalisation: the social losses of failure of systemic institutions exceed by far the

---

[76] Alessandro Barattieri, Laura Moretti and Vincenzo Quadrini, 'Banks Interconnectivity and Leverage' [2018] ESG Montreal Working Paper No. 5, 28.

[77] Andrew Ang, Sergiy Gorovyy and Gregory B van Inwegen, 'Hedge Fund Leverage' (2011) 102 *Journal of Financial Economics* 102.

[78] ESRB, Macroprudential Policy Beyond Banking: An ESRB Strategy Paper, July 2016, www.esrb.europa.eu/pub/pdf/reports/20160718_strategy_paper_beyond_banking.en.pdf, 5.

[79] ECB Occasional Paper, Shadow Banking in the Euro Area: Risks and Vulnerabilities in the investment fund sector, June 2016, www.ecb.europa.eu/pub/pdf/scpops/ecbop174.en.pdf, 26; ESRB EU Shadow Banking Monitor 27 July 2016, 11.

[80] Article 83, UCITS Directive (recast). National authorities often also enact leverage restrictions under Art 25, AIFMD.

[81] AMIC/EFAMA Joint Paper: Use of Leverage in Investment Funds in Europe, July 2017, www.efama.org/Publications/Public/170719_AMIC%20EFAMA%20leverage%20paper.pdf, 4.

[82] EIOPA, 'Discussion Paper on Systemic Risk and Macroprudential Policy in Insurance', 29 March 2019, EIOPA-BoS-19/131, 20–21.

[83] Armour and others (n 15) 489; Fernando Avalos, Ramon Moreno and Tania Romero, 'Leverage on the Buy-Side' [2015] BIS Working Papers No 517, 3.

[84] Fernando Avalos, Ramon Moreno and Tania Romero, 'Leverage on the Buy-Side' [2015] BIS Working Papers No 517, 26; Jeremy Stein, 'Presidential Address: Sophisticated Investors and Market Efficiency' [2009] *Journal of Finance* 5131. See, however, AMIC/EFAMA Joint Paper: Use of Leverage in Investment Funds in Europe, July 2017, www.efama.org/Publications/Public/170719_AMIC%20EFAMA%20leverage%20paper.pdf, 21.

[85] Since the financial crisis it is generally accepted that systemic risk not only arises from the failure of an individual bank (ie the micro-prudential perspective on systemic risk), but can also arise from a wider variety of shocks in markets or financial institutions (ie macro-prudential perspective on systemic risk).

costs incurred by their shareholders.[86] In recognition of this, the FSB has since 2011 published a list of global systemically important banks on its website.[87]

Non-bank financial institutions can present a danger to the financial system as well,[88] and this danger intensifies as financial institutions become more interconnected and leveraged. MiFID II expressly refers to systemic stability considerations as a key driver for governance regulation of investment firms.[89]

Admittedly, insurance companies are considered less risky and less susceptible to runs than banks and are unlikely to have a contagious effect on other financial institutions or the real economy, but in certain situations they can generate systemic risk. This is particularly so if they provide non-traditional insurance products and are interconnected with other SIFIs.[90] The AIG debacle and subsequent bail-out during the crisis serves as the perfect example.[91] The FSB started publishing a list of global systemically important insurance companies in 2013.[92] However, it has recently announced that it will not update this list.[93] In the US, FSOC – which has the authority to designate non-bank financial institutions as systemically important[94] – had originally designated three insurers as systemically important, namely AIG,[95] Prudential,[96] and MetLife.[97] In the literature, the FSOC designations have been critiqued for being too vague, subjective, and inconsiderate of the specifics of the insurance companies in question.[98] Since then, AIG has lost its designation after making significant changes to its business, including reducing the size of its balance sheet and its reliance on short-term funding.[99] MetLife successfully challenged its designation in court, leading to a rescission, because the designation was considered 'arbitrary and capricious'.[100] Finally, on 18 October 2018, Prudential Financial, the last systemically important financial institution, has also been de-designated,[101] even though Prudential did not shrink or simplify itself.[102] This coincides with an announced change of policy by the Trump

---

[86] John Armour and Jeffrey N Gordon, 'Systemic Harms and Shareholder Value' (2014) 6 *Journal of Legal Analysis* 40–41; Paul Davies and Klaus Hopt, 'Non-Shareholder Voice in Bank Governance: Board Composition, Performance and Liability' in Danny Busch, Guido Ferrarini and Gerard van Solinge (eds), *Governance of Financial Institutions* (Oxford, OUP, 2019).

[87] FSB, '2017 List of Global Systemically Important Banks (G-SIBs)' 1.

[88] See Jeremy C Kress, Patricia A McCoy and D Schwarz, 'Regulating entities and activities: complementary approaches to nonbank systemic risk' (2018) *Southern California Law Review* (forthcoming), available at ssrn.com: 'Over the last decade, a consensus has emerged among policymakers and academics that systemic risk is not confined to the traditional banking sector'.

[89] MiFID 2, Recital 5. For criticism, see Jens-Hinrich Binder, 'Governance of Investment Firms under MiFID II' in Danny Busch and Guido Ferrarini (eds), *Regulation of the EU financial markets*: MiFID II and MiFIR (2017) 60–61.

[90] EIOPA, 'Discussion Paper on Systemic Risk and Macroprudential Policy in Insurance', 29 March 2019, EIOPA-BoS-19/131, 12–14 and 21; Armour and others (n 15) 495.

[91] For a detailed analysis of systemic risks in the insurance sector, see Armour and others (n 15) 495–500.

[92] FSB, 'Review of the List of Global Systemically Important Insurers' 1.

[93] FSB, 'FSB statement on identification of global systemically important insurers' (2017), www.fsb.org/2017/11/fsb-statement-on-identification-of-global-systemically-important-insurers/.

[94] Section 113, Dodd-Frank Act.

[95] FSOC, 'Basis of the Financial Stability Oversight Council's Final Determination Regarding American International Group, Inc.' (2013).

[96] Ibid.

[97] FSOC, 'Basis for the Financial Stability Oversight Council's Final Determination Regarding MetLife, Inc.' (2014).

[98] Jacob Wimberly, 'SIFI Designation of Insurance Companies-How Game Theory Illustrates the FSOC's Faulty Conception of Systemic Risk' (2014) 34 *Review of Banking & Finance Law* 337.

[99] FSOC, 'Notice and Explanation of the Basis for the Financial Stability Oversight Council's Rescission of Its Determination Regarding American International Group, Inc. (AIG)' (2017).

[100] *MetLife, Inc. v Financial Stability Oversight Council*, 15-cv-00045 (United States District Court 2016).

[101] FSOC, 'Notice and Explanation of the Basis for the Financial Stability Oversight Council's Rescission of Its Determination Regarding Prudential Financial, Inc.' (2018).

[102] See (very critically): Jeremy C Kress, 'The last SIFI: the unwise and illegal deregulation of Prudential Financial' (forthcoming, 2018) 71 *Stanford Law Review* online, available at ssrn.com.

administration from an entity-based approach to an activities-based approach,[103] although the activities-based regulation has not yet materialised so far. These evolutions demonstrate two things: first, it may not be easy to identify systemically important insurance companies; and second, the insurance companies themselves surely are not neutral towards such qualification, which indicates that it has an impact on their functioning. Nevertheless, the recent trend away from designating systemically important financial institutions (and towards an 'activities-based approach') has received vehement criticism in the literature.[104]

Similarly, the asset management industry is generally not as fragile as banks and entails low levels of systemic risk.[105] However, asset managers vary widely in terms of form and nature of their business. In its 2017 report, the FSB identifies four areas of structural fragility of the asset management business, among which the first two are considered the key issues: '(i) liquidity mismatch between fund investments and redemption terms and conditions for open-ended fund units; (ii) leverage within investment funds; (iii) operational risk and challenges at asset managers in stressed conditions; and (iv) securities lending activities of asset managers and funds.'[106] This brings AIFs, UCITS Directive, pension funds and their managers into the regulatory spotlights of the prudential regulator. The systemic importance of hedge funds, in particular, has been put under scrutiny, especially highly leveraged hedge funds.[107] Less leveraged 'plain vanilla' funds, however, have also been put forward as systemically risky, eg when large redemptions by investors in distressed times can result in asset price movements.[108] Whether or not asset managers and their funds present risks will depend on the specific characteristics of each fund. A highly leveraged hedge fund with illiquid assets is more likely to create systemic instability than a private equity fund where capital is locked-in for, eg, ten years and no liquidity problems can arise.[109]

E. Consequences for Corporate Governance in Financial Institutions

A first conclusion from the above analysis concerns the goal of corporate governance in financial institutions. Against the backdrop of shareholder incentives and ample opportunities to engage in overly risky activities, and the immense societal costs this engenders, the focus of traditional corporate governance on shareholders' interests and stimulating risk taking does not seem appropriate in the context of financial institutions, in particular, but not only, banks. Indeed, stronger

---

[103] US Department of the Treasury, 'Financial Stability Oversight Council Designations – Report to the President of the United States pursuant to the Presidential Memorandum Issued April 21 (2017), 19, www.treasury.gov/press-center/news/Pages/Treasury-Releases-Memorandum-to-the-President-on-FSOCs-Designation.aspx.

[104] Jeremy C Kress, Patricia A McCoy and D Schwarz, 'Regulating entities and activities: complementary approaches to nonbank systemic risk' (2018) *Southern California Law Review* (forthcoming), available at ssrn.com. Their main argument is that an entities-based approach to regulation of systemic risk is complementary to an activities-based approach: certain individual activities may not be risky in isolation, but may contribute to systemic risk in combination with other individual activities and with poor risk management. They argue that '[a]n activities-based approach is inherently blind to this cumulative nature of a firm's systemic risk profile' (p 7), in contrast to the entities-based approach.

[105] Armour and others (n 15) 479 and 503.

[106] FSB, 'Policy Recommendations to Address Structural Vulnerabilities from Asset Management Activities' (2017) 9.

[107] A Kaal Wulf and Timothy A Krause, 'Hedge Funds and Systemic Risk' in H Kent Baker and Greg Filbeck (eds), *Hedge funds : structure, strategies, and performance* (Oxford, OUP, 2017).

[108] IMF, 'The Asset Management Industry and Financial Stability', *Global Financial Stability Report: Navigating Monetary Policy Challenges and Managing Risks* (2015).

[109] For an overview of systemic risk presented by the different types of funds, see Armour and others (n 15) 478–504.

and more shareholder-focused corporate governance structures and boards of directors have been found to be associated with higher levels of systemic risk.[110] Further, banks in which shareholders had stronger shareholder rights were more likely to be bailed out during the financial crisis;[111] bank risk is generally higher in banks that have large shareholders with substantial cash flow rights;[112] shareholder control was associated with higher profits in the years before the crisis but also with larger losses and a higher likelihood of requiring government assistance during the crisis compared to manager-controlled banks;[113] and larger shareholdings of lower-level management and non-CEO higher-level management significantly increase banks' probability of failure.[114] Focusing directors and managers on shareholders' interests had similar effects.[115]

The idea is therefore gaining ground that corporate governance in banks and certain other financial institutions should move from shareholder orientation towards corporate governance that centers around debtholders rather than shareholders, or 'creditor governance'.[116] Such an approach may better reconcile the goals of corporate law with the goals of financial law, namely the stability of both financial institutions and the financial system as a whole. The Basel Committee on Banking Supervision followed suit in the introduction to the Corporate Governance principles for banks, which proclaims: 'The primary objective of corporate governance should be safeguarding stakeholders' interest in conformity with public interest on a sustainable basis. Among stakeholders, particularly with respect to retail banks, shareholders' interest would be secondary to depositors' interest.' In academic literature, proposals have been made to include creditor or supervisory agency representatives on bank boards,[117] but these proposals have also been criticised.[118] Regulators and supervisors can assume the monitoring function of small depositors in their attempts to safeguard financial stability and in so doing partially substitute for insufficient creditor governance.[119] However, for regulators as well it is difficult to ascertain the quality of financial assets and thus to monitor and control bank risk taking.[120] Specifically in the field of corporate governance, regulators also impose suitability requirements on bank

---

[110] Jamshed Iqbal, Sascha Strobl and Sami Vähämaa, 'Corporate Governance and the Systemic Risk of Financial Institutions' (2015) 82 *Journal of Economics and Business* 42.

[111] Daniel Ferreira, David Kershaw, Tim Kirchmaier and Edmund-Philipp Schuster, 'Measuring Management Insulation from Shareholder Pressure' [2016] LSE Legal Studies Working Paper No 01.

[112] Luc Laeven and Ross Levine, 'Bank Governance: Regulation and Risk Taking' (2009) 93 *Journal of Financial Economics* 259.

[113] Reint Gropp and Matthias Köhler, 'Bank Owners or Bank Managers: Who is Keen on Risk? Evidence from the Financial Crisis' [2010] European Business School Research Paper No 10-02 https://papers.ssrn.com/sol3/papers.cfm?abstract_id=1555663.

[114] Allen Berger, Björn Imbierowicz, Christian Rauch, 'The Roles of Corporate Governance in Bank Failures during the Recent Financial Crisis' (2016) 48 *Journal of Money, Credit and Banking* 729.

[115] Rüdiger Fahlenbrach and René M Stulz, 'Bank CEO Incentives and the Credit Crisis' (2011) 99 *Journal of Financial Economics* 11; Shams Pathan, 'Strong Boards, CEO Power and Bank Risk-taking' (2009) 33 *Journal of Banking and Finance* 1340.

[116] Jens Hagendorff, 'Corporate Governance in Banking' in Allen N Berger, Philip Molyneux, and John OS Wilson (eds), *Oxford Handbook of Banking* 2nd edn (Oxford, OUP, 2014) 139, 155; Klaus J Hopt, 'Corporate Governance von Finanzinstituten' [2017] *Zeitschrift für Unternehmens- und Gesellschaftsrecht* 438, 446.

[117] Eg Marco Becht, 'The Governance of Financial Institutions in Crisis' in Stefan Grundmann et al. (eds), *Festschrift für Klaus J. Hopt zum 70. Geburtstag, II* (De Gruyter, 2010) 1625–1626.

[118] For an evaluation see, Paul Davies and Klaus Hopt, 'Non-Shareholder Voice in Bank Governance: Board Composition, Performance and Liability', in Danny Busch, Guido Ferrarini and Gerard van Solinge (eds), *Governance of Financial Institutions* (Oxford, OUP, 2019).

[119] Peter O Mülbert, 'Corporate Governance of Banks' (2009) 10 *European Business Organization Law Review* 429.

[120] John Armour, 'Bank Governance' in Jeffrey N Gordon and Wolf-Georg Ringe, *The Oxford Handbook of Corporate Law and Governance* (Oxford, OUP, 2018) 1113.

shareholders in response to the problem of irresponsible shareholders, although these also have the effect of hampering the discipline of takeovers.[121]

A second lesson for corporate governance in most financial institutions highlights the special importance of sound risk management, in particular when risk may be of a systemic nature. Risk is an integral and unavoidable part of financial institutions, but it must be understood and managed well.[122] According to the OECD, the widespread failure in this regard was perhaps one of the greatest shocks of the financial crisis.[123] There is indeed empirical evidence that bank holding companies with more risk controls took less risk and fared better during the 2008 financial crisis.[124] This led to calls not only for risk committees at board level, but also for risk management functions at manager level and below.[125]

A third lesson follows from the high complexity of the business of many financial institutions, especially – but not only – banks and insurers. Setting correct incentives for directors and management is not the only relevant concern – qualification and experience are equally important. This was all too frequently overlooked during the pre-crisis focus on independence. Many bank board members struggled or failed to understand and handle the complexities and risks of modern banking,[126] a shortcoming which was found to correlate with and even cause losses in certain banks.[127] Independent directors, who did not meet expectations in non-financial corporate governance either, were correlated with *larger* shareholder losses in banks during the financial crisis.[128] More than in non-financial firms, corporate governance of financial firms should pay attention to board composition, specialisation, induction and training of directors and managers.

III. Scope of the Legislative Instruments

Before we delve deeper into a cross-sectoral comparison of the different governance regimes, we briefly sketch the scope of the different legislative instruments. First, at the moment, the corporate governance provisions in CRD IV apply to both banks ('credit institutions') and most investment firms. However, some investment firms are currently excluded from the scope of CRD IV, mainly so-called 'local firms' and firms that provide only certain limited investment services and

[121] Jens Hagendorff, 'Corporate Governance in Banking' in Allen N Berger, Philip Molyneux, and John OS Wilson (eds), *Oxford Handbook of Banking* 2nd edn (Oxford, OUP, 2014) 152; Luc Laeven, 'Corporate Governance: What's Special About Banks?' (2013) 5 *Annual Review of Financial Economics* 71.

[122] Klaus J Hopt, 'Corporate Governance of Banks after the Financial Crisis' in Eddy Wymeersch, Klaus J Hopt and Guido Ferrarini (eds), *Financial Regulation and Supervision* (Oxford, OUP, 2012) 344.

[123] OECD, 'Corporate Governance and the Financial Crisis: Key Findings and Main Messages' (2009) 8.

[124] Andrew Ellul and Vijay Yerramilli, 'Stronger Risk Controls, Lower Risk: Evidence from US Bank Holding Companies' (2013) 68 *The Journal of Finance* 1757. See also, Vincent Aebi, Gabriele Sabato and Markus Schmid, 'Risk Management, Corporate Governance, and Bank Performance in the Financial Crisis' (2012) 36 *Journal of Banking and Finance* 321.

[125] Peter O Mülbert, 'Corporate Governance of Banks' (2009) 10 *European Business Organization Law Review* 433–434; Klaus J Hopt, 'Corporate Governance of Banks after the Financial Crisis' in Eddy Wymeersch, Klaus J Hopt and Guido Ferrarini (eds), *Financial Regulation and Supervision* (Oxford, OUP, 2012) 357–358.

[126] Klaus J Hopt, 'Corporate Governance of Banks after the Financial Crisis' in Eddy Wymeersch, Klaus J Hopt and Guido Ferrarini (eds), *Financial Regulation and Supervision* (Oxford, OUP, 2012) 345.

[127] Harald Hau and Marcel Thum, 'Subprime Crisis and Board (In-) Competence: Private vs. Public Banks in Germany' [2010], www.haraldhau.com/EP_Bank_Governance_83.pdf.

[128] David Erkens, Mingyi Hung and Pedro Matos, 'Corporate Governance in the 2007–2008 Financial Crisis: Evidence from Financial Institutions Worldwide' (2012) 18 *Journal of Corporate Finance* 389. See however, for independent directors on audit and risk committees: Yin-Hua Yeh, Huimin Chung, Chih-Liang Liu, 'Committee Independence and Financial Institution Performance during the 2007–08 Credit Crunch: Evidence from a Multi-country Study' (2011) 19 *Corporate Governance: An International Review* 437. Before the crisis, independent directors did not make much difference: Renée B Adams and Hamid Mehran, 'Bank Board Structure and Performance: Evidence for Large Bank Holding Companies' (2012) 21 *Journal of Financial Intermediation* 243.

do not hold money or securities belonging to their clients (see the definition of 'investment firm' in Article 4(1)(2), CRR). All investment firms are in principle also covered by MiFID II, which also includes some corporate governance provisions. Finally, an exception to the rule that the corporate governance provisions of CRD IV apply to both banks and investment firms is that the rules on the suitability of shareholders only apply to banks, but MiFID II contains equivalent provisions (see further in section IV B).

Under Article 61 of the Investment Firms Directive, CRD IV would be amended to exclude investment firms from its scope, so that investment firms are only governed by the Investment Firms Directive, the Investment Firms Regulation and by MiFID II, all of which contain some governance provisions that apply in principle to all investment firms. Technically, this is done by replacing the word 'institution' with 'credit institution', by striking out the word 'investment firm' in several places, and by redefining 'institution' in CRD IV. However, some types of investment firms will continue to be treated as 'credit institutions' under CRD IV, more specifically, those investment firms that engage in 'dealing on own account' or 'underwriting of financial instruments and/or placing of financial instruments on a firm commitment basis' and that exceed a certain size (in general assets of more than EUR 30 billion). Technically, this is accomplished by changing the definition of credit institution in CRD IV as to include these types of investment firms (see Article 63(3), Investment Firms Regulation).

The UCITS V Directive applies to 'undertakings for collective investment in transferable securities (UCITS) Directive', which can only invest in a limited range of assets (transferable securities and liquid assets, according to the principle of risk-spreading) and should have redeemable units (Article 1, UCITS V Directive). AIFMD applies to 'alternative investment funds (AIFs)', which are all other funds than UCITS funds, but contains some exemptions for (generally speaking) AIFs with assets under management under EUR 100 million, or under EUR 500 million when the AIFs are unleveraged and when redemption rights are only exercisable after more than five years (Articles 1, 3 and 4(1)(a), AIFMD). The IORP Directive applies to pensions funds, called 'institutions for occupational retirement provision (IORPs)' (Article 1), with the definition provided in Article 6(1) and some exemptions in Article 2. Solvency II applies to (life and non-life) insurance undertakings and reinsurance undertakings (Article 2 – with some exemptions in Article 3), but for the purposes of this article, we refer to all of these firms as 'insurance companies'.

Finally, many of the instruments above contain provisions that only apply to certain groups of financial institutions within their scope. The requirement to have a risk, remuneration and nomination committee, eg, only applies to 'significant' institutions under CRD IV (Articles 76, 88 and 95), and the requirement to have a remuneration committee applies only to significant UCITS management companies (Article 14b(4), UCITS V Directive), significant AIFMs (Annex II(3), AIFMD) and significant insurance companies (Article 275(1)(f), Delegated Regulation Solvency II). 'Significant' is typically defined in general terms, referring to the institution's 'size, internal organisation and the nature, scope and complexity of their activities'. For banks and investment firms, these criteria are concretised in the EBA Guidelines on Internal Governance, the EBA/ESMA Suitability Guidelines and the EBA Remuneration Guidelines, as 'global systemically important institutions' (G-SIIs), 'other systemically important institutions' (O-SIIs) (as defined in Article 131, CRD IV) and other institutions that Member States have designated as significant based on their 'size and, internal organisation, and the nature, scope and complexity of their activities'. For AIFMs and UCITS management companies, the criteria are concretised in the respective ESMA Remuneration Guidelines. For insurance companies, Article 275(1)(f), Delegated Regulation Solvency II only stipulates that significance is measured 'in terms of size and internal organisation', without any further specification in guidelines by EIOPA. While the initial commission proposals regarding the Investment Firms Directive just used the concept 'significance' without concretising it, the version adopted by the European Parliament replaced this general concept with a concrete figure regarding asset size that serves as the threshold for application of the provisions.[129] When this chapter uses the term 'significant', it refers to these legally defined concepts. When we refer to a 'systemic' or 'systemically important' institution, on the other hand, we use the term from a functional rather than a regulatory perspective.

The new regime for investment firms takes this approach that distinguishes between significant and non-significant institutions one step further: the largest and riskiest investment firms are subject to the more stringent CRD IV regime, while the so-called 'small and non-interconnected investment firms' are not subject to the corporate governance provisions (Article 25, Investment Firms Directive iuncto Article 12).

IV. A Cross-Sectoral Comparison of Governance in Financial Institutions

A. General Standards of Corporate Governance

Turning to a comparison of the substantive governance provisions, we start with the general standards of corporate governance. Under CRD IV, banks and investment firms are subject to such a general standard: they must have 'robust governance arrangements', including a clear organisational structure and consistent lines of responsibility, effective risk identification and monitoring processes, adequate internal control mechanisms, etc. This standard is subject to a proportionality principle.

Under the new Investment Firms Directive and Investment Firms Regulation, non-systemic investment firms would no longer be subject to CRD IV, but the same standard has been copied almost word for word. However, small and non-interconnected investment firms are excluded from its application.

Insurance companies are subject to a similar general standard for corporate governance, but worded slightly differently: they are to have an 'effective system of governance which provides for sound and prudent management of the business', including 'a transparent organisation structure', 'appropriate segregation of responsibilities', 'regular internal review', etc. A proportionality principle likewise applies. In spite of the similar but nevertheless significantly different wording, little difference seems to have been intended from a substantive point of view. This prompts the question of whether an identically phrased uniform general standard would not have been preferable.

A similar conclusion can be reached for UCITS management companies, AIFMs and IORPs: each of them is subject to an elaborate general standard for corporate governance, and they are all quite similar in content, but worded differently.

In conclusion, the question is whether there are some general governance principles that are common to more than one sector. It should be further looked into whether either a uniformly worded level 1 governance standard could be introduced, whereby the distinctions that are still required are worked out at level 2 or level 3; or alternatively, to increase the cross-sectoral character of the level 3 guidelines. In view of the general nature of this standard and the low level of current convergence, further convergence, though useful, does not seem to be the first priority.

---

[129] See Art 28(4) (on the risk committee) and Art 33(1) (on the remuneration committee) of the Investment Firms Directive, which refer to the criteria in point (a) of Art 32(4).

B. Suitability of Shareholders

Under CRD IV, banks have to inform the competent authorities of the identity of their qualifying shareholders before the start of their activities, and when the shareholders change or further increase their shareholding; the same principle applies to investment firms (under MiFID II) and to insurance companies (under Solvency II). UCITS V Directive also applies the rules for investment firms under MiFID II to UCITS management companies.

The moments in time and the criteria for reviewing shareholders are the same for banks, investment firms, insurance companies and UCITS management companies. The definition of 'qualifying holding' is also identical in CRD IV, UCITS V Directive and Solvency II, while the definition in MiFID II and in AIFMD is nearly identical, except that they refer to the rules of calculation in the Transparency Directive, while the other definitions do not. This high level of convergence is not surprising, as suitability as shareholders for a financial institution is to be tested on the basis of criteria that measure integrity and correctness in behaviour, an approach that seems to be common across sectors.

On the other hand, AIFMD only contains a very limited principle of shareholder suitability: Article 8(1)(d), AIFMD only refers to the condition of shareholder suitability for authorisation and Article 11(c) provides for the possibility for the competent authorities to withdraw the authorisation if this condition is no longer fulfilled. But these provisions only encompass a few sentences, in contrast to the detailed provisions on the time periods, procedure and criteria for shareholder suitability in the other instruments.

Finally, no shareholder suitability is required for IORPs, which is logical, as the members or beneficiaries of IORPs cannot be assimilated to shareholders.

In conclusion, there is a very high level of convergence on the topic of suitability of shareholders for banks, investment firms, insurance companies and UCITS management companies at level 1, with (nearly) identical provisions. This can be explained because Directive 2007/44/EC[130] introduced these provisions for insurance companies, banks and investment firms. Another example of the high degree of cross-sectoral convergence on this topic are the joint EBA/ESMA/EIOPA guidelines (level 3), which explicitly aim at harmonising the framework of shareholders' suitability, so that they are treated in the same manner both in the entire EU and across the three sectors. The guidelines cover the definitions of acting in concert, significant influence, and the decision to acquire, as well as the proportionality principle, the assessment period, the information to be provided (including a harmonised list), and the five assessment criteria. However, of the institutions we study, the guidelines only cover banks, insurance companies and investment firms, but not UCITS management companies or AIFMs. For UCITS management companies, this is especially puzzling, given the fact that UCITS V Directive specifically refers to the MiFID II regime. The gap in the guidelines also shows that the cross-sectoral convergence has not yet been fully extended to AIFMs. It is hard to come up with a good reason why this is the case, especially in comparison to UCITS management companies, and especially since the principle also applies to AIFMs, only in a less detailed manner. One potential explanation is that AIFMs have traditionally been less regulated than UCITS management companies; but for other governance provisions, the regulation of AIFMs is actually more detailed (see further in sections IV C and D, on induction and training, collective suitability, and independence of mind of directors).

---

[130] European Parliament and Council Dir 2007/44/EC of 5 September 2007 amending Council Dir 92/49/EEC and Dirs 2002/83/EC, 2004/39/EC, 2005/68/EC and 2006/48/EC as regards procedural rules and evaluation criteria for the prudential assessment of acquisitions and increase of holdings in the financial sector [2007] OJ L247/1.

Finally, it remains to be seen whether the cross-sectoral convergence that has been accomplished in the legal instruments is also present in supervisory practice. Obviously, the answer could differ depending on whether the suitability of shareholders is assessed by the same (division within) financial supervisors, which shows that this question is also linked with the structure of financial supervision, a topic addressed in another part of this book.

C. Fit and Proper Tests

On 'fit & proper' tests, there appears to be a high level of uniformity between the selected institutions at first sight, as all of the institutions that we study have suitability requirements for their managers. It should be noted that investment firms are covered by the fit & proper rules in both CRD IV and MiFID II, which is relevant considering the fact that CRD IV excludes some types of investment firms from its scope.

Despite the apparent similarity, a closer study reveals that (1) there are many subtle and confusing differences in wording and definitions used and (2) there are some notable differences in the scope of the provisions. In all of the institutions that we study, it is required that managers are assessed by the financial supervisor on an individual basis for their 'sufficiently good repute' (proper) and on an individual and collective basis for their 'knowledge, skills and experience' (fit). There are two exceptions to this last rule: in IORPs, the knowledge, skills and experience are only assessed on a collective (and not individual) basis; in contrast, in UCITS management companies, the knowledge, skills and experience are only assessed on an individual (and not collective) basis. These differences seem arbitrary and no justification is offered for them by the legislator. In our opinion, it is likely that this is the consequence of careless drafting rather than of a conscious policy choice.

In banks and investment firms (both before and after the new investment firms regime), two additional assessment criteria are added: the requirement for managers to possess 'independence of mind' and the requirement to commit 'sufficient time' to the exercise of their function, the latter requirement being further operationalised by specific limits on the number of directorships for significant institutions. For UCITS management companies and AIFMs, the principle that managers should commit sufficient time is mentioned but not operationalised into specific limits. The requirement of independence of mind is also mentioned for AIFMs. Neither of these two additional criteria is mentioned for insurance companies or IORPs. Again, these choices seem highly arbitrary, and the rules should probably be made uniform, as all managers should be independent of mind and should commit sufficient time to their function. On the other hand, one could argue that review of these additional and more stringent requirements by the financial supervisor should only apply to the most important institutions. But even in that case, a case can be made for extending them to systemically important fund managers and insurance companies. In addition, if the idea is one of proportionality, then it makes no sense to apply the additional requirements of sufficient time and independence of mind to all investment firms, even those that are not covered by CRD IV (which will be the case even under the new investment firms regime, as these requirements are stipulated in MiFID II, which refers to CRD IV).

In addition to these differences in the criteria for the fit & proper tests, there is also quite some divergence on the persons to whom they apply. Again, the legislator's choices seem highly arbitrary rather than driven by the nature of the different institutions:

(1) In all of the institutions, it is clear that the fit & proper tests apply to the executive members of the board (in a one-tier system) or to the management board (in a two-tier system).

(2)   There is much more ambiguity on the applicability to the supervisory board (in a two-tier system) or to the non-executive members (in a one-tier system): while for banks and investment firms covered by CRD IV, it is clear that the fit & proper tests apply to supervisory board members and non-executive directors, member states can choose whether or not to apply the fit & proper test to these persons for investment firms covered by MiFID and for insurance companies. Furthermore, for UCITS management companies, AIFMs and IORPs it is unclear whether these persons would be covered by the fit & proper tests.

(3)   In UCITS management companies, AIFMs and IORPs it is also unclear to what extent fit & proper tests apply to the senior managers who are not part of the board, while in insurance companies, banks and investment firms covered by CRD IV, it is explicitly stated that this is the case.

(4)   Finally, there is substantial divergence on whether the heads of the internal control functions are covered by the fit & proper tests: this is the case for banks, investment firms covered by CRD IV, insurance companies and IORPs, but not for investment firms only covered by MiFID 2, UCITS management companies and AIFMs.

In conclusion, there is a lot of convergence on the basic elements of fit & proper testing, such as the individual requirements of 'sufficiently good repute' and 'knowledge, skills and experience' for the managers of the corporation. However, regarding some of the other elements (the requirements of sufficient time and independence of mind, the applicability to supervisory board members and internal control functions, etc) there are still significant differences between the different institutions. The arbitrariness of these differences suggests that they are not likely to be justified by differences in business model or risk, which indicates that a more cross-sectoral approach would be desirable. Of course, this is by itself not yet conclusive on the question (i) whether the uniformisation should lead to an increase or a decrease in the level of details in the tests and (ii) whether a complete uniformisation is desirable.

We would argue, however, that taking the position that the assessment of skills, knowledge and experience should take place both on an individual and on a collective basis in all financial institutions in scope should be uncontroversial. After all, only one regime deviates from each of these requirements (IORPs from the individual basis and UCITS management companies from the collective basis). We would also argue that the fit & proper tests should apply in any case to the executive members of the board(s), a requirement for which Member States only enjoy discretion for investment firms covered by MiFID. Although more controversial, we also believe that the non-executive members of the board or the members of the supervisory board should be subject to (admittedly a possibly different degree of) fit & proper testing, which is already the case under CRD IV, but unclear or optional for the other institutions. This seems logical, given the important role that these members of the board need to fulfill in monitoring executive managers. On the other hand, we acknowledge that an argument can be made that fit & proper testing 'deeper' inside the organisation, and more specifically of senior managers who are not board members and not in charge of internal control functions, could be reserved to only the most important institutions. Currently the fit & proper tests apply to these persons for insurance companies, banks and investment firms covered by CRD IV, but it can be argued that this should be extended to systemic fund managers. Again, we advocate an approach that differs with the level of systemic importance (see further in section V below).

For most of these changes, the regulation at level 1 and level 2 needs to be amended in order to achieve a more cross-sectoral approach. But we do not believe that it should stop there: given the high level of convergence on most aspects of this topic, it should be feasible and more efficient to present a single set of level 3 guidelines, where the three ESAs cooperate, both in the drafting phase and in applying the guidelines, similar to the joint guidelines on the assessment of shareholders. Indeed, some have suggested that there is significant divergence at the level of the supervisory practice,[131] although some steps in this direction are being taken.[132] Eliminating this divergence could take away some of the confusion that this causes and could also help to avoid unnecessary duplication of work. The approach to the suitability of shareholders, with joint guidelines by EBA, ESMA and EIOPA that apply to most (but not all) financial institutions, may offer inspiration here.

D. Induction and Training

Also related to the fit & proper tests is the requirement of induction and training for board members. The principle that the company should devote adequate human and financial resources to the induction and training of members of the board is stipulated for banks, investment firms, and surprisingly also for AIFMs, but not for insurance companies, IORPs or UCITS management companies. It should again be kept in mind that this requirement is also mentioned in MiFID II, which means that it applies to all investment firms. This continues to be the case upon approval under the new investment firms' regime.

The conclusion is the same as for fit & proper tests: one surely can debate about the usefulness of this principle, but the choice of financial institutions to which it applies seems arbitrary at the moment. If there is a reason to apply it even to the smallest investment firms, there does not seem to be a reason not to apply it to insurance companies and UCITS management companies.

E. Board Composition and Structure

In all financial institutions that we cover in this chapter, the composition and structure of the board has hardly been regulated at the European level. There are no requirements for either a one-tier or a two-tier board structure. While one may think at first glance that the European legislator is pretty neutral on the choice – which would be surprising, in view of the necessity to make a distinction between a supervisory and operational function – there is probably another explanation: the indispensable supervisory role to be assumed in financial institutions, either by a part of the board of directors in a monistic system, or by a true supervisory board in a dual system, is required in any case by the EU regulator. In this way it could be left to the Member States to impose or to allow a dual system, leaving room to take into account national sensitivities, as often differences in governance are a consequence of cultural and/or historical elements.[133]

---

[131] Danny Busch and Iris Palm-Steyerberg, 'Fit and proper requirements in EU financial regulation. Towards more cross-sectoral harmonisation?' in Danny Busch, Guido Ferrarini and Gerard Van Solinge, *Governance of Financial Institutions* (Oxford, OUP, 2019) 38.

[132] Eg, after the recently approved review of the ESAs, the regulations of the ESAs (mainly Art 31b of the respective regulations) provide for a system of information exchange between ESMA, EIOPA and EBA regarding fit & proper tests for shareholders, officers and directors. See: European Parliament, Legislative resolution of 16 April 2019 (2019) P8_TA-PROV(2019)0374.

[133] One may think of the German situation where the link between a dual system and employee participation makes it very delicate to tamper with the existing equilibrium. Another good example thereof is the obligation for Belgian banks to install a semi-dual structure: a board of directors focusing on supervision and a management committee focusing on the operational matters, but whose members must be part of the board of directors as well (Art 24 of the Bank Act of

On the topic of independent directors, some European rules do exist. For banks and investment firms, the EBA/ESMA Suitability Guidelines require a 'sufficient number' of independent directors in significant or listed banks and investment firms covered by CRD IV. In addition, for banks and investment firms falling under CRD IV, the EBA Guidelines on Internal Governance and the EBA Remuneration Guidelines require that a majority of the members on the risk committee, the nomination committee and the remuneration committee be independent in 'global systemically important institutions' (G-SII) and in 'other systemically important institutions' (O-SII) (as defined in Article 131, CRD IV); in other significant institutions,[134] there is only a requirement that a majority of the members of the remuneration committee likewise be independent, as well as a requirement of a 'sufficient number' of independent directors on the overall board level. The Audit Directive, which applies to banks, insurance companies and listed firms (so called public interest entities or 'PIEs'– see also below, under section IV F), also requires that a majority of members of the audit committee be independent. Finally, the remuneration committee in significant AIFMs and UCITS management companies should count a majority of independent directors under the respective ESMA Remuneration Guidelines. In conclusion, the instruments mentioned above imply that all of the institutions that we study, except for pension funds and investment firms not covered by CRD IV, are required to have some independent members on their boards. However, it is notable that for some institutions, this obligation is imposed only indirectly through the requirements for the composition of committees. In addition, the committees for which the presence of independent directors is required differ from institution to institution in a highly arbitrary fashion. Finally, if one is convinced that the presence of independent directors can help prevent excessive risk-taking, one could argue that at least systemically important insurance companies or funds should be subject to a bank-like requirement of a majority of independent directors.

Some other elements of the board structure are subject to more detailed regulation at the EU level. All of the financial institutions covered in this chapter are subject to the requirement that the company is run by at least two persons (who also have to meet the fit & proper tests, see above, section IV C). As this is also stipulated in MiFID II, this applies to all investment firms, even those not covered under CRD IV; this continues to be the case under the new investment firms' regime. However, Member States may grant a derogation to investment firms that are natural persons or to investment firms managed by a single natural person, provided that alternative arrangements ensure a sound and prudent management and that the natural person is fit and proper. Member states may grant a similar exception to IORPs, taking into account 'the role of social partners in the overall management of the IORP, as well as the size, nature, scale and complexity of the activities of the IORP'. At first glance this raises the question of whether a similar possibility for an exemption is not justified in other financial institutions, such as insurance companies, UCITS management companies or AIFMs, as well. The answer is probably that the practical relevance for the latter types of institutions of alternative arrangements for a firm that is a natural person or is managed by a single natural person is rather slim.

In addition, banks and investment firms, but none of the other financial institutions, need to have a diversity policy in place. As this is also stipulated in MiFID II, this applies to all investment firms, even those not covered under CRD IV; and this continues to apply under the new

---

25 April 2014): this is an old tradition that was originally imposed by the supervisor, without legal basis, at a moment in time where Belgian practice was not yet familiar with a separation of supervision and operational matters. This principle was then expanded to insurance undertakings (currently Art 45 of the Act on insurance Undertakings of 13 March 2016).

[134] See section III for a precise definition of the term 'significant'. Significant institutions other than the G-SIIs and the O-SIIs are the ones determined by the Member States.

investment firms' regime. The question is again whether, if the requirement is imposed upon banks and investment firms, why it is not the case for other financial institutions. The impact of diversity and more specifically gender diversity is a hotly debated topic,[135] and this is neither the place to continue nor to settle that debate, but once more we want to point to the lack of consistency in the approach. If the rationale behind diversity policies is that they can lead to better monitoring of risk, the question arises whether they should not also be applied to other systemically important financial institutions. If rather the rationale is to promote diversity as a goal in itself, the question arises whether this should not be applied to all financial institutions (of a certain size) or even outside the financial sector.

Finally, in banks and investment firms (but not in other financial institutions), regulation prohibits the combination of the positions of chairman of the board and CEO. As this is also stipulated in MiFID II, this applies to all investment firms, even those not covered under CRD IV, and nothing will change under the new investment firms' regime. Though less so than diversity, the usefulness of this separation of functions is also subject to controversy.[136] However, the question is whether such a requirement – if deemed useful for banks and investment firms – would also be justified in other institutions: again, if the rationale is better monitoring of risk, arguably such a requirement could potentially also be useful for non-bank systemically important financial institutions. To be clear, we take no stance in the debate about whether such a mandatory provision is a good idea, but to the extent that the legislator has reasons to believe that it is for banks and investment firms, it would also be justified for non-bank systemically important financial institutions. In addition, one could argue that applying this requirement to all investment firms, also small and non-risky ones, is an example of over-regulation, if the main justification is better monitoring of risk.

F. Committees within the Board (Risk, Audit, Remuneration and Nomination)

There is significant divergence between financial institutions on the requirements with regard to committees within the board of directors. Only (significant) banks and investment firms are currently subject to the requirement to establish a risk committee, while insurance companies, UCITS management companies, AIFMs, and IORPs are not. Under CRD IV, significant banks and investment firms should have a risk committee composed of non-executive members with

---

[135] For a selection only, and with divergent conclusions, C Post and K 'Biron, Women on Boards and Firm Financial Performance: A Meta-Analysis', AMC 58/5; J Pletzer, R Nikolova, K Kedzior and S Voelpel, 'Does Gender Matter? Female Representation on Corporate Boards and Firm Financial Performance – A Meta-Analysis, PLOS One' [2015] (10:6) (www.ncbi.nlm.nih.gov/pmc/articles/PMC4473005/); B Choudry, 'Gender Diversity on Boards: Beyond Quota's' [2015] *European Business Law Review* 233; L Christiansen, H Lin, J Pereira, P Topalova, and R Turk, 'Gender Diversity in Senior Positions and Firm Performance', IMF Working Paper WP/16/50 (www.imf.org/external/pubs/ft/wp/2016/wp1650.pdf); see also the well known McKinsey series 'Women Matter' (most recent report: *Time to accelerate, Ten years of insights into gender diversity*, October 2017 (www.mckinsey.com/~/media/McKinsey/Featured%20Insights/Women%20matter/ Women%20Matter%20Ten%20years%20of%20insights%20on%20the%20importance%20of%20gender%20diversity/ Women-Matter-Time-to-accelerate-Ten-years-of-insights-into-gender-diversity.ashx), and *Delivering Through Diversity*, January 2018,(www.mckinsey.com/~/media/McKinsey/Business%20Functions/Organization/Our%20Insights/Delivering %20through%20diversity/Delivering-through-diversity_full-report.ashx) most recent *Insight: Still looking for room at the top: Ten years of research on women in the workplace* (www.mckinsey.com/featured-insights/gender-equality/still-looking-for-room-at-the-top-ten-years-of-r.esearch-on-women-in-the-workplace).

[136] Eg, Enriques and Zetzsche have criticised the mandatory separation of the position of chairman and CEO in CRD IV: Luca Enriques and Dirk Zetzsche, 'Quack Corporate Governance, Round III? Bank Board Regulation under the New European Capital Requirement Directive' (2015) 15 *Theoretical Inquiries in Law* 211. They point to a lack of empirical evidence on a correlation between the separation of the positions and performance of banks.

appropriate knowledge, skills and expertise in risk. Financial supervisors may allow a non-significant bank or investment firm to combine the risk committee and the audit committee.[137]

Under the new investment firms' regime, most investment firms would no longer be subject to CRD IV, but the Investment Firms Directive also require significant investment firms to install a risk committee, composed of non-executive members and with appropriate knowledge, skills and expertise in risk. Significance is defined with reference to the size of the assets. Non-significant investment firms may be allowed by the financial supervisors to combine the risk committee and the audit committee. The new provisions also do not apply to 'small and non-interconnected investment firms', which seems logical given the idea that risk committees are only necessary in significant institutions.

According to the Audit Directive, PIEs have to establish an audit committee. One could therefore qualify this Directive as being inherently cross-sectoral in nature, as it is not part of any of the sectoral instruments. The definition of PIE includes listed companies, banks and insurance companies, as well as those entities designated by Member States as PIEs.[138] In SME's and companies with a small market cap (as defined in the Prospectus Directive), however, the board of directors as a whole performs the duties of the audit committee, provided that it is not chaired by an executive member during audit meetings. In addition, there are exemptions for subsidiaries, provided there is an audit committee at the group level, and for non-listed banks which have issued less than EUR 100 million in debt securities and without a prospectus. Member States may also exempt UCITS funds and AIFs.

The audit committee must meet the following requirements:

(a)   it must be entirely composed of non-executive members;
(b)   at least one individual should have a specific competence in accounting and/or audit;
(c)   there should be sufficient collective competence in the sector of the relevant entity; and
(d)   a majority of the members should be independent directors.

A higher degree of convergence is in place on the requirement to install a remuneration committee: it is required for banks, investment firms, insurance companies, UCITS management companies, and AIFMs, but not for IORPs. In each of these cases, however, the duty to have a remuneration committee only applies to 'significant' institutions.[139] Under the new investment firms' regime, a similar provision would apply as under CRD IV, but 'small and non-interconnected investment firms' (would be exempted (as well as other non-significant firms).

For banks, investment firms, UCITS management companies and AIFMs, the applicable regulation stipulates that the remuneration committee should be composed of non-executive members, and guidelines from the supervisors also require that in principle a majority of the members and the chairman of the committee should be independent. For insurance companies, the Delegated Regulation of Solvency II only stipulates that the committee should be 'independent', without specification on how this independence is to be achieved.

Currently, only significant banks and investment firms must establish a nomination committee, as follows from Article 88 of CRD IV. The nomination committee must be composed

---

[137] According to the Q&A, this situation refers to when an institution is not significant but is required to establish a risk committee under the proportionality requirement. It may then combine this risk committee with the audit committee. See: European Banking Authority, 'Single Rulebook Q&A' (question 2013_228 on Art 76(3), CRD IV).

[138] See Accountancy Europe, 'Definition of Public Interest Entities in Europe, State of play after the implementation of the 2014 Audit Reform, Survey, 2017', www.accountancyeurope.eu/wp-content/uploads/171130-Publication-Definition-of-Public-Interest-Entities-in-Europe-1.pdf.

[139] See the definition of 'significance' above in section III and in the remuneration guidelines by the respective supervisors. For insurance companies, however, the definition of 'significance' is not concretised in EIOPA guidelines.

exclusively of non-executive board members. In addition, Article 9, MiFID refers to Article 88 of CRD IV, which means that all investment firms that fall under the scope of MiFID II (which is slightly broader than the scope of CRD IV) are also required to have a nomination committee, and this will not change under the new investment firms' regime.

The picture sketched above of the committees within the board shows some highly arbitrary differences between the different types of financial institutions. If banks are significant, they have to establish all four committees (risk, audit, remuneration and nomination). Significant investment firms have to establish three committees (risk, remuneration, and nomination), both before and after the new investment firms' regime. Insurance companies are required to establish an audit committee and a remuneration committee, while UCITS management companies and AIFMs only have to establish a remuneration committee.

This overview raises consistency questions: where is the logic in subjecting significant investment firms, but not significant insurance companies, to the requirement to have a risk committee, and in subjecting insurance companies, but not investment firms, to the requirement to have an audit committee? And if they are systemically important, should AIFMs and insurance companies not be required to have a risk committee (and potentially the three other committees) as well, given the fact that they can contribute to systemic risk? In addition, it seems an arbitrary anomaly that the independence of the remuneration committee is concretised for banks, investment firms, UCITS management companies and AIFMs, but not for insurance companies. We also note that the fact that the remuneration committee is required across sectors was probably driven by the fact that remuneration has gathered the most public attention, rather than by an actual higher degree of market failure, considering the fact that the other board committees are not applied cross-sectorally to the same extent.

Finally, if a board committee is required, it is almost always only required for significant institutions. This implies that the definition of significance is especially relevant for this topic. It also offers some room to tailor the requirement only to those institutions where the application is justified, assuming at least that significance is defined adequately. This way, the idea behind these rules is similar to the idea of establishing a specific governance regime for all systemically important financial institutions, as we propose in section V.

G. Risk Management Function

At first glance, there is a very high level of convergence on the risk management function. This function is required for banks, investment firms, insurance companies, UCITS management companies, AIFMs, and IORPs. The devil is again in the detail as they do differ between institutions, however.

In banks and investment firms (under CRD IV), the following conditions are stipulated for the risk management function (further concretised in the EBA Guidelines on Internal Governance):

(1) independence from the operational functions;
(2) active involvement in the risk strategy;
(3) headed by an independent senior manager with distinct responsibility;
(4) direct reporting to the management body in its supervisory function;
(5) no removal possible without prior approval of the management body in its supervisory function (ie, in a dual governance structure, the supervisory body, and in a one tier structure, the board of directors where the executive directors are not a majority);

(6) the risk management function is independent from the business unit it oversees and its remuneration is linked to the objective of its function and independent of the performance of the business unit it oversees, and;

(7) the remuneration of the senior officers in the risk management function is directly monitored by the remuneration committee.

The risk management function is regulated in much less detail in insurance companies. Solvency II also comprises the requirement of independence and of reporting directly to the administrative, management or supervisory body, as well as a rule that the remuneration of the control functions is not tied to the performance of the operating units they control, but without all the details prescribed for banks. The rules on dismissal of the risk management function do not have a counterpart in Solvency II.

Similarly, the risk management function in UCITS management companies is also subject to an independence requirement, but companies can deviate from this requirement if appropriate and proportionate. No further regulation is present on level 1 or 2. Interestingly, AIFMs are subject to requirements for the risk management function that are almost as strict as those for banks and investment firms:

(1) independence from the operational functions;

(2) risk managers cannot be supervised by persons belonging to the operating units;

(3) risk managers cannot be not active in any operating unit;

(4) the risk manager's remuneration must be linked to the objective of his function, and independent of the performance of the business unit he oversees;

(5) the remuneration of the senior officers in the risk management function must be directly monitored by the remuneration committee (if there is one).

The ESMA Remuneration Guidelines for UCITS extend the last two principles to UCITS management companies, and they are worded almost identically to the ESMA Remuneration Guidelines for AIFMs.

IORPs must also organise a risk management function subject to an independence requirement, but the Directive allows this function to be combined with other key functions (with the exception of the internal audit function); there is also a requirement that the risk management function must be able to report directly to the administrative, management or supervisory body.

This brings us once more to the question of whether the (admittedly rather limited) differences in the detail of the regulation of the risk management function make sense. Some choices seem especially arbitrary and not the result of logic, but rather of coincidence or of the choice of the moment, without particular concern or consideration for what has already been put into places. Why are, eg, insurance companies subject to much less detail, especially at level 3? Why are the level 1 and 2 rules so different for UCITS management companies and AIFMs, all the more so considering the fact that the level 3 guidelines are extremely similar? In addition, what is the rationale of introducing an appropriateness and proportionality exception to the independence requirement for UCITS management companies, but not for other institutions? Is this a mere consideration of the fact that UCITS management companies may be smaller firms than the other institutions? If so, is that a sufficient reason to allow them not to install a fully independent risk function? And if so, why not extend this flexibility to other smaller firms? We cannot provide well thought-out answers to these questions within the scope of this chapter. We merely plead for an approach that makes more sense from a cross-sectoral perspective. In addition, we would argue that all systemically important financial institutions should have a risk management function that meets the most stringent requirements of CRD IV.

H. Internal Audit Function

CRD IV does not contain an explicit duty for banks and investment firms to establish an internal audit function, which is, to say the least, surprising. CRR does mention the internal audit function a few times, suggesting that it is simply assumed that banks and investment firms have one, but there are no legal requirements to have one at level 1 or level 2. Nevertheless, the internal audit function is required and regulated in detail by the EBA Guidelines on Internal Governance.

Insurance companies, UCITS management companies, AIFMs and IORPs are also required to put into place an independent internal audit function, which implies that the level of cross-sectoral convergence is relatively high. However, for banks, investment firms, UCITS management companies, AIFMs and IORPs, this is only the case to the extent that this is proportionate to their size, nature and complexity, whereas for insurance companies, there is no proportionality exception, which again seems like an arbitrary choice.

For banks, investment firms covered by CRD IV, insurance companies and IORPs – but not for UCITS management companies nor for AIFMs – it is specified that the internal audit function should report directly to the administrative, management or supervisory body.

Finally, for banks, investment firms covered by CRD IV, insurance companies and IORPs, the internal audit function cannot be combined with any of the other control functions. However, insurance companies are allowed to deviate from this prohibition if this would not be appropriate given the nature, scale and complexity of the firm and if the respecting prohibition would lead to disproportionate costs, provided that conflicts of interest can be avoided.

Again, we can raise several questions: is it justified to require all financial institutions to have an audit function, or can a case be made to limit this only to significant institutions? And are the differences in specific regulation really warranted?

I. Compliance Function

As is the case for the internal audit function, CRD IV surprisingly enough does not contain an explicit duty to install a compliance function for banks or investment firms, though the presence of this function is – not surprisingly so – required by the EBA Guidelines on Internal Governance. In addition, CRD IV does regulate the remuneration of the compliance function (which confirms that banks are simply assumed to have one): it must be based on objectives linked to the function, and not on the performance of the business areas the function controls (and of which it should be independent); and the remuneration is directly monitored by the remuneration committee. The Investment Firms Directive and the Investment Firms Regulation do not change anything in this regard: the duty to have a compliance function is not mentioned at level 1 or level 2; its remuneration is regulated in the same way, except, however, that the remuneration is not regulated for small and non-interconnected investment firms.

In insurance companies, the compliance function is required under Solvency II. It should also be independent, it should report directly to the administrative, management or supervisory body, its remuneration should not be linked to the operations that the compliance function controls, and it should have access to all relevant information. There is no similar requirement to the one which exists for banks that the remuneration of the compliance function is to be directly monitored by the remuneration committee.

Similar rules apply to UCITS management companies: they should also have an independent compliance function that should report directly to senior management; it should have access to all relevant information; the compliance function must not be involved in the performance of the services it monitors; and its remuneration may not compromise its objectivity (which is subject to further guidelines by ESMA). However, the latter two requirements do not apply if they are disproportionate. The regime for AIFMs is identical to the one for UCITS management companies.

This raises the following questions: is it really warranted to impose a compliance function on all financial institutions? Is systemic importance a relevant distinguishing criterion, or rather proportionality to the nature, scale and complexity of the firm? And to the extent that a compliance function should be organised, what are the reasons behind the small differences in regulation? Would it not be possible and advisable to make the regulation uniform?

J. Actuarial Function

Under Solvency II, insurance companies are required to have an actuarial function. It has to report directly to the administrative, management or supervisory body. The function should be independent and report directly to the administrative, management or supervisory body. Its remuneration should not be linked to the operations controlled.

IORPs must also have an actuarial function, but only when this is necessary for the business model (ie cover against biometric risks or guarantees of either an investment performance or a given level of benefits). Similarly to insurance companies, if there is an actuarial function, it should be independent and report directly to the administrative, management or supervisory body. For both insurance companies and IORPs, the actuarial function can be exercised by a single person together with other key functions (but not with internal audit).[140]

Other financial institutions are not required to have an actuarial function, and here the reason for the divergence is clear for once, in view of the nature of their respective activities.

K. Applicability of Governance Provisions to Financial Groups

Although this is not the focus of this chapter and certainly requires further study, we also briefly consider the applicability of governance provisions to financial groups. In general, the legislator has decided to apply the governance provisions not only at the level of the regulated entity, but also at a consolidated level.[141] Such an approach certainly makes sense: otherwise, 'bad governance'[142] at the parent level could undermine the effectiveness of good governance

---

[140] Article 24(2), IORP Directive (for IORPs and Recital 32, Solvency II (which only mentions this possibility for small and non-complex insurance companies, however).

[141] See for bank and investment firms groups: Art 92, CRD IV (remuneration), Art 109, CRD IV (many of the other governance provisions) and Art 121. CRD IV (fit & proper requirements for and (mixed) financial holding companies); for insurance groups: Art 246, Solvency II (most governance provisions) and Art 257 (fit & proper requirements for insurance holding companies and mixed financial holding companies); for mixed financial holding companies: Financial Conglomerates Directive, especially Art 13 on fit & proper requirements; for investment firms under the new regime: Art 25(4) Investment Firms Directive (most governance and remuneration provisions, with some exceptions to consolidation) and Art 52 Investment Firms Directive (fit & proper requirements for investment holding companies and mixed financial holding companies).

[142] In this context, 'bad governance' should be understood as governance that is not sufficiently aimed at addressing the market failures in financial institutions. In other words, governance that more strongly aligns management with shareholders could be characterised as 'bad governance' if it encourages excessive risk-taking.

at the subsidiary level.[143] On the other hand, this approach could potentially create overlapping governance regimes in cross-sectoral groups, as multiple and possibly diverging governance regimes could apply, certainly in pan-European groups. Although regulation may contain provisions on which regime takes precedence (see, eg, Articles 120, CRD IV and 213 Solvency II), such provisions risk creating an incentive to structure a group in such a way that the least onerous governance regime applies. In this respect a cross-sectoral approach to corporate governance can truly add value: if the differences in governance requirements are not based on the financial sector, but rather on the degree of risk, the governance requirements applicable at the group level can take into account the riskiness of the whole group. This could eliminate the possibility of regulatory arbitrage within the group, eg if risky activities are conducted within an otherwise less risky group subject to a less onerous governance regime. However, further research is necessary on such a governance regime for cross-sectoral groups, even if we believe that, at first glance, this is an additional argument in favour of a cross-sectoral approach to corporate governance.

V. Making Sense of the Cross-Sectoral Corporate Governance Picture: A New Framework

The above comparison makes clear that, while some governance provisions do apply across sectors, there are still major differences between the sectors. Generally speaking, banks and investment firms are the most heavily regulated institutions, followed by insurance companies and AIFMs. However, on some topics, AIFMs are more strictly regulated (eg risk management function, independence of mind and sufficient time requirements for board members, induction and training, independence of the members of the remuneration committee and of the internal control functions), while on other topics, insurance companies are more strictly regulated (eg composition of the audit committee and independence of its members, suitability of shareholders and fit & proper testing for internal control functions). Do these differences flow from differences in business models and risk levels, or rather from coincidental differences in drafting? Based on our review of all the governance provisions – which revealed many highly arbitrary results – we are inclined to believe that it is often the latter.

Corporate governance in IORPs is generally regulated in a much less stringent way than in other financial institutions, which can probably be justified because of the limited risk that these institutions pose to financial stability. Corporate governance in UCITS management companies is often similar to the regime for AIFMs, although many provisions are less stringent than those for AIFMs (with a notable exception for suitability of shareholders, where the AIFMD regime is highly underdeveloped in comparison to UCITS management companies), which can probably be justified because of the higher level of regulation of the investment strategies of UCITS funds.

Under the new investment firms' regime, only the largest and most significant investment firms will be subject to the more stringent governance regime of CRD IV, making regulation more proportionate to the systemic risk posed by each institution. However, the impact of this change is limited by the fact that MiFID II makes many of the corporate governance provisions in CRD IV applicable to all investment firms, even under the new investment firms' regime. Put differently, there are only a few concrete changes for non-significant investment firms, such

---

[143] For a similar idea, related to the parent company undermining governance of ring-fenced banks, see: Thom Wetzer, 'In two minds: the governance of ring-fenced banks' [2018] *Journal of Corporate Law Studies* 1.

as the abolition of the independence of mind requirement, the abolition of the requirement to have some independent directors, and the abolition of the applicability of fit & proper testing to non-executive directors, senior managers and internal control functions. The rationale of some of these changes is debatable: is meddling with the scope of application of fit & proper tests the right way to deregulate investment firms? Other changes, such as the requirements on independent directors, flow mainly from supervisory guidelines, so they may also continue to be applied to investment firms. This seems to indicate that the intended deregulating of corporate governance in investment firms may be overstated. As the legislator considers such deregulation desirable, changes should probably be made to the Investment Firms Directive and the Investment Firms Regulation to come to an even more proportionate approach.

Assuming a financial stability rationale for governance intervention,[144] it is not surprising that banks and investment firms are subjected to the overall strictest regime. This is especially the case given that CRD IV makes a distinction between significant and not significant firms for many of its corporate governance provisions. Moreover, under the new investment firms' regime, only the largest and most significant investment firms will have to comply with the strictest regime in CRD IV (although the differences with the regime for other investment firms are not as large as they may appear at first sight, something that should perhaps be remedied).

The systemic importance of *large* commercial and investment banks has indeed been the least contested in the aftermath of the crisis. However, as section II makes clear, systemic relevance is not reserved to the business models of the large investment and commercial banks. Neither is it necessarily aligned with the sectoral divide in the EU regulatory structure. A small commercial bank with prudent liquidity management is possibly less systemically important than a highly leveraged and interconnected hedge fund. Nevertheless, the EU governance regime of the former is stricter than that of the latter. Furthermore, there are also significant differences in systemic importance within each sector. As the debacle of Long-Term Capital Management (LTCM) and the resulting private bailout in 1998 made clear, hedge fund failure can pose a threat to systemic stability.[145] Private equity funds, on the other hand, are unlikely to cause systemic risk.[146] The EU regulatory regime, however, subjects both institutions to the same governance regime under AIFMD.

We argue that – given the above analysis – a cross-sectoral governance regime for systemically important financial companies is justified. Such a regime could carve out systemically important financial firms of the existing EU instruments and subject them to a more stringent and harmonised governance regime. The new investment firms' regime serves as inspiration for such a reform. In other words, the proposed approach for investment firms – distinguishing between systemic and non-systemic institutions – may well merit extension to other financial institutions.

In order to achieve this, the EU should adopt cross-sectoral rules applicable to systemically important financial institutions. In an ideal world, such rules could be adopted via a truly high-level cross-sectoral directive or regulation based on – eg – the governance rules in CRD IV. The governance mechanisms used in CRD IV are of such a general nature that – even assuming significant differences in governance needs – they would benefit the governance of all systemically important financial institutions. We appreciate that there may be a need to distinguish between the different business models and the way they present systemic risk. This can, however, be achieved through technical implementation measures at level 2 by the Commission.

---

[144] An assumption that is justified in view of the policy set forward by the EU, see European Commission, 'Green Paper. Corporate Governance in Financial Institutions and Remuneration Policies' (2010) COM(2010) 284 final.

[145] Roger Lowenstein, *When genius failed: the rise and fall of long-term capital management*, (New York, Random House, 2001).

[146] Armour and others (n 15) 491–493.

The problem arises of how systemic institutions can be distinguished from non-systemic institutions, as this requires a case-by-case assessment and cannot be adequately described in a regulatory definition. In the US, FSOC is in charge of designating non-bank financial institutions as systemically important.[147] Despite the fact that the US has recently moved away from the entities-based approach (see above in section II D), some have heavily defended this approach, arguing that it is complementary to an activities-based approach.[148] A similar regime to FSOC could be put in place in Europe. Busch and van Rijn, eg, propose to make the European Systemic Risk Board responsible for designating non-bank financial institutions as systemically important.[149] In their proposals, designated institutions should then be subjected to direct prudential supervision by an EU body and to a tailored prudential regime. We would add that this prudential regime should also include rules on corporate governance that aim to reduce systemic risk.

We also find in the above comparison that many of the current sectoral provisions have the same or a very similar content but are worded slightly or even very differently (see, eg, the general standards on corporate governance, the fit & proper tests, etc). While we do not claim that a sectoral divide between corporate governance regimes can never be justified for other reasons than the rationales discussed above, some of the substantive differences that we found seem very hard to reasonably justify as a response to differences in these other rationales. In addition, a similarly worded provision can be subject to guidelines from different ESAs (EBA, ESMA and EIOPA). For such provision, it is justified to level out the differences in the wording at level 1 and 2, and perhaps to have the ESAs also cooperate at level 3 to ensure that differences, if any, in the guidelines are necessary and justified, and not just the result of different discretionary choices. In the end, it may even be justified to try to come up with cross-sectoral guidelines in some areas, even if the provisions are contained in different level 1 or level 2 instruments with slightly different wording, if the substance of the provisions is similar.

VI. Conclusion

In this chapter we have analysed why financial institutions need special corporate governance and compared the corporate governance provisions for banks, investment firms, insurance companies, UCITS management companies, AIFMs and pension funds. While some authors have argued (and sometimes criticised) that many of the provisions that applied to banks have been blindly transplanted to other institutions, we have found that this has happened in a very inconsistent and arbitrary manner. We concluded that for many of the differences in corporate governance regulation between the sectors no justifications have been advanced. At the same time, many financial institutions are becoming increasingly integrated across sectors. In addition, financial institutions can differ as much within a sector as across sectors. For this reason, we have argued that the European legislator should consider taking a more cross-sectoral approach with regard to corporate governance.

---

[147] Section 113 of the Dodd-Frank Act.

[148] Jeremy C Kress, Patricia A McCoy and D Schwarz, 'Regulating entities and activities: complementary approaches to nonbank systemic risk' (2018) *Southern California Law Review* (forthcoming), available at ssrn.com These authors argue that an activities-based approach fails to take into account the cumulative effect of a financial institution's systemic risk. In this chapter, we do not aim to take a definitive stance in the debate. However, we do believe that there is something in the idea of an entities-based approach, that it deserves more attention in the European Union, and that it is also a useful way of ensuring that corporate governance provisions are tailored to the level of systemic risk.

[149] Busch and van Rijn (n 31).

Our point was not that certain types of financial institutions need more or less stringent corporate governance provisions; rather, we have argued that if the legislator is of the opinion that a governance tool can address a market failure within one financial institution, it could likely do the same in other institutions. In any case, the European legislator should at least justify why it could not. Conversely, if the legislator believes that a governance tool is too far-reaching in one type of financial institution, that may also be true of other financial institutions. Instead of regulation or de-regulation, we argue for a better way of regulating: tailoring governance provisions in a more functional way to the market failures that they aim to address. More concretely, we have argued that systemically important financial institutions should be subject to more stringent cross-sectoral corporate governance provisions. More broadly, the more stringent corporate governance provisions for financial institutions in general should be more proportionate, eg by applying them only to significant institutions and/or by allowing proportionality exceptions. In addition, for some of the 'core provisions', such as the suitability of shareholders and the fit & proper tests for managers, we have argued that the current level of cross-sectoral convergences does allow for a truly cross-sectoral approach, perhaps even with joint level 3 guidelines. Such an approach would be more logical from a cross-sectoral perspective, would eliminate interpretation problems and would reduce compliance costs, especially within cross-sectoral financial groups.

Annex

Table

	Banks	Investment firms	Investment firms (under new regime)	Insurance companies	UCITS management company	AIFMs	IORPs
General standard	Yes (article 74 CRD IV)	Yes (article 74 CRD IV and article 21 Delegated Regulation MiFID 2)	Yes (article 26 Investment Firms Directive and article 21 Delegated Regulation MiFID 2)	Yes (article 41 Solvency II and article 258 Delegated Regulation Solvency II)	Yes (article 12 and UCITS V Directive; article 4 Commission Implementing Directive 2010/43)	Yes (article 18(1) AIFMD and article 57 Delegated Regulation AIFMD 231/2013)	Yes (article 22 IORP Directive)
Suitability of shareholders	Yes (article 14 and article 22–27 CRD IV; 3L3 Guidelines)	Yes (article 10–13 MiFID 2; applies to all investment firms; 3L3 Guidelines)	Yes (article 10–13 MiFID 2; applies to all investment firms; 3L3 Guidelines)	Yes (article 24 and 57–63 Solvency II; 3L3 Guidelines)	Yes (article 8 and 11 UCITS V Directive, which refer to the MiFID regime)	Yes, but not regulated in detail (article 8(1)(d) AIFMD)	No
Fit & proper tests	Yes (article 91(1) and (9) CRD IV; EBA/ESMA Suitability Guidelines)	Yes (article 91(1) and (9) CRD IV applies to all investment firms (article 9 MiFID 2); EBA/ESMA Suitability Guidelines)	Yes (article 91(1) and (9) CRD IV also apply for non-CRD investment firms (article 9 MiFID 2))	Yes (article 42–43 Solvency II; article 258 and 273 Delegated Regulation Solvency II; EIOPA Guidelines on Systems of Governance)	Yes (article 7(1)(b) UCITS V Directive)	Yes (article 8(1)(c) AIMFD and article 21(a) and (c) Delegated Regulation AIFMD 231/2013)	Yes, but should only be collectively fit, but individually proper (article 22 IORP Directive)

(continued)

Table *(Continued)*

	Banks	Investment firms	Investment firms (under new regime)	Insurance companies	UCITS management company	AIFMs	IORPs
Collective suitability	Yes (article 91(7) CRD IV; EBA/ESMA Suitability Guidelines)	Yes (article 91(7) CRD IV applies to all investment firms (article 9 MiFID 2); EBA/ESMA Suitability Guidelines)	Yes (article 91(7) CRD IV applies to all investment firms (article 9 MiFID 2))	Yes (article 258(1)(c) and 273(3) Delegated Regulation Solvency II; EIOPA Guidelines on Systems of Governance)	No	Yes (article 21(a) Delegated Regulation AIFMD 231/2013)	Yes (article 22(1)(a) IORP Directive)
Independence of mind	Yes (article 91(8) CRD IV; EBA/ESMA Suitability Guidelines)	Yes (article 91(8) CRD IV; EBA/ESMA Suitability Guidelines)	No	No	No	Yes (article 21(c) Delegated Regulation AIFMD 231/2013)	No
Sufficient time	Yes, with specific limits on directorships for significant banks (article 91(2)–(6) CRD IV; EBA/ESMA Suitability Guidelines)	Yes, with specific limits on directorships for significant investment firms (article 91(2)–(6) CRD IV; also applies to non-CRD investment firms (article 9 MiFID 2); EBA/ESMA Suitability Guidelines)	Yes, with specific limits on directorships for significant investment firms (article 91(2)–(6) CRD IV also applies to non-CRD investment firms (article 9 MiFID 2))	No	Yes, but only a general principle of sufficient time (article 5 Commission Implementing Directive 2010/43)	Yes, but only a general principle of sufficient time (article 21(b) Delegated Regulation AIFMD 231/2013)	No
Fit & proper test applicable to members of management board / executive directors?	Yes, included in the definition of "members of the management body" (article 91 CRD IV iuncto article 3(7) and (8) CRD IV)	Yes, included in the definition of "members of the management body" (article 91 CRD IV iuncto article 3(7) and (8) CRD IV). For investment firms not covered by CRD IV, see the cell immediately to the right of this one.	Yes, member states can choose which of the two boards or functions (management vs. supervisory) counts as the "management body" (article 4(1)(36) MiFID 2), but fit & proper tests apply in any case to "the persons who effectively direct the business" (article 9(6) MiFID 2)	Yes, included in the definition of "persons who effectively run the undertaking" and potentially in the definition of "administrative, management or supervisory body" (article 42 Solvency II and EIOPA Guidelines on Systems of Governance)	Yes, included in the definition of "the persons who effectively conduct the business of a management company" (article 7(1)(b) UCITS V Directive)	Yes, included in the definition of "the persons who effectively conduct the business of the AIFM" (article 8(1)(c) AIFMD)	Yes, included in the definition of "persons who effectively run the IORP" (article 22 IORP Directive)

(continued)

Table *(Continued)*

	Banks	Investment firms	Investment firms (under new regime)	Insurance companies	UCITS management company	AIFMs	IORPs
Fit & proper test applicable to members of supervisory board / non-executive directors?	**Yes**, included in the definition of "members of the management body" (article 91 CRD IV iuncto article 3(7) and (8) CRD IV)	**Yes**, included in the definition of "members of the management body" (article 91 CRD IV iuncto article 3(7) and (8) CRD IV), but **it depends** for investment firms not covered by CRD IV (see cell immediately to the right of this one).	**It depends**, member states can choose which of the two boards or functions (management vs. supervisory) counts as the "management body" (article 4(1)(36) MiFID 2)	**Yes** in a one-tier structure; **it depends** in a two-tier structure, as member states can choose whether supervisory board falls under the definition of "administrative, management or supervisory body" (article 1(43) Delegated Regulation Solvency II)	**Unclear** whether included in the definition of "the persons who effectively conduct the business of a management company" (article 7(1)(b) UCITS V Directive)	**Yes** in a one-tier board (see the use of "governing body" in article 21 Delegated Regulation AIFMD, as defined in article 1(4); **unclear** in a two-tier board (see use of phrase "the persons who effectively conduct the business" in article 8(1)(c) AIFMD)	**Unclear** whether included in the definition of "persons who effectively run the IORP" (article 22 IORP Directive)
Fit & proper test applicable to "senior managers"?	**Yes**, included in the definition of key function holders (EBA/ESMA Suitability Guidelines)	**Yes**, included in the definition of key function holders (EBA/ESMA Suitability Guidelines).	**Unclear** whether included in the definition of "the persons who effectively direct the business" (article 9(6) MiFID 2)	**Yes**, included in the definition of "persons who effectively run the undertaking" (article 42 Solvency II and EIOPA Guidelines on Systems of Governance)	**Unclear** whether included in the definition of "the persons who effectively conduct the business of a management company" (article 7(1)(b) UCITS V Directive)	**Unclear** whether included in the definition of "the persons who effectively conduct the business of the AIFM" (article 8(1)(c) AIFMD)	**Unclear** whether included in the definition of "persons who effectively run the IORP" (article 22 IORP Directive)
Fit & proper test applicable to heads of internal control functions?	**Yes**, included in the definition of "key function holders" (EBA/ESMA Suitability Guidelines)	**Yes**, included in the definition of "key function holders" (EBA/ ESMA Suitability Guidelines), but **not** for investment firms not covered by CRD IV	**No**	**Yes**, included in the definition of key functions (article 13(29) and 42 Solvency II and EIOPA Guidelines on Systems of Governance)	**No**	**No**	**Yes** (article 22 iuncto article 6(18) IORP Directive
Induction & training	**Yes,** article 91(9) CRD IV; concretized by EBA/ESMA Suitability Guidelines	**Yes,** article 91(9) CRD IV; also applies to non-CRD investment firms (article 9 MiFID 2); concretized by EBA/ESMA Suitability Guidelines	**Yes,** article 91(9) CRD IV also applies to non-CRD investment firms (article 9 MiFID 2)	**No**	**No**	**Yes** (article 21(d) Delegated Regulation AIFMD 231/2013	**No**

(continued)

Table *(Continued)*

	Banks	Investment firms	Investment firms (under new regime)	Insurance companies	UCITS management company	AIFMs	IORPs
Independent directors required?	Yes, EBA/ESMA Suitability Guidelines: "sufficient number of independent directors" for significant banks and for listed banks; at least one independent director for other banks; Audit Directive, EBA Guidelines on Internal Governance and EBA Remuneration Guidelines require independent directors in the audit, risk, nomination and remuneration committee	Yes, EBA/ESMA Suitability Guidelines: "sufficient number of independent directors" for significant and for listed investment firms; EBA Guidelines on Internal Governance and EBA Remuneration Guidelines require independent directors in the risk, nomination and remuneration committee. No requirements for investment firms not covered by CRD IV.	No requirements in the new regime, depends on whether the new guidelines will contain such requirements	Qualified yes, a majority of the members of the audit committee should be independent (article 39 Audit Directive); no other requirements	Qualified yes, a majority of the members of the remuneration committee should be independent (ESMA Remuneration Guidelines UCITS Directive)	Qualified yes, a majority of the members of the remuneration committee should be independent (ESMA Remuneration Guidelines AIFM's)	No
At least two effective managers	Yes (article 13(1) CRD IV)	Yes, but exceptions are possible (article 9(6) MiFID 2; more broadly applicable than CRD IV)	Yes, but exceptions are possible (article 9(6) MiFID 2)	Yes (article 258(4) Delegated Regulation Solvency II)	Yes (article 7(1)(b) UCITS V Directive)	Yes (article 8(1)(c) AIFMD)	Yes, but exceptions are possible (article 21(6) IORP Directive)
Diversity policy?	Yes (article 91(10) CRD IV); concretized by EBA/ESMA Suitability Guidelines	Yes, article 91(10) CRD IV; also applies to non-CRD investment firms (article 9 MiFID 2); concretized by EBA/ESMA Suitability Guidelines	Yes, article 91(10) CRD IV also applies to non-CRD investment firms (article 9 MiFID 2)	No	No	No	No

(continued)

Table *(Continued)*

	Banks	Investment firms	Investment firms (under new regime)	Insurance companies	UCITS management company	AIFMs	IORPs
Separation of chairman/ CEO	**Yes**, unless authorised by the supervisor (article 88(1)(e) CRD IV)	**Yes**, unless authorised by the supervisor (article 88(1) (e) CRD IV); also applies to non-CRD investment firms (article 9 MiFID 2)	**Yes**, unless authorised by the supervisor (article 88(1) (e) CRD IV also applies to non-CRD investment firms (article 9 MiFID 2))	No	No	No	No
Two-tier board	Optional	Optional	Optional	Optional	Optional	Optional	Optional
Risk committee	**Yes**, if significant (article 76(3) CRD IV)	**Yes**, if significant (article 76(3) CRD IV)	**Yes**, if significant in terms of assets (article 28(4) Investment Firms Directive)	No	No	No	No
Audit committee	**Yes**, with limited exceptions (article 39 Audit Directive)	**Optional** for member states, unless listed	**Optional** for member states, unless listed	**Yes** (article 39 Audit Directive)	**Optional** for member states, even if listed	**Optional** for member states, even if listed	**Optional** for member states
Remuneration committee	**Yes**, if significant (article 95 CRD IV)	**Yes**, if significant (article 95 CRD IV)	**Yes**, if significant in terms of assets (article 33 Investment Firms Directive)	**Yes**, if appropriate in relation to the significance (article 275(1)(f) Delegated Regulation Solvency II)	**Yes**, if significant (article 14b(4) UCITS V Directive)	**Yes**, if significant (Annex II (3) AIFMD)	No
Independence of remuneration committee	Only non-executives (article 95 CRD IV); in principle majority of the members and the chairman independent (§49 EBA Remuneration Guidelines)	Only non-executives (article 95 CRD IV); in principle majority of the members and the chairman independent (§49 EBA Remuneration Guidelines)	Only non-executives (article 33 Investment Firms Directive); no guidelines yet on independence.	The committee as a whole must be "independent", but no specific requirements of non-executives or independence (article 275(1)(f) Delegated Regulation Solvency II)	Only non-executives (article 14b(4) UCITS V Directive); in principle majority of the members and the chairman independent (§60–61 ESMA Remuneration Guidelines for UCITS Directive)	Only non-executives (Annex II (2) AIFMD); in principle majority of the members and the chairman independent (§58–59 ESMA Remuneration Guidelines for AIFM's)	/
Nomination committee	**Yes**, if significant (article 88 CRD IV)	**Yes**, if significant (article 88 CRD IV; also applies to non-CRD investment firms (article 9 MiFID 2)	**Yes**, if significant (article 95 CRD IV also applies to non-CRD investment firms (article 9 MiFID 2))	No	No	No	No

(continued)

Table *(Continued)*

	Banks	Investment firms	Investment firms (under new regime)	Insurance companies	UCITS management company	AIFMs	IORPs
Risk management function	Yes (article 76(5) CRD IV and EBA Guidelines on Internal Governance); regulated in detailed (including independence, removal, direct reporting and remuneration). See also article 92(2)(e) and (f) CRD IV.	Yes (article 76(5) CRD IV and EBA Guidelines on Internal Governance); regulated in detailed (including independence, removal, direct reporting and remuneration). See also article 23(2) Delegated Regulation MiFID 2.	Yes, article 23(2) Delegated Regulation MiFID 2; rules on the independence and the remuneration of control functions (article 30 Investment Firms Directive)	Yes, with a general mention of the principle of independence and direct reporting to management body (article 44(4) Solvency II; article 268–269 Delegated Regulation Solvency II); remuneration not linked to operations they control (Article 275(2)(h) Delegated Regulation Solvency II)	Yes, with a general mention of the principle of independence (with a proportionality exception) (article 12 Commission Implementing Directive 2010/43); remuneration regulated in detail by ESMA Remuneration Guidelines for UCITS Directive	Yes, with detailed rules on independence and remuneration (article 39 and 42 Delegated Regulation AIFMD 231/2013); ESMA Remuneration Guidelines for AIFM's are very similar to those for UCITS Directive	Yes, with a general mention of the principle of independence and direct reporting to management body (article 24 IORP Directive)
Compliance function	Yes, not explicitly mentioned in CRD IV, but required in the EBA Guidelines on Internal Governance (taking into account proportionality) including detailed requirements on independence, removal, direct reporting and remuneration	Yes, not explicitly mentioned in CRD IV, but required in article 22(2) Delegated Regulation MiFID 2 and the EBA Guidelines on Internal Governance (taking into account proportionality) including detailed requirements on independence, removal, direct reporting and remuneration	Yes, article 22(2) Delegated Regulation MiFID 2; rules on the independence and the remuneration of control functions (article 30 Investment Firms Directive)	Yes, with a general mention of the principle of independence and direct reporting to management body (article 46 Solvency II; article 268 and 270 Delegated Regulation Solvency II); remuneration not linked to operations they control (Article 275(2)(h) Delegated Regulation Solvency II)	Yes (article 10(2) Commission Implementing Directive 2010/43; remuneration regulated in detail by ESMA Remuneration Guidelines for UCITS Directive, but with a proportionality exception in the level 2 instrument	Yes (article 61(2) Delegated Regulation AIFMD 231/2013; remuneration regulated in detail by ESMA Remuneration Guidelines for AIFM's, but with a proportionality exception in the level 2 instrument	No
Combination of risk management function and compliance function	Yes, taking into account proportionality (§159 EBA Guidelines on Internal Governance)	Yes, taking into account proportionality (§159 EBA Guidelines on Internal Governance)	Not mentioned	Not mentioned	Not mentioned	Not mentioned	/

(continued)

Table *(Continued)*

	Banks	Investment firms	Investment firms (under new regime)	Insurance companies	UCITS management company	AIFMs	IORPs
Internal audit function	**Yes,** not explicitly mentioned in CRD IV, but required in the EBA Guidelines on Internal Governance (taking into account proportionality) including detailed requirements on independence, removal, direct reporting and remuneration	**Yes,** not explicitly mentioned in CRD IV, but required in article 24 Delegated Regulation MiFID 2 and in the EBA Guidelines on Internal Governance, including detailed requirements on independence, removal, direct reporting and remuneration	**Yes,** article 24 Delegated Regulation MiFID 2; rules on the independence and the remuneration of control functions (article 30 Investment Firms Directive)	**Yes,** with a general mention of the principle of independence and direct reporting to management body (article 47 Solvency II; article 268 and 271 Delegated Regulation Solvency II); remuneration not linked to operations they control (Article 275(2)(h) Delegated Regulation Solvency II)	**Yes,** if proportionate (article 11 Commission Implementing Directive 2010/43); remuneration regulated in detail by ESMA Remuneration Guidelines for UCITS Directive	**Yes,** if proportionate (article 62 Delegated Regulation AIFMD 231/2013); remuneration regulated in detail by ESMA Remuneration Guidelines for AIFM's	**Yes,** in a manner that is proportionate (article 24 and 26 IORP Directive)
Combination of internal audit with other key functions?	**No** (§159 EBA Guidelines on Internal Governance)	**No** (§159 EBA Guidelines on Internal Governance)	**Not mentioned**	**No,** unless this would not be appropriate given the nature, scale and complexity of the firm; if it would lead to disproportionate costs; and if conflicts of interest are avoided (article 271(2) Delegated Regulation Solvency II)	**Not mentioned**	**Not mentioned**	**No** (article 24(2) IORP Directive)
Actuarial function	**No**	**No**	**No**	**Yes** (article 48 Solvency II); independence requirement (article 268 Delegated Regulation Solvency II); remuneration not linked to operations supervised (Article 275(2)(h) Delegated Regulation Solvency II)	**No**	**No**	**Yes,** but only to the extent necessary for the business; independence requirement (article 24 and 27 IORP Directive)

8B

A Cross-Sectoral Analysis
of Remuneration Policy Provisions

GUIDO FERRARINI AND MICHELE SIRI

I. Introduction to the Legal Framework

Banks are at the core of the remuneration regime fixed at international and EU levels for the simple reason that they experienced the most serious problems in this area throughout the financial crisis and were also the target of the greatest financial stability concerns as a result of repeated crises both in the US and the EU. However, other institutions are not immune to the problems concerning employees' remuneration and its impact on risk-taking, while the international principles on sound compensation practices apply to all financial institutions. The present chapter, therefore, includes also the EU provisions extending and adapting the remuneration regime to financial institutions other than banks, such as insurance undertakings, asset managers and investment firms.

Policy documents issued after the crisis argue that the recourse to flawed remuneration structures, including the excessive use of short-term incentives for managers and other risk-taking employees, contributed to the failure of many banks and other financial institutions.[1] The EU initially adopted a supervisory approach to remuneration through the Commission Recommendation on remuneration in the financial sector (2009) touching upon the governance and structure of pay along lines similar to those followed by the Financial Stability Board (FSB) principles.[2] At the same time, the Committee of European Banking Supervisors (CEBS) issued high-level principles for remuneration policies at banks.[3] However, subsequent reviews on the

---

[1] See The High-level Group on Financial Supervision in the EU, chaired by Jacques de Larosière, 25 February 2009 (De Larosiére Report), 30 (the excessive level of remuneration and remuneration structure induced too high risk-taking and encouraged short-termism); EBA Regulation, [2009] OJ L120/22 (whilst not the main cause of the financial crisis, inappropriate remuneration practices in the financial services industry induced excessive risk-taking and thus contributed to significant losses of major financial undertakings); Commission Staff Working Document, Corporate Governance in Financial Institutions: Lessons to be drawn from the current financial crisis, Accompanying document to the Green Paper, *Corporate governance in financial institutions and remuneration policies*, Brussels 2.6.2010, SEC(2010) 669, 9; A review of corporate governance in UK banks and other financial industry entities (the Walker Review), 16 July 2009, 90 ff.

[2] Commission *Recommendation on remuneration policies in the financial sector*, C (2009) 3159, (April 2009). In June 2010 the Commission also published a Green Paper on corporate governance in financial institutions and remuneration policies, which analysed the deficiencies in corporate governance arrangements in the financial services industry and proposed possible ways forward; Commission *Green Paper on corporate governance in financial institutions and remuneration policies* (May, 2011).

[3] Committee of European Banking Supervisors (CEBS), *High-Level Principles for Remuneration Policies* (April 2009).

national implementation of these documents revealed shortcomings in several areas,[4] such as the measurement of risk-adjusted performance, the scope of the new standards, proportionality and home/host relationships. Similar differences, together with increased pressure from the media, politicians and the public, led to a change in regulatory approach. The Capital Requirements Directive (implementing the Basel capital requirements) was amended twice also to include provisions on bankers' remuneration: in 2010 when CRD III was enacted[5] and in 2013 when the CRD IV package was adopted, including a new Directive concerning, inter alia, bankers' remuneration.[6] In addition, CEBS issued supervisory guidance in order to facilitate compliance with the remuneration principles included in CRD III,[7] while the European Banking Authority (EBA) issued new Guidelines under the new Directive.[8] The European regulation in this area was deeply overhauled by Directive 2013/36/EU (CRD IV).[9]

In the insurance sector, the provisions on insurers' remuneration policy and its regulation are found in Commission Delegated Regulation (EU) 2015/35 of 10 October 2014 supplementing Directive 2009/138/EC on the taking-up and pursuit of the business of insurance and reinsurance (Solvency II).[10] While not nearly as prescriptive and detailed as CRD IV, the Alternative Investment Fund Managers Directive (AIFMD) or the Undertakings for Collective Investment in Transferable Securities Directive (UCITS V Directive), these requirements include the obligation for the establishment and maintenance of remuneration policies and procedures to avoid conflicts of interest and promote sound and effective risk management. All Solvency II firms have to comply with the remuneration requirements of Article 275 of the Solvency II Regulation and with the European Insurance and Occupational Pension Authority's (EIOPA's) 'Guidelines on the system of governance' finalised on 14 September 2015. In particular, the administrative, management or supervisory body of the undertaking shall establish the remuneration policy for those categories of staff whose professional activities have a material impact on the undertaking's risk profile and is responsible for the oversight of its implementation. An independent remuneration committee shall be created, if appropriate in relation to the significance of the insurance or reinsurance undertakings in terms of size and internal organisation.

In the asset management sector, under Article 14a of UCITS Directive as amended by Directive 2014/91/EU of 23 July 2014 (UCITS V Directive), Member States shall require management companies to establish and apply remuneration policies and practices that are consistent with, and promote, sound and effective risk management and that neither encourage risk-taking which is inconsistent with the risk profiles, rules or instruments of incorporation of the UCITS

---

[4] Commission *Report on the application by Member States of the EU of the Commission 2009/384/EC Recommendation on remuneration policies in the financial services sector*; CEBS, *Report on national implementation of CEBS High-level principles for Remuneration Policies* (June 2010).

[5] CRD III Amending Directives 2006/48/EC and 2006/49/EC as regards Capital Requirements for the Trading Book and for Re-Securitisations, and the Supervisory Review of Remuneration Policies, Official Journal of the European Union, [2010] OJ L329/3.

[6] CRD IV, amending Dir 2002/87/EC and repealing Dirs 2006/48/EC and 2006/49/EC, Official Journal of the European Union, [2013] OJ L176/338.

[7] CEBS, *Guidelines on Remuneration Policies and Practices* (CP42) (December 2010). The CEBS oversaw the implementation of the CRD until the European Banking Authority (EBA) was established in 2011.

[8] EBA, *Guidelines on sound remuneration policies under Articles 74(3) and 75(2) of Directive 2013/36/EU and disclosures under Article 450 of Regulation (EU) No 575/2013*, 21 December 2015.

[9] See, for previous work on this topic, Guido Ferrarini, 'Regulating Bankers' Pay in Europe: The Case for Flexibility and Proportionality', in *Festschrift für Theodor Baums* (Mohr Siebeck, 2017), I, 401–416; Guido Ferrarini, 'CRD IV and the Mandatory Structure of Bankers' Pay', ECGI Law Working Paper No 289/2015, April 2015.

[10] See Michele Siri, 'Corporate Governance of Insurance Firms after Solvency II', ICIR Working Paper Series No 27/2017, Goethe University Frankfurt, International Center for Insurance Regulation (ICIR), https://ideas.repec.org/p/zbw/icirwp/2717.html.

Directive that they manage nor impair compliance with the management company's duty to act in the best interest of the UCITS Directive. The remuneration policies and practices shall include fixed and variable components of salaries and discretionary pension benefits. The AIFMD[11] provides that each AIFM must have remuneration policies and practices for prescribed categories of staff that are consistent with and promote sound and effective risk management and do not encourage risk-taking which is inconsistent with the risk profiles, rules or instruments of incorporation of the AIFs they manage. The AIFM must determine the remuneration policies and practices in accordance with a detailed list of principles set out in Annex II to the AIFMD. The European Securities and Market Authority's Guidelines on Sound Remuneration Policies under the AIFMD sets out guidance explaining how firms may comply with the Annex II Principles.[12]

Investment firms are subject to the regime applicable also to credit institutions (CRD IV), to which MiFID II adds the requirement that the management body has to develop a specific remuneration policy for persons involved in the provision of services to clients so as to 'encourage responsible business conduct, fair treatment of clients as well as avoiding conflict of interest in the relationship with client' (Article 9(3)(c)).[13]

This chapter proceeds as follows. First, we analyse the aims underlying the regulation of remuneration at financial institutions. Second, we discuss the scope of the different legislative instruments. Third, we focus on the various provisions regulating the variable remuneration. Finally, we propose an enhanced role for the proportionality principle, based on a cross-sectoral approach. At the end of this chapter, we also recall the importance of the international dimension which focuses on systemic risk to define the thresholds identifying the institutions (banks, insurance companies, asset managers) which should be subject to the most stringent provisions.

II. Regulatory Aims

In the banking sector, Article 74(1), CRD IV requires institutions to have in place a remuneration policy for all staff, which should comply with the principles set out in Articles 92 and 93 of the Directive and with EBA Guidelines on sound remuneration policies. The remuneration policy should specify all components of remuneration and also include the pension policy. It should be consistent with the objectives of the institution's business and risk strategy, corporate culture and values, long-term interests of the institution, and the measures used to avoid conflicts of interest, and should not encourage excessive risk taking. The remuneration policy should contain the performance objectives for the institution, the methods for the measurement of performance, the structure of variable remuneration, and the ex-ante and ex-post risk-adjustment measures of the variable remuneration.[14]

In the insurance sector, Article 275 of the Solvency II Delegated Regulation provides that, when adopting their remuneration policy, insurance and reinsurance undertakings shall comply with a number of principles, including the following. Firstly, the remuneration policy and remuneration practices shall be established, implemented and maintained in line with the undertaking's business and risk management strategy, its risk profile, objectives, risk management practices and the

---

[11] AIFMD and amending IORP I and UCITS Directive and Regulations CRA and (EU) No 1095/20101.

[12] ESMA, *Guidelines on sound remuneration policies under the AIFMD*, 03.07.2013 | ESMA/2013/232.

[13] See Jens-Heinrich Binder, 'Governance of Investment Firms under MiFID II'', in Danny Busch and Guido Ferrarini (eds), *Regulation of the EU Financial Markets*. MiFID II and MiFIR, (Oxford, OUP, 2017), p 72. Article 27 of the Delegated Council Regulation (EU) 2017/565 of 25 April 2016 supplementing MiFID II provides more detailed requirements.

[14] EBA, *Guidelines on sound remuneration policies*, 14–22.

long-term interests and performance of the undertaking as a whole, and shall incorporate measures aimed at avoiding conflicts of interest. Moreover, the remuneration policy shall promote sound and effective risk management and shall not encourage risk-taking that exceeds the risk tolerance limits of the firm. In addition, the remuneration policy shall apply to the undertaking as a whole and contain specific arrangements that take into account the tasks and performance of the administrative, management or supervisory body, persons who effectively run the undertaking or have other key functions and other categories of staff whose professional activities have a material impact on the undertaking's risk profile.

In the asset management sector, when establishing and applying their remuneration policies, management companies shall comply with the Directive's principles in a way and to the extent that is appropriate to their size, internal organisation and the nature, scope and complexity of their activities (Article 14b). In particular, the remuneration policy must be in line with the business strategy, objectives, values and interests of the management company and the UCITS Directive that it manages and of the investors in such UCITS Directive, and includes measures to avoid conflicts of interest. In addition, the assessment of performance is set in a multi-year framework appropriate to the holding period recommended to the investors of the UCITS Directive managed by the management company in order to ensuring that the assessment process is based on the longer-term performance of the UCITS Directive and its investment risks and that the actual payment of performance-based components of remuneration is spread over the same period. AIFMs are required to comply with a detailed list of principles when establishing and maintaining their remuneration policies and practices. First, the remuneration policy must be consistent with and has to promote sound and effective risk management and does not encourage risk-taking which is inconsistent with the risk profiles, rules or instruments of incorporation of the AIFs they manage. Moreover, the remuneration policy has to be in line with the business strategy, objectives, values and interests of the AIFM and the AIFs it manages or the investors of such AIFs, and includes measures to avoid conflicts of interest.

As to investment firms, Articles 9(3)(c), 23(1), and 24(10), MiFID II require them to define and implement remuneration policies and practices under appropriate internal procedures taking into account the interests of all the clients of the firm, with a view to ensuring that clients are treated fairly, and their interests are not impaired by the remuneration practices adopted by the firm in the short, medium or long term. In addition, remuneration policies and practices shall be designed in such a way as not to create a conflict of interest or incentive that may lead relevant persons to favour their own interests or the firm's interests to the potential detriment of any client.

The multiple goals of the regulation of remuneration policies across the financial sectors justify a certain degree of divergence as to the types of prescriptions. While UCITS Directive, AIFMD and MiFID principles on the remuneration policies are devoted to ensure the consistent and improved implementation of the existing conflicts of interest and conduct of business requirements, the significant homogeneity of prudential regulation between banking and insurance undertakings highlights the possibility and desirability of cross-sectoral convergence, as the following paragraphs will try to demonstrate.

III. Scope

Across the financial sector, cross-sectoral differences become relevant when different types of institutions belong to the same group.

The banking regime initially provided by CRD IV applies on a consolidated basis, i.e. to 'institutions at the group, parent company and subsidiary levels, including those established in offshore financial centres' (Article 92 (1)). The ratio for an EU-wide scope of application is 'to protect and foster financial stability within the Union and to address any possible avoidance of the requirements laid down in this Directive' (67th Recital). In the insurance sector, all entities within the scope of a Solvency II group should have a consistent remuneration policy that is in line with the group's risk management strategies to ensure that Solvency II requirements (including the specific arrangements stipulated in Article 275 of the Solvency II Regulation) are complied with across the group. It does not follow that the same remuneration policy should apply to every group entity, rather that there should be no significant deviation between what applies to the Solvency II firms and other entities in the group.

Many conglomerate groups include banking, insurance and asset management entities which are subject to other regulatory regimes such as the CRD IV, Solvency II Directive, AIFMD and UCITS V Directive, so that different remuneration requirements may need to be applied within the group. A more sophisticated approach emerged with the recent revision of the CRD IV within the so-called Banking Package. Subsidiaries which are not institutions, and therefore not subject to Directive 2013/36/EU on an individual basis, might be subject to other remuneration requirements pursuant to the relevant sector-specific legal acts which should prevail. Therefore, as a rule, remuneration requirements set out for the banking sector should not apply on a consolidated basis to such subsidiaries. However, to prevent possible arbitrage, the remuneration requirements set out in the CRD should apply on a consolidated basis to staff that are employed in subsidiaries that provide specific services, such as asset management, portfolio management or execution of orders, when the same is mandated, regardless of the form such mandate might take, to perform professional activities which qualify them as material risk takers at the level of the banking group. Such mandates should include delegation or outsourcing arrangements concluded between the subsidiary employing the staff and another institution in the same group. At the same time, this requirement signals the need for a better degree of consistency across the various firms to enable the remuneration policy to be applied consistently across the financial institutions which belong to the same groups.

IV. Variable Remuneration

The CRD IV, sub Article 94, paragraph 1 provides several requirements for the variable elements of remuneration. Some of them are rather generic, such as the one requiring performance pay to be based on a combination of the assessment of the performance of the individual and of the business unit concerned and of the overall results of the institution. In addition, performance should be assessed in a multi-year framework in order to ensure that the assessment process is based on longer-term performance and that the actual payment of performance-based components of remuneration are spread over a period which takes account of the underlying business cycle of the credit institution and its business risks. The EBA Guidelines specify that when the award of variable remuneration, including long-term incentive plans (LTIP), is based on past performance of at least one year, but also depends on future performance conditions, institutions should clearly set out to staff the additional performance conditions that have to be met after the award for the variable remuneration to vest.[15] The additional performance conditions should be set for a predefined performance period of at least one year and, when they are

---

[15] EBA, *Guidelines on sound remuneration policies*, 124.

not met, up to 100 per cent of the variable remuneration awarded under those conditions should be subject to malus arrangements.[16]

Still, under Article 94, paragraph 1, CRD IV, the total variable remuneration should not limit the ability of the institution to strengthen its capital base. Furthermore, the fixed and variable components of total remuneration should be appropriately balanced, and the fixed component should represent a sufficiently high proportion of the total remuneration to allow the operation of a fully flexible policy on variable remuneration components, including the possibility to pay no variable remuneration component. Other requirements are more specific, particularly the cap on variable remuneration that the European Parliament asked to include in CRD IV. Also, severance payments are covered by the provision that they will have to reflect performance achieved over time and should not reward failure or misconduct. In addition, remuneration packages relating to compensation or buy out from contracts in previous employment must align with the long-term interests of the institution concerned, including retention, deferral, performance and clawback arrangements.

In general, the measurement of performance used to calculate variable remuneration in the banking sector should include an adjustment for all types of current and future risks and take into account the cost of the capital and the liquidity required. A substantial portion, and in any event at least 50 per cent of variable remuneration shall consist of a balance of (i) shares or equivalent ownership interests, subject to the legal structure of the institution concerned or share-linked instruments or equivalent non-cash instruments, in the case of a non-listed institution; (ii) where possible, other instruments within the meaning of Articles 52 or 63 of CRR or other instruments which can be fully converted to Common Equity Tier 1 instruments or written down, that in each case adequately reflect the credit quality of the institution as a going concern and are appropriate to be used for the purposes of variable remuneration.

In the insurance sector, the EU regulation provides only general principles that set the framework of remuneration policy of insurance undertakings. To start with, the fixed and variable components of remuneration schemes shall be balanced so that the fixed or guaranteed component represents a sufficiently high proportion of the total remuneration to avoid employees being overly dependent on the variable components and to allow the undertaking to operate a fully flexible bonus policy, including the possibility of paying no variable component. Where variable remuneration is performance-related, the total amount of the variable remuneration is based on a combination of the assessment of the performance of the individual and of the business unit concerned and of the overall result of the undertaking or the group to which the undertakings belongs.

In addition, a substantial portion of the variable remuneration shall contain a flexible, deferred component that takes account of the nature and time horizon of the undertaking's business. The deferral period shall not be less than three years and the period shall be correctly aligned with the nature of the business, its risks, and the activities of the employees in question. Financial and non-financial criteria shall be taken into account when assessing an individual's performance. Moreover, the measurement of performance, as a basis for variable remuneration, shall include a downwards adjustment for exposure to current and future risks, taking into account the undertaking's risk profile and the cost of capital. Article 275(2)(c) of the Solvency II Regulation requires firms to defer a 'substantial portion of the variable remuneration component' for a period of not less than three years. There is no flexibility in the Solvency II Regulation for Solvency II firms

---

[16] Ibid.

to elect a shorter period than this specified minimum three-year period, with firms required to ensure that the period (be it three years or longer) is 'correctly aligned with the nature of the business, its risks, and the activities of the employees in question'. The natural life cycle of the business and associated risks should be considered when setting the length of the deferral period.

From a cross-sectoral perspective, it is remarkable that the provision in the Solvency II Regulation is identical to the one in CRD which applies to banks, building societies and investment firms, except that the CRD provision includes a specific 40 per cent minimum deferral threshold. Deferral of variable remuneration allows firms to apply downwards adjustments, in particular by the application of malus prior to the award vesting, to take account of specific risk management failures. Moreover, insurance undertakings should ensure they are able to apply malus during the three-year deferral period required by the Solvency II Regulation.

In the asset management industry, subject to the legal structure of the UCITS Directive and its fund rules or instruments of incorporation, a substantial portion, and in any event at least 50 per cent of any variable remuneration component consists of units of the UCITS Directive concerned, equivalent ownership interests, or share-linked instruments or equivalent non-cash instruments with equally effective incentives as any of the instruments referred to above. The instruments shall be subject to an appropriate retention policy designed to align incentives with the interests of the management company and the UCITS Directive that it manages and the investors of such UCITS Directive.

Furthermore, a substantial portion, and in any event at least 40 per cent, of the variable remuneration component, is deferred over a period which is appropriate in view of the holding period recommended to the investors of the UCITS Directive concerned and is correctly aligned with the nature of the risks of the UCITS Directive in question. This period shall be at least three years. However, the variable remuneration, including the deferred portion, is paid or vests only if it is sustainable according to the financial situation of the management company as a whole, and justified according to the performance of the business unit, the UCITS Directive and the individual concerned. The total variable remuneration shall generally be considerably contracted where subdued or negative financial performance of the management company or of the UCITS Directive concerned occurs, taking into account both current compensation and reductions in pay-outs of amounts previously earned, including through malus or clawback arrangements.

Similar principles apply to Alternative Investment Fund Managers under AIFMD.[17] Article 13 of this Directive provides that Member States shall require AIFMs to have remuneration policies and practices for those categories of staff, including senior management, risk takers, control functions, and any employees receiving total remuneration that takes them into the same remuneration bracket as senior management and risk takers, whose professional activities have a material impact on the risk profiles of the AIFMs or of the AIFs they manage, that are consistent with and promote sound and effective risk management and do not encourage risk-taking which is inconsistent with the risk profiles, rules or instruments of incorporation of the AIFs they manage. The AIFMs shall determine the remuneration policies and practices in accordance with Annex II to the Directive.

As to investment firms, Article 27 of the Delegated Council Regulation (EU) 2017/565 of 25 April 2016 requires that their remuneration policies and practices apply to all relevant persons with an impact, directly or indirectly, on investment and ancillary services provided by the investment firm or on its corporate behaviour, regardless of the type of clients, to the extent that the

---

[17] See Lodewijk van Setten and Danny Busch (eds), *Alternative Investment Funds in Europe. Law and Practice* (Oxford, OUP, 2014); Niamh Moloney, *EU Securities and Financial Markets Regulation* (Oxford, OUP, 2014), p 211, noting that it was the AIFM Directive which influenced the reform of the UCITS Directive as to remuneration.

remuneration of such persons and similar incentives may create a conflict of interest that encourages them to act against the interests of any of the firm's clients. Moreover, because the CRR refers both to investment firms and credit institutions,[18] the same principles for the banking sector apply to the governance aspects of remuneration of investment firms and to the balance between its fixed and variable components.

The EU law has adopted a detailed and stringent regime on the structure, governance, and disclosure of remuneration for the banking sector. Moreover, CRD IV introduced an unprecedented cap to variable remuneration, which may distort incentives and produce unintended consequences on financial institutions' risk-taking. While not nearly as prescriptive and detailed as CRD IV, AIFMD or UCITS V Directive, Solvency II and the EIOPA guidelines differ in significant ways and surprisingly the Solvency II Regulation does not limit variable pay deferral to 'significant' bonuses, therefore including any type of variable remuneration. As this rough rule demonstrates, a cross-sectoral convergence is not only possible but also plausible. To overcome the shortcomings of the European legislation in the banking sector, the area of remuneration regulation should be made more flexible and proportionate, as we discuss in the next paragraph.

V. Proportionality

Under Article 92(2), CRD IV banking institutions comply with the principles just stated and other principles 'in a manner and to the extent that is appropriate to their size, internal organization and the nature, scope and complexity of their activities'. As explained in Recital 66:

> the provisions of this Directive on remuneration should reflect differences between different types of institutions in a proportionate manner, taking into account their size, internal organisation and the nature, scope and complexity of their activities. In particular, it would not be proportionate to require certain types of investment firms to comply with all those principles'.

The EBA Guidelines further specify that the proportionality principle 'aims to match remuneration policies and practices consistent with the individual risk profile, risk appetite and strategy of an institution, so that the objectives of the obligations are effectively achieved'.[19] However, the EBA's Opinion on proportionality expressed the view – shared by the European Commission – that 'the wording of Article 92 (2) does not permit exemptions or waivers to the application of the remuneration principles'.[20]

In the insurance sector, Article 275(3) of the Solvency II Regulation provides for the application of the proportionality principle with the 'internal organisation of the insurance or reinsurance undertaking, and the nature, scale and complexity of the risks inherent in its business' to be taken into account when designing the remuneration policy. Even smaller insurers have to comply with the Solvency II Regulation when setting their remuneration policies. The application of proportionality under Article 275(3) does not permit smaller undertakings to disapply the Solvency II Regulation requirements. These firms have to exercise appropriate judgement to ensure that the specific arrangements for Solvency II staff contained in Article 275(2) are applied proportionally and modified where required to reflect the size and nature of their businesses.[21]

---

[18] See Art 4(1), n 3 of CRR amending EMiR.

[19] Ibid, 75.

[20] EBA, *Opinion on the application of proportionality to the remuneration provisions in Directive 2013/36/EU*, EBA/Op/2015/25, 13.

[21] PRA, *Supervisory Statement 10/16, Solvency II: Remuneration requirements*, London, July 2018.

Nonetheless, it is well known that there are different legal interpretations of the proportionality clause in the EU banking legislation, which have led to different applications of the remuneration principles at the national level. As a result, an action was necessary at the level of the EU institutions in order to ensure that remuneration requirements are applied consistently across the Union. In EBA's view, CRD IV should be amended 'to exclude certain small, non-complex institutions from the requirements to apply the remuneration principles regarding deferral and payment in instruments for variable remuneration, and to limit the scope of those remuneration principles as regards staff who receive low amounts of variable remuneration, including large institutions'.[22] A similar refresh would be appropriate also in the insurance Solvency II Delegated Regulation, which has led to different applications of the remuneration requirements in the Member States implementing national legislation.

The recent revision of the CRD[23] provides for less stringent reporting, disclosure and remuneration requirements to reduce administrative costs for small non-complex institutions without watering down prudential standards. When applied to small and non-complex institutions, some of the principles, namely the requirements on deferral and pay-out in instruments, are too burdensome and not commensurate with their prudential benefits. Similarly, the cost of applying these requirements exceeds their prudential benefits in the case of staff with low levels of variable remuneration, since such levels of variable remuneration produce little or no incentive for staff to take excessive risk.

Consequently, under CRD V all institutions should, in general, be required to apply all the principles to all of their staff whose professional activities have a material impact on their risk profile. However, the revised Directive exempts small and non-complex institutions and staff with low levels of variable remuneration from the principles of deferral and pay-out in instruments. As regards to the scope of the personnel involved, under the revised Article 92(2), the total remuneration policies still have to be applied only for categories of staff whose professional activities have a material impact on the 'institution's risk profile'. However, the new regime is not as over-inclusive anymore as it was before. Essentially, it does not automatically apply any more to any 'senior management, risk takers, staff engaged in control functions and any employee receiving total remuneration that takes them into the same remuneration bracket as senior management'.

It is also worth noting, as mentioned in Recital 8 of Directive 2019/878, that clear, consistent and harmonised criteria for identifying small and non-complex institutions as well as low levels of variable remuneration are necessary to ensure supervisory convergence and to foster a level playing field for institutions and an adequate protection of depositors, investors and consumers across the Union.

A similar regime would be beneficial from a cross-sectoral perspective. The EU legislation should also seek, as far as possible, to limit the potential for outcomes that are disproportionately different across sectors. In the banking and asset management entities (subject to CRD, AIFMD and UCITS V Directive), the prescriptive requirements on deferral may be disapplied under certain conditions. Unfortunately, Solvency II Delegated Regulation Article 275(2) does not provide for the waiver of its provisions in these circumstances. An enhanced application of the proportionality clause would be useful to assess the specific arrangements that firms have put in place for Solvency II staff to comply with Article 275(2). In this sense, a further step toward a more harmonised definition and interpretation of the proportionality clause in the banking and

---

[22] Ibid, 21–22.
[23] Directive (EU) 2019/878 of 20 May 2019 amending CRD IV as regards exempted entities, financial holding companies, mixed financial holding companies, remuneration, supervisory measures and powers and capital conservation measures.

insurance sectors should be considered a priority issue for the smooth functioning of the internal market as well as to foster adequate supervision on the financial institutions as a whole.

VI. Conclusion

A cross-sectoral convergence is not only possible but also conceivable. To overcome the short-comings of the European legislation in the banking sector, the area of remuneration regulation should be made more flexible and proportionate within limits allowed by international princi-ples. A more convergent approach should be adopted for the largest insurance companies when they belong to financial conglomerates. Moreover, it would be wise to focus on systemic risk to define the thresholds identifying the institutions (banks, insurance companies, asset managers) which should be subject to the most stringent provisions as to the setting and monitoring of executive's pay. Lastly, the governance and supervision of pay should emphasise the role of culture in the setting and monitoring of remuneration,[24] for incentives are not set in a vacuum but reflect both the culture prevalent in society and the corporate culture of the individual firm.

---

[24] See Danny Busch and Guido Ferrarini (eds), *Governance of Financial Institutions*, (Oxford, Oxford University Press, 2019).

8C

Ownership Allocation and Stakeholder Representation in Financial Institutions

CARMINE DI NOIA AND MATTEO GARGANTINI*

I. Introduction

Ownership is a key feature in the governance of any enterprise, and financial institutions (FIs) are no exception. Just like any other firm, FIs adopt a broad array of organisational and procedural devices to make sure their management acts in the interest of their shareholders – and of their stakeholders at large, depending on the preferred assumptions on the aim of firm governance.[1] And, once again in line with other firms, FIs' governance is inevitably sensitive to ownership allocation and to the incentives this allocation determines for directors as well as, more indirectly, for managers. Ownership of FIs may protect stakeholders by granting certain powers to them qua shareholders. Next to ownership, other governance tools may ensure stakeholder representation in FI governance, however, regardless of any (additional and more direct) control rights. In this case, corporate governance protects some stakeholders by conferring certain rights upon them qua stakeholders.

This chapter will assess how the corporate governance toolbox adapts to FIs, and to the agency problems they display in different competitive contexts. This includes the role of the boards in ensuring proper management of the enterprise as well as the role of stakeholder representation in all its forms, and particularly through ownership and board membership.

The analysis proceeds as follows. Section II provides a theoretical framework for the allocation of ownership and control in FIs. Section III analyses some alternative models of FIs' ownership, highlighting their relative advantages and disadvantages. Section IV tackles some systems of stakeholder representation within FIs, and explains how these may complement ownership allocation. Section V concludes.

* The opinions expressed are personal. The authors wish to thank Prof Marieke Wyckaert for the useful comments. All errors remain the sole authors' responsibility. Sections I, II and V shall be attributed to Carmine Di Noia; sections III and IV to Matteo Gargantini.
[1] For a recent analysis see, eg, Vikas Mehrotra and Randall Morck, 'Governance and Stakeholders', NBER Working Paper No 23460 (2017).

II. Ownership and Control of Financial Institutions: Theoretical Framework

As we mentioned, allocating firm ownership to a certain constituency is a key governance element in any corporation. However, the role the allocation of ownership plays in FIs, compared to other firms, is particularly important for at least two reasons. The first reason is that the quality of shareholders affects business integrity and firm resilience. Suitability of qualifying shareholders is therefore crucial to ensuring proper FI management, and to facilitate additional capital support in case of financial distress. As a consequence, acquisition of material stakes in FIs' capital is normally subject to supervisory scrutiny, with a view to ensuring that the role of relevant shareholders does not prevent a sound and prudent management of the firm.[2] This aspect of ownership is analysed in depth in Chapter 8A. 'A Cross-Sectoral Analysis of Corporate Governance Provisions' by Tom Vos, Katrien Morbee, Sofie Cools and Marieke Wyckaert.

There is, however, a second reason why ownership is of particular importance to FIs. This has to do with the very nature of share ownership as a governance tool that grants, from a legal point of view, the ability to appoint directors and, consequently, to control the enterprise management. As the new institutional economics has demonstrated, the allocation of ownership over firms is a governance device that helps reduce the costs of firm management.[3] Just like any other assets, ownership can therefore be allocated more or less efficiently, depending on the ability of the owners to minimise those costs. In the case of FIs, key in this respect are the incentives shareholders have due to their nature, because managers will inevitably align to those incentives not to incur the risk of being removed. It is in this second sense that this chapter addresses the issue of ownership allocation within FIs.

What is relevant in our analysis, therefore, is not so much whether an actual or potential shareholder is well-suited to the role but, rather, how the interests of such a shareholder affect the governance of FIs. This influence becomes particularly evident if one considers that FIs under the control of shareholders mainly interested in capital returns are by far the most common form of FIs, but they are not the only existing model. Other FIs are controlled by shareholders whose main interest is, rather, in receiving high quality services at the cheapest price. When this is the case, shareholders are customers of the FIs, and their interest in the remuneration of capital is greatly diminished.

Examples of allocation of ownership to shareholders who contribute input factors other than equity capital are manifold. Take mutual insurance societies as well as mutual savings and cooperative banks as an example. These firms are owned by policyholders, depositors and other customers, and this clearly has an influence on the FI governance. Other examples include financial market infrastructures such as central counterparties (CCPs) and central securities depositories (CSDs), some of which are under the control of their own customers.

Allocation of ownership to customers determines the typical interests that will be represented in the board. Directors will inevitably focus on the price and quality of the financial services the FI provides rather than on returns on equity, as long as the two diverge. This is what makes the allocation of ownership a particularly important element of FIs' governance. As the legal

---

[2] The financial soundness of relevant shareholders belongs to the criteria supervisors assess when assessing the acquisition of qualifying holdings (for banks, see Arts 14(2) and 23(1) Dir 2013/36/EU – CRD IV).

[3] For an overview see Oliver E Williamson, 'The New Institutional Economics: Taking Stock, Looking Ahead', (2000) 38 *Journal of Economic Literature* 595.

and economic theory has demonstrated, the role of stakeholders is in fact a critical issue in FIs' governance.[4]

What does then determine the allocation of ownership, and why are some FIs owned by stakeholders other than mere providers of equity capital? In this regard, Henry Hansmann has explained that ownership will normally pertain, absent external constraints, to the production factor providers (or 'patrons') that minimise the costs of running the firm when in control.[5] These factors of production include equity capital – as is the case with the standard model of FIs – but also business opportunities. More in detail, in line with Ronald Coase's intuition,[6] market contracting and governance (including ownership) are the two basic mechanisms for the allocation of production factors. It is therefore efficient to allocate ownership in a way that minimises the overall costs of governance and market contracting.

There are several market imperfections the costs of which can potentially be reduced by assigning ownership to the affected patrons (ex-ante and ex-post market power, risks of long-term incomplete contracts, asymmetric information, strategic bargaining, and so on). Ownership allows firms to internalise the costs of contracting with one or more category of patrons, and therefore – other things being equal[7] – it is more efficient that this integration occurs with those patrons with whom transacting is more costly. The costs of bargaining with a monopolist are a typical example where internalisation may efficiently occur by allocating ownership to the monopolist's customers.

At the same time, different ownership structures result in different agency costs within the firm. These costs vary with respect to different classes of patrons, as some of them may govern the firm better than others. Of course, patrons that would reduce bargaining costs the most when in control do not necessarily coincide with patrons that would minimise the governance and monitoring costs of ownership. As a consequence, which patron(s) will best suit the role of controlling shareholder(s) will depend on the best combination of the two sources of costs.[8]

As the remainder of the chapter shows, the determinants of the relative advantages and disadvantages of allocating ownership to one or the other groups are manifold. Two are worth mentioning here. The first one is the competitive context where FIs operate. When markets are particularly concentrated and price regulation is difficult, allocating ownership to customers may help reduce the deadweight loss stemming from the distance between marginal revenues and marginal costs.[9] In some markets – such as those involving the provision of clearing and settlement services – FIs have a remarkable market share that gives them a dominant position and, sometimes, a (quasi-) monopolistic power. In those market scenarios, customer-owned FIs are typically less concerned about profit-seeking and, in some cases, they may even adopt a mutualistic governance that only pursues cost-saving and quality-improving strategies.

While customer-owned FIs may reduce the prices charged and increase the production, the break-even constraint will prevent them from applying prices that are equal to marginal costs as long as economies of scale keeps these latter below the average costs for any given level of

---

[4] See especially Mathias Dewatripont and Jean Tirole, *The Prudential Regulation of Banks*, (Cambridge, Mass, MIT Press, 1994). See also infra, section 1.2.

[5] Henry Hansmann, *The Ownership of Enterprise*, (Cambridge, Mass, Harvard University Press, 2000).

[6] Ronald H Coase, 'The Nature of the Firm', (1937) 4 *Economica* 386.

[7] The most relevant of these assumptions is the cost of governance itself stemming from the allocation of ownership to a specific group (see infra).

[8] Hansmann (n 5).

[9] See in general Christopher Decker, *Modern Economic Regulation*, (Cambridge, CUP, 2015), 19–20.

production. As we shall see in section III A, first-best pricing may still be achieved in this context through state-ownership, which may be considered, against this backdrop, as an extreme form of non-profit-maximising organisation.

Next to the competitive context, the second determinant of the relative (dis)advantages of allocating FIs' ownership to a specific stakeholder group is the homogeneity of interests within such a group. If the interests of a class of stakeholders are not homogeneous, that class is likely to increase, relative to more homogeneous classes, the governance costs of the FI. For instance, the relative size of users – or, more precisely, the relative amount of users' transactions with the FI – may skew the users' average preferences as regards the fees' structure FIs adopt when providing their services – these being deposit taking, insurance services, clearing or settlement functions, or investment services. Large users may favour higher, one-off or periodical entry fees, as long as these result in lower fees-per-transaction. Small users are instead more likely to prefer systems where prices proportionally reflect the amount of the volumes transacted, with no rebate for large volumes. The following sections of the chapter will highlight how these conflicts of interest may negatively affect the governance of FIs to the point that it is more efficient to grant control rights to a different class of stakeholders.

Interests may diverge to an even higher extent when shareholders belong to different classes. When this is the case, for instance, shareholders that are seeking for the highest risk-adjusted return on their investment will have different preferences compared to shareholders that have a large volume of transactions, qua customers, with the FI. In our analysis, we refer to FIs whose shareholders all have a 'dual capacity' as owners of (a stake in) the equity capital and as customers as 'customer-owned' FIs. Typically, these FIs have admission requirements in place to make sure all shareholders are sufficiently reliable in their capacity as customers, which further makes the shareholders' features, and interests, more homogeneous. In other models, non-customer shareholders may be allowed, even if customer-shareholders having a dual capacity retain control. We refer to these entities as 'customer-controlled' FIs.[10] Within these FIs, shareholders' interests display a greater degree of divergence, which may on its turn increase governance costs. Consequently, customer-controlled FIs may easily be a transitory condition from a profit-maximising to a customer-owned form, or vice-versa. At the same time, some FIs, whether customer-owned or customer-controlled, may have customers that are not shareholders, while others may provide services to shareholders alone.

III. Ownership and Control of Financial Institutions: Model Analysis

This section highlights some practical implications of the theoretical assumptions sketched out above. It does so by analysing some of the different models for the allocation of control rights over FIs. Each sub-section starts with an example of the relevant model and then briefly delineates the essential features of such a model from the point of view of its ability to address the agency problems we highlighted in section II. In line with the underlying philosophy of the whole chapter, the following analysis is cross-sectoral, as it draws from FIs providing different financial services: banking, insurance, securities settlement, financial data distribution, and others.

---

[10] Carmine Di Noia, 'Customer-Controlled Firms: The Case of Financial Exchanges', in G Ferrarini et al. (eds), *Capital Markets in the Age of the Euro* (Zuidpoolsingel, Kluwer Law International, 2002), 173.

Before starting this exercise, it is however convenient to highlight some features that are common to a remarkable number of FIs that deviate from the standard profit-maximising model, although not to all of them.

Some FIs, and in particular those that qualify as financial infrastructures, manage platforms. This makes them develop network externalities, because their attractiveness depends not only on the quality of the service provided, but also on the number of their (direct and indirect) users.[11] Network externalities are relevant to our analysis because they may sometimes develop into natural monopolies (or into oligopolies) and make competition weaker than in other financial sectors, which on its turn affects shareholder and managerial incentives.[12]

To be sure, recent regulatory developments are endeavouring to increase competition among FIs that operate in oligopolistic markets, such as CSDs and CCPs. Issuers have the right to have their securities – if admitted to trading on a trading venue – recorded at any CSD established in any Member State (Article 49, CSDR). Symmetrically, CSDs enjoy an EU passport that enables them to provide their services in other Member States (Article 23, CSDR). In a similar vein, CCPs authorised to clear an OTC derivative contract can have access to trade feeds from any trading venue where that contract is admitted to trading (Article 8, EMIR), and shall at the same time accept to clear transactions on such contracts on a non-discriminatory and transparent basis, regardless of the trading venue, subject only to operational and technical interoperability (Article 7, EMIR). For the time being, these initiatives have not always proved able to dismantle the existing barriers, however. For instance, CSDs that wish to enter new national markets inevitably have to ensure their customers will be able to comply with the corporate law of the country were the centralised securities are constituted (Articles 23 and 49, CSDR), which means that CSDs have to adopt ad hoc procedures for every jurisdiction they deal with. As harmonisation remains low in this respect, CSDs may have little incentives to enter foreign markets.

Next to affecting competition, platform structures may also play a role in the allocation of ownership as a consequence of their influence on stakeholder interests – one of the determinants of ownership allocation we highlighted above. For instance, two-sided platforms may easily determine conflicting interests between the two user groups they serve. FIs structured as two-sided platforms connect groups of customers that receive different financial services, which are however closely intertwined. The typical example is the credit card industry, which enables payments to take place between shop owners, on one side of the platform, and their customers, on the other side.[13] FIs managing this kind of platform may adopt a pricing structure that receives all the revenues from one side of the platform (profit-making side) and provides free services to users on the other side (loss-leader side).[14] As a consequence, customers on the two sides of the platform have diverging interests, and are less likely to jointly become efficient owners.

Divergent interests may easily affect one-sided platforms, too, especially when not all the relevant stakeholders are direct users. For instance, most investors do not have direct access to a CSD. Rather, they hold their securities accounts through intermediaries, which may on their turn do the same with other intermediaries, and so on until the holding chain reaches the CSD.

---

[11] See Michael L Katz and Carl Shapiro, 'Network Externalities, Competition, and Compatibility', (1985) 75 *American Economic Review* 424.

[12] See, eg, Max Weber, 'Central Counterparties in the OTC Derivatives Market from the Perspective of the Legal Theory of Finance, Financial Market Stability and the Public Good', (2016) 17 *European Business Organization Law Review* 71.

[13] For an analysis see William F Baxter, 'Bank Interchange of Transactional Paper: Legal and Economic Perspectives', (1983) 26 *Journal of Law and Economics* 541; Jean-Charles Rochet and Jean Tirole, 'Two-Sided Markets: A Progress Report', (2006) 37 *RAND Journal of Economics* 645.

[14] Jean-Charles Rochet and Jean Tirole, 'Platform Competition in Two-Sided Markets', (2003) 1 *Journal of the European Economic Association* 990.

In this context, direct users – which are often in such a small number to create an oligopolistic market – may for instance tend to charge indirect users disproportionately for their intermediation.

Even direct users alone may have interests that conflict with those of the platform, in case they carry out a competing business on their own. A bank that is a member of a trading venue may, on its turn, run an MTF or an OTF. In the same vein, a bank that is a participant of a CSD can internalise some settlements, particularly when the buyer and the seller both hold their securities accounts, directly or indirectly, with that same bank (Article 9, Regulation (EU) No 909/2014 – CSDR).[15]

As a consequence, some FIs are subject to competition by their own clients, or even by their own investors. For instance, payment systems and CSDs may enjoy an upstream monopolistic power in their ability to provide centralised services, but may also have an incentive to restrict their clients' ability to provide similar services downstream, at a decentralised level.[16] Whether they compete with their owners or with their clients, some FIs are therefore subject to conflicts of interests that negatively distort their incentives to best serve their principals.

The effect of platform competition on ownership allocation cannot be overestimated, because it explains a remarkable number of deviations from the traditional profit-maximising corporate model in FIs. However, not all FIs that manage platforms are customer-controlled entities, as most of them take the form of profit-maximising entities controlled by equity investors. At the same time, not every customer-controlled FI manages a platform. In the following subsections, we will consider some examples of the possible combinations between these variables in different financial sectors.

A. Stated-Owned and State-Controlled Financial Institutions

The first model we consider is that of FIs that are controlled by a state or by another public entity, whether this fully owns the platform or not. These FIs were much more common in the past, before technological developments and the ensuing competition among new actors[17] led to the privatisation of a number of previously state-owned FIs.[18] Nonetheless, some FIs still display this feature. Among them, the EDGAR (Electronic Data Gathering, Analysis, and Retrieval) system run by the US Securities and Exchange Commission (SEC).

EDGAR is a platform that enables interested parties, including listed companies, to file documents with the SEC and to disseminate them, when the applicable rules so require.[19] As a network that allows dissemination of information subject to mandatory disclosure, EDGAR displays the typical features of a two-sided platform, because it connects regulated entities, on the one side, with investors, on the other side. EDGAR features the characteristics of such a model

---

[15] Salvatore Lo Giudice, 'Settlement Internalization: The Production and Distribution of Services in the (Clearing and) Settlement Industry', (2008) 20 *Journal of Financial Transformation* 127.

[16] Ibid.

[17] Technological developments increased competition by reducing the barriers to entry into the market for FIs, which enlarged the scope of enterprises that could carry out activities developing network effects.

[18] For a recent analysis see OECD, 'Privatisation and the Broadening of Ownership of State-Owned Enterprises Stock-taking of National Practices' (Paris: 2018).

[19] SEC, 'Important information about EDGAR', 16 February 2010, available at www.sec.gov.

in its purest form, because it connects neither regulated entities among themselves, nor investors among themselves, but only the two groups between them.

There may be various reasons why state control can be an efficient governance device for FIs.[20] When FIs are natural monopolies, public ownership or control may reduce the incentives to profit maximisation that characterise other models – including customer-controlled organisations, to some extent – especially when it does not take the form of a profit-maximising corporate structure.[21] This ownership allocation reduces the negative externalities of excessive risk-taking and may optimise production by making prices equal to marginal costs, thus avoiding the under-production problems that are typical to monopolistic market structures.

When marginal costs are lower than average costs due to economies of scale, public control may also, if compared to other models, facilitate state subsidisation, as long as this is considered an objective worth pursuing from a general policy perspective. For instance, the EDGAR platform is accessible for free by investors. Issuers can also file most of their information for free, although they may have to pay a fee when submitting certain documents.[22] To be sure, we have no evidence issuer fees are not sufficient to cover EDGAR operational costs, but the model as such may easily cover imbalances with the general supervisory fees levied on all the supervised entities within a market.

On the flipside of the coin, public control may suffer from well-known efficiency problems, chief among them – if the FI is not subject to competition – reduced incentives to minimise costs and invest in innovation.[23] Regulation normally impose minimum technical standards state-owned FIs have to comply with when they operate in a non-competitive context. Regulation alone might not suffice, however, to foster innovation. Even if the applicable rules reflected the state of the art at any given moment, regulators might not be in the best position to enforce them. The regulators' personnel normally specialise in law or finance and may lack the technical skills required to identify and correct possible shortcomings in the FIs' operation.

B. Customer-Owned and Customer-Controlled Financial Institutions

In the second model of ownership allocation we consider, some customers (or all of them) control, with different legal techniques, the FI that provides financial services to them. As we mentioned, this model can be found both in the realm of financial market infrastructures and in other FIs.

An example concerning a financial market infrastructure is the Depository Trust & Clearing Corporation (DTCC), the holding company of the US DTCC group, which is owned by the customers of its subsidiaries that perform post-trading services within the group.[24] The DTCC

---

[20] For an overview see OECD, 'Ownership and Governance of State-Owned Enterprises A Compendium of National Practices' (Paris: 2018), 16–22.

[21] See section III C below.

[22] SEC, Filing Fee Rate, 1 October 2018, available at www.sec.gov (identifying as fee-bearing documents registration statements under s 6(b) of the Securities Act 1933 as well as statements concerning stock-repurchases and proxy solicitation materials under ss 13(e) and, respectively, 14(g) of the Securities Exchange Act of 1934).

[23] Privatisation is normally associated with better performance: see, eg, William L Megginson and Jeffry M Netter, 'From State to Market: A Survey of Empirical Studies on Privatization', (2001) 39 *Journal of Economic Literature* 321, 356–7.

[24] Paolo Saguato, 'The Ownership of Clearinghouses: When "Skin in the Game" Is Not Enough, the Remutalization of Clearinghouses', (2017) 34 *Yale Journal on Regulation* 101, 107.

group encompasses both CCPs[25] and a CSD,[26] so that the holding company's shareholders are exclusively the users of clearing and settlement services (and of other related services). No external investors can buy shares in the holding company,[27] and the allocation of shares among members is proportional to the overall consideration they pay to the group for the service received.[28] The DTCC is therefore customer-owned according to the taxonomy provided in section II, because all its shareholders have a dual capacity as owners of (a stake in) the equity capital and as customers.

Customer-owned FIs not running a financial market infrastructure include cooperative banks and mutual insurance companies. These FIs are common in most EU countries, and collectively hold a significant market share.[29] Just like with any other cooperative, these entities need to make profits to remain on the market, but profit distribution is not their typical business objective.[30] Profits are not normally distributed, and represent the most important source of capital. The most common voting system of cooperatives adopts the 'one member, one vote' principle, but alternative systems exist (as the DTCC example demonstrates).

While state-owned FIs not having the form of a profit-maximising entity may reduce profits to zero, or even below zero when some subsidisation occurs, customer-controlled FIs typically pursue some kind of stakeholder welfare's maximisation subject to break-even constraints. This is more evident for customer-controlled FIs incorporated as commercial companies, and even for FIs having the same legal form that are fully owned by their customers (also considered in the next section). However, the same applies to some extent to mutualistic entities such as cooperatives, as well, because these cater for their owners-users' need to save on the costs of commercial relationships with such entities. In this case, the incentive is strong for FIs to reduce prices for any given output – or to maximise the output for any given production cost. Whenever the price of a service exceeds the average cost of production, user-shareholders will tend to internalise this difference in their capacity as owners, so that the level of the price will become less relevant for their total welfare. Customer-owned FIs are subject to these incentives regardless of their legal form (profit-maximising entity, cooperative, and others), because owners will always have an interest in purchasing services of the best quality at the cheapest price.

The main agency problem with customer ownership and customer control is that, in these firm models, some of the customers, who consume the services, decide the pricing policy and, in general, the enterprise strategies. In all the examples above, customer-shareholders have contrasting interests: they improve their welfare as the firm's profits (and dividends) increase but also if the prices of the services decrease, because this improves their own consumer surplus. However, ceteris paribus, the firm makes fewer profits in this case. This may lead to perverse effects. Pricing policies that eventually do not lead to maximising profits may represent a problem for dispersed and minority shareholders – whether these are customers or not – who might suffer reduced earnings with little or no influence on the company's strategies.

---

[25] Namely the National Securities Clearing Corporation (NSCC), which provides clearing, settlement, risk management, and central counterparty services to its members for broker-to broker trades involving equities, corporate and municipal debt, exchange-traded funds, and unit investment trusts, and the Fixed Income Clearing Corporation (FICC), which performs comparable functions for the government and mortgage-backed securities markets (DTCC, Condensed Consolidated Financial Statements as of 30 September 2018 and 31 December 2017 and for the three and nine months ended 30 September 2018 and 2017 (1 November 2018), 6, available at www.dtcc.com).

[26] Namely the Depository Trust Company (DTC), which provides central securities depository and settlement services (ibid).

[27] DTCC, 'Financial Market Infrastructures. Building Strength and Resilience for the Future' (2014), 4.

[28] Changes in the ownership structure are made accordingly, at a price determined on the basis of the company's book value (ibid, 5).

[29] Deposits collected by cooperative banks amounted, in 2015, to more than one-fifth of the total EU deposits: Hans Groeneveld, 'Snapshot of European Co-operative Banking 2017', TIAS Working Paper (2017), 20.

[30] Rym Ayadi et al, *Investigating Diversity in the Banking Sector in Europe*, (Brussels, CEPS, 2011), 8 and 11.

By the same token, customers that do not simultaneously qualify as shareholders may also be adversely affected. For example, the management of a FI controlled by large users may structure the pricing policy as a two-part tariff with a large one-shot fee combined with small transaction fees, so that the average fee would be much lower for big intermediaries. Furthermore, non-monetary perverse effects may derive from conflicts of interest involving the decisions to admit new users, which is typical for both FIs operating as self-regulatory organisations and mutualistic or cooperative structures. In particular, stricter (laxer) admission requirements and enforcement standards – for listing, membership, or participation, as the case may be – may lead to a higher (lower) quality of the services provided or may make the FI more resilient, but they may also reduce (increase) shareholder revenues and determine (remove) a barrier to competitors. Finally, conflicts stemming from the dual capacity of customers-owners may also affect investment policies, because investments that would maximise the utility of shareholders may not deliver a similar welfare-maximising effect for large controlling users alone and may therefore be abandoned with a loss of total welfare.[31]

Whether these conflicts lead to suboptimal management of the FI depends on several factors, including the level of homogeneity among customer-shareholders and the level of own funds required. As we clarified in section II, nonhomogeneous interests in a class of stakeholders increase the cost of attributing control powers to such a class. When customer-owned FIs take the form of a cooperative entity, such as cooperative banks and mutual insurance societies, there is another reason why divergent interests among members make firm governance less efficient. This is due to the fact that the 'one member, one vote' principle allocates the pivotal decision-making power to the median shareholder, as opposed to 'one share, one vote' systems that give preference to the average voter. When the preferences of the median and of the average shareholder diverge, the 'one member, one vote' principle therefore leads, by definition, to suboptimal results in terms of shareholder welfare maximisation.[32]

In cooperative banks and mutual insurance societies, shareholders' interests may diverge as a by-product of the legal remedies to the obstacles cooperatives traditionally face when raising own funds.[33] To some extent, the EU rules on prudential requirements are mindful of this limitation and tend to facilitate the formation of own capital by mutualistic FIs through supplementary member calls (see, for mutual insurances, Article 96, Directive 2009/138/EC – Solvency II). When this is not sufficient to meet prudential requirements, some mutualistic FIs may raise funds from external owners,[34] whose interest in profit-maximisation does not coincide with the typical interests of customer-owners.

Competition among customer-shareholders may further exacerbate the governance costs of mutualistic models. On the one hand, having a seat on the board of the company that manages the FI facilitates information exchange among competitors, which may be problematic for the general welfare in case this leads to collusion. On the other hand, and vice-versa, some customer-owners may try to use their influence on FIs' governance to hamper their competitors, or may

---

[31] In the field of securities trading, this conflict has been for years at the heart of (some) stock exchanges' resistance to invest in new technologies enabling electronic trading and remote access (see, eg, Craig Pirrong, 'The Organization of Financial Exchange Markets: Theory and Evidence', (1999) 2 *Journal of Financial Markets* 329).

[32] Oliver Hart and John Moore, 'Cooperative vs. Outside Ownership', NBER Working Paper Series 6421 (1998), 5; see also Hansmann (n 5), 40

[33] For mutual insurers see, eg, Pierre-Charles Pradier and Arnaud Chneiweiss, 'The evolution of insurance regulation in the EU since 2005', in Raphaël Douady et al (eds), *Financial Regulation in the EU: From Resilience to Growth* (Cham, Springer International, 2017), 209.

[34] CEPS (n 30), 14; Jean-Nöel Ory and Yasmina Lemzeri, 'Efficiency and Hybridization in Cooperative Banking: The French Case', (2012) 83 *Annals of Public and Cooperative Economics* 215, 225.

reduce the circulation of sensitive information within the company if they fear that their competitors may take advantage of it.

From the point of view of corporate governance, these conflicts might make two-tier corporate governance systems preferable with a view to reducing, if compared to one-tier structures, the circulation of information among customer-owners, to the benefit of antitrust concerns and of non-colluding competitors. Supervisory boards, which gather the owners' representatives, do not typically deal with day-to-day management, which is left to management boards instead.[35] These latter comprise executives that can be more detached from the shareholders, and may therefore more easily shield sensitive information from them. This way, a two-tier governance may enable customer-owners that are also competitors of the FI to credibly commit, vis-à-vis their fellow peers or even the antitrust authority, not to abuse of free circulation of information within the FI corporate structure.

With regard to financial market infrastructures, possible competition between FIs themselves and their customer-owners may also play a crucial role. As Hart and Moore demonstrate, the level of competition between exchanges and the diversity of interest of the exchange members are the main determinants for FI ownership.[36] Greater competition and greater diversity exacerbate agency costs of customer-controlled firms, making user ownership relatively less efficient. This holds true not only for competition coming from other FIs, but also when customer-owners themselves operate in the same markets, as this increases the conflicts of interests between customer-owners, on the one hand, and the FI, on the other hand.

Things are different when FIs run a financial infrastructure having monopolistic market power. As one of us has demonstrated elsewhere,[37] customer-owned monopolists tend to achieve first-best social outcomes, whilst in customer-controlled monopolists minority shareholders are easily damaged because profits are not necessarily maximised. In particular, customer-owned FIs are welfare-efficient if their customers (listed firms, intermediaries, price vendors, and the like) hold an amount of capital equal to their proportion over the total number of customers.[38] If the ownership is allocated among users in proportion to the quantity of services they purchase – as is the case with the DTCC – price will tend to become irrelevant. If this is not the case, misalignments between the share of company's capital owned and the share of revenues paid to the FIs may skew shareholders' incentives and create conflicts of interests among them, as the interest to profit maximisation may prevail over the consumers' interest, or vice-versa. This is all the more so for customer-controlled entities, where some shareholders do not contribute to the FI's revenues at all.

C. For-Profit (and Listed) Financial Institutions with External Ownership

In this section, we consider FIs that are controlled by external (ie, non-customer) shareholders, which typically combine this feature with the business objective of maximising profits. This is the

---

[35] Reinier Kraakman et al., *The Anatomy of Corporate Law* (Oxford, OUP, 2017), 50–1.

[36] Oliver Hart and John Moore, 'The Governance of Exchanges: Members' Co-operatives versus Outside Ownership', (1996) 12 *Oxford Review of Economic Policy* 53 (addressing stock exchanges in particular).

[37] Di Noia (n 10). For this reason, self-listing of customer-controlled stock exchange may not be an optimal choice, as it may exacerbate investor protection problems (ibid).

[38] For this reason, customer-controlled entities may be less efficient in this respect. Pure shareholders, who do not use the FIs' services, should have equity participation equal to zero, thus turning customer-controlled entities into customer-owned ones.

most common corporate form for FIs, and in particular for those performing banking, investment, and insurance services. But profit-maximising entities are also common among financial market infrastructures, and especially among regulated markets after the demutualisation wave of the late nineties. Today, stock exchanges like the NYSE and Nasdaq have among their shareholders a majority of investors having no, or limited, interest in purchasing their services.[39]

Just like for any other governance structure, the competitive context is a key determinant of the incentives for profit-maximising entities such as FIs with external ownership, as well. It is no coincidence that privatisation of stock exchanges occurred in the aftermath of a wave of technological innovation that opened up competition in markets where incumbent firms could easily display some or all the features of natural monopolists. In a system where the development of network externalities required open outcry on the pits and, later on, direct telephonic connection with the same central matching system, sub-additivity of the cost functions for each trading venue determined a natural tendency towards concentration of trading platforms. In such a context, FIs such as stock exchanges would easily be subject, when under the control of private investors other than users, to technical and x-inefficiency due to weak incentives to maximise outputs for any given inputs.[40] Against this backdrop, external ownership may lead to profit maximisation and, therefore, to suboptimal outcomes in terms of welfare.

Technological innovation may however reduce entry barriers by lowering fixed costs, and by allowing to develop network externalities at cheaper costs.[41] For some financial services, this may easily lead to fully fledged competition, as is the case with trading platforms. For others, competition may only be potential, but market contestability can still produce disciplining effects on firm management that are comparable to those of effective competition.[42] In a context of actual or potential competition, profit-maximising corporate forms may reduce the conflicts of interest among owners that affect customer-controlled (and sometimes even customer-owned) firms, thus fostering investments in new technologies.

In spite of these advantages, FIs that maximise profits are not immune to market failures, either, particularly when profit maximisation leads to suboptimal outcomes due to public good problems and other externalities. Shareholder limited liability and risk-taking incentives, combined with the typically high leverage of banks' balance sheets, are a case in point, along with the systemic impact of major FIs' defaults. These incentive structures lead to a higher risk appetite of for-profit FIs, compared to cooperatives.[43] At the same time, traditional corporate governance tools, such as independent board members, have proven weak in addressing these problems.[44]

When market infrastructures are run as profit-maximising entities, an oft-mentioned drawback for regulated markets is, for instance, a potential interest in relaxing admission to listing

---

[39] As of March 2018, the only three only investors above the 5% threshold in the outstanding capital of Intercontinental Exchange (ICE) – the controlling company of NYSE – were T Rowe Price Associates, Vanguard Group Inc and BlackRock Inc (Intercontinental Exchange, Inc., Notice of 2018 Annual Meeting and Proxy Statement, 29 March 2018, 55). As for NYSE, investors above the threshold are, at the time of writing, Investor AB (controlled by the Wallenberg family), Massachusetts Financial Services Co, Vanguard Group Inc, Blackrock Inc and Capital World Investors (Nasdaq, Ownership Summary, available at www.nasdaq.com).

[40] John R Hicks, 'Annual Survey of Economic Theory: The Theory of Monopoly', (1935) 3 *Econometrica* 1; Harvey Leibenstein, 'Allocative Efficiency vs. "X-Efficiency"', (1966) 56 *American Economic Review* 392.

[41] The ability of new technologies to reproduce network externalities at relatively cheap costs is a common dynamic in most markets, and FIs are no exception. For telecommunications see, eg European Commission, Case M.7217 – Facebook/ WhatsApp – Commission decision pursuant to Art 6(1)(b) of Council Regulation No 139/2004, Brussels, C(2014) 7239 final, 3 October 2014, §§ 127 ff.

[42] William J Baumol, 'Contestable Markets: An Uprising in the Theory of Industrial Structure', (1982) 72 *American Economic Review* 1.

[43] CEPS (n 30), 15–6.

[44] See Dan Awrey et al, *Principles of Financial Regulation* (Oxford, OUP, 2016), 370–80.

standards so as to broaden the number of negotiated stock and the ensuing trading revenues.[45] Whether these concerns are well-grounded or not, it is remarkable that the solution some authors submit to avoid adverse selection problems is a more extensive reliance on admission to listing by a public listing authority.[46] In the light of the analysis above, this would be equivalent to adopting a state-controlled governance for (part of) the functions FIs perform.

Another drawback of profit-maximising FIs may stem from divergent interests between shareholders and users, in contexts where these latter do not have a voice in the FI governance and might not have the possibility of choosing an FI's competitor. For instance, while CCPs' shareholders retain control rights, they are not the residual claimants and primary loss-bearer, because the CCP's default hierarchy of loss-absorption (so called 'waterfall') initially involves members' contributions in the first place.[47] This divergence between voting power and financial exposure may exacerbate the negative externalities that normally accompany limited liability, as shareholders are protected from losses by capital buffers they did not contribute to creating.

This and other similar conflicts of interest make the regulators' role indispensable, as prudential supervision becomes key to curbing excessive risk-taking due to profit maximisation. Absent competition, price regulation may also be needed to ensure FIs supply adequate services at a fair price.[48] However, it is questionable whether regulation can effectively tackle, ex post, issues that better ownership incentives could reduce ex ante.

An extreme form of profit-maximising FIs with external ownership are listed FIs. Going public is a relatively straightforward step for FIs, which in this way can raise at cheaper costs the capital they need to meet their prudential requirements. However, some listings are worth considering here in the light of their peculiar implications. These are the admissions to listing of stock exchanges whose shares are listed – typically[49] – on their same markets (self-listing).

When listing facilitates ownership dispersion, the governance of FIs running a trading platform may be further detached from possible conflicts between owners and customers, because these latter will likely hold (individually, but most likely also collectively) a small amount of the FIs' outstanding capital. Furthermore, (self-)listing may foster the adoption of best governance practices recommended in self-regulatory codes of conduct.[50] On the flipside of the coin, however, (self-)listing may also have negative consequences.[51] Being listed entails some costs, which are normally justified on the basis of companies' funding needs. However, this rationale has been challenged for stock exchanges,[52] due to the normally high level of cash flow these

---

[45] See, eg, Marcel Kahan, 'Some Problems With Stock Exchange-Based Securities Regulation', (1997) 83 *Virginia Law Review* 1509, 1517; Jonathan R Macey, Maureen O'Hara and David Pompilio, 'Down and Out in the Stock Market: The Law and Finance of the Delisting Process', (2008) 51 *Journal of Law and Economics* 683.

[46] For a review see Maureen O'Hara, 'Searching for a New Center: U.S. Securities Markets in Transitions', (2004) 37 *Federal Reserve Bank of Atlanta Economic Review*, 47–51.

[47] Extensively Saguato (n 24).

[48] See text accompanying n 21 above.

[49] Stock exchanges listed on markets run by competitors are rarer. One example was Tradepoint, a UK stock exchange listed on the Vancouver Stock Exchange (see Di Noia (n 10)).

[50] See Art 20, Dir 2013/34/EU on the annual financial statements, consolidated financial statements and related reports of certain types of undertakings.

[51] We are not concerned here with the conflict of interest inherently affecting the (self-)admission to listing and the ensuing (self-)supervision by the regulated market operator.

[52] Di Noia (n 10).

entities enjoy, which reduces the need for external funding.[53] Furthermore, as long as one perceives short-termism as a problem that affects listed companies,[54] a similar concern is all the more justified for all FIs, due to the systemic risks they involve.

IV. Stakeholder Representation

The previous section has analysed the determinants of ownership allocation, in particular in the light of the relative costs and benefits of granting control of FIs to each of the relevant groups of stakeholders. At the same time, the analysis has shown that conflicts of interests among different groups of stakeholders, or within each of those groups, may deliver suboptimal results in terms of agency costs. This may call for some forms of stakeholders' role in the governance, especially – but not exclusively – when competition alone does not provide sufficient incentives to cater for the welfare of all FIs' users.

Besides ownership, representation of stakeholders qua stakeholders – and therefore regardless of any shareholding – is the second device that plays a particular role in FIs' governance. The idea of granting stakeholders, and creditors in particular, some form of representation is far from new. To be sure, some alternatives exist that can deliver creditor protection by way of contractual agreements, such as bond covenants. Other tools can also reduce excessive risk-taking, of course, such as variable remunerations based on CoCo bonds or other similar financial instruments (Article 94(i)(g)(l)(ii), CRD IV). However, all these measures have their drawbacks,[55] which make the agency problem of creditors' interest protection a persistent problem. Having stakeholders' representatives within the companies' bodies may help therefore address some of these concerns, not only within profit-maximising FIs but also elsewhere. For the sake of expositions, this section draws a distinction between stakeholder representation within the board (including through ad hoc internal committees) and stakeholder representation through committees outside the board. The distinction plays a role in defining the representatives' powers, because board membership normally comes with decision-making powers.

However, the difference between intra and extra board representation should not be overestimated. First, access to the board does not necessarily mean full board membership. Participation to board meetings may in fact be sometimes deprived of voting rights, thus resulting in a softened voice. Being part of the board of directors arguably remains a valuable governance tool, if only for the capacity to reduce information asymmetries, but the stakeholders' ability to influence the FI's corporate management is, in this case, softened. It could depend, for instance, on the stakeholders' ability to react to an unsatisfactory board's decision through exit.

Second, representation outside the board never entails direct decision-making powers, but it can sometimes be strengthened by the possibility of drawing the supervisors' attention to stakeholder discontent. The remainder of this section will provide some examples of the various forms of stakeholder representation.

---

[53] See also, more broadly, John Kay, *Other People's Money. Masters of the Universe or Servants of the People?* (London, Profile Books Ltd, 2015), 161–4.

[54] See, eg, Recital 2, Dir (EU) 2017/828 as regards the encouragement of long-term shareholder engagement.

[55] For a recent analysis see Paul Davies and Klaus Hopt, 'Non-Shareholder Voice in Bank Governance', in Danny Busch et al (eds), *Governance of Financial Institutions* (Oxford, OUP, 2019), 126–33.

A. Stakeholder Representation within the Board

The debate on stakeholder – and, in particular, user[56] – representation within the board has gained intensity in the wake of the demutualisation wave of stock exchanges, but has involved other FIs as well, whether demutualised or not.[57] Scholars[58] and market participants[59] have claimed that users' access to the board could reduce the agency costs of FIs' governance and improve the quality and the cost of the services provided. At the same time, others have voiced the concern that enabling FIs' corporate boards to pursue stakeholder interests at large would negatively affect directors' (and managers') accountability, because every decision, even the least sensible, could find a justification as a way to meet some stakeholder need.[60]

An indirect legal coverage for voluntary stakeholder representation may perhaps be traced in provisions requiring board diversity. For instance, the board of regulated market operators and banks that are significant in terms of their size, internal organisation and of the nature, scope and complexity of their activities shall establish a nomination committee composed of non-executive members. As any other nomination committee, this has to identify and recommend to the management body or the general meeting the candidates it deems most suitable to fill management body vacancies. In so doing, the nomination committee takes into account the 'balance of knowledge, skills, diversity and experience of the management body', and sets a gender representation target (Article 88(2)(a), CRD IV; Article 45(4), MiFID II). While none of these elements requires any form of stakeholder representation whatsoever,[61] this would surely be one of the possible ways to reach a proper balance of skills within the management. All the more so as the same law requires that the nomination committee shall try to avoid that the board be dominated by small groups of members to the detriment of the market operator as a whole (Article 88(2), sub-paragraph 2, CRD IV; Article 45(5), MiFID II).

However, direct representation of stakeholders, and of creditors in particular, within the board raises a number of concerns. Just to mention two of them, it remains in the first place unclear how this representation would fit with other – pre-existing or prospective – forms of stakeholder representation. For instance, in countries where labour codetermination is allowed or mandated, the question arises who, between shareholders' and employees' representatives, should free the seats to leave room for creditor representation.[62] Secondly, a more precise identification of the creditor constituency may prove problematic in practice. Depositors would be the obvious main candidates, but their rational apathy might prevent the appointment mechanism from working properly. Furthermore, some other creditors should be excluded, such as other banks that have credits towards their competitors.[63]

Partially because of these uncertainties, stakeholder representation within the board has received scant attention from national and supranational regulatory organisations, with the

---

[56] In this section, we refer to 'stakeholders' and 'users' indifferently.

[57] Mutualistic governance is not immune to issues of stakeholder representation, in fact. These may easily emerge when users' interests are not homogeneous (see section II above; Ruben Lee, *Running the World's Markets* (Oxford, OUP, 2011) 284–7 and 299).

[58] See, eg, Caroline Bradley, 'Technology, Demutualisation and Stock Exchanges: The Case for Co-Regulation', Working Paper, University of Miami School of Law (2002), available at www.ssrn.com; Daniela Russo et al., 'Governance of securities clearing and settlement systems', ECB Occasional Paper No 21 (2004).

[59] Stakeholder representation was invoked, for instance, by UK and French trade associations (Lee (n 57), 288).

[60] Lee (n 57), 291 (also mentioning Prof. Margaret M Blair's opinion).

[61] The same holds true for the ESMA Guidelines on the management body of market operators and data reporting services providers – ESMA70-154-271 (2017).

[62] Davies and Hopt (n 55), 137.

[63] Ibid, 138.

exception of financial infrastructures. The main examples in this area[64] are the Group of Thirty Plan of Action on Clearing and Settlement[65] and the CPSS-IOSCO Principles for Financial Market Infrastructures.[66] Between the two organisations, the Group of Thirty seems to go further in submitting stakeholder representation, as it considers this governance device as indispensable for an infrastructure to pursue users' interests fairly and equitably. To the contrary, the CPSS-IOSCO Principles only consider stakeholder representation within the board as one among many different tools aimed at protecting users' interests. Alternative measures are user committees and public consultation processes.

As for the EU, full board membership of stakeholder representatives does not appear among the governance rules that the law mandates. However, EU law does not completely disregard the matter, either. In particular, a softened form of users' access to the board for some FIs can be traced in FIs managing financial infrastructures, which are once again at the forefront. This is the case, for instance, with CCPs, whose clients' representatives are invited to attend board meetings where some critical matters are discussed, such as prices, fees and rebates as well as asset segregation (Article 27(2), EMIR). While these representatives appear to have no voting power, their presence in the board can enhance their voice and give them an advisory role in the decision-making procedure.

B. Stakeholder Representation Outside the Board

Other forms of users' representation in an advisory capacity may occur outside the board. In the most structured forms, this entails the creation of internal bodies, such as ad hoc committees, where stakeholders have permanent representation. Not only does the creation of committees facilitate the organisation of stakeholder representation, but their permanent nature normally enables those committees to express positions on their own motion. This is a crucial element of stakeholder representation, because it prevents the board from having the exclusive power to define the agenda on the issues that are most sensitive to users.

Once again, EU law mandates some forms of permanent stakeholder representation in the realm of financial infrastructures. For other FIs, concerns that the services' prices or quality may be suboptimal are normally tackled through competition, so the applicable rules do not provide for a legal framework in this respect.

For CCPs, a risk committee is established that comprises representatives of clearing members, independent members of the board of directors, and clients. None of such groups shall have the majority within the committee, but the chairperson should always be an independent director (Article 28, EMIR). The committee advises the board on issues that may affect the CCP's risk management. The list includes 'a significant change in the CCP's risk model, the default procedures, the criteria for accepting clearing members, the clearing of new classes of instruments, or the outsourcing of functions', while the day-to-day management is expressly excluded.

By the same token, CSDs have to establish user committees – one for each securities settlement system they operate – composed of representatives of issuers and of participants (Article 28, CSDR). Along the same lines of CCPs' risk committees, CSDs' user committees

---

[64] Lee (n 57), at 289–90.

[65] Group of Thirty, Global Clearing and Settlement – A Plan of Action (2003), Recommendation 19, 11 (recommending a 'balanced representation of varying stakeholder groups, including users', within the board).

[66] CPSS-IOSCO, Principles for Financial Market Infrastructures, BIS (2012), Principle 2, 31.

advise the management body on some fundamental matters, 'including the criteria for accepting issuers or participants in their respective securities settlement systems and on service level'. This also includes the possibility of submitting, on own motion, opinions on the pricing structures of the CSD.

Finally, to strengthen the voice of the committees of representatives, the CCP or the CSD they belong to has to inform the competent supervisor on any board decision that does not follow the advice of the committees (Article 28(5), EMIR; Article 28(6), CSDR). In the case of CSDs, this alert system can be autonomously activated by the committee itself. While not making the committees' advice binding, triggering this alarm may in practice result in a duty, for the board, to justify its decision in critical cases.

Besides these structured forms of representation, other systems are available to involve stakeholders in the corporate decision-making of financial infrastructures. The most important are consultation mechanisms, which some codifications of best practices recommend either as such or as an alternative to direct representation within the company.[67]

V. Conclusion

This chapter has analysed some drivers of ownership allocation in FIs and has described the EU legal framework on stakeholder representation in those firms. While regulation normally addresses the most typical concerns for stakeholder protection, corporate governance also plays a role in bolstering the regulatory action. Adequate corporate governance can in fact complement the regulatory and supervisory efforts by making FIs more stable and less prone to market failures.[68]

The research object of this chapter goes beyond the typical sectoral divides of FIs. We have analysed allocation of ownership to customers in institutions as diverse as mutual insurance societies, cooperative banks, central counterparties and central securities depositories. In that respect, any legislation that aims to address the specific corporate governance dynamics of such an ownership structure could easily be cross-sectoral.

Proper allocation of ownership enables FIs to reduce – although not to eliminate – transaction costs stemming from divergent stakeholders' interests. Therefore, different ownership structures will lead to equally different benefits in terms of agency problems, but they will also entail specific drawbacks. Stakeholder representation may further contribute to aligning the management of FIs with the needs of their customers, including in contexts where these latter may have no possibility of switching to FIs' competitors. Finally, customer-controlled FIs may take advantage of some corporate governance arrangements, such as a two-tier board structure, to shield information exchange that is necessary for the day-to-day management from potential competitors represented in the supervisory board.

---

[67] See CESR-ECB, 'Recommendations for Securities Settlement Systems and Recommendations for Central Counterparties in the European Union (2009)', Recommendation 13.C.3; CPSS-IOSCO (n 66), Principle 2, § 3.2.18.

[68] This is true not only from a theoretical, but also from an empirical perspective: David A Becher and Melissa B Frye. 'Does regulation substitute or complement governance?', (2011) 35 *Journal of Banking & Finance* 736.

9

Resolution Regimes in the Financial Sector: In Need of Cross-Sectoral Regulation?

To a superficial observer, the resolution of complex, systemically important financial institutions (in the broadest sense, including, for that purpose, also operators of financial market infrastructures) might appear as a problem that has arisen only during, and in the aftermath of, the global financial crisis 2007/2009. That impression would be mistaken, however. As will be discussed in more detail below,[1] work on common standards for resolution regimes, at the international level, had already begun considerably before the crisis. At the national levels, for some sectors, mature regimes for the management of financial institutions' insolvency date back decades ago, while the harmonisation of procedural and substantive frameworks at the European level, in part, has started in the late 1990s. By contrast, the quest for resolution frameworks for application in more than just one sector is a rather new phenomenon. It clearly has been driven by the insight that the financial crisis, among other things, has illustrated not just the modern, globalised financial markets' predisposition for cross-border contagion, but also the interconnection of different parts of financial markets and the resulting potential for cross-sectoral contagion. Among the insights gained from research into the causes and the development of the global financial crisis, the emergence of a comprehensive conceptual understanding of the determinants of systemic risk[2]

[*] The author would like to thank, in particular, Victor de Serière, Danny Busch, Veerle Colaert and other participants in the FinPoSe Workshop at Radboud University, Nijmegen, on 15 and 16 October 2018.

[1] See section I in this chapter.

[2] Cf, in particular, Basel Committee on Banking Supervision (BCBS), 'Global systemically important banks: updated assessment methodology and the higher loss absorbency requirement' (July 2013), available at www.bis.org/publ/bcbs255. pdf; Miquel Dijkman, 'A Framework for Assessing Systemic Risk' (April 2010), *World Bank Policy Research Working Paper* 5282; for a review of the recent economic literature (with a focus on the banking sector) see Olivier De Bandt, Philipp Hartmann and José Luis Peydró, 'Systemic risk in banking. An update', in: AN Berger, P Molyneux and JOS Wilson (eds), *The Oxford Handbook of Banking* (Oxford, Oxford University Press, 2010), p 633; from a legal perspective, Steven L Schwarcz, 'Systemic Risk', (2008) *Georgetown Law Journal* 97, 193. And see International Monetary Fund (IMF), Bank for International Settlements (BIS) and Financial Stability Board (FSB), 'Guidance to assess the systemic importance of financial institutions, markets and instruments: Initial considerations – Joint report to the G20 Finance Ministers and Central Bank Governors' (October 2009), available at www.financialstabilityboard.org/publications/r_091107c.pdf. From an insurance perspective, see, in particular, International Association of Insurance Supervisors (IAIS), 'Insurance and Financial Stability' (November 2011), available at www.iaisweb.org/page/news/other-papers-and-reports//file/34041/insurance-and-financial-stability#; and see Andreas A Jobst, 'Systemic Risk in the Insurance Sector: A Review of Current Assessment Approaches', (2014) *The Geneva Papers* 39, 440. From the perspective of securities regulation, see, in particular, International Organization of Securities Commissions (IOSCO), 'Mitigating Systemic Risk – A Role for Securities Regulators' (February 2011), available at www.iosco.org/library/pubdocs/pdf/IOSCOPD347.pdf.

constitutes a major advancement compared to the pre-crisis literature. It has also been influential in recalibrating the focus of post-crisis financial regulation, by expanding the traditional sector-specific scope to a broader, risk-oriented approach whose perimeter transcends the traditional borders between the various subsectors of financial intermediation and market infrastructure. In the field of financial institutions' insolvency, just as in other areas of prudential regulation, this insight, prima facie, should be expected to foster the development of resolution frameworks whose scope and technical design is informed not by traditional sectoral boundaries, but rather by a functional analysis, leading to the identification of common, or at least, parallel, risks and problems that may or may not occur in more than one sector. Instead of sector-specific resolution frameworks, the expected result would thus be the emergence of cross-sectoral regimes, based on a set of identical conceptual principles and implementing identical technical solutions if and to the extent that the relevant problems are the same. Both at the international level, with the Financial Stability Board's 'Key Attributes of Effective Resolution Regimes for Financial Institutions' of 2011 and 2014,[3] and in European Union law, with the Commission's 2012 'Consultation on a possible recovery and resolution framework for financial institutions other than banks',[4] regulatory initiatives indeed appear to have been moving to that direction for some time. At the same time, however, the bulk of relevant international standards and most legislative initiatives in EU law still continue to be more or less strictly sectoral in scope and nature, and it should be noted that, specifically, the consultation mentioned above has not led to a comprehensive legislative proposal so far (and, indeed, this should not be expected to emerge in the foreseeable future).

Against this backdrop, the present chapter explores the rationale and potential for cross-sectoral regulation in the field of resolution regimes for financial institutions. Starting with a stock-taking exercise of existing initiatives both at the international standard-setting level and in EU law (see section I), the chapter then analyses parallels and residual differences in the technical problems caused by insolvencies in the different sectors of financial markets, as well as in terms of the technical requirements to be met by effective resolution regimes, and the underlying policy objectives (section II). The chapter concludes with a summary (section III).

Two caveats are in place: *First*, given the complex nature of financial institutions' resolution generally, it should be noted from the start that an in-depth, let alone exhaustive treatment of the technical problems to be expected across the different sectors – and potential remedies – cannot reasonably be accomplished within the present context. Instead, this chapter seeks to identify, from a functional perspective, core aspects and challenges that could guide relevant future developments at the level of international standards and/or European harmonisation. *Secondly*, given the global nature of the underlying problems and, indeed, the global roots of international standards in the field of financial regulation, the analysis should, ideally, take into account market structures and regulatory frameworks across a broad range of jurisdictions, including, in particular, the US as one of the most influential drivers of global regulatory convergence. Within the scope of the present project, however, the following analysis, in addition to the applicable international standards as such, will focus mainly on their adoption in European law. Nonetheless, it should be borne in mind that the problems discussed below are part of a broader picture.

---

[3] Financial Stability Board, 'Key Attributes of Effective Resolution Regimes for Financial Institutions' (2011), available at www.financialstabilityboard.org/publications/r_111104cc.pdf; revised version published in 2014, available at www.financialstabilityboard.org/wp-content/uploads/r_141015.pdf.

[4] European Commission, DG Internal Market and Services, 'Consultation on a possible recovery and resolution framework for financial institutions other than banks', 5 October 2012. See, for further information, http://ec.europa.eu/finance/consultations/2012/nonbanks/index_en.htm.

With international standards becoming ever more influential also in the field of financial institutions' insolvency, the question of whether, and under which conditions, cross-sectoral approaches are desirable and/or feasible also in this regard cannot be discussed at an abstract level, but has to build on a careful analysis of the relevant market structures, the risk profiles inherent therein, and the specific channels of cross-sectoral contagion. In view of residual differences between banking, securities and insurance markets as well as market infrastructures, the identification of common, cross-sectoral ground is inevitably intricate. Consequently, any findings that can be offered from a theoretical perspective below (rather than on the basis of a comprehensive, empirical analysis of existing market structures and interlinkages) should be regarded as merely tentative in nature.

I. Taking Stock: Where Do We Stand?

A. International Standards

International standards have addressed problems relating to financial institutions' insolvency in two major waves. Beginning in the 1980s, in response to prominent failures mainly in the banking sector since the 1970s, the first relevant workstreams adopted a *transactional* perspective, and introduced principles for the protection of specific contractual relationships that had been identified as particularly sensitive in the event of a failure of a large financial institution. One aspect where international standards prepared the ground for later European harmonisation concerned problems of finality of transfers in payment and settlement systems,[5] while in the area of minimum standards for the protection of depositors and investors in bank failures, international standards followed only after the harmonisation of the legal framework within the EU.[6] Given the restricted focus on certain transactional aspects, such early initiatives are, as such, outside the focus of the present chapter, but should nonetheless be borne in mind as an integral part of the full picture.

By contrast, the emergence of *institutional* approaches to insolvency management, ie, of procedural and substantive principles for the treatment of insolvent intermediaries as such, took

---

[5] For early initiatives in this regard, carried out by the Committee on Payments and Market Infrastructures and its predecessor established under the auspices of the BIS, see, in particular, BIS, 'Report on Netting Schemes' ('Angell Report') (9 February 1989), available at www.bis.org/cpmi/publ/d02.pdf; id., 'Report of the Committee on Interbank Netting Schemes of the central banks of the Group of Ten countries' ('Lamfalussy Report') (18 November 1990), available at www.bis.org/cpmi/publ/d04.pdf; id., 'Central bank payment and settlement services with respect to cross-border and multi-currency transactions' ('Noëll Report') (9 September 1993), available at www.bis.org/cpmi/publ/d07.pdf; id., 'Real Time Gross Settlement Systems' (March 1997), available at www.bis.org/publ/cpss22.pdf; id., 'Core Principles for Systemically Important Payment Systems' (19 January 2001), available at www.bis.org/cpmi/publ/d43.pdf. For the adoption in European Law, see, in particular, Dir 98/26/EC of the European Parliament and of the Council of 19 May 1998 on settlement finality in payment and securities settlement systems, [1998] OJ L166 of 11 June, p. 45.

[6] Through Dir 94/19/EC of the European Parliament and of the Council of 30 May 1994 on deposit-guarantee schemes, [1994] OJ L135 of 31 May, p 5 (repealed by DGS, [1996] OJ L173 of 12 June, p 149) and ICS, [1997] OJ L84 of 26 March, p 22. For standards published later at the international level, *cf.*, in particular, Financial Stability Forum (as it then was), 'Guidance for Developing Effective Deposit Insurance Systems' (September 2001), available at www.fsb.org/wp-content/uploads/r_0109b.pdf. And see, with a focus on the role of deposit insurance in bank resolution, International Association of Deposit Insurers, 'General Guidance for the Resolution of Failing Banks' (5 December 2005), available at www.iadi.org/en/assets/File/Papers/Approved%20Guidance%20Papers/Guidance_Bank_Resol.pdf; id., 'Funding of Deposit Insurance Systems' (6 May 2009), available at www.iadi.org/en/assets/File/Papers/Approved%20Guidance%20Papers/Funding%20Final%20Guidance%20Paper%206_May_2009.pdf; id., 'Governance of Deposit Insurance Systems' (6 May 2009), available at www.iadi.org/en/assets/File/Papers/Approved%20Guidance%20Papers/Governance%20Final%20Guidance%20Paper%206_May_2009.pdf.

longer to develop. Although the International Monetary Fund and the World Bank, in what was called the Global Bank Insolvency Initiative, had made a first attempt at promulgating standards on the optimal design of bank insolvency management tools in the early 2000s,[7] no further step was taken to promote convergence of relevant practices, procedures and instruments until after the global financial crisis. In 2010, the 'Cross-border Bank Resolution Group', established under the auspices of the Basel Committee on Banking Supervision, then published its 'Report and Recommendations',[8] the development of which – along with the initial version of the FSB's Key Attributes[9] – had an influence on the parallel work on the European Bank Recovery and Resolution Directive (BRRD).[10] Significantly, although the Basel Committee's work recognised the need for the application of such standards also to systemically important non-bank financial institutions,[11] no attempt was made to define cross-sectoral parallels and differences that would have to be taken into account in this regard.

Outside the banking sector, a comprehensive set of standards was first presented for insurance undertakings, with a paper on the challenges of cross-border insolvency management published by IAIS in 2011,[12] whereas insolvency-related problems in investment firms were addressed in a paper on 'Market Intermediary Business Continuity and Recovery Planning', by IOSCO in 2015.[13] Resolution arrangements for financial market infrastructures present a special case in this regard. Certain types of infrastructures had already been addressed by prudential standards in the early 2000s, with an explicit focus on protecting client assets and preventing systemic risk.[14] In 2012, these standards were superseded by a comprehensive package of 'Principles for financial market infrastructures', which specifically address aspects of risk management and business continuity, as well as settlement finality.[15] Since the financial crisis, awareness of the systemic relevance of at least certain types of financial market infrastructures has increased in particular because of the post-crisis trend towards mandatory central clearing requirements for OTC derivatives contracts.[16] Conceived as a means to foster systemic resilience, by shifting default

---

[7] The Initiative's results were published only in 2009, however, see IMF and World Bank, 'An Overview of the Legal, Institutional, and Regulatory Framework for Bank Insolvency' 17 April 2009, www.imf.org/external/np/pp/eng/2009/041709.pdf. And see, for further discussion, Ross Leckow, 'The IMF/World Bank Global Insolvency Initiative – Its Purpose and Principal Features', in DS Hoelscher (ed), *Bank Restructuring and Resolution* (Basingstoke, Palgrave MacMillan, 2006), pp 185–195.

[8] BIS, 'Report and recommendations of the Cross-border Bank Resolution Group' (18 March 2010), available at https://www.bis.org/publ/bcbs169.pdf.

[9] See above, n 3.

[10] BRRD, [2014] OJ L173, 12 June, p 190. See, for a detailed analysis of the roots of that Directive in the national laws of specific jurisdictions and its relationship to the simultaneous emergence of international standards in the field of bank resolution, eg, Jens-Hinrich Binder, 'Resolution: Concepts, Requirements, and Tools', ch 2, in: JH Binder and D Singh (eds), *Bank Resolution: The European Regime* (Oxford, Oxford University Press, 2016), paras 2.05–2.25.

[11] BIS, see above n 8, para 76.

[12] IAIS, 'Issues Paper on Resolution of Cross-border Insurance Legal Entities and Groups' (1 June 2011), available at www.iaisweb.org/page/supervisory-material/issues-papers#.

[13] IOSCO, 'Market Intermediary Business Continuity and Recovery Planning' (December 2015), available at www.iosco.org/library/pubdocs/pdf/IOSCOPD523.pdf.

[14] See, in particular, Committee on Payment and Settlement Systems (CPSS) and Technical Committee of IOSCO, 'Recommendations for securities settlement systems' (November 2001), available at www.iosco.org/library/pubdocs/pdf/IOSCOPD123.pdf; id., 'Recommendations for Central Counterparties' (November 2004), available at www.iosco.org/library/pubdocs/pdf/IOSCOPD176.pdf.

[15] CPSS and Technical Committee of IOSCO, 'Principles for financial market infrastructures' (April 2012), available at www.bis.org/publ/cpss101a.pdf, ss 2.0 and 3.0.

[16] See, in the EU, Arts 4 and 5 of EMiR, [2012] OJ L201 of 27 July, p 1; in the US: Dodd-Frank Wall Street Reform and Consumer Protection Act of 2010, Pub L No 111–203, 124 Stat 1376 (2010), s 723(a)(3) (amending s 2 of the Commodity Exchange Act [7 U.S.C. 2]).

risk from bilateral relations to well-managed central counterparties with mature risk mitigation arrangements, this trend has triggered widespread concerns about the safety of central counterparties and, indeed, their growing significance for global financial stability at large. Such concerns have triggered not just a prolific academic literature,[17] but also prompted a number of international standards on risk mitigation and the management of failures of systemically important financial market infrastructures in general and CCPs in particular.[18]

While the bulk of international standard-setting initiatives thus has been clearly sectoral in scope and content, the only set of standards intended to apply across more than one sector so far have been the FSB's 'Key Attributes of Effective Resolution Regimes for Financial Institutions'.[19] This document presents a particularly interesting case for present purposes. The initial version (published in November 2011), although already addressing not just credit institutions but '[a]ny financial institution that could be systemically significant or critical if it fails' (expressly including financial market infrastructures, for that purpose),[20] was clearly tailored mainly to the needs of failing banks and hardly provided for specific adjustments for sectors other than that. By contrast, the 2014 version, while keeping the original principles (the 12 'Key Attributes') unchanged, was expanded by detailed sector-specific annexes defining implementation and interpretation guidance for FMIs and FMI participants and insurers,[21] recognising that the Key Attributes, as such, should apply across different sectors but need substantial adjustments for application to institutions other than banks.[22]

---

[17] To date, the majority of contributions have been published in the US, with a focus on mandatory central clearing under the Dodd-Frank Act (previous note). See, eg, Julia Lees Allen, 'Note: Derivatives Clearinghouses and Systemic Risk: A Bankruptcy and Dodd-Frank Analysis', (2012) 64 *Stanford Law Review* 1079; Ilya Beylin, 'A Reassessment of the Clearing Mandate: How the Clearing Mandate Affects Swap Trading Behavior and the Consequences for Systemic Risk', (2016) 68 *Rutgers Law Review* 1143; Felix B Chang, 'The Systemic Risk Paradox: Banks and Clearinghouses under Regulation', (2014) *Columbia Business Law Review* 747; Charles Hauch, 'Dodd-Frank's Swap Clearing Requirements and Systemic Risk', (2013) 30 *Yale Journal on Regulation*. 277; Stephen L Lubben, 'Failure of the Clearinghouse: Dodd-Frank's Fatal Flaw?', (2015) 10 *Virginia Law & Business Review* 127; Hester Peirce, 'Derivatives Clearinghouses: Clearing the Way to Failure', (2016) 64 *Cleveland State Law Review.* 589; Mark J Roe, 'Clearinghouse Overconfidence', (2013) 101 *California Law Review.* 1641; Yesha Yadav, 'The Problematic Case of Clearinghouses in Complex Markets', (2013) 101 Georgia Law Review 387. From a European perspective, see, eg, Max Weber, 'Central Counterparties in the OTC Derivatives Market from the Perspective of the Legal Theory of Finance, Financial Market Stability and the Public Good', (2016) 71 *European Business Organization Law Review* 71; Hossein Nabilou and Ioannis G Asimakopoulos, 'Examining the Prudential Regulation and Resolution Regimes for Central Clearing Counterparties in Europe' (1 June 2018), available at https://ssrn.com/abstract=3188844. For a useful comparison between the regulatory frameworks in the EU and the US, see Levon Garslian, 'Towards a Universal Model Regulatory Framework for Derivatives: Post-Crisis Conclusions from the United States and the European Union', (2016) 37 *University of Pennsylvania Journal of International Law.* 941.

[18] See, generally, Committee on Payment and Settlement Systems and Technical Committee of IOSCO, 'Principles for financial market infrastructures', above n 15. And see, in particular, Committee on Payments and Market Infrastructures (CPMI) and Board of IOSCO, 'Recovery of financial market infrastructures' (October 2014, revised in July 2017), available at www.bis.org/cpmi/publ/d162.pdf; FSB, 'Guidance on Central Counterparty Resolution and Resolution Planning' (5 July 2017), available at www.fsb.org/wp-content/uploads/P250717-3.pdf.

[19] See, again, above text and n 3.

[20] FSB, Key Attributes (2011), above n 3, paras 1.1–1.3.

[21] FSB, Key Attributes (2014), above n 3, pp 57–73 (FMI and FMI participants) and pp 75–88 (insurers).

[22] Cf, also ibid, p 2: 'The sector-specific guidance recognises that not all Key Attributes are equally relevant for all sectors and that some require further explanation and interpretation, or some adaptation in order to be effectively implemented in a certain sector. The sector-specific guidance sets out how the Key Attributes should be understood in a sector-specific context. It complements the Key Attributes, and the sector-specific guidance on individual KAs should be considered in conjunction with the KA to which it relates. There should be no inference that a particular KA or element of a KA does not apply simply because there is no supporting provision in the relevant Annex.'

B. European Union

Within the European Union, the emergence of resolution regimes for systemically important financial institutions (in the broadest sense) to date has been exclusively a sectoral phenomenon. The most comprehensive step so far, obviously, has been the adoption of the Bank Recovery and Resolution Directive in 2014 which, in parallel with the Basel Committee's 'Report and Recommendations' and the FSB's 'Key Attributes' introduced a complex harmonised regime for the recovery and resolution of systemically important credit institutions and investment firms for application in the EU as a whole.[23] This Directive has later been adopted as the basis for a separate, more centralised regime for resolution actions within the Single Resolution Mechanism in the Eurozone.[24] For insurers in crisis, by contrast, Title IV, Chapters II and III of the Solvency II Directive[25] provide for some harmonisation of reorganisation and liquidation procedures, but fall short of a comprehensive special regime akin to that developed for credit institutions and investment firms. A Commission proposal for a Regulation establishing a framework for the recovery and resolution of central counterparties,[26] released in 2016, has not yet been formally adopted.

With all existing legislative initiatives confined to specific sectors so far, a move towards cross-sectoral approaches to financial institutions' failure in Europe has yet to materialise. In this respect, it is worth noting that the Commission's 2012 'Consultation on a possible recovery and resolution framework for financial institutions other than banks'[27] has never matured into a legislative proposal. While the proposal for a new framework for CCP resolution discussed before was based on the earlier consultation process,[28] no attempt has been made to develop a comprehensive, cross-sectoral resolution regime. Indeed, the much narrower focus of the CCP proposal may, in itself, be interpreted as an indication that such more ambitious plans stand only little, if any chance to become reality in the foreseeable future.

II. Where to Go from Here? The Case for (and against) Cross-Sectoral Regulation Revisited

A. A Rough Map of Relevant Issues

In order to prepare the ground for a more granular analysis of the rationale, and indeed feasibility, of cross-sectoral resolution regimes for application to a broader range of financial institutions, it should be noted, from the start, that the concept of 'resolution', in the way it has evolved in both international standards and European legislation, should by no means be confused with traditional insolvency procedures. In fact, under the BRRD as well as the SRMR, 'resolution' is conceived as a functional alternative to, and substitute for, traditional means of insolvency management (in particular, liquidation procedures), to be applied specifically in cases where

---

[23] See earlier text and n 10.

[24] See SRM Regulation and amending EBA, [2014] OJ L225 of 30 July, p 1 (hereafter: 'SRMR').

[25] Solvency II (recast), [2009] OJ L335 of 17 December, p 1.

[26] European Commission, Proposal for a Regulation of the European Parliament and of the Council on a framework for the recovery and resolution of central counterparties, 28 November 2016, COM(2016) 856 final. See, for analysis, Randy Priem, 'CCP recovery and resolution: preventing a financial catastrophe', (2018) 26 *Journal of Financial Regulation and Compliance*, 351.

[27] Above n 4.

[28] Commission Proposal, above n 26, p 4.

such traditional means cannot be activated in view of potentially disastrous implications for professional counterparties, depositors, market infrastructures – in short, systemic stability.[29] While the scope of both instruments is not expressly restricted to systemically important institutions, care has been taken to restrict the use of the innovative toolbox to cases where the public interest in the prevention of contagious effects, in the light of the size of the institution in question, its market share, complexity and/or connectedness with other parties, outweighs the disadvantages (eg, the detrimental effects on creditors, as well as potentially higher costs of resolution compared with traditional insolvency liquidation).[30] A set of detailed 'resolution objectives' and 'general principles governing resolution' limit the resolution authorities' discretion and refine the concept of resolution as a functional substitute for traditional insolvency procedures serving broadly similar ends, but affording special protection for the public interest in maintaining a stable, sustainable banking sector subject to market-oriented incentive structures for bank owners, managers, and, indeed, large creditors and investors in bank debt.[31]

This conceptual approach is broadly consistent with the corresponding standards published by the Basel Committee and the FSB and results in a number of specific consequences in terms of both the applicable policy objectives and the technical design of resolution tools. Importantly, while designed so as to prevent contagion by protecting those contractual and economic relationships between an insolvent bank and other parties that could give rise to contagion, 'resolution', as a rule, seeks to preserve the incentive structure of bank owners, investors in bank debt, and managers of banks that would be associated with traditional insolvency liquidation to the extent possible. Particularly with the allocation of losses to shareholders and debt investors facilitated by the combination of what has become known as the 'write-down and conversion' of capital instruments and the 'bail-in' (ie, the cancellation of debt instruments and/or their conversion into equity),[32] the financial burden is to be shifted to those actors who would also have to bear it in traditional insolvency liquidation. 'Resolution', in a nutshell, is an alternative to insolvency liquidation which serves broadly the same ends – permanent solutions for the failure, with losses borne by shareholders and investors – while minimising systemic and fiscal exposure.[33] Through a combination of preventive instruments (including, in particular, the obligation for banks and resolution authorities to engage in proactive recovery and resolution planning)[34] with a complex set of 'resolution tools' and corresponding ancillary 'resolution powers',[35] the BRRD (for the EU as a whole) and the SRMR (for the Eurozone) seek to ensure that future bank failures and, indeed, bank crisis can be managed, as far as possible, without resort to extraordinary, taxpayer-funded bail-outs (which, during the global financial crisis, proved to be quite effective in avoiding systemic repercussions in the short run, but obviously triggered significant negative externalities on public budgets and, arguably, market discipline).

In reviewing the above principles, it seems to be difficult to identify reasons why they – in their entirety – should *not* apply to *any* financial institution whose size, market share, organisational complexity, and/or commercial interrelationship with other market participants or the

---

[29] Cf, in particular, Recitals 5 and 49; see, for further discussion, Binder, above n 10, paras 2.20–2.25.

[30] Cf, Art 32(1)(c), (5) BRRD = Art 18(1)(c), (5) SRMR; see further section II C below.

[31] Cf, Arts 31 and 34 BRRD = Arts 14(2) and 15(1) SRMR.

[32] See Arts 37(3)(d), 43–44, 46–55, BRRD, Arts 21 and 27, SRMR; see also FSB, Key Attributes (2014), above n 3, para 3.2.

[33] Cf, Binder, above n 10, para 2.16.

[34] See ch I (recovery and resolution planning) and ch II (resolvability) of the BRRD; Arts 8–11, SRMR; cf also FSB, Key Attributes (2014), above n 3, paras 10 (resolvability assessments) and 11 (recovery and resolution planning).

[35] Cf, ch IV (resolution tools) and ch VI (resolution powers) BRRD; Art 22(2), 24–27, SRMR; FSB, Key Attributes (2014), above n 3, paras 3.1–3.8.

real economy would give rise to the risk of systemic contagion in the event of a failure. Upon closer inspection, however, differences between the sectors appear to outweigh similarities, casting doubt on the merits of a comprehensive, integrated regime. To be sure, the rationale for the development of functional substitutes to traditional means of insolvency management, as such, is hardly confined to one specific sector, although already at this level, residual differences in terms of business activities result in differences in terms of relevant contagion channels (see section II B). Differences also exist with regard to the need to distinguish between (globally, regionally, or nationally) systemically important financial institutions (which do merit special treatment in insolvency) and others (which do not) (section III C). While recovery and resolution planning, rightly, have been identified as a core element of sustainable resolution frameworks across the board, the scope and content of such preventive measures very much depends on the nature of the respective business activities, indicating that substantial differentiation will be needed for application in various sectors (section II D). Much the same applies with regard to the definition of triggers for resolution (section II E), the design of applicable resolution tools (section II F), and the arrangements in place for the funding of resolution actions (section II G).

B. The Rationale for a Resolution Regime Distinct from General Insolvency Law

Conceptually, the development of special resolution regimes as a substitute for traditional insolvency proceedings reflects the insight that the latter regimes, whether geared towards a forced liquidation or a failing firm or, indeed, its reorganisation under the auspices of an insolvency court and/or an insolvency practitioner, are structurally ill equipped to address the specific problems posed by the insolvency of financial institutions. This is true, in particular, for those institutions, whose size, complexity, market share and/or degree of interconnectedness with other market participants would give rise to concerns that their individual failure may jeopardise the solvency and/or liquidity of their respective counterparties.

Resolution regimes for financial institutions ideally should preserve the principles of loss allocation to shareholders and investors that have been characteristic for the substantive design of traditional insolvency procedures for centuries (in order to realign the incentives of both groups of actors with the objective of long-term sustainability of business models and risk appetites of regulated institutions). Nevertheless, the application of such regimes to failing systemically important financial institutions still has come to be commonly accepted to be impractical. This is partly due to technical features common to traditional insolvency regimes. These include, in particular, (a) the imposition of a temporary ban of payments, a stay of proceedings and a freeze of execution measures in order to protect the insolvent estate prior to the formal commencement of the liquidation or reorganisation procedure as such, and (b) the institutional complexity of court-administered insolvency proceedings, which is incompatible with the need to implement credible reorganisation measures within an extremely short timeframe, so as to remove uncertainty and stabilise market sentiment.[36]

---

[36] See, for further analysis, Binder, above n 10, paras 2.11–2.13; Jens-Hinrich Binder, '"Too-big-to-fail" – can alternative resolution regimes really remedy systemic risk in large financial institutions' insolvency?', in: JR LaBrosse, R Olivares-Caminal and D Singh (eds), *Managing Risk in the Financial Sector* (Edward Elgar, 2011), p 233, at pp 234–240. For a good functional analysis, see also Christos Hadjiemmanuil, 'Bank Stakeholders' Mandatory Contribution to Resolution Financing: Principle and Ambiguities of Bail-In', in: European Central Bank, *ECB Legal Conference 2015* (2015), p 225, at

To some extent, this complexity is attributable to the traditional nature of insolvency proceedings as collective actions involving a high level of creditor participation and creditor control of the economic outcomes, which requires a framework for collective decision-taking that is unnecessary in the event of a purely administrative procedure, where decisions are taken and implemented unilaterally, with no creditor participation. Moreover, the lack of specialised expertise in courts and enforcement authorities may also play a role in this respect. Furthermore, traditional insolvency procedures focus on the solution of a distributional conflict and resulting collective action problems that arise when a firm's assets are no longer sufficient to meet all claims of creditors. Although public interest considerations may (and frequently do) influence substantive principles of insolvency law (particularly in the design of the hierarchy of claims in insolvency, eg, in the form of preferential treatment of workers' claims, tax duties, or social security contributions), the focus, at least in market-oriented insolvency regimes, will be on a fair distribution of assets among creditors, in a way that reflects their contractual and other property rights vis-à-vis the insolvency debtor.[37]

While traditional insolvency procedures allow for only limited room for the protection of interests other than those of the relevant creditors, the need to prevent contagious effects triggered by one particular financial institution's insolvency can, and frequently will, conflict with established principles of creditor participation and, ultimately, even with the established principle of equal treatment of creditors of a given category.[38] As a consequence of these considerations, rather than protecting the failing *institution* as such (eg, through the provision of state aid, which would unduly benefit shareholders and managers, but also investors in wholesale debt, resulting in moral hazard), alternative resolution regimes aim at protecting exclusively those economic *functions* of the relevant institution whose disruption would open contagion channels to other market participants, market infrastructures, and the economy at large. Consequently, ensuring the 'continuity of critical functions' rightly has been identified as the primary 'resolution objective',[39] such functions being defined as

> activities, services or operations the discontinuance of which is likely in one or more Member States, to lead to the disruption of services that are essential to the real economy or to disrupt financial stability due to the size, market share, external and internal interconnectedness, complexity or cross-border activities of an institution or group, with particular regard to the substitutability of those activities, services or operations.[40]

While all resolution objectives[41] are expressly declared to be 'of equal significance', with resolution authorities required to strike a balance, 'as appropriate, to the nature and circumstances of each case',[42] it is obvious that the motive to protect systemically important business activities and the contractual relationships attached thereto – as the potential channels of contagion, the threat of

---

pp 231–236; Gustaf Sjöberg, 'Banking Special Resolution Regimes as a Governance Tool', in: WG Ringe and PM Huber (eds), *Legal Challenges in the Global Financial Crisis* (Oxford, Hart Publishing, 2014), p 187, at pp 188, 194–200.

[37] See, generally, UNCITRAL, 'Legislative Guide on Insolvency Law – Parts I and II' (2005), Pt I, ch I, paras 1 and 13.

[38] On the relevance of both principles for the design of general insolvency laws, see, generally, ibid, paras 11–17.

[39] Article 31(2)(a), BRRD = Art 14(2)(a), SRMR.

[40] Article 2(1)(35), BRRD (applicable to the SRMR by virtue of Art 3(2), SRMR).

[41] See further Art 31(2), BRRD = Art 14(2), SRMR:

> '(b) to avoid significant adverse effects on financial stability, in particular by preventing contagion, including to market infrastructures, and by maintaining market discipline;
> (c) to protect public funds by minimising reliance on extraordinary public financial support;
> (d) to protect depositors covered by Directive 2014/49/EU and investors covered by Directive 97/9/EC;
> (e) to protect client funds and client assets'.

[42] Article 31(3), BRRD = Art 14(3), SRMR.

which will usually motivate the disapplication of ordinary forms of insolvency management in the first place – still plays a special role on top of other considerations that may also be considered in the circumstances.[43]

As such, the fact that none of the above considerations are confined to any particular financial markets subsector hardly needs further explanation. At this rather abstract level, the rationale for the substitution of traditional forms of insolvency procedures with a bespoke regime focusing on the protection of systemically relevant functions therefore certainly qualifies as a potential basis for the development of cross-sectoral resolution regimes. Equally applicable to sectors other than banking are the fundamental objective to protect systemic stability without providing public financial support, and the need to design and implement resolution actions in a way that affords the maximum protection for those counterparties (savers, retail investors) who are incapable of protecting themselves.[44] Finally, at an abstract level, the determinants for the systemic relevance of an institution and, indeed, its economic functions – size and market share, the substitutability of the relevant activities within the given market environment, and the interconnectedness with market participants and market infrastructures[45] – are also sufficiently broadly defined as to provide guidance across the board of financial institutions in the widest possible sense.

On closer inspection, the conclusion that the above findings provide sufficient grounds to support the case for cross-sectoral resolution regimes would be mistaken, however. As such, they hardly extend beyond the insight that traditional forms of insolvency procedures may have to be substituted if and where the key objectives of resolution – including, in particular, the protection of systemically important business functions – cannot be accomplished in ordinary insolvency proceedings. Since both the nature and dimension of what qualifies as systemically relevant functions inevitably differ from sector to sector, the assessment of whether and to which extent such functions cannot be adequately protected by the application of traditional insolvency regimes can also be expected to differ from sector to sector. To give but two examples: First, the highly dynamic nature of a bank's lending, investing and funding arrangements and operations will usually preclude any imposition of a moratorium as part of a resolution strategy aiming at the restoration of the relevant functions on a going-concern basis, lest investors and other counterparties lose confidence in, and run on, the relevant institution, thereby removing any prospect of a sustainable return to normal business operations.[46] For slightly different reasons, moratoria inevitably have to be avoided also in the case of an FMI insolvency, if and to the extent that they would obviously jeopardize the on-going capacity of the FMI to provide its services.[47] The same may not necessarily be the case in the insolvency of a systemically important insurance company, however, where financial relations to other parties are more long-term oriented and therefore more stable and where, as a result, a (selective) moratorium, depending on the circumstances, could be a more useful tool to control the outflow of liquid (always provided that the ban of payments does not in itself trigger domino effects by causing defaults elsewhere in the system).[48] Second, it has to be borne in mind that, in line with residual differences in terms of business

---

[43] This is also reflected in the wording of Recital 1 of the BRRD.

[44] For a formulation of these objectives, cf, again, Art 31(2), BRRD = Art 14(2), SRMR (quoted above at n 44).

[45] Cf, eg, IMF/BIS/FSB, Guidance to assess the systemic importance of financial institutions, markets and instruments: Initial considerations, see above, n 2, pp 8–9.

[46] See, again, above, text and n 36.

[47] FSB, Key Attributes (2014), above n 3, II-1, paras 4.17–4.18.

[48] It is worth noting, in this regard, that the IAIS Issues Paper on insurance resolution discusses traditional winding-up procedures and modifications thereto in rather detailed terms (IAIS, above n 12, paras 48–56), whereas alternative resolution arrangements are only briefly summarised (ibid, paras 57–58).

activities, the sources of contagion differ from sector to sector, which in turn may necessitate special safeguards, both intra-sectoral and inter-sectoral in nature.

All in all, the mere fact that 'systemic relevance' is – rightly – accepted as a phenomenon not restricted to any particular sector is not sufficient to justify the development of cross-sectoral resolution regimes. While the capacity of traditional insolvency procedures to accommodate the characteristics of sector-specific business activities cannot be explored in detail in the present chapter, it is, arguably, precisely the analysis of such details that would have to prepare the ground. If anything, this calls for further, cross-sectoral analysis of the causes of systemic contagion (both inter-sectoral and intra-sectoral) – and of the capacity of traditional insolvency procedures to address these causes. Given the residual differences between the sectors, the rationale for cross-sectoral approaches, in the absence of such research, is far from clear-cut, let alone self-evident.

C. The Scope: Systemically versus Non-Systemically Important Institutions

Even leaving aside the complex and intricate question of whether, despite residual differences in terms of business activities and systemic risk profiles, there is sufficient common ground as to merit the development of cross-sectoral resolution regimes, the delineation of the scope *ratione personae* presents a difficult case from the perspective of a cross-sectoral functional analysis. In the area of banking, a common theme has been the more or less explicit recognition that the quest for special resolution regimes should be confined to those institutions whose size, market share, and interconnectedness make them systemically relevant at a national, regional, or indeed global level, while institutions below that threshold could, and should, be dealt with under different regimes, including, not least, traditional insolvency procedures. For example, the FSB's Key Attributes have been designed with the express purpose to provide a resolution regime for 'financial institution[s] that could be systemically significant or critical' in the event of a failure.[49] Within Europe, although the BRRD, as such, applies to all credit institutions and investment firms regardless of size, complexity, and interconnectedness,[50] the initiation of resolution actions based on the alternative resolution toolbox is subject to a 'public interest test', which is not met if the relevant institution could as well be liquidated under general insolvency law without jeopardising the 'resolution objectives'.[51]

As argued elsewhere, the differentiation – however operationalised – between systemically important institutions (which can be resolved under the new regime), and other institutions (which should be liquidated under general insolvency laws), is by no means accidental. It is also not just attributable to efficiency considerations (from a fiscal perspective, it may be less costly to deal with financial institutions' insolvency within court-administered procedures, making use of the established framework for the solution of corporate insolvencies, including the appointment of private-sector insolvency liquidators). Even more importantly, the restricted scope for the application of alternative resolution regimes ensures that the negative implications of resolution (as opposed to traditional forms of insolvency management) for the creditors of failing financial institutions – in terms of restricted participation in the decision-making process, but also in terms of uncertainty as to the economic outcome – are confined to those cases where

---

[49] FSB, Key Attributes (2014), above n 3, para 1.1.
[50] See Art 1(1), BRRD. In principle, the same applies also to the SRMR, see Art 2, SRMR.
[51] Article 32(1)(c), (5), BRRD = Art 18(1)(c), (5), SRMR. And see also Recitals 45, 46, 49 and 50 of the BRRD.

the public interest in the preservation of financial stability outweighs the private interest of creditors.[52] At the same time, the delineation of the scope of resolution regimes along these lines comes with substantial implications in terms of procedural and institutional complexity. *If*, as under the BRRD/SRMR regime, not all cases qualify for the application of the resolution tool-box, care must be taken to operationalise the choice of procedural regime – and the subsequent implementation – in a way that minimises legal uncertainty. This requires not just a reliable definition of the criteria that determine the choice, but also a clear-cut delineation of responsibilities and powers for the initiation of the respective procedure.[53]

Similar concerns are unlikely to play a role across all sectors. While they are conceivable in the insolvency of insurance companies and investment firms, where similar differences with regard to size, complexity, and interconnectedness exist between individual firms, they are entirely unlikely to play a role in the case of FMI, which are much more homogeneous in terms of systemic relevance, and where the option of a liquidation under traditional forms of insolvency procedures probably has to be ruled out *a limine*. Given the institutional and procedural adjustments necessary to facilitate a smooth interplay between the different levels of crisis management (resolution on the one hand, orderly liquidation on the other), the justification for a genuinely cross-sectoral approach to resolution remains weaker still.

D. Getting Prepared: Recovery and Resolution Planning

On an abstract level, the case for a common, cross-sectoral framework for recovery planning (on the part of the regulated institutions) and resolution planning (by resolution authorities), with the latter retaining responsibility for the assessment of impediments to swift resolution and remedial powers in this regard, appears to be rather clear-cut. For good reasons, the introduction of recovery and resolution planning requirements, and corresponding powers to require changes to existing legal and commercial arrangements so as to prepare the ground for future resolution actions, has been one of the core features of relevant international standards[54] and European legislative initiatives for different sectors to date.[55]

As such, the reasons supporting the implementation of Recovery and Resolution Planning requirements as a building block of cross-sectoral crisis prevention regimes are indeed compelling. While it will be difficult, if not outright impossible, to foresee the specific causes for, and

---

[52] See Jens-Hinrich Binder, 'Proportionality at the resolution stage: Calibration of resolution measures and the public interest test', forthcoming in: (2019) 20 *European Business Organization Law Review*.; id, 'The Relevance of the Resolution Tools Within the SRM', in: MP Chiti and V Santoro (eds), *The Palgrave Handbook on the European Banking Union* (forthcoming 2019).

[53] It should be noted, in this respect, that the need to reconcile both procedural frameworks is amplified under the BRRD/SRMR regime, which refer to traditional insolvency law not just as a functional alternative to resolution in cases where the public interest test (above text and n 50) is *not* met, but also as a benchmark for permissible infringements of creditor rights: Pursuant to Art 60(1), BRRD = Art 17(1), SRMR, creditors' claims are to be treated according to their respective position in the priority of claims under general insolvency laws. Moreover, pursuant to the so-called 'No Creditor Worse Off Rule', creditors must not receive any less as a result of resolution than they would have received had the relevant institution been wound up under general insolvency law (Art 34(1)(g), BRRD = Art 15(1)(g), SRMR).

[54] See, in particular, FSB, Key Attributes (2014), above n 3, paras 11.1–11.12 and Annex 4; IAIS, above n 12, paras 15, 25, 30 and 31; IOSCO, above n 14; CPMI and IOSCO, 'Recovery of financial market infrastructures', above n 18, paras 2.1.1–2.5.7. See also FSB, 'Recovery and Resolution Planning for Systemically Important Financial Institutions: Guidance on Developing Effective Resolution Strategies' (16 July 2013), available at www.fsb.org/wp-content/uploads/ r_130716b.pdf; id, 'Funding Strategy Elements of an Implementable Resolution Plan' (21 June 2018), available at www.fsb.org/wp-content/uploads/P210618-3.pdf.

[55] See, again, ch I (recovery and resolution planning) and ch II (resolvability) of the BRRD; Arts 8–11 SRMR. And see the Commission proposal for a framework for the recovery and resolution of central counterparties (above n 26), ch 1.

characteristics of, a future insolvency, which limits the scope for the development of blueprints for future responses that need only be activated in the event of a failure, the analysis of potential scenarios and problems to be expected in this regard can nonetheless provide both the regulated institutions and the resolution authorities with useful information – information that may not just guide future actions, but also be relied on in the preventive removal of impediments to recovery and resolution by both parties.[56]

At the same time, as Recovery and Resolution Planning, by its very nature, must take place on a case-by-case basis, taking into account, and addressing, firm- and group-specific legal and organisational arrangements, business activities, and risk profiles, it is obvious that its implementation, and the evaluation of the results, beyond a rather abstract framework, can hardly be subjected to a detailed set of principles for cross-sectoral application. Given the residual differences between the sectors in any of the relevant respects, it is, therefore, questionable whether a genuinely cross-sectoral legal framework for Recovery and Resolution Planning would come with added value, compared to the present, sectoral approaches.

E. Triggers for Resolution

The definition of triggers for the initiation of resolution actions clearly constitutes one of the most important design features of resolution regimes in a number of respects. By comparison with traditional insolvency procedures, where the definition of predictable entry criteria is crucial for ensuring a fair balance between the interests of debtors and their creditors,[57] the triggers for resolution do not just determine at which point a collective (rather than individual, focused on bilateral adjudication and enforcement of claims) redress is applied to a firm in financial distress. Even more importantly, the definition of resolution triggers is crucial to ensure that the failure of a systemically important financial institution can – and will – be addressed at an early stage, facilitating effective measures at a point where the relevant firm ideally has not yet reached the point of either balance-sheet insolvency or illiquidity.[58] This certainly explains the reliance on a combination of traditional balance-sheet and liquidity criteria with the relevant firm's failure to sustainably comply with authorisation requirements in the definition of the conditions for resolution under the BRRD and SRMR.[59]

As the authorisation requirements are evidently calculated to provide a solid cushion against losses, infringements of these requirements certainly can be expected to provide a reliable basis for intervention at a moment in time where the creditors' interests are not yet at stake, but can be expected to become endangered within a foreseeable period of time if no remedial action

---

[56] See, for functional analyses, Dalvinder Singh, 'Recovery and Resolution Planning: Reconfiguring Financial Regulation and Supervision', ch 1, in: Binder and Singh, above n 10; Victor de Serière, 'Recovery and Resolution Plans of Banks in the Context of the BRRD and the SRM', ch 10, in: D Busch and G Ferrarini (eds), *European Banking Union* (Oxford, Oxford University Press, 2015). And see, further, Emilios Avgouleas, Charles Goodhart and Dirk Schoenmaker, 'Bank Resolution Plans as a catalyst for global financial reform', (2013) 9 *Journal of Financial Stability*, 210; Jens-Hinrich Binder, 'Resolution Planning and Structural Bank Reform within the Banking Union', in: J Castaneda et al. (eds), *European Banking Union. Prospects and challenges* (Abingdon, Routledge, 2015), p 129; Andrea Minto, 'Banking Crisis Management, Recovery and Resolution Planning, and "New Governance" Theory: Approaching "Living Wills" as a Public-Private Collaborative Form of Regulation', (2018) *European Company and Financial Law Review*, 772.

[57] See, for a detailed analysis, UNCITRAL, see above n 37, Pt I, para 9, Pt II, paras 20–31.

[58] See, for a more detailed analysis, eg, Christos Hadjiemmanuil, 'Special Resolution Regimes for Banking Institutions: Objectives and Limitations', in: Ringe and Huber, above n 36, p 209, at pp 228–230. In a nutshell, these considerations are also captured in FSB, Key Attributes (2014), above n 3, para 3.1.

[59] See Art 32(1)(a), (4), BRRD = Art 18(1)(a), (4), SRMR.

is taken. As such, this rationale arguably is not confined to any specific sector, but should be applicable across the board. Precisely for that reason, however, the rationale for a cross-sectoral restatement of resolution triggers appears to be doubtful. As authorisation requirements inevitably differ from sector to sector, reflecting not just differences in business activities, but also in terms of funding arrangements, it will hardly be possible to define a common standard beyond this very general consensus. If, then, a cross-sectoral definition of triggers would have to be operationalised in entirely different forms for each individual sector, the added value thereby generated can be expected to be rather insignificant.

F. Which Tools?

In addition to common standards for Recovery and Resolution Planning, the emergence of a harmonised set of functional alternatives to traditional forms of insolvency management – the 'resolution toolbox' – forms the core of the post-financial crisis resolution regime: a combination of instruments and powers, some of which have a long tradition in the area of bank insolvency management in a number of jurisdictions, while the 'Bail-In' tool, designed so as to facilitate a conversion of debt into capital instruments, has been designed without precedents in earlier national legislation.[60] While it has to be recalled that a comprehensive, or indeed exhaustive analysis of the suitability of the different tools for cross-sectoral application – due, not least, to their highly technical nature – is outside the scope of the present chapter, already a superficial analysis reveals substantial differences that cast further doubt on the feasibility of a genuinely cross-sectoral regime.

Among the different resolution tools, the transfer of assets and liabilities of, or the shares in, a failing institution to a private sector acquirer or, in order to prepare the basis for a subsequent sale of assets, to a bridge institution (the 'Sale of Business' and 'Bridge Institution' tools, in the terminology of the BRRD and the SRMR),[61] as such, can indeed play a useful role in protecting systemically relevant business functions. For large, globally active institutions and groups of intermediaries, however, the size and complexity of the problem assets may de facto restrict their scope of application. In any event, a successful transfer to a private sector acquirer obviously is contingent on the availability and readiness of a suitable investor to assume the relevant portfolio in the circumstances, which will depend not just on the nature and quality of the relevant assets, but also on the structure of the respective market and market conditions at the relevant time.[62] Against this backdrop, the transfer to private sector acquirers or bridge institutions may turn out to be of limited use particularly in the case of FMI, where suitable and reliable investors will be difficult to find, and where the transfer of the systemically important activities to a bridge institution may be possible, but hardly with the prospect of preparing a gradual winding-down of the relevant business.[63]

---

[60] See, for a detailed analysis of the resolution tools provided by the BRRD and their roots in earlier national legislation and international standards, Binder, above n 10, paras 2.47–2.51.

[61] See Arts 38–39 and 40–41 BRRD, respectively; Arts 24 and 25 SRMR; cf, FSB, Key Attributes, above n 3, paras 3.3 and 3.4.

[62] See, for further discussion, Binder, above n 10, paras 2.47–2.50; id, 'The Relevance of the Resolution Tools …', above n 51.

[63] While Art 27(1)(c) and (d), 40–43 of the Commission Proposal for a framework for the recovery and resolution of central counterparties (above n 26) expressly develop the sale of business and bridge CCP tools as core elements of the proposed resolution toolbox, their practical use remains nonetheless questionable.

For similar reasons, the transfer of certain problem assets to an asset management vehicle (the 'Asset Separation' tool, in the terminology of the BRRD and the SRMR)[64] may have proved a helpful instrument for the restructuring of problem portfolios in past banking crises.[65] Its use in the event of a failing insurance company is far less clear-cut, as it would hardly remove the problem of funding needs in relation to the payout of policies, whereas it is difficult to see how it could be activated in the event of FMI insolvencies at all. It is illustrative, in this regard, that neither the IAIS Issues Paper on insurance resolution[66] nor the Commission Proposal for a framework for the recovery and resolution of central counterparties list asset management vehicles as a possible resolution tool.[67]

Finally, it is also questionable whether the bail-in of debt into capital instruments[68] (in combination with a write-down of the latter) may reasonably be employed in the event of a failure of financial institutions other than banks. As has been discussed intensively in recent years, for the bail-in tool to accomplish its objective – the allocation of past losses to shareholders and creditors, either in the context of a restructuring of the failing institution on a going-concern basis or in conjunction with the transfer of assets and liabilities[69] – a sufficient level of bail-inable debt claims must be present on an on-going basis. Ideally, these should comprise exclusively of designated instruments issued for that very purpose, lest losses are allocated ad hoc to retail creditors and other actors who are incapable of pricing the risk and too dependent on the liquidity of their investments as to be able to afford their conversion into capital.[70]

For reasons that cannot be explored further in the present context, it would appear questionable if these conditions can be met within the context of funding structures of insurance companies and FMI operators. It is worth noting, in this context, that the IAIS Issues Paper on insurance resolution[71] does not expressly refer to bail-ins as a resolution tool, whereas the corresponding sector-specific annex of the FSB's Key Attributes discusses a variety of means to accomplish a restructuring of a failing insurer's liabilities that deviate significantly from standard patterns of the bail-in tool as developed for banks.[72] For FMI operators, the adaptation of the bail-in tool (including, for that purpose, powers to write down capital instruments) would have to take into account the characteristic funding, collateral and loss allocation arrangements that have been developed as standard practice by the industry over decades.[73]

All in all, while certain tools, conceptually, may be of use in more than one sector, the above considerations certainly reinforce, rather than remove, concerns as to the feasibility and adequacy of an integrated cross-sectoral resolution regime for application. While certain elements of the post-crisis toolbox – in particular, the transfer tools – may be of use also in the case of certain

---

[64] See Art 42, BRRD; Art 26, SRMR.

[65] Binder, above n 10, paras 2.51–2.53; id, 'The Relevance of the Resolution Tools …', above n 51.

[66] Above n 12.

[67] Above n. 26.

[68] Articles 37(3)(d), 43–44, 46–55 BRRD, Art 21 and 27 SRMR; see also FSB, Key Attributes (2014), above n 3, para 3.2.

[69] Cf, eg, Art 43(2), BRRD = Art 27(1), SRMR.

[70] For a comprehensive recent discussion, see, Tobias H Tröger, 'Too Complex to Work: A Critical Assessment of the Bail-in Tool under the European Bank Recovery and Resolution Regime', (2018) 4 *Journal of Financial Regulation*, 35; id, 'Why MREL Won't Help Much: Minimum requirements for bail-in capital as an insufficient remedy for defunct private sector involvement under the European bank resolution framework', (2019) 20 *Journal of Banking Regulation*.

[71] Above n 12.

[72] Cf, FSB, Key Attributes (2014), above n 3, II-Annex 2, para 4.4.

[73] Cf, eg, FSB, Key Attributes (2014), above n 3, II-1, paras 4.9–4.11; CPMI and IOSCO, 'Recovery of financial market infrastructures', above n 18, paras 3.2.1–3.2.5 and 3.4.1–3.4.7.

non-bank financial institutions, even they have to be modified substantially in order to address sector-specific characteristics.

G. Funding of Resolution

In international standards[74] as well as in the BRRD[75] and the SRMR (with the creation of a Single Resolution Fund),[76] the funding of resolution actions has been identified and, to some extent, addressed as a major challenge for the successful design and implementation of resolution actions. Given the need to implement resolution actions on short notice, in a dynamic situation where market sentiment will usually be adverse as long as the relevant institution's critical functions have not been stabilised sustainably and credibly yet, funding from market sources in order to meet on-going liquidity needs for the preservation of these functions may be difficult to find. Against this backdrop, there is a trend towards the creation of institutionalised resources, funded by the regulated industry, which ideally should also help to balance out the risk appetite of regulated firms ex ante, before a failure occurs.[77]

While these considerations, as such, can be applied irrespective of sectoral characteristics, the case for a cross-sectoral convergence of funding arrangements is nonetheless limited. As illustrated by the European framework for bank resolution, there is a need to reconcile funding arrangements with existing schemes for the protection of special stakeholders that may or may not exist in the different sectors, which in itself requires sector-specific solutions.[78] A special case, in this regard, are the sector-specific arrangements on loss allocation among participants developed in the FMI sector,[79] which provide further illustration supporting the conclusion that resolution funding arrangements have to be tailored to the need of each particular sector and that 'one-size-fits-all' solutions are clearly inappropriate. Finally, access to central bank funding also has to be taken into account as a potential source of liquidity support, which will not be available across all different sectors.

H. Is there Enough Common Ground?

In summarising the foregoing, it is impossible to escape the conclusion that there is hardly enough common ground as to justify a comprehensive cross-sectoral convergence between the resolution arrangements already in place, or in the process of being developed, for different types of financial institutions, including FMI operators. To be sure, at a very abstract level, the rationale for the disapplication of general insolvency procedures and their substitution with a bespoke regime that is better equipped to protect the public interest in the preservation of key economic functions of financial institutions is the same across all different sectors. Likewise, the rationale for crisis prevention through recovery and resolution planning clearly transcends sectoral

---

[74] See, in particular, FSB, Key Attributes (2014), above n 3, paras 6.1–6.5.

[75] See, in particular, Arts 99–109. And see, for further analysis in this regard, eg, Michael Schillig, *Resolution and Insolvency of Banks and Financial Institutions* (Oxford, Oxford University Press, 2016), paras 12.01–12.35.

[76] Articles 67–79, SRMR.

[77] Cf, again, Schillig, above n 75, paras 12.01–12.03.

[78] Both the BRRD and the SRMR, therefore, address the interplay between resolution funding and deposit insurance; see Art 109, BRRD and Art 79, SRMR, respectively.

[79] See, again, above text and n 73.

borders. Finally, there may well be room for further convergence with regard to specific resolution tools, which cannot be explored in detail within the restrictions of the present chapter. It is worth noting, in this regard, that, while the toolbox for systemically important credit institutions has attracted the attention of a prolific literature, resolution instruments for non-bank financial institutions and FMI operators continue to be far less well-researched, which limits further the basis for cross-sectoral legislation for the time being. Even leaving aside this restriction, however, the above considerations suggest that, while some further convergence in the design of resolution regimes may well be feasible and, indeed, helpful, the residual differences in legal and organisational arrangements, business activities, and the corresponding risk profiles will continue to require substantial sector-specific adjustments – so much so that, in the end, little may be accomplished through the adoption of inevitably broad and abstract common cross-sectoral principles.

III. Conclusions

Examining the rationale for, as well as the technical design of, resolution regimes for different types of financial institutions (in the widest sense), the above findings suggest that, while there is some common ground in terms of underlying policy objectives (the preservation of financial stability, the protection of retail customers, the avoidance of public financial support and the prevention of moral hazard) and even in terms of the technical design of resolution instruments and powers, the basis for genuine cross-sectoral resolution regimes is rather weak. Even a superficial analysis of sector-specific characteristics illustrates that the inevitable adjustments would be manifold, casting doubt on the added value generated by the introduction of inevitably highly abstract common, cross-sectoral principles. Within the European legislative and institutional setting, these conclusions also cast doubt on the merit of a move towards the adoption of general, high-level principles on resolution in a cross-sectoral Level 1 instrument, with subsequent specifications and adjustments left to Levels 2 and 3 of the legislative and regulatory process. If this is true, the question remains if the above analysis has any merit at all beyond that negative finding. In particular, it is worth asking whether the frameworks already in existence should be modified in order to address cross-sectoral problems thus identified. While details are outside the scope of the present contribution, it is at least conceivable that one possible avenue for further research – and, indeed, legislation – in this regard could be the introduction of a more refined set of safeguards against inter-sectoral contagion. Based on enhanced research into the *cross-sectoral* channels of contagion that could be triggered through the initiation of *sectoral* resolution actions, this could inform further refinement of the sector-specific resolution regimes so as to mitigate the risk that resolution actions taken in one sector could disrupt others.[80]

---

[80] To be sure, this aspect has already been addressed in European legislation; cf, eg, Arts 77–80 BRRD (on 'safeguards' for specific financial arrangements in the event of a bail-in and other resolution actions). It should be noted, however, that the effect of such measures on other sectors are not tested, and that similar protective arrangements are not yet in place across the board.

10

Is there a Case for One Cross-Sectoral Compensation Scheme?

VEERLE COLAERT AND GILIAN BENS

I. Introduction

Sectoral guarantee systems. European directives require each Member State to organise both a deposit guarantee scheme and an investor compensation scheme. After the first Deposit Guarantee Directive[1] and the Investor Compensation Scheme Directive[2] had been adopted, there was some optimism that harmonisation of insurance guarantee schemes (IGS) would follow in due course.[3] Although the European Commission advocated the adoption of a European directive on IGS in its 2010 White Paper[4] and the European Parliament recently stressed that the lack of such schemes may reduce consumer confidence,[5] no Commission proposal has been launched yet. Nevertheless, several Member States have in the mean time established an insurance compensation scheme[6] and the European[7] debate on the need for European harmonisation is ongoing.[8]

---

[1] Deposit Guarantee Dir 1994/19/EC, later replaced with Deposit Guarantee Dir (EU) 2014/49.

[2] Investor Compensation Scheme Dir 97/7/EC.

[3] NM Wessel-Aas, 'The Directive on Investor Compensation Schemes' (1999) *European Business Law Review* at 103.

[4] European Commission, White Paper on Insurance Guarantee Schemes, COM(2010) 370 final, 8–10. See for an overview of earlier developments at EU level: Impact Assessment, pp 7–9. Already in 2001 the Insurance Committee set up a working group to analyse IGS related issues. In 2005 a majority of the Member States in the working group were in favour of European coordination, but did not agree on the content and extent of coordination. The European Commission therefore ordered an expert report on IGSs (Oxera, Insurance Guarantee Schemes in the EU, 2008, p 279), held a public consultation, and published the White Paper on IGSs.

[5] Report 17 October 2016 on the Green Paper on Retail Financial Services, nr 15.

[6] As of end February 2018, 20 Member States operated 26 IGSs. See European Insurance and Occupational Pensions Authority's (EIOPA) recently launched 'Discussion paper on resolution funding and national insurance guarantee schemes' (EIOPA-CP-18-003, 30 July 2018) at 23.

[7] Also at the international level, the International Association of Insurance Supervisors (IAIS) and the Financial Stability Board (FSB) are in favour of insurance guarantee schemes. See for an overview: EIOPA, Discussion Paper (fn 6) at 24.

[8] The EIOPA Regulation provides that 'EIOPA may contribute to the need for a European network of national insurance guarantee schemes which is adequately funded and sufficiently harmonized' (Art 26, EIOPA Regulation (EU) 1094/2010. On that basis EIOPA recently launched its 'Discussion paper on resolution funding and national insurance guarantee schemes' (EIOPA-CP-18-003, 30 July 2018). EIOPA seeks feedback, among other things, (i) on its assessment that a minimum degree of harmonisation in the field of policyholder protection in the EU would benefit policyholders, the insurance market and more broadly the financial stability in the EU and (ii) on the design features of national insurance guarantee schemes.

Research Question. In this chapter we raise the question of whether a cross-sectoral compensation scheme for the financial sector would be more effective to achieve the goals of those schemes.[9] The idea of a 'single system of compensation' (for deposits and financial instruments) was already raised by the Economic and Social Committee in 1994.[10] In the end two separate schemes were introduced, but the rules of the Investor Compensation Directive have clearly been based on the equivalent rules of the first Deposit Guarantee Directive.[11] The recent financial crisis has, moreover, shown that financial institutions of all sectors are vulnerable to collapse, to the detriment of their clients. Joining the funds of the three sectoral schemes into one cross-sectoral scheme would allow the use of the proceeds of those funds more flexibly for those financial institutions where they would be most needed at any moment in time, irrespective of their sector.

Structure of the contribution. In order to answer the research question, we will examine the typical business model of credit institutions, investment firms and insurance companies,[12] as well as the function, hierarchy of goals and scope of application of each of the sectoral guarantee schemes. Only if the function and hierarchy of goals of those schemes are sufficiently similar, it would make sense to merge the sectoral schemes into one cross-sectoral scheme.

II. Functions, Hierarchy of Goals and Scope of Deposit Guarantee Schemes (DGS)

Business model of credit institutions – systemic risk. Credit institutions are key to the economy as intermediaries allocating excess money from savers to borrowers in need of money.[13] They typically engage in fractional reserve banking, investing the bulk of deposits and keeping only a small portion of deposits as available financial means. Credit institutions thus provide liquidity and maturity transformation: very liquid and short-term deposits (typically withdrawable on demand) are invested in longer-term and often illiquid assets.[14] As a consequence of the resulting maturity and liquidity mismatch, a credit institution can face serious liquidity and even solvency problems in case of a bank run.[15] Since credit institutions are highly connected with each other

---

[9] In this chapter we do not discuss the question of whether guarantee schemes should be organised at the European or at Member State level. In respect of deposit guarantee schemes, we have discussed this question in another contribution, dealing with the European Commission's proposal for a European Deposit Insurance Scheme (EDIS). See V Colaert and G Bens, 'European Deposit Insurance System (EDIS): Cornerstone of the Banking Union or Dead End', accepted for publication in D Busch and G Ferrarini, *European Banking Union* 2nd edn (Oxford, Oxford University Press, 2019).

[10] See Economic and Social Committee, 'Opinion on the proposal for a Council Directive on Investor Compensation Schemes' (94/C127/01), OJ C127/1-5, 7 May 1994, s 3.2: 'In order not to distort competition between investment firms, according to whether or not hey are also credit institutions, the Economic and Social Committee considers it desirable that there be a single system of compensation able to cover both cash and financial market instruments ...'.

[11] See NM Wessel-Aas (fn 3) at 103, 106 and 107. The author also claims that with the harmonisation of deposit guarantee schemes in the banking sector, it was logical to have an analogous measure in the investment services sector (at 107).

[12] For a more detailed analysis, see chapter 2 of this book.

[13] NJ Ketcha, 'Deposit Insurance System Design and Considerations'. *Bank for International Settlements, Policy Paper* 1999, 221; JD Cummins and MA Weiss, 'Systemic Risk and the Insurance Sector', (2014) *Journal of Risk and Insurance*, 495. See also ch 2 in this book.

[14] NJ Ketcha (fn 14) at 221; Z Pozsar, T Adrian, A Ashcraft and H Boesky, 'Shadow Banking', *FRBNY Economic Policy Review* December 2013, 4; PE Darpeix, 'Systemic Risk and Insurance', *PSE Working Papers* 2015–39, 10; J Armour and others, *Principles of Financial Regulation*, (Oxford, Oxford University Press, 2016), 277; Y Leitner, 'Nontraditional Insurance and Risks to Financial Stability', *Federal Reserve Bank of Philadelphia Research Department* 2018, 18.

[15] B Ruprecht, O Entrop, T Kick and M Wilkens, 'Market Timing, Maturity Mismatch, and Risk Management: Evidence from the Banking Industry', *Deutsche Bundesbank Discussion Paper* 56/2013, 1; J Arifovic, JH Jiang and Y Xu,

and with other financial institutions, the failure of one credit institution can, moreover, cause liquidity problems for other financial institutions (interconnectedness).[16] The failure of one credit institution can also lead to a loss of trust or panic, causing depositors of other credit institutions to retrieve their savings (contagion). In extreme scenarios the entire banking sector and even the whole financial system and economy could plunge into a crisis (systemic risk[17]).[18] Trust that deposits will be paid back to depositors at all times is therefore essential to avoid bank runs and ensure the stability of the banking sector and the economy as a whole.[19]

Function of DGSs. When deposits at a credit institution become unavailable,[20] typically due to (Impending) insolvency,[21] the DGS will need to pay out depositors up to the covered amount, currently set in the EU at (in principle) EUR 100 000 per depositor.[22] With the introduction of DGS Directive (EU) 2014/49, European DGSs can also assist in funding resolution actions.[23]

Hierarchy of goals of DGSs. DGSs are commonly said to serve two goals: protecting depositors against losses in case of insolvency of their credit institution and enhancing the stability of the financial system.[24] It is, however, fair to say that the main goal of DGSs is to ensure bank stability, by reducing the risk that the short-term funding of a credit institution would dry up in

---

'Experimental Evidence of Bank Runs as Pure Coordination Failures', (2013) *Journal of Economic Dynamics & Control*, 2446; X Freixas and J Rochet, *Microeconomics of Banking*, (Cambridge, MIT Press, 2008), 222; H Rockoff, 'Milton Friedman and Anna J Schwartz on the Inherent Instability of Fractional Reserve Banking', in H Rockoff and I Suto (eds) *Coping with Financial Crises: Some Lessons from Economic History*, (Singapore, Springer, 2018) p 126.

[16] H Chen, D Cummins, KS Viswanathan and MA Weiss, 'Systemic Risk and the Interconnectedness between Banks and Insurers: An Econometric Analysis', (2014) *Journal of Risk and Insurance*, 648; PE Darpeix (fn 15) at 10.

[17] Systemic risk can be defined as 'the risk of disruption to financial services that is (i) caused by an impairment of all or parts of the financial system and (ii) has the potential to have serious negative consequences for the real economy'. See FSB, 'Guidance to Assess the Systemic Importance of Financial Institutions, Markets and Instruments: Initial Considerations', October 2009, 5–6. Several factors determine whether an institution is systemically relevant, including size, substitutability and interconnectedness, but also leverage, liquidity risk, maturity mismatches and complexity. See, among others, O Ricci, *Corporate Governance in the European Insurance Industry*, (London, Palgrave Macmillan, 2014) p 82.

[18] JD Angrist and J Pischke, *Mastering Metrics: The Path from Cause to Effect*, (Oxford, Princeton University Press, 2015) p 179; M Brown, ST Trautmann and R Vlahu, 'Understanding Bank-Run Contagion', (2017) *Management Science*, 2280.

[19] JD Angrist and J Pischke (fn 19) at 179.

[20] It means that a deposit that is due and payable has not been paid by a credit institution under the applicable legal or contractual conditions and where (i) the relevant administrative authorities have determined that in their view the credit institution concerned appears to be unable for the time being, for reasons which are directly related to its financial circumstances, to repay the deposit and to have no current prospect of being able to do so or, (ii) a judicial authority has made a ruling for reasons which are directly related to the credit institution's financial circumstances and which has the effect of suspending the rights of depositors to make claims against it (ie a ruling in a bankruptcy or debt suspension procedure), should that occur before the aforementioned determination has been made (Art 8 (1) and 2 (8) Dir (EU) 2014/49).

[21] In a recent case the Court of Justice of the EU ruled, however, that the (old) DGS Directive precluded (i) national legislation according to which the determination that deposits have become unavailable is *concomitant* with the insolvency of that credit institution and the withdrawal of that institution's banking licence and (ii) a derogation from the time limits for determining that deposits have become unavailable and for reimbursing those deposits on the ground that the credit institution must be placed under special supervision. Unavailability of deposits must be determined expressly by the competent national authority and cannot be inferred from other acts of the national authorities nor presumed on the basis of circumstances. A determination that a bank deposit is unavailable can, moreover, not be subject to the condition that the account holder must first make an unsuccessful request for payment of funds from the credit institution. See CJEU Case C-571/16 (4 October 2018). See for a discussion of this case D Busch and S Keunen, 'Is the Statutory Limitation of Liability of the AFM and DNB Contrary to European Union Law?' (SSRN Working Paper id=3346240, 4 March 2019).

[22] Article 6, DGS.

[23] Subject to a number of conditions and limitations. See Art 11(2), DGS and Art 109, BRRD.

[24] Basel Committee on Banking Supervision – International Association of Deposit Insurers, 'Core Principles for Effective Deposit Insurance Systems' (2009), principle 1; A Campbell and P Cartwright, 'Deposit Insurance: Consumer Protection, Bank Safety and Moral Hazard' (1999) *European Business Law Review* at 96.

case of a bank run.[25] Depositors, knowing that their savings are substantially guaranteed, will be less inclined to withdraw their deposits in case of financial turmoil or when rumours regarding financial difficulties of their bank are being spread.[26] The depositor protection goal is therefore instrumental to the main stability goal.[27]

Scope of application of EU deposit guarantee schemes. In view of their contribution to financial stability, all developed financial systems organise some kind of deposit guarantee system. In the EU the DGS Directive requires Member States to establish a DGS in their territory.[28] A credit institution authorised in a Member State should not take deposits unless it is a member of a scheme officially recognised in its home Member State.[29] 'A deposit' is defined as 'a credit balance which results from funds left in an account or from temporary situations deriving from normal banking transactions and which a credit institution is required to repay under the legal and contractual conditions applicable, including a fixed-term deposit and a savings deposit'.[30] Before the introduction of the DGS Directive there was some discussion on the question of whether structured deposits were covered by Member States' DGSs. Under the current definition it is clear that the deposit element of a structured deposit is covered by the competent DGS if the deposit is repayable at par. Also, deposits placed with credit unions are covered by Member States' DGS.[31] The Directive further explicitly includes shares in Irish or UK building societies, apart from those of a capital nature.[32]

Deposits of public authorities and financial institutions are not eligible for coverage. Their limited number compared to all other depositors should minimise the impact on financial

---

[25] V Colaert, 'Deposit Guarantee in Europe. Is the Banking Union in need of a third pillar?' (2015) *European Company and Financial Law Review* 372; European Commission, 'Impact Assessment – Accompanying document to the Proposal for a Directive .../.../EU of the European Parliament and of the Council on DGSs [recast]' (12 July 2010) SEC(2010) 834 final at 27, where the goals of the directive are described as: 'maintaining financial stability by strengthening depositor confidence and protecting their wealth'; R Cerrone, 'Deposit Guarantee Reform in Europe: does European Deposit Insurance Scheme increase Banking Stability' (2018) *Journal of Economic Policy Reform* at 2. See NM Wessel-Aas (fn 3) at 108.

[26] DW Diamond and PH Dybvig, 'Bank Runs, Deposit Insurance, and Liquidity', *The Journal of Political Economy* 1983, 404.

[27] V Colaert (fn 26) at 374; F Allen and E Carletti, 'What is Systemic Risk', (2013) *Journal of Money, Banking and Credit*, 122; J Kerlin, *The Role of Deposit Guarantee Schemes as a Financial Safety Net in the European Union*, (Cham, Springer, 2017) p 35; N M Wessel-Aas (fn 3) at 108. See also, in respect of the European DGS system: European Commission, Impact Assessment Directive .../.../EU of the European Parliament and of the Council on Deposit Guarantee Schemes, 27 and Proposal for a Regulation of the European Parliament and of the Council Amending Regulation (EU) 806/2014 in order to Establish a European Deposit Insurance Scheme, Explanatory Memorandum 1.1.

[28] See for an in depth discussion of this Directive: V Colaert (fn 26) at 372 and J Payne, 'The Reform of Deposit Guarantee Schemes in Europe' (2015) *European Company and Financial Law Review*, 539–562. See on the proposal for a European Deposit Insurance Scheme: V Colaert and G Bens (fn 9).

[29] Article 4(1), Dir (EU) 2014/49.

[30] Article 2, s 1(3), DGS. For the definitions of 'normal banking transactions' and 'temporary situation', see CJEU joint cases C-688/15 and C-109/16, para's 87–94 and para 95 respectively. Credit balances which are in principle not payable at par or only payable at par under a particular agreement or guarantee provided by the credit institution or a third party, however, do not qualify as deposits. Credit balances the existence of which can only be proven by a financial instrument as defined in Annex I, s C of MiFID I are also excluded. See Art 2, s 1(3)b and c, DGS.

[31] A credit institution is defined as 'an undertaking the business of which is to take deposits or other repayable funds from the public and to grant credits for its own account' (Art 4(1)1° of CRR). The credit unions are cooperatives which provide loans, deposit accounts and other services to its members. In general credit unions are smaller than normal banks and invest in less risky products. They sometimes organise a DGS separate from the DGS of other credit institutions. A Cullen, 'Why Do Banks Fail?', SSRN 2011, 46–47.

[32] Article 2(3), DGS. Building societies are owned by their members, and focus on savings and mortgage lending. The fact that they invested in less risky products than traditional banks as well as their focus on serving the interest of their members, are mentioned as reasons why they responded better to the financial crisis. B Casu and A Gall, *Building Societies in the Financial Services Industry* (London, Springer Nature, 2016) at 6.

stability in case of a failure of a credit institution, while authorities also have much easier access to credit than citizens.[33]

III. Functions, Hierarchy of Goals and Scope of Investor Compensation Schemes (ICS)

Business model of investment firms. Investment firms provide a range of investment services to clients in relation to financial instruments – including the execution or transfer of orders, investment advice or portfolio management – and can engage in investment activities on own account – including proprietary trading.[34] The business model of an investment firm is therefore entirely different from the business model of a credit institution. Whereas credit institutions use customers' deposits to offer loans or to make other investments on the credit institution's own account, investment firms are in principle not allowed to use investors' assets on the firm's own account and clients' assets should in principle be kept strictly separate from the firm's own assets.[35] In case of insolvency of an investment firm, the claim of an investor on his or her financial instruments (ownership claim) is therefore typically much stronger than the claim of a depositor on his or her deposits (creditor). As a result, the biggest risk for an investor is not the insolvency of his investment firm, but fraud, negligence or other circumstances resulting in a loss of financial instruments of the client.[36] Moreover, investment firms are typically much less connected to each other and other investment firms than credit institutions. There is, therefore, in principle, hardly any risk of a 'run on investment firms' and resulting systemic risk,[37] even though the crisis has shown that proprietary trading of large investment firms can make them vulnerable to contagion risk under certain circumstances.

Function of investor compensation schemes. The function of ICSs is to protect investors against the risk of theft, embezzlement and other forms of fraudulent misappropriation,[38] but also against the risk of loss of investor assets resulting from unintentional errors, negligence or breakdowns in the firms' systems and controls.[39] In principle, it does not aim to compensate investors for market risk, nor to protect investors against the insolvency of the companies that have issued the financial instruments owned by investors.[40] Since ICS Directive 97/9/EC only aims at minimum harmonisation, Member States can, however, go beyond the requirements of the Directive. The UK's investor compensation scheme, for instance, does provide compensation for losses incurred by investors due to negligent investment advice, when the firm providing the advice is not able to compensate the investor.[41]

Goals of investor compensation schemes. The ICS Directive obliges Member States to establish an investor compensation scheme (ICS) in their territory.[42] The Directive aims at enhancing the

---

[33] Article 5(1) and Recital 31, DGS. Member States may however decide to cover deposits of local authorities with an annual budget of up to EUR 500 000.

[34] See for an overview of investment services and activities: Annex I, A MiFID II (Dir 2014/65/EU).

[35] See the asset segregation rules in Art 16(8), (9) and (10) MiFID II (EU) 2014/65 and Arts 2–8 of MiFID II.

[36] Ibid at 108.

[37] See also NM Wessel-Aas (fn 3) at 105 and 109.

[38] See Recital 3 of ICS; NM Wessel-Aas (fn 3) at 110.

[39] European Commission, Evaluation of the Investment Compensation Scheme Directive – Executive Report (1 February 2005) at 8.

[40] CJEU joined cases C-688/15 and C-109/16 (22 March 2018) para 71.

[41] See Evaluation of ICS (fn 40) at 6.

[42] It should be noted that the evaluation of the Investment Compensation Scheme Directive detected a number of shortcomings (see Evaluation of ICS (fn 40)). In 2010 the European Commission proposed to amend the Directive

internal market and to ensure confidence in the financial system.[43] The idea is that without a minimum level of protection, especially small investors would not be very eager to take investment services from firms established in other Member States.[44] In respect of investor compensation the stability goal is therefore much less important. As mentioned above, there is no, or much less risk of a 'run on investment firms'. Even if investors would lose trust in the financial markets or in a particular investment firm, an investor compensation scheme would not help preventing a run on the investment firm nor a crash in the capital markets, since the scheme, in principle, does not compensate for market risk or for bad advice.[45] The rationale for ICSs is therefore different from the rationale for DGSs. While ICSs mainly focus on investor protection, by providing compensation in case of risk of loss of deposits and financial instruments, which should ultimately facilitate the creation of an internal market, DGSs focus on depositor protection, which should ultimate enhance financial stability.[46]

Scope of application of EU ICSs. No investment firm authorised in a Member State may carry on investment business unless it belongs to an ICS.[47] It should be noted that for purposes of the ICS Directive, 'investment firms' include both investment firms licensed under MiFID II, and credit institutions which are licensed under the Capital Requirements Directive (EU) 2013/36 (CRD IV) and authorised to provide one or more investment services.[48] The ICS should provide cover for claims arising out of an investment firm's inability to (i) repay money owed to or belonging to investors and held on their behalf in connection with investment business, or (ii) return to investors any instruments belonging to them and held, administered or managed on their behalf in connection with investment business,[49] up to an amount of minimum EUR 20 000.[50]

Same deposit covered by both DGS and ICS? Credit institutions which are authorised for providing investment services should be a member of both a DGS and an ICS. In certain circumstances, a client's claim can be brought under both the deposit guarantee system and the investor compensation scheme. In a number of recent cases, brought before the Court of Justice of the European Union[51] a credit institution providing investment services was declared bankrupt, after having received investors' money but before having invested it in financial instruments for account of those investors. The Court of Justice found that those funds were covered both by the ICS – because they are 'money owed to or belonging to investors and held on their behalf in connection with investment business' – and by the DGS – because they were deposits as defined in the (old) DGS Directive 94/19/EC. In such a case the investor can, therefore, choose the most favourable regime (DGSs will typically provide a much higher coverage).[52]

(Proposal for a Directive of the European Parliament and of the Council amending Directive 97/9/EC of the European Parliament and of the Council on investor-compensation schemes (COM/2010/0371 final)) in order to align it with the proposed new Deposit Guarantee Directive (see the Explanatory Memorandum to the proposal, at 3). The proposal was not adopted, however, and was withdrawn on 7 March 2015.

[43] Recital 4 ICS. See also NM Wessel-Aas (fn 3) at 107, where the author gives an overview of the advantages and disadvantages of an investor compensation scheme.

[44] Evaluation of Dir 97/9 (fn 40) at 4.

[45] NM Wessel-Aas (fn 3) at 109. The author adds that if investors decide to withdraw their investments, whether this decision is based on market analysis or the need for liquid assets, they will most likely do so regardless of compensation schemes.

[46] See also the Explanatory Memorandum to the 2010 proposal to amend ICS (fn 43) at 4.

[47] Article 2(1) ICS.

[48] Article 1(1) ICS.

[49] Article 2(2) ICS.

[50] Article 4 ICS.

[51] See CJEU C-671/13 (25 June 2015); CJEU joined cases C-688/15 and C-109/16 (22 March 2018).

[52] CJEU joined cases C-688/15 and C-109/16 (22 March 2018), especially para 71.

IV. Functions, Hierarchy of Goals and Scope of Insurance Guarantee Schemes (IGS)

Business model of insurance companies. Insurance companies assume and diversify risk, pooling risk from their clients and redistributing it across a larger portfolio. Insurance companies basically generate revenue by (i) charging premiums in exchange for insurance coverage; and (ii) reinvesting those premiums in other profit-generating assets. Whereas the banking sector heavily relies on short-term funding (deposits) to finance their long-term investments, insurance activity is based on receiving premiums which are in principle not withdrawable on demand and (the proceeds of) which are used to compensate policyholders when the insured risk occurs.[53] If the insured risk occurs and the insurer needs to pay out policyholders, it can take months before claims are settled and actually paid, reducing liquidity risk.[54] Different from the deposits in fractional reserve banking, insurance liabilities are covered by technical reserves. The occurrence of the insured risk is, moreover, usually independent of the economic cycle, and is statistically relatively predictable. The insurance business is therefore less exposed to economic turmoil.[55] Since claims against insurers typically do not occur all at once, a run on insurance companies is considered to be nearly impossible[56] or at least rare[57] in respect of their core insurance activities. In sum, the insurance sector is less dependent on the trust of their policyholders than banks are on the confidence of their depositors,[58] since 'traditional' insurance activities[59] have the following characteristics: the underwritten risks are idiosyncratic, not correlated and not affected by economic business cycles.[60]

Insurance-based investment products, especially those with a guaranteed return, are generally considered more systemically relevant. Those products are usually redeemable before expiry, even though the policyholder will then typically be required to pay a penalty and may lose tax advantages. Even though those conditions reduce the incentives for early redemption, under certain circumstances policyholders may become immune to any monetary disincentive (eg in case of panic).[61]

---

[53] See also ch 2 in this book (fn 13) and A Van den Hurk and B Joosen, 'Microprudential Regulation' [reference to be added]; AA Jobst, 'Systemic Risk in the Insurance Sector: A Review of Current Assessment Approaches', (2014) *The Geneva Papers*, 447; D Cummins and MA Weiss, 'Systemic Risk and the Insurance Sector', (2014) *Journal of Risk and Insurance*, 500; PE Darpeix (fn 15) at 10; Society of Actuaries, 'Reviewing Systemic Risk within the Insurance Industry?', February 2017, 26; P Bongini, L Nieri, M Pelagatti and A Piccini, 'Curbing Systemic Risk in the Insurance Sector: A Mission Impossible?', (2017) *The British Accounting Review*, 258.

[54] AA Jobst (fn 54) at 445; PE Darpeix (fn 15) at 11.

[55] SE Harrington, 'The Financial Crisis, Systemic Risk, and the Future of Insurance Regulation', (2009) *The Journal of Risk and Insurance*, 804; AA Jobst (fn 54) at 445; P Bongini e.a. (fn 54) at 258; Y Leitner (fn 15) at 18.

[56] O Ricci (fn 18) at 83; PE Darpeix (fn 15) at 12; M Eling and DA Pankoke, 'Systemic Risk in the Insurance Sector: A Review and Directions for Future Research', (2016) *Risk Management and Insurance Review*, 271.

[57] International Association of Insurance Supervisors (IAIS), 'Systemic Risk from Insurance Product Features (previously referred to as Non-traditional Noninsurance activities and products' (16 June 2016) at 16.

[58] AA Jobst (fn 54) at 446; Society of Actuaries (fn 54) at 26.

[59] Even though the distinction between traditional and non-traditional activities is not always clear-cut and has therefore been abandoned by the IAIS (see IAIS, 'Systemic Risk from Insurance Product Features' (fn 58)), we use the term here for ease of reference.

[60] O Ricci (fn 18) at 82; PE Darpeix (fn 15) at 14; M Eling and DA Pankoke (fn 57) at 272. With its core activities the insurance sector is considered to be barely connected to other players of the financial system, again in contrast to the banking sector (M Eling and D Pankoke (fn 57) at 17–18; Y Leitner (fn 15) at 19).

[61] SE Harrington (fn 56) at 788; AA Jobst, (fn 54) at 445; O Ricci (fn 18) at 83; PE Darpeix (fn 15) at 11; C Gollier, 'Long-term Savings: the Case of Life Insurance in France', (2015) *Financial Stability Review (Banque de France)*, 135; M Eling and DA Pankoke (fn 57) at 271; see IAIS, 'Systemic Risk from Insurance Product Features' (fn 58) at 17 and 18. The IAIS states that 'Policies offering protection to holders serve a different economic purpose than products used as a vehicle for saving,

Examples of non-core activities are insurers' underwriting activities to mortgage guarantees or financial guarantees, providing securities lending and derivatives trading.[62] With these activities insurance companies provide services similar to credit institutions and investment firms. They therefore also expose insurance companies to similar risks and make them more interconnected with other financial institutions, increasing their systemic relevance.[63] It should be noted, however, that even though insurance companies may, as part of their investment strategy, engage in non-insurance activities, it would conflict with the EU Solvency II-rules on restrictions for insurers if they would make this part of their core business. Therefore, such non-traditional activities are often performed by a non-insurance subsidiary in EU insurance groups.

Function of IGSs. Although there is no European harmonisation of insurance compensation schemes, several Member States have set up such a scheme – typically as a response to a defaulting national insurance company.[64] Such IGSs step in when an insurance company fails and can no longer fulfill its obligations to policyholders. In such a situation the IGS will compensate policyholders for outstanding claims and/or ensure the continuation of their insurance contracts.[65] Some schemes also have additional functions related to resolution.[66]

Hierarchy of goals of IGSs. According to the European Commission, harmonisation of IGSs would aim at the following goals: the creation of an internal market, policyholder protection, and market stability and the avoidance of systemic risk. Although the White Paper discusses at some length the systemic risk which can result from the absence of an IGS,[67] it finally considers policyholder protection as the main goal of IGSs, and market stability as one of the supporting goals.[68] This is indeed consistent with the general economic perception that the insurance sector is less prone to systemic risk and more resilient to financial crises than the banking sector.

Scope of application of IGSs. The scope of application of national IGSs are very divergent. Certain IGSs only cover 'traditional' insurance products, others only cover insurance-based investment products, and other IGSs cover both.[69]

Covering insurance-based investment products by DGS? During the crisis, the Belgian government decided that a Belgian type of insurance-based investment products, so-called branch

---

which makes them less likely to be seen as deposits. They therefore do not have the same incentives for surrender. ... the substantial liquidity risk may be overestimated for products that are primarily for protection.'

[62] ESRB, 'Report on Systemic Risks in the EU Insurance Sector', December 2015, 14; AA Jobst, 'Systemic Risk in the Insurance Sector: A Review of Current Assessment Approaches', (2014) *The Geneva Papers on Risk and Insurance Issues and Practice*, 447; O Ricci, *Corporate Governance in the European Insurance Industry*, (London, Palgrave Macmillan, 2014), p 85; PE Darpeix, 'Systemic Risk and Insurance', *PSE Working Papers* 2015–39, 14; IMF, 'Global Financial Stability Report: Potent Policies for a Successful Normalization', April 2016, 88; P Bongini, L Nieri, M Pelagatti and A Piccini, 'Curbing Systemic Risk in the Insurance Sector: A mission impossible?', (2017) *The British Accounting Review*, 258.

[63] D Schwarz and SL Schwarz, 'Regulating Systemic Risk in Insurance', (2014) *The University of Chicago Law Review*, 1572; M Dungey, M Luciani and D Veredas, 'Systemic Risk in the US: Interconnectedness as a Circuit Breaker', (2018) *Economic Modelling*, 311; M Billio, M Getmansky, A Lo and L Pelizzon, 'Econometric Measures of Connectedness and Systemic Risk in the Finance and Insurance Sectors' (2012) *Journal of Financial Economics*, 549; AA Jobst (fn 54) at 447; O Ricci (fn 18) at 85; P. Bongini e.a. (fn 54) at 258; Y Leitner (fn 15) at 19.

[64] EIOPA, Discussion Paper (fn 6) at 25–26.

[65] Oxera, *Insurance Guarantee Schemes in the EU*, 2008, I; EIOPA, Discussion Paper (fn 6) at 7 and 22–23.

[66] 11 national IGSs can be used to fund resolution actions. EIOPA, Discussion Paper (fn 6) at 22–23.

[67] European Commission, Impact Assessment Accompanying Document to the White Paper on Insurance Guarantee Schemes, 19.

[68] Ibid at 25–27. For an extensive overview of reasons against and in favour of harmonisation, with a similar hierarchy of goals, see: EIOPA, Discussion Paper (fn 6) at 40–49.

[69] For an overview: EIOPA, Discussion Paper (fn 6) at 29–31. The discussion paper also provides an in-depth overview of arguments in favour of harmonising insurance guarantee schemes.

21 products, would be covered by a newly established guarantee fund for those insurance companies which opted to join the system (not mandatory).[70] In 2011 this fund was merged with the deposit guarantee fund, and participation by Belgian insurers offering branch 21 products to their clients became mandatory. The motivation for covering these insurance-based investment products was that it would help to restore confidence in the Belgian financial system and thus avoid a systemic crisis[71] and that they are considered alternatives to bank deposits.[72] We are, however, of the opinion that those arguments do not justify coverage of those products by the DGS. As shown above, the main reason to establish a DGS is to increase stability of the financial system. Protecting savers is a tool to reach this goal. Even though a 'run' on branch 21 products is theoretically possible, it is much less probable than a run on the bank. As indicated above, these products are long term saving products, and early redemption is sanctioned with high costs and sometimes even tax penalties. Investors are therefore not as likely as traditional depositors to redeem those products upon the first rumour that the insurance company might face a solvency problem. Covering those insurance-based investment products under the DGS would therefore increase policyholder protection, but not substantially reduce systemic risk. On the contrary, it would create serious moral hazard problems. In respect of DGSs critics claim that DGSs result in moral hazard, since it takes away depositors' incentives to seek a prudent bank, while credit institutions will engage in riskier behaviour, allowing them to offer depositors a higher interest rate.[73] Covering insurance-based investment products by the DGS would create moral hazard problems even bigger than in regard of traditional deposits, since (i) insurers benefiting from a DGS guarantee would be incentivised to invest the premiums received in respect of those products in more risky assets, in order to be able to offer a higher return on investment and attract more investors, and (ii) the public at large would be incentivised to invest in those insurance-based investment products rather than depositing their money at the bank, since it would be almost as safe as deposits, while generally generating a higher return. Since in respect of insurance-based investment products the consumer protection goal takes precedence over the stability goal, we are of the opinion that if a Member State (or the EU) would make the policy choice to cover insurance-based investment products, it should do so with a fund separate from the DGS and at conditions which are specific to this type of products.

---

[70] Article 5(3)° Royal Decree of 16 March 2009 regarding the protection of deposits and life insurances by the Guarantee Fund for financial services. Until recently the Belgian Deposit Guarantee System also covered the shares in a number of registered cooperative companies (Art 5(4)° Royal Decree of 16 March 2009 regarding the protection of deposits and life insurances by the Guarantee Fund for financial services). The Council of State has, however, annulled the law introducing such coverage as discriminatory to other investors. The provision had been inserted in the aftermath of the crisis in order to cover the large number of investors who had been lured into putting their savings into cooperative companies closely linked to the failed bank Dexia. After a myriad of legal procedures before the Constitution Court and the European Court of Justice, the Council of State (Raad van State/Conseil d'Etat) has finally annulled this provision (Belgian Council of State, 6 March 2018, No 240.89). The reasons and background of this issue are mainly of a political nature. We will therefore not deal with this in any further detail. For a detailed overview of the background of this provision and the legal procedures aiming at the annulment of this provision, see: V Colaert and T Incalza, 'Report for the European Parliament – Mis-selling of Financial Products: Compensation of Investors in Belgium', (June 2018), www.europarl.europa.eu/RegData/etudes/STUD/2018/618998/IPOL_STU(2018)618998_EN.pdf, at 21–32.

[71] See the explanatory memorandum to the Royal Decree of 14 November 2008 ('Verslag aan de Koning/Rapport au Roi').

[72] See H Debremaeker, 'De depositobescherming in deze tijden van beroering' (2009) *Bank- en Financiewezen* at 132–133.

[73] See in this regard V Colaert (fn 26) at 382–384, section IV, with further references.

V. Conclusion

As from the introduction of the ICS Directive in 1997, the suggestion has been raised to join deposit guarantee and investor compensation schemes into one scheme. In the mean time, several Member States have also introduced insurance guarantee schemes. We have raised the question whether a cross-sectoral deposit, investor and insurance guarantee scheme would be more effective to reach their goals.

A joint cross-sectoral scheme would have more funds available, which in times of crises could be more flexibly attributed across sectors to those financial institutions with the highest needs. However, we found that the functions and goals of the sectoral guarantee schemes are fundamentally different. Therefore, it is entirely justifiable to have three separate sectoral schemes, with different conditions and coverage levels attached to them.

11

The Cross-Sectoral Playing Field in Outsourcing

PETER LAAPER

I. Introduction

A. Overview

Regulation of outsourcing in the financial sector has been in place as from around the year 2000. The various outsourcing regulations that have emerged since were often incomplete and largely inconsistent, resulting in a 'hodgepodge'[1] of sectoral divergences. These regulations are still in full development. Gaps are being filled, often inspired, at least apparently, by solutions from other sectors' outsourcing regulations. New aspects of outsourcing are being covered, too, resulting in ever-growing legal texts.

Yet differences remain and whenever a financial sector's regulatory framework is amended, these modifications never adopt all regulatory solutions from other sectors. As a result, despite all efforts to bridge these gaps, the various outsourcing regulations are still inconsistent from a cross-sectoral point of view.

B. The Concept of 'Outsourcing' in Financial Regulations

Even the concept of 'outsourcing' is not uniformly defined. In fact, the term is not even defined in most sectoral regulations. Even more, in some sectoral regulations, not even the same term is used, as some sectoral regulations use the term 'delegation'. In this chapter, I argue that these differences in themselves have no meaning.[2]

Although this chapter is not about defining the concept of outsourcing, for reading purposes it seems desirable to provide a definition. Based on how outsourcing regulations have evolved over time, a uniform definition of outsourcing for the whole financial sector could be:

> the use of a third party for the performance of any aspect of the outsourcing firm's material functions that would otherwise be undertaken by the entity itself.[3]

---

[1] P Laaper, *Uitbesteding in de financiële sector, in het bijzonder van vermogensbeheer door pensioenfondsen*, (Deventer, Wolters Kluwer 2015). This PhD dissertation contains an English summary but is otherwise in Dutch. The title of the thesis translates into English as: 'Outsourcing in the financial sector, in particular of investment management by pension funds'.

[2] Section VII B.

[3] This definition is based on the findings in P Laaper, *Uitbesteding in de financiële sector, in het bijzonder van vermogensbeheer door pensioenfondsen*, (Deventer, Wolters Kluwer, 2015), p 32–49.

The three defining concepts in the definition are:

Third party	The service provider must be a third party. Hence, delegation of an activity within the firm is not regarded as outsourcing. The third party may be an affiliated entity within a corporate group or an entity that is external to the corporate group.
Own activities	Outsourcing only covers activities that would otherwise be undertaken by the entity itself. Thus, catering and postal delivery of insurance policies are not outsourcing. Own activities are not limited to the firm's regulated activities. Eg, an investment firm using an IT firm for automating some of its processes would still be involved in outsourcing.
Material activities	Not all activities are relevant for supervision. Only activities that must be deemed material for the firm, its clients or for the regulator's supervision, are within the scope of outsourcing. Regulated activities are by definition material. For unregulated activities, the materiality must be assessed on a case-by-case basis. Eg, if an investment firm uses an IT firm for automating some of its processes, it may matter if the IT firm provides a standard application or a tailor-made application.

C. Chapter's Structure

This chapter will first give a quick overview of relevant sources of outsourcing regulation (section II). Then, the 2000 IOSCO report will be discussed, which clearly puts forward the rationale underlying all outsourcing regulations (Section III). It will be explained how this report came to lie at the heart of all outsourcing regulations and how these regulations have cross-pollinated each other (section IV). Then, six general principles of outsourcing regulations will be presented (Section V). After this, we take first a global look at the differences between the various sectoral outsourcing regulations (section VI), followed by a detailed look on a few selected outsourcing topics (section VII). The chapter concludes with a number of policy considerations and recommendations for a more efficient and effective cross-sectoral approach to regulating outsourcing in the financial industry (section VIII).

D. Terminology

In this chapter, the term 'Regulation' will be used exclusively for an EU regulation as in Article 288 of the Treaty on the Functioning of the European Union. The term 'regulations' will be used to describe any set of rules, it being a regulation, a directive, a guideline, a combination of such legal instruments, or only a section of any such legal instrument.

Further, the words 'UCITS Directive', 'AIFMD' and 'IORP II' will be used to refer to the respective Directives, and 'ucits', 'aif' and 'iorp' for the institutions regulated by these Directives.

II. Sources of Outsourcing Regulations

Two types of sources must be distinguished: (1) EU regulations and (2) guidelines of international bodies in which national competent authorities collaborate. These international bodies are the International Organization of Securities Commissions (IOSCO) and a joint forum (hereinafter: Joint Forum) of the Basel Committee on Banking Supervision, IOSCO and the International Association of Insurance Supervisors. The Joint Forum's guidelines were developed to act as a baseline across all sectors. IOSCO's guidelines were created as a supplement, specifically aimed at securities companies. The guidelines of IOSCO and the Joint Forum were very influential in shaping EU regulations and therefore deserve special consideration. Both having been developed in 2005, they will be referred to as '*Joint Forum 2005*' and '*IOSCO 2005*' respectively.

The legal framework governing outsourcing is characterised by the same Lamfalussy structure as most financial regulations in the EU. At level one, a directive contains general outsourcing regulations that may or may not be elaborated upon in a delegated regulation at level two. A European Supervisory Authority (ESA) may also provide level three guidelines on outsourcing. Table 1 provides an overview of the relevant regulations within each financial sector.

Table 1 Financial sector's outsourcing regulations

Type of institution	EU Directive	EU Delegated Regulation	EU Guideline
Ucits	Directive 2009/65/EC ('*UCITS Directive*')	N/A	N/A
Aifs	Directive 2011/61/EU ('*AIFMD*')	Delegated Regulation (EU) No 231/2013 ('*Delegated AIFMD*')	N/A
Banks	Directive 2013/36/EU ('*CRD*')	N/A	EBA Guidelines on outsourcing arrangements, 2019, EBA/GL/2019/0, as published on 25 February 2019 ('*EBA 2019*')*
Payment institutions and electronic money institutions	Directive 2015/2366/EU ('*PSD II*')	N/A	
Investment firms	Directive 2014/65/EU ('*MiFID II*')	Delegated Regulation (EU) 2017/565 ('*Delegated MiFID II*')	
Insurance and reinsurance firms	Directive 2009/138/EC ('*Solvency II*')	Delegated Regulation (EU) 2015/35 ('*Delegated Solvency II*')	EIOPA, Guidelines on System of Governance, EIOPA-BoS-14/253 ('*EIOPA 2013*')
Institutions for Occupational Retirement Provisions (pension funds and the like)	Directive 2016/2341/EU ('*IORP II*')	N/A	N/A

*   In the investment sector, EBA 2019 only applies to investment firms that are within the EBA mandate (hereinafter: '*non-EBA investment firms*'). These are – in short – investment firms that:

(1) provide the investment service of (a) transmitting orders, (b) executing orders on behalf of clients, (c) portfolio management or (d) investment advice, and that are not allowed to (i) keep clients' funds and securities in their possession or (ii) to provide ancillary safekeeping services, and
(2) 'local firms', ie investment firms that (a) deal for their own account on markets in financial futures or options or other derivatives and on cash markets for the sole purpose of hedging positions on derivatives markets, or (b) deal for the accounts of other members of those markets and being guaranteed by clearing members of the same markets, where responsibility for ensuring the performance of contracts entered into by such a firm is assumed by clearing members of the same markets.
(Art 2(1) jo 3(1)(3), CRD jo Art 4(1)(3) jo 4(1)(2), CRR).

III. The 2000 IOSCO Report

An important milestone in the process of regulating outsourcing in the financial sector has been the 2000 IOSCO report on 'Delegation of Functions'.[4] It should be noted that is not the first document to address the issue as it builds on elements from an earlier 1994 IOSCO report.[5] Also, the 1985 UCITS I Directive already contained a very rudimentary regulation concerning outsourcing by the depositaries of investment funds.[6] The 2000 IOSCO report, however, is the first document to contain all of the key elements of the underlying rationale that we find in present-day outsourcing regulations.[7]

The chief concern of the 2000 IOSCO report is the protection of investors. The fear expressed is that by outsourcing tasks, an undertaking sheds responsibility, sometimes even becoming a mere letter-box entity, and considers itself not accountable – towards investors or its supervisor – for shortcomings in the execution of the outsourced tasks or if applicable regulations are not properly observed. The report provides general principles, both for supervisors and outsourcing firms.

IOSCO's approach is that the outsourcer remains fully responsible vis-à-vis investors and supervisors for the acts and omissions of its service provider as if it were its own actions or omissions. In order to be able to meet that responsibility, it must remain 'in control'[8] of the execution of the outsourced activities.

In order to remain 'in control', it is considered necessary that (a) outsourcing does not lead – directly or gradually – to a situation where the outsourcer operates as 'an empty box', (b) that the outsourcer carefully selects a capable service provider with whom it makes a clear agreement, (c) that it effectively supervises the service provider, (d) that it can intervene and, if necessary, does so, and (e) that it can terminate the relationship at any time.

IV. Evolution of Outsourcing Regulations

The rationale presented in the 2000 IOSCO report was highly influential in shaping later outsourcing regulations for other financial subsectors, as it can be found in the regulations for each sector. The rationale consists of the first three general principles presented in section V. These are: (1) retention of responsibility, (2) retention of supervisory powers and (3) retention of control. The pattern of influence is illustrated in Figure 1.

---

[4] IOSCO, Delegation of functions, 2000.

[5] IOSCO, Report on investment management, 1994.

[6] Article 7(2) of Dir 85/611/EEC.

[7] Noteworthy is also the Federal Reserve Bank of New York, 'Outsourcing Financial Services Activities: Industry Practices to Mitigate Risks', 1999. The report presents a similar rationale as the European regulations, showing most of its features. There is no indication that the report has influenced or was influenced by the developments in European regulations on outsourcing. It suggests that the Federal Reserve Bank of New York has independently drawn up its approach and that the rationale, underlying the European outsourcing regulations and the Bank's report is in itself compelling.

[8] 'In control' is not a term used by IOSCO in the report. It is a term used by the Dutch prudential supervisor (DNB) that – to this author's opinion – accurately captures what is expected from the outsourcer.

Figure 1 Influences between outsourcing regulations

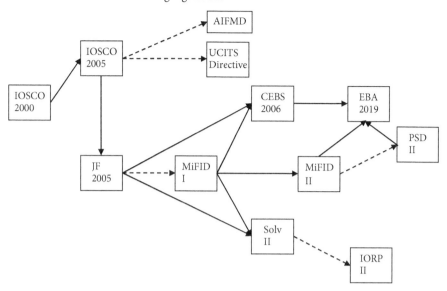

IOSCO 2000	IOSCO, Delegation of functions, 2000	AIFMD	Directive 2011/61/EU (Alternative Investment Fund Managers Directive) and delegated AIFMD
IOSCO 2005	IOSCO, Principles on outsourcing of financial services for market intermediaries, 2005	UCITS Directive	Directive 2009/65/EC (Undertakings for the Collective Investment in Transferable Securities)
JF 2005	Joint Forum, Outsourcing in financial services, 2005	Solv II	Directive 2009/138/EC (Solvency II) and Delegated Solvency II
CEBS 2006	CEBS, Guidelines on outsourcing, 2006	IORP II	Directive 2016/2341/EU (institutions for occupational retirement provision II)
EBA 2019	EBA Guidelines on outsourcing arrangements, 2019 (as published on 25 February 2019)	PSD II	Directive 2015/2366/EU (Payments Services Directive)
MiFID I	Directive 2009/34/EC (Markets in Financial Instruments Directive I) and Delegated MiFID I	MiFID II	Directive 2014/65/EU (Markets in Financial Instruments Directive II) and Delegated MiFID II
1	See IOSCO 2005, footnote 1	2	See Joint Forum, p 8, first bullet
3	See CEBS 2006, p 1, first paragraph	4	Solvency II, Consideration 37
5	See CEBS 2006, p 1, first paragraph	6	Solvency II, Consideration 37
7	MiFID I requirements have remained. New requirements added	8	An update of CEBS 2006. See EBA 2019, p 5
9	See EBA 2019, p 5	10	See EBA 2019, p 4

A	Influence is plausible as IOSCO is the international committee for supervisors of investment funds	B	Influence is plausible as IOSCO is the international committee for supervisors of investment funds
C	Influence is plausible as the Joint Forum is a cooperation of supervisors of investment funds, banks and insurers, and the Joint Forum guidelines have been set up as an industry wide standard	D	Influence is plausible due to resemblances in IORP II and Solvency II, the fact that EIOPA is the European supervisor for both insurers and iorps, and EIOPA has advised the European Commission to apply the material elements of the outsourcing regulations under Solvency II to iorps (see EIOPA's Advice to the European Commission on the review of the IORP Directive 2003/41/EC (EIOPA-BOS-12/015), chapters 17 and 25)
E	Influence is plausible as PSD II's general outsourcing regulations show resemblances with MiFID II's, and EBA has looked at MiFID regulations in the past		

The figure shows that the 2000 IOSCO report laid at the basis of IOSCO's Guidelines of 2005. These, in turn, were probably influential for the outsourcing regulations for aifs and ucits. Continuous lines indicate there is a proven influence from one source to the other. Dashed lines indicate an influence is likely but cannot be proven. The following table provides the sources from which the influence follows (continuous lines) or the argumentation why an influence is likely (dashed lines).

The Joint Forum Guidelines were developed in close co-operation with the IOSCO committee that developed these IOSCO Guidelines. The Joint Forum Guidelines were probably influential in shaping the outsourcing regulations in MiFID I and ultimately MiFID II. The Joint Forum Guidelines and MiFID I outsourcing regulations were certainly influential in shaping the Solvency II outsourcing regulations for (re)insurers and the CEBS Guidelines. The IORP II outsourcing regulations very likely built on the Solvency II outsourcing regulations. The MiFID II outsourcing regulations certainly built on MiFID I's regulations and, in its turn, was probably influential for the PSD II outsourcing regulations. The 2019 EBA Guidelines, finally, built on the CEBS Guidelines, and the MiFID II's and PSD II's outsourcing regulations.

V. General Principles

Overall the sector's regulations, six general principles consistently make an appearance. Although the principles may work out differently because of the nature of a given sector's business or because of sectoral practices, these general principles help fill in the gaps in the hodgepodge of sectoral regulations. Gaps are discussed in section VII.

The first three general principles follow directly from the rationale underlying the outsourcing regulations. They are as follows.

1.   Retention of responsibility

    The main worries for IOSCO were that outsourcing of activities would (1) harm the rights of and the quality of services to clients of the outsourcing institution, and (2) obstruct a supervisor's ability to adequately supervise outsourced activities.[9] In order to counter that

---

[9] IOSCO 2000, Principle 1.1.

risk, the outsourcer must – at the least – retain full responsibility for the execution of the outsourced activities and account for it. It cannot point at its service provider's shortcomings in order to escape responsibility. The concept is still found in other outsourcing regulations.[10]

2.   Retention of supervisory powers

Retention of responsibility of the outsourcing institution is one (important) tool to ward off the risk that the supervisor loses its ability to supervise outsourced activities and – if necessary – enforce regulations.[11] More specific regulatory measures are, for example, an obligation to notify the supervisor of an intended outsourcing[12] or an obligation for the outsourcer to include in the outsourcing agreement third party clauses that allow the supervisor to take supervisory actions vis-à-vis the service provider in relation to the outsourced activities.[13]

3.   Retention of control

In order to meet its responsibilities towards clients and supervisors, the outsourcer must remain 'in control' of its outsourced activities.[14] It is not allowed to become a letter-box entity.[15] Of course, the outsourcer cannot possibly be in *full* control over the outsourced activities. That would mean that the service provider, having to comply with each and every instruction of its client, would lose control over its own organisation. Its management would not be able to meet its own statutory responsibilities towards the legal entity of the service provider, its (other) clients and – if there are – its own supervisors. Moreover, it would be impossible for the service provider to comply with conflicting instructions of different clients. Although the outsourcer cannot retain full control over the outsourced activities, it must therefore retain *sufficient* control to take responsibility vis-à-vis its clients and customers.[16] 'Sufficient control' is an open norm that relates to the concepts of materiality and proportionality (and are discussed hereinafter). Outsourcing regulations often prescribe a minimum set of measures the outsourcer must take.

Other general principles that I discern are:

4.   Proportionality

All outsourcing regulations and guidelines are based on the principle of proportionality.[17] For EU Directives and Regulations, this derives from the Treaty on the Functioning of the European Union,[18] but is also present in the various Guidelines.[19] Proportionality means that when outsourcing entails bigger risks, the outsourcer must take further-reaching

---

[10] Eg, IOSCO 2005, Fundamental precept B; Joint Forum 2005, Principle III; EBA 2019, nr. 35 and 36; Art 13(2), UCITS Directive; Art 20(3), AIFMD; Art 19(6), PSD II; Art 31(1), Delegated MiFID II; Art 49(1) and 49(2)(d), Solvency II; Art 31(2) and 31(3)(d), IORP II.

[11] Eg, IOSCO 2005, p 3, last sentence; Joint Forum 2005, Principle III; EBA 2019, nr. 57, 67(b) and 110; Art 13(1)(b), UCITS Directive; Art 20(1)(e), AIFMD; Art 19(6), PSD II; Art 16(5), MiFID II and Art31(5), Delegated MiFID II; Arts 38(1) and 49(2)(c), Solvency II; Art 31(3(c), IORP II.

[12] Eg, EBA 2019, nr. 58; Art 20(1)(b), UCITS Directive; Art 7(2)(e), AIFMD; Consideration 44 Delegated MiFID II jo Art 21(2), MiFID; Art 5(1)(l), PSD II; Art 49(3), Solvency II; Art 31(6), IORP II.

[13] Eg, IOSCO 2005, topic 7; Joint Forum 2005, Principle III; EBA 2019, nr. 75(n-p); Art 31(2)(h) and (i) jo 31(3), Delegated MiFID II; Art 23(1)(b), PSD II; Art 38(1), Solvency II; Art 50(e), IORP II.

[14] IOSCO 2005, p 2; Joint Forum 2005, Principle II; EBA 2019, nr. 32.

[15] IOSCO 2000, p 3; EBA 2019, nr. 39; Art 13(2), UCITS Directive; Art 20(3), AIFMD.

[16] P Laaper, *Uitbesteding in de financiële sector, in het bijzonder van vermogensbeheer door pensioenfondsen*, (Deventer, Wolters Kluwer, 2015), pp 25–28.

[17] IOSCO 2000, p 4; IOSCO 2005, p 3; Joint Forum 2005, Principles I and II; EBA 2019, Title I; Art 75(e), Delegated AIFMD; Art 16(4), MiFID; Art 11(4), PSD II; Arts 29(3), 41(2) and 41(4), Solvency II; Arts 21(2) and 21(5), IORP II.

[18] Article 5 Treaty on the Functioning of the European Union and Protocol (No 2) on the application of the principles of subsidiarity and proportionality.

[19] IOSCO 2005, p 1; Joint Forum 2005, p 4; CEBS 2006, p 2; EBA 2019, nr. 18.

measures to control these risks. These measures must be proportionate to the risks they aim to control.

In PSD II, Solvency II and EBA 2019, proportionality is also apparent from the distinction that is made between 'regular' outsourcing and outsourcing of 'critical or important activities'.[20] In the latter case, institutions must meet additional requirements.[21]

A consequence of the proportionality principle is that an outsourcer cannot suffice with ticking off specific requirements that may be laid down in regulations. Sectoral requirements are a minimum standard, regardless of the actual size of the risks involved. This is important for financial institutions contemplating outsourcing. It is also important for this study on the regulation of outsourcing across financial sectors. If the *specified* minimum requirements in a sector's regulations are more lenient than the specified minimum requirements in another sector, this does not necessarily mean that less is required from an outsourcer in the former sector.

5.   Materiality

From the principle of proportionality follows the principle of materiality. All regulations explicitly state the principle of materiality. An outsourcing is only considered relevant to supervision if the outsourcing is material. The term 'materiality' is not defined as such but the IOSCO 2005 and Joint Forum 2005 Guidelines do provide an extensive list of factors that may be helpful in determining whether or not a specific outsourcing is to be considered material. Delegated MiFID II gives as examples of immaterial activities: the provision of advisory services to the institution, the provision of other services to the institution that do not form part of its business (such as legal advice, training of personnel, billing and security of premises and personnel), and the purchase of standardised services (such as market information and price feeds).[22] Immaterial activities can be outsourced without the need to comply with outsourcing regulations, although IOSCO and Joint Forum warn that then too, an institution should ensure that what it is buying is appropriate for the intended purpose.[23]

6.   Freedom to outsource

No outsourcing regulation prohibits or requires outsourcing of any activity. UCITS Directive and IORP II take a different approach from other regulations, though. Both regulations do not prohibit outsourcing particular activities as such but they do allow *Member States* to preclude institutions from outsourcing activities.[24] IORP II also allows Member States to require iorps to outsource activities.[25] Thus, with the possible exception of ucits and iorps, institutions enjoy freedom to outsource.[26]

---

[20] Here, too, the wording is not uniform. PSD II refers to 'important operational functions', Solvency II to 'critical or important operational functions' and EBA 2019 to 'critical or important functions'.

[21] It should be noted that MiFID II also uses the term 'critical or important operational functions', but does not oppose that to a 'regular' (yet material) outsourcing. MiFID II opposes the term to the use of a third party that does not constitute an outsourcing within the meaning of the regulation as a result of lack of materiality. EBA 2019 takes a different approach, that leads to a remarkable outcome. See section VII C and the interim conclusion there.

[22] Article 30(2), Delegated MiFID II.

[23] IOSCO 2005, p 1 and Joint Forum 2005 p 4.

[24] According to Art 13(1,) UCITS Directive and Art 31(1), IORP II, Member States can 'allow' or 'permit' institutions to outsource so they can also decide not to.

[25] Article 31(1), IORP II.

[26] See Consideration 43 MiFID. The term 'freedom to outsource' is borrowed from T Czech and E Szlachetka, 'Outsourcing under MiFID', (2009) *Journal of International Banking Law and Regulation*, 24(3), p 151.

Outsourcing may not result in the delegation of an institution's (senior management's) responsibilities.[27] Hence, in spite of freedom to outsource, a senior management's tasks of decision-making and being accountable cannot be outsourced. This one exception – no delegation of senior management's tasks – directly derives from the principle of retention of responsibility.[28]

VI. Topics Covered in Outsourcing Regulations

Table 2 gives an overview of the various topics that are covered *in relation to outsourcing* in the various regulations and guidelines.

When a topic is not covered in relation to outsourcing, applicability of a topic may be inferred. For example: as part of its governance, an iorp must take reasonable steps to ensure continuity of its activities, including contingency plans.[29] This requirement is not mentioned in relation to outsourcing. Hence, the table shows an empty box for business continuity plans of iorps. It may be inferred, though, that if an iorp outsources important activities, good governance will require the iorp to draw up business continuity plans in relation to the outsourced activities.

The table does not show if the topic is covered only partly, or in detail or superficially. UCITS Directive, for example, mentions the concept of a letter-box entity without describing it whereas Delegated AIFMD addresses the concept in a lengthy article. Hence, the table shows an 'X' with regard to letter-box entities for both UCITS Directive and AIFMD.

A. Sectoral Overview

Table 2 shows that there are big differences in coverage between one sector and another. It shows that some regulations or guidelines are rather comprehensive while others show more 'gaps'. In fact, the Electronic Money Directive (EMD)[30] is completely silent on outsourcing and CRD merely touches upon the subject. These institutions are, however, covered by the guidelines of EBA 2019, but these are addressed to supervisory authorities. PSD II and IORP II do not provide much detail on outsourcing requirements either.

Solvency II and, even more so, AIFMD provide a more comprehensive framework show-ing few gaps. EBA 2019 contains extensive guidelines, addressing all topics listed in the table, often at considerable length. This is not surprising. It is the most recent document and, as mentioned before, new regulations tend to pick up topics and solutions from other regulations. This makes EBA 2019 the most complete source of outsourcing regulations, covering 50 pages. Moreover, EBA aimed at ensuring a level playing field for banks, electronic money institutions, payment service providers and investment firms while meeting the requirements of CRD, EMD, PSD II, MiFID II and Bank Recovery and Resolution Directive,[31] and building on the 2006 CEBS guidelines.[32] It was, however, clearly not a project of simply putting the specific outsourcing requirements of CRD, EMD, PSD II and MiFID II together, as EBA 2019 also addresses topics

---

[27] IOSCO 2000, Principle 1.1; IOSCO 2005, p 2; Joint Forum 2005, p 13; EBA 2019, nr. 35–36; Arts 75(a) and 82(1)(b), Delegated AIFMD; Art 31(1)(b), Delegated MiFID II; Art 19(6)(a), PSD II; Art 49(1), Solvency II; Art 31(2), IORP II.

[28] See section V, General Principle 1.

[29] Article 21(5), IORP II.

[30] Directive 2009/110/EC.

[31] Directive 2014/59/EU.

[32] EBA 2019, nr. 15, 16, 19 and p 56.

that are not covered in any of these Directives, such as outsourcing policy and letter-box entities. In fact, EBA 2019 is the only regulation that requires institutions to set up an outsourcing register.[33]

B. Topical Overview

The table can be viewed 'horizontally' as well. A striking observation is that 'outsourcing' is not defined in most sectors' outsourcing regulations. Another observation is that several topics are addressed by the IOSCO, Joint Forum and EBA guidelines, but hardly by the EU Directives and Delegated Regulations. That is the case for the definition of outsourcing, but also for the topics of outsourcing policy, the role of the internal audit function and pre-outsourcing analysis. The opposite is the case for the requirement to notify the institution's supervisory authority of an intended outsourcing, which is not addressed in the IOSCO and Joint Forum guidelines but is mentioned in several sectoral directives or delegated regulations.

If we exclude CRD and EMD, which do not or hardly mention anything about outsourcing, it is clear that some topics are almost invariably addressed. Such topics are a due diligence requirement (not PSD II and IORP II), an oversight requirement (not PSD II), sub-outsourcing (not MiFID, PSD II and IORP II), data security (not UCITS Directive, PSD II and IORP II), access and audit rights (not UCITS Directive), right to change the execution of the outsourced activities (not PSD II and IORP II), termination rights (not UCITS Directive, PSD II and IORP II), exit strategies (not UCITS Directive, PSD II and IORP II) and supervisory powers vis-à-vis the service provider (not UCITS Directive).

Other topics are less often addressed in regulations. Focusing on directives and delegated regulations, such topics include an outsourcing policy (only Solvency II and IORP II), the role of the internal audit function (none), the set-up of an outsourcing register (none), letter-box entities (AIFMD) and the requirement to do a pre-outsourcing analysis (UCITS Directive and AIFMD).

C. Interim Conclusions

From this general overview, some preliminary conclusions can be drawn.

First, there appears to be no good reason why some topics are not covered in some financial sector's regulations. Having supervisory powers directly vis-à-vis a service provider is extremely helpful for supervisors to execute their supervisory tasks. Exercising a due diligence prior to selecting a service provider and maintaining oversight over the execution by the service provider of the outsourced activities, having access and audit rights, the right to effectuate changes in the execution of the outsourced activities (eg via instructions) and the right to terminate the outsourcing contract, are absolutely necessary for an institution to remain in control of the outsourced activities. Given the long and abundant chains of outsourcing, it seems irresponsible for an outsourcing institution not to deal with the issue. Data security is always an important issue, whether it is data about the outsourcing institution or its clients. And these are only topics most often required. For example, although much less often required, it seems irresponsible for an outsourcing institution not to have an exit strategy.

In some cases, a regulatory 'gap' between sectors poses few problems. For example, if an outsourcing institution's minimal requirements are clearly defined and sufficient to actually be

---

[33] EBA 2019, nr. 52–56.

in control, there is no need to define the concept of a letter-box entity. This appears to be the case for MiFID II and Solvency II. An outsourcing policy is a huge contribution to consistently keep control over an intended outsourcing but an outsourcing institution might do without, if it makes a good pre-outsourcing analysis of the associated risks. In a similar vein, setting up an outsourcing register would help keep control, especially when dealing with multiple and inter-related outsourcings and sub-outsourcings, but does not seem to be always necessary to keep control.

Second, combining Table 2 with Figure 1, we can identify 'families' of outsourcing regulations. UCITS Directive and AIFMD have strongly related outsourcing regulations. IORP II's outsourcing regulations are strongly related to Solvency II's. This is not surprising. Institutions covered by UCITS Directive and AIFMD have very similar businesses and are both within the mandate of the same ESA, it being ESMA. The same goes for institutions covered by Solvency II and IORP II, the ESA being EIOPA. This 'familiarity' could have been the result of adaptation to the specific needs and characteristics of strongly related types of business, but this does not appear to be the case. Other 'families' cover topics that seem just as relevant. For example, to have an outsourcing policy seems just as relevant for UCITS Directive and AIFMD institutions as it is for Solvency II and IORP II institutions. On the other hand, a pre-outsourcing analysis seems just as relevant for Solvency II and IORP II institutions as it is for UCITS Directive and AIFMD institutions.

Third, there are several trends that level the playing field. (i) As noted before, when regulations are updated, they tend to pick up topics and solutions that were put forward in other regulations. This inspiration may be drawn from another 'family' of regulations, as illustrated by the influence of the MiFID outsourcing regulations on Solvency II and EBA 2019. (ii) EBA has made a huge step in levelling the differences in outsourcing requirements between the institutions within its mandate. Were it not for the guidelines in EBA 2019, the sectoral differences between CRD, EMD, PSD II and MiFID II would be huge, with MiFID II providing a fairly complete set of regulations and the others little to nothing. It must be noted, though, that EBA 2019 addresses supervisory authorities, not outsourcing institutions themselves.

Fourth, the levelling approach of EBA 2019 creates a new division between sectors. EBA 2019 applies to investment firms within the EBA mandate, but not all investment firms are within the EBA mandate. Thus, although MiFID II provides a fairly complete set of outsourcing regulations, non-EBA investment firms are subject to a less comprehensive regime than investment firms that fall within the EBA mandate.

VII. Some Topics with Sectoral Divergences

From the table, we learned that there are big differences between the various financial sectors' outsourcing regulations that, at least to a large extent, cannot be explained as tailoring regulations according to a given sector's characteristics. The table does not reveal all differences as it does not show whether a topic is covered in detail or only partly or superficially. Therefore, this section highlights some topics to take a more detailed look at sectoral differences.

A. Terminology

The term 'outsourcing' is used in all sectors, except for the sectors of investment funds. In UCITS Directive, AIFMD and the IOSCO documents, the term 'delegation' is used.

Table 2 Topics covered in outsourcing regulations

Topic	IOSCO 2005	Joint Forum 2005	EBA 2019	UCITS Directive	AIFMD and subsequent regulations	CRD	Electronic Money Directive	PSD II	MiFID II and subsequent regulations	Solvency II and subsequent regulations	IORP II
Proportionality	Topic 2	Princ. I	Nr. 18–20		D 75(e)			23(1)	16(5) jo D 30(1). 31(2)(a), 31(2)(d), 32(1)(b)	29(3), 29(4), 49(2)	Consideration 78. Also: 25(2), 26, 47(4)
Definition	p. 1	Ch. III	Nr. 12						D 2(3)	13(28)	
Governance framework											
– outsourcing policy	p. 3	Princ. I	Nr. 41–44							41(3), D 258(2)	21(3)
– conflicts of interests			Nr. 45–47	13(1)(e)	20(2), D 80				D 2(1) jo 29 and 33	D 274(3)(b)	*
– business continuity plans		Princ. VI	Nr. 48–49		D 75(g)				D 31(2)(k)	D 274(4)(e)	
– role of internal audit function	Topic 7	Princ. I	Nr. 51–52		D 79						**
– set-up of an outsourcing register			Nr. 52–56								
– letter-box entity			Nr. 39	13(2)	20(3), D 82				***		
Outsourcing process											
– pre-outsourcing analysis / objective reasons		Princ. I	Nr. 61	13(1), 22a(2)(b)	20(1)(a), 21(11)(b), D 76						
– situations where only a regulated service provider is allowed			Nr. 62–63	13(1)(c)	20(1)(c)				D 32		
– due diligence	Topic 1	Princ. IV	Nr. 69–73	22a(2)(c)	D 98				D 31(2)(a)	D 274(3)(a)	
– notification of outsourcer's national competent authority			Nr. 58–59	13(1)(a)	20(1)			19(6), 28(1)		49(3)	31(6)
– oversight of outsourced functions: ongoing monitoring of the service provider's performance	Topic 1	Princ. II, V	Nr. 100–105	13(1)(f)	20(1)(f), D 75(i)				D 31(2)(e)	D 274(1)	31(4)
– exit strategies	Topic 6	p. 12	Nr. 106–108		D 75(g)				D 31(2)(l)	D 274(4)(d), 274(4)(e)	

Contractual arrangements											
– Sub-outsourcing	Topics 2, 3, 4, 5, 7	Princ. V, VIII	Nr. 76–80	22a(3)		20(3)–20(6), 21(11), D 75(h), 81				D 274(4)(k), 274(4)(l)	
– Data security	Topics 3, 4	Princ. II, VI	Nr. 81–84		D 98(2)(d)			last par. of 5(1)	D 31(2)(j)	D 274(3)(e), 274(3)(f), 274(4)(g)	
– Access and audit rights	Topic 7	Princ. V, VIII	Nr. 85–97	22a(3)(b)(ii), 98(2)(a)	21(11)(d)(ii), D 79		23(1)	D 31(2)(i), 31(3)	38(1)(b), D 274(4)(h)	31(3)(c), 31(7)
– Right to change the execution of the outsourced activities					20(1)(f), D 75(f), 75(h), 75(i)			D 31(3)	D 274(4)(f), 274(4)(j)	
– Liability	Topic 2			13(2), 24	20(3), 21(12)–21(15), D75(a), 83(1)(c), 100–102					
– Termination rights	Topic 6	Princ. V	Nr. 98–99	13(1)(g)	D 75(g), 75(h), 98(7)			D 31(3)	D 274(4)(d), 274(4)(e)	
Outsourcing institution's supervisor's powers vis-à-vis the service provider	Topic 7	Princ. VIII	Nr. 86–89, 111		D 78(3)(b), 79	65(3)(a)(vi)	23(1)	D 31(2)(h), 31(2)(i)	38(1), D 274(4)(b), 274(4)(h), 274(4)(i)	31(7)

In the columns of the various Regulations, references are made to Article numbers (unless explicitly stated otherwise).
In the columns of AIFMD, MiFID II and Solvency II and their subsequent regulations, 'D' refers to Articles in the Delegated regulations.
Article 13 UCITS Directive deals with the ucits' management company. Article 22a and Art 24 UCITS Directive deal with the ucits' depositary.
Article 20 AIFMD and Art 75–82 Delegated AIFMD deal with the aif's management company. Article 21 AIFMD and Arts 83–102 Delegated AIFMD deal with the aif's depositary.
* IORP II does provide regulations on conflicts of interests between an iorp and its depositary, but I consider depositary tasks not to be outsourcing by an iorp as depositary tasks are not tasks that would normally be done by the iorp. See section VII C under 3.
** IORP II does pay special attention to outsourcing of the internal audit function (and other 'key functions'), but not to the role of the internal audit function with regard to outsourcing.
*** A ban on letter-box entities was mentioned in Consideration 19 of Delegated MiFID I (Directive 2006/73). It is not clear why this was not reincluded in (Delegated) MiFID II. Perhaps it was overlooked as it was mentioned in the Considerations instead of in an Article. It seems implausible that letter-box entities would be deemed acceptable under MiFID II.

There appears to be no objective reason for this difference in terminology. Nor does there appear to be a reason to assume a difference in meaning is intended. The rationale underlying the outsourcing regulations is the same and they share a common origin. It appears to be a 'cultural difference' whereby IOSCO started in 2000 with the term 'delegation', while Joint Forum in 2005 chose the then more commonly used term 'outsourcing', and all subsequent outsourcing regulations adopted the terminology of either IOSCO 2005 or Joint Forum 2005, whichever was more relevant to the specific sector.

Although no difference in meaning appears to be intended, the difference in terminology does suggest as much. At the very least, such minor differences are needlessly confusing.

B. Definition

Definitions of outsourcing are given in the outsourcing regulations for investment firms[34] and insurers.[35] No definition is given in UCITS Directive, AIFMD, CRD, EMD, PSD II, IORP II or delegated regulations. However, the guidelines of EBA 2019 contain a definition and are to be applied to banks, payment institutions and electronic money institutions. Other definitions are given in the guidelines of IOSCO 2005 and Joint Forum 2005.[36]

The definitions provided are as follows:

Table 3 Definitions of outsourcing

IOSCO 2005	an event in which a regulated outsourcing firm contracts with a service provider for the performance of any aspect of the outsourcing firm's regulated or unregulated functions that could otherwise be undertaken by the entity itself.
Joint Forum 2005	a regulated entity's use of a third party (either an affiliated entity within a corporate group or an entity that is external to the corporate group) to perform activities on a continuing basis that would normally be undertaken by the regulated entity, now or in the future.
EBA 2019	means an arrangement of any form between an institution, a payment institution or an electronic money institution and a service provider by which that service provider performs a process, a service or an activity that would otherwise be undertaken by the institution, the payment institutions or the electronic money institution itself.
MiFID II	an arrangement of any form between an investment firm and a service provider by which that service provider performs a process, a service or an activity which would otherwise be undertaken by the investment firm itself.
Solvency II	an arrangement of any form between an insurance or reinsurance undertaking and a service provider, whether a supervised entity or not, by which that service provider performs a process, a service or an activity, whether directly or by sub-outsourcing, which would otherwise be performed by the insurance or reinsurance undertaking itself.

---

[34] Article 2(3), MiFID II.
[35] Article 13(28), Solvency II.
[36] A definition was also provided in CEBS 2006, but that guideline was superseded by EBA 2019.

A number of elements in the definitions catch the eye.

1.   The type of relationship

     The definitions use different wordings for the type of relationship of the outsourcer with his service provider ('contract', 'use' or 'arrangement of any form'), but the type of relationship seems to be of no importance.

2   Structural and incidental outsourcing

     Joint Forum 2005 is the only source that defines an outsourcing as one that must be undertaken 'on a continuous basis'. The continuity requirement used to be part of the Dutch supervisor's regulations as well.[37] None of the other outsourcing regulations describe a relevant outsourcing as being performed on a continuous basis. Apparently, the common understanding has become that an outsourcing on a non-continuous basis also needs to be managed appropriately. This appears to be the right approach. Although outsourcing on a non-continuous basis may, in general, be less risky than outsourcing on a continuous basis, the actual risks involved in outsourcing (materiality) are the true reason for regulating it, not the time span of the outsourcing.

     For example, an institution that manages its own investment portfolio decides to change its investment strategy. It subsequently wants to change the composition of its present investment portfolio. It is not uncommon in such a case to appoint a *transition manager* to execute this transition of the portfolio. A transition manager is an investment manager that specialises in transitioning investment portfolio's while minimising costs and managing risks. The appointment of the transition manager is a short-term assignment. Certainly, it is not an outsourcing on a structural basis. There seems, however, to be no good reason to exclude this appointment from the scope of outsourcing.

3.   Activities that would otherwise be undertaken by the entity itself

     In spite of slightly different descriptions, virtually all definitions describe outsourcing as a delegation of activities that would otherwise be undertaken by the institution. IOSCO 2005, however, links outsourcing to activities that *could* otherwise be undertaken by the institution. This wording includes many more activities in the definition. It was, however, never retained by any other guideline or regulation.

Interim Conclusions

The various definitions use somewhat different wordings but these differences do not appear to indicate different criteria. These differences, therefore, only come across as needlessly confusing.

The lack of definitions in UCITS Directive, AIFMD and IORP II make it unclear what interpretation of the term 'outsourcing' is to be adhered to within those sectors and if the same criteria can be used as in regulations that do provide definitions.

---

[37] The Dutch supervisor DNB was one of the first to issue outsourcing regulations, issuing such regulations as early as 2001. They were fairly elaborate and also contained the continuity requirement that Joint Forum 2005 mentions. As the Dutch sources are older, the continuity requirement in Joint Forum 2005 may be inspired on the Dutch regulations. The continuity requirement is still found in Dutch subordinate legislation (in the Decree on prudential regulations (*Besluit prudentiële regels*)) as a condition for the mandatory application of certain outsourcing requirements.

C. The Type and Materiality of Outsourced Activities

Both IOSCO 2005 and the Joint Forum 2005 state that their guidelines 'should be applied according to the degree of materiality of the outsourced activity'.[38] The materiality is determined by the possible negative effects to the institution, its supervisors or its clients, if something goes wrong in the execution of the outsourced activities. Thus, the larger the risks involved, the further-reaching the measures an outsourcing institution should take in order to control these risks. If no material risks are involved, the use of a third party does not constitute outsourcing within the meaning of these guidelines and does not require measures to be taken by the institution. Hence, the distinction these guidelines make with regard to using a third party is between one involving material risks (outsourcing) and one involving immaterial risks (no outsourcing).

The principle of proportionality underlies all European regulations. Thus, an institution making use of a third party, cannot be required to take disproportionate measures. It seems to follow, then, that in any outsourcing regulation, the use of a third party only constitutes an outsourcing if it involves material risks.

In MiFID II, that is the distinction that appears to have been made. Measures are prescribed only when institutions outsource 'critical or important operational functions'.[39] Operational functions are regarded critical or important if a defect in its performance would materially impair compliance with the institution's conditions and obligations, its financial performance, or the soundness or continuity of its investment services and activities.[40]

In other outsourcing regulations, outsourcing is further distinguished in the outsourcing of 'ordinary materiality' and outsourcing of 'critical or important materiality', although the wording is, again, divergent. PSD II makes a distinction between outsourcing of operational functions and outsourcing of important operational functions.[41] Solvency II, in its turn, distinguishes between outsourcing of 'functions or any insurance or reinsurance activity', and outsourcing of 'critical or important operational functions or activities'.[42]

Although the wording in MiFID II, PSD II and Solvency II is fairly similar, the approach in PSD II and Solvency II is different from the approach in MiFID II. MiFID II makes a twofold distinction (either outsourcing of critical or important activities or no outsourcing) whereas PSD II and Solvency II make a threefold distinction (no outsourcing, outsourcing of ordinary materiality, and outsourcing of critical or important materiality). Still, EBA claims in its guidelines that the same approach is taken in all these regulations.[43] On that assumption and in order to create a level playing field for credit institutions, investment firms, payment institutions and electronic money institutions, EBA chooses to use in its guidelines the wording used under MiFID II.[44] Regardless of the merits of pursuing a level playing field, EBA thus ignores that, at least under PSD II and Solvency II, outsourcing may not be 'critical or important' but still involves material risks and thus warrants certain (lighter) measures to be taken.

---

[38] IOSCO 2005, p 1; Joint Forum 2005, p 2.

[39] In two consecutive sentences, MiFID II refers to outsourcing of critical operational functions and outsourcing of important operational functions (Art 16(5), MiFID II), suggesting they are not the same and may need to be dealt with differently. In Delegated MiFID II, however, they are consistently treated the same.

[40] Article 30(1), Delegated MiFID II.

[41] Article 19(6), first vs second paragraph, PSD II.

[42] Article 49(1) vs Art 49(2), Solvency II and Art 274(1) vs Art 274(2), Delegated Solvency II.

[43] EBA 2019, Background note, nr. 20.

[44] EBA 2019, Background note, nr. 20.

UCITS Directive, AIFMD and IORP II also make a distinction between outsourcing of 'ordinary materiality' or 'extra materiality'. Unlike PSD II and Solvency II, they designate specific activities to be of 'extra materiality' when outsourced. For UCITS Directive and AIFMD, it is the outsourcing (delegation) of investment management (portfolio and risk management). For IORP II, it is the outsourcing of 'key functions' (internal audit function, risk management function and actuarial function).

Since IORP II is heavily influenced by Solvency II, and Solvency II too identifies key functions, it seems logical that the outsourcing of key functions by an insurer or reinsurer constitutes outsourcing of 'critical or important operational functions' in terms of Solvency II. Also, key functions help management to remain in control over its activities, whether outsourced or not. Hence, the outsourcing of key functions is automatically of an extra material nature. Other sectoral regulations do not require institutions to set up key functions. Therefore, they do not specifically designate the outsourcing of key functions to be of extra materiality.

Interim Conclusions

Some regulations make a twofold distinction between either outsourcing or not, whereas others make a threefold distinction between no outsourcing, ordinary outsourcing and critical or important outsourcing. These approaches are not necessarily incompatible. The proportionality principle would require less-demanding measures for outsourcing of less materiality. However, if an outsourcing of 'critical or important materiality' under MiFID II has a similar meaning as an outsourcing of 'critical or important materiality' under Solvency II and PSD II (as EBA suggests), then MiFID II does not allow for proportionate measures for an intermediate category of materiality. Then, the EBA 2019 approach with a twofold distinction in either outsourcing or not is not consistent with PSD II.

D. Letter-Box Entities

IOSCO 2000 makes it clear that an institution should not become a letter-box entity as a result of outsourcing because it should remain fully responsible for its operations, whether outsourced or not.[45] An explicit ban on becoming a letter-box entity is taken up, only in UCITS Directive, AIFMD and EBA 2019.[46] MiFID II, Solvency II and IORP II, however, state that an outsourcing institution remains fully responsible for compliance with its regulatory obligations.[47]

PSD II has yet another approach. It forbids an outsourcing to lead to (a) delegation of senior management's responsibility, (b) alteration of the relationship with and obligations to clients, or (c) undermining of conditions on which the institution's authorisation depends.[48] MiFID II, Solvency II and IORP II similarly forbid an outsourcing to lead to such outcomes in order to remain fully responsible and thus not becoming a letter-box entity.[49] It can thus be inferred that PSD II, too, requires an outsourcing institution to remain fully responsible for compliance with its regulatory obligations and hence does not allow an institution to become a letter-box

---

[45] IOSCO 2000, p 8: 'The delegation of a function should not afford the delegator with the means to divest itself of its obligations, especially those concerning operating means, so that it becomes nothing more than an "empty box"'.

[46] EBA 2019, nr. 39; Art 13(2), UCITS Directive; Art 20(3), AIFMD.

[47] Article 30(1), Delegated MiFID II; Art 49(1), Solvency II; and Art 31(2), IORP II.

[48] Article 19(6), PSD II.

[49] Article 30(1), Delegated MiFID II; Art 49(2), Solvency II; and Art 31(3), IORP II.

entity. In any case, in its 2019 guidelines, EBA does not allow payment institutions to become letter-box entities.[50]

In order to prevent becoming a letter-box entity, Delegated AIFMD and EBA 2019 provide a set of more detailed requirements.

Delegated AIFMD holds an institution to be a letter-box entity if it

- no longer retains the necessary expertise and resources to supervise the delegated tasks effectively and manage the risks associated with the delegation;
- no longer has the power to take decisions in key areas which fall under the responsibility of the senior management or no longer has the power to perform senior management functions;
- loses its contractual rights to inquire, inspect, have access or give instructions to its delegates or the exercise of such rights becomes impossible in practice;
- delegates the performance of investment management functions to an extent that exceeds by a substantial margin the investment management functions performed by the AIFM itself.[51]

EBA 2019 considers an institution to be a letter-box entity if it does not or does no longer

- meet all the conditions of its authorisation at all times, including the management body effectively carrying out its responsibilities;
- retain a clear and transparent organisational framework and structure that enables it to ensure compliance with legal and regulatory requirements;
- exercise appropriate oversight and have the ability to manage the risks resulting from the outsourcing (where operational tasks of internal control functions are outsourced); or
- have sufficient resources and capacities to ensure compliance with points (a) to (c).

The requirements of Delegated AIFMD and EBA 2019 appear both to be about an institution not exercising or not being able to exercise sufficient control over the outsourced activities. The sets of requirements of Delegated AIFMD and EBA 2019 seem complementary. In order to exercise sufficient control over outsourced activities, the entity must be able to monitor and manage the service provider and the outsourced activities. It must have disposal of expertise, resources, senior management that carries out its responsibilities,[52] an organisational framework, and contractual rights to monitor and make key decisions. MiFID II names a few contractual rights that an outsourcing investment firm must retain in particular and may serve as a minimum in order to possibly be in control. These are 'instruction and termination rights, rights of information, and right to inspections and access to books and premises'.[53]

One of the requirements presented by EBA 2019 seems far-fetched. EBA 2019 holds that if an institution no longer meets all the conditions of its authorisation, it has become a letter-box entity. For example: a payment institution must hold an amount of capital and must safeguard payment service users' funds, as conditions for authorisation.[54] According to a strict interpretation of EBA 2019, if a payment institution continues to provide payment services but fails to meet one or both of these requirements, it should be deemed a letter-box entity. In our view,

---

[50] EBA 2019, nr. 39.
[51] Article 82(1), Delegated AIFMD.
[52] The requirement of a senior management's responsibilities not being delegated is also found in Art 19(6)(a), PSD II and Art 31(1)(a), MiFID II as one of the forbidden consequences of an outsourcing to result in.
[53] Article31(3), Delegated MiFID II.
[54] Article 5(1)(c) and (d), PSD II.

however, this appears to be a true payment institution, be it one that is in violation of one or two requirements.

EBA made a harmonisation step in drawing up its 2019 Guidelines that will apply to institutions within its mandate (banks, payment institutions, electronic money institutions and many investment firms). ESMA, too, is making a harmonisation step. It considers it essential for national competent authorities to have a harmonised approach for aifs and ucits when assessing if an institution has become a letter-box entity.[55] Yet, investment firms can be regulated by ESMA or by EBA.[56] If their approaches are not identical, an investment firm can be considered a letter-box entity by EBA while it would not be considered as such by ESMA, and vice versa.

Interim Conclusions

Although formulated very differently, it appears that in every regulation an outsourcing institution is not allowed to become a letter-box entity. This is only logical considering the requirement to remain in control.

The essence of what a letter-box entity is appears to be the same over the various sectors' regulations: an outsourcing institution has become a letter-box entity if it cannot or does not exercise sufficient control over the outsourced activities. The criteria used in EBA 2019 and AIFMD and, if you will, PSD II, MiFID II, Solvency II and IORP II turn out to be complementary, rather than exclusive to a given sector.

E. Outsourcing Policy

Apart from the IOSCO 2005, Joint Forum 2005 and EBA 2009 guidelines, only Solvency II and IORP II require outsourcing institutions to adopt and implement an outsourcing policy. Yet, it seems unlikely for an institution to possess 'sound administrative and accounting procedures, internal control mechanisms, effective procedures for risk assessment, and effective control and safeguard arrangements for information processing systems'[57] if it outsources (critical or important operational) functions in the absence of an outsourcing policy.

IORP II requires outsourcing policies to be subject to prior approval by the management board, be reviewed every three years and adapted in view of any relevant and significant change.[58] EBA 2019 adds that this should be done on an individual, sub-consolidated and consolidated basis.[59] IORP II states no requirements as to the contents of the outsourcing policy.

Solvency II states that the outsourcing policy must take into account the impact of outsourcing on the institution's business, and the reporting and monitoring arrangements to be implemented in cases of outsourcing.[60] EIOPA 2013 elaborates on this. It states that the outsourcing policy should cover the institution's approach and processes for outsourcing from the inception to the end of the contract. It should address, in particular: (a) the process for determining whether a

---

[55] ESMA Opinion to support supervisory convergence in the area of investment management in the context of the UK withdrawing from the EU, 13 July 2017 (ESMA 34-45-344), nr. 41.

[56] Investment firms that are subject to CRD are within the mandate of EBA (see Regulation 1093/2010); others are within the mandate of ESMA (see Regulation 1095/2010).

[57] Or similar requirements. See: Art 16(5), MiFID II; Art 12(1)(a), UCITS Directive; Art 18(1), AIFMD; Art 11(4), PSD II.

[58] Article 21(3), IORP II. See also IOSCO 2005, p 3.

[59] EBA 2019, nr. 41.

[60] Article 274(1), Delegated Solvency II.

function or activity is critical or important; (b) how a service provider of suitable quality is selected and how and how often its performance and results are assessed; (c) the details to be included in the written agreement with the service provider; and (d) business contingency plans.[61]

Joint Forum 2005 states that the outsourcing policy should 'include an evaluation of whether, and the extent to which, the relevant activities are appropriate for outsourcing. Risk concentrations, limits on the acceptable overall level of outsourced activities and risks arising from outsourcing multiple activities to the same service provider must all be considered'. Further, the policy should 'ensure its ability to oversee effectively the activity being outsourced'.[62]

EBA 2019 stresses the outsourcing policy should include the main phases of the life cycle of outsourcing arrangements and define the principles, responsibilities and processes in relation to outsourcing. It then gives a detailed list of topics that should be included in the outsourcing policy. These include – in short:[63]

(a) the responsibilities and involvement of the management body, business lines, internal control functions and other individuals in respect of outsourcing arrangements;
(b) defining the business requirements of an outsourcing arrangement;
(c) how to identify if an activity is critical or important;
(d) how to identify, assess and manage risks;
(e) due diligence checks on prospective service providers;
(f) how to identify, assess, manage and mitigate potential conflicts of interest;
(g) business continuity planning;
(h) the ongoing assessment of the service provider's performance;
(i) the procedures for being notified and responding to changes to an outsourcing arrangement or the service provider (such as its financial position, ownership structures or sub-outsourcing);
(j) the independent review and audit of compliance with legal and regulatory requirements and policies;
(k) the renewal processes;
(l) the documentation and record-keeping;
(m) the exit strategies and termination processes.

Interim Conclusions

Regardless of the financial sector an institution is active in, it seems desirable for any outsourcing institution to have an outsourcing policy. Even if an outsourcing institution *can* remain in control over outsourced activities in the absence of an outsourcing policy, its being in control is better ensured if it does have an outsourcing policy. Moreover, the process of outsourcing and subsequent monitoring of the service provider probably increases in efficiency and effectivity if a prior outsourcing policy is written. All in all, it is difficult to see an objective reason against taking up an outsourcing policy requirement in other financial sectors' outsourcing regulations. Nor does there appear to be an objective reason against harmonising the existing requirements for outsourcing policies in IOSCO 2005, Joint Forum 2005, EBA 2019, Solvency II and IORP II.

[61] EIOPA 2013, Guideline 63, nr. 1.116.
[62] Joint Forum 2005, Principle I.
[63] EBA 2019, nr. 42.

F. Instructing or Otherwise Changing the Execution of the Outsourced Activities

It is difficult to imagine how an outsourcing institution can remain in control over its outsourced activities if it cannot somehow alter the way they are executed. Changes in the execution may for example be needed due to regulatory changes, an instruction from the outsourcer's supervisor, or changes in the outsourcer's strategy or policies. Changes may be brought about by an instruction from the outsourcer, but other mechanisms can exist, too. As long as it is the outsourcer that sets the necessary outcomes, it is hard to see why the service provider could not give input on an optimal implementation or even negotiate on the implementation. After all, whatever the outcome, the implementation is to take place in the service provider's business. The service provider needs to remain in control over its business, too, or risk liability issues with its shareholders or – if it is a financial institution – problems with its own supervisor will result.[64] It therefore cannot accept unlimited contractual instruction rights for the outsourcing institution.

There are notable differences on this topic between the various outsourcing regulations. CRD, EMD, PSD II and IORP II do not require the outsourcer to give instructions or at least otherwise effectuate a change in the execution of their outsourced activities. UCITS Directive says that the outsourcing must not prevent the institution from giving further instructions at any time.[65] Delegated AIFMD states that the agreement must set out the manager's instruction rights and, where portfolio management is outsourced, the service provider shall be instructed by the manager on how to implement the investment strategy.[66] Delegated MiFID II provides that the investment firm shall keep its instruction rights.[67] According to Delegated Solvency II, the outsourcing contract must clearly state that (1) the outsourcer may issue instructions concerning the outsourced activities and, further, that (2) the outsourcer must have the right to issue general guidelines and individual instructions as to what has to be taken into account when performing the outsourced activities.[68] The second statement seems redundant after the first.

Interim Conclusions

Where outsourcing regulations state the outsourcer must retain a right to instruct, the obligation to retain such right tends to be general in nature.

There appears to be no objective reason why institutions in some financial sectors would not be required to contractually reserve instruction right for themselves. The desired scope of the instruction right may not be established in general terms. It will depend on the risks involved, which depend on the nature of the industry, but also the nature of the outsourced activity, whether other activities were outsourced, the characteristics of the service provider, the characteristics of the outsourcer (such as its loss bearing capacity) and all risk mitigating measures that have further been taken. However, it remains difficult to imagine why a payment institution or a bank would not need a right to instruct its service provider on the execution of its outsourced activities.

---

[64] See para 1.5 under 3.
[65] Article 13(1)(g), UCITS Directive.
[66] Article 75(f) and (i), Delegated AIFMD.
[67] Article 31(3), MiFID II.
[68] Article 274(4)(j) and (f), Delegated Solvency II.

G. Liability

Except for IOSCO 2005[69] and – apparently – EBA 2019,[70] none of the regulations require the outsourcing contract to contain provisions on the service provider's liability vis-à-vis the outsourcing institution, except where it is a depositary that is outsourcing tasks.[71] Yet, although an outsourcing institution may be fully responsible towards its supervisor and its clients, it does not automatically follow that the outsourcer – in order to remain in control – must hold its service provider fully liable.

Were the outsourcer to hold its service provider fully responsible, it would shed (at least financial) responsibility to the service provider. It would thus loose an important incentive to *actually* be in control over the outsourced activities. Holding the service provider fully liable is thus contrary to the outsourcer's duty to remain in control.

A full liability of the service provider towards the outsourcer may be disproportionate in view of the service provider's fee relative to the possible amount of damages. Also, had the outsourcer not outsourced the activities, it would also have sustained an amount of damages, because no organisation – including the outsourcer's – is perfect so that, inevitably, a number of malperformances would occur. In such cases, the outsourcer would not have a party on who to pass on the damages. Hence, a full liability for a service provider in an outsourcing relationship can be unreasonable.

On the other hand, if the service provider is not or practically not liable for shortcomings in its own services, the outsourcing institution would definitely not be in control. The service provider would have little to no incentive to prevent disturbances in the provision of its services or instances of lower quality of its services.

Worryingly, contracts that limit the service provider's liability to situations where the malperformance was the result of intent or gross negligence, exist. Such thresholds for liability make it virtually impossible for an outsourcer to hold its service provider liable.

Thus, an adequate liability arrangement is somewhere between no liability and full liability. What the arrangement should look like, depends on all the circumstances of the case, such as the nature of the activities, the possible amount of damages, the measures in place to prevent instances where the outsourcer suffers a loss, and the solvency of the service provider. There is also a commercial aspect, as the service provider will raise his fees along with the increase in liability risks he may face. Even though it is impossible to describe in general what a liability arrangement must look like, a liability arrangement should exist.

A liability arrangement is required for depositaries of ucits and aifs that outsource tasks. It should be noted that the use of a depositary by the ucits or aif does not, in my opinion, constitute an outsourcing as depositary tasks are no activities a ucits or aif would otherwise normally undertake.[72] However, where a depositary contracts a third party for material activities that would normally be performed by depositaries, that would be outsourcing.

A ucits' or aif's depositary may outsource its depositary tasks to a sub-depositary. UCITS Directive and AIFMD provide that the sub-depositary must be liable to the depositary in

---

[69] IOSCO 2005, topic 2.

[70] EBA 2019 requires in nr. 75 that the contract states 'the parties' financial obligations. From the EBA feedback on the public consultation it can be inferred that, apparently, this includes a contractual arrangement on the service provider's liability. See EBA 2019, p 112: 'The liability of the service provider is part of the contractual arrangements that should be agreed between the service provider and the institution'.

[71] For depositaries of ucits: Arts 13(2) and 24, UCITS Directive. For depositaries of aifs: Arts 20(3), 21(12)-21(15), AIFMD and Arts 75(a), 83(1)(c) and 100–102, Delegated AIFMD.

[72] See para 1.7.2 under 3.

the same way the depositary is liable to the ucits.[73] They also provide that the depositary is liable for the loss of financial instruments held in custody by either the depositary or a sub-depositary and for all other losses suffered by the ucits or its investors as a result of the depositary or a sub-depositary's negligent or intentional failure to properly fulfil its obligations.[74] Hence, the depositary that outsources tasks to a sub-depositary should make sure contractually that its sub-depositary will indeed be liable accordingly.

Then, the UCITS Directive and AIFMD approaches differ. UCITS Directive provides that the depositary's liability cannot be excluded or limited.[75] It is thus a *full* liability. Because a ucits' (of aif's) depositary must ensure that his sub-depositary is liable in the same way as he is, the sub-depositary must be fully liable too. AIFMD, on the other hand, provides that the depositary shall not be liable if it can prove that the loss has arisen as a result of an external event beyond its reasonable control, the consequences of which would have been unavoidable despite all reasonable efforts to the contrary.[76] Further, AIFMD provides that the depositary may discharge itself of its liability if a number of conditions are met, one of which is the transfer of liability of the depositary to the sub-depositary while making it possible for the aif or its manager to make a claim against the sub-depositary in respect of the loss of financial instruments.[77] Again, this also applies to an aif's sub-depositary.

This difference in liability provisions between UCITS Directive and AIFMD may be explained by the difference in nature of the businesses they regulate. Although they both regulate investment funds, UCITS Directive and AIFMD regulate different varieties. UCITS Directive regulates a more standardised variety where investors should be able to place high trust in the product. AIFMD regulates other varieties that can invest in very risky and exotic markets with exotic structures. That can make it too burdensome for a depositary to have to accept full liability, while the investor may very well know – if duly informed about the characteristics of the aif – that the fund is riskier than a ucits he could invest in.

Interim Conclusion

Liability arrangements are only prescribed for depositaries of ucits or aifs. They are lacking for managers of ucits and aifs and for all other institutions. Levelling this difference seems desirable in so far as a requirement to make a liability arrangement is taken up for institutions presently lacking such a requirement.

Making service providers fully liable, like (sub)-depositaries of a ucits, is not recommendable. Even stipulating the service provider's liability to the same high standard and as detailed as for depositaries in AIFMD, seems undesirable for parties that are not a depositary. Their safekeeping task[78] puts depositaries in a special position of trust that justifies a detailed regulation of a high standard of liability. In other outsourcing relationships, the parties should be able to adjust the liability arrangement to meet their needs. The composition of the liability arrangement should depend on all the circumstances of the case, including a commercial view.

---

[73] Article 22a(3), UCITS Directive and Art 21(11), AIFMD.
[74] Article 24(1), UCITS Directive and Art 21(12), AIFMD.
[75] Article 24(3) and (4), UCITS Directive.
[76] Article 21(12), AIFMD. This provision is worked out in more detail in Art 101, Delegated AIFMD.
[77] Article 21(13)(b) and Art 21(14)(e), AIFMD. This provision is worked out in more detail in Art 102, Delegated AIFMD.
[78] Article 22(5), UCITS Directive; Art 21(8), AIFMD.

H. Termination of the Outsourcing Contract

Many outsourcing regulations require an outsourcing institution to contractually arrange the right to terminate the outsourcing contract with immediate effect if that is in the interest of the clients.[79] Under Solvency II, termination needs to be possible where that is in the interest of the clients, but apparently it does not have to be possible with immediate effect.[80] Delegated MiFID II and Delegated Solvency II add that termination must be possible without detriment to the continuity and quality of its services to its clients.[81] Delegated MiFID II further adds that the continuity and quality of the outsourced activities must be ensured, either by transferring the activities to another service provider or by performing them itself.[82]

A notice period in the event the service provider terminates the outsourcing agreement, is only required under Solvency II. The notice period must be sufficiently long for the institution to find an alternative solution.[83]

IOSCO 2005, Joint Forum 2005 and EBA 2019 draw attention to the need to also contractually arrange for the transfer of information such as client related data, back to the outsourcing institution.[84] EBA 2019 also draws attention to the need to contractually arrange for the service provider to support the outsourcing institution in transferring the outsourced activities to a subsequent service provider.[85]

Interim Conclusion

The sectoral differences seem random. Not all outsourcing regulations require the outsourcing institution to arrange anything in relation to the termination the agreement. Yet, an outsourcer that cannot or cannot at reasonable terms, terminate the outsourcing contract, is not in control over the outsourced activities. It seems desirable to expand these outsourcing regulations on this point.

Still, those outsourcing regulations that do prescribe to make contractual arrangements, differ markedly in what they prescribe. Why would it for outsourcing institutions under Solvency II be of less value to be able to terminate with immediate effect? Or, the other way round, is it always necessary to be able to terminate with immediate effect? Perhaps, a better contractual balance is achieved if termination with immediate effect is possible in cases where the service provider goes bankrupt or seriously underperforms. There seems, however, not always to be a compelling need to be able to terminate with immediate effect.

Some outsourcing regulations make it clear that it is the continuity and quality of the services that need to be ensured after having given notice to the service provider.[86] Not all outsourcing regulations do that, let alone require institutions to make appropriate measures to ensure this.

---

[79] See Article 13(1)(g), UCITS Directive; Art 20(1)(f), AIFMD; Art 31(2)(g), Delegated MiFID II.
[80] Article 274(4)(e), Delegated Solvency II.
[81] Article 31(2)(g), Delegated MiFID II; Art 274(4)(e), Delegated Solvency II.
[82] Article 31(2)(l), Delegated MiFID II.
[83] Article 274(4)(d), Delegated Solvency II.
[84] IOSCO 2005, topic 6; Joint Forum 2005, Principle 5, EBA 2019, nr. 99(a).
[85] EBA 2019, nr. 99(c).
[86] IOSCO 2005, Topic 6; Joint Forum 2005, Principles V and VI; EBA 2019, nr. 106–108; Art 75(g), AIFMD; Art 31(2)(g), Delegated MiFID II; Art 274(4)(d) and 274(4)(e), Delegated Solvency II.

Termination of the contract by the service provider can easily place the outsourcer in a precarious situation if the outsourcer has no immediate alternative. Threatening with termination can thus be a powerful 'weapon' for the service provider in case of a conflict with the outsourcer. It is thus important to have made reasonable arrangements in 'peace time'. Yet, only Delegated Solvency II pays attention to the situation that the service provider terminates the contract.

I. Supervisory Powers vis-à-vis the Service Provider

All regulations either explicitly state or presume that in order to supervise the outsourced activities of a regulated outsourcing institution, a supervisor can address the outsourcing institution, both for information on the outsourced activities and for enforcement measures. Most regulations also require for the supervisor to possess supervisory powers directly to the service provider.

Delegated AIFMD requires that, if portfolio or risk management is delegated to a third country service provider, an agreement must exist between the supervisory authorities of both the home Member State and the third country, that allows the outsourcing institution's supervisor to:

(a) obtain on request relevant information;
(b) obtain access to documents maintained in the third country;
(c) carry out on-site inspections on the premises of the service provider;
(d) receive information from the third country supervisory authority, and
(e) cooperate in enforcement.[87]

Thus, the outsourcing institution's supervisor must obtain these powers through a cooperation agreement with the third country's supervisory authorities.

Delegated MiFID II has a similar approach where an investment firm wishes to outsource functions related to the investment service of portfolio management provided to clients, to a service provider located in a third country. The investment firm can only follow through on its outsourcing plans if a cooperation agreement exists between the supervisors of both the outsourcer and the service provider, whereby the cooperation agreement enables its supervisor to, at least:

(a) obtain on request necessary information necessary to carry out their supervisory tasks;
(b) obtain access to relevant documents maintained in the third country;
(c) receive information from the supervisory authority in the third country;
(d) cooperate with regard to enforcement.[88]

In addition and regardless of what and to where an investment firm outsources activities, Delegated MiFID II also requires an outsourcing institution to ensure:

(a) that the service provider cooperates with the outsourcing institution's supervisor,
(b) that the supervisor has effective access to all relevant data, as well as
(c) effective access to the relevant business premises of the service provider.[89]

---

[87] Article 78(3), Delegated AIFMD.
[88] Article 32(2), Delegated MiFID II.
[89] Article 31(2)(h) and (i), Delegated MiFID II.

It does not state that the outsourcing institution must ensure this by way of a third-party clause to the benefit to the supervisor in an outsourcing contract between outsourcer and service provider, although this seems the obvious way to do.

That is the approach in Solvency II and its delegated act. These require the outsourcing institution to conclude a contract with the service provider which ensures for its supervisor certain powers towards the service provider. These powers to be arranged are that:

(a)   the service provider cooperates with the outsourcer's supervisor;
(b)   the supervisor has effective access to all relevant information;
(c)   the supervisor has effective access to the business premises of the service provider, and
(d)   the supervisor may address questions directly to the service provider to which the service provider shall reply.[90]

PSD II states that Member States must ensure that the outsourcing institution's supervisor is entitled to carry out on-site inspections at any service provider. It does not prescribe Member States on how to ensure this. This can be done by requiring outsourcing institutions to include in their contracts with service providers a third-party clause to the benefit of the supervisor, like in Delegated Solvency II. It can also be done by only allowing an outsourcing if the supervisory authorities have concluded a cooperation agreement, like in Delegated AIFMD. The latter approach, however, seems less suitable as it is intended for outsourcings to third countries. Other Member States' supervisory authorities are required to cooperate on the basis of the EU 'principle of sincere cooperation'.[91]

IORP II requires Member States to ensure that the outsourcing institution's supervisor has the power to request, at any time, information from service providers,[92] and the power to carry out on-site inspections at the premises of a service provider and all subsequent service sub-providers.[93] Like in PSD II, it does not state how Member States are to ensure this, but the most obvious approach would seem to require outsourcing entities to contractually arrange for it.

Interim Conclusions

There are once again marked difference between the various regulations. The powers supervisors are required to have vis-à-vis the service provider, can be:

(a)   addressing questions directly to the service provider (and to which the service provider must reply);
(b)   receive cooperation from the service provider;
(c)   have effective access to all relevant data;
(d)   carrying out on-site inspections at the premises of the service provider (and, to that end, have effective access to the service provider's premises).

---

[90] Article 38(1), Solvency II jo Art 274(4)(b), (h) and (i), Delegated Solvency II.
[91] Article 4(3), Treaty on European Union.
[92] Article 31(7), IORP II.
[93] Article 50(e), IORP II. The relevant text is: 'Member States shall ensure that the competent authorities (...) have the necessary powers and means to (...) carry out on-site inspections at the iorp's premises and (...) on outsourced and all subsequent re-outsourced activities'. It thus suggests inspections 'on premises and activities'. The sentence is grammatically flawed. The main text is my interpretation of what was apparently intended.

Basically, these powers appear to be all about requesting information from the service provider (be it in document form, digital, orally or any other form) and being able to carry out an on-site inspection. Such powers are complementary. A supervisor should be able to verify information it receives from the outsourcing institution or the service provider, and hence be able to carry out an on-site inspection. But it should not be dependent on on-site inspections for obtaining the information it needs to supervise. The right to request information is much less intrusive for the service provider (and much less burdensome for the supervisor).

Both of these rights should thus be conferred on supervisors in all the financial sectors' outsourcing regulations. Yet, some outsourcing regulations do not require supervisors to possess any power vis-à-vis a service provider. IORP II only requires the supervisor to possess the right to carry out an on-site inspection.

The mechanisms to have these rights conferred on the supervisor may diverge. Under Solvency II, the supervisory powers must be arranged in the outsourcing contract between outsourcer and service provider. In other cases 'the outsourcer must ensure' the supervisor is conferred these rights. The only practical way seems to include them in the outsourcing contract.

Under AIFMD another mechanism exists: it is the supervisor that concludes a cooperation agreement with the supervisor of the service provider's country. This is only required for the outsourcing of portfolio or investment management to a third country. If the supervisor fails to conclude such a contract, the outsourcing to a service provider in that third country is not possible. This mechanism is only needed for outsourcings to third countries as supervisors of other Member States are required to cooperate with the outsourcing institution's supervisor on basis of the EU 'principle of sincere cooperation'.

The mechanism whereby the outsourcing contract includes a third-party clause to the benefit of the supervisor has advantages over the AIFMD mechanism whereby the supervisor concludes a cooperation agreement with another country's supervisor:

(1) the supervisor is not dependent on the cooperation of the other country's supervisor, who may or may not be as expeditious as desired;
(2) an institution desiring to outsource to a service provider in a particular country is not dependent on its supervisor concluding (or not concluding) a cooperation agreement with the other country's supervisor. It can just include the necessary third-party clauses to the benefit of its supervisor and source out.

On the other hand, a cooperation agreement between supervisors can have advantages over the 'third party clause mechanism', too:

(1) the supervisor has its powers, even if outsourcer and service provider fail to include the necessary third-party clauses;
(2) the supervisor also has its powers, if the service provider is unwilling to live up to the contractual third-party clause (which may be an issue if enforcing these contractual rights can be frustrated as a result of choice of law and choice of court clauses).

Lastly, a combination of mechanisms can be used, too, as in MiFID II. Under MiFID II, contractual third-party clauses to the benefit of the supervisor are a standard obligation for an outsourcing institution. Where functions of portfolio management provided to clients are outsourced to a third country service provider, the mechanism of the cooperation agreement is prescribed. Perhaps, outsourcings involving portfolio or investment management should be considered extra sensitive, requiring a cooperation agreement between the outsourcer's and service provider's supervisors to be already in place.

VIII. Considerations and Conclusions

There are strong arguments in favour of levelling the various outsourcing regulations. They all share the same underlying rationale and the same general principles.[94] With regard to most topics discussed, no objective reasons were found for differences. Solutions in one regulation often appear perfectly adequate for other regulations that lack these. It is difficult to see why, for example, an institution outsourcing investment management should take different measures depending on being authorised on the basis of a MiFID licence, a banking licence or an AIFMD licence. A similar argument can be made from the perspective of client protection, which is an important aim of outsourcing regulations. If, for example, a pension fund appoints an investment manager who subsequently outsources to a service sub-provider, then why should it matter for the protection of the interests of the pension fund, whether the appointed manager is authorised under UCITS Directive, AIFMD, CRD, MiFID or Solvency II?

It is not surprising, then, that updated regulations usually include (some) new topics and solutions, picked up from other regulations. EBA also acknowledged the desirability of levelling regulations. It produced its EBA 2019 guidelines with the deliberate aim of creating a level playing field for the institutions within its mandate (banks, electronic money institutions, payment institutions and many investment firms). However, a less fortunate side effect of this is that it created an unlevel playing field for investment firms inside and outside its mandate. This should not be exaggerated, as MiFID already provides a fairly complete set of requirements, and the investment firms outside the EBA mandate may very well look at EBA 2019 for inspiration on how to organise their own outsourcing. Still, there appears to be no argument why at least the playing field for investment firms could not be levelled.

Reasons for sectoral differences in outsourcing regulation often have little to do with objectivity and more with pragmatism. Regulations are rarely updated at the same moment. When MiFID was updated to MiFID II, for example, UCITS Directive outsourcing regulations remained unchanged. Another reason is that outsourcing regulations are the outcome of a political negotiating process, where negotiating parties have different (national) interests. Finally, political negotiations can sometimes continue deep into the night, at which time both detail and wording may have lost most of the attention.

Indeed, sectoral differences may have objectively warranted reasons as well. This is the case for the liability of aifs' and, especially, ucits' sub-depositaries. Where such objective reasons exist, these differences should not be set aside. However, such objective reasons are usually not present.

However understandable that sectoral differences exist as a result of reasons that have little to do with objectivity, the situation is less than ideal. Why should, for example, an investment manager meet other requirements – be they more or less demanding – because the manager happens to be licensed in one or another sector? And why should client protection depend on such a chance situation? And even where sectors are fairly unrelated, such as payment services and insurances, it is difficult to see why a payment service provider should not pay attention to, eg, business continuity or due diligence, while such (and other) measures help insurers to be in control over their outsourced activities. The present situation is an unwarranted unlevel playing field.

---

[94] With the possible exception for UCITS Directive and IORP II with regard to the principle of freedom to outsource (see para 1.5 under 6).

EBA has attempted to create a level playing field, at least for the institutions within its mandate. Yet, that attempt itself created an unlevel playing field for investment firms within and outside its mandate. The attempt thus shows that levelling the playing field cannot be done by any supervisory authority alone.

Ideally, a common set of regulations were laid down at level 1. That would guarantee a level playing field. Where objectively substantiated sectoral differences require divergent regulations, such regulations could be laid down at level 2 or 3.

A common set of outsourcing regulations at level 1 may not be expected for the foreseeable future. A pragmatic alternative may be for EBA, EIOPA and ESMA to draw up a common set of outsourcing guidelines together. They would not be dependent on the moment of updating a regulation. They would likely look at all topics and solutions available in all sectors instead of only some. In absence of nightly negotiations, attention for detail and wording may improve as well. Further, as they have all the expertise necessary, they can make sectoral exceptions or additions where desirable.

PART III

Consumer Protection

12

Scope of Protection: Is there a Ground for a Single Criterion?

MARC-DAVID WEINBERGER

I. Introduction

Consumer protection is a well-known reality of contemporary EU Law. It is one of the Union's competences and political missions, and is an important subject-matter of the approximation of laws within the Common Market.[1]

Originated in general contract law, the consumer concept and the protection afforded to consumers evolved and developed in other fields, including most sectors of financial activities. However, the protection of financial services customers appears different throughout its particular regulations.

This chapter intends to examine the scope of protection of the customer of financial services in different sectors of the financial industry, how this scope relates to the general common consumer concept, and whether a cross-sectoral 'financial consumer' concept exists or is needed.

The study will therefore first recall the main principles and laws on (general) consumer protection, and their related possible issues (see section II below). Secondly, it will point out the need for stronger protection in the financial sector and examine the protection of financial services customers through the different *ratione personae* scopes of protection of the main regulations in that sector (below, section III). Thirdly, the incidence of the jurisprudence of the CJEU on the judge's office in relation to consumer protection will be briefly discussed (below, section IV).

II. General Consumer Protection

A. The 'Acquis Communautaire'[2]

As part of the '*acquis*' to date, consumer protection materialises itself through, broadly, two kinds of rules, generally mandatory: first, by requiring various types of precontractual information,

---

[1] Articles 4, 12, 114 and 169 of the Treaty on the Functioning of the European Union (TFEU).
[2] See also the Communication from the Commission to the European Parliament, the Council and the European Economic and Social Committee, 'A New Deal for Consumers', 11 April 2018, COM(2018) 183 final.

they tend to ensure that the consumer's consent is freely given and informed, especially as to his rights and obligations; second, they provide for corrective mechanisms in, and throughout, the contractual relationship. As it is inferred from consumer directives and the jurisprudence of the CJEU,[3] such protection flows from the fundamental postulate that consumers are in an inferior position vis-à-vis the professionals with whom they contract, especially in terms of knowledge (information asymmetry) and bargaining power.[4]

From this perspective, in the EU, consumer protection in general is essentially governed by the following Directives:

–   **Council Directive 93/13/EEC of 5 April 1993 on unfair terms in consumer contracts (UCTD)**. Its purpose is to approximate the laws, regulations and administrative provisions of the Member States relating to unfair terms in contracts concluded between a seller or supplier and a consumer.[5] It is applicable to any consumer contract, though limited to regulating and prohibiting unfair terms.

–   **Directive 2002/65/EC** of the European Parliament and of the Council of 23 September 2002 **concerning the distance marketing of consumer financial services (DMD)**, relates to the remote commercialisation of financial services (ie banking, investment services and insurance activities). It seeks to organise a '"sale method', ie the process of contracting, rather than the contract content as such.[6] Its purpose is to ensure that consumers acquire good knowledge of the contractual conditions and have sufficient time to understand them. The rights granted by this Directive are imperative: the consumer cannot waive them.[7] It is worth pointing out that DMD was the first cross-sectoral consumer regulation applicable to the entire financial industry, showing also the need to organise the protection of the financial customer through more adapted provisions.

–   **Directive 2005/29/EC** of the European Parliament and of the Council of 11 May 2005 **concerning unfair business-to-consumer commercial practices in the internal market (UCPD)**. Its purpose is to contribute to the proper functioning of the internal market and achieve a high level of consumer protection by approximating the laws, regulations and administrative provisions of the Member States on unfair commercial practices harming consumers' economic interests.[8] Like UTCD, UCPD has a limited scope (ie the prohibition of unfair commercial practices) but is generally applicable to all kind of businesses, including financial services (as defined in DMD). For these services however, the Directive's provisions are only of a minimal harmonisation level.[9] It also introduced the notion of 'average consumer': although it aims at protecting all consumers from unfair commercial practices, UCPD takes as a benchmark the average consumer, who is reasonably well-informed and reasonably observant and circumspect, taking into account social, cultural and linguistic factors, as interpreted by the Court of Justice,[10] and contains provisions aimed at preventing

---

[3] In the field of unfair contract terms, see CJEU, 4 June 2009, C-243/08 (*Pannon*) and the quoted decisions. In the field of consumer credit, see CJUE, 21 April 2016, C-377/14 (*Radlinger*).

[4] Consumer protection is provided for where they face special challenges and are particularly vulnerable, for instance due to a peculiar situation in which they conclude an agreement or with regard to a uniquely complex type of contract, see M Lehmann & J Ungerer, 'Save the "Mittelstand": How German Courts Protect Small and Medium-Sized Enterprises from Unfair Terms', (2017) 2 *European Review of Private Law* pp 322–323.

[5] Article 1(1).

[6] Th Bonneau, *Régulation bancaire et financière européenne et internationale*, (Bruylant, 2012), p 275.

[7] Article 12.

[8] Article 1.

[9] Article 3(9), 9).

[10] See notably CJEU, 26 October 2016, C-611/14 (*Canal Digital*).

the exploitation of consumers whose characteristics make them particularly vulnerable to unfair commercial practices;[11]

– **Directive 2011/83/EU** of the European Parliament and of the Council of 25 October 2011 **on consumer rights**.[12] It forms the core of general consumer protection in terms of contract formation process and conditions,[13] regulation of certain fees, and the prohibition of certain practices. However, this Directive does not apply to contracts for financial services,[14] and will therefore not be discussed in this chapter.

Appearing as the complementary *lex generalis* on consumer protection, these four directives determine the now unified EU concept of 'consumer', defined as any natural person who, in the contracts or practices at stake, is acting for purposes which are outside his trade, business, craft or profession.[15] Although seemingly straightforward, this definition has several implications:

(1)   it is exclusive of groups, bodies, corporations, or other legal persons whatever their size and sophistication;

(2)   the consumer notion is objective and functional, ie it does not depend on the finality or subject matter of the contemplated contract or transaction.[16] It is triggered by the simple fact that a natural person is acting outside their professional activities with regard to a professional seller or service provider;[17]

(3)   this in turn implies that the consumer's actual knowledge and experience in the field are irrelevant for the application of the legal protection as such,[18] which is no more subject to the proof of an actual weakness.[19]

B. The Case for Protective Inclusion of Small and Medium-sized Enterprises (SMEs)

As observed above, disparities in contracting situations (such as information asymmetries and the unequal distribution of bargaining power) are a particular challenge for the weaker party to the contract, who typically is a consumer, businesses being excluded. Yet, most reasons

---

[11] Rec 18.

[12] The purpose of this Directive is, through the achievement of a high level of consumer protection, to contribute to the proper functioning of the internal market by approximating certain aspects of the laws, regulations and administrative provisions of the Member States concerning contracts concluded between consumers and traders (Art 1).

[13] It repealed and replaces Dir 97/7/EC of the European Parliament and of the Council of 20 May 1997 on the protection of consumers in respect of distance contracts, which was not applicable to financial services.

[14] Article 3 (3) d).

[15] Article 2(b) of UTCD; Art 2(d) of DMD; Art 2(a) of UCPD and Art 2(1) of Dir 2011/83.

[16] CJEU (ord.), 19 November 2015, C-74/15 (*Tarcău*), § 36.

[17] M Combet, 'Précisions de la notion de consommateur dans les contrats de prêts à la suite d'une novation', (2017) 3 *International Journal of Financial Studies* p 52.

[18] *Traité Pratique de Droit Commercial (belge)*, T. 5, v 1, 2016, p 471.

[19] As pointed out by Advocate General Cruz Villalón in its opinion delivered on 23 April 2015 in the Case C-110/14 (*Costea*), ss 28–29: 'Accordingly, no one can be deprived of the possibility of being treated as a consumer in relation to a contract which is outside his trade, business or profession by reason of his general knowledge or his occupation, and instead regard must be had exclusively to his position vis-à-vis a specific legal transaction. (…) However, those notions of vulnerability and weakness, which generally underlie EU consumer protection law as a whole, were not given concrete form in the legislative expression of the concept of consumer as necessary conditions through its definition in positive law. Thus, neither the definition of consumer nor any other provisions of the Directive make the existence of the status of consumer in a particular situation subject to a lack of knowledge, a lack of information or a genuine position of weakness'.

underlying consumer protection refer to defects in the process of contracting, which can apply also to businesses as well,[20] be it not necessarily in all cases or with the same intensity.[21]

SMEs represent 99 per cent of all businesses in the EU,[22] and are therefore also an important motor of the Single Market economy. Although most corporation models allow for limited liability and the protection of personal assets, their failure can have consequences which are as severe as over-indebtedness is for individuals, and possibly even exacerbated given their potential collateral effects (eg on contractors, employees, etc.)

Still, the basic EU approach on SMEs, including the criteria used to define them, remains largely concerned with encouraging competition and economic growth, especially in terms of access to financing.[23] Even if consideration is now routinely given to the potential impact on SMEs of provisions in legislative proposals as part of the arrangements for conducting impact assessments of proposals leading to new legislation,[24] there is today no legal ground to assimilate SMEs to consumers when applying pure consumer-based legislation.

Financial legislation, conversely, does contain examples of either undifferentiated treatment of natural and legal persons (see below), or of extension of the protection afforded to consumers to microenterprises and SMEs. For instance, under MiFID I,[25] the implementing Directive 2006/73[26] provided that in any case where Article 3(3) of DMD (on distance marketing of consumer financial services) does not otherwise apply, the investment firm complies with the requirements of this provision in relation to the retail (potential) client, as if that client were a 'consumer' and the investment firm were a 'supplier' within the meaning of that Directive.[27] This precision is not taken back under MiFID II as information rules for distance contracting are integrated in that Directive's general provisions on information.[28]

Outside these cases, treating SME's or micro enterprises as consumers seems to be left open to national law. This is not prohibited by EU Law even in the presence of a maximal harmonisation instrument.[29] In some Member States, extensions of protection scopes are currently being discussed or have already been introduced.

In France, for instance, the general provisions of the French *Code de la consommation* and the wording of the *Ordonnance* transposing MCD on credit agreements for consumers relating to residential immovable property have led to a debate on whether the 'civil real estate company'

---

[20] Including transaction costs, competition failure, asymmetric information, lack of bargaining power and spill over effects.

[21] M Lehmann & J Ungerer, 'Save the "Mittelstand": How German Courts Protect Small and Medium-Sized Enterprises from Unfair Terms', (2017) 2 *European Review of Private Law* pp 323–325.

[22] http://ec.europa.eu/growth/smes/business-friendly-environment/sme-definition_en.

[23] See the Communication from the Commission, Review of the 'Small Business Act' for Europe, 23 February 2011, COM(2011) 78 final and the Final Report commissioned by the DG Enterprise and Industry, on the Evaluation of the SME Definition, 2012, https://publications.europa.eu. See also the Commission's proposal for a Regulation on European Crowdfunding Service Providers for Business, 8 March 2018, COM(2018) 113 final.

[24] Cf, the Final Report on the Evaluation of the SME Definition quoted hereabove, pp 21–22.

[25] Directive 2004/39/EC of the European Parliament and of the Council of 21 April 2004 on markets in financial instruments.

[26] MiFIDI implementing Dir 2004/39/EC of the European Parliament and of the Council as regards organisational requirements and operating conditions for investment firms and defined terms for the purposes of that Directive.

[27] Article 29(5)(b).

[28] See Art 46 of the Commission Delegated Regulation (EU) 2017/565 of 25 April 2016 supplementing Dir 2014/65/EU of the European Parliament and of the Council as regards organisational requirements and operating conditions for investment firms and defined terms for the purposes of that Directive.

[29] See CJEU, 12 July 2012, C-602/10 (*Volksbank România*), although this ruling is based on certain recitals of Dir 2008/48 (consumer credit) allowing Member States to apply provisions of this Directive to areas not covered by its scope.

(*Société civile immobilière*) should be included in the scope of protection of the mortgage credit regulation.[30]

The Belgian Law of 25 April 2014 on the status and control of independent financial planners establishes MiFID-inspired conduct of business rules for these intermediaries when dealing with retail clients (as defined in MiFID), and sets out that they should comply with Book VI by treating all retail clients as consumers.[31]

More significantly, Germany has a long-standing tradition of extending the scrutiny of standard terms and conditions[32] in business-to-consumer relations (B2C) to business-to-business contracts (B2B), provided that the clauses were not individually negotiated by the parties.[33] Courts in Germany have rendered many decisions applying the statutory default rules and branding standard terms in contracts between big companies and SMEs as being unfair towards the latter, and consequently void.[34] Belgium followed by adopting, on 21 March 2019, a law introducing in the *Code de droit économique* new rules on unfair contract terms between undertakings.[35]

III. Protection of the Customer of Financial Services

A. Reasons for Increased Protection of the Customer of Financial Services

In its early times, the Common Market for financial services and instruments was essentially conceived for professionals and issuers. Few legal instruments were aimed at their activities with clients, which were therefore poorly considered. This changed considerably as clients' and investors' protection has gained a significant place in the EU and international law.[36] It is inter alia the subject-matter of the OECD G20 High-level Principles of Financial Consumer Protection, and one of the goals of the ESMA.[37]

Like consumers, customers in the financial sector are considered the weaker parties and therefore deserve protection. Another reason is underlying the need for protection: financial services remain contracts, and if clients cannot trust professionals, especially outside their home country, they would not accept to contract, and the freedoms provided for by the Treaties would remain ineffective.

---

[30] C Chombart de Lauwe, 'Réflexions sur l'application du régime du crédit immobilier aux personnes morales', (2016) 2 *International Journal of Financial Services* pp 64–68.

[31] Article 25, s 3.

[32] With a broad conception of the notion of standard terms, leading to a seemingly broad judicial control of such terms.

[33] Control in B2B context was requested because of the idea that not every business could be regarded as having immunity from being put at any disadvantage by standard form contracts. Yet, according to German law, almost all of the specifically void B2C terms must be taken into consideration when assessing 'good faith' and 'reasonableness' as decisive criteria of the fairness test also in B2B relations. On the other hand, when assessing the fairness of B2B terms, it is required that appropriate consideration is given to commercial customs, which serve as a safeguard for the protection of the peculiarities and traditions of business trading (M Lehmann & J Ungerer, 'Save the "Mittelstand": How German Courts Protect Small and Medium-Sized Enterprises from Unfair Terms' (2017) 2 *European Review of Private Law* p 317).

[34] See M Lehmann & J Ungerer, 'Save the "Mittelstand": How German Courts Protect Small and Medium-Sized Enterprises from Unfair Terms', (2017) 2 *European Review of Private Law* pp 313–336, esp. pp 313–314 and 327–329 and the quoted references.

[35] See Projet de loi modifiant le Code de droit économique en ce qui concerne l'abus d'une position dominante significative, Texte adopté en séance plénière et soumis à la sanction royale, *Parl. Doc.*, Chambre 2018–19, n° 54-1451/010.

[36] See Th Bonneau, *Régulation bancaire et financière européenne et internationale*, (Bruylant, 2012) p 254.

[37] Article 5(f) of Reg (EU) N° 1095/2010 of the European Parliament and of the Council of 24 November 2010 establishing a European Supervisory Authority (European Securities and Markets Authority).

The question therefore arises as to who is to be protected. If it seems usual to consider borrowers as consumers, is it necessarily so with regard to investors or other financial services users? This is debatable, as investors do not normally invest so to satisfy daily needs but rather to expect fruitful returns.[38] On the contrary, it can be argued that the mobilisation of savings has become a common need, as such, for individuals and households, indeed even for legal persons, and that financial products and services are now commercialised quite like other goods and services.

The 2008 financial crisis generated a new approach of the commercialisation of financial products, and at the same time the protection of products users has been completed with additional information and advice duties, supervision and/or (prior) authorisations of products, best execution rules, reporting obligations, rules on conflict of interests, mandatory warnings, etc. These mechanisms and their reach vary depending on the subject-matters and goals of the regulation, and can be either limited (eg the Prospectus and PRIIPs Regulations, where information is the main means of achieving protection), issued from a broad set of protection rules (eg MiFID II), or somewhere in between (eg the UCITS Directive legislation[39]).

This evolution has also led to a sliding in semantics from the 'investor' notion to 'consumer of financial products' notion, implying inter alia that if the investor is considered a consumer, increased supervision of financial products appears highly desirable.[40]

As noted below, certain legal instruments do assimilate customers of financial services with consumers, although others recognise that not all and any clients/investors deserve the same (level of) protection.[41] Before examining these instruments, it is worth recalling the main reasons commending a broader protection for the 'financial consumer'.

B. General Consumer Protection is Insufficient in the Financial Sector

Because of the nature of financial services and products, stronger protection appears as an essential pillar to increase trust of customers of financial services and therefore contributes to well-functioning financial markets and reinforces financial stability.[42]

Except for their subject-matter, financial products and services differ from non-financial goods and services because the consequences of issues and problems are likely to be much more drastic. Strong(er) consumer protection therefore appears necessary to prevent such disruptive impacts. Financial products and services are disruptive for consumers when the economic and financial consequences of mis-selling, inappropriate selling, the crystallisation of the risk(s) embodied in a financial product or service, and the non-respect of the contractual obligations by the consumer may be such that the financial health of consumers is seriously impaired, and consumers may be pushed into a state of acute financial vulnerability.[43]

---

[38] Th Bonneau, *Régulation bancaire et financière européenne et internationale*, (Bruylant, 2012) p 255.

[39] In regard of UCITS Directive, investors are 'shareholders' or 'co-owners' with no management powers. This passivity leads to protection requirements, organised through many legal instruments due to the great variety of UCITS Directive. These are not examined in this chapter.

[40] P-H. Conac, 'La nouvelle règlementation des produits financiers dans l'Union européenne: une révolution dangereuse', in Joly et al (eds) *Mélanges en l'honneur de Jean-Jacques Daigre*, (2017) p 506.

[41] For instance, IOSCO 'Suitability Requirements With Respect To the Distribution of Complex Financial Products', Final Report, January 2013, FR01/13.

[42] OECD, 'G20 High-Level Principles on Financial Consumer Protection', October 2011, p 4.

[43] Study, 'Consumer Protection Aspects of Financial Services', Directorate-General for Internal Policies, 2014. According to the Study, financial products and services are also considered to have the potential to be highly disruptive to the

Even in the absence of mis-selling or inappropriate selling, the acquisition of various types of financial products or services is particularly challenging for many consumers. The reason for this is explained in a 2014 Study for the European Parliament on Consumer Protection Aspects of Financial Services, being understood that information asymmetry and lack of bargaining power are common to both the 'regular' consumer and the 'financial' consumer.[44] Interesting is to note that the Study addresses SMEs as consumers.

First, most consumers do not buy (new) financial products and services on a regular basis. Therefore, when buying a new financial product or service, they do not have much past knowledge or experience to rely on for taking decisions.

Second, many financial products and services can be rather complex and opaque, and putting together the information required for making an informed choice is very time-consuming. As a result, consumers may acquire new financial products or services based on only limited information.

Third, many financial products and services have a relatively long duration, and the problems and issues that they potentially cause for consumers, may manifest themselves only in the distant future. It is therefore difficult for consumers to properly asses the true cost of a financial product and its riskiness at the time of the agreement.

Fourth, the venues open to consumers to address financial problems once they have occurred may be close to nil in some cases or may be costly, take a long time and yield a result which is uncertain at the outset.

Fifth, a number of consumers also have limited financial literacy skills and exhibit behavioural biases which tend to amplify the issues described above.

Sixth, the failure of a financial firm can be more disruptive to a consumer than the failure of a non-financial firm. This is due to the fact that amounts involved with financial firms are often bigger, information transfers may not be frictionless or costless, financial firms are often involved in long-term relationships with customers, and the financial firm has a fiduciary commitment to the customer.

C. Legislative Responses to the Peculiarities of the Financial Sector

From what can be observed *de lege lata*, EU Law addresses the differences between the 'regular' consumer and the 'financial' consumer through different ways of legislating in the various fields of the financial sector.

In terms of protection scope, one may distinguish: (i) pure consumer-based financial regulations, which are legislative instruments aimed at adapting and/or amplifying the '*consumer acquis*' in a particular field, whether general or specific, although dedicated to the consumer only (below, i); financial regulations with a broader scope while maintaining special rules for consumers (below, ii); and financial regulations with a broader scope, but without specific consideration of the consumer (below, iii).

Single Market where the consequences of inappropriately selling or mis-selling may (i) cause financial instability (in some cases a particular product may have the potential to result in both significant financial harm for some consumers and wider financial instability, or (ii) affect a large number of individual consumers in national markets, or (iii) directly impact negatively on cross-border trade in financial services ('Consumer Protection Aspects of Financial Services', Study of the Directorate-General for Internal Policies (European Parliament), February 2014, PE 507.463, p 10).

[44] The following is quoted from the Study 'Consumer Protection Aspects of Financial Services', Directorate-General for Internal Policies, 2014, pp 10–12 and pp 41–42, available at www.europarl.europa.eu/RegData/etudes.

i. Credit Services: Pure 'Consumer-Based' Protection

Consumer credit is one field where the European legislator has intervened early (1986 for the first directive). Directive 2008/48/EC of the European Parliament and of the Council of 23 April 2008 on credit agreements for consumers (CCD) aims at (fully) harmonising certain aspects of the laws, regulations and administrative provisions of the Member States concerning agreements covering credit for consumers.[45]

Again, CCD is purely consumer-based, and refers to the two usual cumulative criteria of the consumer notion[46] being (i) the nature of the borrower (natural person), and (ii) the purpose of the credit (non-professional). It is the destination of the good or service acquired with the credit which determines the professional or non-professional capacity of the borrower. The protection under CCD lies essentially on three pillars which are (i) (precontractual) information, (ii) the APRC, and (iii) the assessment of the borrower's creditworthiness. It also regulates the retraction right and the early repayment of the credit.

Directive 2014/17/EU of the European Parliament and of the Council of 4 February 2014 on credit agreements for consumers relating to residential immovable property (MCD). The purpose of MCD is to lay down a common framework for certain aspects of the laws, regulations and administrative provisions of the Member States concerning agreements covering credit for consumers secured by a mortgage or otherwise relating to residential immovable property.

MCD defines the consumer by referring to the definition contained in CCD.[47] But the protection under MCD differs from that of CCD, first of all because the credit agreement is not contemplated as such, and no retraction right is provided for. Second, because the creditworthiness assessment of the borrower can lead to a refusal to grant a credit, which is not the case under CCD. Third, the regulation of the indemnity for early repayment is entirely left to the Member States.[48]

ii. Payment Services: Broader 'User-Based' Protection with Specific (Mandatory) Rules for Consumers

Directive (EU) 2015/2366 of the European Parliament and of the Council of 25 November 2015 on payment services in the internal market (PSD II) establishes rules for distinguishing between different categories of payment service providers,[49] and rules concerning the transparency of conditions and information requirements for payment services. It sets out the respective rights and obligations of the payment service users and the professionals who provide payment services as a regular occupation or business activity.[50] Overall, PSD II aims at improving the security of payments chains, and the payment service users trust and protection.[51]

In terms of scope of protection, PSD II relies essentially on a definition of the 'payment service user', being any person making use of a payment service in the capacity of payer, payee, or both.[52]

---

[45] Article 1.

[46] Article 3(a) defines the consumer as a natural person who, in transactions covered by this CCD, is acting for purposes which are outside his trade, business or profession.

[47] Article 4(1).

[48] Th Bonneau, *Régulation bancaire et financière européenne et internationale*, (Bruylant, 2012), p 297.

[49] Article 1(1).

[50] Article 1(2).

[51] See Recs 4, 6, 28, 29, 33, 63, 73, 95.

[52] Article 4(10). See also Rec 7, 13, 28, 54, 69 to 74, 81 to 85 and 99.

It is therefore a broad notion which covers natural persons as well as legal persons, whether or not acting for private or professional purposes.[53] Given the *Grüber* case,[54] when a natural person initiates mixed payment transactions, ie for private as well as professional purposes, he will not qualify as a consumer unless the professional use is marginal in the context of these operations.[55]

Still, PSD II uses the (traditional) definition of the consumer[56] – ie a natural person acting for purposes outside its professional activities – who appears as a particular category of payment service users.[57] Indeed, for consumers, either specific rules shall apply (eg rules on the value date of cash placed on payment accounts,[58] and a mission for the Commission to inform the consumers about their rights and obligation[59]), or certain exemptions allowed by the Directive when the user is not a consumer are prohibited (namely in terms of information requirements, fees, liability in case of fraudulent use of payment instruments and more generally for the performance of payment transactions).[60]

The Directive does not give much explanation about the differentiated treatment of the consumer. The only rationale to be found is that non-consumers are generally in a better position to assess the risk of fraud and take countervailing measures.[61] But while considering that consumers and undertakings are not in the same position, and do not need the same level of protection,[62] PSD II nevertheless allows Member States to treat microenterprises as consumers.[63] To define microenterprises, the Directive refers to Commission Recommendation 2003/361/EC, which is more competition-law based and does not comment on the differences between consumers and microenterprises.

Finally, the PSD II provisions are without prejudice to the application of other directives (such as CCD) and other relevant Union law or national measures regarding conditions for granting credit to consumers,[64] regarding precontractual information (though it aims at clarifying its cumulative application with DMD),[65] and regarding unfair or misleading practices.[66] In the absence of further specification in the Directive as to this cumulative application, the different scopes *ratione personae* of these other instruments should be borne in mind, as they generally only apply to consumers.

iii. *Investment and Insurance Services: Functional '(Retail) Client-Based' Protection*

Directive 2014/65/EU of the European Parliament and of the Council of 15 May 2014 on markets in financial instruments (MiFID II) applies to investment firms, market operators, data reporting services providers, and third-country firms providing investment services or performing

---

[53] *Traité Pratique de Droit Commercial (belge)*, T. 5, v 1, 2016, p 256.
[54] CJEU, 20 January 2005, C-464/01 (*Grüber*), §39 and ff.
[55] PE Berger and S Landuyt, 'Het toepassingsgebied van de wet betalingsdiensten en de wet betalingsinstellingen', in *Financiële regulering in de kering*, (Antwerpen-Cambridge, Intersentia, 2012), p 131.
[56] Article 4(20).
[57] See Recs 13, 42, 53, 59, 61 to 63, 66, 72, 73, 75 and 101.
[58] Article 85.
[59] Article 106.
[60] See Arts 38(1), 40, 41, and 61(1).
[61] Rec 73.
[62] Rec 53.
[63] Articles 38(2) and 61(3), and Rec 53.
[64] See Art 61(4).
[65] See Art 39.
[66] See Rec 55.

investment activities through the establishment of a branch in the Union. It establishes requirements in relation to (a) authorisation and operating conditions for investment firms; (b) provision of investment services or activities by third-country firms through the establishment of a branch; (c) authorisation and operation of regulated markets; (d) authorisation and operation of data reporting services providers; and (e) supervision, cooperation and enforcement by competent authorities.[67]

Although not obviously flowing from the definition of its scope, an important part of the MiFID II device is dedicated to investor protection, essentially through conduct of business and best execution rules. The conduct of business rules are detailed essentially in the Commission Delegated Regulation (EU) 2017/565 (hereafter 'the Regulation').[68]

While MiFID II mentions the consumer in a couple of its recitals,[69] and provisions,[70] it is not consumer-based. Instead, it organises an original and rather sophisticated clients' categorisation system, according to which the level of protection afforded by the Directive is modulated.[71]

Under MiFID II, a client is any natural or legal person to whom an investment firm provides investment or ancillary services.[72] Among the clients, a distinction is made between professional and retail clients: professional clients are those meeting the (objective and quantitative) criteria laid down in Annex II of the Directive,[73] based on the consideration that such clients possess the experience, knowledge and expertise to make their own investment decisions and properly assess the risks incurred. As it flows from Annex II, professional clients include professionals of the financial sector, governmental bodies and very large companies.

By contrast, retail clients are all and any clients who do not qualify as professional clients.[74] Being defined by opposition to professional clients, they are clients who do not possess the experience, knowledge and competence to take investment decisions on their own and to assess the correlative risks. Retail clients are actually protected through a great(er) set of rules (than for professional clients), especially information obligations *sensu lato*, which remind of the core consumer protection techniques.

Retail clients therefore appear as a residual category, likely to encompass many persons, with a great range of difference in terms of knowledge and experience in investment services and products. This is common with the general consumer concept (see above), but with this important difference that retail clients may be legal persons and groups without legal personality.

Both the consumer and the retail client concepts depart from a collective and global approach. Whereas the actual knowledge or competence of the 'regular' consumer is absolutely irrelevant (above section II), there has been some discussion on this question in respect of the MiFID scope of protection. MiFID II imposes specific duties on investments firms to profile their individual clients (also known as the 'Know your Customer' obligations[75]), even those who would otherwise qualify as a consumer. The reach of this profiling obligation depends on the type of services

---

[67] Article 1(1) and (2).

[68] Commission Delegated Regulation (EU) 2017/565 of 25 April 2016 supplementing Dir 2014/65/EU of the European Parliament and of the Council as regards organisational requirements and operating conditions for investment firms and defined terms for the purposes of that Directive.

[69] Recs 77, 81, 156 and 166.

[70] Essentially Arts 74 (right of appeal) and 75 (consumers complaints).

[71] See Rec 86.

[72] Article 4(1), 9).

[73] Article 4(1), 10).

[74] Article 4(1), 11).

[75] Article 25 of MiFID II. For a cross-sectoral analysis of the know-your-customer requirements, see Chapter 14B of this book, 'An Assist-Your-Customer Obligation' for the Financial Sector?' by Danny Busch, Veerle Colaert and Geneviève Helleringer.

offered or provided and on the client's category. At the top, the 'suitability test' obliges firms offering or providing portfolio management or investment advice to gather sufficient information about the retail client's knowledge and experience in the investment field relevant to the specific type of product or service, that person's financial situation including his ability to bear losses, and his investment objectives including his risk tolerance so as to enable the investment firm to recommend to the client or potential client the investment services and financial instruments that are suitable for him and, in particular, are in accordance with his risk tolerance and ability to bear losses.[76]

Does that profiling obligation imply that, based on the client's profile, the investment firm may evaluate under its own responsibility which information is to be communicated to the retail client, or should all retail clients receive the same and all of the information provided for in MiFID II? Some authors plead in favour of this first point of view, arguing that 'common sense' would allow the conclusion that more selective information can be transmitted to clients having a certain competence and who, because of their experience in financial markets or professional activity, do not need particular explanation.[77]

The MiFID I and MiFID II provisions, however, seem to dictate adherence to the second point of view, at least from a supervisory perspective.[78] The clients' categorisation is designed so that all clients appertaining to the same category would benefit from the same protection. In terms of information, only professional clients may be presumed to have sufficient knowledge to decide on their own. Certainly, the Regulation states that the information to be provided to clients shall be sufficient for, and presented in a way that is likely to be understood by the *average member of the group* to whom it is directed, or by whom it is likely to be received,[79] which allows for a certain degree of standardisation, but is not an exemption basis. The only possible limitation resulting from the text relates to the description of the risks associated with the financial instruments, which shall include information 'where relevant to the specific type of instrument concerned and the status and level of knowledge of the client'.[80] Besides, the level of detail of the information to be provided may vary according to whether the client is a retail client or a professional client and the nature and risk profile of the financial instruments that are being offered, but should always include any essential elements.[81]

The profiling obligation under MiFID II is therefore not conceived as a means of derogating from the conduct of business rules; it is aimed at ensuring that suitable services or financial instruments are acquire by, or recommended to, the client.[82]

Another originality of the MiFID II clients' categorisation system is that it allows for changes in categories, either through opting-out, or opting-in the retail client category. This is a significant

---

[76] Article 25(2), MiFID II.

[77] Ph Bourin, 'L'investisseur privé serait-il devenu un simple consommateur?', in *Droit bancaire et financier au Luxembourg*, (Limal, Anthemis, 2014), pp 705–748, especially pp 738–742. This was the case at least before the entry into force of MiFID I, as ruled by the Belgian Supreme Court (Cour de cassation) in a recent decision (Cass. (Bel.), 22 June 2018, C.17.0017.F, www.cass.be. In free translation: 'The ambit of the information duty of the financial intermediary in relation to a transaction on financial instruments is to be assessed according to the degree of the professional knowledge of the client to whom the information is intended'.

[78] Failure to provide the legally required information would therefore be a fault. However, in a private lawsuit, this will not impair a court to decide that there are no damages, or that there is no causation with the damages, if the retail client is shown to already know the relevant information he did not receive.

[79] Article 44(2)(d).

[80] Article 48 (especially (2)) of the Reg.

[81] Rec 64 of the Reg.

[82] R Price, 'Conduct of Business Standards – Fair Dealing with Clients', in M Elderfield (ed) *A Practitioner's Guide to MiFID*, (Old Working, City & Financial, 2007), p 166.

difference with the consumer regime, as consumers cannot opt out of their protected status,[83] and non-consumers cannot opt into the consumer status.

As opting-out implies a reduction of the protection level, it is subject to the strict procedure and conditions laid down in Annex II of MiFID II. Technically, a retail client who is a natural person investing for private purposes (therefore a consumer) and meets the criteria of Annex II, may be treated as a professional client and therefore waive part of the protection conferred by MiFID II.

The MiFID II clients' categorisation has inspired other financial regulations. For instance, Regulation (EU) n° 1286/2014 of the European Parliament and of the Council of 26 November 2014 on key information documents for packaged retail and insurance-based investment products (PRIIPs), which lays down uniform rules on the format, content, and provision of the key information document to be drawn up by PRIIP[84] manufacturers in order to enable retail investors to understand and compare the key features and risks of the PRIIP,[85] is entirely dedicated to the retail investor, defined either as a retail client under MiFID II, or as a customer within the meaning of IMD,[86] where that customer would not qualify as a professional client under MiFID II.[87]

The MiFID professional client notion is also used in the Prospectus Regulation[88] to define qualified investors,[89] as well as in the Directive on Insurance Distribution.

Directive (EU) 2016/97 of the European Parliament and of the Council of 20 January 2016 on insurance distribution (IDD) is aiming essentially at laying down rules concerning the taking-up and pursuit of the activities of insurance and reinsurance distribution in the Union.[90]

IDD sets out rules on registration of insurance intermediaries or undertakings, and their freedom to provide services and freedom of establishment. It then provides for organisational requirements,[91] as well as information requirements[92] and conduct of business rules, which are largely MiFID-inspired[93] (including general principles to act honestly, fairly and professionally in accordance with the best interests of their customers, fairness of information, and remuneration surveillance).[94]

The scope of protection of IDD is rather ambiguous, but also seems to favour a broad scope of protection, which is not based on the 'consumer' concept. Although IDD is part of the set of

---

[83] Still, as most of consumer rights are of an imperative nature, they may generally waive their rights once the event triggering protection has occurred and they are aware of their rights.

[84] PRIIPs are packaged retail and insurance-based investment products, ie one or both of the following: (a) a PRIP ('packaged retail investment product' being an investment, including instruments issued by special purpose vehicles, where, regardless of the legal form of the investment, the amount repayable to the retail investor is subject to fluctuations because of exposure to reference values or to the performance of one or more assets which are not directly purchased by the retail investor); (b) an insurance-based investment product (an insurance product which offers a maturity or surrender value and where that maturity or surrender value is wholly or partially exposed, directly or indirectly, to market fluctuation), cf, Art 4(1)–(4) of PRIIPs.

[85] Article 1.

[86] Former IDD, see below.

[87] Article 4(6).

[88] Regulation (EU) 2017/1129 of the European Parliament and of the Council of 14 June 2017 on the prospectus to be published when securities are offered to the public or admitted to trading on a regulated market.

[89] Article 2(1), (e) (iv), and (2).

[90] Article 1(1).

[91] Articles 10 and fl.

[92] Articles 18, 21, and 23.

[93] *Adde* Arts 19 (transparency on conflicts of interests); 20 (advice, and standards for sales where no advice is given); 24 (rules on cross-selling); 25 (product oversight and governance requirements); and 26–30 (additional requirements in relation to insurance-based investment products, including assessment of suitability or appropriateness (with an 'execution-only' exemption similar to MiFID II), and reporting.

[94] Article 17.

laws promoted by the European Commission with the view to restoring the confidence of the consumer in financial services and increasing its protection level,[95] it uses the word consumer essentially in its recitals, as a reminder of the need for (adequate and high-level) consumer protection whatever the insurance distribution channel.[96] Despite Recital 43, according to which '[a]s this Directive aims to enhance consumer protection, some of its provisions are only applicable in 'business to consumer' relationships, especially those which regulate conduct of business rules of insurance intermediaries or of other sellers of insurance products', the consumer is not the subject of any specific substantial rules under IDD.[97]

The word 'investor' also appears on a few occasions,[98] as well as the word 'client',[99] but it is the word 'customer' which is definitely the most used by IDD.[100]

In fact, *none* of these concepts are defined in Article 2 of IDD. As such, they appear to have no distinct meaning, suggesting interchangeability.[101]

Moreover, the specific care for consumers as contemplated by Recital 43 (above) seems in fact to be absorbed, and expressed in a quite limitative way, by Article 22(1) of IDD, which contains a flexibility clause allowing Member States to provide that certain information[102] need not be provided to a professional client as defined in MiFID II. This seems to be the only legally binding indication of the scope of protection of IDD. It seems to mean that the scope of protection of IDD is not limited and includes any customer, retail or not, but that Member States have the option to limit the scope of protection of certain provisions to retail clients (as defined in MiFID) only.

The intertwining of the customer- and the MiFID-client concept indicates that customers under IDD may be any natural or legal persons. This is also indirectly confirmed by the definition of the retail investor in the PRIIPs Regulation (above).

IV. An Issue at Stake: The '*Pannon*' Jurisprudence

As seen above, variations in protection scopes raise several issues. One of them relates to the apprehension of consumers' and other protected persons' rights by national courts.

In the field of consumer protection, the jurisprudence of the CJEU has shaped the judge's office, through several decisions first rendered under Directive 93/13 on unfair terms. Since the *Pannon* case,[103] the Court orders national judges to control ex officio the possible unfair nature of contract terms when sufficient elements de jure and de facto are provided by the parties.

---

[95] M Hostens, 'De richtlijn verzekeringsdistributie en de impact op het Belgisch recht', (2016) 10 *T.B.H.* pp 926–927.

[96] See Recs 6, 7, 10, 15, 16, 19, 21, 34, 43, 52 and 68.

[97] The word consumer appears in Arts 5(1) and (2), 8(3) and (4), 9(2), 10(7), 11(2) (publication of 'general good' rules), (14) (complaints, where the consumer seems to be a sub-category of the customer), 23(7), 24(7) (Possibility for the Member States to intervene to prohibit the sale of insurance together with an ancillary service or product which is not insurance, when they can demonstrate that such practices are detrimental to consumers), and 41(1).

[98] See Recs 33, 56 and 61 and Arts 2(17) and 41(2).

[99] See Rec 51 and Arts 22 and 29.

[100] See Recs 3, 5, 8, 10, 12, 14, 15, 33, 36 to 42, 44 to 53, 55 to 57 and 63, and Arts 1(4), 2(1), (2), (15), and (18), 10(6), 14, 15, 17 to 20, 22 to 25, 27 to 30 and 34.

[101] Only Rec 49 sets out that in the case of group insurance, 'customer' should mean the representative of a group of members who concludes an insurance contract on behalf of the group of members where the individual member cannot take an individual decision to join, such as a mandatory occupational pension arrangement.

[102] Ie, the information referred to in Arts 29 and 30 of IDD, relating to insurance-based investment products.

[103] CJEU, 17 September 2009, C-143/09 (*Pannon*), following 27 June 2000, C-240/98 (*Oceano Grupo*) and C-244/98 (*Salvat Editores*); adde CJEU, 26 October 2016, C-611/14 (*Canal Digital*).

Such duty relies patently, and essentially, on the principle of effectiveness applied to the protection granted to consumers, based on the Court's consideration of the contractual imbalances faced by the latter, their ignorance of their rights and the deterrent effect for them of the litigation costs. The Court seems also reluctant to leave it to national judges to appreciate when to intervene ex officio.

Often reiterated, the *Pannon* ruling is considered to be general, and therefore transposable to other consumer directives, even more broadly to any situations where consumers are ignorant of their rights.[104] This is confirmed by subsequent case-law of the CJEU,[105] as similar rulings appeared in the field of consumer credit for instance.[106]

Would this modern approach of the judge's office remain limited to consumers' cases or will it extend to other persons protected by the financial regulation?

This question arises particularly in relation to the MiFID-retail clients' category, as these clients may not necessarily be consumers strictly speaking (see above). As such, given the background and finality of the MiFID rules on investors protection, and the reasons underlying the *Pannon* decision, it cannot be excluded that ex officio control on these rules shall be required whomever the retail client is.[107]

This is probably less clear for those financial directives or regulations whose personal protection scopes are broader, whether or not including specific rules for consumers. In the absence of a common 'financial consumer' concept, the active intervention of the judge would likely require a case-by-case analysis of the rationale and purpose of the protective rights and duties consecrated by these instruments. The imperative nature of such rights (where applicable) may, at least, be an indication of the need for ex officio control.

V. Conclusions

From this short overview, one will notice that the 'customer of financial services' who deserves protection does not coincide with any unique or unequivocal legal notion. When it comes to financial regulation, the common consumer concept tends to dissolve itself, entirely or partially, within the various scopes of personal protection. These scopes are quite heterogeneous, and appear to be circumscribed by the EU legislator on a case-by-case basis, according to the particular field covered, though without a connecting thread. Overall, there are no, or few, explanatory statements on the reasons for choosing one way or the other. The outcome of this disparity is that certain customers of financial services are protected by, for instance MiFID, PSD or IDD, but not by the Unfair Contract Terms Directive, while other customers are protected by both the financial law directives and the Unfair Contract Terms Directive.

At least, it is observable that the consideration of the greater complexity, opaqueness, or riskiness of certain financial services or products leads to designing protection scopes which extend beyond the sole natural persons. In general, the distinctions between, firstly, natural

---

[104] L Van Bunnen, 'L'office du juge stimulé par le droit européen', (2015) *Revue critique de jurisprudence belge* p 157.

[105] See also the analyses of A Michel, 'Un office du juge (encore plus) étendu: l'hypothèse du consommateur défaillant', (2018) 118 *Droit de la consommation - Consumentenrecht*, pp 118 to 129; C Delforge, 'Clauses abusives, office du juge et renonciation', (2008) 3 *Revue de Jurisprudence de Liège, Mons et Bruxelles*; D Busch, *MiFID II/MiFIR: nieuwe regels voor beleggingsondernemingen en financiële markten*, (Wolters Kluwer Nederland, 2015), pp 227–228.

[106] CJEU, 4 October 2007, C-429/05 (*Max Rempion*) and CJEU, 21 April 2016, C-377/14 (*Ernst Georg Radlinger*).

[107] See D Busch, *MiFID II/MiFIR: nieuwe regels voor beleggingsondernemingen en financiële markten*, (Wolters Kluwer Nederland, 2015), pp 227–228; M-D. Weinberger, 'MiFID I & II. Portée générale des règles destinées à la protection des investisseurs', (2017) VI *Dr. Banc. Fin*, p 402.

persons and legal entities, and, secondly, private or professional purposes, which lie at the heart of the traditional consumer concept, are receding in financial regulation. MiFID II contains strong arguments in that direction when recognising that even professionals need a certain degree of protection, and removing municipalities and local public authorities from the list of the per se professional clients.[108]

Once it is seen that the complexity and riskiness of financial services and products are equally challenging for, at least, the smaller businesses, might there be a ground for the emergence of a unique and simplified 'financial consumer' notion?

One possible solution would be to generalise the extension of consumers protection rules to SME's.[109]

The question would naturally remain of the criteria to properly map the vulnerable businesses, as it seems impossible to derive the necessity of protection of small companies only from the number of their employees or annual turnover.[110]

Should the presence of an in-house lawyer or legal department be a decisive factor? Possibly in regards to information asymmetry, though not necessarily to redress the lack of bargaining power. For some authors, a suitable criterion should refer to what is usual practice for the respective line of business. Where both professional parties to a contract belong to the same line of business, it can be assumed that they are equally familiar with trade practices and conditions and there is consequently a lesser need for protecting either side.[111] The adequacy of this criterion is however relative given the different subject-matters of financial legislation. It is nevertheless used as part of the MiFID II clients' categorisation, which is probably the most comprehensive and inclusive one to date. A generalisation of this system, including its opting out possibility, may lead to benefits in terms of predictability, simplification, and cost efficiency.

Unfortunately, there seems to be no background thinking on, or willingness to simplify the different personal scopes of protection in financial legislation. This is attested especially by the March 2018 Commission proposal for a regulation on crowdfunding:[112] despite close links with the regulation of financial services (at least for investment-based crowdfunding), the proposal adopts its own terminology which does not coincide with the MiFID II analogous rules, including in terms of personal protection scope.

Moreover, and as a matter of fact, the consumer notion itself is passing through an 'existential crisis',[113] torn between its traditional abstract and contractual approach, the realities of the contemporary markets and competition policies, and the national initiatives allowing extensive application of consumers protective rules to SME's.

---

[108] Rec 104 of MiFID II.

[109] In Belgium, a 2014 Royal Decree (*Arrêté royal du 23 mars 2014 visant à prendre des dispositions particulières et à déroger à l'application de certaines dispositions du livre VI du Code de droit économique pour certaines catégories de services financiers*) has rendered the general legal provisions on consumer protection (Book VI of the *Code de droit économique*) largely applicable to financial services, though without paying sufficient attention to the differences in the ratione personae scopes of protection. This has been seen as a missed opportunity to use a single criterion, such as the MiFID retail client notion (See V Colaert, 'De toepassing van Boek VI van het Wetboek Economisch Recht op de financiële sector', in *De levenscyclus van bank-, beleggings-, en verzekeringsproducten*, (Larcier, 2014), pp 160–161).

[110] M Lehmann & J Ungerer, 'Save the "Mittelstand": How German Courts Protect Small and Medium-Sized Enterprises from Unfair Terms', (2017) 2 *European Review of Private Law*, pp 335–336.

[111] Ibid, p 334.

[112] Commission's proposal for a Regulation on European Crowdfunding Service Providers for Business, 8 March 2018, COM(2018) 113 final.

[113] Th Bourgoignie, 'Droit de la consommation: une mutation salutaire?', in J Rogge (ed) *Liber Amicorum Jean-Luc Fagnart*, (Anthemis, 2008), pp 845–866.

13

Product Information for Banking, Investment and Insurance Products

VEERLE COLAERT

I. Introduction

Sectoral Product Information rules ... Until recently financial regulation in regard of product information was typically sector- or even product-specific: a 'standard European consumer credit information form' should be made available in respect of consumer credit;[1] a 'European Standard Information Sheet' for mortgage credit;[2] a prospectus and summary prospectus for securities offered to the public or admitted to trading;[3] a separate prospectus regime applied and a Key Investor Information Document (KIID) should be made available in respect of Undertakings for the Collective Investment in Transferable Securities (UCITS) Directive funds;[4] whereas no harmonised information obligations applied in respect of other funds, nor in respect of bank deposits or insurance products.[5]

... until the PRIIPs Regulation. On 26 November 2014 the European Parliament and the Council, however, adopted the so-called PRIIPs Regulation, or 'Regulation on key information documents for Packaged Retail and Insurance-based Investment Products'.[6] It marked a clear change in the approach to financial regulation, being the first EU regulation to take a cross-sectoral approach. Indeed, the scope of application of the PRIIPs Regulation is not defined in terms of the sector to which a product belongs. Instead, it targets all *complex* ('packaged') products which can be sold to a retail public and have the same economic purpose (investment), such as structured deposits, structured securities, investment funds and insurance-based investment products. The PRIIPs Regulation introduces a standardised three page 'key information document' or 'KID' for all these products.[7] The Regulation thus aims at enhancing investor

---

[1] Article 16 and Annex I to CCD.

[2] Article 14 and Annex II to MCD.

[3] Prospectus Dir 2003/71/EC was recently replaced by Prospectus Regulation (EU) 2017/1129 (see Art 1(1)).

[4] Articles 69 and 78, UCITS Directive and Commission Regulation (EU) No 583/2010.

[5] The IDD recently introduced the 'Insurance Product Information Document' (IPID) for insurance products. See Art 20(4)–(7) and Commission Implementing Regulation (EU) 2017/1469.

[6] Regulation (EU) No 1286/2014 of the European Parliament and of the Council of 26 November 2014 on key information documents for packaged retail and insurance-based investment products (PRIIPs) [2014] OJ L352/1.

[7] Articles 5–12 of the PRIIPs Regulation determine the content and format of the KID. See for a critical discussion: V Colaert, 'The Regulation of PRIIPs: Great Ambitions, Insurmountable Challenges', (2016) 2(2) *Journal of Financial Regulation* 2 (2).

protection by: (i) improving the quality of investor information in respect of those products,[8] and (ii) improving the comparability of financial products with similar economic features, even when they have a different legal qualification.[9]

The first goal, improving investor information, should be seen against the backdrop of the long-established law and economics problem of information overload. The KID is put forward as an answer to this problem. In this chapter we will not assess whether a prospectus, or a short and standardised information document, are indeed efficient investor protection techniques. On the basis of established law and economics and behavioural finance literature, we have expressed doubt in this respect in previous contributions. Behavioural finance has indeed wiped the floor with the very foundations of the information paradigm. It has been shown that even if more compact product information is readily available, investors are likely to ignore or misinterpret it. A plethora of psychological heuristics and biases steer the behaviour of the investor and explain why they do not optimally use the information provided.[10]

Goal of this chapter. For purposes of this chapter, we will not deal with those issues, but take as a given that the European legislator sees product information as one of the building blocks of protection of financial consumers and that information documents are here to stay. Starting from this premise, we will assess (i) whether the scope of application of the PRIIPs Regulation is wide enough, or whether it should, on the contrary be further broadened to other investment products, currently not covered; and (ii) whether an even more cross-sectoral approach to product information in respect of banking and insurance products would be efficient and desirable.

Structure of this chapter This chapter is therefore structured as follows. In a first section the scope of application of the PRIIPs proposal is critically discussed in view of the UCITS Directive KID, the prospectus summary and the PEPP KID. In a second section the Standard European Consumer Credit Information Form, the European Standard Information Sheet for mortgage credit and the Insurance Product Information Document will be examined in order to answer the second research question.

---

[8] See already European Commission, 'Feedback Statement on contributions to the call for evidence on "substitute" retail investment products' (March 2008) 20: 'A generic and cross-cutting problem, highlighted by all stakeholders, was that of the danger of overloading consumers with information that is irrelevant, overly technical or presented inappropriately with some responses advocating simplification of disclosures to retail investors. The issue is not felt to be ... whether there is "enough" information but whether the information will be read and understood by the consumer'. The argument was repeated in the Explanatory Memorandum to the Proposal COM(2012) 352 (fn 9), at 8–9; in recitals 2 and 15 to the PRIIPs Regulation and in the Final Draft RTS (JC/2016/21) (fn 9) at 6.

[9] See Recitals 1, 6 and 17 to the PRIIPs Regulation; Joint Committee of the European Supervisory Authorities, 'Final draft regulatory technical standards (JC/2016/21) at 6. Also: Consumer Markets Scoreboard SEC(2010)1257 of the European Commission, 'Making Markets Work for Consumers' (4th edn, October 2010). This report shows that the market for 'investments, pensions and securities' performs worst out of the 50 sectors examined, amongst other things with respect to comparability of products and services (p 15). An earlier Consumer Markets Scoreboard came to the following conclusion: 'A recent survey found that ... information which is presented in too many different ways when comparing between different offerings are ... important barriers to cross-border shopping of financial services quoted by European consumers' and 'As evidenced by a series of surveys, a well-drafted set of standardised information facilitates clearly the comparability of competing offers, and help ensure that consumers understand and can use information e.g. for switching providers. ... In a Eurobarometer survey, 79% of European citizens thought that it would be useful if all financial services providers used a standardised information sheet. ...' (European Commission, 'Commission Staff Working Document on the Follow up in Retail Financial Services to the Consumer Markets Scoreboard' (SEC (2009)1251 22 September 2009) 6 and 9).

[10] See on this issue: V Colaert, 'The Regulation of PRIIPs' (fn 7) at 217–219 and 221–222 and V Colaert, 'Building Blocks of Investor Protection: Ever expanding regulation tightens its grip' (2017) *Journal of European Consumer and Market Law* at 229–230 and 232–233, with ample further references.

II. Scope of the PRIIPs Regulation

Comparability of information on investment products. As mentioned above, the second goal of the PRIIPs Regulation is to provide the investor with easily accessible, understandable and comparable information, which should improve comparability of substitute products. The PRIIPs Regulation therefore takes a horizontal,[11] cross-sectoral approach. It applies to a range of products with similar features, 'regardless of their form or construction'[12] since '(t)he level of protection afforded to the retail investor should not vary according to the legal form of these products.'[13] The question arises, however, whether *all* products which can be considered substitutes are indeed covered by the PRIIPs Regulation.

Scope of application of the PRIIPs Regulation. From the outset, the proposed PRIIPs Regulation targeted four product families: investment (or mutual) funds; investments packaged as life insurance policies; retail structured securities; and structured term deposits[14].[15] One of the goals of the legislature was, however, to transcend the *legal* qualification of such products and to define the scope of application of the Regulation on the basis of the economic purpose of the product.[16] The PRIIPs Regulation therefore defines a 'Packaged Retail investment Product' or 'PRIP' as 'an investment … where, regardless of the legal form of the investment, the amount repayable to the retail investor is subject to fluctuations because of exposure to reference values or to the performance of one or more assets which are not directly purchased by the investor'.[17] Many other products than the aforementioned product families are therefore covered, including all derivatives.[18]

The original proposal for a 'PRIPs' Regulation only featured this definition.[19] In the final stage of the legislative process, and without much explanation, the acronym 'PRIPs' was changed into 'PRIIPs' ('Packaged Retail Investment and Insurance-based Products'). A definition of 'insurance-based investment product' was added, as 'an insurance product which offers a maturity

---

[11] European Commission, 'Consultation by Commission Services on legislative steps for the Packaged Retail Investment Products Initiative' (26 November 2010) 2.

[12] Recital 6 to the PRIIPs Regulation.

[13] Communication of the Commission to the European Parliament and the Council, 'Packaged Retail Investment Products' (COM(2009)204, 30 April 2009) at 1. See also the Explanatory Memorandum to the Proposal for a PRIPs Regulation (fn 8) at 2: 'Existing disclosures vary according to the legal form a product takes, rather than its economic nature or the risks it raises for retail investors. The comparability, comprehensibility and presentation of information vary, so the average investor can struggle to make necessary comparisons between products.'

[14] According to Commission Communication COM(2009)204 (fn 13) at 4, 'structured term deposits offer a combination of a term deposit with an embedded option or an interest rate structure. They are designed to achieve a specific payoff profile, which they achieve through transactions in derivatives such as interest rate and currency options'. Although the PRIIPs Regulation does not feature a definition, MiFID II 2014/65/EU does. Structured deposits are defined in Art 4 (1)43° of MiFID II as '*deposits*' in the meaning of Art 2(1)(c) of the DGS (ie 'a credit balance which results from funds left in an account or from temporary situations deriving from normal banking transactions and which a credit institution is required to repay under the legal and contractual conditions applicable, including a fixed-term deposit and a savings deposit'), which are 'fully repayable at maturity on terms under which interest or a premium will be paid or is at risk, according to a formula' involving certain underlying financial instruments or indexes.

[15] CESR/10-1136, CEBS 2010 196, CEIOPS-3L3-54-10, 'Report of the 3L3 Task Force on Packaged Retail Investment Products (PRIPs)' (6 October 2010) at 3, n° 3. Recital 6 of the PRIIPs Regulation reiterates those four product families.

[16] Commission Communication COM(2009)204 (fn 13) at 2; Explanatory Memorandum to Proposal COM(2012)352 (fn 9) at 2.

[17] Article 4(1), PRIIPs Regulation.

[18] See for an indicative list of products in scope of the PRIIPs Regulation: Joint Committee of the ESA's, 'Discussion Paper: Key Information Documents for Packaged Retail and Insurance-Based Investment Products' (PRIIPs) (JC/DP/2014/02, 17 November 2014) at 12–14.

[19] See the definition of 'investment product' in Art 4(a) of Proposal COM(2012)352 (fn 9).

or surrender value and where that maturity or surrender value is wholly or partially exposed, directly or indirectly, to market fluctuations' (Article 4(2) PRIIPs Regulation). We have previously argued that this addition is regrettable, as it undermines the goal of the legislature to abandon an approach based on legal form and focus on economic substance instead. In our opinion 'insurance based investment products' are PRIPs as defined in the Regulation, so that, the addition of a separate definition or 'insurance based investment products' blurs the scope of what a PRIP is, rather than clarifying the scope of the PRIIPs Regulation.[20]

The distinguishing feature of both types of PRIIPs is in any event that they are 'packaged' or 'manufactured':[21]

> [A] firm constructs the PRIP, by packaging or structuring different elements together, for instance by wrapping a financial asset or assets within another structure, or by providing investment management through a collective investment scheme, or by devising a financial instrument that creates exposure to other financial instruments, indices or reference values.[22]

Because of their layered structure, the European legislature considers packaged products the most difficult to understand for retail investors – even though they are not necessarily the most risky products. The manufacturing process moreover can lead to a fundamentally identical investment proposition taking different legal forms and being offered across different industry sectors.[23] This situation was seen as a fertile breeding ground for regulatory arbitrage: increased offering of the least regulated product or service or, worse, repackaging of products in order to avoid the more burdensome legislation.[24] The PRIIPs Regulation has been explicitly presented as an answer to the problems which regulatory arbitrage creates for retail investors.[25]

Products out of scope. 'Simple' products, the value of which does not derive from some underlying product, are by definition excluded from the scope of application of the Regulation.[26] The choice to limit the scope of the PRIIPs Regulation to packaged products only, was based on the argument that a regulatory regime designed for 'all possible assets' would be difficult to develop, especially in the area of product disclosure requirements, 'as very different measures would be needed for packaged investment products, compared with the full range of possible investments that might be made in underlying assets themselves.'[27] The additional complexities triggered by the packaged element were seen as justifying a specific regulatory regime.[28]

---

[20] See in this sense Veerle Colaert, 'European banking, securities and insurance law: cutting through sectoral lines?' (2015) *Common Market Law Review* at 1599.

[21] Recital 6 to the PRIIPs Regulation.

[22] See European Commission, 'Consultation by Commission Services on legislative steps for the Packaged Retail Investment Products Initiative' (26 November 2010) 5.

[23] Explanatory Memorandum to the Proposal for a PRIPs Regulation (fn 8) at 7.

[24] There has indeed been some evidence of regulatory arbitrage in the retail investment services sector. See for concrete examples: Niamh Moloney, *EU Securities and Financial Markets Regulation* (Oxford, OUP, 2014) 780, fn 71; European Commission, 'Open Hearing on Retail Investment Products' (2008) at 11, indicating that in France, sales of unit-linked life insurance have increased following the implementation of MiFID; see also, at 16–17, for several examples of regulatory arbitrage in the Netherlands, and, at 18, for a quote of Eddy Wymeersch, chairman of CESR at the time, arguing that regulatory arbitrage has been seen on a massive scale through the growth of the certificate market.

[25] Commission Communication COM(2009)204 (fn 13) at 2; European Commission, 'Consultation by Commission Services on legislative steps for the Packaged Retail Investment Products Initiative' (26 November 2010) at 5. See for a more extensive overview of the genesis of the PRIIPs Regulation: Colaert, 'European banking, securities and insurance law' (fn 20) at 1594–1597.

[26] Article 2(2)(c) of the PRIIPs Regulation also explicitly excludes simple deposits, although this seems superfluous in view of the definition of a PRIP, which clearly does not cover such deposits.

[27] European Commission, 'Consultation by Commission Services on legislative steps for the Packaged Retail Investment Products Initiative' (26 November 2010) at 6.

[28] Ibid.

The PRIIPs Regulation further explicitly excludes non-life insurance contracts and 'pure protection' life insurance contracts,[29] a number of securities which are excluded by the Prospectus Directive (such as securities issued or guaranteed by public authorities) and a range of pension products.[30]

The PRIIPS Regulation moreover granted a transitional period of five years during which the PRIIPs Regulation is not applicable to UCITS Directive funds.[31] The reason for this temporary exemption was that a Key Investor Information (KII) document very similar to the KID had been in use for UCITS Directive funds since 2011.[32] The legislator first wanted to evaluate the use of the PRIIPs KID, before requiring the UCITS Directive industry to change to a new type of information documents. The UCITS Directive exemption has recently been extended until 31 December 2021.[33] The legislator nevertheless seems to agree in principle on the idea that UCITS Directive funds should in the long run be subject to the PRIIPs Regulation, which would indeed increase the comparability of UCITS Directive funds with other comparable products, currently subject to the PRIIPs Regulation.

Scope too limited? One of the main reasons for introducing the PRIIPs Regulation was the lack of accessible and harmonised information documents for financial products (except for UCITS Directive funds), making it very difficult for retail investors to assess and compare the risks, costs and other features of products across the different sectors of the financial industry. If increasing transparency and comparability of substitute investment products is indeed one of the main goals of the PRIIPs Regulation, the European legislature's choice to only cover 'packaged' products is regrettable. Although the structure of a 'simple' (in the sense of non-packaged) product may be easier to comprehend, the often lengthy and technical terms and conditions may make it quite hard to figure out the exact costs, risks and other features of those simple products. A 'packaged' product will moreover often be a substitute for a 'simple' product. By excluding simple products from its scope of application, the PRIIPs Regulation does not allow easy comparison between the costs, risks and other features of a layered product and its simple counterpart. In our opinion the limitation of the scope of the PRIIPs Regulation to packaged products is therefore a missed opportunity.[34] Two examples are telling in this regard.

Simple deposits. Only so-called 'structured deposits'[35] are covered by the Regulation. Holders of 'simple' deposits with fixed or floating rates do not benefit from any harmonised product information. The terms and conditions of even ordinary savings accounts, however, often feature complicated interest calculations and hidden costs, making those products far from transparent and therefore hard to compare.[36] Consumers may moreover have an interest in comparing

---

[29] Ie life insurance contracts where the benefits under the contract are payable only on death or in respect of incapacity due to injury, sickness or infirmity (see Art 2 2)(a) and (b). These products are not covered by the definition of PRIP or of insurance-based investment product, so that an explicit exclusion seems superfluous.

[30] See Art 2(2) PRIIPs Regulation.

[31] Recital 35, Arts 32(1) and 33(1) PRIIPs Regulation.

[32] See fn 4.

[33] The PRIIPs review has been postponed for one year, in view of the fact that the PRIIPs Regulation has entered into force one year later than originally planned. Therefore, the UCITS Directive exemption has also been extended, to allow the legislator to take into account the results of the review when deciding on the application of the PRIIPs KID to UCITS Directive funds. See Art 17 of Regulation (EU) 2019/1156 of the European Parliament and of the Council of 20 June 2019 on facilitating cross-border distribution of collective investment undertakings and amending Regulations (EU) No 345/2013, (EU) No 346/2013 and (EU) No 1286/2014; see also Joint Committee of the ESAs, 'Final Report following joint consultation paper concerning amendments to the PRIIPs KID' (JC 2019 6.2, 8 February 2019) at 4.

[34] See Colaert, 'European banking, securities and insurance law' (fn 20) at 1599–1600.

[35] See fn 14.

[36] On top of a fixed interest rate, there are often loyalty or other premiums if certain conditions are fulfilled, or use is made of temporary higher rates, making it hard to compare the conditions of different simple saving deposits. Recital 18 of the PRIIPs Regulation refers to 'a teaser rate followed by a much higher floating conditional rate' which 'takes advantage

structured deposits with simple deposits.[37] Inclusion of simple deposits into the scope of the PRIIPs Regulation would not only increase transparency of these products, it would also facilitate such very relevant comparison. It should further be noted that today several Member States already impose information requirements for deposits (be they simple or structured) at national level. As simple deposits fall outside the scope of the PRIIPs Regulation, Member States are not obliged to align their national regime for simple deposits with the PRIIPs information regime.[38] Having different disclosure regimes in place for products which can clearly be substitutes from a saver's perspective, does not only complicate comparability for consumers, it also adds unnecessary costs for financial institutions. They may have to implement two different information models (one for PRIIPs and another for non-PRIIPs subject to a national regime). If financial institutions engage in cross-border activities they may even need to produce different information sheets in different Member States for those non-harmonised products.[39]

Simple securities. Securities are a second example of the limited scope of application of the PRIIPs Regulation. Structured securities are subject to the PRIIPs Regulation, whereas no KID needs to be available for 'simple' securities. Should a retail investor wish to compare a structured security (eg a convertible bond) with a simple security (eg a simple bond), there will be no KID for the simple security to facilitate such comparison. Economically they may however well be regarded as substitutes.[40]

Even though the Prospectus Regulation attempted to model the new summary prospectus on the PRIIPs KID,[41] it does not refer to the PRIIPs provisions, let alone widen the scope of application of the PRIIPs Regulation, but creates a new format. Interestingly, for products which are covered by both the Prospectus Regulation and the PRIIPs Regulation, the issuer may opt or Member State authorities may require to replace part of the prospectus summary with the content of the PRIIPs KID for efficiency reasons.[42] Key information on the issuer and the offer to

---

of retail investors' behavioural biases' and which prompt a comprehension alert to be inserted in the KID for structured products. Many 'simple' deposits use the exact same technique, taking advantage of the same behavioural biases, without a KID being available for the protection of consumers of those simple deposits.

[37] A recent FCA study shows the importance of stimulating such a comparison. It found that 'although all five structured deposits in the survey would have been unlikely to return more than simple fixed-term cash deposits, our respondents did not recognize this. Investors required relatively high rates of return on risk-free cash deposits to value them over and above structured deposits' and 'behavioural biases, combined with features of structured deposits that can exploit these biases, may lead investors to have unrealistically high expectations of product returns and impede their ability to evaluate and compare structured products to each other and against other deposit-based alternatives'. The result is that many retail investors prefer structured deposits to less risky alternatives with higher returns. See Financial Conduct Authority, 'Two plus two makes five? Survey evidence that investors overvalue structured deposits' (Occasional Paper No 9, March 2015) at 4 and 5. See also at 10: 'exponential compounding bias may distort the comparison of structured products, whose returns are often expressed over a five-year period, to cash term deposits with annual interest rates.'

[38] Recital 8 to the PRIIPs Regulation.

[39] See V Colaert, 'The Regulation of PRIIPs' (fn 7) at 208–209.

[40] The fact that simple securities are not covered by the PRIIPs Regulation, played a role in the discussions on MiFID II, level 2 texts. In a reaction to the consultation on MiFID II, level 2 measures, many respondents were of the opinion that the MiFID II product governance rules should not apply to shares and bonds since they are not 'manufactured' by the issuer and are not issued for a designated target market. Nevertheless, a few respondents, including consumer and investor associations, noted that including products such as shares and bonds was crucial from an investor protection standpoint considering that such products are out of the scope of PRIIPS. ESMA agreed with the latter view (ESMA, Final Report – ESMA's Technical Advice to the Commission on MiFID II and MiFIR (19 December 2014 ESMA/2014/1569) at 53–54, para 12).

[41] Recital 32 Prospectus Regulation.

[42] Recital 32 and Art 7(8) *in fine* Prospectus Regulation. Already when introducing the PRIIPs KID, the Commission had considered that the KID might replace the summary prospectus for PRIIPs covered by the Prospectus Directive (European Commission, 'Consultation by Commission Services on legislative steps for the Packaged Retail Investment Products Initiative' (26 November 2010) at 21). At the time this idea did not make it since the information obligations of the prospectus summary was deemed to serve additional purposes not covered by the KID, such as market transparency

the public or admission to trading on a regulated market of the securities concerned should then be added in accordance with the requirements of the Prospectus Regulation.[43] Since, apparently such an approach is deemed sufficiently informative for these complex products, it is not clear why the PRIIPs KID, extended with such additional information, has not been chosen as the format of the prospectus summary for all securities (it being understood that the PRIIPs level 2 regulation could, if necessary, differentiate[44]).

PEPPs. It was positive from this perspective that the original proposal for a PEPP Regulation explicitly referred to the PRIIPs Regulation for the content and format of the PEPP KID.[45] This would have ensured maximum comparability between PRIIPs and PEPPs – which the European legislator clearly considers as possible substitutes.[46] The European Parliament has, however, heavily amended the original Commission Proposal. In its final version, the PEPP Regulation creates a totally independent legal regime for the PEPP KID.[47] Even though it is clearly based on the PRIIPs regime, it does not refer to the PRIIPs Regulation any more and there are a number of major differences with the PRIIPs KID. While the PEPP Regulation introduces a number of information elements particular for PEPPs in view of the nature of the product (eg a description of the retirement benefits), this could have been dealt with within the framework of the PRIIPs Regulation (for instance in level 2 regulation[48]). Other elements which will feature in the PEPP KID would on the other hand also be very relevant information in regard of all PRIIPs, such as the information related to the performance of the PEPP provider's investments in terms of ESG factors.[49] The Sustainability Action Plan of the European Commission will probably also entail an

---

or a full picture of all details in relation to a proposed contract. For this reason, the PRIIPs requirements applied independently from, and in addition to existing information duties resulting from the Prospectus Dir (Art 3 of the PRIIPs Regulation. See also Explanatory Memorandum to the Proposal for a PRIPs Regulation (fn 8) at 12.

[43] Recital 32 and Art 7(8) *in fine* Prospectus Regulation.

[44] The PRIIPs Regulatory Technical Standards adopted by Commission Delegated Regulation (EU) 2017/653 already differentiate the exact content of the PRIIPs KID for different types of products. Similarly, Commission Delegated Regulation in regard of key financial information in the summary prospectus differentiates between different types of products. See Commission Delegated Regulation (EU) 2019/979 of 14 March 2019 supplementing Regulation (EU) 2017/1129 of the European Parliament and of the Council with regard to regulatory technical standards on key financial information in the summary of a prospectus, the publication and classification of prospectuses, advertisements for securities, supplements to a prospectus, and the notification portal, and repealing Commission Delegated Regulation (EU) No 382/2014 and Commission Delegated Regulation (EU) 2016/301 (C(2019) 2022 final, 14 March 2019).

[45] Article 23 of Commission proposal for a regulation on a pan-European personal pension product, COM(2017) 343 final.

[46] See, eg, Recital 4 PEPP Regulation (EU) 2019/1238: 'By channeling more of Europeans' savings from cash and bank deposits to long-term investment products, such as voluntary pension products with a long-term retirement nature, the impact would therefore be beneficial both for individuals ... and for the broader economy' and Recital 7: 'Personal pensions are important in linking long-term savers with long-term investment opportunities.'

[47] Articles 26–28, PEPP Regulation (EU) 2019/1238.

[48] See fn 44.

[49] Article 28(3)(c)(xii), PEPP Regulation. Art 8(3)(c)(ii) PRIIPs Regulation only states that 'where applicable, specific environmental or social objectives targeted by the product' should be mentioned. Art 8(4) adds that 'the Commission shall be empowered to adopt delegated acts ... specifying the details of the procedures used to establish whether a PRIIP targets specific environmental or social objectives.' See also the Joint Committee of the ESAs, 'Joint Technical Advice on the procedures used to establish whether a PRIIP targets specific environmental or social objectives pursuant to Article 8(4)' (JC 2017 43, 28 July 2017). The Joint Committee only urged the European Commission to further detail how to disclose in a clear and specific way the environmental or social objectives, if any, while the Joint Committee saw no need for a delegated act in respect of (i) how PRIIPs manufacturers should specify environmental or social objectives as part of their investment policy, (ii) governance procedures and controls, nor (iv) the review of progress in respect of those objectives. The Joint Committee is of the opinion that existing legislation in the UCITS, AIFMD, IDD and MiFID II framework sufficiently caters for the latter aspects. So far, the European Commission has not implemented this technical advice into a delegated act, even though the European Parliament in May 2018 explicitly urged the European Commission to make use of its powers to introduce delegated acts under art. 8(4) of the PRIIPs Regulation as soon as possible and before developing the sustainability taxonomy (see European Parliament, Resolution of 29 May 2018 (2018/2007 (INI)) at point 11).

update of the PRIIPs framework in respect of ESG factors.[50] It would, however, have been more efficient if one regulation would have dealt with product information in respect of all investment products in the widest sense, which would be the only regulation to be updated in view of new insights.

EIOPA has been given a mandate to conduct consumer testing in regard of the details on format and length of the PEPP KID.[51] This means that also in this respect the end result will most probably be different from the PRIIPs KID, undermining one of the main goals of the PRIIPs Regulation: creating one tool allowing easy comparison of products which serve a similar economic purpose.

Crowdfunding. Also the Proposal for a Regulation on European Crowdfunding Service Providers (ECSP) for business[52] creates a new 'Key Investment Information Sheet', without referring to the PRIIPs KID. The proposal implicitly justifies this choice, by stating that '[i]nvestments in products marketed on crowdfunding platforms are not comparable to traditional investments products or savings products and should not be marketed as such' (Recital 30). We are of the opinion, however, that it is artificial to draw a distinction between 'traditional' and 'innovative' investment and saving products. Crowdfunding platforms are just one other way of financial intermediation and many investors do consider crowdfunding products to be alternatives to other investment and saving products.[53] The purpose of the Key Investment Information Sheet is also very similar to the purpose of the PRIIPs KID and of the prospectus and prospectus summary: 'to enable investors to make an informed investment decision' (Recital 31). Still, a different name and different terminology are used, as well as a different, although similar, content and order of items,[54] while no standardised format seems to be required.[55] Furthermore no authorisation by a competent authority is necessary prior to the use of those information sheets (Recital 33), even though Member States may require prior notification to the competent authority.[56]

We believe it would be much more efficient from a legislative as well as investor protection perspective if the Proposed Crowdfunding Regulation would refer to the PRIIPs KID, and only make amendments and / or additions where necessary. Similar to the prospectus summary, key information on the issuer and the offer of products concerned should then be added to the PRIIPs KID.[57] Other additions (eg warnings) or adaptations may be needed in view of the different

---

[50] The European Commission's Action Plan mentions this very briefly: 'Criteria would have to be identified for specific financial products offered to retail investors (such as Packaged Retail Investment and Insurance Products)'. See European Commission, 'Action Plan: Financing Sustainable Growth' (COM(2018) 97 final, 8 March 2018) at 5. See also previous footnote.

[51] Article 28(5), PEPP Regulation (EU) 2019/1238.

[52] Commission Proposal on European Crowdfunding Service Providers (ECSP) for Business (COM(2018)113, 8 March 2018), amended by the European Parliament European Parliament in its 'Legislative resolution of 27 March 2019 on the proposal for a regulation of the European Parliament and of the Council on European Crowdfunding Service Providers (ECSP) for Business' (COM(2018)0113 – C8-0103/2018 –2018/0048(COD)). On 24 June 2019 the Council of the European Union came up with a compromise proposal ('Proposal for a Regulation of the European Parliament and of the Council on European Crowdfunding Service Providers (ECSP) for Business and amending Regulation (EU) No 2017/1129 – Mandate for negotiations with the European Parliament – Compromise proposal' (Council 10557/19).

[53] In the same sense, see E Macchiavello in ch 4 of this volume.

[54] Article 16 and Annex I of the Compromise Proposal (Council 10557/19).

[55] Even though the Commission receives a mandate to adopt delegated acts specifying, among other things, the requirements for and content of the model for presenting the information (Art 16(9)).

[56] Moreover, the crowdfunding services provider should have in place procedures to verify the completeness and clarity of the information contained in the Key Investor Information Sheet (Arts 16(5) and 10(2)(mb) of the Compromise Proposal (Council 10557/19).

[57] See fn 43. The latest version of the Crowdfunding compromise proposal states that where prospective investors are provided with a key investment information sheet, the crowdfunding service providers and the project owners shall be considered as satisfying the obligation to draw up a key information document in accordance with the PRIIPs Regulation

platform via which the product is bought. Nevertheless, by using one and the same format, especially retail investors – or in the words of the Crowdfunding Proposal 'non-sophisticated investors'[58] – would be able to compare crowdfunding products with other investment and saving products much more easily. With one look on the PRIIPs KID summary risk indicator, for instance, it would be clear for investors that most crowdfunding products are much riskier than most so-called 'traditional' investment and saving products.

Extending the scope. It can be argued that, from a retail investor's point of view, the need for product transparency and comparability is not limited to PRIIPs as defined in the PRIIPs Regulation, but extends to any saving and investment product available to the investor or saver, including simple deposits, simple securities, PEPPs and crowdfunding products. The current limitations in scope seem quite arbitrary in this respect.

Recital 8 to the PRIIPs Regulation states that the European Supervisory Authorities should monitor the products which are excluded from the scope of the PRIIPs Regulation and, where appropriate, issue guidelines to address any problem which is identified. Such guidelines should be taken into account in the review on the possible extension of the scope and the elimination of certain exclusions.[59] The review will be held in 2019–2020. Whereas there is good hope that the UCITS Directive exemption will in the end be eliminated, there does not seem to be much political impetus to extend the scope of the PRIIPs Regulation to any other financial products. It is to be regretted that neither the Prospectus Regulation, nor the PEPP Regulation nor the Proposed Crowdfunding Regulation has bothered to take the PRIIPs KID as the model for providing information to retail customers. The political reluctance to further broaden the scope of the PRIIPs KID may stem from the current difficulties to create informative and non-misleading risk and performance indicators for all products covered by the PRIIPs Regulation.[60] However, creating new types of information sheets for substitute products currently out of scope of the PRIIPs Regulation does not solve that problem, and exacerbates the problem of non-comparability of products with very similar economic functions.

III. Other Standardised Information Documents in Financial Regulation

Beyond investment products, other financial legislation also requires financial institutions to provide their customers with standardised information sheets.

A. Credit Information

Different function of credit and investment products. The Consumer Credit Directive features a Standard European Consumer Credit Information (SECCI),[61] and the Mortgagee Credit

---

(Art 16 (8a) of the Compromise Proposal (Council 10557/19)). This provision confirms that the purpose and set-up of the key investment information sheet and the PRIIPs KID are very similar. On the other hand, the PRIIPs KID is not deemed to suffice for selling a PRIIP via crowdfunding. The key investment information sheet is indeed more elaborate (it can be up to 6 sides of A4 pages – see Art 16(3) of the Compromise Proposal (Council 10557/19 – contrary to the PRIIPs KID which can only be up to 3 pages) and also contains information on the issuer and the offer, similarly to the prospectus summary, as well as a number of additional warnings.

[58] Recital 29c and Art 3(1)(ga) of the Compromise Proposal (Council 10557/19). See also chapter 14B of this book.

[59] Recital 8 of the PRIIPs Regulation.

[60] See in this regard Joint Committee of the ESAs, 'Joint Consultation Paper concerning amendments to the PRIIPs KID' (JC 2018 60, 8 November 2018) at 10, 23–24 and 26–27.

[61] Article 5(1) and Annex II to CCD.

Directive requires creditors to provide a European Standardised Information Sheet (ESIS).[62] Credit products clearly serve other functions than investment products. They allow customers short of money to buy goods they cannot afford on the basis of their own funds, whereas investment and saving products allow customers with an excess of money to grow their own funds and/or save them for the future. With those different functions come different types of risk and different information needs. The use of different information sheets therefore seems justified.[63]

Differences between credit information sheets. The Consumer Credit Directive and the Mortgage Credit Directive, however, provide for two totally different information sheets – for consumer credit on the one hand, and mortgage credit on the other. There are indeed obvious differences between those two types of credit, mainly in respect of the purpose of the credit: consumer credit allows the consumer to buy any type of movable good or service between EUR 200 and EUR 75 000,[64] whereas mortgage credit typically allows the consumer to buy or (re)build immovable property, and/or grants a mortgage or similar security on immovable property to the creditor.[65] Nevertheless the risks for the consumer, and the type of information he or she needs is very similar. If one compares the two information sheets, it is indeed clear that many information items overlap. However, the ESIS also features information elements which are not included in the SECCI. Sometimes this is clearly the result of differences in the product,[66] other differences do not seem justified and would also seem helpful information in respect of consumer credit.[67] Moreover, the two information sheets have a different format,[68] use a different terminology,[69] and a different order,[70] without any obvious justification for those differences.

Need for one credit information sheet. One could argue that those differences are not problematic, since consumer credit and mortgage credit are no substitutes, and there is therefore no need for consumers to compare a consumer credit with a mortgage credit. However, in view of the similarities between consumer and mortgage credit, which present similar risks for consumers (eg in terms of understanding the costs of the credit, the risk of over indebtedness, the consequence of non-compliance), it would nevertheless be beneficial for consumers to receive information documents with substantially the same format, terminology and look and feel for the two types of credit. Consumers who already took one or more consumer credits, would already be familiar with the information sheet when they would later be looking for a mortgage credit (or vice versa). Also, from a legislative efficiency perspective, it would be more efficient to create

---

[62] Article 14(2) and Annex II to MCD.

[63] It should moreover be noted that, contrary to the information documents discussed in the previous section, the SECCI and the ESIS are personalised in function of the situation of the consumer (interest rates may differ in function of the creditworthiness of the consumer, duration of the credit will depend on the preferences of the consumer, …).

[64] Article 2(2)(c), CCD.

[65] Articles 1 and 3, MCD.

[66] For instance, the 'maximum available loan amount relative to value of property' is only relevant for a credit with a security on the immovable property financed by the credit.

[67] Ie, the following information elements of ESIS: 'Currency and implication on the credit'; 'Risk of variable interest rates' and 'Risk of changes in income'.

[68] The SECCI uses a table, whereas the ESIS uses plain text.

[69] The SECCI uses for instance the following concepts: 'credit product', 'APR' and 'late payment'; whereas the ESIS uses the concepts 'loans', 'APRC' and 'non-compliance with commitments'. Whereas 'non-compliance with commitments' is clearly a broader concept than 'late payment', it is not clear why the consumer credit client wouldn't need information on what happens when he or she does not comply with other commitments than timely payment.

[70] The SECCI deal with more elements under general sections, such as 'main features' and 'costs', whereas the ESIS uses more sections. In the SECCI for instance, 'late payments' and 'obligation to enter into ancillary contracts' are elements of the 'cost of the credit', and 'instalments' is part of the 'main features', whereas the ESIS features separate sections on 'non compliance with payments', 'additional obligations' and 'instalments'. The SECCI also uses a different order for the main features than the ESIS (in the SECCI the type of credit is the first element and the duration of the loan is the last element, whereas in the ESIS the type of loan is only the third element, whereas 'duration' is the second element.

one common credit information sheet, the format and content of which would be optimised in the light of behavioural finance insights. Obviously differentiation could still be needed for one type of credit or the other by adding certain information elements, or changing the order of the information, but the differences should not go beyond what is necessary.

It should be noted that certain types of credit to consumers are still not covered by EU legislation – notably credit to consumers via Peer-to-Peer platforms.[71] It would make sense to have those credits to consumers also covered by the same credit information sheet.

B. Insurance Information

IPID. Also in the insurance sector a short product information sheet has recently been introduced. Article 20(4)–(7) of the Insurance Distribution Directive features the Insurance Product Information Document (IPID), the format of which has been developed in level 2 Regulation (EU) 2017/1469. This information document should be produced for non-life insurance products and life insurance products without investment or saving purpose (insurance-based investment products being covered by the PRIIPs KID). The function of such insurance products is to eliminate the uncertainty of an unexpected and sudden financial loss, and is indeed different from the function of saving and investment products or credit products. The content of the IPID is therefore obviously quite different from the PRIIPs KID and the credit information sheets, including information on what is insured and what is not, what the restrictions on coverage are, where the insurance is valid, etc.

IV. Need for Cross-Sectoral Consistency

No case for one cross-sectoral product information document. It is clear that the functions and risks of investment products, credit products and insurance products are very different, and that therefore also client information needs in respect of those products are substantially different. Even though there is room for a less scattered landscape of information documents, by using one format and content for all retail investment products, another for all credit products, and a third for all insurance products, there is no case for one cross-sectoral information document.

But need for cross-sectoral efficiency and consistency. Nevertheless, we are of the opinion that there is room for more cross-sectoral consistency in terms of format and terminology used. The formats of the PRIIPs KID, the SECCI, the ESIS and the IPID indeed look very different. Whereas the ESIS uses plain text, all other information sheets use some kind of table. Contrary to the ESIS and the SECCI, the PRIIPs KID uses visual indicators, and the IPID uses pictograms and vivid colours. Even though the content of the different information sheets needs to differ, their formats could be more aligned. All information sheets discussed in this chapter are addressed to retail customers or consumers.[72] The goal of the format used is to appeal to that target group and increase the chance that they will actually read and understand the information provided to them. If, for instance, the use of colors and pictograms (as in the IPID), would be more effective for retail customers or consumers to read and understand the information provided to them,

---

[71] See O Cherednychenko and J-M Meinderstma, 'Consumer CreditMis-selling of Financial Products' (Study requested by the European Parliament IP/A/ECON/2016-17, June 2018), at 24.
[72] For the difference, see the contribution by Marc-David Weinberger in this book.

this should inspire an update of the PRIIPs KID and the credit information sheets. Similarly, the PRIIPs KID approach of heading each section with a question rather than a word (eg 'what is this product' rather than 'main features of the product') might be more appealing to the target group. Also the maximum number of pages of the information sheets could be tested with the target group, to check what length is perceived as information overload. It should be noted that whereas the PRIIPs KID has a maximum length of three A4 pages,[73] the IPID has a maximum length of two A4 pages,[74] while the credit information sheets have no maximum length. Finally, the European Commission should come up with a common cross-sectoral terminology to be used in all information sheets, so that the same concepts are consistently referred to with the same terminology across sectors.

Consumer testing. The format and terminology of information sheets for financial products could, however, be more harmonised across sectors. The more recent information documents, including the UCITS Directive KIID, PRIIPs KID and IDD IPID are based on consumer testing (and consumer testing is also announced for the PEPP KID). This results in markedly more attractive and accessible information sheets. The progressive insights resulting from consumer testing and behavioural finance should be used in all standard information documents for financial products.

V. Conclusion

Goal of this chapter. In this chapter, we have examined whether a more cross-sectoral approach to product information in respect of banking, investment and insurance products would be efficient and desirable. This chapter did not go into the question of whether product information is actually an efficient means of retail client protection, but we took as a given that the European legislator sees product information as one of the building blocks of protection of financial consumers. Starting from that premise, we came to the following conclusions.

Need for a functional definition of 'investment product'. The PRIIPs Regulation is at first sight a good example, '*avant la lettre*', of the research hypothesis of this project: the same level 1 regulation applies to a range of financial products with similar economic features. Where needed in function of the differences in products covered by the PRIIPs Regulation, the level 2 Regulation differentiates. The PRIIPs Regulation has therefore often been described as a 'cross-sectoral' regulation. With its definition of 'Packaged Retail Investment Product', the PRIIPs Regulation is indeed the first to have introduced a functional definition of investment product, covering products which are formally insurance (insurance-based investment products) or banking products (structured deposits), but are functionally investment products. In our opinion, the PRIIPs Regulation is, however, 'functionally sectoral' rather than cross-sectoral, since it only attempts to cover (packaged) investment products.

PRIIPs KID should apply to all investment products. Even though this functional approach is clearly an improvement, the scope of the PRIIPs Regulation is, in our view, still too limited. It should cover all financial products with a primary investment purpose, including UCITS Directive funds, simple securities, PEPPs and crowdfunding products. It is important for retail investors to be able to compare packaged with non-packaged products, and products sold via traditional intermediation channels with crowdfunding products. The proliferation of information

---

[73] Article 6(4), PRIIPs Regulation.
[74] Exceptionally 3. See Art 3 of Regulation (EU) 2017/1469.

documents which are inspired by the PRIIPs KID, but the final format and content of which is likely to deviate more or less substantially from the PRIIPs KID, is therefore to be regretted.

PRIIPs KID should also apply to all saving products. The PRIIPs Regulation should, moreover, be extended to simple deposits to allow for easy comparison between structured deposits and simple deposits. The PRIIPs Regulation should indeed use a broader functional definition of 'Retail Saving and Investment Product', so that substantially the same information sheet, subject to small modifications and/or additions (to be specified in the level 2 regulation), would be used for all saving and investment products in the broadest sense.

Differentiation necessary for credit and insurance products … Information sheets for other financial products can, and should, differ in function of the specificities of these products. It is indeed quite obvious that the content of the PRIIPs KID should differ from the content of the Insurance Product Information Document and the standardised information sheets in respect of consumer credit and mortgage credit. Nevertheless, there should, in our opinion, be one standardised information sheet for all retail loan agreements (even though level 2 rules could differentiate between consumer and mortgage credit information where necessary).

… but 'look and feel' could be more harmonised cross-sectorally. Even if a different content is necessary in view of the different functions and risk of functionally different products, using a consistent terminology and a similar 'look and feel' for all information sheets across the financial industry, would increase the familiarity of retail customers with this type of information sheets and the information they contain. Moreover, the results of consumer testing of the optimal format of an information sheet, could and should benefit all information sheets cross-sectorally.

14

Service Quality (Conduct of Business) Rules

14A

Is there a Case for a Cross-Sectoral Duty of Care for the Financial Sector?

VEERLE COLAERT AND MAARTEN PEETERS

I. Introduction

General standards of behaviour in civil law/common law. Most Member States provide a general duty of care and/or fiduciary duties[1] in their civil or common law systems.[2] Such duties function as positive, open standards against which legally relevant behaviour is measured to determine contractual or non-contractual liability. Such behaviour is typically required to be honest, fair and, in the case of an economic actor, professional.

Sectoral financial regulation duties of care. Apart from those general duties of care that apply to any and all types of activity or actor, several pieces of financial regulation contain particular duties of care, providing an overarching standard governing the relationship between a certain type of financial institution on the one hand and their customers on the other.

Consumer law prohibition of unfair commercial practices. Moreover, the Unfair Commercial Practices Directive 2005/29/EC (UCPD) has introduced an EU-wide prohibition of unfair commercial practices in the business-to-consumer relationship, which could also be perceived as a general duty of care.

Research questions. This raises the following questions: (i) Is there a need for financial regulation duties of care in addition to the – by nature cross-sectoral – national civil/common law duties of care, and if so, why? (ii) If there is indeed such a need, is there a case for a single cross-sectoral duty of care in financial regulation? (iii) If there is indeed a need for a cross-sectoral duty of care, is there a need to have a cross-sectoral financial regulation duty of care, on top of the harmonised consumer law prohibition on unfair commercial practices, which applies already cross-sectorally?

---

[1] On the role of fiduciary duties in the financial sector, see I MacNeil, 'Rethinking Conduct Regulation' 2015 *Butterworths Journal of International Banking and Financial Law* at 415–416, with further references. In what follows we use the expression 'civil or common law duties of care' in the largest sense, including fiduciary duties.

[2] See D Busch and C Van Dam, *A Bank's Duty of Care* (Oxford, Hart Publishing, 2017), including chapters on Germany, Austria, France, Italy, Spain, the Netherlands, England and Wales and Ireland. Very often a breach of a duty of care will lead to claims for damages in tort. See W Van Gerven e.a., *Cases, Materials and Text on national, supranational and international Tort Law* (Oxford, Hart Publishing, 2001) at 2–5. For the UK, see among others: K Alexander, 'Bank Civil Liability for Mis-selling and Advice' in D Busch and C Van Dam, *A Bank's Duty of Care* (Oxford, Hart Publishing, 2017) at 259 and 278 and following.

Structure of this chapter. In order to answer these questions, we will start by listing and comparing the directives and regulations in EU financial regulation that contain duties of care, and briefly discuss the approach taken in those financial law directives and regulations that do not feature a duty of care. This overview will allow us to discover the nature, meaning and variances of the duty of care in EU financial regulation, and to draw a preliminary conclusion on whether one cross-sectoral financial regulation duty of care would be preferable (section II). In the next section, we will examine the interaction of these financial regulation duties of care with national civil/common law duties of care, in order to discover whether financial regulation duties of care have an added value next to those national duties. In the fourth section we will examine the interaction of the prohibition of unfair commercial practices with financial regulation duties of care, in order to decide on the need for one or more financial regulation duties of care on top of the UCPD prohibition of unfair commercial practices.

II. Duties of Care in EU Financial Legislation

Conduct of business versus prudential regulation? The duty of care in financial regulation is typically the first in a list of conduct of business rules, requiring honest, fair and professional conduct in the best interest of clients and/or market integrity. Conduct of business rules are defined as 'those principles of conduct which should govern the activities of financial services firms in protecting the interest of their customers and the integrity of the market'.[3] Their main purpose is indeed customer protection and market integrity. They are usually opposed to prudential rules, which can be defined as 'preventive measures intended to ensure the soundness and safety of individual institutions (micro-perspective) and of the system as a whole (macro-perspective)',[4] and the main purpose of which is financial stability. It is clear, however, that client protection and market integrity on the one hand, and market stability on the other, are two sides of the same coin: honest, fair and professional dealing will not only protect clients, but also increase trust in the market, and therefore increase market stability; market stability on the other hand is a necessary condition for honest, fair and professional client transactions. Moreover, the distinction between conduct of business rules and prudential rules is often not entirely clear-cut. Prudential requirements regularly use wording that is highly similar to the terminology of financial regulation duties of care, eg requirements for management to be of good repute (honesty) and to have a high level of knowledge and skill (professionalism), and organisational requirements to avoid conflicts of interest (fairness). Those requirements clearly contribute to the ability of financial institutions to comply with the duty of care.

In this section we will discuss the origin and nature of financial regulation duties of care, as well as their different appearances – or lack thereof – in financial regulation. For an overview visualising the differences in approach, see Figure 1.

---

[3] IOSCO, 'International Conduct of Business Principles' (July 1990) nr 18.
[4] L Dragomir, *European Prudential Banking Regulation and Supervision: the legal dimension* (London, Routledge, 2010) at 2.

A. EU Securities Legislation

Origin and nature of the duty of care in securities regulation. The concept of duty of care in EU financial regulation has originated in securities regulation, and more particularly in the 1993 Investment Services Directive (ISD). The ISD introduced six general rules of conduct, including a requirement for investment firms to act '*honestly and fairly*' and a requirement to act '*with due skill, care and diligence*'. Both requirements were followed by the wording 'in the best interests of its clients and the integrity of the market'.[5] These two obligations represented two bullet points in a list also mentioning – in the briefest of wordings – a know your customer obligation, an information duty, a conflict of interest rule and a reference to compliance with 'all regulatory requirements'.

The original and the adapted Commission Proposals for the ISD did not contain any rules of conduct.[6] They were inserted into the text only in the last phase of the legislative proceedings, in order to reflect a recent 'agreement reached at international level by IOSCO'.[7] The Technical Committee of IOSCO 'had in mind rules applying to financial intermediaries designed to promote the primacy of the interests of the client and the integrity of the market.' IOSCO saw a need for conduct of business rules on account of two developments that started in the 1970's. The first was internationalisation, which posed challenges from a (national) supervisory point of view. The second was institutionalisation, whereby smaller retail investors were in need to see their interests protected when dealing with large financial services firms. The principles were thought to contribute to retail investors' 'confidence in the integrity of the market and in the firms with which they deal', thus supporting the 'continued participation' of retail investors in financial markets.[8] The IOSCO report pointed out that they 'are frequently determined by the professionals themselves, may be applied only to them and may lead only to professional or civil – not criminal – sanctions.'[9] IOSCO for the first time set international common standards for business conduct and encouraged supervisors to implement these standards in their supervisory practice.[10]

In its 1990 principles, IOSCO defined two principles. The honesty and fairness principle was defined as follows: 'In conducting its business activities, a firm should act honestly and fairly in the best interests of its customers and the integrity of the market.' The diligence requirement was

---

[5] Article 11 Council Dir 93/22/EEC of 10 May 1993 on investment services in the securities field.

[6] See Commission Proposal of 3 January 1989 for a Council Directive on investment services in the securities field, (COM/88/778 final), and Amended proposal of 8 February 1990 (COM/89/629 final). Art 9, s 1, last bullet of the COM/88/778 proposal did, however, feature 'prudential rules', including a requirement to be organised in such a way that conflicts of interest are reduced to a minimum. This was amended in Art 11, s 1, last bullet of the COM/89/629 proposal, requiring investment firms to be organised in such a way that conflicts of interest do not result in clients' interests to be prejudiced.

[7] IOSCO, 'Resolution on International Conduct Of Business Principles' (November 1990). As the Commission explains, it considered a 'list of general principles of conduct … a useful addition to the Common Position [on the Directive]. … The rules may only be applied insofar as they are justified by the general good. Therefore, Member States must ensure that professional traders are not subjected to an unnecessary degree of protection, which could constitute a barrier to freedom of services.' (European Commission, 'Communication to the European Parliament on the Council's Common Position on the Directive on Investment Services in the Securities Field' (SEC(93) 75 final SYN 176, 14 January 1993) at 11.

[8] See IOSCO, 'Report of the Technical Committee on International Conduct of Business Principles' (9 July 1990) at 3, para 12.

[9] Ibid at 5, para 20.

[10] Ibid at 3, para's 12–13, and at 6, conclusion.

worded as a duty to 'act with due skill, care and diligence in the best interests of its customers and the integrity of the market'. The wording in the ISD was near identical.

MiFID. The Commission proposal for the MiFID I Directive integrated both the honesty and fairness principle and the diligence requirement into one general duty of care, requiring 'an investment firm [to] act honestly, fairly and professionally in accordance with the best interests of its clients'. The requirement to promote market integrity was the subject of a separate provision.[11] The MiFID also introduced a clear hierarchy in the conduct of business rules, which the ISD lacked. It states that firms should comply with the duty of care 'and comply, *in particular*, with the principles set out in paragraphs 2 to 8'. This makes clear that the principles set out in paragraphs 2 to 8 do not exhaust the general duty, but rather specify a number of rules that have to be complied with in any case in order to abide with the duty of care. Therefore, the MiFID duty of care has both a 'container' or 'umbrella' nature – all other conduct of business rules are instances of what it means to comply with the duty of care – and a 'catch-all function', in the sense that any conduct which is not caught by a more specific conduct of business rule, will be covered by the MiFID duty of care. This wording not only survived the MiFID I legislative process in one piece, but remained identical in MiFID II.[12] The duty of care with a view to market integrity has been moved to the MiFIR.[13]

The MiFID II duty of care applies to investment firms and credit institutions whenever they provide 'investment services or, where appropriate, ancillary services to clients'. Interestingly, investment firms may bring about or enter into transactions with eligible counterparties without being obliged to comply with most of the conduct of business rules of Article 24.[14] A slightly differently worded duty of care applies in such case: investment firms will need to 'act honestly, fairly and professionally'[15] but there is no obligation to act in the best interest of the client. The reason for this difference in wording would be that parties to an arm's-length transaction in the wholesale market do not normally protect each other's interests, unless otherwise agreed.[16]

Investment funds. The UCITS Directive and AIFM Directives contain duties of care that are worded in a similar way as in the 1993 ISD, not the more recent (2004) MiFID I. The 2009 UCITS Directive copies the ISD with two separate requirements: acting 'honestly and fairly' as well as acting 'with due skill, care and diligence', both of which 'in the best interests of the

---

[11] 'An investment firm should act honestly, fairly and professionally and in a manner which promotes the integrity of the market' (Art 25(1), MiFID I).

[12] Article 19(1), Dir 2004/39/EC of 21 April 2004 on markets in financial instruments (MiFID I); Art 24(1), Dir 2014/65/EU of 25 April 2014 on markets in financial instruments (MiFID II). The legislator introduces a number of references to the general duty of care with a slightly different wording. As such, we find several mentions of 'acting in' the interest or best interest(s) of the client(s) in Art 24, Dir 2014/65/EU. For a detailed discussion, see L Enriques and M Gargantini, 'The overarching duty to act in the best interest of the client in MiFID II' in D Busch and G Ferrarini (eds) *Regulation of the EU financial markets. MiFID II and MiFIR* (Oxford, OUP, 2017) at 88. There is no indication however that these minor variations in wording pertain to a difference in meaning (V Colaert, 'MiFID II en de zorgplicht: niets nieuws onder de zon?' in I De Meuleneere, V Colaert e.a. (eds), *MiFID II & MiFIR: Capita Selecta* (Antwerpen, Intersentia, 2018) at 102).

[13] Article 24(1), MiFIR 600/2014: 'competent authorities … shall monitor the activities of investment firms to ensure that they act honestly, fairly and professionally and in a manner which promotes the integrity of the market.'

[14] Article 30, 1 MiFID II.

[15] 'and communicate in a way which is fair, clear and not misleading, taking into account the nature of the eligible counterparty and of its business.' Art 30, 1 MiFID II.

[16] L Enriques and M Gargantini (fn 12) at 90. These authors explain this double standard ('honestly, fairly and professionally') and ('in the best interest of the client') as an attempt of the European legislator to reflect both the civil law duty of care and the common law concept of fiduciary duties – with 'the best interest of the client' as important reference – into this first conduct of business rule (see nr 4.16).

UCITS Directive it manages and the integrity of the market'.[17] The 2011 AIFMD takes a different approach and groups the requirements of acting 'honestly, with due skill, care and diligence and fairly in conducting their activities' in one sentence[18] and then continues to make separate mention of the obligation to 'act in the best interests of the AIFs or the investors of the AIFs they manage and the integrity of the market'.[19] The AIFMD variant of the duty of care also applies to European long-term investment funds and Money Market Funds through a reference in the respective directives governing these funds.[20]

European venture capital funds and European social entrepreneurship funds are governed by separate directives that take a similar approach to stipulating the duty of care as the AIFM directive. These funds are required to 'act honestly, fairly and with due skill, care and diligence in conducting their activities'. In separate points of the same article, these funds are also put under the obligation to (among other things) possess adequate knowledge, treat investors fairly and 'conduct their business activities in such a way as to promote the best interests of the qualifying (…) funds they manage, the investors therein and the integrity of the market'.[21]

EMIR. The 2012 regulation on OTC derivatives, central counterparties and trade repositories (EMIR)[22] imposes a general duty of care on central counterparties: '(…) a CCP shall act fairly and professionally in accordance with the best interests of [its] clearing members and clients and sound risk management'.[23] Sound risk management is a typical prudential requirement. As an element of a financial regulation duty of care, it is unique to the aforementioned regulation.

Remarkably, this duty of care only applies to CCPs. Although EMIR features rules on conflicts of interest and professional management in respect of trade repositories,[24] no general duty of care applies to the latter.

Credit rating agencies and CSDs. Similarly, the 2009 Credit Rating Agencies Regulation does not impose a general duty of care on credit rating agencies, even though it imposes specific obligations regarding conflicts of interests and appropriate knowledge and experience of rating analysts.[25]

---

[17] Article 14, 1(a) and (b) of Dir 2009/65/EC of 13 July 2009 on the coordination of laws, regulations and administrative provisions relating to undertakings for collective investment in transferable securities (UCITS) Directive.

[18] Article 12, 1(a) of Dir 2011/61 of 8 June 2011 on Alternative Investment Fund Managers.

[19] Article 12, 1(b) of Dir 2011/61. Art 16 of the AIFMD Delegated Regulation (EU) nr. 231/2013 provides that '[w]hen assessing the AIFM's compliance with Article 12(1) of Directive 2011/61/EU, the competent authorities shall use at least the criteria laid down in this Section'. Busch and Van Setten hold that the AIFMD duty of care thus only aims at minimum harmonisation (see D Busch and L Van Setten, 'The Alternative Investment Fund Managers Directive' in L Van Setten and D Busch (eds), *Alternative Investment Funds in Europe – Law & Practice* (Oxford, Oxford University Press, 2014) para 1.214. We are of the opinion that this provision does not deal with the level of harmonisation of the duty of care. Rather, it confirms that the AIFMD duty of care is an open catch-all provision: the more detailed provisions or the Delegated Regulation should at least be complied with, but other types of behaviour can also be brought under the AIFMD duty of care.

[20] Article 7 (2) of Dir 2015/760/EU of 29 April 2015 on European long-term investment funds. Money market funds follow the UCITS Directive or AIFM regime depending on their type of authorisation. Art 1(1)(a) of Dir 2017/1131/EU of 14 June 2017 on money market funds. Neither the ELTIF nor the MMF Directives contain a separate stipulation on the duty of care.

[21] Article 7(a), (c), (e) and (f) of both Dir 2013/345 of 17 April 2013 on European venture capital funds and Dir 2013/346 of 17 April 2013 on European social entrepreneurship funds.

[22] Article 78(2) and (6) of Regulation 648/2012 of 4 July 2012 on OTC derivatives, central counterparties and trade repositories (EMIR).

[23] Article 36(1), EMIR. In addition to the general duty of care, CCPs also face specific obligations on conflicts of interest and professional behaviour, among other things.

[24] Article 78(2) and (6).

[25] Articles 6, 7 and Annex I of Dir 2009/1060 of 16 September 2009 on credit rating agencies.

CSDs. The 2014 Regulation on central securities depositories (CSD) provides for 'general' provisions with regard to organisational requirements, conduct of business rules, CSD services and prudential requirements.[26] However, none of these 'general' provisions contain a general duty of care, even though the general provisions on the organisational requirements do include provisions on conflicts of interests and the good repute and experience of senior management. The 'conduct of business rules' in Section II of Chapter II of the CSD are somewhat remarkably introduced with the following 'general provision': 'A CSD shall have clearly defined goals and objectives that are achievable, such as in the areas of minimum service levels, risk-management expectations and business priorities.' No reference is made to acting fairly and professionally in accordance with the best interests of participants.

Crowdfunding service providers. Looking at envisaged future securities legislation, the crowd-funding proposal[27] contains a general duty of care that resembles the one in MiFID I, even if it is not explicitly set up as a catch-all requirement with reference to other requirements that should be '*particularly*' complied with: 'Crowdfunding service providers shall act honestly, fairly and professionally in accordance with the best interests of their clients and prospective clients.'[28]

PEPP Regulation. Similarly in the Regulation on a pan-European Personal Pension Product, it is held that '[w]hen carrying out distribution activities for PEPPs, PEPP providers and PEPP distributors shall always act honestly, fairly and professionally in accordance with the best interests of their PEPP customers.'[29]

B. EU Banking Legislation

No general duties of care. The majority of EU banking regulation – the Capital Requirements Package[30] – is prudential in nature and does not contain a duty of care, even though some of those prudential requirements will indeed be important prerequisites for credit institutions to be able to treat customers honestly, fairly and professionally (such as the requirement of good repute and skill or professional behaviour of management, and the rules on the management of conflicts of interest.)[31] Obviously, if a credit institution provides specific services, it may be subject to a duty of care specific to that service (eg MiFID II if it provides investment services; Mortgage Credit Directive if it provides a mortgage credit (see section II.B.)).

---

[26] Articles 26 (3); 27 (1); 32, 36 and 42 of CDS Regulation.

[27] Commission Proposal on European Crowdfunding Service Providers (ECSP) for Business (COM(2018)113, 8 March 2018), amended by the European Parliament European Parliament in its 'Legislative resolution of 27 March 2019 on the proposal for a regulation of the European Parliament and of the Council on European Crowdfunding Service Providers (ECSP) for Business' (COM(2018)0113 – C8-0103/2018 –2018/0048(COD)). On 24 June 2019 the Council of the European Union came up with a compromise proposal ('Proposal for a Regulation of the European Parliament and of the Council on European Crowdfunding Service Providers (ECSP) for Business and amending Regulation (EU) No 2017/1129 – Mandate for negotiations with the European Parliament – Compromise proposal' (Council 10557/19).

[28] Article 4(2) of the Crowdfunding Proposal. This provision remained unchanged throughout the legislative process.

[29] Article 22 Regulation (EU) 2019/1238 of the European Parliament and of the Council of 20 June 2019 on a pan-European Personal Pension Product (PEPP).

[30] CRD IV, and CRR.

[31] Articles 23(1)b and 91 of CRD IV.

PSD 2 and CCD: lex specialis in regard of UCPD. The general duty of care is equally absent from the 2015 Payment Services Directive (PSD 2)[32] and the Consumer Credit Directive,[33] even though those Directives can be qualified as directives with a focus on customer protection and conduct of business rules. The reason is that those Directives are considered a lex specialis in regard of the Unfair Commercial Practices Directive 2005/29/EU,[34] which features a general prohibition on unfair commercial practices. This prohibition can, in our opinion, be considered a general duty of care (see section IV.A.).

Except in the Mortgage Credit Directive. It is somewhat surprising, therefore, that the Mortgage Credit Directive, even though it also explicitly refers to the Unfair Commercial Practices Directive,[35] does feature a general duty of care. Creditors, credit intermediaries and appointed representatives are required by the Mortgage Credit Directive to act 'honestly, fairly, transparently and professionally, taking account of the rights and interests of the consumers.'[36]

C. EU Insurance Legislation

Insurance Distribution Directive. The 2002 Directive on Insurance Mediation (IMD), the predecessor of the Insurance Distribution Directive (IDD), predated MiFID I by 16 months. It did not contain a general duty of care. In 2014, MiFID II inserted a Section III A in the IMD in relation to insurance-based investment products. This resulted in the aging IMD being upgraded with a general duty of care provision for this type of product only. The wording was practically the same as in Article 24 of MiFID II, with a reference to acting 'honestly, fairly and professionally in accordance with the best interests of its customers.' The IDD, which fully replaced the IMD in 2016, extended the scope of the duty to the activity of insurance distribution as a whole, without a limitation to insurance-based investment products, whilst retaining the wording.[37]

Prudential insurance and pension regulation. For the sake of completeness it should be noted that insurance prudential legislation (Solvency II and IORP Directive) does not feature a general duty or care, but does contain a 'prudent person rule', as a general standard for investment decisions by institutions for occupational retirement provision (IORPs) and insurance and reinsurance undertakings. In this respect, the IORP Directive also refers to a duty to invest in the 'best long term interests of members and beneficiaries as a whole.'[38]

---

[32] Directive 2015/2366/EU of 25 November 2015 on payment services in the internal market (PSD II).

[33] CCD.

[34] See Recital 18 of the CCD and Recital 55 PSD II.

[35] The references relate to unfair or misleading advertising (Recital 37) and correct information on costs and ancillary services (Recital 50).

[36] Article 7(1) of MCD.

[37] 'Member States shall ensure that, when carrying out insurance distribution, insurance distributors always act honestly, fairly and professionally in accordance with the best interests of their customers.' Art 17(1) of IDD.

[38] Solvency II states that 'Member States shall ensure that insurance and reinsurance undertakings invest all their assets in accordance with the prudent person rule, as specified in paragraphs 2, 3 and 4.' (Art 132(1) of Solvency II.

In the 2016 IORPs Directives (as in the previous version of 2003) we read that *'Member States shall require IORPs registered or authorised in their territories to invest in accordance with the 'prudent person' rule and in particular in accordance with the following rules: a: 'the assets shall be invested in the best long-term interests of members and beneficiaries as a whole. (…)'*. Art 19(1) of Dir 2016/2341 of 14 December 2016 on the activities and supervision of institutions for occupational retirement provision (IORPs).

Figure 1 (Elements of) a general duty of care

EU SECURITIES LEGISLATION	1993 ISD	2004 MiFID/ MiFIR	2009 UCITS Directive	2009 CRA	2011 AIFM	2012 EMIR – TR	2012 EMIR – CCP	2013 EVCF	2013 EuSEF	2014 MiFID II	2014 CSD	2015 ELTIF	2018 Crowd-funding
Honest	v	v	v		v					v			v
Fair	v	v	v		v		v			v			v
Skill, care and diligence	v		v		v			v	v				
Professional		v					v			v			v
In particular		v								v			v
Best interest of the client	v	v	v		v		v	v	v	v, with exceptions			
Market integrity	v		v		v			v	v				
Transparency													
Prudent person principle													
Good repute	v	v	v	v	v	v	v	v	v	v	v		v
Knowledge and experience	v	v	v	v	v	v	v	v	v	v	v	v	v
Conflicts of interest	v	v	v	v	v	v	v	v	v	v	v	v	v

EU INSURANCE LEGISLATION	2002	2009	2016	2016
	IMD	Solvency II	IDD	IORP
Honest			✓	
Fair			✓	
Skill, care and diligence				
Professional			✓	
In particular				✓
Best interest of the client		✓	✓	✓
Market integrity				
Transparency				
Prudent person principle		✓		✓
Good repute	✓		✓	✓
Knowledge and experience	✓		✓	✓
Conflicts of interest			✓	

EU BANKING LEGISLATION	2008	2013	2014	2015	2017
	CCD	CRD	MCD	PSD2	PEPP
Honest			✓		✓
Fair			✓		✓
Skill, care and diligence					
Professional			✓		✓
In particular					
Best interest of the client			✓		✓
Market integrity					
Transparency			✓		
Prudent person principle					
Good repute		✓	✓	✓	✓
Knowledge and experience		✓	✓	✓	✓
Conflicts of interest		✓	✓		✓

D. Nature, Meaning and Variances of the Duty of Care in EU Financial Legislation

The overview of the various instances of the duty of care in financial legislation leads to the following preliminary conclusions.

Incidence. The duty of care is mostly present in securities and insurance legislation, the mortgage credit directive being a notable exception in banking legislation. Several regulations and directives lack a duty of care altogether. In some cases, as for the Consumer Credit Directive and the Payments Services Directive, this can be explained by the fact that those directives are considered a lex specialis in relation to the UCPD. Other financial law directives and regulations lacking a general duty of care, do typically feature specific prudential and/or organisational requirements which are closely related to the ability of financial institutions to comply with the different aspects of a typical duty of care, namely honesty (good repute), fairness (conflict of interests) and professionalism (knowledge and experience).

The duty of care is typically the main conduct of business rule which a financial institution needs to respect in its direct relationship to its clients, and especially its *retail* clients. Financial institutions which only deal with wholesale clients, such as CRA's, trade repositories and CSDs, do not face a financial regulation duty of care. In MiFID I, the duty of care did not apply in respect of transactions on MTFs and regulated markets and between eligible counterparties.[39] MiFID II has softened this approach and only removes the best interest requirement from the relationship with eligible counterparties, retaining the obligation to act honestly, fairly and professionally.[40]

Catch-all and container function. MiFID is the only directive explicitly expressing the catch-all and container function of its duty of care, using the wording 'in particular'.[41] IDD uses the MiFID II wording without the 'in particular' addition. Other pieces of legislation, such as the UCITS Directive and AIFM, have bullet lists lacking a hierarchy or other relation between the duty of care and subsequent specific requirements in the same list. In view of the general scope of the duty of care in all directives and regulations which feature such a duty, it is fair to assume, however, that all duties of care in EU financial regulation at least implicitly have such a catch-all and container function.

'Best interest of the client' and/or 'market integrity'? All expressions of the duty of care in financial regulation refer, with some variations, to the 'best interests of the client'.[42] Whereas MiFID I also referred to the 'integrity of the market', just as the MiFIR and the UCITS Directive, AIFM, EVCF and EUSEF Directives do, the more recent directives and regulations featuring a duty of care do not refer to market integrity anymore. However, it seems self-evident that market integrity should be considered a key concern of all financial institutions.

Significance of variances? Figure 1 shows that there are other small variances in the wording of the duty of care in the different directives and regulations. Overall, however, it appears correct to assume that most of the variety in the ways in which the duty care is stipulated throughout EU financial legislation does not appear to be related to a difference in meaning, and simply seems to point to a lack of rigour in legislative drafting.

---

[39] The precise terms of the exemptions can be found in Arts 14(3); 24 (2) and 42 (3) of MiFID (I).

[40] Article 30(1) of MiFID II.

[41] Although the IORP Directive seems to operate in a similar way with the use of the 'prudent person principle' and of the wording 'in particular', the IORP Directive does not feature the terms 'honest', 'fair' or 'professional', so we are dealing with a different type of care here.

[42] Enriques and Gargantini relate this expression to the common law tradition where it is often associated with fiduciary relationships. See Enriques and Gargantini (fn 12) at 86, para 4.04.

E. Need for One Cross-Sectoral Financial Regulation Duty of Care?

Need for a cross-sectoral duty of care? Certain Member States already feature a cross-sectoral duty of care in their national financial regulation.[43] In view of the findings above, we ask the question of whether it would be advantageous to introduce at EU-level a harmonised cross-sectoral duty of care for the financial sector as a whole, covering all financial institutions, services and products. There are, in our opinion, a number of important arguments in favour of such an approach.

Unsubstantiated differences lead to legal uncertainty and inefficient duplications. We have come to the conclusion that the differences in wording of the duty of care in the many directives and regulations regulating the financial industry, can typically not be explained on the basis of differences between the institutions to which they apply, or the services or products they provide. Such differences, therefore, seem unsubstantiated in most cases. However, those differences in terminology create legal uncertainty as to the exact meaning of the duty in different legal instruments, which is inefficient for the financial institutions subject to this duty. Moreover, different European Supervisory Authorities (EBA, ESMA and EIOPA) are competent for interpreting these duties of care, each in their sector. This might lead to diverging interpretations of the standard of care required in each of the sectors. Finally, if a discussion on the meaning of a duty of care would become the subject of a judgment by the Court of Justice of the European Union, one might assume that this interpretation also applies to the other duties of care, but, again, this requires interpretation, especially when the wording of the different duties of care differs. If there would be one cross-sectoral duty of care for the financial sector, ESMA, EBA and EIOPA would have to cooperate when interpreting this duty with further guidelines or Q&A's; and a preliminary ruling by the Court of Justice of the EU on such a cross-sectoral duty would automatically apply for all financial institutions subject to this duty.

Limited scope of application of duties of care in financial regulation. In EU financial legislation, duties of care are typically limited to specific institutions or even specific services of a regulated entity. The 'general' nature of the duty of care should therefore be properly understood: the duty will always be confined to the limits of the instrument in which it is enshrined and can, obviously, not be invoked against parties that are not in scope of the piece of legislation. Many financial

---

[43] In the UK the cross-sectoral 'treat your customer fairly' Initiative already dates back to 2006 (see FSA, 'Treating customers fairly – towards fair outcomes for consumers' (July 2006) www.fca.org.uk/publication/archive/fsa-tcf-towards. pdf, and a duty of care has been enshrined in the cross-sectoral FSA and later FCA Handbook (Principles for Business) even before that date (www.handbook.fca.org.uk/handbook/PRIN/2/?view=chapter). See Principle 1: 'A firm must conduct its business with integrity'; principle 2: 'A firm must conduct its business with due skill, care and diligence'; Principle 6: 'a firm must pay due regard to the interests of its customers and treat them fairly'. Those principles already applied to almost all financial services providers; as from 1 August 2019, they will also apply to payment services provided and electronic money institutions (see FCA, 'General standards and communication rules for the payment services and e-money sectors' (Policy Statement PS19/3, February 2019).

As from 1 January 2014, the Netherlands also introduced a general duty of care for financial services providers in Art 4:24a of the Dutch Law on Financial Supervision, even though not all financial activities are covered: investment firms and investment funds, for instance are covered by their sector-specific EU duty of care. See in this respect, among others, KWH Broekhuizen and CE du Perron, 'De zorgplicht in twee gedaanten', in D Busch and MP Nieuwe Weme (eds), *Christels koers. Liber Amicorum Prof.mr.drs. CM Grundmann-van de Krol* (Deventer Kluwer, 2013) 149–162; D Busch, 'Contouren van een generieke zorgplicht in de Wft' in EM Dieben and FMA 't Hart (eds), *Klantenbelang Centraal* (Financieel Juridische Reeks 4, Amsterdam NIBE-SVV, 2012) at 97–106.

In Belgium the MiFID II duty of care has been implemented with a much wider scope of application than MiFID II requires: Art 27, s 1 of the Belgian Law on Financial Supervision not only applies in respect of investment and ancillary services, but should apply to credit institutions and investment firms when 'offering or providing financial products or services'. See V Colaert, 'MiFID II en de zorgplicht: niets nieuws onder de zon?' (fn 12) at 107–111.

institutions and services are therefore not covered by a financial regulation duty of care. A cross-sectorally applicable duty of care would apply to the entire financial sector. It would therefore not only have a gap-filling, but also a 'virtue signalling' function.[44]

Cross-sectoral duty of care? In view of the findings above, we can draw the preliminary conclusion that having one cross-sectoral duty of care for the financial sector could be regarded as advantageous. It would cover all financial institutions, services and products, thus avoiding any gaps. This would render the 'catch-all' function of the duty more meaningful, as more types of behaviour could be caught,[45] and it would have an important virtue-signalling function. Moreover, unsubstantiated differences in wording, which create uncertainty as to the exact meaning of the duty in different legal instruments, a multiplication of interpretation and translation efforts, and the risk of different standards for similar services provided by the different financial institutions, would be avoided. In the next sections we will seek to answer the question of whether existing cross-sectoral duties of care, which are not specific to the financial sector, suffice, or whether there is an added value to having one cross-sectoral financial regulation duty of care.

III. Need for Financial Regulation Duty or Duties of Care on Top of Civil/Common Law Duties of Care?

Civil/common law. Member States typically already have a general, non-sector specific duty of care and/or fiduciary duties in their civil or common law. This raises the question what the added value of (a) financial regulation duty(ies) of care would be. To answer this question, we should first determine the relationship between the duties of care in financial regulation on the one hand, and the duties of care in national civil or common law on the other hand. This is a much-debated question.

A. Relationship between Duties of Care in Financial Regulation and Duties of Care in National Civil or Common Law

i. *Nature of Financial Regulation Duties of Care*

Public law? In respect of the MiFID conduct of business rules, many authors have argued that they provide for public law standards and therefore, only maximally harmonise the relationship between the investment firm and the supervising authority. Even though most authors accept that those public law standards also influence civil/common law standards,[46] national judges would

---

[44] In his letter to the Chair of the Second Chamber of the Dutch Parliament, J Dijsselbloem, Minister of Finance of the Netherlands at the time, explicitly mentioned those two reasons (among other reasons) for the introduction of a general duty of care for the entire financial sector in the Netherlands: it should function as a catch-all clause on the basis of which the Autoriteit Financiële Markten (AFM) would be able to enforce if there are no more specific rules in Dutch financial regulation; and it was to support the change of culture which the AFM was aiming to achieve. See J Dijsselbloem, 'Evaluatie algemene zorgplicht Wet op het financieel toezicht' (letter of 30 December 2016), www.zorgkennis.net/downloads/kennisbank/ZK-kennisbank-Kamerbrief-Evaluatie-algemene-zorgplicht-4424.pdf, at 2–3 and 6.

[45] Naturally, the less narrowly defined duty could also be regarded as problematic by financial institutions subject to supervision on the basis of such a duty. See below, section III.A.

[46] Especially in Germany, the courts have been very reluctant to recognise any private law effect of the MiFID conduct of business rules, even though this jurisprudence has met with opposition in legal doctrine. For an overview, see

not be limited by the MiFID conduct of business rules when judging on the behaviour of investment firms towards their clients in a case based on civil/common law duties. The MiFID duty of care would then only set a minimum, but not necessarily a maximum standard.[47]

Private law nature of conduct of business rules. We do not agree with this view. Even though most Member States distinguish between private law and public law in their legal systems, the European legislator does not make any determination on the public or private law nature of its rules. All national rules which go against – or in case of maximum harmonisation – go beyond the European rules, should be abolished or (if it is an open norm) interpreted in accordance with the EU rules. Most Member States have implemented the MiFID conduct of business rules in laws which they label as 'public law'. However, conduct of business rules regulate the relationship between two *private* parties: the financial institution and their clients; they create obligations for one private party (the financial institution) and rights for the other (the client).[48] Therefore, we have previously argued that the MiFID conduct of business rules are in essence of a private law nature.[49] The only public law aspect is the fact that EU law requires that compliance with those rules should be supervised, and if necessary enforced, by a public authority. Even though this public enforcement is obviously of a public law nature, this does not render the supervised relationship between two private parties of a public law nature (similarly in respect of the unfair commercial practices rules, see section IV.B.).[50]

Enforcement of compliance with conduct of business rules. EU financial regulation only harmonises the behavioural standards for financial institutions, and the *public enforcement* of those standards.[51] It does not harmonise the *private enforcement* of compliance with those standards. However, the Court of Justice of the EU has shed some light on the role of the MiFID conduct of business rules in a private law legal dispute. The *Genil* case dealt, among other things, with

---

J Binder, 'Germany' in D Busch and C Van Dam, (fn 2) at 72–74. The author concludes that the regulatory and contractual obligations of intermediaries vis-vis their clients are subject to two separate regimes, each associated with separate enforcement regimes. This is rather ironic in view of the comments made on German law in this respect during the MiFID I legislative process, see fn 54. See in this respect also, equally critical of the position of the German courts: S Grundmann, 'The Bankinter Case on MiFID Regulation and Contract Law' 2013 *European Review of Contract Law* 267–280.

[47] Among others: O Cherednychenko, 'European Securities Regulation, Private Law and the Investment Firm-Client Relationship' (2009) *European Review of Private Law*, at 925; more nuanced: D Busch, 'The private law effect of MiFID: the Genil case and beyond' (2017) *European Review of Contract Law*, 70–93; D Busch, C van Dam and Bart van der Wiel, 'Netherlands' in D Busch and C Van Dam, (fn 2) at 211–212.

[48] V Colaert, *De rechtsverhouding financiële dienstverlener – belegger* (Brugge, die Keure, 2011) at 24–30. The public law – private law distinction is used in almost all jurisdictions, and is always defined in more or less the same way: private law regulates the relationship between two private parties; public law regulates the organisation of government or the relationship between government and a private party. See in this respect amongst others: J Merryman, 'The Public Law – Private Law Distinction in European and American Law' (1986) *Journal of Public Law*. at 5–7; C Saiman, 'Public Law, Private Law and Legal Science' (2008) *American Journal of Comparative Law*. at 692.

[49] V Colaert, *De rechtsverhouding financiële dienstverlener – belegger* (fn 48) at 136–146. In the same sense, even though hesitantly: European Commission (Civic Consulting) 'Study on the application of Directive 2005/29/EC on Unfair Commercial Practices in the EU, Part 1 – Synthesis Report' (22 December 2011) at 31: 'The extent to which Directive 2004/39/EC is of relevance to the contractual relationship between the investor and the investment firm is entirely unclear. The Directive itself only talks of harmonisation aiming at mutual recognition of authorisations by the competent authorities. Indeed, it does not seem to make much sense to harmonise rules on, for example, inducements for matters of prudential supervision law whilst leaving it to the Member States to prohibit the identical practices under contract or tort law. As recital (2) of Directive 2004/39/EC prominently confirms, the Directive aims to facilitate crossborder investment services. Thus, where Directives 2004/39/EC and 2006/73/EC contain specific rules on a particular issue, they would imply maximum harmonisation of related private law as well. This is however anything but clear and would have ultimately to be decided by the CJEU.'

[50] Compare to S Grundmann (fn 46) at 278 and 280, who is of the opinion that the MiFID conduct of business rules have to be seen in their full amount 'also' as contract (or tort) law standards.

[51] Article 70(1) and (3) a, x MiFID II.

the question of contractual consequences (in national contract law) of non-compliance with MiFID I obligations in the absence of EU legislation on those consequences. The Court held that 'it is for the internal legal order of each Member State to determine the contractual consequences of non-compliance with those obligations, *subject to observance of the principles of equivalence and effectiveness*.'[52] As a consequence, in a private claim for damages caused in the MiFID sphere, clearly the fully MiFID harmonised standard of care is relevant in judging the case, as the effectiveness of the MiFID rules needs to be safeguarded. The question arises whether national judges can go beyond the standards set by the MiFID duty of care in a private enforcement case. We are of the opinion that they cannot, since MiFID fully harmonises the standards of behaviours for financial institutions, also when enforced on the basis of a breach of civil/common law duties of care or fiduciary duties (or even on the basis of the UCPD, see section IV).

Scope of harmonisation. In previous contributions we have indeed argued that in case a directive fully harmonises the behavioural standard, such directive also fully harmonises any civil/common law behavioural standard in the regulated relationship.[53] The fact that the MiFID conduct of business rules would have such an impact on civil law rules in the Member States, was explicitly recognised by the European Parliament.[54] And the European Commission even chose for an implementing directive rather than an implementing regulation:

> [i]n order to enable Member States, when transposing its provisions into national law, to not only adjust its requirements to the specificities of their particular market but also ensure coherence with other bodies of law. For example, the provisions dealing with the conduct of business regulate the relationship between investment firms and their clients, an area that is also governed by Member States' civil law. However, this should not imply that legal provisions in other existing areas of law which are inconsistent

---

[52] EUCJ, judgment of 30 May 2013, *Genil*, C-604/11, para 57. For discussions, see D Busch, 'The Private Law Effect of MiFID: the Genil Case and Beyond' in D Busch and G Ferrarini (eds) *Regulation of the EU financial markets. MiFID II and MiFIR* (Oxford, OUP, 2017), A Tenenbaum, 'Les contrats financiers complexes et les obligations d'information: partition d'un dialogue subtil entre la CJEU et les juges nationaux' 2014 (Revue des Contrats) at 123; V Michel, 'Note sous CJUE, 4° ch., 30 mai 2013, aff. C-604/11' 2013 (LexisNexis Jurisclasseur); S Grundmann (fn 46) 267–280.

[53] V Colaert, *De rechtsverhouding financiële dienstverlener – belegger* (fn 48) at 321 and following, nrs. 688 and following; V Colaert, 'Les règles de conduite MiFID, le droit de la consommation et le droit civil: une relation complexe' (2012) *RPS*, at 271–310; European Commission, 'Study on the application of Directive 2005/29/EC (fn 49) at 31 (see also previous footnote). In the same sense, even though these authors do not take position on the public or private law nature of the conduct of business rules: S van Baalen, 'Aansprakelijkheid als gevolg van een schending van de Wft-regels' in D Busch et al (eds), *Onderneming en Financieel Toezicht* (Deventer, Kluwer, 2010) at 1024; CMJ Lieverse, annotation N°12 under HR 5 June 2009, *JOR 2009/199* (Treek/Dexia Bank Nederland); CMJ Lieverse, 'Oneerlijke handelspraktijken en handhaving van consumentenbescherming in de financiële sector: taken en bevoegdheden van de AFM' in CMJ Lieverse en J Rinkes, *Oneerlijke handelspraktijken en handhaving van consumentenbescherming in de financiële sector – Preadvies voor de Vereniging voor Effectenrecht 2010* (Deventer, Kluwer, 2010) at 115–116; PO Mülbert, 'Auswirkungen der MiFID-Rechtsakte für Vertriebsvergütungen im Effektengeschäft der Kreditinstitute' (2008) *ZHR*, 172; I Riassetto and JF Richard, 'Luxembourg' in D Busch and DA DeMott (eds), *Liability of Asset Managers* (Oxford, Oxford University Press, 2012), 178, No 6.63.

[54] See the justification to amendment 23 of the European Parliament to the MiFID Proposal: 'This amendment is necessary to make clear that the new EU framework supersedes traditional pre-existing civil liability. Without such clarification, investment firms in countries such as Germany could be subject to a double layer of regulation, with the old case-based rules undermining the distinction drawn in the ISD between professional and retail investors.' Similarly the justification to amendment 139 to the MiFID Proposal: 'In some Member States, such as Germany, much investor protection is carried out via civil liability in the courts. With the codification of investor protection in the ISD, it should be made clear that the new EU framework supersedes traditional pre-existing civil liability. Without such clarification, investment firms in Germany could be subject to a double layer of regulation, with the old rules undermining the distinction drawn in the ISD between professional and retail investors.' See European Parliament, 'Report on the proposal for a European Parliament and Council directive on Investment services and regulated market, and amending Council Dir 85/611/EEC, Council Dir 93/6/EEC and European Parliament and Council 2000/12/EC' (A5-0287/2003, 4 September 2003) at pp 20 and 88.

with the provisions of the implementing Directive should not be repealed or adjusted to ensure proper implementation.[55]

Impact on national case law and civil/common law duty of care. It is important not to interpret this as if a judge would be placed in a 'MiFID straitjacket' when applying the duty of care in a dispute on the basis of a civil/common law duty of care. Financial regulation duties of care are themselves open standards. Since the legislator and regulator can never foresee each eventuality, it is the prerogative of national case law to make concrete the MiFID behavioural standard.[56] The restrictions that are brought about by EU financial regulation aiming at full harmonisation, are of a more formal nature. First, as said above, the effectiveness of the EU standard will need to be preserved: a judge cannot be less strict than the MiFID standard requires when applying a civil or common law duty of care. Secondly, there may be relevant regulatory guidance that the judge should take into account when making concrete the behavioural standard in a specific case, such as supervisory guidelines, best practices or supervisory decisions. Thirdly the civil law judge could (and should) submit a preliminary question to the Court of Justice of the EU if interpretation questions arise while applying a common or civil law duty of care to a case the facts of which are in scope of EU financial legislation.[57] In this way financial regulation duties of care indirectly (fully) harmonise the civil and common law duties of care in relationships subject to a financial regulation duty of care.[58]

Finally, it goes without saying that the harmonised financial regulation duties of care only harmonise the behavioural standard of care which a financial institution should respect in its relationship with its clients. They have no implications on the determination of damages and causation in accordance with the laws on tort or contract, nor on the intricacies of national procedural rules (including law of evidence).[59] Therefore, even though the behavioural standard of civil/common law duties of care are in our opinion also (fully) harmonised by the financial regulation duties of care, whether and what kind of remedies a client will actually receive in a private enforcement case in the different Member States, can still widely vary.

---

[55] European Commission, 'Background Note – Draft Commission Directive implementing Directive 2004/39 of the European Parliament and of the Council as regards record-keeping obligations for investment firms, transaction reporting, market transparency, admission of Financial instruments to trading, and defined terms for the purposes of that Directive' (6 February 2006) at 2.2.

[56] Busch raises a very interesting question in this regard in D Busch, 'The private law effect of MiFID I and MiFID II: the Genil case and beyond' in D Busch and G Ferrarini, *Regulation of EU Financial Markets – MiFID II and MiFIR* (Oxford, Oxford University Press, 2017) para 20.20: If specific conduct of business rules allow a certain behaviour (eg provide a *standardised* warning that a product is inappropriate) can a judge then still be stricter on the basis of the more general MiFID duty of care (and eg hold that the financial institution should have given a personalised warning)? We are of the opinion that he cannot. The specific conduct of business rules should in our opinion be considered a 'lex specialis' in relation to the more general MiFID duty of care. In our opinion, only if a certain behaviour cannot be brought under a more specific conduct of business rule, the judge (or a supervisor for that matter) can assess the behaviour under the more general MiFID duty of care.

[57] German courts generally found that MiFID conduct of business rules have no impact on civil law, and therefore do not see a need to refer civil law cases in which there may be a violation of a MiFID conduct of business rule for a preliminary ruling to the Court of Justice of the EU (S Grundmann (fn 46) at 277). In 2011 a Spanish court, however, famously asked for a preliminary ruling on the application of MiFID (EU CoJ, judgment of 30 May 2013, *Genil*, C-604/11, para 26). In our opinion, this case shows that the MiFID conduct of business rules, as interpreted by the Court of Justice of the EU, indeed also harmonise the standard of behaviour based on civil and common law duties of care, even though the burden of proof, the sanctions in case of violation of this standard, and the other conditions to conclude whether a sanction should be imposed (such as proof of causality) obviously remain unharmonised.

[58] See V Colaert, *De rechtsverhouding financiële dienstverlener – belegger* (fn 48) at 584.

[59] Even the burden of proof should probably not be such that it undermines the effectiveness of the EU rules.

Maximum versus minimum harmonisation in financial regulation. It should be noted that the private or public law nature of the financial regulation duties of care is less of an issue if seen with respect to financial regulation duties of care which do not aim at *maximum* harmonisation (such as the IDD duty of care). In such cases a civil law judge can in any event go beyond the interpretation of the financial regulation duty of care.

B. Added Value of Financial Regulation Duties of Care on Top of Civil/Common Law Duties of Care

Overview. In our opinion, the added value of (a) financial regulation dut(y)ies of care in addition to national civil law and common law duties, is not to be found in the exact content or wording of these rules. Rather, (i) they contribute to the harmonisation of an EU-wide standard of behaviour in the internal market and (ii) they provide a legal basis for the supervisor to provide more detailed guidance on how to comply with such a standard of behaviour in particular circumstances, and to impose administrative sanctions in case of non-compliance with this standard.

Harmonising the level of care throughout the EU. First, the added value of having financial regulation duties of care is that they allow for harmonisation of the standards of behaviour of specific types of financial institutions towards their clients. Even though several attempts have been made in the past, the idea of a full harmonisation of the civil law of the Member States is currently still unfeasible.[60] However, national civil/common law standards of care result in rather different standards for careful behaviour in the different Member States. In order to create an internal market for financial services, the European Union has opted to harmonise the legal regimes applicable to financial institutions, including, for many financial institutions, the standard of care to be observed in the relationship with their clients. In order to achieve harmonisation of the standard of care of financial institutions throughout the Union, financial regulation duties of care were thus necessary on top of existing civil and common law duties of care. As a result, if questions arise on the meaning and scope of the concepts of this duty of care (eg 'honesty', 'fairness', 'average client', …), the European Court of Justice can be requested to provide a preliminary ruling in order to harmonise the interpretation of those concepts across the Member States (see section III.A.i.).

Legal basis for supervisory guidance and enforcement. Secondly, financial regulation duties of care also serve as the legal basis for financial supervisory authorities to (i) provide guidelines on the exact scope of this duty for specific financial institutions, and to (ii) sanction non-compliance with administrative sanctions. Article 24 of MiFID II for instance, which contains the duty of care, is one of the infringeable articles listed explicitly in the Directive. As a result, Member States must ensure that 'their competent authorities may impose administrative sanctions and measures (…)' and 'shall take all measures necessary to ensure that they are implemented. Such sanctions and measures shall be effective, proportionate and dissuasive (…)'.[61] Nevertheless, in view of legal certainty ('*lex certa* principle'), one would expect the supervisor to abstain from imposing sanctions on the sole basis of a general duty of care, considering this is an open norm.[62]

---

[60] For an extensive overview of the history, and a comparison of all initiatives, see N Jansen and R Zimmerman, *Commentaries on European Contract Laws* (Oxford, OUP 2019).

[61] Article 70(1) and (3) a, x MiFID II.

[62] A report from the Netherlands indicated that up to that point, no administrative supervisory cases had been brought forward on the basis of the Dutch general financial legislation duty of care (even though it mentions a number of civil

The situation would naturally be different if, on the basis of the financial regulation duty of care, the supervisor would either first warn a financial institution that, in the opinion of the supervisor it is violating its duty of care, so that it can change its behaviour and avoid administrative sanctions,[63] or adopt clear guidelines, Q&As and other preventive supervisory tools on how to behave in particular situations, particularly in light of new market developments. Regulatory guidance directly based on a general financial regulation duty of care is, to our knowledge, scarce.

IV. General Duty of Care in the Unfair Commercial Practices Directive

A. Does the Prohibition of Unfair Commercial Practices Amount to a Duty of Care?

Prohibition of unfair practices. In 2005, the Unfair Commercial Practices Directive (UCPD) introduced an EU-wide prohibition of unfair commercial practices in the relationship between businesses and consumers.[64] Article 5 of the UCPD provides that a commercial practice shall be unfair if it is contrary to 'the requirements of professional diligence',[65] while 'professional diligence' is defined as 'the standard of special skill and care which a trader may reasonably be expected to exercise towards consumers, commensurate with honest market practice and/or the general principle of good faith in the trader's field of activity'.[66] Article 5, UCPD names two particular types of unfair practices: misleading, and aggressive practices. Annex II of the UCPD features a black list of practices which are in all circumstances considered to be unfair. Recital 13 explains that '[t]he general prohibition is elaborated by rules on the two types of commercial practices which are by far the most common, namely misleading commercial practices and aggressive commercial practices.'[67]

Duty of care? One could wonder whether a *prohibition* of unfairness can be considered equivalent to a *duty* to act honestly, fairly and professionally. Although at first sight not an open, positive

law cases and a number of cases before the ombudsservice Kifid which make use of the general financial legislation duty of care). Therefore, the report did not draw any conclusions on the practical effects and efficacy of having such a duty of care in financial legislation. See J Dijsselbloem (fn 44) at 2. Also other authorities have, to our knowledge, not yet enforced a financial regulation duty of care as such, without also referring to more concrete rules which the financial institution would have breached.

[63] For this reason the Dutch Autoriteit Financiële Markten (AFM) (i) can only sanction on the basis of the general duty of care in case of 'evident' abuses, and (ii) should always first give a warning, after which the AFM can only take a sanction in case of non-compliance with this warning (Art 4:24a, Wft). Moreover, the Mr Dijsselbloem is of the opinion that it would be a good idea for the AFM to publish guidelines on its enforcement policy on the basis of concrete cases, if the case may be. See in this respect J Dijsselbloem (fn 44) at 4 and 7.

[64] For a discussion of UCPD, see J Stuyck, E Terryn and T Van Dyck, 'Confidence through fairness? The new Directive on Unfair Business-to-Consumer Practices in the Internal Market' (2006) 43 *CML Rev* 107; S Weatherill and U Bernitz, *The Regulation of Unfair Commercial Practices under EC Directive 2005/29* (Oxford, Hart Publishing, 2007).

[65] For a practice to be considered unfair, it should also materially distort or be likely to materially distort the economic behaviour with regard to the product of the average consumer whom it reaches or to whom it is addressed, or of the average member of the group when a commercial practice is directed to a particular group of consumers.

[66] Article 2(h), UCPD.

[67] The Court of Justice of the EU has clarified the relationship between the general prohibition and the more specific prohibitions. It held that the wording 'in particular' does not imply that general requirements are to be applied in addition to more specific ones. On the other hand, a party cannot rely on complying with one or more requirements, for instance professional diligence, to refute a claim that it infringed a more specific requirement from the UCPD, for instance the prohibition on misleading commercial practices (CJEU, judgment of 19 September 2013, *CHS Tour Services GmbH v Team4 Travel GmbH*, C-435/11, para 39, 40 and 45).

norm to act honestly, fairly and professionally, the definition of what constitutes an unfair prac-tice in Article 5, UCPD does use the open norm of *'professional diligence'*, which refers to the elements of honesty, good faith and professionalism – the typical ingredients of a duty of care. Therefore, the approach of Article 5, UCPD can rightly be considered a general EU duty of care[68] that should govern every business-to-consumer relationship.

B. Application of the UCPD to the Financial Industry?

Lex specialis derogat legi generali. Article 3(4), UCPD provides that in case of conflict between the provisions of the UCPD and other Community rules regulating specific aspects of unfair commercial practices, the latter shall prevail and apply to those specific aspects. Recital 10 states it somewhat differently and provides that the UCPD applies only insofar as there are no specific Community law provisions regulating specific aspects of unfair commercial practices, such as information requirements. It provides protection for consumers where there is no specific sectoral legislation at Union level and should be seen as a complement to the acquis, which is applicable to commercial practices harming consumers' economic interests. This is stated to be particularly important for complex products with high levels of risk to consumers, such as certain financial services products.

This provision and recital raise the question whether the UCPD duty of care still applies when there is a duty of care in a specific piece of EU legislation. In the next sections, we will use the prototype financial regulation duty of care of the MiFID as an example in order to make the analysis more concrete, and seek an answer to the question of whether one would be obliged in the MiFID sphere to apply the MiFID duty of care to the exclusion of the UCPD.

Public or private law nature of the rules? To answer this question, we should first establish whether the UCPD and MiFID set rules of the same 'nature'. After all, the UCPD's *lex generalis* rule could not be applied between two sets of rules of a different nature.[69] Consumer law is generally considered to be of a private law nature since it regulates the relationship between two private parties (businesses and consumers).[70] Member States are free, however, to 'choose the enforcement mechanisms which best suit their legal tradition, as long as they ensure that adequate and effective means exist to prevent unfair commercial practices.' … 'Most systems … combine elements of public and private enforcement'.[71] As discussed above (in section III.A.i.),

---

[68] See European Commission, 'Staff working document – Guidance on the implementation/application of directive 2005/29/EC on unfair commercial practices' (SWD(2016) 163 final, 25 May 2016) at 148: 'Article 5(2)(a)UCPD on the requirements of professional diligence seems particularly relevant to traders acting towards consumers within the fields of immovable property and financial services. If the trader does not act with the standard of skill and care which can reasonably be expected from a professional within these fields of commercial activity, the consumer might suffer significant economic consequences.'

[69] See on this theme, in more detail, V Colaert, *De rechtsverhouding financiële dienstverlener – belegger* (fn 48) at 6–7.

[70] European consumer law has often been considered as a first step towards harmonisation of contract law. See for instance E Hondius, 'The Protection of the Weak Party in a Harmonised European Contract Law: A Synthesis', (2004) *Journal of Consumer Policy*, 245: 'Consumer Protection has been developed especially on the European level and indeed it provides the best example of harmonization of private law.'; S Weatherilll, *EU Consumer Law and Policy*, (Cheltenham, Edward Elgar, 2005), 116: 'Most of all, it opened up a new potential 'growth area' – European (or at least EC) private law.' The Netherlands has, moreover, transposed the UCPD into their national Civil Codes. See on this question also V Colaert, *De rechtsverhouding financiële dienstverlener – belegger* (fn 48) at 193–195.

[71] See European Commission, 'First Report on the application of Directive 2005/29/EC' (COM 2013/139, 14 March 2013) at 26: 'Under Article 11 of the UCPD, Member States are free to choose the enforcement mechanisms which best suit their legal tradition, as long as they ensure that adequate and effective means exist to prevent unfair commercial prac-tices. On the basis of Article 13 of the UCPD, it is also left to the Member States to decide what type of penalties should be applied, as long as these are 'effective, proportionate and dissuasive. … Most systems, however, combine elements of

in our opinion the MiFID conduct of business rules intrinsically have the same private law nature, since they set standards of how financial institutions should behave in relation to their clients, even though they can typically be enforced either by public authorities or in private law proceedings.

Application of the lex generalis rule? Since the MiFID conduct of business rules and the UCPD share the same private law nature,[72] we can consider the question of how to apply the UCPD's *lex generalis* rule in a MiFID context. One could argue that since MiFID applies to a more specific subject matter than the UCPD and both feature a duty of care, the MiFID duty of care would always take precedence over the UCPD. We believe such interpretation to be incorrect on the basis of two textual arguments in the UCPD. First, Article 3(4) of the UCPD only states that the other Community rules shall prevail 'in case of conflict' between the provisions of the UCPD and those other Community rules.[73] Even though many MiFID conduct of business rules overlap, there does not seem to be any conflict.[74] Second, Article 7, UCPD prohibits misleading omissions, ie leaving out information which is essential for the consumer to be able to make an informed decision. In order to facilitate the appreciation of what constitutes essential information, the Article refers to Annex II to the UCPD for a list of EU rules providing information obligations which should be deemed essential information. This list also mentions Article 19, of MiFID I (which contained the MiFID I conduct of business rules). This means that the EU legislator had no doubt that an investor-consumer would be in a position to invoke the UCPD when an investment firm had made a misleading omission. Therefore, the fact that the MiFID contains a duty of care and a requirement on non-misleading information, does not lead to the conclusion that the UCPD would no longer apply in the relationship between an investment firm and an investor-consumer. The MiFID conduct of business rules rather fine-tune the interpretation of the UCPD rules.[75,76]

---

public and private enforcement.' See also EUCJ, judgment of 16 April 2015, UPC Magyarország, C 388/13, paras 56 and 57 and the case-law cited there. See for an overview of enforcement mechanisms in the different Member States: European Commission, 'Study on the application of Directive 2005/29/EC (fn 49) at 33–34. This study explicitly mentions 'that consumers may of course have individual remedies stemming from Community or national contract or tort law' (at 35).

[72] European Commission, 'Study on the application of Directive 2005/29/EC' (fn 49) at 53 states: 'At EU level, commercial practices in the area of investment services are subject to Directive 2004/39/EC on markets in financial instruments.' Similarly, the former UK Financial Services Authority (currently replaced by the Financial Conduct Authority, FCA) stated upon the implementation in the UK of the UCPD: 'We consider that our Handbook and our regulatory approach already address any unfair commercial practices in the area of financial services' (FSA, 'Reforming Conduct of Business Regulation' (Consultation Paper 06/19) at 28.8.

[73] The text of this Article should prevail over the seemingly more stringent wording of Recital 10 (stating that the UCPD 'only' applies if there are no specific Community law provisions).

[74] V Colaert, *De rechtsverhouding financiële dienstverlener – belegger* (fn 48) at 281–282; V Colaert, 'Financiële diensten en de Wet Marktpraktijken. Enkele knelpunten' 2011 (*Droit Bancaire et Financier*) at 100.

[75] See in this respect also European Commission, 'Study on the application of Directive 2005/29/EC (fn 49) at 29: 'from a trader's perspective it does not really matter whether the prohibition of an activity that he or she wants to engage in forms part of the law of unfair commercial practices or of (public) trading law. In fact, country reports recognise this overlap. They mention a number of absolute prohibitions or restrictions that can be clearly classified as trading laws; yet the country reports also treat them as commercial practices rules in that they mention them as examples of national legislative prohibitions not contained in the blacklist of the UCPD' and in respect of the regulation of professions (at 30): 'The respective laws may form part of public law or contain private law rules. They are often enforced by public law means. They can however also be seen as concretising the 'professional diligence' standard from UCPD Article 5(2). Thus, a breach of such professional regulation may at the same time be an unfair commercial practice in terms of Article 5(2) UCPD; provided that the other requirements of Article 5(2) UCPD are met'.

[76] One could even consider the MiFID conduct of business rules as 'codes of conduct' in the sense of Art 10 and Recital 20 of the UCPD. The latter recital states that '[i]t is appropriate to provide a role for codes of conduct, which enable traders to apply the principles of this Directive effectively in specific economic fields. In sectors where there are specific mandatory requirements regulating the behaviour of traders, it is appropriate that these will also provide evidence as to the requirements of professional diligence in that sector. The control exercised by code owners at national or Community

Cumulative application. In our view this means that the financial regulation duties of care and the UCPD shall both apply in the relationship between a financial institution and an investor-consumer. Depending on national law,[77] the authority or private party taking the initiative,[78] and the goal of the procedure,[79] either the UCPD, a financial regulation duty of care or the civil or common law duty of care will serve as legal basis for an enforcement procedure. The interpretation of the behavioural standard of the financial institution should nevertheless always be the same:[80] the UCPD should be interpreted taking into account the MiFID conduct of business rules (including more specific conduct of business rules and supervisory guidelines and interpretations); the MiFID duty of care should be interpreted taking into account the UCPD rules (specific practices which are blacklisted in Annex I to the UCPD should, for instance, also be considered contrary to the MiFID duty of care).[81]

---

level to eliminate unfair commercial practices may avoid the need for recourse to administrative or judicial action and should therefore be encouraged.' Even though the provision on codes of conduct is typically interpreted as applying to self-regulatory codes, one could see the MiFID conduct of business rules as 'specific mandatory requirements regulating the behaviour of traders', which provide 'evidence of the requirements of professional diligence in that sector'. It should be noted in this respect that MiFID-like codes of conduct indeed existed in certain Member States as self-regulatory tools before the introduction of the ISD. This interpretation would further confirm that the conduct of business rules of the financial sector do not overrule the UCPD rules as a *lex specialis*, but provide relevant input as to how to interpret the UCPD rules.

[77] In most Member States different authorities are competent for enforcing consumer law and financial law. In certain jurisdictions agreements clarify what Authority should take action and on what legal basis in case of overlap, in other jurisdictions this may be less clear. According to Dutch law, for instance, the Autoriteit Financiële Markten (AFM) should enforce a breach of the national implementation of the UCPD in the area of financial services or activities (see CWM Lieverse, 'Oneerlijke handelspraktijken en handhaving van consumentenbescherming in de financiële sector' (fn 53) at 17–25. In case certain behaviour falls in scope of both the national implementation of the UCPD and financial regulation, the AFM should enforce on the basis of financial regulation (at 111–113; see also the judgment of the court of Rotterdam, 20 July 2015, JOR 2016/62 (Sdu Jurisprudentie Onderneming & Recht), aflevering 3, 2016, and annotation of CWM Lieverse). In Belgium the Economic Inspection (FOD Economie, Middenstand en Energie) is the competent authority for enforcing the national implementation of the UCPD. If a specific case would also fall in the remit of financial regulation, for the enforcement of which the Financial Services and Market Authority (FSMA) is the competent authority, the FSMA and the Economic Inspection will consult each other in order to decide who will take action (see V Colaert, *De rechtsverhouding financiële dienstverlener – belegger* (fn 48) at 289). In the UK a 'concordat' between the Office of Fair Trading (OFT) and the Financial Conduct Authority (FCA), previously the FSA, deals with the matter: 'The FSA expects to address unfair commercial practices in financial services using its existing Handbook and other regulatory tools. The OFT and the FSA will work together to ensure that a consistent and co-ordinated approach is taken ... in relation to unfair commercial practices and to agree which of them is best placed to lead in each case' (Memorandum of Understanding between the Office of Fair Trading and the Financial Conduct Authority (2 April 2013), Annex C at 23.

[78] The consumer law Authority will enforce on the basis of the UCPD; the financial law Authority will enforce on the basis of financial regulation. Consumer organisations, moreover, may want to start an action for injunction, which requires a violation of one of the consumer law directives mentioned in Annex I to Directive 2009/22/EC of the European Parliament and of The Council of 23 April 2009 on injunctions for the protection of consumers' interests. In this situation, a consumer organisation will base its action against a financial institution on a violation of the UCPD.

[79] Stopping the violation via an action for injunction, sanctioning the financial institution, claiming damages, ...

[80] See also European Commission, 'Staff working document – Guidance on the implementation/application of directive 2005/29/EC on unfair commercial practices' (SWD(2016) 163 final, 25 May 2016) at 16 states in this respect: '... in order to ensure the proper enforcement of EU consumer protection laws, Member States should ensure coordination in good faith between the different competent enforcement authorities. In those Member States where different authorities are responsible for enforcing the UCPD and sector-specific legislation, the authorities should closely cooperate to ensure that the findings of their respective investigations into the same trader and/or commercial practice are consistent.'

[81] V Colaert, *De rechtsverhouding financiële dienstverlener – belegger* (fn 48) at 287; J Rinkes, 'Oneerlijke handelsprak-tijken en handhaving van consumentenbescherming in de financiële sector: een consumentenrechtelijk perspectief' in C Lieverse en J Rinkes, *Oneerlijke handelspraktijken en handhaving van consumentenbescherming in de financiële sector – Preadvies voor de Vereniging voor Effectenrecht 2010* (Deventer, Kluwer, 2010) at at 272, nr. 8. It also means that even though the UCPD only aims at minimum harmonization in respect of financial services (Art 3(9), UCPD), the maximum harmonisation character of the MiFID conduct of business rules, means that Member States should not go beyond the provisions of MiFID and the UCPD in the relationship between investment firms and their investor-clients (V Colaert, *De rechtsverhouding financiële dienstverlener – belegger* (fn 48) at 280).

Other financial regulation duties of care. The above reasoning can, in principle, also be made in respect of other financial regulation duties of care. The idea of a cumulative application is even explicitly confirmed in the IDD, which provides that the prohibition of misleading information is without prejudice to the UCPD (Article 17(2)). It should be noted, however, that the scope of protection of the UCPD is limited to 'consumers', ie 'any natural person who is acting for purposes which are outside his trade, business, craft or profession' (Article 2(a)). Whereas many retail clients qualify as such, professional clients will usually not be consumers. The UCPD duty of care will therefore not be relevant for, among others, central securities depositaries, central counterparties, trade repositories and credit rating agencies, which only deal with professional clients (see also section IV.C.).

C. Added Value of Financial Regulation Duties of Care on Top of the UCPD?

Overview. The UCPD contains a general duty of care which in principle also applies to the financial sector. At first sight, the UCPD's general prohibition of unfair commercial practices could therefore function as a cross-sectoral duty of care for the financial sector.[82] It is indeed a harmonised duty, so that the European Court of Justice can ensure a harmonised interpretation via preliminary rulings. The UCPD has, however, two characteristics which make the UCPD duty of care unsuitable to function as the cross-sectoral duty of care for the entire financial sector.

Supervision. First, we have established that the added value of financial regulation duties of care on top of civil or common law duties of care, is, among other things, that they are the legal basis for supervisory guidance and supervision (see section III.B.). It should be pointed out, however, that whereas supervisory authorities are competent to monitor compliance with relevant financial legislation, they do not enjoy the same competence with regard to the UCPD.[83] For the UCPD standards to function as a cross-sectoral duty of care for the financial sector, each relevant financial regulation directive or regulation would have to explicitly provide that (i) national and European financial supervisors could use the UCPD prohibition of unfair commercial practices to provide further guidance on the interpretation of the standard of professional diligence for particular financial institutions, and (ii) that those supervisors could also enforce non-compliance with the UCPD with administrative sanctions.

Scope of protection. Second, the scope of protection of most financial regulation duties of care differs from the scope of protection of the UCPD. As mentioned above, the UCPD intends to protect the 'consumer', ie 'any natural person who … is acting for purposes which are outside his trade, business, craft or profession'. Most financial legislation defines the protected party more broadly. MiFID for instance protects the much larger category of retail and professional clients; IDD protects all 'customers' of insurance intermediaries; and the UCITS and AIFM Directives protect all investors in those funds, without distinction.[84] For the UCPD prohibition of

---

[82] In this sense: I MacNeil, (fn 1) at 414–415: 'In principle it would seem that consumer law could do much of the work of conduct regulation while the integration of financial services into mainstream consumer law would align standards of conduct in financial services with other commercial activity' and 'since the practices targeted by the CPRs include a broadly framed general prohibition against unfair commercial practices, they have the capacity to take on a role similar to the FCA Principles for Business'.

[83] In MiFID II, for instance, the supervisory authority has a duty to 'monitor the activities of investment firms so as to assess compliance with the operating conditions provided for in this Directive.' (Art 22, MiFID II).

[84] See on this issue the contribution of MD Weinberger in this book.

unfair commercial practices to adequately function as the cross-sectoral duty of care in the areas regulated by those directives, those directives would have to explicitly provide that for purposes of the services and activities regulated in those directives, the UCPD has a broader scope of protection. Such a technique has indeed been used in the past already.[85] More problematic is that other financial institutions, such as central securities depositaries, central counterparties, trade repositories and credit rating agencies, only have professional clients and not 'consumers' in the sense of the UCPD. They are therefore not subject to the UCPD at all. The UCPD could therefore not function as a duty of care for those financial institutions.

Conclusion on the UCPD duty of care. Applying the UCPD-standard instead of the panoply of financial duties of care, could work in respect of financial services provided to consumers. Additional financial regulation should then, however, remedy the above shortcomings. This option would therefore not simplify the current situation.

V. Conclusion

Unsubstantiated differences in financial regulation duties of care. From the above overview we can conclude that not all actors on the financial markets are subject to a financial regulation duty of care. In those directives and regulations that do feature a duty of care, their core concepts and content have remained the same over the past 20 years, even though the precise wordings have varied. It is not clear whether these differences relate to an actual difference in the scope of the duty of care, or are simply the result of a lack of care and precision on the part of the legislator when drafting and/or translating the relevant provision in the different pieces of financial regulation. Our research did in any event not reveal any justification by the legislator of such differences, which leads us to conclude that they are mostly unsubstantiated.

Relevance of financial regulation duties of care alongside national civil/common law duties of care. Next to 'virtue signalling', we have found at least two types of added value of having financial regulation duties of care alongside national civil/common law duties of care. First, they allow to harmonise the standard of behaviour of financial institutions in relation to their clients, in contrast to the national civil or common law duties of care, which lead to different national interpretations of the standard of behaviour without the Court of Justice of the European Union having any competence to come up with common interpretations. Second, financial regulation duties of care are also a supervisory tool, and provide a legal basis for preventive supervisory guidance, especially in light of new market developments, and public enforcement.

Is there a need for one cross-sectoral duty of care for the entire financial sector? These two types of added value do not necessarily depend on having *one* cross-sectoral financial regulation duty of care. On the other hand, having one cross-sectoral duty of care would avoid unsubstantiated differences in wording which can create uncertainty as to the exact meaning of the duty in different legal instruments, and duplicate interpretation and translation efforts. Moreover, a cross-sectoral duty of care would have a catch-all function: all financial institutions, activities and

---

[85] Under the MiFID I-regime, implementing Dir 2006/73/EC provided that in any case where Art 3(3) of Dir 2002/65 on distance selling of financial services did not otherwise apply, the investment firm should comply with the requirements of that article in relation to the retail (potential) client, as if that client were a 'consumer' and the investment firm were a 'supplier' within the meaning of that Directive. In Belgian law, Art 25, s 3 of the law of 25 April 2014 on financial planners provides that when providing advice on financial planning, financial planners should comply with the Belgian provisions on consumer protection and market practices (Book VI of the Code of Economic Law), and act as if all their retail clients were consumers as defined in Belgian consumer law.

services would be covered by a financial regulation duty of care, avoiding any gaps. If one agrees that there is an important added value to having a financial regulation duty of care in client-facing relationships, it does not make much sense that certain areas of the financial sector are not subject to such a duty.

Can the UCPD prohibition of unfair commercial practices function as cross-sectoral duty of care for the financial industry? We have argued that the UCPD's prohibition of unfair commercial practices could in principle function as a cross-sectoral duty of care for financial institutions providing services to consumers. This solution would, however, also have a number of shortcomings. First, financial regulation would need to broaden the UCPD's scope of protection beyond 'consumers' to all clients of a financial institution. Second, financial regulation would have to explicitly provide that the national and European financial supervisors could use the UCPD prohibition of unfair market practices as a legal basis for fine-tuning the standard of professional diligence in the financial sector, and for enforcing non-compliance with the UCPD with administrative sanctions. For financial institutions providing services to professional clients only, the UCPD could, however, not function as the cross-sectoral duty of care. We have therefore concluded that this option would hardly simplify the current situation.

Is not having a common cross-sectoral duty of care for the financial sector problematic? As mentioned above, we are of the opinion that at least in theory a single cross-sectoral financial regulation duty of care would be preferable to the current situation, considering the inconsistent way in which the duty of care has been implanted into several pieces of financial legislation and to avoid gaps. Nevertheless, the current panoply of financial regulation duties of care does not seem to create substantial interpretation problems in practice. Moreover, for financial institutions dealing with consumers, the UCPD remains an important fall back directive in areas of the financial industry which do not (yet) have a sector-specific duty of care (such as crowdfunding or the sale of virtual currencies). Therefore, even though a single cross-sectoral duty of care would increase legal coherence and consistency, such benefit seems in itself insufficient to embark on cross-sectoral law-making on this specific issue. Naturally, if other topics of legislation would warrant such an effort, it would seem an obvious choice to also include the duty of care in a cross-sectoral piece of legislation.

14B

An 'Assist-Your-Customer Obligation' for the Financial Sector?

DANNY BUSCH, VEERLE COLAERT AND GENEVIÈVE HELLERINGER[1]

I. Introduction

The first part of this chapter (section II) compares four sets of similar 'know-your-customer' (KYC) rules in respect of investment products in the largest sense, namely those covered by the Markets in Financial Instruments Directive II (MiFID II), the Insurance Distribution Directive (IDD), the Regulation on a pan-European Personal Pension Product (PEPP)[2] and the (proposed) Crowdfunding Regulation.[3] The latter three sets of know-your-customer rules have been inspired by the original MiFID I rules. There are, however, a number of differences. The first part of the chapter will assess the similarities and differences to decide whether they are justified or not.

The second and third part of the chapter (sections III and IV) will compare the various know-your-customer requirements with a number of 'assist-your-customer' requirements in the banking and insurance sectors. While these latter requirements have (mostly) originated independently from the MiFID I KYC-rules, they share with them a comparable function or goal, ie assisting the customer in taking decisions adapted to his needs. We will first explore the 'demands and needs' analysis applicable to insurance and pension products under IDD and the PEPP Regulation. We will then turn to the duty of assistance, the advice test, and the responsible lending requirement of the Consumer Credit Directive (CCD) and the Mortgage Credit Directive (MCD). In those parts, we will assess how far the similarities in approach go, and should go.

By way of conclusion (section V) we will answer the question whether and to what extent a more cross-sectoral 'assist your customer rule' is warranted.

[1] The authors are very grateful to Eugenia Macchiavello and Michele Siri for their most valuable comments to an earlier draft of this text.

[2] Regulation (EU) 2019/1238 of the European Parliament and of the Council of 20 June 2019 on a pan-European Personal Pension Product (PEPP).

[3] Commission Proposal on European Crowdfunding Service Providers (ECSP) for Business (COM(2018)113, 8 March 2018), amended by the European Parliament European Parliament in its 'Legislative resolution of 27 March 2019 on the proposal for a regulation of the European Parliament and of the Council on European Crowdfunding Service

II. 'MiFID-Like' Know-Your-Customer Requirements for Investment Products in the Broad Sense

A. Overview

i. *MiFID II & IDD*

Suitability assessment. MiFID II contains a 'suitability assessment' for firms providing investment advice[4] or portfolio management services[5] to clients in connection with financial instruments and structured deposits.[6] IDD contains an almost identical suitability assessment for insurance undertakings and insurance intermediaries providing advice to customers on insurance-based investment products.[7]

Appropriateness assessment. In addition to the 'suitability assessment', MiFID II also contains an 'appropriateness assessment' which in principle applies to firms that provide 'execution-only services', that is, (1) reception and transmission of orders, (2) execution of orders, or (3) underwriting or placing of financial instruments, whether on a firm commitment basis or otherwise.[8] IDD contains a similar appropriateness assessment which in principle applies to insurance intermediaries and insurance undertakings that carry out insurance distribution activities in relation to sales of insurance-based investment products where no advice is given ('non-advised sales' or 'execution-only services').[9]

ii. *PEPP Regulation*

Only advised sales. Recital (30) of the PEPP Regulation states the following:

> Advice should be given to prospective PEPP savers by PEPP providers or PEPP distributors prior to the conclusion of the PEPP contract taking into account the long-term retirement nature of the product, the individual demands and needs of the PEPP saver and the limited redeemability. Advice should particularly aim at informing a PEPP saver about the features of the investment options, the level of capital protection and the forms of out-payments.

In view of this, the sale of PEPPs must necessarily be combined with advice.

Suitability assessment. It is therefore logical that the PEPP Regulation only contains a suitability assessment for financial undertakings that advise PEPP savers on pan-European

---

Providers (ECSP) for Business' (COM(2018)0113 – C8-0103/2018 – 2018/0048(COD)). On 24 June 2019 the Council of the European Union came up with a compromise proposal ('Proposal for a Regulation of the European Parliament and of the Council on European Crowdfunding Service Providers (ECSP) for Business and amending Regulation (EU) No 2017/1129 – Mandate for negotiations with the European Parliament – Compromise proposal' (Council 10557/19). Please note that in this chapter we discuss the Compromise Proposal of 24 June 2019 (Council 10557/19). This is not necessarily the final text that will be adopted. Where relevant, we will contrast the Compromise Proposal with the version of the text as adopted by the European Parliament on 27 March 2019.

[4] Defined as: 'the provision of personal recommendations to a client, either upon its request or at the initiative of the investment firm, in respect of one or more transactions relating to financial instruments, (see Art 4(1)(4), MiFID II).

[5] Defined as: 'managing portfolios in accordance with mandates given by clients on a discretionary client-by-client basis where such portfolios include one or more financial instruments' (see Art 4(1)(8), MiFID II).

[6] Article 25(2), MiFID II (for structured deposits read in conjunction with Art 1(4), MiFID II).

[7] See Art 30(1), IDD.

[8] Article 25(3), first paragraph, first sentence, MiFID II.

[9] Article 30(2), first paragraph, first sentence, IDD.

Personal Pension Products (PEPPs).[10] There exists no such concept as a PEPP appropriateness assessment for the non-advised sale of a PEPP.

iii. (Proposed) Crowdfunding Regulation

Entry knowledge test. Finally, crowdfunding service providers[11] must assess whether and which crowdfunding services offered are 'appropriate' for the prospective non-sophisticated investors.[12] This assessment within the meaning of the (proposed) Crowdfunding Regulation is referred to as an 'entry knowledge test'.[13] Thus, it applies at the level of the service in general, i.e., on a more abstract level than the MiFID II, IDD and PEPP Regulation suitability and appropriateness tests, which necessarily relate to specific investment products. Once the investor has access to one or more of the crowdfunding services offered, no further suitability or appropriateness tests apply, although the (proposed) Crowdfunding Regulation does provide for a number of other protective measures for non-sophisticated investors, including investment limits and warnings, and a reflection period.[14]

Crowdfunding services. After the 'entry knowledge test' has been complied with, the investor may be granted access to one or more of the crowdfunding services offered. 'Crowdfunding services' means the matching of business funding interest of investors and project owners through the use of a crowdfunding platform and which consist of any of the following: (1) the facilitation of granting of loans; (2) the placing without firm commitment as referred to in Annex I.A of MiFID II of transferable securities and admitted instruments for crowdfunding purposes issued by project owners or a special purpose vehicle, and the reception and transmission of investor orders, as referred to in Annex I.A of MiFID II, with regard to those products.[15]

Relationship with MiFID II. Even though individually, the reception and transmission of investor orders and placement of transferable securities without firm commitment match investment services covered by MiFID II, it is the joint provision of those services on a public platform that provides unrestricted access to investors that are the key features of crowdfunding services.[16] Crowdfunding service providers falling under the scope of the (proposed) Crowdfunding Regulation will be exempted from the application of MiFID II.[17] In a previous version of the proposal, also investment advice as referred to in Annex I.A of MiFID II with regard to transferable securities or the facilitation of loans issued by project owners, was considered a crowdfunding service.[18] In the Compromise Proposal investment advice is no longer regarded

---

[10] Financial undertakings entitled to advise on PEPPs are: credit institutions, insurance undertakings engaged in direct life insurance, institutions for occupational retirement provision (IORPs), investment firms providing portfolio management, UCITS Directive or UCITS Directive management companies, and EU alternative investment fund managers (EU AIFMs).

[11] 'Crowdfunding service provider' means a legal person who provides one or more crowdfunding services and has been authorised for that purpose by the relevant national competent authority in accordance with Art 10 of the (proposed) Crowdfunding Regulation. See Art 3(1)(c) Crowdfunding Regulation Compromise Proposal.

[12] Article 15(1) Crowdfunding Regulation Compromise Proposal.

[13] See the title of Art 15 of the Crowdfunding Regulation Compromise Proposal: 'Entry knowledge test and simulation of the ability to bear loss.'

[14] Article 15b and 15c of the Crowdfunding Regulation Compromise Proposal.

[15] See Article 3(1)(a) Crowdfunding Regulation Compromise Proposal.

[16] Recital 9 of the Compromise Proposal.

[17] Recital 44 of the Compromise Proposal refers to an unidentified Directive which will provide for such exemption.

[18] Article 4(a) of the text adopted by the European Parliament on 27 March 2019 (fn 3).

as a crowdfunding service. This means that a crowdfunding platform should not provide investment advice in respect of products which can be qualified as financial instruments or structured deposits under MiFID II, unless it is authorised as a MiFID II investment firm (or qualifies under one of the MiFID II exemptions).

B. Products in Scope

i. MiFID II and IDD

Financial instruments and structured deposits. The MiFID II suitability assessment applies (1) to advice and portfolio management with respect to *financial instruments* and (2) to advice with respect to *structured deposits*.[19] 'Financial instruments' are transferable securities (such as shares and bonds), money-market instruments, units in collective investment schemes, most derivatives products, and emission allowances.[20] A 'structured deposit' is a deposit on which the interest to be paid is not determined by reference to an interest rate (such as Euribor), but is instead dependent, for example, on the position of the AEX index.[21] The MiFID II appropriateness assessment applies to execution-only services solely with respect to financial instruments.[22]

Insurance-based investment products. The IDD suitability assessment applies to advice with respect to insurance-based investment products.[23] 'Insurance-based investment products' (or 'IBIPs') are defined as insurance products which offer a maturity or surrender value, where that value is exposed to market fluctuations.[24] The IDD appropriateness assessment applies to non-advised sales with respect to insurance-based investment products.[25]

Common denominator. The common denominator is that financial instruments, structured deposits and insurance-based investment products are all investment products, as they are all, in whole or in part, and directly or indirectly, exposed to market fluctuations.

---

[19] See Art 25(2) (financial instruments), read in conjunction with Art 1(4), MiFID II (structured deposits).

[20] See Art 4(1)(15) read in conjunction with Annex I, Section C of MiFID II.

[21] See Art 4(1)(43), MiFID II read in conjunction with Art 2(1)(c) of DGS, OJ L173/149, 12 June 2014 (Deposit Guarantee Schemes Directive).

[22] Does MiFID II extend the appropriateness assessment to (1) the reception and transmission of orders in 'structured deposits', and (2) the execution of orders in respect of a 'structured deposit' on behalf of a client? Strictly speaking, Art 1(4), MiFID II merely provides that the KYC rules must be complied with in *providing advice* on structured deposits and in their *sale*. The *sale* of a structured deposit means, basically, that a credit institution or investment firm acts purely as the buyer's contractual counterparty (dealing on its own account). Such a transaction does not result in (1) the reception and transmission of orders in relation to structured deposits, and/or (2) the execution of orders in relation to a structured deposit on behalf of the client. On the other hand, it is perhaps conceivable that the European legislator would not wish to exclude the application of the appropriateness assessment to the reception and transmission of orders in structured deposits and the execution of orders in structured deposits on behalf of the client. The term 'sale' should therefore be broadly interpreted in relation to structured deposits. Another approach would be to reclassify the sale of a structured deposit as the execution of an order in a structured deposit on behalf of the client, by analogy with the manner in which this happens in the sale of a financial instrument issued by the credit institution or investment firm itself. See Art 4(1), at (5), MiFID II. In one of these ways the appropriateness assessment could also be applicable to the sale of structured deposits.

[23] See Art 30(1), first paragraph, IDD.

[24] See Art 2(1)(17), IDD. The following products are, however, excluded from the definition: (i) non-life insurance products, (ii) life insurance contracts where the benefits under the contract are payable only on death or in respect of incapacity due to injury, sickness or disability, and (iii) pension products. See Art 2(1)(17), IDD.

[25] See Art 30(2), first paragraph, first sentence, IDD.

ii. PEPP Regulation

PEPP. If advice is provided on *pan-European Personal Pension Products*, the PEPP suitability assessment applies. A 'pan-European Personal Pension Product' or 'PEPP' is an individual, non-occupational pension product subscribed to voluntarily by a PEPP saver in view of retirement, and which has no or strictly limited possibility for early redemption.[26] A PEPP is to be qualified as a long-term investment product.[27] It is therefore an investment product, alongside financial instruments, structured deposits and insurance-based investment products.

iii. (Proposed) Crowdfunding Regulation

Loans and transferable securities. Crowdfunding services necessarily relate to business loans transferable securities or so-called 'admitted instruments for crowdfunding purposes'.[28] Transferable securities (such as shares and bonds) are naturally investment products. They are included in the broader category of financial instruments in the sense of MiFID II. Nevertheless, the (proposed) Crowdfunding Regulation also applies to loans which cannot be qualified as transferable securities. Loans granted to project owners (ie businesses) through the facilitation of a platform and admitted instruments are in our view sufficiently close to other investment products such as (listed) bonds and shares to qualify them as investment products.[29] 'Admitted instruments for crowdfunding purposes' are shares of a limited liability company, provided that the transfer of such shares is not subject to restrictions which would effectively prevent the shares from being transferred.[30]

C. Scope of Protection

i. MiFID II

Professional clients. MiFID II gives an exhaustive list of parties classified as professional clients. They include banks, investment firms and other authorised or regulated financial institutions such as undertakings for collective investment in transferable securities (UCITS) Directive and alternative investment funds (AIFs). Undertakings that meet certain quantitative requirements ('large undertakings'), national and regional governments and a number of international or supranational institutions and organisations, and institutional investors whose main activity is to invest in financial instruments, are also classified as professional clients.[31]

---

[26] See Recital (20) and Art 2 sub (2) PEPP Regulation (EU) 2019/1238.

[27] See, eg, Recitals (1), (4), (11), and (16) PEPP Regulation (EU) 2019/1238.

[28] See Art 3(1)(g) Crowdfunding Regulation Compromise Proposal, where 'investor' is defined as any person that, through a crowdfunding platform, grants loans or acquires transferable securities or admitted instruments for crowdfunding purposes.

[29] In Belgium the term 'investment instrument' is already used in the Prospectus Law to also cover, among other things 'all other instruments which allow making a financial investment' (Art (3), s 1 11° of the Prospectus Law of 11 July 2018). This has been interpreted as including standardised loan agreements.

[30] See Art 3(1)(aa), (i) and (ia) Crowdfunding Regulation for definitions of 'loans', 'transferable securities' and 'admitted instruments for crowdfunding purposes'.

[31] An undertaking is categorised as large if it meets two of the following size requirements on a company basis: (1) a balance sheet total of EUR 20 million; (2) net turnover of EUR 40 million; and (3) own funds of EUR 2 million. For a complete list of parties categorised as professional clients, see Annex II to MiFID II.

Retail clients. All clients not classified as professional clients are deemed to be *retail clients*. These include private clients and undertakings that do not meet the quantitative criteria for large undertakings (ie SMEs).[32]

Eligible counterparties. Under MiFID II, there is, finally, the possibility for the first category of professional clients to be treated as 'eligible counterparties'.[33] This category is applicable only in relation to the execution of orders on behalf of clients, dealing on own account and receiving and transmitting orders, or ancillary services directly relating to such transactions.[34] The category of eligible counterparty is therefore not relevant to, amongst others, portfolio management and investment advice. In respect of the latter services, there are only two possibilities for the investment firm: to classify the client either as a retail client or as a professional client.

Changing client category. Under MiFID II, clients may, if certain conditions are fulfilled, switch to a different category either on a trade-by-trade basis or for the provision of the service in general. Such a request may be made for more protection (opting down) or for less protection (opting up). A firm should inform its clients of the possibility of opting up and opting down, and about how this will lower or raise the level of protection.[35]

ii. IDD

Customers. The scope of protection of IDD is rather ambiguous.[36] Despite the use of the (non-defined) term 'consumer' in Recital (43), the legally binding provisions of the IDD mostly use the (equally undefined) term 'customer'. The IDD in any event does not distinguish between retail and professional customers, but does refer to a Member States' option to soften certain information requirements in relations with professional clients. The IDD further empowers the Commission to adopt delegated acts with respect to the KYC requirements, taking into account, among other things, 'the retail or professional nature of the customer or potential customer'.[37] However, Commission Delegated Regulation (EU)2017/2359, which implements the IDD KYC requirements, does not make any such distinction.

iii. PEPP Regulation

PEPP saver. A 'PEPP saver' means a natural person who has concluded a PEPP contract with a manufacturer or distributor of PEPPs.[38]

---

[32] Article 4 (1)(11), MiFID II.

[33] Article 45(1) Commission Delegated Regulation (EU) 2017/565. The list of eligible counterparties is virtually identical to the list of professional clients, save for two exceptions (one of which is the large undertakings). Art 30(2), first paragraph, MiFID II.

[34] Article 30(1), MiFID II.

[35] For more detail and the exact conditions for opting up and opting down, see: Art 45 Commission Delegated Regulation (EU) 2017/565 MiFID II, Art 30(2), second paragraph, MiFID II, Annex II at II, MiFID II, Art 71 Commission Delegated Regulation (EU) 2017/565 MiFID II.

[36] See in more detail chapter 12 of this book.

[37] Recital 51 and Arts 22(1) and 30(6), IDD. With respect to conflicts of interest, Art 28(3) requires that the disclosure include 'sufficient detail taking into account the nature of the customer'. It is not clear whether this refers to a professional or retail classification, or to any other aspects which define the nature of the customer. Interesting in this regard is that, for purposes of the PRIIPs regulation, a 'retail client' is defined as (a) a retail client as defined in Art 4(1)11, MiFID II, or (b) a customer within the meaning of IDD, where that customer would not qualify as a professional client as defined in MiFID II (Art 6(4), PRIIPs Regulation).

[38] See Art 2(3) PEPP Regulation (EU) 2019/1238.

iv. (Proposed) Crowdfunding Regulation

Investor. Under the (proposed) Crowdfunding Regulation, 'investor' is defined as any person that, through a crowdfunding platform, grants loans or acquires transferable securities.[39] Even though previous versions of the proposal did not differentiate between different types of investors, the Compromise Proposal distinguishes between non-sophisticated and sophisticated investors. This distinction builds on the distinction between professional clients and retail clients established in MiFID II, but also considers experience and knowledge of potential investors in crowdfunding.[40] In fact the (proposed) Regulation draws a new distinction, which is clearly inspired by the MiFID II distinction, but with different, more lenient criteria. For instance, the criteria for non-sophisticated investors to opt-up and become a sophisticated investor are much more flexible than for retail investors to be requalified as a professional investor under MiIFD II.[41] Likewise, large undertakings under MiFID II are considered sophisticated investors under the proposed Crowdfunding Regulation,[42] but a 'large entity' – which should only meet much lower criteria – can also request an opt-up and be requalified as a sophisticated investor.[43]

v. Cross-sectoral Perspective

Unjustified differences between MiFID, IDD and the Crowdfunding Regulation. The scope of protection of the IDD differs substantially from the MiFID II know-your-customer requirements. If insurance-based investment products are indeed substitutes for many MiFID II financial instruments, this different approach seems hard to justify.[44] In relation to crowdfunding, however, levelling the cross-sectoral playing field for investor protection is not the only consideration. The EU legislator is of the opinion that in order to make crowdfunding work, the regulation must strike a balance between investor protection and easy market access for SMEs, particularly for start-ups. In view of the latter consideration, the regulator has attempted to reduce the costs and therefore the compliance burden for crowdfunding services. The new distinction in the proposed Crowdfunding Regulation between sophisticated and non-sophisticated investors could stem from this concern. It seems contradictory, however, that the group of 'non-sophisticated investors' for purposes of crowdfunding services is smaller than the group of 'retail investors' for 'traditional' MiFID investment services, while the risks of crowdfunding investments are higher. Those differences seem unjustified.

Justified difference in respect of PEPP Regulation. In respect of the PEPP Regulation, on the other hand, the difference in scope of protection seems fully justified in view of the nature of the product, since only natural persons save for their pensions.

---

[39] Article 3(1)(g) Crowdfunding Regulation Compromise Proposal.

[40] Recital 29c, Art 3(1)(ga) and (gb) and Annex II of the Crowdfunding Regulation Compromise Proposal.

[41] See Annex II.I.B of the Crowdfunding Regulation Compromise Proposal, compared to Annex II.II.1. MiFID II.

[42] Annex II.III of the Crowdfunding Regulation Compromise Proposal.

[43] See Annex II.I.A of the Crowdfunding Regulation Compromise Proposal (at least two of the following criteria should be met: own funds of own funds of at least EUR 100,000; net turnover of at least EUR 2,000,000; balance sheet of at least EUR 1,000,000) compared to large undertakings in Annex II.I.(2) of MiFID II (at least two of the following criteria should be met: balance sheet total: EUR 20,000,000; net turnover: EUR 40,000,000; own funds: EUR 2,000,000).

[44] In a recent case dealing with the same issue under current Belgian law, the Belgian Constitutional Court held contrary to the constitutional principle of equal treatment, the fact that unlike investment services providers, insurance services providers had no possibility to distinguish between retail and professional clients (and therefore had to comply with the demanding conduct of business regime for retail clients in respect of all customers) (Belgian Constitutional Court, Judgment No 89/2016 (9 June 2016), www.const-court.be/public/n/2016/2016-089n.pdf).

D. Suitability Assessment in MiFID II, IDD and PEPP Regulation

i. Scope of the Assessment

a. MiFID II & IDD

Level 1. Under MiFID II, with respect to 'retail clients' (ie consumers and SMEs) the suitability assessment requires the firm to obtain information regarding (a) the (potential) retail client's *knowledge and experience* in the investment field relevant to the specific type of product or service, (b) his *financial situation* (including his ability to bear losses) and (c) his *investment objectives* (including his risk tolerance), so as to enable the firm to recommend to the (potential) retail client the investment services and products that are suitable for him (and, in particular, are in accordance with his risk tolerance and ability to bear losses).[45] IDD imposes almost exactly the same suitability assessment with respect to 'customers'.[46]

Level 2 legislation. Under MiFID II, the information to be obtained from the (potential) retail client is further specified in level 2 legislation. The information about the retail client's *knowledge and experience* includes, where relevant, information on (a) the types of services, transactions and products with which the retail client is familiar, (b) the nature, volume, and frequency of the retail client's transactions in products and the period over which they have been carried out, and (c) the level of education, and profession or relevant former profession of the (potential) retail client.[47] The information about his *financial situation* includes, where relevant, information on (1) the source and extent of his regular income, (2) his assets (including liquid assets, investments and real property), and (3) his regular financial commitments.[48] The information about *investment objectives* includes, where relevant, information on (i) the length of time for which the retail client wishes to hold the investment (investment horizon), (ii) his preferences regarding risk taking (risk tolerance), (iii) his risk profile, and (iv) the purposes of the investment.[49] Again, IDD has adopted almost precisely the same further specifications in level 2 legislation.[50] The IDD Delegated Regulation, however, adds that where information required for the IDD suitability assessment has already been obtained for the purposes of the demands and needs analysis (see section III of this chapter), the insurance intermediary or insurance undertaking need not request it anew from the customer.[51] A similar provision is not included in MiFID II, since it does not feature a demands and needs analysis (regarding whether the IDD demands and needs analysis is useful on top of the IDD suitability assessment, see section III of this chapter).

Level 3. The Suitability Guidelines published by the European Securities and Market Authority (ESMA) provide much more detail concerning MiFID II.[52] In respect of IDD, however, the European Insurance and Occupational Pensions Authority (EIOPA) has not yet come up with further guidelines on suitability. It would have been preferable for ESMA and EIOPA to have

---

[45] Article 25(2), first paragraph, MiFID II. See also Art 54(2) Commission Delegated Regulation (EU) 2017/565.
[46] Article 30(1), first paragraph, IDD. See also Art 9(1) and (2) Commission Delegated Regulation (EU) 2017/2359.
[47] Article 55(1) Commission Delegated Regulation (EU) 2017/565.
[48] Article 54(4) Commission Delegated Regulation (EU) 2017/565.
[49] Article 54(5) Commission Delegated Regulation (EU) 2017/565.
[50] Article 17(1), Art 9(3), first sentence, and Art 9(4), first sentence, Commission Delegated Regulation (EU) 2017/2359.
[51] Article 17(3) Commission Delegated Regulation (EU) 2017/2359.
[52] See ESMA35-43-1163 (6 November 2018).

cooperated to come up with common guidelines. Indeed, it not only seems rather inefficient for EIOPA to duplicate the work done by ESMA, it also increases the chances of unsubstantiated differences.

Treatment of professional clients. Under MiFID II, if an investment firm provides investment advice or portfolio management services to a 'professional client' (including an opt-up professional client), the firm is entitled to *assume* that the client has the necessary experience and knowledge to understand the risks involved in the transaction.[53] In providing investment advice (but not portfolio management services), the firm is also entitled to assume that a professional client (but not an opt-up professional client) is able to bear any financial losses that may occur.[54] This means, therefore, that information needs to be obtained only concerning the client's risk tolerance and investment objectives. Since the IDD does not distinguish between retail and professional clients (see section II.C.ii. above), the full suitability test will need to apply in respect of customers that would qualify as professional clients under MiFID II, unless Member States have made use of the option to soften certain requirements in respect of professional customers. There does not seem to be any justification for this difference between MiFID II and IDD.

ESG preferences. Finally, it is noteworthy that the European Commission recently launched its Sustainable Finance Action Plan. One of the concrete actions included in the Action Plan concerns the incorporation of sustainability considerations when providing advice or portfolio management services under MiFID II and IDD. According to the European Commission, a client's preferences as regards sustainability are often not sufficiently taken into account when advice is given or portfolio management services are provided. For this reason, the Commission proposes that MiFID II and IDD firms should ask about their clients' preferences (such as environmental, social and governance (ESG) factors) and take them into account when assessing the range of financial instruments and investment-based insurance products to be recommended, ie in the product selection process and suitability assessment.[55] In view of this, the Commission has launched a consultation to assess how best to include ESG considerations in the advice that investment firms and insurance distributors offer to individual clients. The aim is to amend delegated acts under MiFID II and IDD.[56] Both ESMA and EIOPA came up with technical advice to the Commission in this respect. Encouragingly, EIOPA and ESMA report having closely liaised during the preparation of the technical advice to ensure consistency across sectors.[57] Meanwhile, ESMA already addressed the topic in paragraph 28 of its updated Guidelines on certain aspects of the MiFID II suitability requirements of 6 November 2018 by stating that

> ESMA considers it would be a good practice for firms to consider non-financial elements when gathering information on the client's investment objectives, and [...] collect information on the client's preferences on environmental, social and governance factors.[58]

---

[53] Article 54(3), first paragraph, Commission Delegated Regulation (EU) 2017/565.
[54] Article 54(3), second paragraph, Commission Delegated Regulation (EU) 2017/565.
[55] European Commission, Action Plan: Financing Sustainable Growth, COM(2018) 97 final (8 March 2018), p 6–7.
[56] Commission Delegated Regulation (EU) .../... of XXX, amending Delegated Regulation (EU) 2017/2359 with regard to environmental, social and governance preferences in the distribution of insurance-based investment products, Ref Ares(2018)2681527 – 24/05/2018, and Commission Delegated Regulation (EU) .../... of XXX amending Regulation (EU) 2017/565 supplementing Directive 2014/65/EU of the European Parliament and of the Council as regards organisational requirements and operating conditions for investment firms and defined terms for the purposes of that Directive, Ref Ares(2018)2681500 – 24/05/2018.
[57] EIOPA, 'Technical Advice on the integration of sustainability risks and factors in the delegated acts under Solvency II and IDD' (EIOPA-BoS-19/172 30 April 2019) at 4, para 8; ESMA, 'Final Report – Technical advice to the European Commission on integrating sustainability risks and factors in MiFID II' (ESMA35-43-1737, 30 April 2019) at 7.
[58] See ESMA35-43-1163 (6 November 2018), at No 28. For the Commission's invitation to ESMA to address this, see: European Commission, Action Plan: Financing Sustainable Growth, COM(2018) 97 final (8 March 2018), p 7. Regarding

In its consultation paper dated 19 December 2018 on integrating sustainability risks and factors in MiFID II, ESMA proposes to strengthen its approach by clarifying that firms 'should' collect information from clients in relation to their ESG preferences.[59] As mentioned above, EIOPA has not yet come up with suitability guidelines in respect of IDD.

b. PEPP Regulation

IDD suitability rules. When PEPPs are advised by (1) insurance undertakings engaged in direct life insurance or (2) insurance intermediaries, the IDD suitability rules for advice on insurance-based investment products apply.[60] This means that the IDD suitability rules described under section a. above apply to PEPPs advised by such financial undertakings, including ESG considerations.

MiFID II suitability rules. When PEPPs are advised by investment firms that did not create the relevant PEPPs, the MiFID II suitability rules for investment advice to retail clients apply.[61] This means that the MiFID II suitability rules described under section a. above apply to PEPPs advised by such investment firms, including ESG considerations.

PEPP suitability rules. All other manufacturers and distributors advising on PEPPs than those discussed above, must comply with the suitability rules for advice which are included in the PEPP Regulation itself.[62] According to these suitability rules, such a PEPP adviser must ask the prospective PEPP saver to provide information regarding (a) that person's *knowledge and experience* in the investment field relevant to the PEPP offered or demanded, (b) that person's *financial situation* (including his or her ability to bear losses), and (c) his or her *investment objectives* (including his or her risk tolerance, so as to enable the PEPP provider or PEPP distributor to recommend to the prospective PEPP saver one or more PEPPs that are suitable for that person and, in particular, are in accordance with his or her risk tolerance and ability to bear losses. The PEPP suitability rules are much less detailed than the IDD and MiFID II suitability rules. Moreover, the PEPP Regulation does not currently provide for the possibility to adopt level 2 legislation to provide more detail on suitability assessments.

ESG considerations. Also, the PEPP suitability rules included in the PEPP Regulation do not contain an explicit reference to ESG considerations. It should, however, be pointed out that in recital (8), such considerations are mentioned in a more general sense:

> [the PEPP Regulation] enables the creation of a personal pension product which will have a long-term retirement nature and will take into account environmental, social and governance (ESG) factors a referred to in the United Nations-supported Principles for Responsible Investment, insofar as possible (…).[63]

Cross-sectoral perspective. It follows from the above that different rules will apply to savers, depending on the intermediary selling the PEPP. From the perspective of a cross-sectoral, level playing field, this approach is difficult to accept.

---

the Commission's Sustainable Finance Action Plan, see: D Busch, G Ferrarini & A Van den Hurk, The European Commission's Sustainable Finance Action Plan, in: F-J. Beekhoven van den Boezem, C Jansen & B Schuijling (eds), *Sustainability and Financial Markets* (Law of Business & Finance Volume 17, Wolters Kluwer, 2019), p 35–58.

[59] See for further details ESMA35-43-1210 (19 December 2018), pp 21–25 in respect of para 28 of the Suitability Guidelines.

[60] Article 23(1)(a) PEPP Regulation (EU) 2019/1238, read in conjunction with Art 30, IDD.

[61] Article 23(1)(b) PEPP Regulation (EU) 2019/1238, read in conjunction with Art 25, MiFID II.

[62] Article 23(1)(c) and Art 34(4) PEPP Regulation (EU) 2019/1238.

[63] See also Recitals (47) and (51).

ii. Who is Subject to the Suitability Assessment (Legal Persons, Groups and Representatives)?

a. MiFID II

Who is subject to the suitability assessment? Under MiFID II, where (1) a client is a legal person, (2) a client consists of a group of two or more natural persons, or (3) one or more natural persons are represented by another natural person, the investment firm must establish and implement a policy as to who should be subject to the suitability assessment and how this assessment will be done in practice, including from whom information about knowledge and experience, financial situation and investment objectives should be collected. The investment firm must record this policy. Where a natural person is represented by another natural person or where a legal person having requested treatment as a professional client in accordance with Section 2 of Annex II of MiFID II is to be considered for the suitability assessment, the financial situation and investment objectives must be those of the legal person or, in relation to the natural person, the underlying client rather than the representative. The knowledge and experience, on the other hand, must be those of the representative of the natural person or the person authorised to carry out transactions on behalf of the underlying client.[64]

b. IDD

No rules similar to MiFID II. Similar rules to the MiFID II rules discussed under a. above are not included in IDD. While many IBIPs are only useful for natural persons, there are also IBIPs which can be bought by legal persons. Moreover, situations can in any event arise where one natural person is represented by another person. The lack of rules in IDD to regulate who should be subject to the suitability assessment in such cases seems, therefore, unjustified.

Group insurance. However, IDD does contain a provision on the related topic of suitability assessments in relation to group insurance. With regard to group insurance, the insurance intermediary or insurance undertaking must establish and implement a policy as to who will be subject to the suitability assessment in case an insurance contract is concluded on behalf of a group of members and each individual member cannot take an individual decision to join. Such a policy must also contain rules on how the assessment will be done in practice, including from whom information about knowledge and experience, financial situation and investment objectives must be collected.[65] This difference is clearly warranted in view of the nature of the product.

c. PEPP Regulation

Independent PEPP savers associations. An independent PEPP savers association can also subscribe to PEPPs on behalf of its members, as provided by Recital (24) of the PEPP Regulation:

> A PEPP contract might also be concluded by the representative of a group of PEPP savers, such as an independent savers association, acting on behalf of that group provided that this is done in compliance with [the PEPP Regulation] and applicable national law and that PEPP savers subscribing in this way obtain the same information and advice as PEPP savers concluding a PEPP contract either directly with a PEPP provider or through a PEPP distributor.

---

[64] Article 54(6) Commission Delegated Regulation (EU) 2017/565.
[65] Article 13 Commission Delegated Regulation (EU) 2017/2359.

This means that in the case where an independent PEPP savers association subscribes on behalf of its members, the PEPP suitability assessment must be undertaken on an individual basis.

iii. Cross-selling

MiFID II. Under MiFID II, cross-selling exists when an investment service is offered together with another service or product as part of a package or as a condition for the same agreement or package.[66] Where a firm recommends such a package of services or products to retail or professional clients, the overall bundle should be suitable.[67]

   IDD. In a similar vein, IDD defines cross-selling as the practice by which an insurance product is offered together with an ancillary product or service which is not insurance, as part of a package or the same agreement.[68] IDD applies (almost) verbatim the MiFID II rule with respect to an insurance intermediary or insurance undertaking providing investment advice recommending a package of services or products to customers.[69]

   PEPP Regulation. As discussed above, the MiFID II suitability assessment applies when PEPPs are advised by investment firms which did not manufacture the relevant PEPPs, whereas the IDD suitability assessment applies when PEPPs are advised either by insurance undertakings engaged in direct life insurance or by insurance intermediaries. In such cases, the MiFID II or IDD cross-selling rules for advice on insurance-based investment products apply. All other manufacturers and distributors advising on PEPPs must comply with the suitability rules for advice that are included in the PEPP Regulation itself. Unfortunately, the PEPP Regulation itself does not include rules on cross-selling. From the perspective of a cross-sectoral, level playing field, this approach is difficult to accept.

iv. Where Insufficient Information is Provided/None of the Services or Products are Suitable

MiFID II. Under MiFID II, if a firm fails to obtain the specified information, it may not recommend investment services or products to a (potential) retail client.[70] Similarly, where none of the services or products are suitable for the retail or professional client, the firm may not recommend or decide to trade.[71]

   IDD. Again, IDD applies (almost) exactly the same rules to insurance intermediaries and insurance undertakings in the context of the IDD suitability assessment with respect to customers.[72]

   Proposed PEPP Regulation. As discussed above, the MiFID II suitability assessment applies when PEPPs are advised by investment firms that did not manufacture the relevant PEPPs, whereas the IDD suitability assessment applies when PEPPs are advised by insurance undertakings engaged in direct life insurance or by insurance intermediaries. In such cases, the rules

---

[66] See for further detail Art 24(11), MiFID II. For an elaborate discussion of the different rules on cross-selling in financial regulation, see: V Colaert, 'Cross-selling practices in the financial sector: Whose cross to bear?' (KU Leuven Working Paper, 2019).

[67] Article 25(2), second paragraph, MiFID II.

[68] Article 24(1) IDD. See for further detail Art 24 IDD.

[69] Article 30(1), second paragraph, IDD.

[70] Article 54(8) Commission Delegated Regulation (EU) 2017/565.

[71] Article 54(10) Commission Delegated Regulation (EU) 2017/565.

[72] Article 9(5) and (6) Commission Delegated Regulation (EU) 2017/2359.

discussed above will apply when insufficient information is provided or when none of the services or products are suitable to a PEPP saver. The PEPP Regulation does not provide anything for such situations for all other manufacturers and distributors advising on PEPPs. This may, however, be the subject of a level 2 text at a later stage.

v. How to Obtain Reliable Information

MiFID II. Under the MiFID II suitability test, a firm is entitled to rely on the information provided by its (potential) retail clients, unless it is or should be aware that the information is manifestly out of date, inaccurate or incomplete.[73] It must, however, take reasonable steps to ensure that the information collected about its clients is reliable. This includes (but is not limited to) (a) ensuring clients are aware of the importance of providing accurate and up-to-date information; (b) ensuring all tools employed in the suitability assessment process, such as risk assessment profiling tools or tools to assess a client's knowledge and experience, are fit-for-purpose and are appropriately designed for use with its clients, with any limitations identified and actively mitigated through the suitability assessment process; (c) ensuring questions used in the process are likely to be understood by clients, capture an accurate reflection of the client's objectives and needs, and solicit the information necessary to undertake the suitability assessment; and (d) taking steps, as appropriate, to ensure the consistency of client information, such as by considering whether there are obvious inaccuracies in the information provided by clients.[74] The ESMA suitability guidelines[75] provide further guidance in this respect.

IDD. Again, IDD applies (almost) exactly the same rule to insurance intermediaries and insurance undertakings in the context of the IDD suitability assessment.[76] However, as mentioned above, EIOPA has not yet taken action in this area.

Proposed PEPP Regulation. Since the MiFID II suitability assessment applies when PEPPs are advised by investment firms that did not manufacture the relevant PEPPs, and the IDD suitability assessment applies when PEPPs are advised by insurance undertakings engaged in direct life insurance or insurance intermediaries, the abovementioned rules apply in respect of the reliability of information. Again, the proposed PEPP Regulation does not provide any rules in this respect for all other manufacturers and distributors advising on PEPPs. This may, however, be the subject of a level 2 text at a later stage.

vi. Switching Investments

MiFID II. Under MiFID II, when providing investment advice or portfolio management services that involve switching investments (either by selling a product and buying another, or by exercising a right to make a change in regard to an existing product), the firm must collect the necessary information on the client's existing investments and the recommended new investments. The firm must also undertake an analysis of the costs and benefits of the switch, so as to reasonably be able to demonstrate that the benefits of switching are greater than the costs.[77]

---

[73] Article 55(3) Commission Delegated Regulation (EU) 2017/565.
[74] Article 54(7) Commission Delegated Regulation (EU) 2017/565.
[75] See ESMA35-43-1163 (6 November 2018).
[76] Articles 10 and 17(4) Commission Delegated Regulation (EU) 2017/2359.
[77] Article 54(11) Commission Delegated Regulation (EU) 2017/565.

IDD. IDD applies almost word for word the same rules when insurance intermediaries and insurance undertakings provide advice that involves switching between underlying assets.[78]

Proposed PEPP Regulation. Again, since the MiFID II suitability assessment applies when PEPPs are advised by investment firms that did not manufacture the relevant PEPPs, and the IDD suitability assessment applies when PEPPs are advised by insurance undertakings engaged in direct life insurance or insurance intermediaries, the abovementioned rules apply in respect of the switching of investments. The proposed PEPP Regulation does not provide any rules in this respect for all other manufacturers and distributors advising on PEPPs. This may, however, be the subject of a level 2 text at a later stage.

vii. Suitability Reports and Suitability Statements

MiFID II. Under MiFID II, when providing investment advice, firms must provide a report to the *retail client* that includes (a) an outline of the advice given and (b) how the recommendation provided is suitable for the retail client, including how it meets (i) the retail client's objectives and personal circumstances with reference to the investment term required, (ii) the retail client's knowledge and experience, and (iii) the retail client's attitude to risk and capacity for loss.[79] Firms must draw retail clients' attention to and must include in the suitability report information on whether the recommended services or instruments are likely to require the retail client to seek a periodic review of their arrangements.[80] Where a firm provides a service that involves periodic suitability assessments and reports, subsequent reports issued after the initial service is established may only need to cover changes in the services or instruments involved and/or the circumstances of the client.[81]

IDD. IDD has adopted very similar provisions.[82]

Proposed PEPP Regulation. Again, the MiFID II or IDD suitability assessment applies in the circumstances discussed above, including the respective rules regarding suitability reports and statements. The proposed PEPP Regulation does not provide any rules in this respect for all other manufacturers and distributors advising on PEPPs. This may, again, be the subject of a level 2 text at a later stage.

viii. Automated Advice and Automated Portfolio Management

MiFID II. Under MiFID II, where investment advice or portfolio management services are provided in whole or in part through an automated or semi-automated system, the responsibility to undertake the suitability assessment still applies, and lies with the firm providing the service.[83] ESMA's suitability guidelines provide further guidance in this respect.[84]

IDD. Again, IDD applies almost exactly the same rule to insurance intermediaries and insurance undertakings in the context of automated or semi-automated advice to customers on

---

[78] Article 9(7) Commission Delegated Regulation (EU) 2017/2359.
[79] Article 54(12), first paragraph, Commission Delegated Regulation (EU) 2017/565.
[80] Article 54(12), second paragraph, Commission Delegated Regulation (EU) 2017/565.
[81] Article 54(12), third paragraph, Commission Delegated Regulation (EU) 2017/565.
[82] Article 14(1), (2) and (3) Commission Delegated Regulation (EU) 2017/2359.
[83] Article 54(2) Commission Delegated Regulation (EU) 2017/565.
[84] See in particular paras 6, 7, 20, 21, 32 and 51 of ESMA35-43-1163 (6 November 2018).

insurance-based investment products.[85] As mentioned above, EIOPA has, however, not yet come up with suitability guidelines.

PEPP. Again, since the MiFID II or IDD suitability assessments apply in the circumstances discussed above, also the respective abovementioned rules on automated advice will apply in those circumstances. The proposed PEPP Regulation itself also stipulates that the responsibilities of the PEPP provider may not be reduced due to the fact that advice is provided in whole or in part through an automated or semi-automated system.[86] This safeguards that a similar rule applies to all other manufacturers and distributors advising on PEPPs, even though it remains to be seen whether EIOPA will develop level 3 guidance similar to the ESMA guidance in regard of MiFID.

E. Appropriateness Assessment: MiFID and IDD

As mentioned in section II.A.ii., PEPPs can only be sold in an advised context, meaning that the PEPP Regulation only features a suitability test and no appropriateness test.

i. Scope of the Assessment

Level 1. Under MiFID II, with respect to 'retail clients' (ie consumers and SMEs)[87] the appropriateness assessment requires the firm to ask the (potential) retail client to provide information regarding that person's *knowledge and experience* in the investment field relevant to the specific type of product or service offered or demanded so as to enable the investment firm to assess whether the investment service or product envisaged is appropriate for the client.[88] IDD applies (almost) verbatim the same appropriateness assessment with respect to 'customers'.[89]

Level 2. The information to be obtained from the (potential) retail client on his *knowledge and experience* is further specified in MiFID II and IDD Level 2 legislation (see section D.i.a. above). Moreover, the MiFID II Delegated Regulation provides that the appropriateness assessment need not be applied in relation to professional clients and eligible counterparties.[90] Since IDD does not distinguish between retail and professional customers, the appropriateness assessment also needs to apply to customers that would qualify as 'professional' under MiFID II, unless Member States have made use of the option to soften the know-your-customer requirements in relation to professional customers.

ii. Cross-selling

Bundled package should be appropriate. Under MiFID II, if a firm provides execution-only services where a bundle of services or products is envisaged (cross-selling), the assessment must consider

---

[85] Article 12 Commission Delegated Regulation (EU) 2017/2359.
[86] Article 34(5) PEPP Regulation (EU) 2019/1238.
[87] See Art 4(1)(11) read in conjunction with Annex II, MiFID II.
[88] Article 25(3), first paragraph, first sentence, MiFID II.
[89] Article 30(2), first paragraph, first sentence, IDD.
[90] See Art 56(1), second paragraph, Commission Delegated Regulation (EU) 2017/565 (professional clients); Art 30(1), first paragraph, in conjunction with Art 25(3), MiFID II (eligible counterparties).

whether the overall bundled package is appropriate.[91] IDD applies (almost) exactly the same rule to cross-selling by an insurance intermediary or insurance undertaking.[92]

iii. *Service or Product is Not Appropriate/No Information is Provided*

Product or service is not appropriate. Under MiFID II, where the firm considers that based on the information it has received on the (potential) retail client's knowledge and experience, the product or service is not appropriate to the (potential) retail client, the firm must warn the client. That warning may be provided in a standardised format.[93] Substantially similar rules apply under IDD.[94]

Insufficient information. Under MiFID II, where a (potential) retail client (a) has not provided information regarding their knowledge and experience, or (b) where the information provided is not sufficient, the firm must warn the (potential) retail client. The warning may again be provided in a standardised format.[95] IDD has adopted almost precisely the same rules.[96]

iv. *Exemption for Non-complex Products*

MiFID II. MiFID II exempts certain non-complex products from appropriateness assessments. In particular, exemptions apply to the reception and transmission of client orders in financial instruments, and to the execution of orders in financial instruments on behalf of a client, provided that: (1) the service relates to orders in non-complex financial instruments as listed in Article 25(4)(a), MiFID II, and as interpreted in Article 57 of the Delegated Regulation, (2) the service is provided at the initiative of the client, (3) the bank or investment firm has clearly informed the client before the start of the service that in the provision of that service the investment firm is not required to assess the appropriateness of the financial instrument or service provided or offered and that therefore the client does not benefit from the corresponding protections of the relevant conduct of business rules, *and* (4) the investment firm complies with its obligations in respect of conflicts of interest.[97] For the sake of clarity, it should be noted that this exception is important only in relation to retail clients, as the appropriateness assessment does not apply to professional clients and eligible counterparties.

IDD. IDD contains a similar exemption which is subject to substantially the same conditions in the case that an insurance intermediary or insurance undertaking provides execution-only services with respect to non-complex insurance-based investment products.[98] Obviously, the determination of when a product is deemed 'complex' is different under IDD in view of the differences in the products' scope. IBIPs can be considered non-complex when they only provide investment exposure to financial instruments deemed non-complex under MiFID II and do not incorporate a structure which makes it difficult for the customer to understand the risks involved.[99]

---

[91] Article 25(3), first paragraph, second sentence, MiFID II.
[92] Article 30(2), first paragraph, second sentence, IDD.
[93] Article 25(3), second paragraph, MiFID II.
[94] Article 30(2), second paragraph, IDD.
[95] Article 25(3), third paragraph, MiFID II.
[96] Article 30(2), third paragraph, IDD.
[97] See Art 25(4)(a)-(d), MiFID II and Art 57 Commission Delegated Regulation (EU) 2017/565.
[98] Article 30(3)(a)-(d), IDD and Art 16 Commission Delegated Regulation (EU) 2017/2359.
[99] See for a more in-depth discussion of this issue K Noussia and M. Siri, 'The Legal Regime and the Relevant Standards' in P Marano and I Rokas, *Distribution of Insurance-Based Investment Products* (Cham, Springer, 2019) at 46.

Moreover, an important difference is that the exemption from the IDD appropriateness rules with respect to non-complex, insurance-based investment products is formulated as a Member State option, the exemption in MiFID II is an option that is directly applicable and therefore may be exercised by the firm itself. The inevitable result of this difference is that MiFID II firms may use the exemption across the Union, whereas insurance intermediaries or insurance undertakings may only use the exemption in those Member States that exercised the Member-State option.[100] This difference does not seem to be justified on the basis of a difference in the nature of the products.

v. Records

MiFID II. In terms of record-keeping requirements, MiFID II requires firms to retain a record of the result of the appropriateness assessment. If the investment service or product purchase was assessed as potentially inappropriate for the retail client, the records must show (a) whether the firm warned the retail client about this, (b) whether the retail client asked to proceed with the purchase despite the warning, and (c) where applicable, whether the firm accepted the retail client's request to proceed with the transaction. If a retail client failed to provide sufficient information to enable the firm to undertake an appropriateness assessment, a record must be kept showing (a) whether the firm warned the client about the missing information, (b) whether the retail client asked to proceed with the transaction despite this warning, and (c) where applicable, whether the firm accepted the retail client's request to proceed with the transaction.[101]

    IDD. Again, IDD contains almost precisely the same rules.[102]

F. Entry Knowledge Test: (Proposed) Crowdfunding Regulation

i. Scope of the Assessment

General. As mentioned previously, according to the (proposed) Crowdfunding Regulation, crowdfunding service providers must assess whether and which crowdfunding services offered are 'appropriate' for prospective non-sophisticated investors, before giving full access to invest in their crowdfunding projects.[103] Given that sophisticated investors are, by definition, aware of the risks associated in crowdfunding projects, there is no merit in applying the test to those investors.[104]

    Substantive test. For the purposes of the abstract 'entry knowledge test', crowdfunding service providers must request information about the prospective investor's basic knowledge and understanding of risk in investing in general and in the types of investments offered on the crowdfunding platform, including information about: (a) past investments in transferable securities, admitted instruments for crowdfunding purposes or loan agreements, including in early or expansion stage businesses; (b) any relevant knowledge or professional experience in relation to crowdfunding investments.[105]

---

[100] See explicitly on the latter: Art 30(3), last paragraph, IDD.
[101] Article 56(2) Commission Delegated Regulation (EU) 2017/565.
[102] Article 19(3) Commission Delegated Regulation (EU) 2017/2359.
[103] Article 15(1) Crowdfunding Regulation Compromise Proposal.
[104] Recital 30a of the Crowdfunding Regulation Compromise Proposal.
[105] See Art 15(2) Crowdfunding Regulation Compromise Proposal.

Entry knowledge test and appropriateness tests. Even though the 'entry knowledge test' resembles the MiFID II and IDD 'appropriateness assessment' in requiring an assessment of knowledge and experience, the 'entry knowledge test' is, fundamentally different. Whereas the MiFID II and IDD appropriateness assessments relate to specific investments, the entry knowledge test applies on a more abstract level, before a prospective non-sophisticated investor is given access to crowdfunding services. One could argue that an 'entry knowledge' test offers investors less protection, since it applies on an abstract level and not in relation to a specific investment, while investors only receive a warning and can still invest if the test turns out negative. As mentioned above (see Section II.C.v.), the reason for this fundamentally different approach seems to be the desire of the regulator to strike a balance between investor protection and easy market access for SMEs, particularly for start-ups. The abstract 'entry knowledge' test could be the result of a compromise in this respect. On the other hand, it should be noted that the (proposed) Crowdfunding Regulation offers additional means of investor protection that are absent from MiFID II, IDD and the PEPP Regulation.

Cap of EUR 8,000,000. First, in view of the risky nature of investing through crowdfunding, and for the sake of investor protection, the scope of the (proposed) Crowdfunding Regulation is limited. It applies only to crowdfunding offers with a consideration equal to or less than EUR 8,000,000 per crowdfunding offer, which is calculated over a period of 12 months with regard to a particular crowdfunding project.[106] This cap, however, only reduces the total potential damage to investors in a single project. But, it does not reduce the total damage for individual investors, who can still invest quite a lot through crowdfunding.

Loss simulation. Second, crowdfunding service providers must at all times offer (prospective) investors the possibility to simulate their ability to bear loss, calculated as 10 per cent of their net worth, based on the following information: (a) regular income and total income and, and whether the income is earned on a permanent or temporary basis; (b) assets, including financial investments, personal and investment property, pension funds and any cash deposits; and (c) financial commitments, including regular, existing or future. Irrespective of the results of the simulation, (prospective) non-sophisticated investors should not be prevented from investing in crowdfunding projects. The non-sophisticated investor should acknowledge the results of the simulation.[107]

Investment limits. In the Council Compromise proposal of 24 June 2019, two further investor protection techniques have been added. First Member States have the option to introduce a limit to the amount of money non-sophisticated investors can invest into an individual crowdfunding project. The amount of this limit cannot be lower than EUR 1,000 per crowdfunding project.[108]

Reflection period. The Compromise Proposal also introduces rules in respect of the 'time interval' which should be respected regarding crowdfunding offers, consisting of a number of steps. One of the steps is that the prospective investor expresses an interest via the crowdfunding platform to invest into the crowdfunding project.[109] The crowdfunding service provider should provide for a reflection period of 7 calendar days, during which the non-sophisticated investor may at any time revoke this expression of interest, without incurring a penalty or giving a reason.[110]

---

[106] Article 2(2)(d) Crowdfunding Regulation Compromise Proposal.
[107] Article 15(5) Crowdfunding Regulation Compromise Proposal.
[108] Article 15a Crowdfunding Regulation Compromise Proposal.
[109] Article 15b(0) Crowdfunding Regulation Compromise proposal.
[110] Article 15b(1) Crowdfunding Regulation Compromise proposal.

ii. Mandate for Level 2 Legislation

L2 legislation. Finally, it should be noted that the Commission may adopt delegated acts to specify the arrangements necessary to (i) carry out the 'entry knowledge test'; (ii) carry out the simulation; (iii) provide the information needed for the 'entry knowledge test'.[111]

iii. Service is Not Appropriate/No Information is Provided for Purposes of 'Knowledge Entry Test'

Risk warning. Where prospective non-sophisticated investors do not provide the information required, or where crowdfunding service providers consider, on the basis of the information received pursuant to the abstract 'entry knowledge' test, that (i) the prospective non-sophisticated investors have insufficient knowledge, crowdfunding service providers must inform them that the services offered on their platforms may be inappropriate for them and give them a risk warning. The investor should expressly acknowledge that they have received and understood the warning.[112]

iv. Cross-sectoral Perspective

Comparison with MiFID II, IDD and PEPP Regulation. As shown above, the 'knowledge entry test' resembles the appropriateness test, but is fundamentally different since it applies at a more abstract level. Moreover, the (proposed) Crowdfunding Regulation does not contain any rules on the question of who should be subject to the entry knowledge test if the client is a legal person or a group, or represents another person. Nor does the (proposed) Crowdfunding Regulation contain any rules on cross-selling, on how to obtain reliable information, on switching, or on reporting. It is arguable that some of these rules should also apply, at least to a certain extent, to (certain) crowdfunding services; some may well pop up in future level 2 crowdfunding legislation. However, as previously remarked (see section II.C.v. and II.F.i. above), in respect of crowdfunding the EU regulator wanted to strike a balance between investor protection and easy market access for SMEs, particularly for start-ups. In view of the latter consideration, the regulator is of the opinion that the costs and therefore the compliance burden should not be too high. From a retail investor's perspective, however, one could wonder why the same investors should receive different protection depending on the distribution channel. One could even argue that in this way there is an unlevel playing field between crowdfunding platforms, on the one hand, and traditional investment firms on the other. In our opinion, SME access to funding is indeed a legitimate concern. Nevertheless, easier access to funding should ideally be realised independent of the distribution channel.

G. Degree of Harmonisation

MiFID II. The MiFID II suitability rules for investment advice aim at maximum harmonisation.
    IDD. Recital (3) IDD makes it clear that IDD, on the contrary, is only 'aimed at minimum harmonisation and should therefore not preclude Member States from maintaining or

---

[111] Article 15(6) Crowdfunding Regulation Compromise Proposal.
[112] Article 15(4) Crowdfunding Regulation Compromise Proposal.

introducing more stringent provisions in order to protect customers, provided that such provisions are consistent with Union law, including [IDD]'. In view of this, individual Member States are free to introduce rules that are stricter than the IDD KYC rules. From the perspective of investor protection, this is perhaps good news, but from the viewpoint of a cross-sectoral level playing field for investment products in the broad sense, this is of course less ideal.

Proposed PEPP Regulation. In view of the fact that the IDD suitability rules for advice on insurance-based investment products amount to minimum harmonisation, this feature of the rules also applies to PEPPs advised by (1) insurance undertakings engaged in direct life insurance or (2) insurance intermediaries. This is made explicit in the PEPP Regulation, which stipulates that '[the IDD suitability rules] shall apply only to the extent that there is no more stringent provision in the applicable national law (…)'.[113] In view of the fact that the MiFID II suitability rules for investment advice require maximum harmonisation, it seems that this feature of the rules also applies to PEPPs advised by investment firms that did not manufacture the relevant PEPPs. In such cases, Member States are not allowed to introduce stricter or more lenient rules. For other PEPP advisors, the PEPP Regulation is directly applicable.

(Proposed) Crowdfunding Regulation. The original proposal for a Crowdfunding Regulation created an optional (opt-in) regime: platforms not opting in would be subject to MiFID II or ad hoc national crowdfunding regimes (or other rules), depending on the regulatory approach to crowdfunding adopted by the Member States where they have their seats. For platforms that would opt in, Member States would not be allowed to adopt stricter or more lenient rules.[114] The Compromise Proposal has, however, changed this approach and intends to introduce a mandatory regime for crowdfunding services providers in the EU.

H. Evaluation

MiFID, IDD and PEPP Regulation: similar, but with unsubstantiated differences. It follows from the above comparison that the MiFID II, IDD and PEPP KYC rules are very similar, but that there are still many differences which are difficult to justify from the perspective of a cross-sectoral level playing field. A first major difference is the level of harmonisation. While the proposed PEPP and Crowdfunding rules are part of a regulation, MiFID II aims at maximum harmonisation and IDD only aims at minimum harmonisation. National rules in respect of IBIPs can therefore differ widely between Member States. There does not seem to be a logical explanation for these varying levels of harmonisation, which might best be explained as arising from successful lobbying efforts by the insurance sector. Moreover, while MiFID II and the (proposed) Crowdfunding Regulation draw a distinction between different client categories in determining the scope of protection, IDD and the proposed PEPP Regulation do not. Whereas the nature of a PEPP explains why the PEPP Regulation rules only apply to natural persons, the reason why IDD does not distinguish between client categories and why MiFID II and the (proposed) Crowdfunding Regulation use different distinctions, is not obvious. Since financial instruments and insurance-based investment products and crowdfunding products are substitutes for many investors, these differences seem difficult to justify. As a last example, concerning the suitability test, the PEPP Regulation provides for similar rules as MiFID II and IDD at level 1, but does not give a mandate to the

---

[113] Article 23(2) PEPP Regulation (EU) 2019/1238.
[114] COM(2018) 113 final, p 6.

European Commission to develop those rules at level 2. Since investment firms and insurance intermediaries distributing PEPPs must comply with MiFID II and IDD respectively, but other PEPP advisors need only comply with the much less developed rules of the PEPP Regulation, this leads to an unlevel playing field and numerous unjustifiable differences.

Even if at level 1 and level 2, the rules of MiFID II, IDD and the PEPP Proposal are fairly similar, there is no guarantee that the level 3 guidelines will be sufficiently similar or diverge only where needed in view of differences in the regulated products. The same issue may arise in Member States that may have a sectoral or at least non-integrated approach to supervision.

Crowdfunding: is the radically different entry knowledge test substantiated? The KYC crowd-funding rules take a radically different approach than the MiFID II, IDD and PEPP KYC rules, by introducing an entry knowledge test. This entry knowledge test resembles the appropriateness test, but applies on a more abstract level. Many differences between the crowdfunding rules and other regulations seem to stem from the idea that the costs and therefore the compliance burden in respect of crowdfunding should not be too high. However, if one agrees that crowdfunding is, in the end, just another distribution channel through which investors get access to investment products, major differences in the level of protection of those investors, compared with MiFID II, IDD and the PEPP Proposal, do not seem warranted.

Inefficiencies of four sets of rules for investment products. The four sets of rules discussed in this section have in common that they regulate assist-your-customer obligations in respect of invest-ment products, broadly construed. Having different rules applicable to those products depending on their legal form (MiFID financial instruments or structured deposits versus insurance-based investment products or personal pension products) or distribution channel (crowdfunding plat-forms versus traditional banks and investment firms) leads to duplication of legislative work at levels 1, 2 and 3 of the Lamfalussy procedure, and an accordingly increased translation burden. Moreover, legislative innovations are often only introduced in the latest piece of legislation. The proposed Crowdfunding Regulation, for instance, introduces a simulation approach to losses, which could be useful in other instances. In the current legislative approach, a new regulatory insight in respect of investment products would require amendments to four legislative texts.

The current legislative approach therefore seems hugely inefficient and leads to unsubstanti-ated differences, which can, moreover, trigger regulatory arbitrage.

Need for level playing field for investment products. In our opinion, it would be more efficient to have a common set of know-your-customer rules in one piece of legislation applicable to all investment products, broadly construed. This would avoid unsubstantiated drafting, lobbying and translation differences as well as differences merely resulting from new insights at the time the latest directive or regulation was introduced. MiFID II would be the obvious candidate for such a 'cross-sectoral' piece of legislation for investment products. Of course, there should be room for variation at level 1, 2 and/or 3 to reflect substantiated differences, for example in view of the distribution channel (eg crowdfunding platforms) or in view of the specificity of a certain product (eg pension products). MiFID II already shows that such an approach is feasible, with, for instance, specific rules based on various distribution channels (eg robo-advice[115]) or products (eg UCITS Directive and PRIIPs,[116] or leveraged products[117]).

From a pragmatic perspective, widening the scope of application of MiFID II in this manner may seem difficult to achieve. As a second-best alternative, the PEPP-proposal technique of

---

[115] Article 54(1), second paragraph, Commission Delegated Regulation (EU) 2017/565.
[116] Article 46 Commission Delegated Regulation (EU) 2017/565.
[117] Article 62(2) Commission Delegated Regulation (EU) 2017/565.

referring to the MiFID II (and IDD) suitability tests, is preferable to the IDD-technique of dupli-cating MiFID II, with a number of unsubstantiated differences, especially at levels 2 and 3. A great advantage of the PEPP-proposal technique is that it avoids having to duplicate and trans-late all level 2 and 3 rules. This technique thus reduces the risk of unsubstantiated differences. It may, however, be considered less user-friendly than one 'cross-sectoral' set of KYC-rules, even though this may be less of a problem in a world in which legislative texts are more and more often consulted on a computer screen. Adding suitable hyperlinks may well be able to remedy this difficulty.

III. Demands & Needs Analysis

A. Introduction

Source. Even though 'MiFID-like' know-your-customer requirements only apply in respect of *investment-based* insurance products (IBIPs), the IDD provides for another type of duty of assis-tance for *all* insurance contracts, including IBIPs: the 'demands and needs analysis'. The PEPP Regulation has introduced a similar requirement for PEPPs.

   Concept. The demands and needs analysis requires the insurance distributor/PEPP provider or distributor to (i) specify, on the basis of information obtained from the customer, the demands and the needs of that customer, (ii) provide the customer with objective information about the insurance product to allow that customer to make an informed decision and (iii) ensure that any contract proposed is consistent with the customer's insurance/PEPP demands and needs.[118] An insurance distributor/PEPP provider or distributor that provides advice prior to the conclusion of a contract must also 'provide the customer with a personalised recommendation explaining why a particular product would best meet the customer's demands and needs.'

   Goal. The demands and needs test is intended to protect customers by avoiding mis-selling.[119]

B. Relationship with Know-Your-Customer Rules

Cumulative application. In respect of insurance products other than life insurance, the needs analysis is the only applicable assist-your-customer test. However, when an insurance distributor or a PEPP provider/distributor gives advice on insurance-based investment products or PEPPs, it must also apply a suitability test.[120] As discussed in Section II.D.i., this means that the insur-ance distributor should obtain the necessary information regarding the customer's knowledge and experience, financial situation, and objectives. If an insurance distributor provides no advice in respect of IBIPs, it should perform an appropriateness test, and obtain the necessary informa-tion on the customer's knowledge and experience in respect of the relevant product or service.

---

[118] Article 20 (1) IDD and Art 25, PEPP Proposal.

[119] Recital 44, IDD. In Belgium, this is interpreted as an insurance contract which would over-, under- or inadequately insure the customer. See, ie, the explanatory statement to Art 4 of the Belgian Royal Decree of 21 February 2014 amend-ing the law of 27 March 1995 on insurance and reinsurance mediation and the distribution of insurance, Belgian Official Gazette, 7 March 2014 at 20133; Circular FSMA_2015_14 (1 September 2015) at 40.

[120] Article 30, IDD; Art 25(3), PEPP Proposal. See also section II.D.i.a.

Article 30(1) and (2) IDD explicitly state that the suitability and appropriateness tests are '*without prejudice*' to the requirement to perform a demands and needs analysis;[121] in the PEPP Regulation, cumulative application of the demands and needs analysis and the suitability test in an advice context, is clear from the set-up of Article 25.

No advice. In case the insurance distributor merely sells an IBIP without giving advice, the situation is clear: the demands and needs analysis is supplemented with the appropriateness test, which requires an assessment of whether the customer has sufficient knowledge and experience with the product to understand the risks involved.

Advice. The situation is more complicated when the demands and needs analysis is to be combined with the suitability test. The industry has raised the question of whether the suitability test 'absorbs' the demands and needs analysis – in other words, whether compliance with the suitability test can be considered to automatically result in compliance with the demands and needs analysis. The Belgian Financial Services and Markets Authority (FSMA) addressed this question in 2014,[122] and in 2018 EIOPA answered this question in the context of IDD.

FSMA position 2014–15. The Belgian Financial Services and Markets Authority (FSMA) ruled that an insurance services provider that complies with the suitability test in respect of insurance-based investment products can reasonably assume that the product or service in question also meets 'the demands and needs' of that client and therefore complies with the demands and needs analysis. According to the FSMA, no separate needs analysis is required to be performed in such circumstances.[123]

EIOPA position 2018. EIOPA was asked to answer almost the same question in its IDD Q&A.[124] The question posed was what 'in practical terms […] is the scope of the demand and needs test' in 'the case of a personal recommendation for an Insurance-based Investment Product (IBIP), where a suitability test as well as a demands and needs test must be performed'? In such cases, 'can one assume that, if an IBIP is suitable for a customer, this IBIP is also consistent with the customer's demands and needs?'

EIOPA's answer is long, and somewhat enigmatic. It first makes clear that the scope of the demands and needs test is not prescribed in the Directive nor in the Delegated Regulation and that it is subject to national implementation. It then proceeds to give 'some guidance' regarding

---

[121] See also Recital 7 of Commission Delegated Regulation (EU) 2017/2359.

[122] The question arose early in Belgium, since the Belgian implementation of MiFID I, including the suitability test, had been extended to the insurance sector, in which a demands and needs analysis also already applied.

[123] Circular FSMA_2014_02 (16 April 2014) at 39, later replaced with Circular FSMA_2015_14 (1 September 2015) at 38–39. Critics of this FSMA position claim that the suitability test and the demands and needs analysis have different goals. The demands and needs analysis is a means of ensuring that adequate products are sold to clients and avoiding mis-selling. In Belgium, this has been interpreted as a requirement to avoid that a client would be over- or under- or inadequately insured. The demands and needs analysis would thus gear the insurance product or service to the insured risk. The suitability test on the other hand, gears the product or service to the qualities and objectives of the client. In the context of insurance-based investment products, however, the two positions do not seem to differ that much. Insurance-based investment products are investment products rather than insurance products. Analysing whether the client would be 'over- or under- or inadequately insured', when buying such a product therefore seems to boil down to analysing whether such a product would be adequate for the client, also in view of the investment products already in the client's portfolio. This would come very close indeed to an analysis of the question whether the insurance-based investment product matches the investment objectives of the client, where the advisor would, obviously, also need to take into account the other products already in the portfolio of the client.

[124] EIOPA, 'Questions & Answers on the Application of the Insurance Distribution Directive' (10 July 2018) question 1638, available via https://eiopa.europa.eu/Pages/News/EIOPA-publishes-first-set-of-Questions--Answers-on-the-Application-of-the-Insurance-Distribution-Directive.aspx.

minimum expectations for this test and how it may relate to the assessment of suitability.[125] EIOPA points out a number of clear differences between the demands and needs test, on the one hand, and the suitability test, on the other. Among these differences, (i) the demands and needs test has to be performed prior to the conclusion of the contract and is 'distinct from the suitability assessment in advised cases', whereas the suitability assessment can also be provided at any time during the customer relationship; (ii) the assessment of demands and needs is required whether or not advice is being provided; and (iii) the specification of the demands and needs would not amount to a suitability assessment. While this is all clear, it still does not answer the converse question of whether a qualitative and timely suitability assessment would also cover the demands and needs test, or whether, on the contrary, the demands and needs test would require a different approach.

EIOPA goes on to give some guidance on the content and goal of the demands and needs analysis: the main information concerning the customer's demands and needs would typically include personal information (age, profession, place of residence, etc) and information particularly linked to the type of product requested. This information should be designed to enable the insurance intermediary or insurance undertaking to assess whether certain products can be offered or not, 'according to their capacity of meeting the demands and needs of the customer'. This could lead to a selection of a range of comparable products for consideration during the suitability assessment where advice is being given or during the appropriateness assessment where no advice is given. EIOPA concludes that depending on national implementation, where advice is being provided, the demands and needs test and assessment of suitability could be seen as 'a continuum, rather than as a break'. EIOPA emphasises that where the customer is provided with advice, the suitability test requires the insurance distributor to obtain information that is more detailed and specific, like the customer's financial situation, his ability to bear losses, his investment objectives, his risk tolerance, and other correlated information. The final outcome should be a personalised recommendation in which it is specifically explained why a particular product best meets the customer's demands and needs.

No general answer on relationship between suitability and demands and needs assessment. All elements mentioned by EIOPA as typical examples of information the company should request from the client to assess his demands and needs are typically also requested in a suitability assessment. While the suitability assessment can indeed be performed after conclusion of the contract and the demands and needs analysis should, according to EIOPA, be performed before the conclusion of the contract, in practice the suitability assessment is often performed before conclusion of the contract. The Belgian FSMA has maintained its position since the EIOPA answer. While in our opinion, nothing in EIOPA's answer precludes such a national interpretation, it is clearly not the only valid answer national authorities could give to the question. Since EIOPA has explicitly stated that the exact scope of the demands and needs test is not prescribed and is subject to national implementation, it is indeed impossible to answer the question whether compliance with the suitability assessment would also constitute compliance with the demands and needs analysis in general terms. The answer may differ from Member State to Member State and will indeed depend on the national scope of the demands and needs analysis. This is obviously regrettable from a legal certainty and internal market perspective.

---

[125] EIOPA indeed extensively refers to the recitals and articles of the IDD and the IDD implementing regulation in respect of the IDD conduct of business rules, which do not, however provide an answer to the question. See Recital 7 of Commission Delegated Regulation (EU) 2017/2359 and Art 30(1), IDD, which both clarify that the assessments of suitability and appropriateness are without prejudice to the obligation to consider and specify prior to the conclusion of any insurance contract, the demands and needs of the customer on the basis of information obtained from the customer.

No guidance on the content of the needs analysis. The main problem is indeed that EIOPA deems the scope of the demands and needs test to be subject to national implementation. This is in sharp contrast to the very detailed EU implementation of the suitability test, which has been extensively clarified by level 2 and, in the case of MiFID II, even level 3 rules. The EIOPA answer in the Q&A is in our opinion a missed chance to clarify the demands and needs analysis, as well as its relationship with the suitability requirement.

C. Cross-sectoral Point of View

Products which fulfil the same function need to be subject to the same rules. If insurance-based investment products are indeed investment products, rather than insurance products, they should be subject to the same rules as other investment products, in order to avoid regulatory arbitrage. The same is true for PEPPs. IDD and the PEPP Regulation have indeed substantially aligned the rules for IBIPs and PEPPs to the MiFID II rules.

Applying demands and needs test to IBIPs and PEPPs is an anomaly. In our view, applying the demands and needs analysis to IBIPs and PEPPs in addition to the suitability or appropriateness test is not justified. Indeed, for the sake of regulatory consistency, the same rules should apply to functionally equivalent products. Imposing both tests makes the regulatory framework for IBIPs and PEPPs stricter than for other investment products. From that perspective, the FSMA interpretation eschewing cumulative application of the suitability test and the demands and needs analysis seems reasonable.

In case of a non-advised sale of IBIPs, however, no such interpretation is possible. The appropriateness test only requires an evaluation of the client's knowledge and experience. The demands and needs analysis, however, requires an additional inquiry, which may in practice come close to a test of the objectives of the client.[126] The extra requirement of a demands and needs analysis on top of the appropriateness test therefore creates a difference in treatment between, on the one hand, non-advised customers buying IBIPs and, on the other hand, non-advised customers buying other investment products. This difference is not justified in the IDD's explanatory memorandum or other preparatory documents. In our opinion it is indeed an unjustifiable difference, which stems from the fact that the demands and needs analysis was a tool created to avoid mis-selling of insurance contracts *other* than IBIPs, for which no other regulatory tools exist to avoid mis-selling. IBIPs and PEPPs, however, are in fact investment products, to which the suitability test or the appropriateness apply to avoid mis-selling (alongside a range of other measures). Therefore, the demands and needs analysis should in our opinion not also apply to those products.

Information gathering and communication with customers. In a situation where an insurance distributor is selling or giving advice on non-IBIP insurance products, the demands and needs analysis may have a valid role to play. Even then, there are a number of issues where aspects of the demands and needs analysis could be aligned with the know-your-customer rules discussed in section I. More specifically, the rules on information gathering and processing, developed

---

[126] In the ESMA's Consultation Paper on Draft guidelines on MiFID II product governance requirements, 'objectives' and 'needs' of the client in respect of the product were two distinct categories (see ESMA/2016/1436, at 6, para 11). In the final guidelines, objectives and needs were put in one category, since it was too difficult to distinguish between them (See ESMA35-43-620, at 7, para 18, e).

in conjunction with the know-your-customer requirements, could be extended to the demands and needs test, including the rules on the reliability of information gathered from clients in the context of the suitability test (see section II.D.iv.). Those same rules would, in our opinion, be very helpful in the context of information gathering for purposes of the demands and needs test.

IV. Duty of Assistance & Responsible Lending Requirements

A. Introduction

Context. In the banking sector, there are two types of 'assist-your-customer' rules. First, both the Consumer Credit Directive and the Mortgage Credit Directive feature rules requiring creditors and credit intermediaries to provide adequate explanations to the consumer in order to place the consumer in a position enabling him to assess whether the proposed credit agreement is adapted to his needs and to his financial situation ('duty of assistance'). Second, both in the Consumer Credit Directive and in the Mortgage Credit Directive, creditors are also subject to a duty to 'lend responsibly', meaning that they must assess whether the consumer to whom a credit is to be granted will be reasonably able to pay back the loan. Both sets of rules are discussed in more detail below.

B. Duty of Assistance

i. *What is it?*

Concept. Both Article 5(6), CCD and Article 16, MCD impose a duty of assistance upon creditors and credit intermediaries, in practically the same terms. Creditors, and, where applicable, credit intermediaries must provide adequate explanations to the consumer, in order to place the consumer in a position enabling him to assess whether the proposed credit agreement is adapted to his needs and to his financial situation. Where appropriate, this can include explaining the pre-contractual information, the essential characteristics of the products proposed and the specific effects they may have on the consumer, including the consequences of default in payment by the consumer.

Explanation in a personalised manner. Although this may seem to be an enhanced information obligation, Recital (27) of the CCD makes very clear that it truly is a duty of assistance. The reason for this duty is that 'despite the pre-contractual information to be provided, the consumer may still need additional assistance in order to decide which credit agreement, within the range of products proposed, is the most appropriate for his needs and financial situation'. The recital also clarifies that it does not suffice to provide general information on the different types of products on offer. The relevant pre-contractual information should be explained 'in a personalised manner so that the consumer can understand the effects which they may have on his economic situation'.

Only in respect of products on offer. The additional assistance thus relates to the products proposed by the creditor, and seems to require an explanation of all products on offer by the creditor. The duty does not extend to alternative credit products offered by competitors, even if those would be more 'adapted' to the needs or financial situation of the consumer.

Goal. The ultimate goal of the duty of assistance is to place the consumer in a position where the consumer is able to assess whether the proposed credit agreement is adapted to his needs and to his financial situation.

Advice? This duty of assistance applies in all circumstances, irrespective of whether the creditor or credit intermediary intends to give advice on the credit agreement. The CCD does not provide anything in particular for the situation where advice is given to the consumer on what credit product to choose. Article 22(3), MCD, however, does provide for an additional advice standard on top of this duty of assistance,[127] which is clearly inspired by the MiFID suitability test: if advisory services are provided to consumers, the creditor, credit intermediary or appointed representative must obtain the necessary information regarding (i) the consumer's personal and financial situation, and (ii) his preferences and objectives, so as to enable the recommendation of suitable credit agreements. Such an assessment must be based on information that is up to date at that moment in time and must take into account reasonable assumptions as to risks to the consumer's situation over the term of the proposed credit agreement.

ii. Comparison with the Know-Your-Customer Rules

Self-assessment by the client. The most important difference between the duty of assistance in respect of credit services, and the know-your-customer rules discussed in section I, is that the assessment of whether a credit agreement is 'adapted' to the needs and financial situation of the consumer is ultimately left to the consumer, whereas in respect of the know-your-customer requirements, the assessment should be made by the financial institution. Only if the creditor provides advice on mortgage credit, an additional 'advice standard' applies, which requires the *creditor* to assess the situation of the client.

Two tests applicable in all circumstances. The duty of assistance should facilitate two self-tests by the consumer: whether the credit is adapted to (i) his needs and (ii) his financial situation. The duty applies in all circumstances, irrespective of whether the financial intermediary gives advice or not. This is very different from the know-your-customer requirements, where in a non-advised context only the client's knowledge and experience must be tested (appropriateness).

It is quite understandable that the duty of assistance in respect of credit services does not refer to knowledge and experience, since the goal of this duty is precisely to make sure that the customer understands the credit agreement on offer and its consequences. The duty of assistance does refer to a self-assessment by the consumer of his financial situation – the same test as in the suitability test – and of his needs. At first sight, the latter test would seem closer to the 'demands and needs' assessment discussed in the previous section, than to the 'objectives' assessment in section I. In reality, however, no further explanation is given on how exactly the 'needs' concepts should be interpreted.

Additional test in case of mortgage advice. Only the MCD provides for specific rules in respect of mortgage credit advice beyond the duty of assistance. Where mortgage advice is provided, the creditor should obtain information on (i) the consumer's personal and financial situation, and (ii) his preferences and objectives. The elements to assess are largely the same as in respect of the duty of assistance, although worded slightly differently. Instead of 'financial situation' in the duty of assistance, the advice test requires information on the consumer's 'personal and financial

---

[127] See Art 22(7), MCD, which provides that Art 22 is without prejudice to Art 16 and to Member States' competence to ensure that services are made available to consumers to help them understand their financial needs and which types of products are likely to meet those needs.

situation'. We assume, however, that the information on the 'personal situation' should relate to the financial situation of the client or his or her preferences or objectives. Indeed, personal circumstances such as whether a person has children, is married or divorced, or has a job, substantially affect his or her financial situation and may also influence that person's borrowing preferences or objectives. Instead of 'needs' in the duty of assistance, the advice test requires information on 'preferences and objectives'. Again, no further explanations are given on those concepts, which seem to cover largely the same kind of assessment as the 'needs' in the duty of assistance.

As pointed out above, the main difference between the duty of assistance, on the one hand, and the advice test in case of mortgage credit, on the other, is that in case of advice, the *financial institution* must make this assessment. Once the financial institution has made its recommendation, it must still comply with the duty of assistance and provide personalised information to the consumer to allow him to assess for himself whether the proposed credit agreement is indeed adapted to his needs and financial situation.

iii.   *Cross-sectoral Point of View*

A number of conclusions can be drawn from the above discussion in terms of cross-sectoral consistency.

Different services may need different rules. First, it is clear that credit services are substantially different from investment services. It may, therefore, be justified for the legislator to implement a different approach to consumer protection.

Different wording of the tests not always substantiated. Nevertheless, the requirement for mortgage credit providers to perform an advice test in case of mortgage advice is clearly inspired by the MiFID suitability test. Even though the different wording of the suitability test can be partially explained by the difference in product on which advice is given, there are also a number of unsubstantiated differences. First, the MCD requires information on the 'personal situation' of the client. This is not explicitly mentioned in any of the other suitability tests we reviewed in section I, even though, in practice, the customer's personal situation is obviously also very important for the assessment of suitability under those other regulations, and should be considered implicitly covered by the suitability tests for investment products (as stated above, a person's personal situation has a big impact on his or her financial situation). Second, the MCD does not require an assessment of knowledge and experience. Some mortgage credit products are, however, quite complex, in view of which such a test would be quite useful. Third, the MCD requires a test of the 'preferences and objectives' of the client, whereas the other suitability tests call for an inquiry into the client's 'objectives'. 'Preferences' are, however, again at least implied in the objectives assessment in the other suitability tests.

It would add to the consistency of the regulatory framework if such differences would always have a clear meaning, and would be explained in the preparatory documents of the legislation.

Quality and shelf life of information. Finally, the MCD states that the assessment credit providers undertake 'shall be based on information that is up to date at that moment in time and shall take into account reasonable assumptions as to risks to the consumer's situation over the term of the proposed credit agreement.' The MiFID II rules on the quality and shelf life of the information requested from the client are much more elaborate. Information gathering and processing indeed seems an area where cross-sectoral rules would add consistency and increase legal certainty and efficiency.

The same services need substantially the same rules. The rules on duty of assistance in the CCD and the MCD are substantially the same. The only major difference is that the MCD provides for an advice test in relation to mortgage credit advice, which is clearly inspired by the MiFID suitability test. There does not seem to be a reasonable justification for not having such a suitability test in respect of consumer credit. One could argue that the fact that the amounts involved in consumer credit are usually much lower, could justify the difference. Nevertheless, the amounts involved in consumer credit may still be considerable (eg for a car loan) and extensive jurisprudence shows that mis-selling is a key problem in this area. A more plausible explanation is that the MCD is of a much later date than the CCD. The MCD was adopted at a time when MiFID II had almost been finalised, and the suitability test was considered of high value in that context. The MCD seems to have profited from those new insights.[128]

C. Responsible Lending

i. *What is it?*

Concept. On top of the duty of assistance, both the CCD and the MCD provide for a duty of responsible lending, which requires financial institutions to assess the creditworthiness of the consumer.

Goal. The goal of responsible lending requirements is to avoid consumer overindebtedness resulting from consumers taking up loans which they cannot reasonably be expected to repay on the basis of their available income. The expression of this goal, however, differs somewhat between the CCD and the MCD. The CCD focuses on the consumer protection aspect.[129] The MCD – which was introduced after the devastating consequences of the US housing bubble on financial stability had become clear – hinges on both consumer protection and stability goals to justify its responsible lending rule.[130] Interestingly, whereas the CCD focuses on the responsibility of the creditor in responsibly lending,[131] the MCD also requires the borrower to engage in 'responsible borrowing'.[132]

Comparison between CCD and MCD. The CCD and the MCD both require the creditor to assess the consumer's creditworthiness before the conclusion of the credit agreement, and before any significant increase in the total amount of the credit.[133] The MCD, contrary to the CCD, elaborates in further detail what this means: the assessment must take appropriate account of factors relevant to verifying the ability of the consumer to meet his obligations under the credit agreement. The MCD additionally requires that the procedures and information on which the assessment is based, be established, documented and maintained,[134] and deals with the hypothesis

---

[128] This hypothesis is substantiated by the fact that other and new MiFID II elements have been inserted in the MCD, such as the rules on inducements and the distinction between independent and limited advice (see Art 22 (1)–(2) and (4)-(5), MCD).

[129] Recital 26, CCD.

[130] Recitals 3 and 5, MCD.

[131] Recital 26, CCD does mention that 'consumers should also act with prudence and respect their contractual obligations', but this is not reflected in the articles of the CCD.

[132] See Recital 4, MCD. Although the articles of the MCD do not put an explicit obligation on the consumer, the MCD does provide for heavy consequences of, irresponsible borrowing, due to providing false information or being unwilling to provide the necessary information in the responsible lending process. See Art 20(3) in fine and Art 20(4), providing that in the first case, Member States may allow the termination of the credit agreement by the creditor where it is demonstrated that the consumer knowingly withheld or falsified the information; and that in the second case, the credit cannot be granted.

[133] Article 8, CCD; Art 18, MCD.

[134] Article 18(2), MCD.

in which the assessment of creditworthiness of the client was incorrectly conducted.[135] Whereas the CCD does not explicitly state what a creditor must do in case of a negative creditworthiness assessment,[136] the MCD clearly states that the creditor should only make the credit available to the consumer where the result of the creditworthiness assessment indicates that the obligations resulting from the credit agreement are likely to be met in the manner required under that agreement.[137]

Both the CCD and the MCD deal with database consultations by the creditor in order to retrieve creditworthiness data, but again the MCD is more elaborate and stricter.[138] The MCD further describes the information upon which the creditworthiness assessment must be based, what sources of information can be used, and how the information should be verified.[139]

Furthermore, the MCD provides that the creditor should warn the consumer that if the creditor is unable to carry out an assessment of creditworthiness because the consumer chooses not to provide the information or verification necessary for an assessment of creditworthiness, the credit cannot be granted.[140] The CCD does not mention any consequences of a consumer not providing sufficient information.

Moreover, EBA has developed the MCD rules on responsible lending in level 3 guidelines,[141] whereas it has not given any guidance on the CCD rules.

Only one difference between the CCD and MCD versions of the responsible lending requirement seems clearly linked to the different purpose of the credit: the MCD requirement that the assessment of creditworthiness in relation to a mortgage credit should not rely predominantly on the value of the residential immovable property exceeding the amount of the credit, or the assumption that the residential immovable property will increase in value, unless the purpose of the credit agreement is construction or renovation.[142]

ii. Comparison with the Know-Your-Customer Rules

The creditworthiness assessment requires the creditor to test the financial situation of the client, which is substantially the same test as the second test of the MiFID, IDD and PEPP suitability assessment discussed in section II.D.i. Although the product which is sold to the client is different, the goal of the test is largely the same: avoiding financial distress to the client caused by acquisition of a product, the financial consequences of which he is not able to bear. Additionally, however, responsible lending is also important for the stability of the creditor. The crisis has indeed shown that when large scale irresponsible lending gives rise to numerous credit defaults, this can result in bank failures and systemic risk.

iii. Cross-sectoral Point of View

Need for the same rules for the same services. There are numerous differences between the CCD and the MCD. Some differences are justified in view of the different nature of the credit agreement

---

[135] Article 18(4), MCD.
[136] This is left to the Member States to decide (see Art 23).
[137] Article 18(5)(a), MCD.
[138] Articles 8(1) in fine and 9 CCD and Art 18(5)(b) and (c) and (6) and Art 21, MCD.
[139] Article 20(1)–(3), MCD.
[140] Article 20(4), MCD.
[141] EBA, 'Guidelines on Creditworthiness Assessment' (EBA/GL/2015/11, 19 August 2015).
[142] Article 18(3), MCD.

(eg the requirement that the assessment of creditworthiness should not rely predominantly on the value of the residential immovable property exceeding the amount of the credit). Other differences, where the MCD sets more elaborate or stricter standards than the CCD, might be justified in view of (i) the fact that mortgage credits typically represent larger amounts of money and bind the consumer for a much longer period of time, and (ii) the fact that the MCD responsible lending rules are based on market stability concerns as well as consumer protection concerns, whereas the CCD rules are only based on a consumer protection rationale.

Such explanations are, however, not warranted on the basis of the preparatory documents of the MCD. Many differences seem, on the contrary, largely the result of the fact that the MCD is a post-crisis directive, which was introduced at a time (i) when stricter regulation in the credit market was seen as necessary and therefore much easier to introduce than it was at the time of introduction of the CCD, and (ii) when there was already substantial experience with a number of rules in other directives, such as the suitability test and the rules on inducements under MiFID. Indeed, the majority of differences seem to be the result of new insights in respect of financial regulation or the credit market generally, rather than based on a deliberate choice to introduce different rules for mortgage credit and consumer credit. On the basis of our research on the duty of assistance and the responsible lending requirement, we are of the opinion that one directive on credit services for consumers would be much more efficient, and avoid gaps or the need to duplicate guidelines, even though specific exemptions, differentiations or specifications may need to apply in relation to specific types of credits and/or distribution channels.[143]

Alignment between CCD and MCD creditworthiness test and suitability assessment? Since the goals of the creditworthiness assessment and the assessment of the financial situation of the client in the suitability test are the same, both assessments could, in our opinion, be more streamlined. In the context of the suitability test, there are well-developed rules on how the client's financial situation is to be tested, and what information is to be requested from the client (see section II.D.i.). The EBA guidelines on creditworthiness repeat some of those rules to a limited extent, but are much less elaborate. In the CCD and even more so in the MCD, on the other hand, there are a number of rules on database consultation and informing the client of decision-making on the basis of automated processing.[144] Those are themes that are not developed in the context of the KYC rules discussed in section I. Also, the rules on disclosure and verification of consumer information could and should be more streamlined. These are areas where more cross-sectoral consistency – and even one cross-sectoral piece of legislation – seems warranted.

V. Conclusions

Assist-your-customer obligations in all traditional sectors. From this chapter it is very clear that the traditional 'caveat emptor' principle no longer holds in the financial sector; 'assist-your-customer' rules apply in all traditional sectors. We have distinguished three main types of assist-your-customer rules, which mainly correspond with the traditional sectors: investing, lending and insurance.

Investment services. First, MiFID II, IDD, the PEPP Regulation and the proposed Crowd-funding Regulation each feature some kind of 'know-your-customer' rules for products with an

---

[143] It seems, for instance, very inefficient that the EBA guidelines on the creditworthiness assessment only relate to the MCD.

[144] Articles 8–9 Consumer Credit Dir and 18(5)c), Mortgage Credit Dir.

investment purpose. We have argued that it would make sense to have one set of common know-your-customer rules for all those investment products, for instance in MiFID II. This would avoid duplication of legislative and translation work at levels 1, 2 and 3, as well as unsubstantiated differences which can trigger regulatory arbitrage. In view of certain product specificities (for instance, leveraged products, pension products or IBIPs) or specific distribution channels (for instance, robo-advice or crowdfunding), certain variations in the level 1, 2 or 3 texts would nevertheless be necessary, and already exist today.

Insurance services. In respect of insurance services, the typical assist-your-customer requirement consists of a 'demands and needs analysis'. We have argued that the demands and needs analysis is especially relevant for traditional insurance products, but much less so for insurance-based investment products and PEPPs. The latter products are, in fact, investment products for which more elaborate know-your-customer rules already apply. Cumulative application of the demands and needs analysis and those know-your-customer rules currently leads to unnecessary uncertainty. It would make more sense to confine the demands and needs analysis to traditional insurance products in the strict sense and not to apply it to IBIPs, which are already covered by know-your-customer rules.

Credit services. In respect of credit services, there are currently two sets of assist-your-customer rules. First, both the Consumer Credit Directive and the Mortgage Credit Directive feature a duty of assistance, which applies in all circumstances and should allow the client to self-assess whether a credit is adapted to his needs and financial situation. When the creditor provides advice in respect of mortgage credit, the creditor should, moreover, assess substantially the same elements for the client. Second, both the Consumer Credit Directive and the Mortgage Credit Directive feature a 'responsible lending' test, requiring the credit institution to check whether the client will reasonably be able to pay back the credit. In respect of those tests, we have established that there are a number of differences between the rules applicable to consumer credit and mortgage credit. Even though some of those differences can be explained by differences in the product (for instance, the fact that in respect of mortgage credit there is typically a security on real estate), most of the differences do not seem substantiated. Most importantly, the fact that an advice test only applies with respect to mortgage credit seems merely to be based on the fact that the Mortgage Credit Directive was introduced at a later stage than the Consumer Credit Directive. We argue that it would be more efficient to have one set of common rules for all credit services, with specific exemptions, differentiations or specifications for specific types of credits and/or distribution channels. Arguably, such common rules should also include crowdlending to consumers, even though further research on this question is needed.[145]

Answer to research question. Finally, in respect of our research question – whether and to what extent a more cross-sectoral 'assist your customer rule' is warranted – we come to the following conclusions.

First, it is clear that investment services, insurance services and credit services are substantially different. Therefore, a different approach on the question of what type of assist-your-customer rule is needed for each of those services can be justified. Whether or not more or less assistance is needed in each of the sectors comes down to a policy choice. Nevertheless, it is important that the scope of each of the sectors is properly defined in order to ensure that substantially the

---

[145] The Consumer Credit Directive and Mortgage Credit Directive typically do not apply to crowdlending, if the creditor is a consumer. Nevertheless, on the borrower side, the same consumer protection concerns apply as in a traditional lending business. If a platform acts as a crowdlending intermediary, it would therefore arguably be a good idea to extend the traditional duty of assistance and responsible lending requirements to the platform.

same rules are applicable to substantially similar products.[146] Insurance-based investment products and personal pension products, for instance, are mainly investment products, and should therefore not be treated as an insurance product: MiFID-like know-your-customer tests apply and should apply, whereas there is not much of a case to apply an additional demands and needs analysis. As set out above, we are of the opinion that it would be more efficient if one common set of rules would apply to all investment products. Similarly, we think that one common set of rules should apply to all credit products. IDD already creates a common set of rules for insurance products.

Secondly, there is room for more cross-sectoral consistency, which could be achieved in at least two ways. First, the terminology used in the different directives and regulations should be more aligned. If differing terminology is deemed necessary, the regulator should set forth explicitly how the underlying concepts are different (eg 'demands and needs' versus 'needs and preferences' versus 'objectives'). Second, all assist-your-customer rules discussed in this chapter (except for the duty of assistance in respect of credit services) are based on information gathering and processing by the financial institution. Under MiFID II and its level 2 and 3 texts, rules relating to information gathering and processing are developed in quite some detail (including rules on how to ensure reliability of information, on the use of automated processes, …). The Consumer and Mortgage Credit Directive features rules on the use of databases in the information gathering process. Regulators from different sectors have much to learn from each other in this area. Cross-sectoral guidance on information gathering and processing would indeed be very helpful for financial institutions subject to assist-your-customer rules of any kind.

---

[146] On this point, see: V Colaert, 'MiFID II and investor protection: picking up the crumbs of a piecemeal approach', in D Busch and G Ferrarini, *Regulation of the EU Financial Markets: MiFID II and MiFIR* (Oxford, Oxford University Press, 2017) 610–611.

15

Conflicts of Interest and Inducements in the Financial Sector

VEERLE COLAERT AND THOMAS INCALZA*

I. Introduction

Unbridled gain is the devil's workshop. If an idle brain is the devil's playground,[1] unbridled gain is his workshop. While in a free market system every player's individual pursuit of profit may be the starting point for encouraging economic growth, market failures such as information asymmetry and behavioural biases require certain restrictions on laissez-faire capitalism. In financial regulation, one of the most obvious situations calling for such restrictions is where the personal interests of a service provider are at odds with its client's. Due to the information asymmetries inherent to financial services,[2] the expected outcome of such conflicts of interest, if unregulated, would be that the service provider will place its own benefit above the client's. Notable examples are the *Cirio* and *Parmalat* cases where banks mitigated their own risk at the expense of (mostly small) investors by dumping bonds in their clients' portfolios on which they had inside information that the companies involved were likely to go bankrupt.[3]

Inducements. A very particular type of conflict of interest is the one caused by the receipt or payment of 'inducements'. An inducement is 'any fee, commission or any non-monetary benefit' provided by or paid to a service provider in connection with the provision of a financial service.[4] Naturally, such benefits pose a real risk of presenting the service provider with an incentive to promote and/or sell certain products over others in order to benefit from the inducement, rather than because it is in the best interest of the client. The EU's legislative answer to 'inducements' is threefold. It typically builds on the more general duty of care and conflicts of interest rules,[5]

* The authors would like to thank Caroline Van Schoubroeck (KU Leuven) for her valuable comments and suggestions.

[1] Meredith Willson, *The Music Man* (Broadway, 1957).

[2] For information asymmetries in general and in financial markets in particular, see Eva Becker, *Knowledge capture in financial regulation* (Munich, Springer, 2016) 171 ff.

[3] Alberto Alesina and Francesco Giavazzi, *The future of Europe: reform or decline* (Cambridge (MA), MIT Press, 2008) 112–113; Guido Ferrarini and Paolo Giudici, 'Financial scandals and the role of private enforcement' in John Armour and Joseph A McCahery (eds), *After Enron: improving corporate law and modernising securities regulation in Europe and the US* (Oxford, Hart Publishing, 2006) 162–186; Marc Kruithof, 'Conflicts of interest in institutional asset management' in Luc Thévenoz and Rashid Bahar (eds), *Conflicts of interest: corporate governance and financial markets* (Alphen aan den Rijn, Kluwer Law International, 2007) 296.

[4] For more detailed definitions, see below III.A.

[5] Lachlan Burn, 'The European Directives relating to issue and trading of securities' in Raj Panasar and Philip Boeckman (eds), *European Securities Law* (Oxford, Oxford University Press, 2010) 82.

topped off with inducement-specific rules. The EU legislature has first introduced specific rules in relation to inducements in respect of investment and ancillary services in MiFID I[6] and further enhanced these rules in MiFID II.[7] Over the years, separate inducements regimes have been included in other instruments like IDD,[8] regulating insurance intermediaries and undertakings, MCD,[9] focusing specifically on mortgage credit, the new PEPP Regulation,[10] targeting distributors of Pan-European Personal Pension Products and, most recently, the Crowdfunding Regulation Compromise Proposal.[11] Other instruments, such as the CCD,[12] covering consumer credit, do not contain any rules on inducements, even though this area seems to be confronted with similar problems.

Structure of this contribution. First, the purpose and function of each of these three layers – (1) duty of care, (2) conflicts of interest, and (3) inducements – are briefly described. Then, the specific inducements definitions and rules are compared between MiFID II, IDD, MCD, and the PEPP Regulation, briefly referring, whenever useful, to the upcoming rules of the Crowdfunding Regulation Compromise Proposal.

II. The EU's Layered Approach to Regulating Inducements in the Financial Industry

The base: a general duty of care. The first, most basic rule by which the behaviour of financial institutions paying or receiving inducements should be judged, is the general duty of care,[13] requiring the service provider to always act honestly, fairly and professionally in accordance with the best interests of the client. For investment firms, this basic principle was already laid down in Article 19(1) of MiFID I of 21 April 2004[14] and can now be found in

---

[6] Directive 2004/39/EC of the European Parliament and of the Council of 21 April 2004 on markets in financial instruments amending Council Dirs 85/611/EEC and 93/6/EEC and Dir 2000/12/EC of the European Parliament and of the Council and repealing Council Dir 93/22/EEC [2004] OJ L145/1 (hereinafter: 'MiFID I').

[7] Directive 2014/65/EU of the European Parliament and of the Council of 15 May 2014 on markets in financial instruments and amending Dir 2002/92/EC and Dir 2011/61/EU [2014] OJ L173/349 (hereinafter: 'MiFID II').

[8] Directive (EU) 2016/97 of the European Parliament and of the Council of 20 January 2016 on insurance distribution (recast) [2016] OJ L26/19 (hereinafter: 'IDD').

[9] Directive 2014/17/EU of the European Parliament and of the Council of 4 February 2014 credit agreements for consumers relating to residential immovable property and amending Dirs 2008/48/EC and 2013/36/EU and Regulation (EU) No 1093/2010 [2014] OJ L60/34 (hereinafter: 'MCD').

[10] Regulation (EU) 2019/1238 of the European Parliament and of the Council of 20 June 2019 on a pan-European Personal Pension Product (PEPP) [2019] OJ L198/1 (hereinafter: 'PEPP Regulation').

[11] Commission Proposal on European Crowdfunding Service Providers (ECSP) for Business (COM(2018)113, 8 March 2018), amended by the European Parliament European Parliament in its 'Legislative resolution of 27 March 2019 on the proposal for a regulation of the European Parliament and of the Council on European Crowdfunding Service Providers (ECSP) for Business' (COM(2018)0113 – C8-0103/2018 – 2018/0048(COD)) (hereinafter: 'proposed Crowdfunding Regulation'). On 24 June 2019 the Council of the European Union came up with a compromise proposal ('Proposal for a Regulation of the European Parliament and of the Council on European Crowdfunding Service Providers (ECSP) for Business and amending Regulation (EU) No 2017/1129 – Mandate for negotiations with the European Parliament – Compromise proposal' (Council 10557/19). Unless explicitly mentioned otherwise, references in this chapter to the 'Crowdfunding Regulation Compromise Proposal' should be read as references to the Council's Compromise Proposal.

[12] Directive 2008/48/EC of the European Parliament and of the Council of 23 April 2008 on credit agreements for consumers and repealing Council Dir 87/102/EEC [2014] OJ L133/66 (hereinafter: 'CCD').

[13] For a detailed cross-sectoral analysis of the duty of care in financial institutions, see chapter 14A of this book by Veerle Colaert and Maarten Peeters: 'Is there a case for a cross-sectoral duty of care for the financial sector?'.

[14] Article 19(1) of MiFID I.

Article 24(1) of MiFID II.[15] As Silverentand, Sprecher and Simons put it, 'this general duty forms the basis for all conduct rules applicable to the provision of investment services'.[16] For the insurance sector, this requirement was not included in the original Insurance Mediation Directive (IMD) of 9 December 2002.[17] It was only introduced, for the first time, by Article 17(1) of the current Insurance Distribution Directive (IDD) of 20 January 2016.[18] Article 22 of the PEPP Regulation contains the exact same duty of care provision for PEPP providers and distributors. The same goes for Article 4(2) of the Crowdfunding Regulation Compromise Proposal. MCD's duty of care, however, takes a slightly different approach. In the first place, Article 7(1) of MCD contains a *broader* duty of care as it not only expects mortgage creditors and credit intermediaries to act 'honestly, fairly and professionally' but explicitly requires them to act 'transparently' as well. In the second place, the wording of MCD's duty of care is also more *limited* than the former since it only requires 'taking into account' the rights and interests of the consumers, thereby holding a significantly lower standard than effectively *acting* in their *best* interests would take.[19]

The middle: a specific obligation to identify and control or disclose conflicts of interest. Legal instruments addressing inducements specifically usually also contain a second legislative layer composed of specific conflicts of interest rules. Whereas the duty of care is a conduct of business requirement, applicable only when actually providing services to clients, this second layer contains continuous, organisational conflicts of interest rules, regardless of whether services are provided or not.[20]

Those rules state that the service provider, once licensed to provide financial services, should take all appropriate steps to (a) *identify* and (b) *prevent or manage* conflicts of interest between a client and themselves (including their managers, employees and tied agents, or any person directly or indirectly linked to them by control) or between one client and another.[21] Where organisational or administrative arrangements are not sufficient to ensure that risks of damage to client interests will be prevented, such conflicts of interest should be (c) clearly *disclosed* to the client. Again, this requirement had already been introduced for investment firms in Articles 13(3) and 18 of MiFID I, which would later become Articles 16(3) and 23 of MiFID II.[22] According to Article 7(4) of the proposed Crowdfunding Regulation, crowdfunding service providers will be subject to a similar regime.

---

[15] Article 24(1) of MiFID II.

[16] Larissa Silverentand, Jasha Sprecher and Lisette Simons, 'Inducements' in Danny Busch and Guido Ferrarini (eds), *Regulation of the EU financial markets: MiFID II and MiFIR* (Oxford, Oxford University Press, 2017) 205.

[17] Directive 2002/92/EC of the European Parliament and of the Council of 9 December 2002 on insurance mediation [2003] OJ L9/3 (hereinafter: 'IMD').

[18] Article 17(1) of IDD.

[19] Article 7(4) of MCD, however, specifies that, when providing advisory services, the remuneration structure of the staff may not prejudice their ability to act in 'the consumer's best interest' (eg by being contingent on target sales), implying that, at least when actually providing advice, such a duty does exist (see also Art 22(3)(d) and Recital (31) of MCD only requiring 'advice' to be given in the best interests of the customer).

[20] Stefan Grundmann and Philipp Hacker, 'Conflicts of interest' in Danny Busch and Guido Ferrarini (eds), *Regulation of the EU financial markets: MiFID II and MiFIR* (Oxford, Oxford University Press, 2017) 179 ff.

[21] In this final example, a conflict of interest between two clients will, in effect, naturally amount to a conflict of interest between the service provider itself and the 'less-attractive' client.

[22] Although MiFID I's conflicts of interest rules have not been 'radically overhauled in MiFID II, they are tightened and clarified in various respects', such as by stressing that the disclosure of a conflict of interest is a measure of last resort to be used 'only where the effective organisational and administrative arrangements put in place by the investment firm to prevent or manage conflicts of interest are not sufficient to ensure, with reasonable confidence, that the risks of damage to the interests of the client will be prevented' (see Danny Busch, 'Conduct-of-business rules under MiFID I and II' in Danny Busch and Cees van Dam (eds), *A bank's duty of care* (Oxford, Hart Publishing, 2017) 50 ff).

In the insurance sector, however, this rule was only imposed in 2016 by Articles 27 and 28 of IDD.[23] Although the obligation to (a) *identify* and (b) *manage* conflicts of interest is imposed on all insurance intermediaries and insurance undertakings (Article 28), the obligation to *prevent* conflicts of interest seems to be limited to those carrying on the distribution of insurance-based investment products (IBIPs)[24] (Article 27).

At first glance, the PEPP Regulation may appear not to contain any specific conflicts of interest regime comparable to MiFID II's or IDD's. Article 23, however, provides that, for the distribution of PEPPs, both (a) insurance undertakings and intermediaries, and (b) investment firms are to comply with their respective sector-specific distribution regimes (ie the national laws giving effect to the relevant provisions of either IDD or MiFID II and their respective delegated acts). The articles referred to explicitly include the respective MiFID and IDD provisions on conflicts of interest. MiFID II's distribution regime is moreover extended, by that same provision, to (c) 'all other PEPP providers and PEPP distributors'. Article 41(1)(a) contains a specific rule covering also the investment phase, providing that '[i]n the case of a potential conflict of interest, a PEPP provider, or the entity which manages its portfolio, shall ensure that the investment is made in the sole interest of PEPP savers'.

MCD, however, does not contain any such pairing provision and merely states that a mortgage creditor's or credit intermediary's 'remuneration policy'[25] should incorporate measures to avoid conflicts of interest (Article 7(3)(b)) and that those claiming to provide 'independent advice' 'shall not be remunerated for those advisory services by one or more creditors' if 'the number of creditors considered is less than a majority of the market' (Article 22(4)).[26]

The topping: a detailed regulation of 'inducements'. A third and final rule intends to control inducements, which, as mentioned above,[27] can give rise to a particular type of conflict of interest. As inducements pose a high risk of clouding the service provider's objective judgment – which, pursuant to the base rule, should always be made in accordance with the best interests of the client[28] – more detailed requirements were deemed necessary. It should come as no surprise by now that the IMD did not mention anything about inducements. Under MiFID I an inducements regime was introduced in the MiFID I Implementing Directive[29] as an implementation of the MiFID I duty of care. Thus, Article 26 of the MiFID I Implementing Directive clarified that investment firms should be regarded as not fulfilling their duty of care 'if, in relation to the provision of an investment or ancillary service to the client, they pay or are paid any fee or commission, or provide or are provided with any non-monetary benefit', except in a number of cases. This rule

---

[23] It should be noted, however, that although the IMD did not contain a specific conflicts of interest regime, Art 132(2) of Solvency II did already provide, in very general terms, that '[i]n the case of a conflict of interest, insurance undertakings, or the entity which manages their asset portfolio, shall ensure that the investment is made in the best interest of policy holders and beneficiaries' (see Dir 2009/138/EC of the European Parliament and of the Council of 25 November 2009 on the taking-up and pursuit of the business of Insurance and Reinsurance (Solvency II) [2009] OJ L335/1).

[24] See also below section III.B.ii. ff.

[25] Contrary to MiFID II and IDD, MCD appears to use the term 'remuneration' not only in the strict sense of a firm's (internal) compensation structure, a topic addressed in the contribution of Guido Ferrarini and Michele Siri in this book (see Chapter 8B), but also to refer to benefits received from (external) third parties, ie 'inducements' (see below section III.A.).

[26] It should be noted, however, that Art 88(1) of CRD IV requires that 'the management body defines, oversees and is accountable for the implementation of the governance arrangements that ensure effective and prudent management of an institution, including [...] the prevention of conflicts of interest'. Many mortgage credit providers are credit institutions that would need to comply with this requirement.

[27] See above section I.

[28] See above section II.

[29] Commission Dir 2006/73/EC of 10 August 2006 implementing Dir 2004/39/EC of the European Parliament and of the Council as regards organisational requirements and operating conditions for investment firms and defined terms for the purposes of that Dir [2006] OJ L241/26 (hereinafter: 'MiFID I Implementing Directive').

has been upgraded to an independent level 1 rule by Articles 23 and 24 of MiFID II. In the insurance sector, the top tier of inducements regulation is now governed by Article 29 of IDD which, however, takes an approach opposite to MiFID II's.[30]

Interestingly, the Commission's initial proposal for a PEPP Regulation did contain a specific provision devoted to inducements. Article 20 of that proposal referred to the MiFID II rules '[w]ith regard to the payment or reception of fees or commissions or the provision or reception of non-monetary benefits in connection with the distribution of a PEPP to or by any party except the PEPP saver'.[31] As mentioned above,[32] Article 23 of the final text extended this referral to IDD's and MiFID II's entire distribution regime, with a few exceptions, absorbing the Commission's original inducements-specific provision. MCD only imposes information requirements regarding the existence of inducements (Article 15(1)(g)). Article 7(4), however, allows Member States '[to] impose more stringent requirements in relation to the use of the terms "independent advice" or "independent advisor" by creditors, credit intermediaries or appointed representatives, including a ban on receiving remuneration from a creditor'. Article 4(3) of the proposed Crowdfunding Regulation takes yet another approach by restricting crowdfunding service providers from paying or accepting 'any remuneration, discount or non-monetary benefit' but only if such inducements are paid or accepted 'for routing investors' orders to a particular crowdfunding offer made on theirs platform or to a particular crowdfunding offer provided on a third party platform'.

A three-tier cake. The EU's layered approach to regulating inducements in the financial industry can therefore be depicted as a three-tier cake albeit one with very different toppings.[33] Regarding the application of this layered regime, it should be noted that ESMA's predecessor, CESR, explained that the conflicts of interest rules (ie the 'middle') and the inducements rules (ie the 'topping') 'are complementary and not substitutes or alternatives',[34] stressing that '[c]ompliance with the conflicts rules does not provide a safe harbour from the inducements rules' and that '[c]ompliance with the inducements rules does not provide a safe harbour from the conflicts rules'.[35]

III. Sectoral Divergences in Inducements Regulation[36]

Overview. Overall, the EU legislature seems to look much less askance at inducements in the insurance and mortgage credit market than it does in the investment sector (including PEPPs distributed by other intermediaries than insurance intermediaries). This different degree of distrust becomes apparent by pointing out the three main dissimilarities in inducements regulation: (1) how inducements are technically defined; (2) whether inducements are 'banned unless permitted', 'permitted unless banned' or 'banned unless sufficient players'; and (3) whether they aim at minimum or maximum harmonisation.

---

[30] See below section II.A. ff.

[31] European Commission, 'Proposal for a Regulation of the European Parliament and of the Council on a pan-European Personal Pension Product (PEPP)', COM(2017) 343 final, 29 June 2017, 35.

[32] See above section II.

[33] See figure below, further explained in section IV.

[34] CESR, 'Inducements: Good and poor practices', *Consultation Paper*, 22 October 2009, CESR/09-958, 12.

[35] CESR, 'Inducements under MiFID', *Second Consultation Paper*, April 2007, CESR/07-228b, Annex III, para 17.

[36] See also Veerle Colaert, 'MiFID II in relation to other investor protection regulation: picking up the crumbs of a piecemeal approach' in Danny Busch and Guido Ferrarini (eds), *Regulation of the EU financial markets: MiFID II and MiFIR* (Oxford, Oxford University Press, 2017) 595 ff.

A. Definition

Various legislative techniques leading to the same description. Although MiFID II does not explicitly define the term 'inducement', the word 'inducements' is used several times throughout the text, eg in Articles 16(3), 23(1), 24(13)(d) and 27(2). Remarkably, Article 24(9), the most relevant inducement-specific provision, does not use the word at all. Instead, Article 24(9) of MiFID II contains a lengthy description, originating from Article 26 of the former MiFID I Implementing Directive, referring to 'any fee or commission, or provide or are provided with any non-monetary benefit in connection with the provision of an investment service or an ancillary service, to or by any party except the client or a person on behalf of the client'. The same expression is used in Article 11 of MiFID II Delegated Directive which, again, does not technically *define* the term. This is different in the insurance sector where, for purposes of the IDD, Article 2(2) of the IDD Delegated IBIPs Regulation[37] does contain a definition of an 'inducement' as 'any fee, commission, or any non-monetary benefit provided by or to such an intermediary or undertaking in connection with the distribution of an insurance-based investment product, to or by any party except the customer involved in the transaction in question or a person acting on behalf of that customer'. This description seems to overlap with IDD's own level-1 definition of a 'remuneration' as, according to Article 2(1)(9), 'any commission, fee, charge or other payment, including an economic benefit of any kind or any other financial or non-financial advantage or incentive offered or given in respect of insurance distribution activities'. It appears, however, that in IDD, the term 'remuneration' is reserved for internal benefits, provided within the insurance company to, for example, its employees, whereas the term 'inducements' should be used for external benefits, provided by a third party to the insurance company. MCD has adopted the word 'inducements' in Article 15(1)(g), without ever defining it, while Article 7(4) refers to 'commissions' included in the 'remuneration structure of the staff' which here, apparently, can also entail remuneration from a creditor. The PEPP Regulation does not even use the word 'inducement' but instead refers to the relevant provisions under IDD and MiFID II.[38] Finally, the Crowdfunding Regulation Compromise Proposal does not use the term 'inducement' either, but prohibits the payment or acceptance of any remuneration, discount or non-monetary benefit for routing investors' orders. All eventually leading to virtually the same description (except for the Crowdfunding Regulation Compromise Proposal, the scope of which seems to be more limited – cf below), there appears to be no substantive reason for this intersectoral panoply of legislative techniques to simply define inducements.

B. Banned-Unless-Permitted (MiFID II), Permitted-Unless-Banned (IDD) or Banned-Unless-Sufficient-Players (MCD)

Overview. A second, this time major difference, mainly between MiFID II and IDD, is that formally the ban on commissions is the rule in investment but the exception in insurance. A general prohibition of inducements had already been introduced by MiFID I[39] and was further

---

[37] Commission Delegated Regulation (EU) 2017/2359 of 21 September 2017 supplementing Dir (EU) 2016/97 of the European Parliament and of the Council with regard to information requirements and conduct of business rules applicable to the distribution of insurance-based investment products [2017] OJ L341/8 (hereinafter: 'IDD Delegated IBIPs Regulation').

[38] See above section II. ff.

[39] See below section II.B.i. ff.

enhanced by MiFID II.[40] In IDD, however, the general rule to date remains that inducements are allowed, on certain conditions.[41] Since the PEPP Regulation refers back to IDD and MiFID II, only the latter two will be discussed below, followed by a brief comparison with the approach taken by MCD.

i. MiFID II: Banned Unless Permitted

MiFID I. In MiFID I, the prohibition of inducements was not an absolute injunction but a mere starting point. As such, the ban on inducements in Article 26 of the MiFID I Implementing Directive was immediately followed by three exceptions:[42] (i) 'direct fees', ie when the inducement is paid to or by the client (or on his behalf); (ii) 'quality-enhancing fees', ie when the inducement is paid to or by a third party, provided that the inducement is disclosed to the client in a comprehensive and understandable manner prior to the provision of the investment service; that the inducement is designed to enhance the quality of the relevant service; and the inducement does not impair the firm's duty of care; and (iii) 'proper fees', ie when the inducement consists of fees necessary for the provision of the investment service (such as custody costs, settlement and exchange fees, regulatory levies and legal fees[43]), provided they do not impair the firm's duty of care. The second exception was clearly the most generous one, but also gave rise to a lot of questions. CESR therefore provided for a number of general factors to be taken into account in determining whether or not a given arrangement enhances the quality of the service:[44] (a) the type of service and any specific duties the firm owes to the client; (b) the expected benefit for the client as opposed to the expected benefit for the firm; (c) whether there will be an incentive for the firm not to act in the client's best interest; (d) the relationship between the investment firm and the entity receiving or providing the benefit; and (e) the nature of the item, the circumstances in which it is paid and whether any conditions attach to it. Under this second exception the EU legislature excluded, most generously, 'the receipt by an investment firm of a commission in connection with investment advice or general recommendations, in circumstances where the advice or recommendations are not biased as a result of the receipt of commission'.[45] This recital prompted CESR to consider that other situations may be treated in a similar way. For example, 'where an issuer or product provider pays an investment firm for distribution where no advice or general recommendation is provided'.[46] The (questionable) reasoning behind this recommendation was that, in the absence of payment by the product provider or issuer, these services, most likely, would not be provided at all.

MiFID II. Due to its rather broad exceptions, the MiFID I prohibition of inducements has in practice not been experienced as a real injunction.[47] In order to strengthen investor protection, the EU legislature thought it appropriate 'to further restrict the possibility for firms providing the service of investment advice on an independent basis and the service of portfolio management

---

[40] See below section II.B.i. ff.

[41] See below no section II.B.ii. ff.

[42] See also the important level 3 guidance: CESR, 'Inducements under MiFID', Recommendations, May 2007, CESR/07-228b, 6–7, para 10; CESR, 'Inducements: Good and poor practices', *Consultation Paper*, 22 October 2009, CESR/09-958, 12; CESR, 'Inducements: Report on good and poor practices', *Report*, 19 April 2010, CESR/10-2995, 15, para 40.

[43] Danny Busch and Cees van Dam, *A bank's duty of care* (Oxford, Hart Publishing, 2017) 54.

[44] CESR, 'Inducements under MiFID', *Recommendations*, May 2007, CESR/07-228b, 9, Rec. 4.

[45] Recital (39) of the MiFID I Implementing Directive.

[46] CESR, 'Inducements under MiFID', *Recommendations*, May 2007, CESR/07-228b, 9–10, para 21.

[47] Rosemarijn Labeur, 'Provisieverbod beleggingsondernemingen: een blik terug en een blik vooruit' (2014) 12 *Tijdschrift voor Financieel Recht* 502.

to accept and retain fees, commissions or any monetary and non-monetary benefits from third parties, and particularly from issuers or product providers.'[48]

MiFID II: Standard inducements regime for limited advice and execution only services.[49] If the firm does not claim the advice to be provided on an independent basis, it is merely giving 'limited advice', subject to the 'standard' inducements regime, largely comparable to the former MiFID I rules. Article 24(9) of MiFID II retains the explicit legal presumption that, as a rule, investment firms providing or accepting benefits 'are regarded as *not fulfilling* their obligations' under Article 23 (regarding conflicts of interest) or Article 24(1) (duty of care). Although differently worded, in effect, Article 24(9) of MiFID II contains the same exceptions as Article 26 of the MiFID I Implementing Directive, excluding 'direct fees',[50] 'quality-enhancing fees'[51] and 'proper fees'.[52] However, MiFID II introduces a much stricter interpretation of 'quality-enhancing fees'. Article 11 of the MiFID II Delegated Directive now explains that a fee shall be considered to be quality enhancing only if: (a) it is justified by an additional or higher level of service; (b) it does not directly benefit the recipient firm without tangible benefit to the client; and (c) an ongoing inducement is justified by an ongoing benefit to the client.[53] These *cumulative* 'conditions' are much stricter than the *alternative* 'criteria' previously listed in CESR's guidance with regard to the MiFID I Implementing Directive.[54] As an effect, the burden of proof has shifted to the investment firm, which will have to show that the benefit consisted either of direct, quality-enhancing or proper fees.

MiFID II: Enhanced inducements regime for independent advice and portfolio management. If the investment firm claims to be providing 'independent' advice or if it provides portfolio management, it has to comply with stricter rules. In that case MiFID II requires that the firm should not 'accept and retain fees, commissions or any monetary or non-monetary benefits paid or provided by any third party or a person acting on behalf of a third party in relation to the provision of the service to clients' (Articles 24(7)(b) and (8) of MiFID II). This ban only affects benefits that are 'accepted' by the firm, excluding payments by the firm to a third party, and those 'retained' by the firm, excluding the ones immediately retroceded to the client.[55] Apart from those exemptions only 'minor non-monetary benefits' are allowed, provided that they are *quality enhancing* and do not impair the firm's *duty of care*. According to Article 12(3) of the MiFID II Delegated Directive, such 'acceptable minor non-monetary benefits' include: (a) generic information relating to a financial instrument or an investment service; (b) written material from a third party that is commissioned and paid for by an issuer to promote a new issuance or to produce such material on an ongoing basis, provided that relationship is duly

---

[48] Recital (74) of MiFID II.

[49] Article 30(1) of MiFID II provides that 'investment firms authorised to execute orders on behalf of clients and/or to deal on own account and/or to receive and transmit orders, may bring about or enter into transactions with eligible counterparties *without being obliged to comply with the obligations under Article 24*, with the exception of paragraphs 4 and 5'.

[50] First section of Art 24(9) of MiFID II: '[…] to or by any party except the client or a person on behalf of the client […]'.

[51] Article 24(9)(a) and (b) of MiFID II and second section of Art 24(9) of MiFID II.

[52] Third section of Art 24(9) of MiFID II.

[53] Article 11 of the Commission Delegated Dir (EU) 2017/593 of 7 April 2016 supplementing Dir 2014/65/EU of the European Parliament and of the Council with regard to safeguarding of financial instruments and funds belonging to clients, product governance obligations and the rules applicable to the provision or reception of fees, commissions or any monetary or non-monetary benefits [2017] OJ L87/500 (hereinafter: 'MiFID II Delegated Directive').

[54] See above section III.B.i.

[55] Recital (74) of MiFID II; Larissa Silverentand, Jasha Sprecher and Lisette Simons, 'Inducements' in Danny Busch and Guido Ferrarini (eds), *Regulation of the EU financial markets: MiFID II and MiFIR* (Oxford, Oxford University Press, 2017) 217; Rosemarijn Labeur, 'Inducements' in Danny Busch and Kitty Lieverse (eds), *Handboek beleggingsondernemingen* (Deventer, Wolters Kluwer, 2019) 625.

disclosed; (c) participation in training events; (d) hospitality of a reasonable de minimis value, such a food and drink during a business event; and (e) other minor non-monetary benefits as determined by the national legislature, provided they are quality enhancing and do not impair the firm's duty of care. Evidently, according to the Commission, minor non-monetary benefits meeting those criteria can safely be said to enhance the quality of service provided to the client as required by Article 29 of MiFID II.

MiFID II: Investment research. It is not uncommon in the investment sector for third parties to provide 'investment research' to investment firms. As such research has an economic value, it would in principle qualify as an inducement, especially if it is provided free of charge or at a discount.[56] During ESMA's consultation, the then proposed enhanced inducements regime of MiFID II prompted fears from market players and Member States that 'rules would be imposed that would hinder investment firms' access to research and would pose concerns for the viability of firms providing research'.[57] That is why the European Commission added an extra exception in Article 13 of the MiFID II Delegated Directive (EU) 2017/593[58] providing that 'research by third parties to investment firms providing portfolio management or other investment or ancillary services to clients shall not be regarded as an inducement' in two situations. The first is when the research is received in return for direct payments by the investment firm out of its own resources. This is only logical as in that case, there is no real 'benefit' to be feared. The second is when it is paid for by a separate research payment account and a number of strict conditions are met, including a specific research charge to the client, regular assessments of the research budget and the development of quality criteria. It is important to note that both situations require that the research is paid for. Investment research provided entirely free of charge will therefore still qualify as an inducement.[59] Provided that it is not substantial and does not include any substantive analysis, such free research can, however, still constitute an acceptable minor non-monetary benefit, excluding it from the enhanced inducements rules.[60]

ii. IDD: Permitted Unless Banned

The problem of IBIPs: a 'level' playing field without the 'same' requirements? Given the EU's sectoral approach to financial regulation, the MiFID rules only apply to the investment and not the insurance sector. Over the past few decades, however, it has become common practice for insurance companies and intermediaries to offer their clients 'insurance-based investment products'.[61] Economically, these 'IBIPs' often function as substitutes for certain financial instruments subject to MiFID. Legally, however, they are treated as insurance products.[62]

---

[56] Larissa Silverentand, Jasha Sprecher and Lisette Simons, 'Inducements' in Danny Busch and Guido Ferrarini (eds), *Regulation of the EU financial markets: MiFID II and MiFIR* (Oxford, Oxford University Press, 2017) 223; Rosemarijn Labeur, 'Inducements' in Danny Busch and Kitty Lieverse (eds), *Handboek beleggingsondernemingen* (Deventer, Wolters Kluwer, 2019) 628.

[57] Ibid.

[58] This provision does not define 'research' but a description can be found in Recital (28) of the MiFID II Delegated Directive.

[59] In practice, the distinction between research that has to be paid for (no inducement) and research that can be provided free of charge (acceptable minor non-monetary benefit) is not always clear (see Frank Dankers, 'MiFID II en de 'undbundling' van beleggingsresearch' (2016) 18 *Tijdschrift voor Financieel Recht* 9).

[60] Recital (29) of the MiFID II Delegated Directive.

[61] For more information on the development of IBIPs, see Pierpaolo Marano and Ioannis Rokas (eds), *Distribution of insurance-based investment products* (Cham, Springer, 2019).

[62] Danny Busch, 'MiFID II: Stricter conduct of business rules for investment firms' (2017) 12 *Capital Markets Law Journal* 340, 343.

In Recital 56 of IDD the legislature explicitly acknowledges that 'insurance-based investment products are often made available to customers as potential alternatives or substitutes to investment products subject to Directive 2014/65/EU' and that '[t]o deliver consistent investor protection and avoid the risk of regulatory arbitrage, it is important that insurance-based investment products are subject, in addition to the conduct of business standards defined for all insurance products, to specific standards aimed at addressing the investment element embedded in those products. Such specific standards should include [...] restrictions on remuneration.'

IDD: the tables turned. Despite claiming to level the playing field for IBIPs and other investment products, IDD's approach to inducements is entirely opposite to MiFID's. Even though it provides more detailed guidance for IBIPs, the IBIPs-regime is hardly more aligned to MiFID II. While under MiFID II, inducements are banned unless explicitly permitted, Article 29(2) of IDD has adopted the legal presumption that, if insurance intermediaries or undertakings accept or provide benefits, as a rule, they 'are regarded as *fulfilling* their obligations' under Article 17(1) (regarding the duty of care) and Articles 27 and 28 (regarding conflicts of interest). This means that, in the insurance sector, inducements are permitted, albeit on certain conditions. This approach leaves the burden of proof with the client or supervisor, who will have to demonstrate that the benefit either impairs the service provider's duty of care or has a 'detrimental impact' on the quality of the service. In respect of the distribution of IBIPs, the European Commission has come up with more detailed rules on what is to be considered 'a detrimental impact' (Article 8 of the IDD Delegated IBIPs Regulation). This will mainly depend on the nature and the scale of the inducement. The firm should moreover perform an overall analysis taking into account the following criteria: (a) whether the inducement could provide an incentive to offer or recommend a particular insurance product or service despite the fact that the service provider would be able to offer a different one which would better meet the customer's needs; (b) whether the inducement is based on quantitative rather than qualitative criteria reflecting compliance with applicable regulations, the quality of the service and customer satisfaction; (c) the value of the inducement in relation to the value of the product or services; (d) whether the inducement is paid at the moment of conclusion of the contract or extends over the whole term; (e) the existence of an appropriate reclaiming mechanism; and (f) the existence of a value accelerator which is unlocked by attaining a sales target. This technique of listing *alternative* 'criteria' for assessing whether an inducement is detrimental to the quality of the service seems more liberal than the current MiFID II approach containing *cumulative* 'conditions' for a fee to be quality enhancing.[63] Member States can, however, decide to introduce a stricter inducements regime.[64]

No enhanced inducements regime. On top of this reversal of the burden of proof, IDD does not contain an enhanced inducements regime, comparable to MiFID's, for insurance intermediaries or companies claiming to be providing advice on an independent basis. It is interesting to note that the Commission, in its original draft, favoured a much more MiFID-like approach in proposing a general ban on inducements for independent advice in the insurance sector as well.[65] This provision, however, was deleted by the European Parliament maintaining that '[t]he directive should not discriminate specific remuneration systems which have established themselves

---

[63] See above section III.B.i. ff.

[64] See below section III.C.

[65] Article 24(5)(b) of the draft IDD, as proposed by the Commission, said, in a wording comparable to MiFID II's, that '[w]hen the insurance intermediary or insurance undertaking informs the customer that insurance advice is provided on an independent basis, the insurance intermediary or insurance undertaking shall [...] not accept or receive fees, commissions or any monetary benefits paid or provided by any third party or a person acting on behalf of a third party in relation to the provision of the service to customers'.

in the market and which ensure insurance coverage for citizens'.[66] It is up to the Member States to decide whether or not to introduce specific rules for independent advice. And even if they choose to do so, Member States are not required to provide an enhanced inducements regime for independent insurance advice. According to Article 29(3) of IDD, Member States *may* provide that the intermediary claiming to be independent 'shall assess a sufficiently large number of insurance products available on the market which are sufficiently diversified'. It should be noted that the inducements regime of Article 29 of IDD moreover only applies to the distribution of IBIPs. For the distribution of other insurance products, Article 22(3) of IDD merely states that Member States *may* additionally 'limit or prohibit the acceptance or receipt of fees, commissions or other monetary or non-monetary benefits paid or provided to insurance distributors by any third party, or a person acting on behalf of a third party'. Evidently, commissions are still considered 'normal' in the insurance sector. Due to this market structure, the EU legislature appears to be primarily concerned with the risk that, if inducements would be banned in respect of independent insurance advice, less fortunate citizens would no longer be able to afford it.[67]

Assumptions may be legally flawed. Some disagree with this view. It has been argued that, economically, the costs of inducements are already borne by the end client and that a ban on inducements would therefore not have a big impact.[68] More research would be needed to substantiate such claims. However, the idea that insurance coverage will decrease due to the introduction of a MiFID-like ban on inducements in the insurance sector might also be legally flawed. It appears to stem from the assumption that, if inducements were banned for independent advice, small insurance companies and intermediaries would automatically disappear, as their main source of revenue would dry up. This is not necessarily the case. After all, '[t]here is a significant possibility that many investment advisers working with a remuneration structure geared towards third-party commissions would simply cease to selfdescribe as being independent and switch their business to the provision of non-independent advice (in that making the nature of their business more transparent to clients)'.[69]

---

[66] European Parliament, 'Report on the proposal for a directive of the European Parliament and of the Council on the insurance mediation (recast)', *Plenary sitting*, A7-0085/2014, 5 February 2014, 129.

[67] George Papaconstantinou, 'Investment bankers in conflict: the regime of inducements in MiFID II and the Member States' Struggle for Fairness' (2016) 12 *European Review of Contract Law* 356, 390.

[68] This statement was made, for example, in the impact assessment of MiFID II where an Italian trade association explained that 'reduction in the use of inducements has resulted in an increase in the charges levied on investors [so as] to compensate the portfolio managers for the revenues lost' while stressing that 'previously the customer would have borne these charges implicitly as the product provider would have charge (sic) higher fees in order to enable him to pay commissions to the portfolio manager and these fees would have been deducted from the investment returns achieved' (see European Commission, 'Impact assessment accompanying the document Proposal for a Directive of the European Parliament and of the Council one Markets in financial instruments [Recast] and the Proposal for a Regulation of the European Parliament and of the Council on Markets in financial instruments', *Commission Staff Working Paper*, Brussels, 20 October 2011, SEC(2011) 1226 final, 68). From this, the Commission concluded that the net impact of the ban on inducements, for portfolio managers, would be neutral as 'the inducements on packaged products could be passed on to the end clients who would (in theory) be exactly compensated for the increased charges made by the portfolio managers'. If the Commission's reasoning is correct, a MiFID-like ban on inducements in the insurance sector would increase intermediaries' independence without them suffering any real economic losses, refuting the argument that insurance coverage for citizens would decrease. Although the overall cost of product management may very well increase due to possible diseconomies of scale, a MiFID-like ban in the insurance sector would then not automatically involve a surge in prices for independent advice by the same amount the inducements cost the sector today.

[69] European Commission, 'Impact assessment accompanying the document Proposal for a Directive of the European Parliament and of the Council one Markets in financial instruments [Recast] and the Proposal for a Regulation of the European Parliament and of the Council on Markets in financial instruments', *Commission Staff Working Paper*, Brussels, 20 October 2011, SEC(2011) 1226 final, 68.

It is indeed important to point out that the enhanced MiFID II inducements rules are, essentially, part of the provisions on 'information to clients'.[70] That is why Recital (74) of MiFID II only cites them as 'strengthen[ing] the protection of investors and increas[ing] clarity to clients as to the service they receive'. This means that, in effect, the severe MiFID II return-to-client sanction for independent advisors is, to large extent, a rule of disclosure.[71] The enhanced regime only applies when the investment firm wants to *claim* that it provides 'independent advice'. If it would simply acknowledge the fact that, due to the inducements received, it is no longer independent, there is no real 'ban' on inducements in regard of advice, even in MiFID II. Provided the firm complies with the standard regime, it can continue to give (limited) advice, even though it can no longer claim to be independent, the inducements will need to comply with the heavy quality enhancement test, and the firm will need to disclose the inducements to the client. Only when providing portfolio management the return-to-client rule would result in an actual ban on inducements.

No exceptions for research. IDD nor the IDD Delegated IBIPs Regulation contain any exceptions with regard to research. This exception, however, is directly linked with MiFID II's *enhanced* inducements regime.[72] Although Article 13 does not expressly limit its scope of application, it is primarily concerned with firms providing independent advice or portfolio management. Recitals (27) and (28) of the MiFID II Delegated Directive also consistently refer to investment firms providing investment advice on an independent basis or portfolio management services, for whom 'further clarifications in relation to the payment or reception of research should be provided'. As IDD, contrary to MiFID II, has not adopted an enhanced inducements regime, naturally, there was no need to introduce a similar exception in the insurance sector.

iii. *MCD: Banned for Independent Advice Unless Sufficient Players*

In between MiFID II and IDD. Interestingly, MCD takes an entirely different approach to inducements. Here, Article 22(4) provides that Member States may prohibit the use of the term 'advice' and 'advisor' or similar terms when the advisory services are being provided to consumers by creditors, tied credit intermediaries or appointed representatives of tied credit intermediaries. Member States who do not prohibit the use of the term 'advice' should at least restrict the use of the term 'independent advice' to creditors, credit intermediaries or appointed representatives providing advisory services that (a) consider a sufficiently large number of credit agreements available on the market; and (b) shall not be remunerated for those advisory services by one or more creditors. The second condition, which basically comes down to a ban on inducements, comparable to MiFID II's, however, only applies 'where the number of creditors considered is less than a majority of the market'. This approach is more lenient than MiFID II's, not only because of this provision, but also because, for tied advisors and non-advised sales, it does not

---

[70] Jeremy Burke and Angela A Hung, 'Financial advice markets: a cross-country comparison', *Report to the Department of Labor* (Cambridge, RAND Corporation, 2015) 22.

[71] This is more clearly phrased, for example, in MCD where Art 22(4) restricts the *use* of the term 'independent advice' or 'independent advisor' to creditors and credit intermediaries that consider 'a sufficiently large number of credit agreements available on the market' and which are 'not [...] remunerated for those advisory services by one or more creditors'. The result, however, is the same. The injunction only affects those *claiming* to be 'independent'.

[72] George Papaconstantinou, 'Investment bankers in conflict: the regime of inducements in MiFID II and the Member States' Struggle for Fairness' (2016) 12 *European Review of Contract Law* 356, 390.

even contain a standard inducements regime. It is, however, much stricter than IDD's, as it explicitly *requires* Member States to introduce these rules for those claiming to provide 'independent advice'.

iv. *Crowdfunding Regulation Compromise Proposal: Banned if Paid or Accepted for Routing Orders to a Particular Offer*

A broader ban with a stricter scope. Finally, the Crowdfunding Regulation Compromise Proposal uses yet another technique for banning unwanted inducements. Article 4(3) prohibits crowdfunding service providers from paying or accepting inducements 'for routing investors' orders to a particular crowdfunding offer made on their platform or to a particular crowdfunding offer provided on a third party platform'. This ban appears to have a stricter *scope* than MiFID II's or even IDD's, limiting its application to those payments that have the purpose of routing orders to a particular offer. If this is the case, however, Article 4(3) of the proposed Crowdfunding Regulation allows for no exceptions at all, prohibiting 'any remuneration, discount or non-monetary benefit', rendering the *ban* itself, at the same time, stricter than MiFID II's and certainly IDD's. It remains to be seen, however, how this provision would be interpreted by the supervisors and competent courts, should it become law.

C. Maximum Harmonisation versus Minimum Harmonisation

MiFID II, Crowdfunding Regulation Compromise Proposal and PEPP Regulation: maximum harmonisation. The sectoral divergences in inducements regulation are highlighted even more by the fact that MiFID II aims to achieve maximum harmonisation, whereas IDD only contains minimum rules. Pursuant to Article 24(12) of MiFID II, Member States are only allowed to impose additional requirements on investment firms 'in exceptional cases' which must be objectively justified and proportionate to the specific risks to investor protection, subject to a strict notification procedure to the European Commission.[73] Being a regulation, the Crowdfunding Regulation Compromise Proposal also aims at achieving maximum harmonisation. The same is true for the PEPP Regulation, it being understood that when insurance intermediaries distribute PEPPs, they will be subject to the national implementation of the IDD regime, which only aims at minimum harmonisation.

IDD and MCD: minimum harmonisation ... IDD, however, explicitly aims at minimum harmonisation. According to Article 22(3) of IDD Member States may limit or prohibit the acceptance or receipt of inducements paid or provided to insurance distributors in relation to the *distribution* of insurance products in general. In respect of IBIPs, Article 29(3) of IDD moreover allows Member States to impose stricter rules in relation to the provision of investment *advice*, in the sense that 'where an insurance intermediary informs the client that advice

---

[73] Recital (76) of MiFID II explicitly confirm the possibility to impose such additional requirements in respect of inducements, provided they comply with these conditions and procedures, 'may include prohibiting or further restricting the offer or acceptance of fees, commissions or any monetary or non-monetary benefits paid or provided by any third party or a person acting on behalf of a third party in relation to the provision of service to clients'. This allowed the Netherlands, for example, to retain their more general ban on inducements (see also Larissa Silverentand, Jasha Sprecher and Lisette Simons, 'Inducements' in Danny Busch and Guido Ferrarini (eds), *Regulation of the EU financial markets: MiFID II and MiFIR* (Oxford, Oxford University Press, 2017) 210–211 and 221–222).

is given independently, the intermediary shall assess a sufficiently large number of insurance products available on the market'. This optional extension would be very similar to the above-mentioned requirement for 'independent' mortgage creditors and credit intermediaries under Article 22(4)(a) of MCD to 'consider a sufficiently large number of credit agreements available on the market'.[74] Under IDD, even if Member States opt to introduce the concept of independent advice, they are not obliged to establish an enhanced inducements regime in that respect. Nevertheless, several Member States have made use of the IDD's minimum harmonisation character and introduced a regime very similar to the MiFID II regime to the insurance sector, or at least to the distribution of IBIPs. In the UK, for example, 'the FCA is extending some MiFID II requirements to the distribution of IBIPs, which might cause some additional work for insurance manufacturers and distributors, e.g. [...] the requirement that inducements have to enhance the quality of the service and not just have no detrimental impact (PS18/1, Ch. 3)', meaning that '(insurance) intermediaries are not allowed to receive any commissions for investment products including life insurance policies'.[75] In the Netherlands, with regard to retail investors, a general inducement ban, affecting investment and insurance firms alike,[76] has already been in effect since January 2014.[77] The unlevel playing field resulting from the minimum harmonisation character of IDD is even more remarkable considering the fact that stricter national requirements for the IBIPs inducements rules in Article 29 of IDD have to be complied with by *all* insurance intermediaries and undertakings 'including those operating under the freedom to provide services or the freedom of establishment'. This is an important exception to the overall home-state-control principle generally adhered to in EU financial regulation.[78] The minimum harmonisation character of IDD could therefore significantly hamper the creation of a true internal market.[79]

... *potentially lowering investor protection.* One may wonder why a cross-sectorally unified approach to regulating inducements in the same way for all investment products and services was possible in the UK and in the Netherlands but not at EU level. Not only has IDD missed the opportunity of truly levelling the playing field, its minimum harmonisation character has actually *reduced* investor protection in some Member States. This happened in Belgium, for example, where the authors of the draft bill transposing IDD originally proposed to retain the banned-unless-permitted rule from the existing Belgian AssurMiFID regime.[80] Cabinet, however, decided to change this presumption into a permitted-unless-banned rule, claiming that, although the existing framework contributes to a higher level of investor protection, it preferred to align the

---

[74] See above section III.B.iii.

[75] Annette Hofmann, Julia K Neumann and David Pooser, 'Plea for uniform regulation and challenges of implementing the new Insurance Distribution Directive' (2018) 43 *The Geneva Papers* 740, 752; FCA, 'Changes to the use of dealing commission rules: feedback to CP13717 and final rules', *Policy Statement*, May 2014.

[76] Danny Busch, 'MiFID II: Stricter conduct of business rules for investment firms' (2017) 12 *Capital Markets Law Journal* 340, 378, fn 212.

[77] Article 168a of the Decree on Conduct of Business Supervision on Financial Undertakings AFS (Besluit gedragstoezicht financiële ondernemingen Wft); Larissa Silverentand, Jasha Sprecher and Lisette Simons, 'Inducements' in Danny Busch and Guido Ferrarini (eds), *Regulation of the EU financial markets: MiFID II and MiFIR* (Oxford, Oxford University Press, 2017) 205.

[78] Larisa Dragomir, *European prudential banking regulation and supervision: the legal dimension* (London, Routledge, 2010) 165 ff.

[79] Veerle Colaert, 'MiFID II in relation to other investor protection regulation: picking up the crumbs of a piecemeal approach' in Danny Busch and Guido Ferrarini (eds), *Regulation of the EU financial markets: MiFID II and MiFIR* (Oxford, Oxford University Press, 2017) 597.

[80] Article 27(5)–(7) of the Act of 2 August 2002 on the supervision of the financial sector and on financial services [OJ 4 September 2002] 39121, as amended by the Act of 21 November 2017 on the infrastructure of markets in financial instruments and transposing Dir 2014/65/EU [OJ 7 December 2017] 107933.

new Belgian insurance regime to the text of the IDD.[81] This means that, in spite of it only imposing *minimum* rules, IDD resulted in Belgium effectively *lowering* investor protection by shifting the burden of proof back to the client or supervisor. Unsurprisingly, this decision was met with harsh criticism from opposition benches.[82]

IV. Conclusion

Sectoral divergences. From this chapter, it can be concluded that the EU's current three-tier approach to regulating inducements contains a number of sectoral divergences which seem to grow more apart from bottom to top (see figure below). The first layer contains virtually the same basic duty to act in the best interest of the client, for investment firms, insurance distributors, PEPP distributors and, subject to some variations, mortgage credit providers. More sectoral differences can be found in the second layer, focusing on conflicts of interest between the service provider and its client. Although the same organisational requirements apply to investment firms, insurance distributors and PEPPs distributors, MCD hardly contains any conflicts of interest rules at all,[83] merely providing that a creditor's remuneration policy should incorporate 'measures' to avoid them. The most substantial differences, however, are situated in the third layer, regulating inducements specifically. The MiFID and IDD main approach to inducements is completely opposite: under MiFID II, inducements are 'banned unless permitted', while for insurance distributors they are 'permitted unless banned'. Contrary to MiFID II, IDD moreover does not contain an enhanced inducements regime for independent advice. These sectoral discrepancies extend to the distribution of PEPPs, since the PEPP Regulation refers to either the IDD or MiFID II regime, depending on who is the PEPP distributor. MCD, finally, does contain binding obligations for Member States to restrict the use of the term 'independent advice', but, contrary to MiFID II, the ban on inducements for MCD independent advisers is lifted if the number of creditors considered is more than a majority available on the market and MCD does not feature any inducements rules in respect of tied advice or non-advised sales. A final important difference between these inducements regimes, is their level of harmonisation. Whereas MiFID II aims at maximum harmonisation, IDD and MCD only achieve minimum harmonisation of their inducements regimes, and the PEPP Regulation refers to the national implementation of MiFID II and IDD respectively. The proposed Crowdfunding Regulation, should it become law, risks complicating the current framework even more, being a maximum harmonisation instrument employing an entirely different technique for banning inducements, which is conditional on the question whether the payment is made or accepted for routing investors' order to a particular offer.

---

[81] Projet de loi transposant la directive (UE) 2016/97 du Parlement européen et du Conseil du 20 janvier 2016 sur la distribution d'assurances, Exposé des motifs, *Doc. parl.*, Chambre 2017–18, DOC 54-3297/001, 8–9.

[82] Projet de loi transposant la directive (UE) 2016/97 du Parlement européen et du Conseil du 20 janvier 2016 sur la distribution d'assurances, Rapport, *Doc. parl.*, Chambre 2017–18, DOC 54-3297/003, 7: 'dans le secteur de l'assurance, ce système d'incitations a déjà donné lieu par le passé à divers abus: dîners, voyages d'agrément dans tous les sens du terme et autres; même la FSMA a tiré la sonnette d'alarme concernant ces pratiques à l'occasion de l'élaboration de la réglementation MiFID.' Free translation to English: 'in the insurance sector, this system of incentives has already given rise to various abuses in the past: dinners, pleasure trips in every sense of the word and so on; even the FSMA has sounded the alarm about these practices during the development of MiFID regulations.'

[83] See, however, fn 25.

Figure The EU's current three-tier approach to regulating inducements

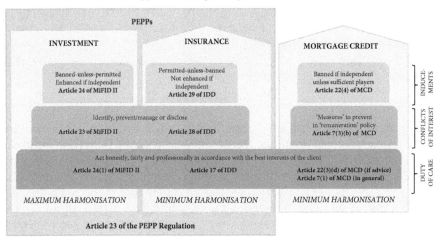

Do differences in products and markets justify a different inducements regime? Investment products, insurance products and loans are entirely different products, which on certain points clearly need different legislation. The question is whether the inducements regime is one of those points. The reason for regulating inducements is the same in all the sectors: avoiding that clients would be harmed by conflict of interests resulting from inducements. Empirical research should clarify whether the specific characteristics of the market structure in each sector would indeed justify differences in the applicable inducements regimes. The explanatory documents introducing those regimes do not seem to contain any indication in that direction. The question then arises whether it is problematic to have different inducements regimes in the different sectors.

The same regime should apply to functionally equivalent products and services. Even though loans and traditional insurance services are clearly different from MiFID financial instruments, IBIPs, PEPPs and MiFID financial instruments can all be considered investment products in the broad sense. The same credit institution can indeed offer its clients a choice between MiFID II financial instruments, IBIPs or PEPPs, which may in certain circumstances be considered valid alternatives for a client wishing to save for his pension. Since the IDD regime is more lenient, such a financial institution will be able to receive inducements when advising that client on an independent basis to invest in an IBIP (unless the national IDD legislation is stricter, while it will not be able to receive the same inducements when advising that client on an independent basis to invest in a MiFID financial instrument. This creates a real risk of regulatory arbitrage. In order to curb that risk, the same inducements framework should apply at least to all investment products in the broad sense.

Cross-sectoral alignment to reduce technical complexity. Regulatory arbitrage will not be a risk between products which are not functionally equivalent, eg insurance, investments and credit agreements, or mortgage credits and consumer credits. Even between those different products, levelling the cross-sectoral playing field would, however, lead to more legal coherence. Many differences between the inducements regimes do not seem very substantial. The various legal ways in which the term 'inducements' has been defined (or not defined), for instance, amount to technical but not substantive differences. And even the opposite approach in the standard inducements regime of MiFID II and the IDD inducements regime may in the end not lead to a different judgment on whether a given scenario is admissible or not. This different approach will in our opinion mainly result in a shift of the burden of proof of compliance with the duty to act in the best interest of the client. Those differences do not seem substantial, and therefore it would be hard to argue that they are substantiated by differences in products or market structure in the different sectors. The PEPP Regulation in fact confirms that the differences between the MiFID II and IDD inducements rules are not necessary in view of the specific characteristics of the product. The PEPP Regulation indeed applies different inducements regimes to the distribution of the same product, depending on the sector to which the PEPP distributor belongs.

Lemon makes the milk curdle. Although the EU legislature seems to have expressed its preference for MiFID II in the PEPP Regulation, declaring that all PEPP providers and distributors other than insurance undertakings or intermediaries should comply with the MiFID II rules, this contribution did not intend to answer the question as to *which* of the different inducements regimes should be preferred in the top layer, whether the stricter MiFID regime, the more lenient IDD rules or even the MCD approach keeping the middle between the two. To a hungry person, a lemon topping is just as tasty as a creamy one. They should not be unduly mixed though. That would make the milk curdle, and cracks would begin to show in the surface.

16

Product Intervention:
A Cross-Sectoral Analysis

VEERLE COLAERT

I. Introduction

Product intervention as an investor protection technique. For a very long while, the idea to prohibit a category of investors to acquire certain products, was considered extremely paternalistic and an unacceptable infringement of the freedom of choice of investors. The recent crisis has however led to increasingly wide support for product intervention as an investor protection technique. Over the past couple of years, many Member States have issued some kind of product-intervention measure. Four different types of product intervention can be distinguished: (1) an outright ban to sell certain product categories to a category of clients (usually retail clients); (2) a ban on certain product features; (3) a ban on the marketing of certain products; (4) and extra information or warnings in respect of certain products.[1]

Competences of the European Supervisory Authorities (ESAs). After the European Banking Authority (EBA) and the European Securities and Markets Authority (ESMA) had been using their consumer protection competences to issue warnings against certain products, the MiFIR and the PRIIPs Regulation have finally provided the legal basis allowing further steps to be taken. MiFIR and the PRIIPs Regulation indeed attribute direct 'product intervention powers' to ESMA, EBA and EIOPA in their respective fields of competence: MiFIR attributes such powers to ESMA with respect to financial instruments and to EBA in respect of structured deposits;[2] the PRIIPs Regulation attributes exactly the same competences to EIOPA with respect to insurance-based investment products. Each authority can in its field of competence and on certain

---

[1] Securities and Markets Stakeholder Group, 'Own Initiative Report on Product Intervention under MiFIR' (16 June 2017, ESMA 22-106-264) at 4. The annex to this report gives an overview of all national measure which have been taken up to May 2017.

[2] See in this respect: D Busch, 'Product governance and product intervention under MiFID II/MiFIR' in D Busch and G Ferrarini (eds), *Regulation of the EU Financial Markets. MiFID II and MiFIR* (Oxford, OUP 2017) 123–146; V Colaert, 'Product intervention: Keystone of the EU investor protection regime' (KU Leuven Working Paper, July 2019) available at http://ssrn.com/abstract=3440557.

conditions, temporarily[3] prohibit or restrict in the EU (a) the marketing, distribution or sale of certain products or (b) a type of financial activity or practice.[4]

Competences of Member States' Authorities. The MiFIR and the PRIIPs Regulation moreover explicitly allow Member States' competent authorities, upon certain conditions, to (continue to) prohibit or restrict (a) the marketing, distribution or sale of certain such products or (b) a type of financial activity or practice.[5] ESMA, EBA or EIOPA, respectively, shall in such circumstances perform a facilitation and coordination role. They shall ensure that action taken by a competent authority is justified and proportionate and that where appropriate a consistent approach is taken by the competent authorities.[6] The typical 'comply or explain' approach applies in this matter: the competent European Supervisory Authority can give an opinion on whether it deems action by the national authority appropriate; if the national authority does not comply with such opinion, it should immediately publish on its website a notice fully explaining its reasons.

Need for a cross-sectoral approach? The competences of the three ESAs in respect of product intervention are, at first sight, very similar. In this chapter we examine whether it would be feasible and more efficient to regulate product intervention in a one cross-sectoral piece of EU legislation. To that end we will, in a first section, carefully compare the level 1 and level 2 texts with regard to the MiFIR and PRIIPs product intervention provisions. Any differences that are detected will be carefully considered in order to decide whether or not they are substantiated in view of differences between the sectors. In a second section we raise a number of more fundamental issues that follow from the fact that the product intervention powers of the three ESAs have been regulated in two different regulations. In a third section we relate this research to the sectoral architecture of the ESAs.[7] A last section concludes.

II. Unsubstantiated Differences between the MiFIR and PRIIPs Product Intervention Provisions

A. Different Scope of Application

Scope of application of MiFIR product intervention powers. Article 1(1)(e) of MiFIR mentions with respect to 'subject matter and scope' that the MiFIR 'establishes uniform requirements in relation to … product intervention powers of competent authorities, ESMA and EBA …'.

Article 1(2) states that '[t]his Regulation applies to investment firms, authorised under Directive 2014/65/EU and credit institutions authorised under Directive 2013/36/EU of

---

[3] Currently the ESAs can take product intervention measures for a maximum of three months. Those measures are renewable. As explained in section III.B., ESMA has issued two product intervention measures, both of which have been renewed several times. This renewal process creates a heavy burden on the competent ESA, which should each time examine and justify such prolongation. In the ESA Review the ESA product intervention measures remain temporary, but the renewal burden is softened somewhat. The ESA should review the decision at appropriate intervals and at least every six months. Following at least two consecutive renewals and based on proper analysis in order to assess the impact on the consumer, the ESA may decide on the annual renewal of the prohibition.

[4] Articles 40–41, MiFIR; Art 16, PRIIPs Regulation.

[5] Article 42, MiFIR; Art 17, PRIIPs Regulation.

[6] Article 43, MiFIR; Art 18, PRIIPs Regulation.

[7] On the need for a cross-sectoral architecture of financial supervision in the EU, see also chapter 17 of this book.

the European Parliament and of the Council when providing investment services and/or performing investment activities and to market operators including any trading venues they operate.'

On the basis of this last provision, it been argued that the product intervention powers of ESMA and the NCA's under MiFIR only apply to products marketed and distributed by credit institutions and investment firms and that a product intervention measure under MiFIR will therefore not apply to fund management companies which distribute units in investment funds directly.[8] We believe, however, that there are good arguments for a wider interpretation of the MiFIR product intervention provisions, since the product intervention provisions are clearly not addressed at any financial institution, but at the authorities at national level, ESMA and EBA. The product intervention powers attributed to these authorities are also clearly not limited to products marketed and distributed by credit institutions and investment firms, but apply in respect of the marketing, distribution or sale of financial instruments and structured deposits, irrespective of the distributor.[9] The first, strict interpretation is, however, ESMA's reading of this provision.[10]

Comparison with the scope of application of the PRIIPs Regulation. If this would indeed be the correct interpretation of the scope of application of the MiFIR product intervention powers, it would mean that the scope of the product intervention powers granted to EBA and ESMA would be more restrictive than the product intervention powers given to EIOPA in the PRIIPs Regulation. Article 2(1) of the PRIIPs Regulation indeed does not limit the scope of application of the PRIIPs Regulation. It states that '(t)his Regulation shall apply to PRIIP manufacturers and persons advising on, or selling, PRIIPs.' The limitation of the scope of application of the MiFIR would be a clearly unsubstantiated – and inefficient – difference.

B. Other Differences

Level 2 provisions. The level 2 texts develop the criteria and factors which the ESAs need to take into account when issuing a new product intervention measure. Separate provisions apply to each of EBA,[11] ESMA[12] and EIOPA,[13] although the three provisions are largely similar.

Substantiated differences and similarities. If there are differences between the three provisions, they are usually easy to explain in view of differences in underlying products. The EBA criteria and factors in respect of structured deposits, for instance, refer to the deposit guarantee system,[14]

---

[8] Eg, JP Servais, 'Les pouvoirs d'intervention sur les produits reconnus aux superviseurs: un nouvel outil en vue de la protection des investisseurs' in I De Meuleneere, V Colaert et al. (eds), *MiFIR II and MiFIR: Scope, Investor Protection, Market Regulation and Enforcement* (Antwerp, Intersentia, 2018) at 233.

[9] See Arts 39–42, Recital 29. See for further arguments also SMSG, 'Advice to ESMA – Own Initiative Report on Product Intervention under MiFIR' (ESMA22-106-264, 16 June 2017); V Colaert, 'Het toepassingsgebied van de MiFIR productinterventiemaatregelen' (2017) *TRV-RPS*, 965–969.

[10] ESMA, 'Impact of the exclusion of fund management companies from the scope of the MiFIR Intervention Powers' (ESMA50-1215332076-23, 12 January 2017). ESMA therefore believes that the EU institutions should address the risk of arbitrage between MiFID firms and fund management companies. It states that, in particular, in addition to the powers available under MiFIR, NCAs and ESMA should have the powers to apply restrictions/prohibition directly to fund management companies.

[11] Article 20 of Commission Delegated Regulation (EC) 2017/567.

[12] Article 19 of Commission Delegated Regulation (EU) 2017/567.

[13] Article 1 of Commission Delegated Regulation (EU) 2016/1904.

[14] Article 20(2)(b) and (c) last bullet of Commission Delegated Regulation (EC) 2017/567.

whereas the ESMA criteria and factors in respect of financial instruments refer to the bid/ask spread, the frequency of trading availability, the issuance size and size of the secondary market, the presence or absence of liquidity providers or secondary market makers and the features of the trading system,[15] as well as to the trading, clearing and settlement systems.[16] The EIOPA criteria and factors in respect of insurance-based investment products refer to the coverage level defined in national insurance guarantee schemes law and to the value of the technical provisions.[17]

It should be pointed out that the use of the *same* language can in certain circumstances be problematic. Certain respondents to the EIOPA consultation in regard of the criteria and factors to be taken into account when issuing a new product intervention measure, expressed critical views on the use of the terms '*investor*' or '*switch an instrument*'. They claimed EIOPA should have used insurance-specific language such as 'policyholder' or 'converted contract'. EIPOA justified its choice of language by referring to the fact that the PRIIPs Regulation also uses this wording, and that the policyholders in respect of products in scope of the product intervention products, are in fact always investors. A use of the term 'policyholders' might, in EIOPA's opinion, be misinterpreted to expand the scope of its powers under the PRIIPs Regulation.[18]

Unsubstantiated differences. The number of differences in language are unsubstantiated, but seem unimportant.[19] Other differences in factors and criteria do seem to have a different meaning, without clear justification of why such a different assessment of the need for product intervention measures in respect of products of the three sectors would be necessary. For instance, for the three ESAs, one of the factors to take into account when deciding to issue a product intervention measure is the degree of transparency of the financial product, activity or practice. For EBA this includes, amongst other things, 'the use of product names or of terminology or other information that is misleading by implying product features that do not exist', whereas for ESMA and EIOPA it includes 'the use of product names or terminology or other information that imply a greater level of security or return than those which are actually possible or likely, or which imply product features that do not exist'.[20] In the EIOPA factors and criteria an additional factor is, moreover, added in respect of the assessment of the degree of transparency, 'whether there was insufficient, or insufficiently reliable, information about an insurance-based investment product to enable market participants to which it was targeted to form their judgment, taking into account the nature and type of insurance-based investment products'.[21] No equivalent criterion is mentioned in the EBA and ESMA texts. On the other hand, the EBA and ESMA factors mention 'the fact that the value of any underlying is no longer available or reliable',[22] whereas the EIOPA factors do not mention this. The difference in products do not seem to justify those seemingly random differences in wording and criteria. In the next sections, we will examine the causes of those differences and possible solutions.

---

[15] Article 19(2)(g) of Commission Delegated Regulation (EC) 2017/567.

[16] Article 19(2)(t) of Commission Delegated Regulation (EC) 2017/567.

[17] Article 1(2)(b) last two bullets and (c) last bullet.

[18] EIOPA, 'Final Report on Product Intervention Powers under the Regulation on Key Information Documents for Packaged Retail and Insurance-Based Investment Products' (EIOPA-15/569, 29 June 2015) at 67.

[19] For instance, Art 19(2)(d), fourth bullet of Commission Delegated Regulation (EC) 2017/567 refers, in respect to the criteria and factors which ESMA should take into account, to 'the nature of risks and transparency of risks', whereas Art 20(2)(d), fourth bullet refers to 'the type and transparency of risks' in respect of the criteria and factors which EBA should take into account; Art 19(2)(g) refers to 'the ease and cost', whereas Art 20(2)(g) refers to the 'costs and ease'.

[20] Articles 19(20)(d), fifth bullet and 20(2)d), fifth bullet of Commission Delegated Regulation (EC) 2017/567, and Art 1(2)(d), fifth bullet of Commission Delegated Regulation (EU) 2016/1904.

[21] Article 1(2)(d) last bullet of Commission Delegated Regulation (EU) 2016/1904.

[22] Article 19 (2)(e) last bullet and Art 20(2)(e) last bullet of Commission Delegated Regulation (EC) 2017/567.

III. Fundamental Issues Resulting from Regulating Product Intervention in Two Different Sets of Rules

While the differences mentioned above may seem futile and may not result in problems in practice, there are in our opinion a number of more fundamental issues resulting from the fact that product intervention is regulated in two different sets of rules.

A. Inefficiencies

Cross-sectoral PRIIPs Regulation only gives powers to EIOPA. First, it is contra-intuitive that, although the PRIIPs Regulation covers financial products originating from the three sectors – and its implementing legislation is prepared by the joint committee of the three ESAs – it only gives product intervention competences to EIOPA, whereas ESMA and EBA have been given the exact same competences in the MiFIR.[23] It would certainly have been more elegant if one provision in the horizontal PRIIPs Regulation would have attributed such competence to the three European Supervisory Authorities, each in their respective sectoral field of competence.

Risk of unsubstantiated – and therefore inefficient – differences. Also from a legislative efficiency perspective, the current approach is sub-optimal. If the level 1 rules on product intervention need to be adapted, two different legislative texts need to be changed, and the legislator may simply omit to adapt one of the two regulations. This is what happened recently during the ESA review, when only the MiFIR was updated to reflect the need for the ESAs to be able to take temporary product intervention measures for longer periods of time, whereas the equivalent PRIIPs rules, conferring the same powers to EIOPA, have – for no apparent reason – not been updated.[24] Moreover, the two different level 1 texts need to be implemented in two different level 2 texts, following different legislative processes, with different authorities involved. Each of the ESAs has for instance been given the competence to develop their own technical advice on 'criteria and factors to be taken into account in applying product intervention powers'.[25] As discussed in section I above, this resulted in two Commission Regulations, with, indeed, a number of unsubstantiated differences in the criteria and factors to be taken into account by EBA, ESMA and EIOPA. It should be noted that the Commission, when it asked for EIOPA's advice after the advice from ESMA and EBA had already been received, has shown awareness of this problem and attempted to alleviate it. The Commission indeed invited EIOPA 'to cooperate closely and take into account the result of the work which has been already undertaken by ESMA and EBA in the context of the product

---

[23] It seems that the idea to provide the ESAs with product intervention powers came up during the discussion on MiFID II/MiFIR. The original idea seems to have been to insert the equivalent powers for EIOPA in the IDD. In that way there would have been a legislative parallel between the conduct of business rules – introduced in MiFID II for financial instruments and structured deposits, and in IDD in respect of insurance-based investment products – and the product intervention competences for EBA and ESMA (in MiFIR) and EIOPA (in IDD). The adoption of IDD, however, took much longer than the adoption of MiFID II, while the legislative process of the PRIIPs Regulation seemed to end at a similar moment as MiFID II.

[24] New Art 40(6) MiFIR for ESMA; new Art 41(6) for EBA. See Art 6(8) and (9) of the Regulation of the European Parliament and of the Council amending a range of regulations and directives in view of the ESA review (COM(2018)0646 – C80409/2018 – 2017/0230(COD)) as approved by Council and Parliament on 16 April 2019.

[25] ESMA, 'Final Report – ESMA's Technical Advice to the Commission on MiFID II and MiFIR' (ESMA/2104/1569, 19 December 2014) 187–196; EBA, 'Technical advice on possible delegated acts on criteria and factors for intervention powers concerning structured deposits under Articles 41 and 42 of Regulation(EU) No 600/2014 (MiFIR)' (EBA Op/2014/13, 11 December 2014); EIOPA, 'Technical Advice on criteria and factors to be taken into account in applying product intervention powers' (EIOPA-15/564 29 June 2015).

intervention powers under Regulation (EU) No 600/2014'.[26] In response to the consultation preceding EIOPA's technical advice, several respondents nevertheless pointed out unsubstantiated differences with the ESMA and EBA criteria and factors.[27] EIOPA seems to have taken these comments into account, and has justified in its feedback statement certain remaining differences on the basis of technical differences between life insurance products and other investment products.[28] We have shown above, however, that there are still a number of differences in the level 2 texts, which are hard to justify on the basis of differences in relevant products.

Inefficient triplication of efforts. This process furthermore leads to triplications in efforts by the three ESAs, which consult separately on substantially the same criteria and factors. Moreover, each of the level 1 and level 2 texts, need to be translated into all the languages of the Union. With a range of often unsubstantiated differences, this creates an unnecessary burden on the Union's translation service and a risk of further translation differences.

No procedural safeguards for cooperation between the ESAs on product intervention. The fact that the ESAs have, in regard of the criteria and factors to be taken into account when deciding on product intervention measures, finally come up with substantially the same 'criteria and factors' and have clearly benefited from each other's efforts in creating such technical advice, is reassuring. There are however no procedural safeguards for the future in this regard.

One legislative text on product intervention would be more efficient. It is clear therefore, that if there would be one level 1 text on product intervention, this would have structurally ensured that the ESAs would cooperate in the Joint Committee in the implementation of the product intervention measures at the level 2. This could have resulted in one and the same level 2 text, which could still have differentiated where necessary in view of differences in products, as was the case in the level 2 text on the PRIIPs KID.[29]

B. Avoiding Regulatory Arbitrage

Product intervention measure should not create risk of regulatory arbitrage. The ESAs can only take a product intervention measure if a range of conditions are fulfilled and precautions taken. One of those precautions is that the ESA which takes the measure, should ensure that the measure does not create a risk of regulatory arbitrage,[30] ie the risk that if the distribution or marketing of one product is prohibited or curtailed, an economically similar product would be created, which possibly falls under the remit of another ESA.

Impossibility for the ESA issuing the measure to avoid regulatory arbitrage. It is strange that this provision has been drafted as a precaution that should be taken by the ESA who takes the measure. It is quite obvious that the ESA who intends to take a measure cannot, on its own, avoid regulatory arbitrage. In order to fulfil this condition, the ESAs need to cooperate: they need to notify each other of every new product intervention measure which they intend to take, upon which the other ESAs should consider whether they also need to take a product intervention

---

[26] European Commission, letter to the chairman of EIOPA (30 July 2014) https://eiopa.europa.eu/Publications/Requests%20for%20advice/C238A332.pdf.

[27] See, ie, the feedback statement in EIOPA, 'Technical Advice on criteria and factors to be taken into account in applying product intervention powers' (EIOPA-15/564, 29 June 2015) at 8: 'Other respondents welcomed the close alignment with MiFIR and questioned why EIOPA, for example, added "significantly" to criterion iii.e when referring to selling outside the target market, which would be less strict than rules for other sectors'.

[28] Ibid.

[29] On the PRIIPs KID, see chapter 13 of this book.

[30] See, for ESMA: Art 40(3), MiFIR, for EBA Art 41(3), MiFIR and for EIOPA Art 15(3), PRIIPs Regulation.

measure in their field of competence in order to avoid regulatory arbitrage. But there is no legal basis for such a requirement.

EIOPA's reaction to ESMA's first product intervention measures. EIOPA appears to have explicitly made such a consideration in respect of the first product intervention measures issued by ESMA. On 22 May 2018, ESMA took the following measures: (i) the marketing, distribution or sale of contracts for differences (CFDs) to retail clients was restricted;[31] and (ii) the marketing, distribution or sale of binary options to retail clients was prohibited. The measures applied as of 2 July 2018 for binary options and as of 1 August 2018 for CFDs.[32] Interestingly, ESMA explicitly prohibits to participate, knowingly and intentionally, in activities the object or effect of which is to circumvent those product intervention measures.[33] This indeed seems its only possibility to contribute to avoiding regulatory arbitrage. The measures have been lifted on 1 and 31 July respectively.[34]

EBA and EIOPA did not yet take any product intervention measures. However, EIOPA did issue a statement on 1 July 2018 confirming that EIOPA is supportive of the EU-wide measures taken by ESMA, and expects insurance undertakings to avoid instruments for which ESMA has issued a ban or restriction as possible direct underlyings of insurance-based investment products. It further states that, in general, product intervention powers in one sector should never be circumvented by repackaging the instruments that have been banned or restricted for offer in another sector. EIOPA did not take any product intervention measures in this regards, since it considered that there is at this juncture no evidence of direct policyholder exposure to CFDs or binary options, for instance, as sole underlyings of units offered in unit-linked insurance contracts, and that the possibility of such policyholder exposure to CFDs or binary options developing does not seem highly probable.[35]

This EIOPA statement makes clear that EIOPA indeed did consider the possible need to take measures to avoid regulatory arbitrage after ESMA's product intervention measures, even though,

---

[31] The marketing, distribution or sale to retail clients of CFDs is restricted to circumstances where at least all of the following conditions are met:

    (a) the CFD provider requires the retail client to pay the initial margin protection;
    (b) the CFD provider provides the retail client with the margin close out protection;
    (c) the CFD provider provides the retail client with the negative balance protection;
    (d) the CFD provider does not directly or indirectly provide the retail client with a payment, monetary or excluded non-monetary benefit in relation to the marketing, distribution or sale of a CFD, other than the realised profits on any CFD provided; and
    (e) the CFD provider does not send directly or indirectly a communication to or publish information accessible by a retail client relating to the marketing, distribution or sale of a CFD unless it includes the appropriate risk warning specified by and complying with the conditions in Annex II.

[32] ESMA, 'Notice of ESMA's Product Intervention Decisions in relation to contracts for differences and binary options' (ESMA35-43-1135). See also ESMA, 'Questions and Answers On ESMA's temporary product intervention measures on the marketing, distribution or sale of CFDs and Binary options to retail clients' (ESMA35-36-1262). Both measures had been taken for the maximum period of three months; both measures have been renewed (and slightly adapted) on several occasions since, until 1 and 31 July 2019 respectively (see fn 34).

[33] ESMA, 'Notice of ESMA's Product Intervention Decisions in relation to contracts for differences and binary options' (ESMA35-43-1135), Art 3.

[34] On 1 July 2019, ESMA announced that it would cease to renew its product intervention measures relating to binary options, as most national competent authorities had at that time taken permanent national product intervention measures that are at least as stringent. Later that month, on 31 July 2019, it also announced that it would cease to renew its product intervention measures relating to contracts for differences for the same reason. See ESMA's press-site: www.esma.europa.eu/press-news/esma-news/esma-ceases-renewal-product-intervention-measure-relating-binary-options; www.esma.europa.eu/press-news/esma-news/esma-ceases-renewal-product-intervention-measures-relating-contracts.

[35] EIOPA, 'Statement on consumer detriment resulting from policyholder exposure to contracts for differences and binary options' (EIOPA-18/251, 1 June 2018), https://eiopa.europa.eu/Publications/Statements/EIOPA-18-251%20Statement%20on%20contracts%20for%20differences%20and%20binary%20options.pdf.

strictly speaking, ESMA is the ESA who should avoid regulatory arbitrage when considering taking a product intervention measure. Again, while it is reassuring that EIOPA spontaneously did engage in a regulatory arbitrage assessment, it was not legally obliged to do so. There is, moreover, no evidence of EBA having made a similar assessment.

Need for legal requirement for ESAs to cooperate to avoid regulatory arbitrage. It would be more coherent if all ESAs would be legally required (i) to inform the other ESAs when they intend to take a product intervention measure, and (ii) to assess whether further action is needed to avoid regulatory arbitrage, each time one of them intends to take a product intervention measure. Even though one cross-sectorally applicable legal text in respect of product intervention is not strictly necessary to achieve this result, it would have resulted more naturally in cooperation on product intervention in the Joint Committee of the ESAs.

IV. Structure of Financial Supervision

Risk of gaps and overlaps. The sectoral division of competences between the three ESAs in this area may create supervisory gaps: if new products are created, will it always be evident which Authority is competent to take action? Today for instance, it is not very clear whether different types of 'tokens', created in the context of virtual currencies and ICO's, are financial instruments, payment instruments, or something else.[36] The risk of supervisory overlaps in the same situation may be less problematic from a consumer protection point of view, but they are inefficient.

One cross-sectoral ESA. For product intervention purposes, one cross-sectorally competent ESA – be it an integrated or twin peaks authority – would indeed be more efficient.[37]

V. Conclusion

Need for cross-sectoral product intervention powers and supervisory approach. The fact that the product intervention powers have been regulated in two different pieces of EU regulation, seems nothing more than accidental. It would certainly have been more elegant if one provision in the horizontal PRIIPs Regulation would have attributed the product intervention competences to the three European Supervisory Authorities, each in their respective sectoral field of competence. It would have avoided the allegedly different scope of application of MiFIR and the PRIIPs Regulation in respect of product intervention. It would moreover have structurally ensured that the ESAs would cooperate in the level 2 and 3 implementation of the product intervention measures, avoiding unsubstantiated differences at levels 2 and 3. It would also have allowed to require the three ESAs in one and the same provision to cooperate in order to avoid regulatory arbitrage.

The current sectoral legislative and supervisory approach to product intervention is therefore suboptimal. A cross-sectoral legislative, and arguably also supervisory approach to product intervention would indeed be more efficient.

---

[36] See, ie, ESMA, 'Securities and Markets Stakeholder Group – Own Initiative Report on ICOs and crypto-assets' (ESMA22-106-1338, September 2018); ESMA, 'Advice. Initial Coin Offerings and Crypto-Assets' (ESMA50-157-1391, 9 January 2019) at 18–21.

[37] See on this issue more generally, chapter 17 of this book.

PART IV

Supervision and Internal Market

17

A Holistic Approach to the Institutional Architecture of Financial Supervision and Regulation in the EU

WOLF-GEORG RINGE, LUIS MORAIS AND DAVID RAMOS

I. Introduction

The 2008/09 global financial crisis resulted in a major reconsideration of many rules and assumptions underpinning financial systems across the globe. Whilst much of the reforms have focused at addressing these problems through imposing new substantive rules,[1] there has also been recognition that the institutional setup in place before 2008 was partly responsible and failed to mitigate the extreme effects of the crisis.[2] This has led to a renewed emphasis on improving the regulatory and supervisory framework in many jurisdictions. Much praise, for example, has been made for the 'twin peaks' approach to financial supervision, as pioneered among others in Australia and the Netherlands, in which financial conduct and prudential regulation are carried out by two separate regulatory agencies.[3] To be sure, there is a vivid academic debate on the merits of the twin-peaks approach as well as on the relevance of the institutional framework, more generally. Some commentators argue in fact that the particular form of regulatory institutional infrastructure has little to do with the ability to detect problems or to prevent or mitigate the effects of financial crises.[4] Conversely, there is a growing empirical evidence for the relevance

---

[1] New substantive rules for the financial sector have been put in place to counter the main regulatory and supervisory shortcomings exposed by the crisis. Lastra and Wood identified ten different groups of explanations for the global financial crisis. See RM Lastra and G Wood, 'The Crisis of 2007-09: Nature, Causes, and Reactions' in T Cottier, JH Jackson and RM Lastra (eds), *International Law in Financial Regulation and Monetary Affairs* (Oxford, OUP, 2012) 9.

[2] See, eg, L Garicano and RM Lastra, 'Towards a New Architecture for Financial Stability: Seven Principles' in T Cottier, JH Jackson and RM Lastra (eds), *International Law in Financial Regulation and Monetary Affairs* (Oxford, OUP, 2012) 72.

[3] J Cooper, 'The integration of financial regulatory authorities – the Australian experience' *Paper presented to the Comissão de Valores Mobiliários (Securities and Exchange Commission of Brazil) at the 30th Anniversary Conference 'Assessing the Present, Conceiving the Future'*, 4-5 September 2006. Available at: download.asic.gov.au/media/1339352/integration-financial-regulatory-authorities.pdf; A Godwin, S Kourabas and I Ramsay, 'Twin Peaks and Financial Regulation: The Challenges of Increasing Regulatory Overlap and Expanding Responsibilities' (2016) 49 *The International Lawyer* 273.

[4] See, eg, SC Bair, 'The Case Against a Super Regulator' *New York Times* (31 August 2009). Available at: www.nytimes.com/2009/09/01/opinion/01bair.html; S Keen, 'Australia versus the US and UK: the Kangaroo Economy' in SJ Konzelmann and M Fovargue-Davies (eds), *Banking Systems in the Crisis: The Faces of Liberal Capitalism* (Oxford, Routledge, 2013), 210–216. See also D Calvo, D Crisanto, J Carlos, S Hohl and OP Gutiérrez, 'Financial supervisory architecture: what has changed after the crisis?' (2018) *Financial Stability Institute – FSI Insights on Policy Implementation,*

of the institutional architecture,[5] and it is now widely accepted that institutional design remains important in mitigating financial crises.[6]

Whilst a number of countries within the European Union (including the UK, Belgium, Ireland, and the Netherlands), but also outside, like Australia, New Zealand and South Africa, have introduced new institutional architectures due to their experiences during the crisis and in light of such academic support,[7] the European framework for financial regulation and supervision was not significantly altered. True, the post-crisis reform wave that shook the EU has led to a revamp of the previous 'college-based' architecture towards genuine EU agencies.[8] Through a reform process of Europeanisation of financial supervision,[9] the resulting three European Supervisory Authorities (ESAs) – the European Banking Agency (EBA), the European Securities and Markets Agency (ESMA), and the European Insurance and Occupational Pensions Authority (EIOPA) – replicated and cemented the 'tripartite' organisation that had already been adopted by their 'college' predecessors.[10] Put differently, at a moment of great momentum in terms of regulatory reform, the EU did not choose to adopt the 'twin peaks' model that was – and still is – generally considered 'state of the art', albeit not fully exempt of risks (eg as regards the potential externalisation of conflicts between the prudential and market conduct perspectives of financial supervision). Rather it chose to remain in a 'silo' architecture with three separate bodies responsible for banking, securities and insurance. The major risk of such a sectoral architecture is that separate agencies may fail to recognise any cross-sectoral problems and risks that are evolving, may fail to adequately address financial conglomerates, and may more generally encounter fundamental challenges in adopting a more holistic approach to financial regulation and supervision.[11]

This chapter examines the case for adopting a twin-peaks architecture in the EU, or other options oriented towards a more integrated and better coordinated institutional setup able to

---

No 8, Bank for International Settlements: Basel. Available at: www.bis.org/fsi/publ/insights8.pdf; and L Morais, 'Models of Financial Supervision in Portugal and the European Union – Executive Summary – Part VI of White Paper on Regulation and Supervision of the Financial Sector' (2017) *Paper published by Banco de Portugal/Bank of Portugal*. Available at: www. bportugal.pt/sites/default/files/anexos/pdf-boletim/livro_branco_web_en.pdf.

[5] See, eg, W Shon and I Vyshnevskyi, 'The "Twin Peaks" model of post-crisis banking supervision' (2017) 24 *Applied Economics Letters* 571.

[6] See J Hill, 'Why did Australia fare so well in the global financial crisis?' in E Ferran and others (eds), *The Regulatory Aftermath of the Global Financial Crisis* (Cambridge, Cambridge University Press, 2012), 203–300; D Masciandaro, R Vega Pansini and M Quintyn, 'The Economic Crisis: Did Financial Supervision Matter?' (2011) *IMF Working Paper No WP/11/261*, 4; EF Brown, 'A Comparison of the Handling of the Financial Crisis in the United States, the United Kingdom and Australia' (2010) 55 *Villanova Law Review* 509, 574–575.

[7] For an analysis of different Twin Peaks implementations among selected case studies, see A Godwin, T Howse and I Ramsay, 'A Jurisdictional Comparison of the Twin Peaks Model of Financial Regulation' (2017) 18 *Journal of Banking Regulation* 103.

[8] For an interesting study exploring the politics and architecture of the institutionalisation and rationalisation of the EU regulatory space and providing for an explanation for the evolution from EU networks of national authorities to EU agencies, see D Levi-Faur, 'Regulatory networks and regulatory agencification: towards a Single European Regulatory Space' (2011) 18 *Journal of European Public Policy* 810.

[9] M Scholten and A Ottow, 'Institutional Design of Enforcement in the EU: The Case of Financial Markets' (2014) 10 *Utrecht Law Review* 81.

[10] The three ESAs replaced the previously existing networks of national supervisors: namely, (i) for banking, the Committee of European Banking Supervisors (CEBS) established by Decision 2004/5/EC of 5 November 2003; (ii) for insurance and pensions, the Committee of European Insurance and Occupational Pensions Supervisors (CEIOPS) established by Decision 2004/6/EC of 5 November 2003; and (iii) for securities, the Committee of European Securities Regulators (CESR) established by Commission Decision 2004/7/EC of 5 November 2003 and amending Decision 2001/527/EC.

[11] See, eg, V Colaert, 'European Banking, insurance and investment services law: Cutting through sectorial lines?' (2015) 52 *Common Market Law Review* 1576; and N Moloney, 'EU financial market regulation after the global financial crisis: more Europe or more risks' (2010) 47 *Common Market Law Review* 1317.

achieve more efficiency in fulfilling supervisory tasks and, thus, prevent as much as possible regulatory and supervisory failures, especially in situations that require expedite communication flows and combined interventions of supervisors. Ten years after the crisis, we will discuss the present political window of opportunity for implementing a novel approach in the peculiar EU architecture, triggered importantly by Brexit and by a high-level review process of the ESAs. As we shall see, EU and national lawmakers were not only unable to seize opportunities for reform but have also let those opportunities pass by when they presented themselves. The present political climate does not leave us to expect any significant reform anytime soon. Rather, we strongly argue that the reform architecture of the EU should be modified incrementally, and without need for Treaty revision. Hence, if, in order to redesign the EU institutional architecture of financial supervision, a top-down approach looks unfeasible, we will assess the possibility for a bottom-up experimentalist approach as a viable path towards the implementation of a twin peaks model, or, possibly as a more viable and desirable path, a hybrid model that nevertheless preserves some of its main advantages. Acknowledging the difficulty of such a radical transformation in the EU institutional paradigm of financial supervision, these proposals can inform attempts towards any possible alternative solution, which – by preferring to emphasise substance over form – may ultimately constitute a model that delivers the same benefits as twin peaks in substance, even without replicating the dual institutional structure in form (and avoiding at the same time some of the disadvantages of such structure).

This chapter is organised as follows. Section II provides a brief description of the current EU model of financial supervision and regulation, reviews alternatives that were adopted elsewhere and discusses the reasons why no fundamental reform was adopted in Europe in the wake of the crisis. Section III considers the current and renovated momentum for reform and concludes that several present opportunities for changing the institutional setup have not been seized. Part IV explores how incremental changes can be implemented without major Treaty reform. Section V concludes.

II. The EU Architecture and the Case for Reform

A. The Present Landscape

The current EU architecture arises from the reforms proposed in the de Larosière Report, adopted in 2009 in the wake of the financial crisis.[12] Even at a moment when the dire state of financial markets had called for bold measures to strengthen financial stability through enhanced coordination arrangements, moving from a mere system of coordination (implemented through the Level 3 Lamfalussy Committees) to a direct allocation of regulatory/supervisory competences to European authorities was anything if not a clear change in the existing consensus. This resulted in an extremely careful language, which proposed to balance a potentially momentous shift with a narrow list of tasks in principle, and with a decentralised approach in practice.[13] The newly envisaged supervisory structure also tried to reconcile different ideas: national

---

[12] J de Larosière and others, *Report by the High Level Group on financial supervision in the EU* (Brussels, 25 February 2009) ('de Larosière Report'). Available at: http://ec.europa.eu/info/system/files/de_larosiere_report_en.pdf.

[13] The de Larosière Report did its best to allay fears over a possible 'Europeanisation' of financial supervision, to the point of maintaining an ambivalence of language between the reference to 'authorities' and to 'committees'. In the Report's

authorities, European authorities, and supervisory colleges, each of which are reflective of a different philosophy.[14] This understandably avoided the turmoil (operational and political) that might have ensued, had the proposal solely consisted in a re-allocation of competences. Instead, the key words were reassuringly European-oriented, such as the 'harmonisation' of rules and standards, as well as 'coordination' and 'cooperation' in the exercise of national competences.

Coordinating different territorial supervisory levels was not the only critical aspect in the de Larosière Report: the financial crisis had exposed the shortcomings of a system that lacked both a clear macro-prudential perspective, as well as adequate information flows to coordinate it with the micro-prudential side. Thus, aside from creating three authorities (EBA, ESMA, EIOPA) from the pre-existing committees, with the ability to coordinate supervision, and supervisory standards,[15] the report also recommended the creation of a European Systemic Risk Board (ESRB), formed by the chairs of the three ESAs, as well as the ECB and the European Commission.[16]

With the focus on (i) coordination between national and European authorities, and (ii) coordination between micro and macro-prudential supervision, predictably, (iii) inter-sectoral coordination took a secondary role, albeit not fully forgotten. In fact, the report advised that the review, which should take place within three years after the new supervisory framework

---

own words: 'The ESFS should constitute an integrated network of European financial supervisors, working with enhanced level 3 committees ('Authorities'). Therefore the ESFS would be a largely decentralised structure, fully respecting the proportionality and subsidiarity principles of the Treaty. So existing national supervisors, who are closest to the markets and institutions they supervise, would continue to carry-out day-to-day supervision and preserve the majority of their present competences'. See de Larosière Report (n 12) 47 at para 184.

[14] Recommendation 18 of the de Larosière Report is a testimony of a European talent for compromise (if one is an advocate) or muddle-through solutions (if one is a critic). According to Recommendation 18: 'A European System of Financial Supervisors (ESFS) should be set- up. This ESFS should be a decentralised network:

- existing national supervisors would continue to carry-out day-to-day supervision;
- three new European Authorities would be set up, replacing CEBS, CEIOPS and CESR, with the role coordinate the application of supervisory standards and guarantee strong cooperation between the national supervisors;
- colleges of supervisors would be set up for all major cross-border institutions.
- The ESFS will need to be independent of the political authorities, but be accountable to them. It should rely on a common set of core harmonised rules and have access to high-quality information.' See de Larosière Report 48.

[15] Recommendation 22: In the second stage (2011-2012), the EU should establish an integrated European System of Financial Supervision (ESFS).

- The level 3 Committees should be transformed into three European Authorities: a European Banking Authority, a European Insurance Authority and a European Securities Authority.
- The Authorities should be managed by a board comprised of the chairs of the national supervisory authorities. The chairpersons and director generals of the Authorities should be full-time independent professionals. The appointment of the chairpersons should be confirmed by the Commission, the European Parliament and the Council and should be valid for a period of 8 years.
- The Authorities should have their own autonomous budget, commensurate with their responsibilities.
- In addition to the competences currently exercised by the level 3 committees, the Authorities should have, inter alia, the following key-competences: i) legally binding mediation between national supervisors; ii) adoption of binding supervisory standards; iii) adoption of binding technical decisions applicable to individual financial institutions; iv) oversight and coordination of colleges of supervisors; v) designation, where needed, of group supervisors; vi) licensing and supervision of specific EU-wide institutions (e.g. Credit Rating Agencies, and post-trading infrastructures); vii) binding cooperation with the ESRC to ensure adequate macro-prudential supervision.
- National supervisory authorities should continue to be fully responsible for the day-to-day supervision of firms.' See de Larosière Report 55–56.

[16] de Larosière Report 57.

entered into force, should evaluate the possibility of moving towards a twin-peaks structure, with a prudential and a market conduct authority as the first point in the agenda.[17]

As it often happens, however, planning did not anticipate all circumstances, and the 2007–2009 crisis was followed, after 2010, by a Eurozone sovereign debt crisis that drastically exposed the dangerous liaisons between sovereign and banks. In this context, the ECB announced its readiness to stand behind the euro,[18] but this caused a row with the Federal Constitutional Court in Germany and could not be the long-term answer.[19] To sever the link between banks and sovereigns the solution could not be the ECB's implied promise that, at the moment of truth, it would act to support the market in sovereign bonds (liquidity backstop). Rather, there should have been a Eurozone deposit insurance scheme (solvency backstop) for bank deposits that prevented bank runs and did not ultimately rely on individual Member States' financial resources. Yet, it was feared that this could increase the problem of moral hazard for Member States, which would then have less incentive to duly monitor their national champions. Thus, a system had to be put in place to ensure that the decisions concerning the supervision of banks, as well as the crisis management measures in case those banks reached a point of non-viability were adopted at a European level. Ironically, as of today, the resulting Banking Union includes a Single Supervisory Mechanism (SSM), headed by the ECB, and a Single Resolution Mechanism (SRM), headed by the Single Resolution Board (SRB); while it still lacks a Single Deposit Insurance Scheme,[20] and where the transformation of the European Stability Mechanism (ESM), originally created as an institution separate from the EU,[21] into a European Monetary Fund (EMF)[22] inside the Eurozone crisis-management infrastructure is still uncertain.

Therefore, while rich in institutions and rules, the resulting system appears quite poor in terms of backstops. The problem is that the new rules and institutions do not fit into the picture originally envisaged in the de Larosière Report. In the early stages of the recession, indeed, the debate was still dominated by some American traits, such as derivatives, the connections between traditional and parallel banking (or shadow banking[23]), or the participation of (some) insurance companies as key players in the market.[24] Cross-sectoral convergence not only made sense – and

---

[17] 'Recommendation 24: The functioning of the ESFS should be reviewed no later than 3 years after its entry into force. In the light of this review, the following additional reforms might be considered:

  – Moving towards a system which would rely on only two Authorities: the first Authority would be responsible for banking and insurance prudential issues as well as for any other issue relevant for financial stability; the second Authority would be responsible for conduct of business and market issues [...]'. See de Larosière Report 58.

[18] On this point, the actual tone of the authoritative statement by ECB's President Mario Draghi during his speech at the Global Investment Conference in London on 26 July 2012 (ie 'Within our mandate, the ECB is ready to do whatever it takes to preserve the euro') is emblematic.

[19] Cf, C-62/14 *Gauweiler and Others v Deutscher Bundestag* of 16 June 2015, ECLI:EU:C:2015:400.

[20] European Commission, 'Proposal for a Regulation of the European Parliament and of the council amending Regulation (EU) 806/2014 in order to establish a European Deposit Insurance Scheme' (Strasbourg, 24 November 2015), COM(2015) 586 final.

[21] Treaty Establishing the ESM, signed on 2 February 2012. Available at: www.esm.europa.eu/legal-documents/esm-treaty.

[22] European Commission, 'Proposal on the establishment of the European Monetary Fund' (Brussels, 6 December 2017), COM(2017) 827 final.

[23] US Financial Crisis Inquiry Commission, *Final Report of the National commission on the Causes of the financial and Economic Crisis in the United States* (25 February 2011). Available at: www.govinfo.gov/content/pkg/GPO-FCIC/pdf/GPO-FCIC.pdf.

[24] ibid, xxiv-xxv and 23–24.

still does – but also looked urgent.[25] Yet, as the crisis moved to Europe, it acquired its uniquely European traits and, as a consequence, the problem concentrated in traditional banking (and sovereigns), parallel banking and insurance did no longer look so urgent anymore. The limited political capital had to be invested in a (more drastic) reallocation of competences, only this time with banks as protagonists. Cross-sectoral convergence and coordination had relatively lost importance or urgency, as well as other initiatives, such as shadow banking.[26]

B. Alternative Approaches to Supervision

The advent of the last global financial crisis highlighted the importance of the institutional architecture of financial supervision and regulation in promoting financial stability. The models adopted in different jurisdictions can be roughly classified into four categories:[27]

(1) a '**single regulator**' structure, built around a single integrated authority responsible for the regulation and supervision of the entire financial system;
(2) a '**sectoral model**', or a tripartite architecture with three different authorities responsible for banking, insurance (and pensions), and securities, respectively;
(3) the '**twin peaks**' approach, or a dual agency structure in which one authority is responsible for market conduct integrity and consumer protection, while the other for the stability of the financial system;[28]
(4) at a different level, in a growing number of cases '**hybrid models**' have been developed combining elements of various approaches and with a key focus on mechanisms of coordination between different supervisory functions and tasks.[29]

Notably, the current institutional architecture of financial supervision and regulation in the EU follows the **tripartite** model, with the three ESAs as protagonists: EBA (formerly in London and now in Paris) for banking, ESMA (in Paris) for securities, and EIOPA (in Frankfurt) for insurance and pensions. Additionally, the European Systemic Risk Board (ESRB) has a macro-prudential mandate. Furthermore, adding an extra layer of *complexity* to the EU architecture, within the Euro area the core of prudential supervision has been gradually concentrated within the hands of the ECB. One possible question, therefore, is why the EU did not seize the momentum of post-crisis reform to move to more innovative supervisory structures.

---

[25] Yet in Europe the issue of re-allocation of competences was considered even more urgent, and, institutionally speaking, it was easier to transform the existing 'Committees' in 'Authorities', with the possibility of merging them in the future, rather than creating new authorities with new mandates from scratch.

[26] The issue of shadow banking received attention only initially. See European Commission, 'Green Paper. Shadow Banking' (Brussels, 19 March 2012), COM(2012) 102 final; and European Commission, 'Communication from the commission to the Council and the European Parliament. Shadow Banking – Addressing New Sources of Risk in the Financial Sector' (Brussels, 4 September 2013), COM(2013) 614 final. These documents were followed by proposals that did not drastically alter market practice and structure. One concerned money market funds, proposed in 2013, and adopted in 2017, with important changes from the original text; the other, securities financing transactions (SFT), which introduced new transparency rules, but no obvious limitations on this type of transactions. See Regulation (EU) 2017/1131 of the European Parliament and of the Council of 14 June 2017 on money market funds, and Regulation (EU) 2015/2365 of the European Parliament and of the Council of 25 November 2015 on transparency of securities financing transactions and of reuse and amending Regulation (EU) No 648/2012 [2017] OJ L169/8.

[27] For an overview about the first three listed categories of supervisory models, see generally: E Wymeersch, 'The structure of financial supervision in Europe: about single, twin peaks and multiple financial supervisors' (2007) 8 *European Business Organization Law Review* 239.

[28] F Restoy, 'The Organization of financial supervision' (26 January 2016) *Central bankers' speeches*, Madrid: Bank for International Settlements. Available at: www.bis.org/review/r160126b.pdf.

[29] For a recent view on these categories and variations of such categories see D Calvo, D Crisanto, J Carlos, S Hohl & OP Gutiérrez (n 4); and also L Morais (n 4).

C. Why did the EU Stick to the Sectoral or Tripartite Approach?

The discussion outlined above shows the main reasons why the EU stuck to the tripartite approach: path dependence and minimisation of transaction costs. The evolution of this peculiar institutional supervisory architecture (here, considered broadly to also include resolution) is not the result of a top-down approach and careful planning followed by a linear execution. It rather underlies a path-dependent process, with important doses of improvisation, where each move tried to adapt to the latest source of the crisis following the path that was more cost-effective. Undoubtedly, the creation of the ESAs, mainly focused on financial *regulation stricto sensu* and not so much on day to day financial *supervision*,[30] was a major achievement in terms of reallocation of competences. However, reshaping the former 'Committees' as 'Authorities' with a limited list of competences was one thing; whereas, creating new authorities *ex novo* with open-ended mandates on prudential supervision and market conduct would not have been feasible absent a major catastrophe.

Yet, such a catastrophe seemed to manifest with the bank-sovereign crisis, but by then the problem had mutated into a 'narrower' banking crisis. This justified the move towards the Banking Union, not at all a drastic overhaul of the whole supervisory system. Furthermore, although far-reaching in its effects, the move did, again, follow an institutional path of minimum resistance. In the understanding of most Member States, indeed, monetary and bank supervisory functions were closely associated. In addition, in its monetary capacity, the ECB already retained a powerful role to coordinate, when not dictating important decisions that directly affected banks, with a legal basis on the Treaties (eg payment systems)[31] or by its operational practice (eg in the determination of eligible counterparties, eligible collateral, conditions to extend liquidity assistance, etc). Major as the re-allocation of competences under the SSM was, there had been, however, some pre-existing structures to build upon.

As to resolution, the whole framework, structure and agencies were created from scratch, but with almost no fully developed national regimes predating the European one.[32] One reason is the chronology: countries, which had created national resolution regimes and authorities before the adoption of the SRM rules, had done so recently and already in the wake of the financial crisis. Thus, there had been no time to develop a strong institutional mentality, which could have resulted in resistance against a re-allocation of those competences. For Member States, and their resolution authorities, it was difficult to oppose losing what they were not aware they had.

The second chief reason is a legal one. Even if EU institutions had managed to muster the political support to undertake not only a territorial, but also a functional overhaul of powers, it is unclear whether the re-allocation of functions along prudential and market conduct lines to newly created agencies would have been legally admissible. In its *Meroni* doctrine, the CJEU had

---

[30] On the conceptual distinction between financial *regulation* and financial *supervision*, see de Larosière Report 38: 'The present report draws **a distinction** between **financial regulation** and **supervision**: Regulation is the set of rules and standards that govern financial institutions; their main objective is to foster financial stability and to protect the customers of financial services. Regulation can take different forms, ranging from information requirements to strict measures such as capital requirements. **On the other hand, supervision is the process designed to oversee financial institutions in order to ensure that rules and standards are properly applied**. This being said, in practice, regulation and supervision are intertwined and will therefore, in some instances, have to be assessed together (…)' (emphases added).

[31] Article 127(2) TFEU.

[32] One interesting exception concerns the Portuguese case in which, in the context of the external economic intervention of 2011, leading to a Memorandum of Understanding (MoU) concluded with the European Commission, the International Monetary Fund and the European Central Bank, a national regime of banking resolution was adopted in 2012 following already what might be considered as the new EU paradigm that would be established later under the Banking Recovery and Resolution Directive (BRRD) – [2014] OJ L/173/190.

clearly stated that agencies and bodies (ie no institutions) could not be granted discretionary powers,[33] and completed this in its *Romano* ruling by saying that agencies could not enjoy the power to dictate acts of general application (ie regulatory power).[34] In third place, the clarification of competences after the Lisbon Treaty seemed to contemplate the exercise of delegated and implementing powers of legislation for the European Commission only.[35]

Naturally, these constraints were to an appreciable extent re-shaped after the CJEU decision in the *Short selling* case.[36] On that occasion, although not expressly overruling its *Meroni* and *Romano* doctrine, the Court interpreted it in a way that acquired a completely new meaning. In fact, the Court was ready to admit that the power of an EU authority (ESMA in that case) to dictate a ban on short selling was rule-bound, and thus non-discretionary. This, particularly because ESMA was subject to a series of conditions envisaged in the law, despite those conditions meant that it had to interpret the existence of a 'threat to the orderly functioning and integrity of financial markets or to the stability of the whole or part of the financial system',[37] which does not establish a clear-cut limitation of mandate. The Court was also ready to state that the *Romano* doctrine could not result in more stringent conditions than those formulated under its judgment in *Meroni*[38] (thus, de facto depriving the *Romano* ruling of any autonomous significance). Finally, the Court was ready to interpret the delegated and implementing powers of the Commission as non-exclusionary, ie the fact that the Commission could exercise delegated or implementing powers of legislation did not mean that other bodies could not be conferred such powers.[39] An interpretative stretch, when one considers that, as a consequence of the ruling, the Commission, an EU institution would be subject to legal constraints envisaged in the Treaty, whereas a body or authority that is not even contemplated in the Treaty would not.

Still, none of these circumstances were known at the time when the ESAs reform was adopted (2010), and even during the Banking Union reforms the implications of the new CJEU case law were not fully settled. Indeed, even today the legislative role of the ESAs is exercised through the elaboration of regulatory and implementing technical standards (RTS and ITS), which then have to be adopted as delegated or implementing regulations by the European Commission.[40] Even today the most critical decision the SRB can make (ie the adoption of a resolution scheme for a failing financial institution) is in a way subject to the final say of the Commission. The latter has the power to challenge the assessment of the more discretionary component in the decision, ie the presence of a public interest,[41] an aspect where the Council can also weigh in.[42] This raises important questions as to who these decisions belong to, as well as about the binding nature, and justiciability (ie challengeability) of preparatory instruments or even soft law ones.

[33] Case 9/56 *Meroni v High Authority* of 13 June 1958, 151–154. ECLI:EU:C:1958:7.
[34] Case 98/80 *Giuseppe Romano v Institut national d'assurance maladie-invalidité* of 14 May 1981, ECLI:EU:C:1981:104, at para 20.
[35] Articles 290 and 291 TFEU.
[36] C-270/12 *UK v Parliament and Council* of 22 January 2014, ECLI:EU:C:2014:18 (*Short Selling*).
[37] *Short selling*, at paras 46–47.
[38] *Short selling*, at para 66.
[39] *Short selling*, at paras 77–86.
[40] Recitals (21)–(25) and Arts 8(2)(a)-(b), 10, and 15 of Regulations (EU) No 1093/2010, 1094/2010 and 1095/2010 of the European Parliament and of the Council of 24 November 2010 establishing the three ESAs: respectively EBA, EIOPA, and ESMA, [2010] OJ L331/12.
[41] Article 18(5) and (7) of Regulation 806/2014 of the European Parliament and of the Council of 15 July 2014 establishing uniform rules and a uniform procedure for the resolution of credit institutions and certain investment firms in the framework of a Single Resolution Mechanism and a Single Resolution Fund and amending Regulation (EU) No 1093/2010 [2014] OJ L225/1 (SRM Regulation).
[42] Article 18(8), SRM Regulation.

Yet, even if the more benign interpretation of the CJEU in the *Short Selling* case had been settled, the challenges of implementing a twin peaks structure would have been formidable. Had supervisory and regulatory competences not only been allocated to EU authorities, but also re-distributed along functional (rather than sectoral) lines, new allocative questions would have immediately arisen. For instance, there might be doubts about authorities' competences to interpret their own mandates, as well as their leeway. For instance, which authority would have the competence to adopt rules on the portfolio composition or leverage of hedge funds or money market funds? Or what about Basel framework rules on market discipline? Here, the problem would seem to rely less on the issues themselves (which could have been resolved) than in the risk of any Member State, or party affected by the measures to turn a technical issue into a constitutional one. This does not justify the current system, and its shortcomings, it merely helps to explain it.

Hence, although the EU's challenge of cross-sectoral, or post-sectoral supervisory policy is often defined in terms of the ESAs system, that is not the only, or even the most important challenge. In our view, the path-dependent process followed during and after the successive crises has created at least three scenarios for friction to achieve a post-sectoral approach.[43]

(1) Horizontal, between the three ESAs themselves, which need to coordinate their policies.
(2) Vertical, between the ESAs and NCAs, which, as the historically important supervisors within their respective jurisdictions, are still keen to preserve their competences.
(3) Horizontal, between a Euro area framework, which is strongly centralised and focused on banks/states, and an EU-based one, which instead is decentralised and divided along sectoral lines.

D. Institutional Experimentalism: The Proposals for the Supervision of Central Counterparties (CCPs)

In the context of the review of the governance and operations of the ESAs, the Commission presented, among other things, a proposal for a regulation aiming at introducing a more integrated approach to the oversight of central counterparties (CCPs). CCPs are frequently interposed between counterparties to a derivative contract, becoming the buyer to every seller and the seller to every buyer. In doing so, CCPs become the focal point for derivative transactions and crucially reducing the market risks stemming from counterparty default. The so-called EMIR 2.2 proposal related to CCPs which serve businesses in more than one Member State and thus have a Union dimension.[44]

Importantly, the proposal has the effect to enhance ESMA's supervisory powers. Since its inception, ESMA has already enjoyed some limited supervisory powers in the regulation of the

---

[43] See, eg, V Colaert (n 11).
[44] See European Commission, 'Proposal for a Regulation of the European Parliament and of the Council amending Regulation (EU) No 1095/2010 establishing a European Supervisory Authority (European Securities and Market Authority) and amending Regulation (EU) No 648/2012 as regards the procedures and authorities involved for the authorisation of CCPs and requirements for the recognition of third-country CCPs' (Strasbourg, 13 June 2017), COM(2017) 331 final; and its amendment (Brussels, 20 September 2017), COM(2017) 539 final (hereinafter EMIR 2.2). The proposal builds on an extensive assessment of Regulation (EU) No 648/2012 of the European Parliament and of the Council of 4 July 2012 on OTC derivatives, central counterparties and trade repositories (the European Market Infrastructures Regulation – or EMIR Regulation) and on two public consultations promoted by the Commission: the first on the ESAs' mandate and the other on the Capital Market Union Mid-Term Review.

financial sector, namely concerning credit rating agencies (CRAs),[45] short selling of credit default swaps (CDS),[46] and trade repositories (TRs).[47] Thus, by conferring supervisory competences to ESMA, the EU tripartite model has lost both functional and organisational symmetry among the three ESAs.[48] EMIR 2.2 goes beyond this, as it envisages the creation of a new supervisory mechanism and body within the ESMA organisation to assume supervisory tasks over EU and third-country CCPs. ESMA is granted broad extraterritorial supervisory powers in respect to Tier 2 third-country CCPs.[49] Extending the competences and powers of ESMA follows the trend of previous approaches (CRAs, CDS, and TRs). This process can be interpreted using alternative, partially complementary, views.

One view is to see the process as an example of continued path dependence. If the current tri-partite structure of the ESAs can be explained as a consequence of the evolution from the previous Committee structure, following the path of minimum resistance, a similar rationale could explain the asymmetric evolution of the new allocation of competences among the ESAs. From a vertical perspective, additional EU competences resulting from the regulation of newly established subject matters (such as CRAs, TRs, now CCPs) are less likely to encounter resistance from national authorities, who have not yet become accustomed to exercising the relevant authority. From a horizontal perspective, the overhaul of bank regulation has put the ECB front and centre (thus leaving EBA in a decidedly secondary role in terms of re-allocation of powers). Since securities markets have been next in terms of the level of legislative activity, this has placed ESMA in the best position to be the main beneficiary among the ESAs.

A second possibility would be to adhere to the view of the de Larosière Report that there is a tendency to centralise market conduct supervision in the hands of a single agency,[50] and ESMA is well-placed to assume that role, for reasons that go beyond path dependence. Given its competences over TRs and CRAs, ESMA would potentially become the main central data repository and supervisor of financial data. Since data gaps were identified as one of the shortcomings of existing supervisory structures (even at a global level[51]) some commentators believe that ESMA's role should become more prominent within the EU architecture of financial supervision. Given the increased need for information exchange among different institutional levels (ESMA vis-à-vis NCAs but also ESMA vis-à-vis ECB), this also has the potential to make the

---

[45] Regulation (EU) No 462/2013 of the European Parliament and of the Council of 21 May 2013 amending Regulation (EC) No 1060/2009 on credit rating agencies [2013] OJ L146/1.

[46] Regulation (EU) No 236/2012 of the European Parliament and of the Council of 14 March 2012 on short selling and certain aspects of credit default swaps [2012] OJ L86/1.

[47] EMIR Regulation (n 44).

[48] R D'Ambrosio and M Lamandini, 'The maintenance of the structural and functional parallelism among ESAs' (2018) *Presentation at the CIRSF Annual International Conference 2018,* Lisbon, 6 June 2018. Available at: ebi-europa. eu/wp-content/uploads/2018/01/Raffaele-D%E2%80%99Ambrosio-The-maintenance-of-the-structural-and-functional-parallelism-among-ESAs-despite-the-misalignment-in-the-current-and-proposed-allocation-of-supervisory-tasks.pdf.

[49] The EMIR 2.2. proposal envisages a two-tier system for classifying third-country CCPs. Entities may be defined as 'substantially systemically important CCPs', thus falling under direct supervision of ESMA, and be subject to stricter requirements, including compliance with relevant EU prudential requirements and agreement to provide ESMA with all applicable information and allow for on-site inspections.

[50] M Lamandini, 'A supervisory architecture fit for CMU: Aiming at a moving target?' (2018) *ECMI Commentary No 55,* 9 August 2018, 4. Available at: http://aei.pitt.edu/94353/1/ECMI_Commentary55_ML_SupervisoryArchitecture CMU.pdf.

[51] See, eg, FSB-IMF The Financial Crisis and Information Gaps, *Report to the G-20 Finance Ministers and Central Bank Governors.* Prepared by the IMF Staff and the FSB Secretariat (29 October 2009). Available at: www.imf.org/external/np/ g20/pdf/102909.pdf. Currently the 'Data Gaps Initiative' is in its Second Phase. See FSB-IMF The Financial Crisis and Information Gaps, *Second Phase of the G20 Data Gaps Initiative (DGI-2). Third Progress Report.* Prepared by the IMF Staff and FSB Secretariat (September 2018). Available at: www.fsb.org/wp-content/uploads/P250918.pdf.

system of supervision more coordinated as a whole, as it is the case for the supervision of the EU banking system.[52]

Yet a third possibility is to consider the projected reform of CCP supervision not only as a step in the process of reforming the vertical allocation of competences, or the trend to give ESMA a prominent role among ESAs, but also as an example of institutional experimentalism, because it takes a traditionally market conduct authority into a field closely related to financial stability, such as clearing and settlement.

This can also explain why the governance structure for these supervisory competences try to reconcile the needs of the broader ESAs reform, with the unique features of CCPs, and their relevance for financial stability. On one hand, it is true, the reform of CCP supervision cannot be understood without the broader context of the reform of ESAs; with the pervading idea of supplementing the looser structure of the Board of Supervisors, prone to a cacophony of national interests, with a more centralised body, the Executive Board, formed by full members, to ensure that genuinely European interests are also taken into consideration.[53] In line with this, the reforms intend to create a new body within ESMA, the 'CCP Supervisory Committee', or 'CCP Executive Session' (depending of the version of the proposal[54]). Yet CCP supervision has been considered different enough (and important enough) to establish a body different from the Executive Board, also in its (slightly contrived) structure, which includes:

– Permanent voting members, including a Chair, a Vice-Chair, as well as four Directors.
– Permanent non-voting members, such as one representative from the ECB and one from the European Commission;
– Non-permanent voting members, such as the representative(s) from the relevant (domestic) competent authorities relevant for the specific CCP) and;
– Non-permanent, non-voting members, such as the representative(s) from the central(s) bank(s) of issue relevant for the specific CCP.

This complexity is compounded by the fact that the previous supervisory structure, based on home country authorities and supervisory colleges is kept. Trying to seek a smooth transition to the new structure, the newly proposed rules state that the Chair of the CCP Committee/Session should chair and manage colleges, and permanent members, as well as the ECB, should attend them, but only the former would have a vote.[55] This is completed with the requirement of consultation of certain decisions with the central bank of issue.[56] Furthermore, the latest proposals

---

[52] Lamandini (n 50) 7.

[53] See Amended Proposal for a Regulation of the European Parliament and of the Council Brussels amending, inter alia, Regulations (EU) No 1093/2010, 1094/2010, and 1095/2010 establishing the three ESAs (Brussels, 12 September 2018), COM(2018) 646 final 2017/0230 (COD). In particular, Recital (21) states, in no uncertain terms, that: '[w]ithin the founding regulations of the ESAs it was provided that competent authorities would play a key role within their governance structure. It was also specified in those regulations that in order to prevent conflicts of interest, the members of the Board of Supervisors and of the Management Board would act independently and in the sole interest of the Union. The initial governance structure of the ESAs did not however provide sufficient safeguards to ensure that conflicts of interest be entirely avoided which can affect the ESAs' ability to take all the decisions necessary in the area of supervisory convergence and to ensure that their decisions take the broader Union interests fully into account.'

[54] The initial European Commission Proposal for a Regulation (n 44) referred to the 'CCP Executive Session' within the Board of Supervisors; whereas the European Parliament Report on the same proposal, A8-0190/2018 of 25 May 2018, refers to the 'CCP Supervisory Committee'.

[55] Articles 18, 19, and 21 of EMIR, as they would be modified by European Commission proposal (n 44).

[56] New Art 21(a) as envisaged by European Commission proposal (n 44), in the version proposed by the European Parliament. See A8-0190/2018.

emphasise the fact that domestic authorities would continue to exercise their current supervisory responsibilities, and, to put some order into the potential chaos, they distinguish decisions where domestic authorities need ESMA's prior consent, those where they need to consult ESMA, and those for which they would be solely responsible.[57] ESMA's broader powers concern third-country CCPs, with the possibility of exercising direct supervision over them if they meet a certain threshold, and are thus, considered 'Tier 2' CCPs.[58]

E. Towards an EU Twin Peaks Structure?

The foundation of the tripartite architecture (the division of financial activity in sectors[59]) is increasingly becoming dysfunctional in the face of the financial industry reality. This is exemplified by the advent of conglomerate financial institutions, ie multi-sector companies that would fall into two or more 'silos' of the tripartite structure. Consequently, the downsides of the current European framework (eg regulatory overlaps and regulatory arbitrage) might become even more relevant in the future, which calls for a revision of this structure.[60] New requirements of scrutiny of systemic risk also qualitatively transform the landscape of the institutional architecture of financial supervision in connection with functions that are not *stricto sensu* of financial supervision, but a profound interplay with it – mainly resolution functions.

The failure of the single authority model and the recent regulatory structure changes in several countries demonstrate that the adoption of the Twin Peaks model could be an interesting option for the European Union.[61] Even if this model did not prevent supervisory failures in the recent crisis, its lessons and implications should be critically assessed.[62] However, considering the different models of financial supervision adopted by different jurisdictions around the world, one fundamental question necessarily arises: which one would be the most appropriate for the EU financial system? What is the real viability of its adoption?

Even if a post-sectoral approach makes sense under current circumstances, it is not difficult to see that any evolution in that direction should address the reality of the current institutional architecture and allocation of competences at different levels. As said earlier, the major challenge does not lie with a re-distribution of the still-limited competences of the ESAs, but in the re-allocation of competences between NCAs and ESAs, and between the ESAs and the Banking Union. None of the avenues to achieve this looks easy, or even, in some cases, feasible.

---

[57] Newly proposed Art 21(a) EMIR, in relation to new Recital (20a) as envisaged by European Commission proposal (n 44), in the version proposed by the European Parliament. See A8-0190/2018.

[58] See newly proposed para 2(a) of Art 25 and Art 25(b) EMIR as envisaged by European Commission proposal (n 44).

[59] To be sure, the reality is no longer a 'pure' separation model, since it has gradually been combined with functional elements concerning the oversight of certain financial instruments, and is thus no longer conducted on strictly sectoral terms.

[60] The choice of a particular architecture of financial supervision should be indeed forward-looking and, thus, also anticipate how supervised entities will react to the new framework. See, in this sense, the study by JE Colliart, 'Optimal supervisory architecture and financial integration in a banking union' (2015) *ECB Working Paper Series No 1786*, April 2015. Available at: www.ecb.europa.eu/pub/pdf/scpwps/ecbwp1786.en.pdf?dfd7be4b6e182a5d7f4fbb8ee943e548.

[61] See, eg, D Schoenmaker and V Nicolas (2017). 'EBA relocation should support a long-term "twin peaks" vision' (Bruegel Blog Post, 5 April 2017). Available at: bruegel.org/2017/04/eba-relocation-should-support-a-long-term-twin-peaks-vision.

[62] See on this Morais (n 4). Most notably, the very recent Royal Commission into Misconduct in the Banking, Superannuation and Financial Services Industry – Commonwealth of Australia (2019) presents a very negative image of the performance of the Australian Twin Peaks model, which is usually presented as one of the reference or paradigmatic applications of such model – See the *Final Report* (Commonwealth of Australia, 2019). Available at: http://treasury.gov.au/publication/p2019-fsrc-final-report.

(1) The first possibility would be for the EBA to assume the competences of the SSM, which looks unfeasible: operationally, because this would involve transferring all expertise and resources from one body to another, but also adjusting for the severed link between monetary and supervisory policy; politically, only the opposition of the ECB itself suggests this is a no go; and legally, where apart from the necessary changes in SSM legislation, the transfer of supervisory competences to the ECB was made on the basis of Article 127(6) TFEU, which expressly refers to the ECB, and not EBA, and it is unclear whether the same competences that were transferred under the aegis of Article 127(6) could be re-assigned to EBA using a different provision.

(2) The second possibility would be to try to turn either the ECB or the ESRB into a prudential supervisor for the whole EU. Yet this poses major difficulties: both political, since all EU Member States would have to adopt the euro or sign an agreement to attribute such competences to the ECB or ESRB;[63] and legal as it would require a change in Article 127(6) TFEU, to enable the ECB to supervise insurance undertakings. If all of this was surmounted (a mountain-size 'if'), there would still be the difficulty of transforming one of the ESAs (arguably ESMA) into a sufficiently powerful market conduct supervisor to balance the priorities of the EU supervisory system, and ensure that it is not too skewed towards prudential supervision. This would be difficult to achieve, especially without a change in the Treaties, to acknowledge the role of the new authority (and possibly to grant it independence from the European Commission).

The above analysis demonstrates what the actual, and formidable, obstacles that a twin peaks approach to financial supervision would have to confront in the operational, political and legal arena. This is not impossible, but not too realistic either, at least in an economic and financial landscape where the phantom of a financial crisis (correctly or not) does no longer look a clear and present danger (political crises are another story) and the lack of cross-sectoral coordination does not look like a sufficiently powerful reason on its own. At the risk of sounding dismal, the best chance for a full-scale reform that could implement a twin peaks approach would be another large crisis that cut across the banking and insurance sectors.

Nevertheless, in case this model will not be adopted: what are possible alternatives to improve the current EU system of financial supervision? How may different institutional models at EU Member State level and at EU (supranational) level coexist?[64] These questions cannot be answered without a further reflection on the forces underpinning the preference for a twin peaks model, or for alternative hybrid models addressing issues of cross-sectoral coordination, and their meaning.

III. The Current Political Climate

Despite the strong economic case for reform, as discussed above, this section intends to demonstrate that the current political appetite for moving to a twin-peaks structure is not realistic. Worse, we will show that the very recent past presented a number of opportunities, which would

---

[63] Article 7 of Council Regulation (EU) No 1024/2013 of 15 October 2013 conferring specific tasks on the European Central Bank concerning policies relating to the prudential supervision of credit institutions [2013] OJ L287/63 (SSM Regulation).

[64] Eg, the dual model/architecture at EU level of a banking resolution authority (SRB) vis-à-vis a banking supervision authority (SSM) is not replicated in most EU Member States.

have facilitated switching to a more integrated structure; but lawmakers failed to seize these opportunities.

A. Brexit, ESAs Reform, and their Impact on EU Financial Supervisory Architecture

Some critical factors are set to affect the balance of supervisory power in the EU. Brexit is one, and the ESAs reform is another. Since the current design of financial regulation in Europe was based on the allocation of supervisory powers among France, Germany, and UK, the prospective Brexit agreement created a unique political opportunity to reshape the European architecture of financial regulation. Furthermore, the reform of ESAs constitutes an important shift in EU financial supervision, with further transfers of supervisory powers to the supranational level. These factors, in different ways, could create an opportunity to open a debate on the desirability of moving towards something akin to a twin peaks model or, alternatively, to some kind of hybrid model. Realistically speaking, however, that outcome looks now even less likely than it did when the process began. The more relevant considerations are as follows.

i. EBA Relocation

Brexit will involve a relocation of EBA to the EU27, and policy makers have now chosen Paris as its future home.[65] Instead of just moving the EBA out of London, this moment could have been seized to revamp the entire system by replacing the current authorities with a prudential supervisor and a market conduct agency. Frankfurt is already the home of EIOPA and the European Central Bank, whose building is also the ESRB's headquarters. Thus, it would have been a natural place for hosting the prudential supervisor, while Paris could have become the home of the market conduct agency.

ii. Review of the Operation of the ESAs

It so happens that the EU Commission has recently been conducting a review of the operation of the ESAs.[66] The initial goal of the review process was to evaluate their operations and to see whether they are delivering their goals, with a view of potential reform. It is exactly in this process that a functional reconsideration of the entire supervisory structure might be implemented. This should be considered in interplay with the feedback obtained, by the end of 2016, from the Public Consultation on macro-prudential control.[67]

The current proposals try to ensure that there is a continuity in the work of the ESAs decision-making, which also reflects European views, through the transformation of the Management

---

[65] See EBA's press release of 6 March 2019, 'EBA will sign today its new headquarters agreement with French authorities'. Available at: eba.europa.eu/-/eba-will-sign-today-its-new-headquarters-agreement-with-the-french-authorities.

[66] Regulations establishing the ESRB and the ESAs contain provisions for the Commission to publish a review report on the operations of the new authorities, on the mission and organisation of the ESRB, and of the entire ESFS architecture. See Art 81 of ESAs Regulations (EU) Nos 1093/2010; 1094/2010 and 1095/2010. Following the result of a public consultation, the Commission submitted a proposal to reform ESAs, see COM(2017) 536 final. After intense discussion, the Commission decided to present a second, amended proposal in 12 September 2018. See COM(2018) 646 final.

[67] See European Commission, 'Summary of responses to Consultation document – Review of the EU Macro-Prudential Policy Framework' (2017). Available at: http://ec.europa.eu/finance/consultations/2016/macroprudential-framework/docs/summary-of-responses_en.pdf.

Board into an Executive Board, with permanent members that are not conflicted by national interests, and are appointed on the basis of merit by the Council, from a list elaborated by the Commission and approved by the European Parliament.[68] The reform also tries to centralise part of the decision-making, by allocating to the Executive Board a number of relevant tasks,[69] including the exercise of supervisory powers.[70]

However, the vertical tensions stirred by national authorities' reluctance to lose control over the process have shaped the process, and postponed, yet again, a thorough debate on the need for a more rational horizontal allocation of supervisory functions among the authorities. In the newest proposal, supervisory powers over money laundering have been allocated to EBA,[71] in what may be considered a victory of European over domestic positions, but one that takes the sectoral logic as a given. If one conclusion can be reached in this respect, it is that EU institutions do not seem ready to pledge resources and political capital pursuing a horizontal re-allocation of supervisory competences in the name of a more rational distribution of functions, when the very idea of EU-level supervisors is not yet mature, and the realm of competences allocated to that EU level has not yet settled into a distinctive supervisory practice, where lessons may be drawn, and further reforms considered.

iii. Regulatory Competition

Brexit is expected to cause a reorganisation of the European capital market, which is currently highly concentrated in London.[72] Several financial institutions may be expected to move to other Member States, and this might create a regulatory race to the bottom among the remaining members.[73] In line with the subsidiarity principle, this problem could be avoided by an efficient and robust regulatory framework at the European level, which would also contribute to the competitiveness of the EU27 capital market against third countries (such as post-Brexit UK). Seeing, however, the direction the ESAs reform is pointing to, one can surmise that such efforts to enhance the regulatory framework would pile up competences on the ESAs following the same sectoral rationale that has so far been assumed as common ground, rather than redistributing competences between them.

B. Other Contributing Factors

The adoption of a twin peaks model in Europe faces a range of hard political and legal barriers. Notably, also powerful interest groups and lobby influence the decision-making process in the EU and the adoption of a holistic supervision might not be in their best interest. However, in addition to Brexit other factors might contribute to a change in the EU model.[74]

---

[68] Newly proposed Art 45 for ESAs Regulations as envisaged by European Commission proposal (n 44).

[69] Newly proposed Art 47 for ESAs Regulations as envisaged by European Commission proposal (n 44).

[70] Newly proposed Art 47(3), with reference to new Arts 35(b) to (h) of ESAs Regulations as envisaged by European Commission proposal (n 44).

[71] Newly proposed Arts 9(a) and (b) of Regulation (EU) 1093/2010 (EBA Regulation) as envisaged by European Commission proposal (n 44).

[72] See WG Ringe, 'The Irrelevance of Brexit for the European Financial Market' (2018) 19 *European Business Organization Law Review* 1.

[73] ESMA, 'ESMA response to the Commission Consultation Document on Capital Markets Union Mid-Term Review 2017' (4 April 2017) ESMA31-68-147.

[74] See, eg, N Véron, 'Charting the Next Steps for the EU financial Supervisory Architecture' (2017) *Policy Contribution Issue No 6*, Bruegel. Available at: http://bruegel.org/wp-content/uploads/2017/06/PC-16-2017-1.pdf.

i. Political Momentum

The implementation of a Twin Peaks model in Europe might require deep reforms in EU legislation (especially Treaty revision) that until some time ago were seen as unfeasible. Yet recent political events in the main Member States appear to shift this belief. After the financial crisis had created a more vocal opposition to the EU, also galvanised by Brexit, pro-European parties have had to become more proactive by highlighting the virtues of further (but also more rational) integration showing that the EU is not only a useful entity to lay the blame, but also an inspiring political idea. The latter has not only turned out to be popular among many voters, but also revamped the European project, which has regained momentum increasing the political feasibility of a deep reformulation of the current financial supervision and regulation model, especially towards a more holistic system.[75]

ii. Trend Towards Centralisation

The recent implementation of the Single Supervisory Mechanism (SSM) was the first step in creating a banking union.[76] Regulation 1024/2013 establishing the SSM clearly states that it intends to contribute to 'the safety and soundness of credit institutions and the stability of the financial system'.[77] If this goal were to be extended to all financial intermediaries, the SSM objective would look very similar to one of a prudential authority in the twin peaks model. Indeed, since the borders of financial activities are blurring, a reinforced prudential supervisory mandate within the ECB would both facilitate the conduction of the monetary policy and financial supervision. Still, an extended mandate of the ECB in terms of financial supervision and financial stability considered from a prudential perspective would not translate foreseeably into a prudential arm of a European Twin Peaks model given the lack of a normative mandate for supervision of investment firms and insurance companies.[78] This would require Treaty change. Even then, it would be a real challenge to insert this massive Eurozone prudential supervisor inside a looser EU-wide prudential supervisory structure. Beyond the centralisation versus decentralisation dichotomy, the fact that centralisation of supervisory powers occurred with a very specific Treaty base (Article 127(6) TFEU), instead of choosing a broader, internal market competence (eg Article 114 TFEU) has put a cap (temporary at least) on the objective and territorial expansion of such centralisation.

iii. Capital Markets Union

The formation of a truly integrated European capital market by 2019 was a key element in the previous Commission's investment plan.[79] An efficient and robust regulatory framework at the

---

[75] Cf, D Masciandaro, 'Politicians and financial supervision unification outside the central bank: Why do they do it?' (2009) 5 *Journal of Financial Stability* 124. The author provides a political economy model to analyse the determinants of the institutional architecture of financial supervision, according to which changes in the political orientation of a government may stimulate the implementation of reforms.

[76] See, eg, J Gordon and WG Ringe, 'Bank Resolution in the European Banking Union: A Transatlantic Perspective on What It Would Take' (2015) 115 *Columbia Law Review* 1297.

[77] Recitals (30) and (65) and Art 1 of the SSM Regulation.

[78] See M Goldmann, 'Monetary Policy and Prudential Supervision – From Functional Separation to a Holistic Approach?' (2018) *SAFE Policy Letter No 63*. Available at: www.econstor.eu/bitstream/10419/172554/1/1010350943.pdf.

[79] European Commission, 'Communication on Capital Market Union: time for renewed efforts to deliver for investment, growth and a stronger role of the euro' (Bruxelles, 28 November 2018) COM(2018) 767 final.

European level seemed essential for this plan to succeed. However, unlike the Banking Union project, the Capital Markets Union looks so far like Pirandello's *Six characters in search of an author*. The number of specific projects included within the agenda for a Capital Markets Union not only lack a unifying idea; but they also lack a specific institution that, in a way similar to the ECB and SRB for the Banking Union, can transform those ideas into an institutional reality, which helps to achieve market unification in practice.[80]

C. Institutional, and a Principles-Based Perspective: The Quest for Meaning

The above sections may be read as painting a dismal picture: (i) a twin picture structure seems the best-suited for a post-sectoral world; (ii) however, as today, the difficulties to its introduction look insurmountable; and (iii) the best chance for such step change happening lies in political developments that may be largely disruptive in other respects (eg Brexit), look increasingly out of reach (eg horizontal re-allocation of competences between ESAs) or require Treaty change (eg using the SSM as a basis to create an EU-wide prudential supervisor).

Still, the discussion about a twin peaks structure and, more generally, about a post-sectoral approach to financial supervision, is grounded on assumptions that may still benefit from further discussion. First, it is important to reflect on the reasons why a twin peaks approach may be preferable, and their implications from a jurisprudence perspective. Second, we need to reflect on the cost that such implications may have in terms of the exploration of further alternatives.

Beginning with the first point, the case for a twin peaks structure is grounded on the existence across the different financial sectors of functionally similar risks, from a prudential perspective (ie solvency, liquidity, leverage) or market conduct perspective (eg mis-selling to retail investors). This has the potential to create: (i) regulatory arbitrage; (ii) contradictory rules; and (iii) duplication and overlapping of efforts and requirements.

From a jurisprudence-based perspective, these problems are encompassed by the idea of consistency, or integrity, of the supervisory system,[81] conceived as a whole. If the system pursues a set of goals (policies) that cut across the different sectors, it thus becomes important: (i) that such goals are made clear, and pervade the main rules underpinning the system's institutional structure; and (ii) that the system's goals are reflected through the proper principles, which, in this case, can be allocative principles that define the institutions' mandates, or their supervisory purview.[82]

Bearing in mind this perspective, *if* the priority in a post-sectoral landscape is to evolve towards a function-based, or risk-based, model, the important thing is not the formal definition of the activity (banking, securities, insurance) but the kind of risks that the activity can actually pose. If those risks are similar, then the way to deal with them should be too. Now, if one looks at the foundations of the financial system, there are relevant similarities among different financial activities. From a prudential perspective, for example, the risks of banks and investment

---

[80] Concerning the deficiencies of the CMU agenda, see WG Ringe, 'Capital Markets Union for Europe – A Political Message to the UK' (2015) 9 *Law & Financial Markets Review* 5.

[81] The 'inconsistency' problem of law has been highlighted by R Dworkin, *Law's Empire* (Oxford, Hart Publishing, 1986).

[82] For a difference between policies and principles, see R Dworkin, *Taking Rights Seriously* (London, Duckworth, 1977).

firms are addressed through the same rules.[83] The rules for insurance firms, while having to deal with risks that present some appreciable qualitative differences (eg liquidity is a less relevant risk, whereas the protection of policyholders is much more important than the system itself and its interconnectedness) are based on comparable underpinning principles (even though the business models at stake differ in a manner that require somehow dissimilar technical models in prudential terms).[84] It is, however, once one descends into the details that the differences can become more salient.[85]

At this point the importance of aspects of institutional design and, in particular, of the allocation of competences becomes more salient. Financial regulation and supervision require a high level of coordination from the top-down. Indeed, the acknowledgement of this aspect resulted in the Lamfalussy process, and its four levels (framework acts, delegated and implementing acts, guidelines and recommendations, and supervisory practice). This strategy was used to ensure the harmonisation of measures at an EU level but was agnostic as to the substance of what had to be harmonised. If a sectoral approach was adopted, the four levels should ensure that insurance, banking, or securities rules are harmonised. But, conversely, this creates the risk of institutional drift *between* the matters subject to harmonisation: even if different pieces of level 1 legislation are grounded on similar principles (eg CRR/Solvency II), their implementation as well as their interpretative guidelines and supervisory practices are institutionally designed to drift apart. Especially because, under the current EU architecture, there is every incentive to ensure vertical consistency, but too little to ensure a horizontal one.

The above helps to identify the sources of friction. One is the asymmetry between the need for clarity about the different policies/goals of financial regulation that transcend sectoral divisions, and the lack of a more explicit legislative acknowledgement of those goals, and the relationship between them. Another is the orientation of the current policymaking strategy towards ensuring consistency *within* each legislative project (eg MiFID, or CRD/CRR) and its four levels. The unintended consequence of this may be to enhance the risk of inconsistencies *between* legislative projects, especially if levels 2–4 are in the hands of separate authorities.

In our view, the ideal solution should be to have levels 2–4 of projects that address a functionally similar problem (ie prudential rules and market conduct rules) to be coordinated by the same authority. However, we have also pointed to the need to be realistic about the legal, political, and operational feasibility of this solution. Thus, rather than concentrating in what may possibly be the best, but unfeasible solution, it may be more useful to understand what makes it best, and what possibilities there may be to preserve its benefits even within a different institutional setting. This is done in section IV below.

Another important aspect is the need to reflect more deeply about the implications and risks of *any* structure, which, like the twin peak structure, theoretically claims to be superior by achieving better consistency in the application of the rules. The reasoning in favour of twin peaks is somehow as follows: financial firms, and the activities they pursue, have converged towards models that pose similar risks and challenges. Those risks and challenges are primarily tackled

---

[83] Indeed, CRD IV, amending Dir 2002/87/EC and repealing Dirs 2006/48/EC and 2006/49/EC (CRD), as well as Regulation (EU) 575/2013 of the European Parliament and of the Council of 26 June 2013 on prudential requirements for credit institutions and investment firms and amending Regulation (EU) No 648/2012 (CRR) are applicable to both credit institutions and investment firms.

[84] Solvency II [2009] OJ L335/1.

[85] For a comprehensive comparison between the regulatory framework for banks and insurance companies, see N Gatzert and H Wesker, 'A Comparative Assessment of Basel II/III and Solvency II' (2012) 37 *The Geneva Papers on Risk and Insurance – Issues and Practice* 359.

through two types of rules (prudential and market conduct), which are differentiated by the type of risks they address. Put this way, the approach sounds linear and elegant, especially in contrast with the messy evolution of the current system as described in prior sections. However, we would fail in our aim to assess a twin peaks structure on the grounds of consistency/integrity if we did not also point out some of the risks that such a view based on consistency/integrity entails.

The philosophical grounds of the contrast between the current approach and any alternative design (twin peaks or otherwise), where supervisory competences are allocated through a top-down design that reverts to first-level principles, are well captured in the debate, during the 1990s and beyond, between Ronald Dworkin[86] on one side, and Richard Posner[87] and Cass Sunstein[88] on the other. The former, the philosopher, argued that law is interpretative in nature, and that truly hard cases, ie those that cannot be resolved through the exegetic construction of the law, need a deeper reflection about the underpinning principles (which he calls 'justificatory ascent') to differentiate the 'true' and 'false' propositions.[89] The latter, self-styled pragmatists argued that such construction was not possible. Posner considered that notions of 'true' and 'false' did not apply to legal (and moral) issues, and thus legal and moral truths were local in nature.[90] Sunstein, for his part, argued that relying on a 'theory' to address an issue could actually bring more harm than good, since the quest to ensure the consistency of a decision with first-order principles may actually compromise a general agreement as to the correct solution, with a justification on principles that may itself be controversial.[91] He also argued that the 'justificatory ascent' ignores the actual institutional capacities of those entrusted with the task of finding a solution be them courts or agencies.[92]

Although these considerations may look far away from the present debate, they lie at its very core. Accordingly, a twin peaks structure is only in principle preferable if one can conclude that the Law of Finance is organised around sets of rules and criteria that pivot around first-order principles, which reflect prudential and market conduct dimensions, and thus the regulatory/supervisory structure should be aligned with that division. We believe that, in light of the information available at present, this might be the case (although acknowledging, at the same time, that more than one institutional design could cope with such division). Nevertheless, the 'pragmatist' objection would ask: 'what if is it not?' That is, what if Financial Law can be organised around a set of principles that do not neatly fall into the 'prudential' and 'market conduct' categories? If this were so, some issues where there may be consensus as to their solution could be mired in a controversy as to the 'correct' allocation of competences. Conversely, if there were principles or goals that could not be classified amongst the two existing categories (eg think about the need to promote financial innovation, or competition in the financial sector), those could receive a secondary treatment. A pragmatist answer would then suggest construing a solution that looks apt to the concrete case, and perhaps dares to experiment a bit, until the more robust solutions, the ones that can be applied generally, emerge as a result of practice and experience. Another answer would be to rely on 'incompletely theorised agreements', where players focus on

---

[86] See R Dworkin, 'In Praise of Theory' (1997a) 29 *Arizona State Law Journal* 353; R Dworkin, 'Reply' (1997b) 29 *Arizona State Law Journal* 431; and R Dworkin, 'Darwin's New Bulldog' (1998) 111 *Harvard Law Review* 1718.

[87] See RA Posner, 'Conceptions of 'Legal Theory': A Response to Ronald Dworkin' (1997) 29 *Arizona State Law Journal* 377; RA Posner, 'The Problematics of Moral and Legal Theory' (1998) 111 *Harvard Law Review* 1637.

[88] See CR Sunstein, 'From Theory to Practice' (1997) 29 *Arizona State Law Journal* 389; CR Sunstein, 'Incompletely Theorized Agreements' (1995) 108 *Harvard Law Review* 1733; and CR Sunstein and A Vermeule, 'Interpretation and Institutions' (2003) 101 *Michigan Law Review* 885.

[89] R Dworkin (n 86) (1997a; 1997b; and 1998).

[90] RA Posner (n 87) (1997).

[91] CR Sunstein (n 88) (1995 and 1997).

[92] CR Sunstein and A Vermeule (n 88).

the specific solution, without ascending to the alternative sets of principles that could justify it (which may consume resources, and breed controversy).[93]

It is interesting to note that the Dworkin-Posner/Sunstein debate, while having general reach, ultimately focused on the role of courts and their approach to hard cases, as a testbed. In that context, however, the pragmatist position is more clearly vulnerable: truths may be local in nature and courts may be overworked and under-resourced, but the application of the law by courts rests on the understanding that, when parties present opposing arguments, there is one right solution for each case. A solution that is consistent with the system's general principles, regardless of whether the connection with those principles is made explicit or not. The field of administrative agencies, on the other hand, lends itself more easily to a pragmatist approach. In the regulation and supervision of financial services the notions of 'true' and 'correct' do not have the same significance as in court rulings. The role of discretion is more widely acknowledged. Indeed, a part of the current debate lies exactly in determining how and to what extent to limit such discretion, and what is the role of courts. In the EU, the original case law in *Meroni* may have obscured this, but the revision in the *ESMA* ruling clarified that an agency's decisions remain valid if there is a legal framework of reference to assess their validity, but that framework does not ultimately require a single correct solution.

In light of the above, we may consider that there is a case for the adoption of a twin peaks structure, given the currently available information, the structure of EU financial legislation and its underpinning logic. However, we also acknowledge there is room to consider alternative solutions that properly address the overriding concerns underlying the twin peaks structure and its underlying principles. Conversely, the current system, messy as it may look, is the result of a path-dependent process that has responded to *real* problems. Thus, a solution that departs from the current structure to face the new challenges may have some benefits as well:

(1)   It does not lose sight of the priorities that justified each of the reforms, eg the Banking Union is not complete, and it may never be fully satisfactory, but such completion, especially the more controversial issues, such as the European Deposit Insurance Scheme, would be abandoned if the energies shifted towards a re-design of the regulatory/supervisory system.

(2)   The understanding that the current structure is inadequate for new issues with a post-sectoral dimension (eg FinTech) can spur agencies to achieve common solutions through coordination in order to avoid criticism, thus safeguarding their institutional reputation.

(3)   An admittedly incomplete system with duplications, imperfect allocation and potential inconsistencies can also be a test bed for experimental solutions, in both technical and organisational matters.

(4)   Last but not least, twin peak structures have been introduced in contexts where there were already existing supervisory authorities with experience to draw from, in terms of the most efficient allocation of competences. The ESAs, in contrast, were established in legal regulations adopted in 2010, and they have been vested with supervisory competences even more recently, and these are far from broad (their more prominent role is still associated to the preparation of regulatory work), and the centralisation of functions via the Executive Board is, at the time of writing, still a legislative project. Surely it is possible to rely on the experience with different structures in other jurisdictions, including Member States, but the ESAs themselves lack historical experience of their own, and mistakes to learn from. It is difficult to foresee with full accuracy what kind of problems will affect the future performance of

---

[93] CR Sunstein (n 88) (1995).

tasks by ESAs; some such problems may mirror those faced by national supervisors, and some might be attributable to a sub-optimal allocation of tasks, but others may be uniquely European, and/or arise from a combination between horizontal *and* vertical misallocations. Indeed, the widespread view that the system is still a work-in-progress may help render it more malleable when the need for substantial reform arises. Perhaps that is not necessarily a worse scenario than one where EU institutions were already under the impression that this time they 'just got it right', or one where so much political capital had been spent that any further calls for change would to meet a pervading sense of reform fatigue.

The above does not change our main conclusion: under the present circumstances we believe that a twin peaks model or an equally functional hybrid model, ensuring proper and efficient coordination *within* the prudential and market conduct dimensions of financial supervision (without neglecting coordination *between* these two dimensions), would be preferable in terms of institutional design. However, since for the reasons discussed above such structure looks presently unfeasible, it is important to be aware about the benefits of the messier, imperfectly sectoral, current approach in a constantly shifting financial landscape, as well as the reasons why we consider the twin peaks model an important paradigm in terms of financial supervision, to see if the latter can somehow be replicated within a sectoral model.

IV. Possible Alternatives for Improvement

Considering the possibility that a twin peaks model might not be adopted in view of the identified hurdles, but also due to its own potential limitations, alternative options and various scenarios should be considered to improve the EU supervisory structure in line with a more holistic approach to regulation and supervision. In a similar direction, the French Autorité des marchés financiers (AMF) has recently set out its proposals for the new 2020–2024 EU legislature.[94] Among these are a number of pragmatic proposals to promote greater convergence in the supervision of actors and developing a framework for day-to-day relations between supervisors (considering the effect of Brexit and the coexistence of several financial centres).[95]

In this spirit, the present section analyses how the current EU financial regulatory framework could be incrementally improved without an overall re-writing of its institutional design.

Among others, topics to be considered are as follows.

A. Improve Cooperation and Coordination between the ESAs

In the absence of any political appetite of moving towards a Twin Peaks structure, or of other reasons disavowing such a move, a more straightforward substitute could be seen in a reinforced system of cooperation between the ESAs. This would be a simple fix to address the downsides of a tripartite 'silo' structure with its lack of a holistic approach to supervision. The present system

---

[94] Autorité des Marchés Financiers, EU2024: 'Shaping EU27 Capital Markets to Meet Tomorrow's Challenges – Focus areas and initial proposals of the French AMF' (June 2019), available at www.amf-france.org/technique/multimedia?docId=78900687-9efe-4fd0-88db-fd7c83738a7b.

[95] See also Robert Ophèle, AMF Chairman, speech at FIA's International Derivatives Expo Conference – 'Shaping EU27 capital markets to meet tomorrow's challenges', London, 4 June 2019.

allows for some elements of cooperation between the three ESAs, but complementary ways of making this system more efficient and functional should be explored, eg building on the current structures for that coordination which may be further developed.

Within this context, the role of the Joint Committees of European supervisory authorities, which already have a mandate oriented towards the goal of ensuring that the three ESAs 'shall cooperate regularly and closely and ensure cross-sectoral consistency'[96] should be reinforced. A good illustration of this role that the joint committee may perform in order to enhance cross-sectoral consistency and coordination can be found, eg, in the principles set out in its Joint Position and Guidelines regarding 'manufacturers' product oversight and governance processes'.[97] The Chairpersons of the three ESAs could play a prominent role in such coordination efforts.[98]

The goals of Joint Committees are defined in a sufficiently broad way to allow for the kind of symbiosis that could result in a coordination along prudential and market conduct goals. If the work of such committees becomes more prominent, coordination needs could dictate a top-down specialisation of prudential and market conduct units in each of the authorities. Were this so, there would be no pressing need to restructure the ESAs to create new authorities to group the specialised units: a fluid exchange and workflow coordination would take care of that. Furthermore, the specialisation would be achieved in an incremental, iterative way, where things other than a post-sectoral allocation of tasks could be considered in the process.

As things stay now, these prospects look uncertain. Inward-looking institutional inertia could render Joint Committees ineffective, and changes in policy priorities could impose a piecemeal approach, where the Joint Committee would be occupied on the issues of the moment, rather than be an instrument to further a prudential-market conduct specialisation agenda. Currently proposed rules emphasise the Joint Committee's role in coordinating money laundering tasks with other tasks.[99] The other risk is that they may be oriented towards an issue-by-issue approach, but our goal is to lay out the possibilities by which post-sectoral views could find their way inside the current institutional structure, with or without twin peaks.

B. Improve Coordination between Micro and Macro Policies

In the present framework, the ESAs are responsible for micro level while the ESRB is in charge of macro level oversight. Although the ESAs are part of the ESRB, the current structure favours the

---

[96] Article 54 of EBA Regulation, and in corresponding provisions of the EIOPA and ESMA Regulations.

[97] See Joint Committee of the European Supervisory Authorities, *Joint Position of the European Supervisory Authorities on Manufacturers' Product Oversight and Governance Processes* (2013) JC-2013-77. Available at: https://eiopa.europa.eu/Publications/Administrative/JC-2013-77__POG_-_Joint_Position_.pdf.

[98] The Board of Supervisors can delegate specific tasks to internal committees, but also to the Executive Committee, or its Chairperson, which provides another source of coordination powers, aside from its role in the Executive Committee itself. See newly proposed Art 41 of Regulations 1093/2010, 1094/2010, and 1095/2010 as envisaged by European Commission proposal (n 44).

[99] Newly proposed para 2(a) of Art 54 in Regulations 1093/2010, 1094/2010 and 1095/2010 as envisaged by European Commission proposal (n 44). Interestingly, the explanatory part of the Amended proposal states that: 'The proposed amendments to the Regulation governing the European Insurance and Occupational Pensions Authority and the Regulation governing the European Securities and Markets Authority remove Directive 2015/849 on the prevention of the use of the financial system for the purposes of money-laundering or terrorist financing from the scope of activities of those two authorities and clarify that the Joint Committee should be used as a forum for cooperation on matters related to the *interaction between prudential, and anti-money laundering* and countering financing of terrorism aspects' omitting any mention to market conduct issues.

macro agenda in detriment to topics such as consumer protection. We admit that better inter-action can be achieved in this domain. Such enhanced and qualitatively improved interaction should involve – as contemplated in the pending reform – the introduction of adjustments in the functioning of ESRB making it more efficient and improving its governance, also improving its interplay with the ECB and the structures it has put in place to deal with macroprudential supervision. In fact, in various national architectures of financial supervision (eg Germany or France, albeit with different institutional overall designs) new structures entrusted with scru-tiny of systemic risk and macroprudential supervision tend also to play a role as a conduit for enhanced *coordination* between either sectoral perspectives and prudential and market conduct perspectives. An incremental role of a reformed ESRB, with significant operational interplay with ECB and also a reinforced interplay with ESAs preferably through their *Joint Committee*, which could include a segment more dedicated to such interplay oriented towards cross-sectoral macroprudential considerations, would be a step in the right direction.

As well as top-down coordination between micro and macro policies, new insights could be gained from a bottom-up approach, in those cases where supervisory tasks require the joint input of authorities with 'macro' and 'micro' approaches. Thus far, the more interesting experiment in this sense is the reform of CCP supervision. As discussed above,[100] the currently proposed structure introduces a CCP Executive Session/Supervisory Committee within ESMA, with a composition that includes permanent voting members, permanent non-voting, non-permanent voting, and non-permanent non-voting, to streamline decision-making.[101] This accompanies the more relevant role given to ESMA, which has to give its consent on numerous supervi-sory decisions,[102] and exercises direct supervisory responsibilities over systemically important (Tier 2) CCPs from third-countries.[103]

The more interesting innovation is the presence, within the Committee, of a representative of the ECB, as well as other relevant central banks of issue. This is supplemented by central banks' relevant role in the aspects related to the CCP's payment and settlement arrangements, as well as their liquidity risk, and the requirement to obtain the central bank's consent on a series of relevant decisions.[104] A similar scheme is proposed with regard to third-country CCPs, where the proposed rules vest ESMA with direct supervisory powers,[105] in agreement with the third country supervisory authorities,[106] but also reserve a relevant role for the central bank of issue, and require its consent for certain decisions.[107]

While this system of 'vetocracy' creates a risk of paralysis, it provides an even greater incentive for ESMA and central banks to engage in a fluid exchange of information, which can improve ESMA's understanding of the links between macro and micro dimensions. This may improve not

---

[100] See II.D above.

[101] Newly proposed Arts 18 and 21, EMIR, as envisaged by European Commission proposal (n 44).

[102] On access to a CCP, access to a trading venue, authorisation of a CCP, extension of activities and services of a CCP, capital requirements, withdrawal of authorisation, review and evaluation, shareholders and members with qualifying holdings, information to competent authorities, review of models, stress testing and back testing, and approval of inter-operability arrangements. See newly proposed Art 21(a), EMIR, as envisaged by European Commission proposal (n 44).

[103] Newly proposed Art 25(a), as envisaged by European Commission proposal (n 44).

[104] On authorisation of a CCP, extension of activities and services of a CCP, withdrawal of authorisation, margin requirements, liquidity risk controls, collateral requirements, settlement and approval of interoperability arrangements. See newly proposed Art 21(b), EMIR, as envisaged by European commission proposal (n 44).

[105] Newly proposed Arts 25(b)–(n), as envisaged by European Commission proposal (n 44).

[106] Newly proposed Art 25(7), as envisaged by European Commission proposal (n 44).

[107] Eg, margin requirements, liquidity risk controls, collateral requirements, settlement and approval of interoperability arrangements. See newly proposed Art 25(b)(2), EMIR, as envisaged by European Commission proposal (n 44).

only the performance of the specific tasks, but also the authorities' understanding of the interplay between different regulatory goals.

C. Coordination with National Authorities, Access to Information, and ESAs Mandates

The current model requires a close cooperation between the ESAs and the national authorities. However, in the present legal structure, the ESAs rely on their national counterparts' will of cooperation and capabilities to perform their tasks. In particular, the ESAs rely on the national authorities to obtain data and information from the institutions that they regulate.[108] Information is a key input in the regulatory process, thus we will discuss the possibility of allowing the ESAs to directly request data from financial institutions.

D. Extension of the ESAs' Mandates

While the ESAs can adopt standards, they lack the real power to enforce them. Indeed, truly supervisory power is more an exception (such as in the case of rating agencies) than a real ability of the ESAs in the current framework. Further study should explore how their power could be extended.

E. Issues Transversal to Further Integration and Coordination between ESAs, also Involving the SSM

We will examine information flows between supervisors in a context of further integration and coordination as contradictory requirements may be at play here, on the one hand, towards maximum public disclosure of certain types of information and, on the other hand, towards reserve on sensitive information.

V. Conclusion

This chapter has primarily argued that (a) a post-sectoral logic suggests that a twin peaks model or a functional equivalent may be the optimal supervisory solution; (b) that solution poses seemingly insurmountable political and legal problems, which make it unfeasible; so (c) we should rather concentrate our efforts on what is feasible.

Such synthesis, however, would be not only simplified, but simplistic, first, because it offers an unnecessarily dismal picture; second, because it is in the nuances where some of the main lessons may be drawn. Taking the first point, the twin peaks model sits better with a post-sectoral logic, and yet it cannot offer a magic formula of success. Supervisory gaps and overlaps can also arise

---

[108] E Becker, *Knowledge Capture in Financial Regulation: Data, Information and Knowledge in the US Financial Crisis* (Berlin, Springer, 2016).

within a twin peaks structure, which also does not guarantee that the prudential supervisor will measure risk more accurately, or the conduct supervisor will be sufficiently alert.

Going to the second point, the twin peaks model faces obstacles that are extremely hard to overcome, but this is not only due to caprice or interest groups. The idea of an 'EU model' for financial supervision is not in the Treaties, and the only provision (Article 127(6) TFEU) hints at the ECB, but only for policies of prudential supervision, and restricted to banks. The drafters did not have in mind a massive reallocation of supervisory powers to the EU. Even if the need for a more rational distribution of powers looks like a necessity now, the absence of a very clear Treaty basis should give us pause for reflection. For one, this should mean that every re-allocation that has EU institutions as its beneficiaries should be properly justified, which means that the path followed will be that of minimum resistance, which risks producing solutions that are less efficient, but are, perhaps, perceived as more legitimate due to their gradualism. Furthermore, the lack of a clear model outlined in the Treaties permit the secondary rulemaker to experiment with different models.

Thus, going to the third point, since political and legal realities seem to impose a view characterised by restraint and gradualism (and thus incompatible with the massive overhaul a twin peak structure would require), we should exploit the advantages of this approach, and be less afraid of an experimental approach.[109] Twin-peak structures have, by now, a track record to back them, even if not free of problems, but the supranational supervisory structure of the EU is something unseen before. This suggests that, if the two are combined, it will be hard to fully extrapolate the conclusions from domestic experience. Instead, further reforms that try to promote a post-sectoral approach should try to think more in functional, rather than structural, terms. Functionally speaking, what is needed is greater coordination between the regulatory and supervisory tasks that, even though performed by different authorities (or units) pursue the same goals. There exist channels, both formal (Joint Committee and sub-committees, which can be incrementally reinforced) and informal (enhanced coordination and information flows), that can be used to achieve that goal. If the EU lawmakers wished to help, they could more clearly differentiate the goals (prudential and market conduct) that the different authorities are supposed to fulfil (especially in the case of ESAs, since SSM rules do that). But mostly, the authorities themselves should partake the conviction that a post-sectoral view is not just an academic exercise, but a source of supervisory consistency and efficiency.

---

[109] See also AMF (n 94).

18

What Happens when an EU Financial Institution Crosses Borders? Time for Consistency?

EMANUEL VAN PRAAG[1]

I. Introduction

EU financial institutions can serve clients resident in other EU Member States that are not where their headquarters are based. This is arranged for in various EU financial services directives (and regulations). In this chapter I will discuss the similarities and differences in how these directives regulate cross border activities. I will answer the following two key questions:

(1) When is an EU financial institution deemed to be active in another Member State (hereafter: the 'host state') rather than the Member State where its headquarters are (hereafter: the 'home state'). This question is relevant, because only if a financial institution is deemed to be active in the host state, the supervisory authorities of the host state have the right to project some power over the financial institution. Because the powers of the host state supervisory authorities differ depending on the qualification of the cross-border activities, I will also discuss the various ways that a financial institution can be active across borders. (in section II).

(2) I will then delve into the division of competences between the home state supervisory authorities and the host state supervisory authorities. When active across borders, to what extent is the financial institution supervised by the home state supervisory authorities and to what extent by the host state supervisory authorities? (in section III)

In section IV I will evaluate the findings and provide suggestions to improve the EU financial services directives.

---

[1] This chapter is based on Emanuel's Dutch book and PhD thesis EJ van Praag *Europees financieel toezicht Bevoegdheden in het Europees financieel toezicht*, (Boom Juridisch Den Haag, 2017).

With the term 'financial institution' I do not mean to refer to a defined term, eg financial institution as defined in the Capital Requirements Regulation (CRR).[2] I merely refer to the companies that are the subject of this comparative study. These are listed in the table below.

Type of company	Sector
Credit institutions[3]	Saving/deposit taking and lending
Mortgage credit intermediaries[4]	Lending
UCITS Directive and their managers[5]	Investing
AIFs and their managers[6]	Investing
Investment firms[7]	Investing
Insurance companies[8]	Insurance
Insurance intermediaries[9]	Insurance
Payment institutions[10]	Payments

This selection is made of all applicable financial services directives (and regulations), because as depicted in the table above, together they cover the four main retail financial products (saving/deposit taking and lending, investing, insurance and payments).

II. When is a Financial Institution Active in the Host State?

Before we discuss which host state rules and supervision apply to a financial institution active in a host state, we first need to find out when exactly this financial institution is deemed to be active in the host state.[11] The EU financial services directives arrange for three modes of cross border activity: via a branch (see section II.A.), via the provision of services (section II.B.) and via agents (section II.C.). A fourth mode is provided for by the Directive on electronic commerce (section II.D.), which operates outside of the scope of the EU financial services directives but which is nevertheless relevant for this study.

A. What is a Branch?

As we will discuss in more detail in section III below, the powers of the host state supervisory authorities are most extensive when the financial institution is operating in the host state

---

[2] CRR, 575/2013/EU.
[3] CRR, 575/2013/EU and CRD IV, 2013/36/EU.
[4] MCD, 2014/17/EU.
[5] UCITS IV Directive, 2009/65/EU.
[6] AIFMD, 2011/61/EU.
[7] MiFID II, 2014/65/EU and MiFIR, 600/2014/EU.
[8] Solvency II, 2009/138/EC.
[9] IDD, 2016/97/EU.
[10] PSD II, 2015/2366/EU.
[11] For a more extensive discussion see EJ van Praag, 'What happens when an EU financial institution crosses borders? Time for an update?', (2019) *Tijdschrift voor Financieel Recht* p 36–48. This section II is partly based on this journal article.

through a branch (office). Therefore, it is relevant to investigate what is meant with a branch. I must emphasise that the difference between the provision of services and the establishment of a branch is a fine line and that Member States have different interpretations.[12]

The definition of a branch in CRR is:[13] 'A place of business which forms a legally dependent part of an institution and which carries out directly all or some of the transactions inherent in the business of institutions.' The other EU financial services directives use similar definitions.[14] The essence of the definition of a branch is, that a local office only qualifies as a branch if it performs work that is normally performed by the financial institution and for which the financial institution is authorised. The emphasis on the word 'transaction' in the English language version of the definition of a branch of a credit institution is a bit deceiving, as it suggests that the branch should conclude transactions. The other language versions (using words like *Tätigkeit* or *operations or werkzaamheden*) show that a branch of a credit institution can already qualify as such if it performs work that is typically undertaken by and reserved to credit institutions, such as deciding on loans to be granted, informing clients on their financial situation and accepting orders.[15] Also the definitions in the other EU financial services directives point towards this conclusion.

On the other hand, a back office of a credit institution is not a branch. All language versions of the CRR definition of a branch contain the word 'directly' (*unmittelbar* or *directement* or *rechtstreeks*). I conclude from this that a branch office can only qualify as such, if it services clients/ is market facing. For example, an administrative outsourcing centre in a Member State does not qualify as a branch, provided that it does not interact with any clients or markets directly, even if it has a back office role in serving clients (eg checking and verifying documents).[16] For the other financial institutions no such reference to 'directly' is made. Still my judgement would be that a mere back office not facing the financial markets or clients would not be a branch.

A branch must serve local clients. For example, a call centre located in another Member State other than the home state is only a branch if it serves local clients or interacts with the market

---

[12] See for the Dutch interpretation the fine by the AFM for Novum Bank of 18 October 2018, ps://www.afm.nl/~/profmedia/files/maatregelen/boetes/2018/novum-bank.pdf where the AFM explains in detail why the local office qualifies as a branch and Rb. Rotterdam 20 December 2018, ECLI:NL:RBROT:2018:10909. See for a recent EU document Opinion of the European Banking Authority on the nature of passport notifications regarding agents and distributors under Dir (EU) 2015/2366 (PSD2), Dir 2009/110/EC (EMD2) and Dir (EU) 2015/849 (AMLD), 24 April 2019, EBA-Op-2019-03, p 2.

[13] CRR, Art 4(1) 17.

[14] See for an overview of these definitions in other financial services directives E.J. van Praag, *Europees financieel toezicht Bevoegdheden in het Europees financieel toezicht*, (Boom Juridisch Den Haag, 2017), p 250 and the website of the FCA here: www.handbook.fca.org.uk/handbook/glossary/G113.html.

[15] If the office performs no activities that are typical for banking work, it is not a branch office. Therefore, an office only performing marketing activities, market research and/or general provision of information about the banking services offered, is not considered a branch office, but a 'representative office'. See, eg, for France Code monétaire et financier – Art OJ L511-19 and the positions of the ACPR https://acpr.banque-france.fr/en/authorisation/banking-industry-procedures/licensing-authorisation-and-registration/representative-office for Spain and the position of the Banco de Espana see www.bde.es/bde/es/secciones/servicios/Instituciones_fi/autorizacion-de-/Entidades_extra_b2b445b0957db51.html, and for Germany Art 53a of German Kreditwesengesetz – KWG and for the position of the Bafin see www.bafin.de/SharedDocs/Veroeffentlichungen/EN/Merkblatt/mb_050401_grenzueberschreitend_en.html;jsessionid=08C7DDE3FCBD8B674DB309F29EA29AC8.2_cid381?nn=9451720#doc7857716bodyText2; for the Netherlands and the position of DNB see www.toezicht.dnb.nl/3/50-225790.jsp and see for Italy, eg Circolare n 285 del 17 dicembre 2013, p 65 and 69. See for ESMA about representative offices under MiFID extensively Questions and Answers Relating to the provision of CFDs and other speculative products to retail investors under MiFID 31 March 2017, ESMA35-36-794, p 84–86.

[16] See also ECJ, 15 September 2011, C-347/09 (*Dickinger and Ömer*), paras 35–36 where the fact that clients could not see any local presence was a reason to conclude that the activity was covered under the freedom of services.

where it is based. So, if a Dutch credit institution were to serve the French market via a call centre in Brussels, this call centre does not qualify as a branch in France, because this call centre is not based in France but in Belgium. This call centre is not a branch in Belgium either, because it does not serve any Belgian-based clients. In that case the Dutch credit institution would be deemed to provide the freedom of services from the Netherlands into France directly, regardless of the role of the Brussels office.[17]

B. What are Cross Border Services

If a financial institution acts under the freedom to provide services as opposed to via a branch, it is significantly less exposed to local regulation and supervision, but nevertheless may need to take some local regulation and supervision into account. Below I explore what is covered by the freedom of services.

i. *The Place of Characteristic Performance or the Initiative Test?*

The freedom of services under CRD IV, MCD, MiFID II and PSD II, is triggered per the text of these directives when the services are provided 'within' the territory of another Member State or 'in the host Member States'. I quote by way of example CRD IV:[18] 'Any credit institution wishing to exercise the freedom to provide services by carrying out its activities *within the territory of another Member State* for the first time shall notify the competent authorities of the home Member State of the activities on the list in Annex I which it intends to carry out.' Unfortunately none of these directives make explicit when a service is exactly provided 'within' the territory of another Member State.[19] This has led to considerable debate within the EU where there are two main opposing views.[20] On the one hand there is the European Commission and some Member States such as the UK[21] who consider the place of the 'characteristic performance' determinative. They look at where the characteristic performance is physically taking place to determine if a service is provided in the host state. I quote the European Commission:[22]

> A bank may have non-resident customers without necessarily pursuing the activities concerned within the territory of the Member States where the customers have their domicile.

---

[17] See with respect to MiFID the European Commission document: 'Supervision of branches under MiFID' of 18 June 2007, MARKT/G/3/MV D(2007) 2386, where the Commission considered that the supervisory authority of the host state should be responsible for the supervision of clients that are in the host state. For the supervision of client relationships that are outside of the host state, the home state should be solely responsible regardless of the fact that the work is done in the branch office. See also Commission, Interpretative Communication: 'Freedom to provide services and the interest of the general good in the Second Banking Directive', (97/C 209/04), p 13.

[18] CRD IV, Art 39. See for comparable phrases MCD, Art 32(1), UCITS IV Directive, Art 16(1), MiFID II, Art 34(1), IDD, Art 4(1) and PSD II, Art 28(1).

[19] In the same vein EBA, EIOPA, ESMA Report on cross-border supervision of retail financial services, 9 July 2019, JC/2019-22 p 23

[20] See for an extensive analysis, EJ van Praag *Europees financieel toezicht Bevoegdheden in het Europees financieel toezicht*, (Boom Juridisch Den Haag, 2017), p 233. See also the ESMA letter to European Commission of 26 September 2018 Ref: 'MiFID II / MiFIR third country regimes, provision of investment services and activities at the exclusive initiative of the client and outsourcing of functions to third country entities', p 4.

[21] FCA handbook SUP App 3.1 Application www.handbook.fca.org.uk/handbook/SUP/App/3/?view=chapter, 18 October 2018.

[22] See Commission, Interpretative Communication: 'Freedom to provide services and the interest of the general good in the Second Banking Directive', (97/C 209/04), p 8. EBA still referred to the Commission's interpretive communication in the EBA Discussion Paper 'Draft requirements on passport notifications for credit intermediaries under the Mortgage Credit Directive', 11 December 2014, EBA/DP/2014/03, p 6.

Consequently, the fact of temporarily visiting the territory of a Member State to carry on an activity preceding (e.g. survey of property prior to granting a loan) or following (incidental activities) the essential activity does not, in the Commission's view, constitute a situation that is liable in itself to be the subject of prior notification. [...]

Furthermore, the Commission considers that the fact of temporarily visiting the territory of a Member State in order to conclude contracts prior to the exercise of a banking activity should not be regarded as exercising the activity itself. [...]

If, on the other hand, the institution intends to provide the characteristic performance of a banking service by sending a member of its staff or a temporarily authorized intermediary to the territory of another Member State, prior notification should be necessary.

Taken to the extreme, under the 'characteristic performance' test a financial institution can launch a website and set up an internet campaign to offer services to clients in another Member State without being deemed to be active there. I quote the European Commission from 1997:[23] 'Lastly, the provision of distance banking services, for example through the Internet, should not, in the Commission's view, require prior notification, since the supplier cannot be deemed to be pursuing its activities in the customer's territory.'

On the other hand, there are Member States that look at who took the initiative for the service provision.[24] If the financial institution took the initiative to service a client in the host state, the financial institution is deemed to be active in the host state. These Member States apply the 'initiative test' or 'original solicitation test'. Such a country applying the original solicitation test is the Netherlands.[25] For the Dutch AFM the key question is who took the initiative for the relationship. If that is the client, that implies no cross-border service provision. If the financial institution took the initiative, the financial institution is providing cross-border services in the Netherlands even if all the work is carried out outside of the Netherlands. On the other hand, as long as the client took the initiative, it does not seem to matter that part of the work is carried out in the Netherlands.

To conclude: depending on the position of the relevant Member State, services are provided in the host state if the financial institution took the initiative to provide services to local clients or alternatively if the characteristic performance takes places in the host state.

---

[23] See Commission, Interpretative Communication: 'Freedom to provide services and the interest of the general good in the Second Banking Directive', (97/C 209/04), p 8.

[24] See communication from the Commission, 'The Application of Conduct of Business Rules under Article 11 of the Investment Services Directive', (93/22/EEC), 14 November 2001, COM(2000) 722 final, p 11. J Welch, 'The sophisticated investor and the ISD', in: G Ferrarini, KJ Hopt en E Wymeersch (eds), *Capital markets in the age of the euro: cross-border transactions, listed companies and regulation*, (Den Haag, Kluwer Law International, 2002), p 105 and N Moloney, *EC Securities Regulation*, 2nd edn (Oxford, Oxford University Press, 2008), p 439. Examples are Germany, see Bafin 'Notes regarding the licensing for conducting cross-border banking business and/or providing cross-border financial services' April 2005, www.bafin.de/SharedDocs/Veroeffentlichungen/EN/Merkblatt/mb_050401_grenzueberschreitend_en.html Italy, see Circolare n 285 del 17 dicembre 2013, p 93, France, see AAth. Gkoutzinis, *Internet Banking and the Law in Europe*, (Cambridge, Cambridge University Press, 2006), p 246–248 and the Czech Republic, see 'Interpretation of what constitutes providing financial services in the Czech Republic', 6 November 2013, at www.cnb.cz/miranda2/export/sites/www.cnb.cz/en/faq/providing_financial_services_in_czech_republic.pdf. See extensively about the application of the initiative test outside of the EU AAth. Gkoutzinis, *Internet Banking and the Law in Europe*, (Cambridge, Cambridge University Press, 2006), p. 64–67 and 232–237 and IOSCO, 'Report on Securities Activity on the Internet II', June 2001, p 5, 66 and 103. Also some EU directives use the initiative test when determining whether a third country firm is active in the EU. See MiFID II, Art 42 and Recital 111, MiFIR, Art 46(5) and Recital 43.

[25] AFM 'Markets in Financial Instruments Directive' In 82 vragen door de MiFID Tweede herziene druk Amsterdam januari 2008. See with respect to investment services Rb. Rotterdam 24 april 2007, *JOR* 2007/149 and Hof Amsterdam 14 January 1999, *JOR* 1999/35 and Rb. Rotterdam 11 July 2016, ECLI:NL:RBROT:2016:6829, r.o. 5.4. See with respect to banking services Rb. Rotterdam, 8 August 2005, ECLI:NL:RBROT:2005:AU0663, r.o. 2.4.2.

ii. Specific Rules in Directives and Regulations to Determine Whether Cross Border Services Take Place

As set out above in section II.B.i for credit institutions, mortgage credit intermediaries, investment firms and payment institutions there are no clear and detailed rules in the relevant EU financial services directives that stipulate when such a financial institution is deemed to be active across borders, which is why Member States have diverging interpretations. For UCITS Directive and their managers, AIFs and their managers and insurance companies and insurance intermediaries however there are specific rules provided in the directives.

a. UCITS Directive and their Managers

For UCITS Directive and their managers it is relatively clear when they are active on a cross border basis.[26] Either if they manage a UCITS Directive fund that is domiciled in another jurisdiction or when they market a UCITS Directive in another Member State. As each UCITS Directive must have a manager and inform their supervisory authorities thereof, it is easy to determine when this manager is from abroad. Marketing is not defined in the UCITS Directive itself, but it suggests some active decision on behalf of the UCITS Directive manager to approach a market. Put differently it encapsulates the initiative test, as marketing on itself requires an initiative. One does not market by accident.[27]

b. AIFs and their Managers

Just like with the UCITS Directive also under the AIFMD, managers can perform cross border activities either via managing foreign AIFs[28] or by marketing their own AIFs.[29] Marketing is defined as 'a direct or indirect offering or placement at the initiative of the AIFM or on behalf of the AIFM of units or shares of an AIF it manages to or with investors domiciled or with a registered office in the Union.'[30] Here it is crystal clear in the Directive itself that marketing includes an initiative to approach a market.[31]

c. Insurance Companies

Solvency II explicitly states that 'for life and non-life insurance, the Member State of the provisions of services means, respectively, the Member State of the commitment or the Member State in which the risk is situated, where that commitment or risk is covered by an insurance undertaking or a branch situated in another Member State.'[32] So the relevant question becomes what

---

[26] UCITS IV Directive, Art 16.

[27] See, eg the AFM 'Beleidsregel Actief zijn in Nederland', (2013) *Stcrt.*, 29981, 28 October 2013 where the Dutch AFM has provided guidance on when a UCITS Directive manager or AIF manager has approached the Dutch market.

[28] AIFMD, Art 33.

[29] AIFMD, Art 32.

[30] AIFMD, Art 4(1) x.

[31] See on how this has been implemented in various Member States for the Netherlands the AFM 'Beleidsregel Actief zijn in Nederland 2013', (2013) *Stcrt.*, 29981, 28 October 2013. For Germany Kapitalanlagegesetzbuch, Absatz 293 and the website of the Bafin in Häufige Fragen zum Vertrieb und Erwerb von Investmentvermögen nach dem KAGB, www.bafin.de/SharedDocs/Veroeffentlichungen/DE/FAQ/faq_kagb_vertrieb_erwerb_130604.html?nn=2821494 and ESMA's opinion to the European Parliament, 'Council and Commission and responses to the call for evidence on the functioning of the AIFMD EU passport and of the National Private Placement Regimes', 30 July 2015, ESMA/2015/1235, p 16.

[32] Solvency II, Art 13(9).

is meant with 'member state of the commitment' or 'Member State in which the risk is situated'. Fortunately both are defined in Solvency II.

According to Solvency II the term 'Member State in which the risk is situated', means any of the following:[33]

a.   the Member State in which the property is situated, where the insurance relates either to buildings or to buildings and their contents, in so far as the contents are covered by the same insurance policy;

b.   the Member State of registration, where the insurance relates to vehicles of any type;

c.   the Member State where the policy holder took out the policy in the case of policies of a duration of four months or less covering travel or holiday risks, whatever the class concerned;

d.   in all cases not explicitly covered by points (a), (b) or (c), the Member State in which either of the following is situated:

(i)   the habitual residence of the policy holder; or

(ii)   if the policy holder is a legal person, that policy holder's establishment to which the contract relates;"

And defines the term 'Member State of commitment', as:

a.   'the habitual residence of the policy holder;

b.   if the policy holder is a legal person, that policy holder's establishment, to which the contract relates;

d. Insurance Intermediaries (EIOPA)

For insurance intermediaries EIOPA has defined when cross-border services are deemed to be provided. I quote:[34]

An Intermediary or Ancillary Intermediary is operating under freedom to provide services if it intends to provide a policyholder, who is established in a Member State different from the one where the Intermediary or Ancillary Intermediary is registered, with an insurance contract relating to a risk situated in a Member State different from the Member State where the Intermediary or Ancillary Intermediary is registered.

Put differently an insurance intermediary only provides cross-border services when the policyholder and the insurance risk are based in another Member State. EIOPA does not make this explicit, but I would assume that in determining where the risk is based, the same rules should be applied as set forth in Solvency II.

C. Can the Financial Institution Operate Abroad via Agents?

Some of the EU financial services directives provide for the possibility to access the market in another Member State via a separate legal entity (an agent) which is not part of the financial institution. Although legally separate, agents are often assimilated to a branch or treated as a branch of the financial institution itself. We will see which EU financial services directives allow for this possibility and which do not.

---

[33] Solvency II, Art 13 sub 13. See ECJ 14 June 2001, C-191/99 (*Kvaerner/Ministerie van Financiën*).

[34] EIOPA, Decision of the Board of Supervisors on the cooperation of the competent authorities of the Member States of the European Economic Area with regard to Directive (EU) 2016/97 of the European Parliament and of the Council of 20 January 2016 on insurance distribution, EIOPA-BoS/18-340 28 September 2018, p 14.

i. Credit Institutions

CRD IV does not explicitly provide for the possibility for credit institutions to use agents in the home state or a host state. Nevertheless, credit institutions can access the host state markets via intermediaries. These intermediaries will as a starting point require an authorisation based on national law, unless as we will explain below, they can act under MiFID II, the MCD or PSD II. Put differently the credit institution itself has a passport based on CRD IV, but CRD IV does not provide any rights or passport to agents of credit institutions.

However, the credit institution itself can also be deemed to be active via a branch if it uses intermediaries to serve clients in the host state. Whether the activity via the intermediaries would make the activity of the credit institution qualify as a branch depends on the degree of independence of the intermediaries. I quote the European Commission:[35] 'for the use of an intermediary to result in a bank possibly falling within the scope of the right of establishment, three criteria must be met at one and the same time:

- the intermediary must have a **permanent mandate**;
- the intermediary must be subject to the **management and control** of the credit institution he represents. In order to ascertain whether this condition is met, it is necessary to check whether the intermediary is free to organize his own work and to decide what proportion of his time to devote to the undertaking. A final pointer is whether the intermediary can represent several firms competing to provide the service concerned or whether he is, on the contrary, bound by an exclusive agreement to one credit institution;
- the intermediary must be able to **commit the credit institution**. A credit institution may be committed via an intermediary even if that intermediary cannot sign contracts. For example, if the intermediary can make a complete offer on behalf of an institution but only the bank itself has the power to sign the contract, the criterion of commitment may still be met. If the credit institution can reject the proposal submitted by the intermediary and signed by the customer, the criterion of the commitment capacity is not met.

The presence of an intermediary leads to the conclusion that a credit institution acts via a branch, when the intermediary can act on behalf of the credit institution and is controlled by the credit institution on a permanent basis (so not just once like, eg a lawyer holding a power of attorney or credit institution working together in a syndicate, but repeatedly).[36] Intermediaries that do not act on behalf of the credit institution but only on behalf of the client, are no branch of the credit institution.

ii. Mortgage Credit Intermediaries

The MCD provides for two kind of intermediaries without their own licence, because they are covered by the licence of another legal entity. These are the tied credit intermediary, which is a credit intermediary who acts on behalf of and under the full and unconditional responsibility of one creditor, normally a credit institution,[37] and the appointed representative, which is an

---

[35] Commission, Interpretative Communication: Freedom to provide services and the interest of the general good in the Second Banking Directive, (97/C 209/04), p 12. See also the definition of a branch in Solvency II, art 13 (11) where this is made explicit.

[36] See, eg, for Italy Circolare n 285 del 17 December 2013, p 93.

[37] MCD, Art 4(7). These tied credit intermediaries can also act for or a limited amount of creditors, but for the sake of simplicity we ignore this.

intermediary that is acting on behalf of and under the full and unconditional responsibility of only one credit intermediary.[38]

The tied credit intermediary can operate across borders, but should be supervised directly when operating outside of its home state. The appointed representative is always supervised via the credit intermediary.[39] The appointed representative however can only operate across borders to the extent the host state also provides for the possibility to use appointed representatives (this is a national discretion).

The MCD is silent on the question of whether a tied credit intermediary or appointed representatives can also operate under the licence of a foreign credit intermediary or creditor. Put differently: a credit institution in the Netherlands may appoint a tied credit intermediary based in the Netherlands who also distributes mortgages in Belgium and who can establish a branch office for this purpose. It is unclear however whether this tied credit intermediary can be based in Belgium, but act under the responsibility of a Dutch credit institution.

iii. UCITS Directive and their Managers and AIFs and their Managers

Both the UCITS Directive and AIFM Directives do not foresee the possibility of appointing agents or anything equivalent.

iv. Investment Firms

MiFID II provides for the possibility to use tied agents to access foreign markets. A MiFID tied agent is a natural or legal person who, under the full and unconditional responsibility of only one investment firm (or credit institution) on whose behalf it acts, promotes investment and/or ancillary services to clients or prospective clients, receives and transmits instructions or orders from the client in respect of investment services or financial instruments, places financial instruments or provides advice to clients or prospective clients in respect of those financial instruments or services.[40] Tied agents can operate across borders via the freedom to provide services.[41] MiFID II also explicitly provides for the possibility that an investment firm or credit institution appoints tied agents in an host state.[42] For example, a Dutch investment firm may appoint a tied agent that is based in Belgium. In that case this is equated to the situation that the Dutch investment firm would establish a branch in Belgium. In a recent court ruling the ECJ explained that tied agents can be directly subject to supervision based on rules of national (non-EU) origin on top of the supervision on the investment firm itself and the responsibility of the investment firm to make sure that tied agents act in accordance with MiFID rules.[43]

v. Insurance Companies

Solvency II does not explicitly provide for the possibility for insurance companies to use agents in the home state or a host state. Nevertheless, insurance companies can access the local

---

[38] MCD, Art 4(8).
[39] MCD, Art 32(2).
[40] MiFID II, Art 4(1) 29 and Art 29.
[41] MiFID II, Art 34(2).
[42] MiFID II, Art 35(2) and ESMA, 'MiFID Questions and Answers Investor Protection & Intermediaries', 22 June 2012, ESMA/2012/382 p 8. Under MiFID I only investment firms could appoint tied agents, credit institutions could not. This editorial mistake has been corrected under MiFID II.
[43] ECJ 8 May 2019, C-53/18 (*Mastromartino*).

market via agents. These agents will – as a starting point – require independent authorisation under national law, unless as we will explain below, they can act as an agent of the insurance company under IDD.[44]

Additionally, via these intermediaries the insurance companies can also be considered active via a branch itself. Whether the activity of the intermediaries would make the activity of the insurance companies qualify as a branch depends on the degree of independence of the intermediaries. We refer to what has been said about this above with respect to credit institutions.[45]

vi. Insurance Intermediaries

There are two kind of insurance intermediaries that do not have their own separate licence.

Firstly, there are ancillary insurance intermediaries who act under the responsibility of the insurance company and that are themselves out of scope of IDD.[46] As these intermediaries are out of scope of IDD, they do not hold an EU passport. To the extent they want to operate across borders they have to rely on the national implementation of exemptions in each Member State.

Secondly there are insurance intermediaries that act under the responsibility of an another insurance intermediary or an insurance company. Notwithstanding the fact that they are under the responsibility of another entity, they qualify as insurance intermediary themselves. Therefore they can fully exploit all possibilities offered by IDD including the EU passport.

The IDD is silent on the question of whether an insurance intermediary can also operate under the licence of a foreign insurance intermediary or insurance company. Put differently: an insurance intermediary or insurance company in the Netherlands may extend its licence over an insurance intermediary based in the Netherlands who also distributes insurance policies in Belgium. It is unclear, however, whether this foreign insurance intermediary can be based in Belgium, but act under the responsibility of a Dutch insurance intermediary or Dutch insurance company.

vii. Payment Institutions

PSD II explicitly provides for the possibility to use agents. An agent is a natural or legal person who acts on behalf of a payment institution in providing payment services.[47] A payment institution that appoints agents in other Member States is subject to the same rules as a payment institution establishing a branch itself.[48] On the other hand PSD II does not rule out that an

---

[44] In the Netherlands agents of insurance companies would normally require a licence as '*gevolmachtigde agent*' based on Dutch national law 'pursuant to Art 2:92 FSA.

[45] Reference is made to the Commission interpretative communication freedom to provide services and the general good in the insurance sector (2000/C 43/03), pp 9–11 which to a great extent copies the Commission, 'Interpretative Communication: Freedom to provide services and the interest of the general good in the Second Banking Directive', (97/C 209/04), p 12 quoted above.

[46] IDD, Art 1(3) and (4).

[47] PSD II, Art 4(38). See extensively on this definition 'Opinion of the European Banking Authority on the nature of passport notifications regarding agents and distributors under Directive (EU) 2015/2366' (PSD2), Dir 2009/110/EC (EMD2) and Dir (EU) 2015/849 (AMLD), 24 April 2019, EBA-Op-2019-03, p 5.

[48] PSD II, Arts 29 and 30.

agent can be appointed that does not qualify as an establishment.[49] PSD explicitly provides for the possibility that an agent is appointed outside of the home state of the payment institution.[50] Interestingly, PSD II does not provide for the opportunity for credit institutions to appoint agents to provide payments services.[51]

D. Directive on Electronic Commerce

Next to the EU financial services directive there is another possibility for cross border service delivery, namely based on the Directive on electronic commerce.[52] The scope of the Directive on electronic commerce is not limited to financial services and, as we will see, the Directive on electronic commerce does not apply when a situation is already dealt with in the EU financial services directives. The Directive on electronic commerce applies when two conditions are met.

Firstly, the service is provided as an Information Society service, that is to say, any service normally provided for remuneration, at a distance, by electronic means and at the individual request of a recipient of services.[53] For the purposes of this definition:

(i)   'at a distance' means that the service is provided without the parties being simultaneously present;

(ii) 'by electronic means' means that the service is sent initially and received at its destination by means of electronic equipment for the processing (including digital compression) and storage of data, and entirely transmitted, conveyed and received by wire, by radio, by optical means or by other electromagnetic means;

(iii) 'at the individual request of a recipient of services' means that the service is provided through the transmission of data on individual request.

Secondly the Directive on electronic commerce is only relevant, if an activity is not covered by the EU financial services directives.[54] If the activity is subject to an EU financial services directive, the rules of this directive also apply if the service would otherwise qualify as an Information Society service. An example: the rules of the Directive on electronic commerce do apply to the online intermediation in consumer credit,[55] as there is no EU directive providing a passport for this, but would not apply to the online intermediation in mortgage credit. Mortgage credit specific rules on cross border activity are provided in the MCD and take precedence.[56]

---

[49] Commission Delegated Regulation (EU) 2017/2055 of 23 June 2017 supplementing Dir (EU) 2015/2366 of the European Parliament and of the Council with regard to regulatory technical standards for the cooperation and exchange of information between competent authorities relating to the exercise of the right of establishment and the freedom to provide services of payment institutions, Art 10 lid 1 sub d.

[50] PSD II, Arts 19(5) and 28(1)(d).

[51] See about this extensively the EBA Q&A at https://eba.europa.eu/single-rule-book-qa/-/qna/view/publicId/2013_190.

[52] Directive 2000/31/EC of the European Parliament and of the Council of 8 June 2000 on certain legal aspects of information society services, in particular electronic commerce, in the Internal Market ('Directive on electronic commerce').

[53] Directive on electronic commerce, Art 2(a) jo. Dir 98/48/EC of the European Parliament and of the Council of 20 July 1998 amending Dir 98/34/EC laying down a procedure for the provision of information in the field of technical standards and regulations, Art 1(2). Cf, ECJ 10 April 2018, C-320/16 (*Uber France SAS*).

[54] See EJ van Praag *Europees financieel toezicht Bevoegdheden in het Europees financieel toezicht*, (Boom Juridisch Den Haag, 2017), pp 248–250 and FCA Handboek SUP App 3.3.10 Background, available here www.handbook.fca.org.uk/handbook/SUP/App/3/?view=chapter. K Taylor, 'Legal update The impact of the E-Commerce Directive in the area of financial services', (2002) *Journal of Financial Services Marketing*, p 393, Communication from the Commission to the Council and the European Parliament E-Commerce And Financial Services7 February 2001, COM(2001)66 final, p. 6, 18 and 19; en AAth. Gkoutzinis, *Internet Banking and the Law in Europe*, (Cambridge, Cambridge University Press, 2006), p 288, Ph Athanassiou, 'Towards pan-European Hedge Fund Regulation? State of the Debate', (2008) *Legal Issues of Economic Integration*, p 18. Directive on electronic commerce, Recital 11 and 27.

[55] See, eg, Rb. Rotterdam 2 February 2018, ECLI:NL:RBROT:2018:645.

[56] MCD, Art 32.

The relevance of the Directive on electronic commerce is, that it contains a so-called country of origin clause.[57] Based on this country of origin clause, supervision is solely allocated to the supervisory authorities of the home state of the online service provider without even a notification being required. Only in rather exceptionally cases, if justified by valid reasons and when the relevant procedural requirements are met, Member States can take measures against companies acting under the country of origin clause of the Directive on electronic commerce.[58]

III. Which Rules are Subject to Home State Supervision and Which to Host State Supervision

Now that I have established how financial institutions can act across borders, I will evaluate which rules are subject to home state supervision and the observance of which rules is subject to host state supervision. Supervisory authorities always apply their own national law. So if I conclude that a certain activity is subject to host state supervision, this automatically implies that this activity is also subject to host state laws (or more precisely the host state implementation of the EU financial services directives).

The starting point is that financial institutions are only supervised by their home state supervisory authorities. There are three main exceptions to this rule:

(1) Host state authorities may enforce rules that are outside of the scope of the EU financial services directives.[59] Eg CRD IV deals with prudential requirements. CRD IV does not say anything about fighting money laundering, dealing fairly with clients or tax. Therefore unless otherwise provided in other EU legislation, host state supervisory authorities may supervise observance of these rules based on their national rules.

(2) Many EU financial services directives provide for emergency procedures in case a financial institution is obviously misbehaving and thereby endangering the integrity of the financial markets in the host state.[60] This is however limited to emergencies only and does not provide host state supervisory authorities the right to supervise the financial institution on a day to day basis.

(3) In many EU financial services directives it is provided, that specific rules are supervised by the host states. As we will see below this predominantly concerns observance of the conduct of business rules by branch offices.

In this chapter I will only deal with category 3. Even then it is impossible to give a detailed overview of all rules for all financial institutions. Therefore in line with the cross-sectoral approach of this book I will concentrate on the main differences between otherwise comparable types of financial institutions.

---

[57] Directive on electronic commerce, Art 3.

[58] Directive on electronic commerce, Art 3(4). Communication from the Commission to the Council and the European Parliament E-Commerce And Financial Services7 February 2001, COM(2001)66 final, p 8. See extensively A-G Szpunar 30 April 2019, C-390/18 (*AIRBNB*), paras 128–148.

[59] See EJ van Praag *Europees financieel toezicht Bevoegdheden in het Europees financieel toezicht*, (Boom Juridisch Den Haag, 2017), p 175.

[60] See ECJ 27 April 2017, C-559/15 (*Onix Asiguari SA/IVASS*) and EJ van Praag, 'Noot bij HvJ EU 27 april 2017', (2016) *Ondernemingsrecht*, pp 494–498.

A. Consistency in the Investment Industry between UCITS Directive, AIFMD and MiFID II

Firstly I will compare investment firms, UCITS Directive managers and AIF managers with each other. This comparison makes sense, because these three types of financial institution all invest on behalf of clients.

i. Rules that Apply to the Investment Firm and Fund Managers

MiFID II takes as a starting point that all rules and requirements are subject to home state supervision. As an exception to this rule however, for a branch, the following conduct of business rules are subject to host state supervision:[61]

- (i) providing information about the investments to clients;
- (ii) obtaining information from clients as part of the know your client requirements (ie for the suitability and appropriateness test);
- (iii) the suitability of the advice/portfolio management;
- (iv) remuneration and training of client-facing staff;
- (v) ban on/rules about inducements;
- (vi) recording agreements in the client file; and
- (vii) best execution-rules.

The logic behind this is that these conduct of business rules can more easily be supervised by the host state supervisory authorities since those authorities are closest to the branch, and are better placed to detect and intervene in respect of infringements of rules governing the operations of the branch.[62] For the important product governance rules it is unclear whether these are subject to home state or host state supervision, as they are as well based on an article subject to home state supervision[63] as an article subject to host state supervision.[64]

UCITS IV Directive deliberately aims to follow MiFID II.[65] A UCITS Directive manager that manages a fund via its branch office is subject to host state supervision for conduct of business rules that apply to the manager, such as the fiduciary obligation to act in the best interest of the UCITS Directive funds and to act with due care and diligence and rules regarding conflicts of interests.[66] Also for AIF managers that manage a fund via a branch office the fiduciary obligation to act in the best interest of the AIF and rules regarding conflict of interests are subject to host state supervision.[67] So far MiFID II, UCITS IV Directive and AIFMD are pretty well in line with each other.

---

[61] MiFID II, Art 35(8). Also various rules relating to market integrity are subject to host state supervision. We will not discuss them here.

[62] MiFID II, Recital 90.

[63] MiFID II, Art 16, sub 3.

[64] MiFID II, Art 24.

[65] CESR's advice to the European Commission on the UCITS Management Company Passport, October 2008, CESR/08-867, p 14.

[66] UCITS IV Directive, Art 17(4)(5) jo. Art 14.

[67] AIFMD, Art 45(2) jo. Arts 12 and 14.

ii. *Rules that Apply to the Funds*

The picture becomes complicated and less consistent when we look at the rules that also concern the investment funds next to the managers. Here we see a noticeable difference between the UCITS Directive and AIFM regime. The reason for this is that the UCITS Directive regime historically addressed funds[68] whereas the AIFM regime was drafted only for managers. Therefore, the UCITS Directive regime prescribes rules to be followed by the funds whereas the AIFM regime only sets rules for the managers. I explain how this leads to inconsistencies.

If a UCITS Directive or AIF manager manages a fund domiciled in another Member State, then that second state does not only qualify as the host state of the manager but also as the home state of the fund. To the extent that rules apply to the fund directly, these rules are subject to the supervision of the home state of the fund (which is the host state of the manager).[69] In practice of course it is up to the manager to abide to these rules, as the fund is merely a legal construct to hold the assets.[70] This implies that it matters a lot whether the rules are addressed to the fund or the manager, when the manager is managing a fund domiciled abroad. As we will see in the list below, there are many rules that are addressed to the manager within the AIFM regime which are addressed to the fund in the UCITS Directive regime.

Rule	UCITS Directive	AIFM
Rules regarding the risk management of the fund	Fund[71]	Manager[72]
Rules regarding the liquidity management of the fund	Fund[73]	Manager[74]
Rules regarding the investment in securitisation positions	Fund[75]	Manager[76]
Rules regarding the valuation of the assets (determining the NAV)	Fund[77]	Manager[78]
Rules regarding the role of and supervision on the depositary	Fund[79]	Manager[80]
Rules regarding the provision of information to investors	Fund[81]	Manager[82]

In the case of a manager managing a fund domiciled in another Member State, the rules listed above are supervised by the supervisory authorities of the home state of the manager in case of

---

[68] UCITS IIIA Directive, Art 5 etc (2001/107/EC).

[69] UCITS IV Directive, Art 19 lid 3 t/m 5.

[70] UCITS IV Directive, Recital 6.

[71] UCITS IV Directive, Art 19 lid 4. See also CESR's advice to the European Commission on the UCITS Management Company Passport, October 2008, CESR/08-867, p 13.

[72] AIFMD, Art 15.

[73] UCITS IV Directive, Art 19 lid 4. See also CESR's advice to the European Commission on the UCITS Management Company Passport, October 2008, CESR/08-867, p 13.

[74] AIFMD, Art 16.

[75] UCITS IV Directive, Art 19 lid 4. See also CESR's advice to the European Commission on the UCITS Management Company Passport, October 2008, CESR/08-867, p 13.

[76] AIFMD, Art 17.

[77] UCITS IV Directive, Art 19 lid 4. See also CESR's advice to the European Commission on the UCITS Management Company Passport, October 2008, CESR/08-867, p 13.

[78] AIFMD, Art 19.

[79] UCITS IV Directive, Art 5(2) and (4).

[80] AIFMD, Art 21.

[81] UCITS IV Directive, Ar. 19 lid 4. See also CESR's advice to the European Commission on the UCITS Management Company Passport, October 2008, CESR/08-867, p 13 and UCITS IV Directive, Art 82.

[82] AIFMD, Arts 22 and 23.

an AIF. However, if the fund is a UCITS Directive, the rules listed above are supervised by the supervisory authorities of the home state of the fund, which is the host state of the manager.

iii. *Information Provision in Case of Cross Border Distribution of UCITS Directive Funds*

In the case of cross-border distribution of investment funds more inconsistencies come to the fore especially when compared with the cross-border activities of investment firms. In case of cross-border distribution of UCITS Directive without a branch office the way information is provided by the UCITS Directive manager is subject to host state supervision.[83] This is peculiar, because if an investment firm makes available information about the same UCITS Directive, this is only subject to home state supervision. Within the AIFM regime information provision is a rule imposed on the manager directly and therefore only subject to home state supervision.

B. Consistency in Conduct of Business Rules between MCD, MiFID II, IDD and PSD II

MCD, MiFID II, IDD and PSD II, all contain rules regarding the protection of clients. Therefore it is relevant to evaluate whether the division of competence is consistent amongst these directives.

i. *Cross Border Provision of Services*

PSD II as well as MiFID II do not allocate any supervisory responsibilities to the host state in case of cross border service provision.[84]

With the MCD this is also the starting point. However, to a certain extent the host state can impose requirements for the knowledge and competence of staff on a mortgage credit intermediary.[85] To me this seems logical, as these knowledge and competence requirements relate to the peculiarities of the local housing market. They concern amongst others knowledge about procedures to acquire real estate, the taking of collateral and the operation of the local land register. The MCD is however silent on which supervisor should see to these requirements.[86] The MCD only contains a general statement that Member States should cooperate and which enables Member States to delegate tasks and responsibilities, but without delineating which supervisor is formally responsible.[87] This will need to be solved in practice.[88]

Also, with IDD as a starting point no supervisory competences are allocated to the host state in case of mere cross-border services. However, the host state supervisory authorities may enforce the rules of general interest.[89] These rules are outside of the harmonised area.

---

[83] UCITS IV Directive, Art 94.

[84] The only exception is that with PSD II the host state has a role in the notification process. See PSD II, Art 28(7).

[85] MCD, Art 9 lid 3 sub b and preamble 33.

[86] The ESAs seem to have the view that this is the host state. See EBA, EIOPA, ESMA Report on cross-border supervision of retail financial services, 9 July 2019, JC/2019-22 p 52.

[87] MCD, Art 5.

[88] In one draft of the MCD this power was clearly allocated to the host state. However, this phrasing did not make the final version, which suggests that somewhere in the negotiations this phrasing was removed/altered. See Proposal for a Directive of the European Parliament and of the Council on credit agreements relating to residential property – Presidency compromise proposal, 20 October 2011, 15777/11 2011/0062 (COD), Art 6(3) sub (ii).

[89] IDD, Arts 9 and 11. See for an overview of these rules in the various Member States EIOPA Report Insurance Distribution Directive – Report Analysing National General Good Rules, 22 July 2019.

Interestingly IDD explicitly indicates, that Member State rules requiring that some insurance products are only sold within an advisory relationship and rules on inducements are outside of the harmonised area.[90] Put differently: this is something Member States can decide on themselves. This also means that if a Member State decides to set stricter rules on inducements these also apply to cross border services provision into that Member State. This is interesting because within MiFID II, Member States may also set stricter rules on inducements, but these will not apply in case of mere inbound cross border service provision.

ii. Branches

For branches the starting point for all four Directives, MCD, MiFID II, IDD and PSD II, is that the conduct of business/client protection rules are subject to home state supervision. Examples of conduct of business rules are rules relating to information provision, fiduciary duty, the quality of advice and the knowledge and competence of staff (see more extensively for MiFID section III.A. above).[91] Rules that are more of an organisational or prudential nature remain subject to home state supervision, eg about the fit and proper testing of directors, procedures for risk management and the management of conflicts of interest. However, in the actual implementation of this design principle in specific directives inconsistencies do occur. The explanation for this is, that there is no hard and clear line between conduct of business rules and rules that are of a more organisational nature. For example, the important product governance rules are within the MiFID II (and in my analysis also within MCD) part of the organisational rules and therefore subject to home state supervision whereas within IDD they are conduct of business rules and therefore subject to host state supervision. On the other hand rules about knowledge and competence of staff are within the MCD and MiFID II part of the conduct of business rules and therefore subject to host state supervision,[92] whereas within IDD they are part of the organisational requirements and therefore subject to home state supervision.[93] On the other hand the rules on cross selling are within MiFID II a conduct issue and therefore subject to host state supervision whereas within MCD it is part of the organisational requirements and therefore subject to home state supervision.

C. Consistency between Product Producers (Credit Institutions and Insurance Companies) and Intermediaries (Mortgage Credit Providers, Payment Institutions, Investment Firms and Insurance Intermediaries)

It is also relevant to compare between product manufacturers who may distribute their own products and intermediaries who distribute the same products but then manufactured by another party. For example, a credit institution can distribute the mortgages it originates itself or a mortgage credit intermediary can distribute its mortgage loans. Naturally you would expect that the same rules apply independently of who is distributing the mortgage loans. So it should not matter from the perspective of the consumer whether he gets the mortgage loan directly from the credit institution or via a mortgage credit intermediary. Therefore the rules in the MCD also apply to

---

[90] IDD, Arts 22(2) and 29(3) and Art 30(3).
[91] MCD II, Art 34(2), MiFID, Art 35(8), IDD, Art 7(2) and PSD II, Art 100(4).
[92] See MiFID II, Art 25(1) jo. MiFID II, Art 35(8) and MCD, Art 9(3).
[93] IDD, Art 10(2) jo. IDD, Art 7(2).

credit institutions distributing loans directly.[94] In the same vein a insurance company can act as a direct writer or the insurances it underwrites can be distributed by an insurance intermediary. IDD applies to both situations.

Naturally one would also expect that the rules for supervisory competence apply in the same manner. For instance, if a branch of a credit institution or a branch of a mortgage credit intermediary would breach the same rule in the MCD, one would expect the supervisory competence and powers of the host state to be the same. As we will see below this is not clearly laid down in the MCD and the IDD.

i. MCD

As set out above the host state is responsible for supervising the conduct of business rules for branches of mortgage credit intermediaries.[95] The MCD however is silent on how supervisory competences are allocated with respect to branches of creditors rather than intermediaries. The relevant article does not mention creditors (such as credit institutions) at all. In my opinion this is a rather frustrating omission, but I see no other option than that branches of credit institutions are subject to host state supervision in the same manner as branches of credit intermediaries. Otherwise this would lead to the rather bizarre conclusion that a credit institution that infringes a rule in the MCD (eg the obligation to properly inform the client), would be subject to laws of another Member State and subject to supervision of the supervisory authorities of another Member State than a branch of a credit intermediary that would break the same rules.

ii. IDD

Unfortunately the same mistake has been made in IDD, which also applies to insurance companies distributing their own products directly. Once more the legislator has not made clear which supervisory authority supervises branches of insurance companies with respect to IDD rules. Once more I come to the conclusion that the same rules and the same supervisory competence should apply as for insurance intermediaries.

iii. MiFID II and PSD II

For MiFID II and PSD II it is clear that as far as the supervisory competence for the conduct of business rules is concerned credit institutions providing investment services or payment services are treated similarly as investment firms and payment institutions.[96]

IV. Concluding Thoughts and Suggestions

Having evaluated the cross-border rules for the financial institutions subject to either CRD IV, MCD, UCITS Directive, AIFMD, MiFID II, Solvency II, IDD and PSD II, I come to the following practical suggestions.

---

[94] See, eg, MCD, Arts 7 and 9.
[95] MCD II, Art 34(2).
[96] Eg, MiFID II does make clear how the competences are divided with credit institutions, see MiFID II, Art 1(3) c and d and PSD II, Art 100(4) that relates to payment service providers, which term includes payment institutions and credit institutions offering payment services.

A. Arrange for a Passport for Deposits Intermediation and Consumer Credit Intermediation

In discussing what is there, it also becomes apparent what is missing. Core services for credit institutions include the offering of deposits and consumer credit. Credit institutions can do this based on their CRD IV passport. However, there is not an intermediary passport for such activities. This means that whereas for example a mortgage intermediary or insurance intermediary can be active across borders based on an EU financial services passport, there is no such possibility for parties wanting to intermediate in deposits and consumer credit. These parties have to meet the national rules and will be subject to local supervision in every Member State where they want to be active, unless their activities qualify as Information Society service in scope of the Directive on electronic commerce. I recommend arranging for an EU passport for consumer credit and deposits intermediation as well. Thus would lead to the further completion of the *EU financial services acquis*.

B. Arrange for Clear Definitions of When a Financial Institution is Active Across Borders

As discussed above, many of the EU financial services directives are not clear as to the question of when a financial institution is active across borders in the first place, leading to two opposing positions in the EU. Some Member States apply the initiative test, others the test of the characteristic performance.

Also to the extent directives do clearly determine when a financial institution is active across borders, they are not consistent amongst each other either. I give an example. Imagine a Dutch inhabitant who wants to buy a second home in Belgium. He goes to his Dutch intermediary to get a mortgage and insurance. The intermediary approaches a Dutch bank. This Dutch bank can offer the mortgage without being active in Belgium, because both under the initiative test and the characteristic performance the bank is only active in the Netherlands.[97] A Belgian bank would be more complex, because a Belgian bank may not actively market in the Netherlands. The insurance intermediary will also arrange for home insurance. For the home insurance a Belgian insurer will need to be found, because Dutch insurers can only insure the house when notified in Belgium. A Dutch insurer will need to offer the life insurance policy, because if the client lives in the Netherlands a Belgian insurer will deemed to be active in the Netherlands when offering this insurance. Besides this being a regulatory constraint for the involved financial institution, this also makes cross border consumption of financial services more complex for the EU citizens.

It is my expectation that more and more cross border situations will occur when the big tech firms such as Apple, Amazon or Google enter into financial services. For example, even when Apple would not actively market on the Dutch market, it cannot easily isolate the Dutch market either. For such big online firms it is impossible to contain their marketing or products in specific markets, unless they block clients.[98] Unless Apple would consciously decide to refuse

---

[97] The Dutch bank can however not renew or change the mortgage contract later on if the client decides to reside in Belgium permanently, because this will often be seen as the conclusion of a new mortgage contract in Belgium.

[98] Eg, Dutch clients of Bunq bank were also using Apple pay even though it was only officially introduced in Spain and Italy. https://tweakers.net/nieuws/136495/bunq-maakt-apple-pay-via-work-around-beschikbaar-in-nederland.html.

Dutch clients, it would get a significant Dutch client base without meeting the initiative test or characteristic performance test.

I suggest the following clear and easy to impose rules:

(a) If the financial institution has a direct contract with the client, it is deemed to be active across borders when the client lives abroad when concluding the contract. This would normally be the case when offering deposits or loans and/or intermediating in these products, providing investment services and when offering and/or intermediating in insurance products. All financial institutions offering these products normally know who their clients are and where they live. The only carve out should be for insurances for clients that are on holiday, eg when renting a car on holiday and perhaps for nationals living abroad.[99]

(b) If the financial institution has no direct contract with the client, it is deemed to be active across border when he is actively promoting the product. This would relate to UCITS Directive and AIFM funds which are normally not directly distributed to the end client by the UCITS Directive and AIF managers.

A related issue is how to distinguish between activities performed based on the freedom to provide services or via a branch. Due to the proliferation of digital means this distinction becomes increasingly harder to make and to justify. Elsewhere I already explained that physical presence should be substituted for commercial presence to determine to what extent the host state supervisory authority should be involved in the supervision.[100]

C. Arrange for Cross Sectoral Consistency for the Use of Agents

Except from UCITS Directive and AIFMD all directives in some manner or form allow agents to be used. However, there are many differences in the details. Some agents can be covered by the licence of the principal, eg agents of payments institutions. Some agents cannot, eg agents of banks intermediating in deposits or consumer credit. Some directives explicitly allow for the agent to be covered by the licence of the principal who is based in another Member State, eg MiFID II tied agents that connect to a licence from an investment firm in another Member State. Some do not, for instance IDD that does not make explicit if the main financial institution can be from another Member State. I recommend two suggestions:

(a) All agents can be covered by the licence of the main financial institution.
(b) Agents can also be covered by the licence of the main financial institution, when this main financial institution is established in another Members State.

D. Arrange for Consistency between the UCITS Directive and AIFM Framework

As explained in section III.A., similar rules are applied by different supervisory authorities in case of the cross-border management of funds. This is caused by the fact that the UCITS Directive

---

[99] Personally, I do not see a problem in German banks serving the German migrant workers in the Netherlands solely based on German rules and supervision, but this is in practice hard to delineate.

[100] EJ van Praag, 'What happens when an EU financial institution crosses borders? Time for an update?', (2019) *Tijdschrift voor Financieel Recht* p 47. This problem is also noted in EBA, EIOPA, ESMA Report on cross-border supervision of retail financial services, 9 July 2019, JC/2019-22 p 10 and 56.

regime was originally drafted for and primarily addressed funds, whereas the AIFM regime was drafted for and only addressed managers. Because many managers manage UCITS Directive and AIF simultaneously, this leads to the bizarre conclusion that for the cross-border management of AIF funds rules are applied by the home state whereas with the cross-border management of UCITS Directive funds similar rules are applied by the host state.

Therefore I suggest to work towards a consistent model, where the jurisdiction rules are the same.

E. Arrange for Consistency between the MCD, MiFID II, IDD and PSD II

MCD, MiFID II, IDD and PSD II all aim to achieve client protection. All are based on the general principle that conduct of business supervision is subject to home state supervision in case of cross-border services. However, various carve outs have been implemented within MCD and IDD. Some of them seem justified, eg because of particular local market knowledge required for distributing mortgages and insurance products. However, some seem less logical, eg inducements rules that within IDD would be subject to host state supervision whereas within MiFID II they would be subject to home state supervision.

For branches, all four Directives have as a general principle in common that conduct of business rules are subject to host state supervision, but organisational rules remain subject to home state supervision. However, in practice this principle has not consistently been put through, because some rules seem to have been qualified as organisational in some directives but are considered a conduct of business rule in others.

Therefore I suggest working towards a consistent model, where the jurisdiction rules are the same.

F. Make Explicit that Credit Institutions and Insurance Companies are Supervised in the Same Way as Mortgage Credit Intermediaries and Insurance Intermediaries for Conduct of Business Rules

When acting as distributor themselves credit institutions and insurance companies are subject to MCD and IDD respectively. However, the Directives are silent on which supervisory authority supervises credit institutions and insurance companies with respect to these rules when active cross border. I would consider it logical that this is aligned with the intermediaries performing the same services, but nevertheless I recommend that this should be made explicit.

Apart from these practical suggestions I also have a concluding remark. The EU financial service directives often deal with similar issues and aim to achieve similar goals via similar rules. For example, MCD, MiFID II and IDD have similar know your client requirements and similar knowledge and competence requirements for staff. It seems logical that the supervisory authorities supervising the observance of these know your client requirements and knowledge and competence requirements for staff should be the same too, also in cross-border situations. This has merit, because additional supervisory authorities supervising the same rules, leads to more compliance costs with financial institutions as financial institutions will have to interact with respect to the same rules with more authorities. When the supervisory authorities also have distinct views, thus requiring different processes, it will require even more resources from the financial institution. It should be borne in mind that many financial institutions deal with different products simultaneously. For example, when buying a house the advisor will normally look at the mortgage itself but also related investments and insurance products, thus acting as mortgage credit intermediary, investment firm and insurance intermediary simultaneously. There should be one supervisory authority supervising the whole process with respect to the same aspect. Currently inconsistencies in the EU financial services directives thwart this policy goal.

PART V

Summary and Conclusions

19

Summary and Conclusions

VEERLE COLAERT AND DANNY BUSCH

In the first chapter of this book, we put forward the research hypothesis that there is a sufficient degree of similarity in functions, problems and regulatory goals to make it feasible to apply a number of common concepts and principles across the financial industry, even though certain differences in functions, characteristics and risks may still require different detailed requirements, on top of, or even deviating from, common concepts and principles.

By way of conclusion, this chapter provides a summary of the main research conclusions of this book, with a view to concluding to what extent our initial research hypothesis has been confirmed or refuted.

I. Conceptual Framework for a Cross-Sectoral Approach to Financial Regulation

The first part of this book has laid down the foundations of a cross-sectoral approach to financial regulation. In this part we have sought to answer the question of whether there is, in general, sufficient ground to embark on a more detailed cross-sectoral analysis of financial regulation.

In a first chapter Monika Marcinkowska has set out the functioning of the financial industry and the extent to which its *manifold functions* are fulfilled by different actors of the industry, including the shadow banking industry. She has found that the financial industry is complex and changing quickly. Nevertheless, all financial institutions and venues largely perform the same three basic functions – collection, allocation and deployment of capital – albeit in different ways and to different degrees. The author concludes that effective regulation should take into account those changing realities, and should ideally regulate economic functions, rather than a specific institution, structure or architecture.

In a second chapter Eddy Wymeersch has established the *configuration of objectives of financial regulation*. The author finds that the three objectives of financial regulation correspond to three layers of financial regulation: the relationship of a market participant with an institution corresponds to the customer protection objective, the regulation of the financial institution as such corresponds to the micro-prudential stability objective, whereas the protection of societal interest corresponds to the macro-prudential objective. Those three layers and objectives are present in all sectors of financial regulation, alongside the market integration objective, which is an important overarching objective of EU financial regulation. The author concludes that the financial regulatory system is very complex, with not only sectoral rules, but also many layers of regulation, and national divergences. This sometimes resulting in different rules for identical issues. The author argues for a common rulebook via an interactive website, where different levels of regulation are accessible via links. He further pleads for single definitions, the merger of duplicative or similar provisions across sectors and even for the harmonisation of contract and tort law in order to avoid regulatory arbitrage in respect of investor protection. He predicts that a common 'core' or rules should be feasible in many areas, such as, notably, corporate governance and rules for the protection of the financial consumer.

In a third chapter, Eugenia Macchiavello has evaluated whether and to what extent (sectoral) regulation appropriately covers different types of financial innovation (*FinTech*). She finds that the current approach to FinTech is to develop separate regulatory regimes for new technologies. She argues that a more efficient and effective regulatory framework would focus on functions and transcend not only sectors, but also the technology employed to provide services or products. Nevertheless, there could be a need for fine-tuning in regard of particular technologies, and the proportionality principle should play a prominent role. She concludes that only when new technologies create truly new functions or businesses, there could be a need to establish a new regulatory regime (eg, DLT).

Finally, Kitty Lieverse and Victor de Serière embark on a study of the problems and limitations encountered by *national attempts to restructure financial regulation in a more cross-sectoral manner*, on the basis of their experiences with the Dutch approach. They conclude that the Dutch approach is not ideal, but seems to work reasonably well, especially for the cross-sectorally structured national supervisory authorities. Remarkably, they find that the main downside of a national cross-sectoral approach to financial regulation is the fact that EU regulation is structured in a sectoral manner. Even if different pieces of EU regulation have topics in common that would in principle be suitable for a cross-sectoral implementation at the national level, such topics are not arranged in exactly the same consistent manner, resulting in tensions for Member States aiming to implement such comparable but not similar provisions on a cross-sectoral basis. In case of minimum harmonisation, such a Member State can opt to implement the cross-sectoral approach at the level of the highest standard, which, however, leads to goldplating. This has the benefit of national cross-sectoral consistency, but the downside of disturbing the European sectoral level playing field. The current EU tendency to increasingly use regulations instead of directives further complicates a cross-sectoral approach to regulation at the national level.

From this first part we conclude that the functions of the different sectors of the financial industry and the goals of financial regulation for each of the sectors are sufficiently similar to predict that many problems which lead to regulation are the same or highly similar in the three sectors, and that at least in some areas a more cross-sectoral approach to EU financial regulation could be feasible and more efficient. Moreover, FinTech evolutions would, in general, benefit from an approach where the regulatory framework not only transcends sectors, but also the technology employed to provide services or products. The Dutch experience with a partially cross-sectoral approach to legislation has, finally, shown that such an approach is feasible and can in principle work well, even though it would be much easier to uphold if a cross-sectoral approach to financial regulation would also apply at EU-level.

II. A Cross-Sectoral Perspective on Financial Stability

In the second part of this book, the main aspects of prudential regulation have been systematically compared in order to assess what differences are substantiated on the basis of different functions, characteristics or risks of various types of financial institutions, and what differences are accidental, unjustified and potentially detrimental to efficiency.

First, Danny Busch and Mirik van Rijn have assessed the current approach to *macro-prudential stability* in search for cross-sectoral consistency. They find that gaps in the coverage of regulation and supervision have led to an inconsistent regulatory treatment of equivalent products and/or services, causing an un-level playing field, encouraging regulatory arbitrage and a build-up of systemic risk in the less regulated or unregulated parts of the system. They conclude that there is a need for cross-sectoral consistency, especially for institutions that pose systemic risk, which should be brought within a regulatory perimeter consistent with the risk they pose to financial stability. They argue that a European body should be in charge of monitoring financial institutions active in the EU, and identify institutions which pose systemic risk. This means that also non-bank systemically important financial institutions should come under stricter European supervision, ideally within the perimeter of an expanded European 'Banking' Union.

Second, Arthur van den Hurk and Bart Joosen have critically compared the *capital requirements* for banks, investment firms and insurance firms. They conclude that even though financial regulation in those three areas features the same three pillar model and similar concepts and practices, differences in business models, risk profile and stakeholder interests of those institutions require substantially different capital requirements. Nevertheless, they see a number of areas where more convergence is feasible, such as the supervisory review process in the second pillar, capital requirements in view of systemic risk, and group supervision.

Third, the *corporate governance rules* for different types of financial institutions have been scrutinised. Tom Vos, Katrien Morbee, Sofie Cools and Marieke Wyckaert first establish the relationship between general corporate governance on the one hand and corporate governance for financial institutions on the other. They then meticulously compare the different elements of corporate governance (including fit and proper tests for directors, board composition, suitability of shareholders, etc) in the numerous pieces of financial regulation for different types of financial institutions. They find that while certain governance provisions do apply in all sectors, there are also major differences. Generally speaking, banks and investment firms are most heavily regulated, followed by insurance companies and AIFMs. With a few exceptions, those differences do not seem to flow from differences in business models and risk levels, but are rather coincidental drafting differences. Since financial institutions are increasingly integrated in cross-sectoral groups and can differ as much within a sector as across sectors, the authors argue that the EU legislator should consider a more cross-sectoral approach with regard to corporate governance. This would eliminate interpretation problems and reduce compliance costs, especially within cross-sectoral groups. Moreover, systemically important financial institutions should be subject to a more stringent and harmonised governance regime. Guido Ferrarini and Michele Siri have come to very similar conclusions with regard to the corporate governance rules dealing with remuneration: cross-sectoral convergence is conceivable, while a focus on systemic risk should inform thresholds to identify the institutions, across the sectors, which should be subject to the most stringent provisions in respect of executive pay. Carmine di Noia and Matteo Garantini, finally, discuss two other particular aspects of corporate governance: ownership allocation and stakeholder representation. They find another cross-sectoral divide, in terms of the ownership structure of financial institutions: each financial sector displays all the main models of ownership allocation, as the underlying rationales supporting one or the other model are far from being sector-specific. This suggests that an adequate regulatory approach to ownership (and to stakeholder representation as well) should equally be cross-sectoral.

Fourth, Jens Binder discusses the *resolution regimes* in the financial sector from a cross-sectoral perspective. He finds that there is common ground in terms of underlying policy objectives as well as the technical design of resolution instruments and powers for different types of financial institutions. The author nevertheless concludes that the basis for a genuine cross-sectoral resolution regime is rather weak, since sector-specific characteristics would in such an approach require manifold adjustments. Further research should, however, be conducted into the cross-sectoral channels of contagion that could be triggered through the initiation of sectoral resolution actions, which could inform further refinement of sector-specific resolution regimes so as to mitigate the risk that resolution actions taken in one sector would disrupt other sectors.

Fifth, Veerle Colaert and Gilian Bens have compared the scope, goals and functions of the *guarantee systems* available in the banking, investment and insurance sectors, in order to answer the question of whether there is a case for one cross-sectoral guarantee system. They conclude that the goals and functions of deposit guarantee systems, investor compensation schemes and insurance compensation schemes are fundamentally different, and that there is, therefore, no ground for the introduction of a cross-sectoral scheme.

Finally, Peter Laaper has discussed *outsourcing* from a cross-sectoral perspective. He concludes that there are strong arguments in favour of harmonising the various outsourcing regulations, since they all share the same rationale and are based on the same principles, while he did not find any objective reasons to differentiate. He argues that, ideally, a common set of rules would be laid down at level 1, while objectively substantiated sectoral differences could be laid down at levels 2 or 3. While this may be difficult to achieve in the foreseeable future, a pragmatic alternative might be for the Joint Committee of the three ESAs to establish a common set of outsourcing guidelines.

From the second part we conclude that many rules aiming at increased stability of financial institutions are sector-specific with good reason. Differences in business models and risk profile of different types of financial institutions require substantially diverging capital requirements and resolution regimes, while the sectoral guarantee systems also have distinct functions and goals and should therefore not be merged. In certain areas, which relate less to the specificity of the business model or risks of specific financial institutions and more to organisational matters, there is much more ground for a cross-sectoral approach. This conclusion was most clearly established in respect of the different areas of corporate governance and in regard of outsourcing. The goals and overall design of those rules are highly similar across sectors, while the authors find that divergences of specific rules for different actors are typically unsubstantiated. A more cross-sectoral approach to corporate governance and outsourcing would therefore be feasible. The chapters on corporate governance further point to the importance of the proportionality principle, and the need to introduce more stringent cross-sectoral rules for systemically important financial institutions. More generally a cross-sectoral divide emerges in this Part, between systemic and non-systemically important financial institutions. In almost all areas and sectors examined in this Part, authors conclude that different rules already apply, or should apply in function of this divide. Financial stability regulation would, therefore, especially benefit from a more cross-sectoral approach to systematically important financial institutions, across sectors, with one macro-prudential European body in charge of identifying and monitoring all financial institutions which pose systemic risk.

III. A Cross-Sectoral Perspective on Customer Protection

In a third part different aspects of customer protection have been systematically compared between sectors, in order to assess what differences are substantiated, and what differences are accidental, unjustified and potentially detrimental to efficiency. In doing so, also the relationship with general consumer law and civil law – which are by nature cross-sectoral – has been established.

In a first chapter Marc-David Weinberger has compared the *scope of protection* of different rules of EU financial regulation and general consumer law. He finds that in view of the greater complexity and riskiness of certain financial services and products, the scope of protection in EU financial regulation typically extends beyond the traditional consumer concept, even though there is no unique scope of protection for all financial services. The author argues that there might be a ground for a unique and simplified 'financial consumer' notion, which would include vulnerable businesses, and discusses a number of possible criteria to assess which businesses should be protected, such as annual turnover, presence of an in-house lawyer, or specialisation in a certain line of business.

Second, Veerle Colaert has examined whether a more cross-sectoral approach to *product information* in respect of banking, investment and insurance products would be feasible. She finds that the current proliferation of information documents for investment products hampers the comparison of functionally equivalent products, and therefore argues that the PRIIPs KID should be the standard for all investment and saving products in the largest sense. She further argues that it would enhance customer protection to also introduce one information sheet for all retail loan agreements. While she finds that the format and content of information sheets for investment, credit and insurance products differ and should indeed differ in function of the specific goals and functions of those products, she argues that the EU legislator could harmonise the 'look and feel' of all information sheets across sectors in order to increase the familiarity of retail customers with this type of information sheets.

Third, service quality rules (with respect to investment services often referred to as '*conduct of business rules*') in different pieces of financial regulation have been assessed, with a focus on the various expressions of the general duty of care and the different assist-your-customer rules. Veerle Colaert and Maarten Peeters find that numerous, but not all, actors on the financial markets are subject to financial regulation *duties of care*, often slightly differently worded, without there being any obvious justification for those differences. They have found that even though all jurisdictions have duties of care in their civil or common law systems, financial regulation duties of care allow for an EU-wide harmonisation of the standard of behaviour of financial institutions, and provide a legal basis for supervisory guidance and enforcement. The prohibition of unfair commercial practices in Directive 2005/29/EU already functions as a cross-sectoral duty of care, but only in relation to consumers and without financial supervisors being necessarily able to provide guidance or enforce on that basis (depending on national legislation). The authors conclude that even though the current panoply of financial regulation duties of care does not seem to have created substantial problems in practice, one cross-sectoral duty of care for the financial sector would increase legal coherence and consistency and avoid interpretation problems and possible gaps. The case for a cross-sectoral duty of care would, however, be much stronger if other topics of conduct-of-business legislation would also warrant such an effort. In the next chapter, Danny Busch, Veerle Colaert and Geneviève Helleringer have compared the different *assist-your-customer obligations* in EU financial regulation. They find that it would make sense to have one common set of know-your-customer rules for all investment products in the largest sense, for instance in MiFID II, even though variations may be necessary in view of certain product specifics or specific distribution channels. Similarly they argue for one responsible lending, assist-your-customer and advice test in respect of all credit services to consumers, replacing the similar, but diverging tests of the Mortgage Credit Directive and the Consumer Credit Directive. In respect of insurance services, they argue that the demands and needs analysis should be reserved for 'traditional' insurance services and not apply to insurance-based investment products, which are mainly investment products, and are already subject to know-your-customer rules. They conclude that investment services, insurance services and credit services are different and differences in assist-your-customer rules across the sectors can therefore be warranted. Nevertheless, terminology should be more consistent across sectors and cross-sectoral standards on information gathering and processing would improve the current situation.

Fourth, Veerle Colaert and Thomas Incalza examined the approach to *conflicts of interest and inducements* in the different sectors. They find that even though the conflicts of interests regimes are substantially similar across sectors, the inducements regimes differ substantially, especially between MiFID II, the Insurance Distribution Directive (IDD), the Mortgage Credit Directive (MCD) and the (proposed) Crowdfunding Regulation. The IDD and MCD moreover only aim at minimum harmonisation of the inducements regime, whereas MiFID II and the (proposed) Crowdfunding Regulation aim at maximum harmonisation. The authors conclude that the fact that financial instruments and structured deposits, insurance products, credit agreements and crowdfunding products are subject to diverging inducements regimes can only be justified if further research would show that the risks, market functioning and the impact of the inducements regime on the specific market would differ – no such evidence exists today. The risks of having diverging inducements regime, are, however, limited if the nature of those products is such that there is no risk of regulatory arbitrage between them (eg insurance and loan products). The fact that insurance-based investment products are potentially subject to a more lenient inducements regime than other investment products (unless Member States would have levelled the playing field in their national legislation) could, however, lead to regulatory arbitrage, when an intermediary could receive inducements in regard of the sale of insurance-based investment products, which he cannot receive in regard of MiFID II investment products. The authors therefore argue for a level playing field, at least between all investment and saving products in the largest sense.

Finally, Veerle Colaert has made a cross-sectoral analysis of the *product intervention* competences and measures of supervisory authorities in the EU. She finds that there is no good reason for attributing those product intervention competences in two different pieces of EU regulation. If those competences would have been attributed on the basis of one single provision, most logically in the horizontal PRIIPs Regulation, (i) the allegedly different scope of application of MiFIR and the PRIIPs product intervention measures would have been avoided; (ii) cooperation between the ESAs in the level 2 and level 3 implementation of the product intervention powers would have been structurally ensured, avoiding unsubstantiated differences; and (iii) the three ESAs could have been required in one and the same provision to cooperate in order to avoid regulatory arbitrage. She concludes that the current sectoral legislative and supervisory approach to product intervention is suboptimal, while a cross-sectoral legislative, and arguably also supervisory approach to product intervention would be more effective.

From the third part we conclude that in the field of investor protection there is ground for a cross-sectoral approach in respect of the regulatory duties of care, conflicts of interests rules and the rules on information gathering and processing for purposes of the assist-your-customer rules. For other customer protection aspects sector-specific legislation seems warranted, subject to two important caveats. First, within one sector there is room for more 'cross-sectoral' consistency: products with the same economic function should be subject to the same regulatory treatment in order (i) to avoid regulatory arbitrage, (ii) to meet the legitimate expectations of customers in regard of their regulatory protection; and (iii) to increase the familiarity of customers with the scope of their regulatory protection. In this regard several chapters have pleaded for 'cross-sectoral' consistency between MiFID II financial instruments, insurance-based investment products, PEPPs, crowdfunding investment products and even saving products such as bank deposits. Those products are today indeed subject to different sectoral legislation. Those pleas for 'cross-sectoral' consistency actually come down to a plea for the proper definition of the scope of application of each sector and regulatory document. This scope of application should be defined on the basis of the economic function of a product or service, rather than its formal legal qualification. Second, and closely related to the previous point, also within one sector there is room for more 'sectoral' consistency. There are, for instance, a number of unsubstantiated differences between the consumer credit and the mortgage credit directives, while consumers borrowing via crowdfunding platforms are currently often not at all protected. Finally, we can also conclude from this part that general consumer law has an important role to play in the background as cross-sectoral rules applicable to the entire financial industry, albeit only in the relationship with natural persons acting outside the scope of their business or profession ('consumers'), and even though financial supervisory authorities often have no competence to enforce or provide further guidance in respect of general consumer law.

IV. Supervision and Internal Market

In the last part of the book the supervisory architecture and the internal market rules in financial regulation have been examined from a cross-sectoral perspective.

Georg Ringe, Luis Morais and David Ramos examined the different models for an *institutional architecture of EU financial supervision* from a more 'holistic' perspective. They find that a cross-sectoral logic suggests that a twin peaks model may be the best supervisory solution, but poses seemingly insurmountable political and legal problems. They argue that promoting a cross-sectoral approach should therefore be based on functional rather than structural reforms: the current sectoral EU supervisory model needs greater coordination between the regulatory and supervisory tasks that pursue the same objective, even if performed by different sectoral authorities. Both formal and informal channels can be used to achieve that goal. They conclude that even if EU lawmakers could more explicitly differentiate the objectives of regulation and supervision by each of the authorities (prudential and market conduct), mostly the authorities themselves should partake the conviction that a cross-sectoral view is not just an academic exercise, but a source of supervisory consistency and efficiency.

In the last chapter of the book, Emanuel van Praag has compared the rules on the supervision of cross-border services for financial institutions subject to different regulatory frameworks. He finds that the relevant rules in CRD IV, MCD, UCITS Directive, AIFMD, MiFID II, Solvency II, IDD and PSD II substantially diverge, while there are no passport provisions for deposit and consumer credit intermediation. Moreover, even the definitions of when a financial institution is active across borders substantially differ. While different types of rules (eg prudential rules versus conduct of business) may require a different internal market approach, the author has identified important areas where greater consistency would lead to a much more efficient regulatory framework.

V. Assessment of the Research Hypothesis and Outlook

The research hypothesis of this project was that there is a sufficient degree of similarity in functions, problems and regulatory goals to make it feasible to apply a number of common concepts and principles across the financial industry, even though certain differences between financial institutions, products and services may still require different detailed requirements, on top of, or even deviating from, common concepts and principles.

A. Assessment of the Research Hypothesis

The above summary shows that the research hypothesis has been confirmed, even though the extent to which differs markedly depending on the specific area of research.

The hypothesis is most valid in regard to *regulation of* a more *organisational nature*. The most promising areas for a cross-sectoral approach are indeed corporate governance and outsourcing. Diverging pieces of legislation were typically found to be unsubstantiated and a cross-sectoral approach would be feasible relatively easily. Similarly, the internal market rules organising the supervision of cross-border services would benefit from more consistency across the different pieces of financial regulation.

In areas of financial regulation dealing with *customer protection*, cross-sectorally applicable consumer protection rules already exist in general consumer law (such as Unfair Commercial Practices Directive 2005/29/EC, Unfair Contract Terms Directive 1993/22/EU and Distance Selling of Financial Services Directive 2002/65/EC). Additional rules for the protection of the customer of financial services then tend to be rather detailed and sector-specific. Unsubstantiated 'cross-sectoral' differences in the field of customer protection often seem to stem from an overlay limited definition of the scope of application of a certain piece of regulation, with the result that new pieces of regulation are created to address functionally equivalent products. Therefore, functionally equivalent products are often subject to similar, yet different rules.

With regard to important areas of financial regulation dealing with *financial stability*, such as capital requirements, resolutions procedures and guarantee systems, there is little room for a cross-sectoral approach and the research hypothesis seems to be largely refuted. Those areas of regulation are most closely related to the specific business activities of financial institutions and the related solvency risks. However, a cross-sectoral divide has emerged between systemic and non-systemically important financial institutions. Distinct rules apply or should apply in function of this divide and cross-sectoral supervision of systematically important financial institutions would be desirable.

This brings us, finally, to the *architecture of financial supervision* more generally. Supervision is already organised in line with the cross-sectoral twin peaks model in many Member States. Supervisors have indeed an important role to play in levelling the cross-sectoral playing field – even if they are unable to go against the wording of level 1 or 2 texts. While a twin peaks model matches a cross-sectoral approach to financial regulation, there does not currently seem to be sufficient political will to realise such a structural reform of the European Supervisory Authorities (ESAs). The authors of the relevant chapter argue that this should, however, not overly hamper the ESAs' efforts in advancing a cross-sectoral approach, since they already have many formal and informal tools at their disposal to actively promote cross-sectoral consistency and efficiency. Even within the current EU supervisory architecture, a more cross-sectoral approach to regulation and supervision is therefore feasible.

The overall conclusion of this book is therefore that in a number of areas a cross-sectoral approach to financial regulation would at least in theory be feasible, in view of the similarity of regulated problems, functions of the financial industry and goals of regulation in each of the sectors.

B. Benefits of a Cross-Sectoral Approach

The next question which arises is whether it would also be more efficient, ie whether the benefits of a cross-sectoral approach outweigh the costs. A full-blown cost-benefit analysis would be required to answer this question, and even then it is very questionable whether such an analysis would lead to a conclusive answer. It is indeed almost impossible to accurately quantify the potential short- and long-term costs and benefits at stake.

Nevertheless, the research in this book allows us to put forward a number of important observations which inform the question of whether a more cross-sectoral approach to financial regulation would be more efficient than the current approach in the areas identified above.

On the one hand, path dependency always favours the status quo. Indeed, a cross-sectoral approach would require a regulatory change, the upfront cost of which, in terms of regulatory effort but also in terms of re-adjustment by the financial industry, would be considerable.

On the other hand, this research has identified a number of benefits which a cross-sectoral approach to regulation would likely bring.

First, applying cross-sectoral regulatory concepts and principles would be beneficial in terms of *regulatory efficiency*. Cross-sectoral regulation would avoid the need to duplicate regulatory efforts for the same or very similar problems in different sectors of the financial industry. Moreover, the use of very similar – but slightly divergent – concepts, definitions and rules in several pieces of EU financial regulation on the same issue, would be avoided and different cost-benefit-analyses could be replaced by one enhanced cost-benefit analysis. Translation work would be reduced to one cross-sectoral directive or regulation only, and therefore also the risk of unsubstantiated differences resulting from translation would decrease. In case new insights or developments – eg the recently increased focus on sustainable finance – would require a change in regulatory approach to a certain problem, only one piece of legislation would need to be amended, instead of different pieces of sectoral regulation (with, again, the risk that not all sectoral legislation would be properly amended or translated). This research has shown that differentiation is sometimes needed to deal with sector- or institution-specific aspects, even in areas which are prone to cross-sectoral regulation. This is obviously also feasible in one cross-sectoral piece or legislation, at level 1, level 2 or even level 3, as long as the common core remains sufficiently substantial.

Second, reducing unsubstantiated differences in regulatory answers to similar problems would *increase transparency*. If the same basic principles would apply throughout the financial industry, it would become easier for both financial institutions and their customers to get familiar with basic rights and obligations. Likewise, if documents and information would always be structured in the same manner and use the same terminology where possible, it would be easier for customers to find information and to understand how those documents work.

Third, reducing unsubstantiated differences between sectoral regulation would *reduce compliance costs*. Certain functionally similar institutions, products or services are regulated differently for no other reason than that the texts went through a separate legislative process, with different people and different lobbying groups involved. The consequence of such differences is that diverging compliance tools need to be set up, which is expensive and time-consuming. This is clearly inefficient if those differences cannot be justified on the basis of differences in function, characteristics or risks of products, services or institutions.

Fourth, cross-sectoral common principles which only differentiate where this is needed on the basis of differences in functions, characteristics or risks, would seriously *reduce the risk of regulatory arbitrage*.

Fifth, in an industry that is continuously innovating at a pace that legislators and financial supervisors can hardly keep up with, a cross-sectoral approach to regulation would reduce the risk that new products, services or institutions would slip through the net as not fitting in any of the existing sectoral legislative frameworks. By formulating high-level cross-sectoral concepts and principles, the *risk of gaps* would be *reduced*: new ways of intermediation and new financial products or services would be naturally covered by those cross-sectoral level 1 principles. Further fine-tuning could then, if needed, be developed in a later stage at levels 2 and 3 of the Lamfalussy procedure.

As mentioned above, it would be a great challenge to objectively answer the question of whether a cross-sectoral approach to financial regulation would in the end be more efficient than the current sectoral approach. However, on the basis of the research performed in this book, we can conclude that in important areas of financial regulation the indices are clearly positive. Moreover, certain new challenges for the financial sector in the field of sustainable finance are also plainly cross-sectoral in nature.[1] In the end whether we will witness a move towards a more cross-sectoral financial regulation, depends on a rising awareness among all stakeholders involved, of the shortcomings of the current, and of the benefits or a more cross-sectoral approach. We hope this book may contribute to raise such awareness and ultimately lead to an improved financial regulation for the European Union.

---

[1] Next to a number of changes to sectoral pieces of legislation, the European legislator recently adopted a new cross-sectoral Regulation on disclosures relating to sustainable investments and sustainability risks, which applies to financial market participants and financial advisors of the banking, investment and insurance sectors. See Regulation of the European Parliament and of the Council on sustainability-related disclosures in the financial services sector (2018/0179 (COD)), final text agreed on 23 October 2019, not yet published in Official Journal. In view of its very recent adoption, this Regulation has not been discussed in this book.

INDEX